P9-CJI-613

THE PAPERS
of
JOHN C. CALHOUN

Edwin Hemphill is a graduate of Hampden-Sydney College, Emory University, and the University of Virginia. During 1950 he was director of the History Division of the Virginia State Library. Since 1959 he has been the editor of the South Carolina Department of Archives and History, in which position he has devoted most of his time to editing the papers of Calhoun.

THE PAPERS

of

JOHN C. CALHOUN

Volume III, 1818-1819

Edited by

W. Edwin Hemphill

Published by the University of South Carolina Press
for the South Caroliniana Society, *Columbia, 1967*

Library of Congress Catalog Card Number: 59–10351
Manufactured in the United States of America

CONTENTS

Preface	vii
Introduction	xiii
The Papers of John C. Calhoun	1
August, 1818	3
September, 1818	85
October, 1818	177
November, 1818	248
December, 1818	324
January, 1819	446
February, 1819	532
March, 1819	623
Symbols	715
Bibliography	731
Index	735

PREFACE

This third volume of *The Papers of John C. Calhoun* is much like its predecessor. Volume II comprehended the first eight months (minus about one week) of the South Carolinian's service as Secretary of War. Volume III covers the next eight months of his career in the same office—August, 1818, through March, 1819. Because the previous volume presents much information, particularly in its introductory matter,[1] that is relevant also to this one, the editor needs only to call attention to differences between the two.

In this edition of Calhoun's *Papers,* they are defined as comprising both his outgoing and his incoming mail, together with comparatively few other documents written neither by nor to him but concerning which he had some demonstrable responsibility or in which he had some probable interest. Readers who know how the National Archives during the past 30 years has made accessible millions of documents that had previously been unavailable will not be astonished that so inclusive a definition makes the number of Calhoun's extant papers quite large. This volume alone cites an estimated 4,000 or 5,000 of them—perhaps 6,000 to 8,000 if all distinct versions in manuscript and in print are counted.

All papers written by Calhoun himself that are known to have survived from the eight months are included, together with a large selection of his official papers as well. The extant personal papers are quite few in number, and each is published in complete, verbatim transcription. The official papers are so numerous, however,

[1] W. Edwin Hemphill, ed., *The Papers of John C. Calhoun,* Volume II, *1817–1818* (Columbia: University of South Carolina Press for the South Caroliniana Society, c. 1963), pp. xi–xciv. Hereafter, except when numerals must be used to designate also volume numbers and issue numbers in periodicals, the volumes and pages of published and manuscript books will be cited in the form illustrated by the following examples: 2:xi–xciv, 12:158–162, and E:392.

that to print each is utterly impracticable. Only those that seem most important to the editor, for one reason or another, are reproduced in full. Many of the remaining official documents appear only in condensed abstracts; but the reader is told where he can examine them in unabbreviated form if he wishes to do so.

Not mentioned in any way are some 2,000 more official Calhoun papers that were abstracted or transcribed during the course of preparing this volume. These omitted items, of a highly-routine nature having little foreseeable value to scholars, can be described as being largely of four kinds:

(1) Hundreds deal with comparatively unimportant personnel matters. In most instances, these comprise or concern applications, recommendations, appointments, promotions, transfers, pensions, and the like for individual soldiers, veterans, or would-be soldiers, militiamen, Cadets or prospective Cadets, the heirs of soldiers, and civilians who had government employment or sought it. Samples of such documents are included, however, especially if they were written in behalf of multiple individuals or if a vacant position concerned was of a high level.

(2) Hundreds of others deal with individual claims and financial transactions. Omitted papers of this type include requests and requisitions for remittances, announcements that checks or drafts had been issued against the War Department, transfers of its funds from one appropriation to another, reports that a voucher had been paid, and similar documents. Enough of these financial papers, especially those that involve multiple transactions or comprehensive appropriations, have not been excluded, however, to reveal reasonably well, the editor believes, some of the financial straits through which Calhoun passed in his official course.

(3) Scores of the omitted items comprise routine reports submitted to the War Department at regular intervals by subordinates. Addressed to Calhoun by name simply as a matter of form, these reports most likely were relayed from his office to the appropriate bureaus within the War Department without having received even casual inspection by him. Examples of such monthly or quarterly reports are those sent by the Southern Division's Deputy Commissary of Purchases John McKinney at Newport, Kentucky; by McKinney's counterpart in the Northern Division, Darby Noon at New York City; by two officials of the United States Armory at Harpers Ferry, Virginia (later West Virginia), Superintendent William McGuire and Armorer Armstead Beckham; by two officials of

the corresponding manufacturing facility at Springfield, Massachusetts, Roswell Lee, its Superintendent, and John Chaffee, its Paymaster and Military Storekeeper; and by Bvt. Maj. Sylvanus Thayer, the Superintendent of the United States Military Academy at West Point, New York. Such routine documents, chiefly financial in nature, usually reported receipts, disbursements, the arms produced, and similar details.

(4) Although Calhoun served as Acting Secretary of the Navy during October, November, and December, 1818, hundreds of the Navy documents have been omitted, especially if they were not addressed to Calhoun by name. Some Navy officers never learned that Calhoun served in this capacity until he had ceased to do so; many sent communications directed to the Secretary of the Navy by title only, without mention of any person's name; and some began to address their letters to Smith Thompson as Secretary of the Navy as much as a month before he assumed his place in the President's Cabinet on January 1, 1819. Comparatively few letters known to have been dispatched from the Navy Department in the name of Calhoun as its Acting Secretary have been omitted; even so, these may total a few scores.

To summarize, only a few hundred letters signed by Calhoun have been deleted, and these include none that was written and signed in his own hand; but many hundreds of documents addressed to him have been excluded because of sheer necessity, although these doubtless contributed directly or indirectly to the total body of information upon which he formulated his executive decisions.

Speaking figuratively, the editor's heart has bled each time he has decided that he must delete from publication any document relevant to Calhoun. Some comforting considerations, however, have reduced his anguish, and these same thoughts can be reassuring to readers.

Included is every appropriate document of the period that is known to be preserved in any repository other than the National Archives. Those in that institution that have been excluded have been selected from only about 25 series of manuscripts within about 10 of its Record Groups, chiefly Record Groups 45, 94, and 107. These are among the National Archives' most orderly manuscripts; the letterbooks have indexes, and the loose papers are arranged in personnel files or by some other system that a researcher can master rather quickly. Moreover, many of the approximately 25 series can be surveyed outside the National Archives, because microfilm copies have been published at nominal cost and distributed widely. For example, hundreds of incoming letters in Record Group 107 (Records of the Office of the Secretary of War) and in the voluminous file known as Letters Received by the Secretary of War, Registered Series, 1801–1860, have been omitted in this edition; but these documents can be found in Microcopy 221.

It is reassuring, too, that the Calhoun editorial office does all that it can to make accessible even those Calhoun papers that it cannot possibly publish. Efforts are made continuously to bring its collection of photocopies to virtual completeness. One evidence of steady progress toward this lofty goal can be seen by comparing the list of "Symbols" in this book with the corresponding appendix in Volume II. All incoming photocopies are accessioned, both by their respective dates and by the names of the correspondents other than Calhoun who sent or received the documents. Similarly, abstracts and transcriptions of all Calhoun papers excluded from this volume are filed in the office both chronologically and alphabetically. Research in the collection is permitted without any unusual restriction of any kind. Within readily imaginable, reasonable limits, as a last resort for the benefit of scholars who are not able to visit the editorial office for research, its staff will answer specific inquiries by mail.

Quite representative samples of the types of Calhoun papers that do not clutter the pages of the present volume appear within its predecessor. Because readers of Volume II are afforded ample opportunity to evaluate the flood of routine documents that engaged Calhoun's attention as Secretary of War, the contents of Volume III have been made more selective. Volume III has thus been enabled to present more documents in the form of complete transcriptions, more words actually written by and to John C. Calhoun.

Many persons have made distinctive contributions to the progress of the Calhoun *Papers* project during its 15-year history. Many continue to do so. Their interest and help is appreciated both personally and as evidence of the unselfish spirit that generally pervades the fraternity of scholarship. Particularly useful and pleasant have been the editor's relationships with the personnel of one distant and three local agencies.

The National Historical Publications Commission, which has its office in the National Archives, continues to render invaluable services that would otherwise be unavailable to the Calhoun editorial office and to other *Papers* projects. Dr. Oliver W. Holmes, the Commission's Executive Director, has been always understanding and ever willing to go a second mile. This volume embodies some of the first fruits of financial grants made to the Calhoun project in and since 1965. The good effects of this supplementary support will become much more evident in future volumes.

The assembling and publication of Calhoun's papers continue to have three local sponsors—the South Carolina Department of Archives and History, the University of South Carolina, and the South Caroliniana Society. Policy-making and staff personnel of these sponsors include colleagues and friends whose vision, occasional counsel, and steady encouragement make possible results that are of national and international importance, not merely of local value. Chief among these gratifying friends, these benefactors of human knowledge, are Charles E. Lee, Director of the South Carolina Department of Archives and History, and E. L. Inabinett, Librarian of the University's South Caroliniana Library and Secretary-Treasurer of the South Caroliniana Society.

In portions of the labors that are brought to completion in this book, I have enjoyed the patient, loyal assistance of several associates. Miss Mary Esther Donelan has shared the work with me since mid-December of 1962; she has served the project both in its office and in the National Archives. Miss F. Helen Beach has searched for Calhoun documents, on a part-time basis, ever since 1952, first as an employee of the National Historical Publications Commission and now for more than a year as a valued member of the Calhoun editorial staff. Miss Ruth Elizabeth Clark (now Mrs. Richard G. Stone, Jr.) pioneered during six months of 1965 in a renewed effort to discover Calhoun documents systematically in the National Archives. Assistants in the editorial office have included Mary Lynn (Mrs. Douglas H.) Engel during 1961–1964 and Dr. Jack S. Mullins during 1965–1967. Since mid-November, 1964, Gothedon (Mrs. James Thomas) Wheat has been the office's faithful and intelligent typist, except during the summers of 1965 and 1966, when Miss Diana Bliss Kelley efficiently replaced Mrs. Wheat.

All of these friends have heightened whatever merits are embodied within this book. Its deficiencies can properly be attributed to me, because I have been freer than many another editor to decide how best to present documents so rich, so unique, as these Calhoun papers are. It has been my privilege to work with these Calhoun documents through a longer period of time than any of my colleagues, to edit more of them personally, and to review the work done by each of my associates. I have gained the greatest familiarity with the Calhoun papers, and I accept full responsibility for their presentation. But it is quite possibly more important for me to testify that I see in them a unity, an integrity, a comprehensive wholeness. This volume omits some parts of that whole and condenses other parts; and it does not include, of course, the documents postdating its terminus that I have already edited for inclusion in later volumes of this series. Readers will not, therefore, see this book from the same vantage point. But I hope that, nevertheless, they will find themselves enabled to correlate bits of scattered information and to sense in a heartening, even thrilling way the unity and orderly procedures with which public servants during 1818–1819 made democracy work while our nation was yet young.

W. EDWIN HEMPHILL.

South Carolina Department of Archives and History
Columbia, South Carolina
May 1, 1967

INTRODUCTION

John C. Calhoun served as Secretary of War from December 8, 1817, through March 3, 1825. When he entered this extremely useful period of his long career, he was only 35 years old. The War Department before his tenure has been considered at best a mediocrity, at worst a disgrace. He converted it into a vital, efficient, respected unit. Under his leadership a stagnant, cumbersome power—the largest executive agency of the United States—was transformed into a moving, disciplined, creative, progressive force for national strength and expansion.

The effects of Calhoun's outstanding service as an administrator can be seen from two viewpoints. One is that of the man himself. He gained in the Secretaryship of War perspectives and experiences that confirmed his earlier dedication to nationalism. The other viewpoint is that of the federal Union. The unifying impact of Calhoun's achievements during 1817–1825 helped to regain the loyal support of thousands of outraged citizens who, as recently as the Hartford Convention of 1814, had openly threatened to disrupt the Union by secession.

These thoughts are, of course, broad generalizations and, as such, can be challenged and debated. But they are also in general accord with past and present understandings of the South Carolinian's contributions to the national welfare as a member of the Cabinet of President James Monroe.[1] They are being substantiated by more abundant documentary evidence than ever before in *The Papers of John C. Calhoun,* this first multivolume edition of his correspondence.

Amid such generous documentation you can discover many intriguing items, some of which will be merely isolated or curious

[1] The standard biographies of Calhoun and some other appraisals of his career are listed in *The Papers of John C. Calhoun,* 2:459–467.

specimens and others of which will be typical components of an intrinsic unity. You may welcome, therefore, an introductory view of some themes about which you may wish to be alert while you meander through the following pages. This essay will make your trail clear by identifying 16 topics characteristic of Calhoun's papers of 1818–1819.

Unprecedented Prosperity

The first of these topics will remind you of an underlying fact. About the end of the year 1818 the economy of the United States reached its high-water mark of postwar prosperity before receding into the Panic of 1819. President Monroe expressed on November 16, 1818, the temper of the times in his second annual message to Congress about the state of the Union. "The auspicious circumstances under which you will commence the duties of the present session," he assured the assembled Senators and Representatives, "will lighten the burdens inseparable from the high trust committed to you. The fruits of the earth have been unusually abundant, commerce has flourished, the revenue has exceeded the most favorable anticipation, and peace and amity are preserved with foreign nations on conditions just and honorable to our country. For these inestimable blessings we can not but be grateful to that Providence which watches over the destiny of nations." [2]

The general prosperity of the last months of 1818 and the first quarter of 1819 was not, however, universal throughout the nation. Nor did the Panic of 1819 begin simultaneously throughout the vast extent of the country. You may detect within the textual pages of this book a few hints that the economic tide was beginning to turn as early as March, 1819.

Acting President of the United States

Throughout the first seven or eight weeks after July, 1818, President Monroe was away from Washington. So also was the Secretary of the Navy, Benjamin W. Crowninshield; indeed, he

[2] James D. Richardson, *A Compilation of the Messages and Papers of the Presidents, 1789–1902* (10 vols. [Washington:] Bureau of National Literature and Art, 1903), 2:39.

never resumed the duties of his office after having left the capital in May of 1818 for a crisis-abbreviated trip with Monroe and Calhoun to inspect defense sites in the Chesapeake Bay area. With the exception of Calhoun, every other member of the Cabinet—Secretary of State John Quincy Adams, Secretary of the Treasury William H. Crawford, and Attorney General William Wirt—was absent from the seat of government for at least one interval during August and early September, 1818.

Under these circumstances Calhoun served, in effect, as the Acting President of the United States. To the absent Monroe he wrote frequently. He handled the most urgent business of executive agencies other than his own, especially that of the Department of State. And he did so at a time of national crisis.

Not all citizens agreed with the administration's decision of about July 20 to return Pensacola and other Spanish posts in the two Floridas that had been captured before June by Maj. Gen. Andrew Jackson, under an unexpectedly liberal interpretation of the orders given to him by Calhoun. A war intended to subdue the Seminoles had been converted by Jackson into a war of conquest against the Spanish. Successful negotiation of a long-pending treaty with Spain concerning several important issues had been made precarious by Jackson's unforeseen application of his authority. War with Spain was a penalty that might conceivably be suffered as a result of the indignity that he had heaped upon that weak nation's head. Moreover, he had committed an insult against Great Britain, by executing summarily two citizens of that empire—and this, too, at a time when the renewal of a profitable commercial treaty with that more feared power was hanging in the balance. (The negotiations with Spain were protracted until the latter part of February, 1819. Those with Great Britain were concluded on October 20, 1818.[3])

The letters written and received by Calhoun during this critical juncture toward the end of the summer of 1818 reveal him to have been temporarily the key figure in putting into effect the administration's policy that had been adopted in the third week of July. What is more, he is seen to have acted loyally, even though he

[3] Richard Peters, ed., *The Public Statutes at Large of the United States of America* . . . [Including Private Laws, Indian Treaties, and Treaties with Foreign Powers, 1789–1845] (8 vols. Boston: Little, Brown and Company, c. 1846), 8:248–273. For Monroe's summation of relationships with Great Britain and with Spain as of mid-November, 1818, see Richardson, *Messages and Papers of the Presidents,* 2:39–44.

had not been at first in total agreement with that policy. He observed alertly the public's reactions; he even helped to shape public opinion in favor of the administration policy. Amid the issues of international importance, he was attentive enough to routine matters of a merely individual nature, however, to give promptly to Nicholas P. Trist the appointment as a Cadet that President Monroe recommended.

Acting Secretary of the Navy

During the last three months of 1818 the Secretary of War served also as Acting Secretary of the Navy. The executive of the Navy Department, Benjamin W. Crowninshield, had arrived at his Massachusetts residence on July 7, remained there for a long time, took no part in the Cabinet's discussions during the remainder of the summer, and resigned perhaps early in October as of September 30.[4] No letter of his resignation has chanced to come to the present editor's attention. Nor has the editor discovered any letter or commission appointing Calhoun as Acting Secretary of the Navy or directing him to serve as *ad interim* head of the Navy Department. There is, therefore, a looseness or informality about Calhoun's connection with the Navy Department, although one official report states unequivocally that the South Carolinian served as a temporary replacement for Crowninhield from October 19 through December 31, 1818.[5]

One thing is clear: Calhoun's papers in the following pages include a letter signed by him as Acting Secretary of the Navy as early as October 17.[6] Already heavily burdened with pressing business in the War Department, Calhoun naturally and obviously permitted the Chief Clerk of the Navy Department, Benjamin Homans, to receive and to answer many letters in the Navy office. To do more than Calhoun did was doubtless not expected of him.

[4] See the *Correspondence between Gen. Andrew Jackson and John C. Calhoun, President and Vice-President of the U. States, on the Subject of the Course of the Latter, in the Deliberations of the Cabinet of Mr. Monroe, on the Occurrences in the Seminole War* (Washington: printed by Duff Green, 1831), p. 31. Compare Robert Brent Mosher, compiler, *Executive Register of the United States, 1789–1902 . . .* (Senate Document No. 196, 58th Congress, 3rd Session. Washington: Government Printing Office, 1905), p. 90.

[5] Mosher, *Executive Register*, p. 90.

[6] See Calhoun's letter of October 17, 1818, to Commodore D[aniel] T. Patterson, below, p. 217.

Many items of business that were not transacted overtly in Calhoun's name but which he influenced through frequent or even daily conferences with Homans may not appear within the covers of this book. Every Navy document that is included, however, is a contribution to knowledge previously unknown to Calhoun's biographers, not one of whom has ever reported that the South Carolinian assumed any responsibility over this other branch of the nation's defense forces. Under Calhoun, for a while, these forces were unified in somewhat the same way that they have been since the Second World War under the Secretary of the Department of Defense.

Congress in Session

Another guidepost is the fact that the second session of the Fifteenth Congress convened on November 16, 1818, and continued through March 3, 1819. For months prior to its opening Calhoun kept himself and his subordinates busy with the preparation of reports to be submitted to Congress about various subjects. During the long session he and they were frequently overwhelmed by the importunate pressures that descended upon them from or through Congressmen by mail and in person.

When the session had ended and while the Monroe administration was proceeding through the first month of its third year, War Department officials tackled their share of the follow-up work that fell to their lot, for it was their duty to execute or to assist in executing many of the new laws that had been enacted. Only at the end of March, 1819, did Calhoun and other high-ranking officials of the administration feel that their clean-up labors were under a reasonable degree of control. Then they began what history knows as President Monroe's "Southern tour." (And that point has been chosen as a logical terminus for this installment of the Calhoun *Papers*.)

Report on Indian Trade

Three of Calhoun's reports to the House of Representatives within this session must be accorded rank much above the level of the ordinary. On December 5, 1818, he reviewed the history and appraised with judicious reserve the successes and limitations of the government-operated Indian trading houses, which were usually called "Factories." Calhoun preferred to see the Factory system continued. But prominent businessmen and some Congressmen wanted profits from the Indian trade to go to private enterprisers. If the government should relinquish its monopoly, Calhoun argued persuasively, it should do so only to licensed, corporate entrepreneurs large enough to engage in the business responsibly under regulations that would protect the Indians' and the nation's interests.

Congress did not yield to the insistent pressure of the business community. The Factory system expired, by law, on March 1, 1819; but the Indian trading houses were revived and extended by a new statute that was approved two days later. This new law embodied some improvements that may have originated with Calhoun. For one thing, it was more flexible. The old statute of April 20, 1818, had designated specifically the only locations at which Indian Agents and Factors might be stationed. Its effect was to make the system unadaptable to changing needs; Factories could not be moved with the Indians when the frontier advanced. The corrective statute of March 3, 1819, made it possible to transfer these government officials and services "to such other places as the public service may require."

In addition, the new act authorized the appointment, with the consent of the Senate, of an Indian Agent for the Upper Missouri at the comparatively high salary level of $1,800 annually.[7] Both the increase in the number of Agents and the pay granted to the new appointee hinted that something unusually important was in the making. On that same third day of March troops and supplies were being mustered for a major movement into the almost-totally-unknown Northwest—an effort often called the Yellowstone Expedition but more realistically known as the Missouri Expedition. More will be said about this pioneering Army maneuver in a later section of this Introduction.

Report on Reduction of the Army

On December 11, 1818, Calhoun advocated the maintenance of a professional Army sufficiently large, especially in the number of its commissioned officers, to provide civilian benefits during times

[7] Peters, ed., *The Statutes at Large,* 3:514.

of peace and to afford effective leadership for nonprofessional soldiers in times of war. In other words, he argued against reduction of the Army. He based his persuasive appeal on a contention that the Army's growth was merely proportional to its enlarged responsibilities in a rapidly expanding nation. The Union's thousands of miles of borders and the Army's dispersal among widely-scattered posts meant, he insisted, that professional soldiers need not be feared as a potential threat to republican institutions. Convinced, Congress did not reduce the authorized strength of the Army.

Calhoun also availed himself of the the same opportunity to recommend increased flexibility and other reforms—more fresh vegetables, for example—in the rations that had been rigidly prescribed by law. The following pages show that much of what he said about the legal ration had been suggested by his forward-looking, science-minded appointee to the office of the Army's Surgeon General, Dr. Joseph Lovell.

Report on Roads and Canals

On January 7, 1819, Calhoun completed and dated a major treatise on the relationship between the Army and national development. It argued that the United States should build roads and canals because these transportation facilities would be of value in war or in peace. What little the Army had been doing thus to strengthen the nation was, in Calhoun's opinion, a mere pittance.

Opposition to such internal improvements at federal expense, even as a means of keeping soldiers busy when they had no enemy to fight, was so widespread that Calhoun's plea was made largely in vain. Constitutional doubts permeated many minds—among them, that of President Monroe. He had given to Congress in 1817 a long explanation of his belief that federal funds could not be appropriated for internal improvements until the Constitution was amended to grant to Congress an express authority to designate tax revenues for such uses.[8]

There is evidence, derived largely from the memoirs of John Quincy Adams, that Calhoun's advocacy of roads and canals in his report was originally written in stronger terms but was later moderated by Calhoun because of Monroe's opposition. When the President learned how ardently Calhoun's proposed report, not yet

[8] Richardson, *Messages and Papers of the Presidents,* 2:17–18.

released, urged internal improvements, Monroe called his Cabinet into conference on January 12. Calhoun read his intended statement. Monroe objected that it was inconsistent with his own publicly-announced view; and he contended that, since the heads of the federal agencies were officers serving under himself as chief executive, what they proposed to Congress should not be in conflict with his own known stance. (Making a minor point, Monroe argued also that it was not proper for the House of Representatives to have called upon Calhoun directly, rather than through Monroe, for the report in question.) Adams supported the President.

Calhoun then readily agreed to omit all passages in his proposed report that implied that Congress had a duty to finance internal improvements. Moreover, Calhoun pointed out that his proposed draft had specifically disclaimed any consideration of the question of constitutional authorization.[9] The next-to-last paragraph of the document as we know it embodies just such a disclaimer. We can only guess what passages may have been deleted, in fulfillment of Calhoun's offer, before the report was submitted to the House on January 14. But it is entirely conceivable that what Calhoun had written under the date of January 7 may have been revised, without changing the dateline, before the document was received by the House a week later.

Private Laws

Literally scores of the decisions of Congress affected Calhoun. For example, not less than three of every five of the session's batch of 47 private laws, enacted to grant various forms of relief to individuals, seem to have involved Army men or War Department accounts.[10] One authorized the Treasury Department's auditors to settle the claim of Monsieur Poirey for his services as secretary and aide-de-camp to Maj. Gen. Lafayette during the American Revolution[11]—a claim about which Calhoun and Thomas Jefferson had been corresponding. Another private law directed that a claim by Aquila Giles dating back to 1782 should be paid.[12] Others ordered

[9] This issue is summarized (and Adams's most pertinent words are quoted and cited) in Leonard D. White, *The Jeffersonians: a Study in Administrative History, 1801–1829* (New York: The Macmillan Company, c. 1951), pp. 67–68.

[10] Peters, ed., *The Statutes at Large,* 6:216–235.

[11] *Ibid.,* 6:225.

[12] *Ibid.,* 6:230.

the settlement on principles of equity of the disputed accounts of Joseph Wheaton, a Quartermaster officer during the War of 1812,[13] and of William B. Lewis, who had served as Deputy Quartermaster General in the Tennessee militia units that had successfully but somewhat irregularly enabled Andrew Jackson to become a military hero in the same war.[14]

Another private law ordered the War Department to increase the pensions that it had already granted to 17 individuals, including one Timothy Mix, and to add 11 new names to its rolls of disabled pensioners. Among these 11, for example, were Peter Francisco, popularly known as "The Giant of Virginia," who had distinguished himself in an exploit against Banastre Tarleton's cavalrymen during the Revolution, and Solomon Van Rensselaer of New York, whose service as a Captain under Maj. Gen. Anthony Wayne in a battle against Indians in 1794 was rewarded.[15]

Appropriations to the War Department

The major act of 1819 appropriating funds to the War Department provides over-all insights into its operations that can be seen only piecemeal in the textual portion of this book. That statute itemized allotments totaling more than $7,180,000. One million dollars were made available for the salaries of soldiers, almost as much for their food, more than half a million for their transportation, and $400,000 for their clothing. Half a million dollars were designated for the construction of fortifications under direction of the Army Engineers. Ordnance officers were allotted about half a million for purchases of guns and ammunition, for the building or completion of several arsenals and other storage facilities (perhaps most notably a new powder magazine at Baton Rouge), and similar outlays. The sum of $375,000 was appropriated to the armories at Springfield, Massachusetts, and at Harpers Ferry, which were government-operated manufacturing plants for the production of rifles and other small arms. The Military Academy received more than $35,000.

Ten thousand dollars were assigned for the extra pay of the Army's noncommissioned officers and enlisted men who were "em-

[13] *Ibid.*, 6:232.
[14] *Ibid.*, 6:217.
[15] *Ibid.*, 3:526–528.

ployed in the construction and repairs of military roads." Allotments related to various surveys included $6,500 to finance the special costs of Topographical Engineer Stephen H. Long's intended explorations of unknown or little-known areas drained by rivers northwest of the Ohio and, more especially, west of the Mississippi. For current expenses of the Indian Agents, including some overdue costs of negotiating past Indian treaties, almost a quarter of a million dollars were appropriated. More than half a million dollars were earmarked for disabled veterans and for half-pay pensions to the widows and ophans of veterans; more than $1,800,000 were made available for pension payments in 1819 to Revolutionary veterans under the statute that had been enacted on March 18, 1818.[16]

There were several other acts of appropriation that were important to Calhoun. From the personal viewpoint, the chief of these must have been those which raised the salary of the Secretary of War by one-third to $6,000 annually, from the beginning of the year 1819, and placed him on a par with the Secretaries of the State, Treasury, and Navy Departments.[17] An appropriation act approved on the final day of the Congressional session, March 3, 1819, provided funds for other civilian salaries and for office expenses in the bureau of the War Department, which amounted to much less than $100,000 annually—an extremely low ratio of administrative cost compared with the approximately ten million dollars for which they and their Army-officer colleagues were responsible.

One interesting revelation can be found in such itemized provisions for the War Department's housekeeping expenses. The specific figures include references to the new headquarters of the Department. Construction funds had been appropriated in April, 1818, for two new office buildings. One, to be built on the east side of the White House, was to house the State and Treasury Departments. The other, equidistant from the President's residence but to the west of it, was intended for joint use by the War and Navy Departments.

As early as August, 1818, Calhoun queried his subordinates about how much space they would need in the new building for

[16] *Ibid.*, 3:480–481. The total of more than $900,000 for the Army's subsistence or rations included $200,000 that had been made available on December 16, 1818. *Ibid.*, 3:478.

[17] *Ibid.*, 3:484 and 498. Compare *The Papers of John C. Calhoun,* 2:xl–xli.

their respective quarters. Among the appropriations that were made available on March 3, 1819, were almost $23,300 to cover expenses "attending the occupancy of the new executive buildings" and $10,000 for roofing "with slate the two executive buildings now occupied by the State, Treasury, War, and Navy Departments."

Another statute of the same day provided funds for completing the rebuilding of the United States Capitol, which had been burned by the British in 1814; for making some improvements at the White House; for "enlarging the offices west of the President's house" at a cost of $8,137; and for providing a water system for the White House and the two executive office buildings.[18]

These appropriations narrow the limits within which the new Army–Navy building must have been first occupied. The office of the Secretary of War and many other War Department bureaus probably moved into it as early as February or March, 1819. That time is as much as a year and a half earlier than the approximate time reported by a major historian of the War Department.[19]

Indian Treaties, Annuities, and Civilization

Eleven treaties negotiated with Indian tribes were ratified by the Senate. Ten were drafted during August, September, and October, 1818, at locations near the tribes' residences; these were intended chiefly to accomplish cessions of Indian lands to the United States. One was concluded on February 27, 1819, in Washington by Calhoun himself. Its principal object was to encourage better and larger-scale compliance on the part of the Eastern Cherokees with the principles that had been embodied in earlier Cherokee treaties within the previous two years. Some Eastern Cherokees were thus given additional incentive to exchange their lands in the mountainous area of the Southeast for real estate in the Arkansas River area, to which they would emigrate. Those who declined to choose that alternative were given new assurances and protective procedures under which they would receive rights to tenure in individual, not tribal, holdings in the Southeast.[20]

[18] Peters, ed., *The Statutes at Large,* 3:496–502, 516.

[19] See *The Papers of John C. Calhoun,* 2:xliii–xlvi, and the references, particularly the last, cited therein.

[20] These 11 treaties have been published, among other places, in Peters, ed., *The Statutes at Large,* 7:176–200.

The costs of negotiating an Indian treaty were usually compounded by the financial obligations stipulated in it. Such documents often specified that the Indians were to receive, in compensation for the lands they ceded, a certain sum of money annually for a certain number of years. The appropriations of the 1818–1819 session included $50,000 to cover the 1818 deficit in Congressional provision for these annuities and almost $135,000 for these obligations in 1819.[21]

A separate allotment of $10,000 was made on March 3, 1819, "for the civilization of the Indian tribes." It authorized the President, with the consent of the Indians, "to employ capable persons of good moral character, to instruct them in the mode of agriculture suited to their situation" and "for teaching their children in reading, writing, and arithmetic."[22] This was an annual appropriation, renewed automatically. Calhoun began after 1819 to expend it effectively not in salary payments to government employees but as grants-in-aid for schools that were operated by Christian missionaries.

Veterans' Benefits

This volume includes many bits of evidence that James L. Edwards and other Clerks in the War Department's Pension Office were swamped during the autumn of 1818 by an unexpected, overwhelming backlog of approximately 20,000 applications from Revolutionary veterans. Congress reacted promptly. A statute of December 5 empowered Calhoun to employ as many at 12 additional Clerks for one year and appropriated $12,000 "for their compensation."[23]

Several other new laws also dealt with veterans' benefits. Calhoun received an extension through March 3, 1824, of his authority to issue warrants for military land bounties to soldiers of the War of 1812.[24] The right of a soldier's heirs to relinquish his land bounty and to receive in lieu thereof a pension was extended for three years.[25] To prevent disability payments to former soldiers who were no longer invalids, medical testimony certifying the continu-

[21] *Ibid.*, 3:478 and 517–520, respectively.
[22] *Ibid.*, 3:516–517.
[23] *Ibid.*, 3:477.
[24] *Ibid.*, 3:487.
[25] *Ibid.*, 3:524.

ance and extent of each disability was required periodically after 1818 of all such pensioners except those whose stipends recognized Revolutionary service and those who had suffered some absolutely irremediable disability, such as an amputation.[26]

Some Miscellaneous Laws

Several other public laws enacted by Congress during 1818–1819 dealt with miscellaneous matters. Noncommissioned Army officers and enlisted men employed "at work on fortifications, in surveys, in cutting roads and other constant labour, of not less than ten days," were to receive for such extra service 15 cents and an extra gill of whisky per day.[27] The military road from Huntsville, Alabama, to Madisonville, Louisiana, was designated to become a mail route upon completion.[28] Calhoun was directed to cause to be sold every military site that had become or should later become "useless for military purposes."[29] He was authorized also to sell to one John Preacher the Keep-Tryst Furnace tract of 220 acres in Jefferson County, Virginia (later West Virginia), near the armory at Harpers Ferry; the price might be whatever sum Calhoun might consider "most conducive to the interest of the United States."[30]

To care better for the needs of pensioners in East Tennessee, Calhoun was empowered to appoint a second pension agent in that State.[31] In keeping with his quest for clarity and directness in administrative procedures, responsibility for "all unsettled accounts arising out of Indian affairs," other than those related to Indian trade (which Fifth Auditor Stephen Pleasonton handled), was vested in Calhoun and in Third Auditor Peter Hagner, to the exclusion of Second Comptroller Richard Cutts.[32]

The Militia

We can imagine that Calhoun found one of the most plaguing problems that he faced during 1818 and 1819 to be the court-martial

[26] *Ibid.*, 3:514–515.
[27] *Ibid.*, 3:488.
[28] *Ibid.*, 3:508.
[29] *Ibid.*, 3:520.
[30] *Ibid.*, 3:521.
[31] *Ibid.*, 3:521.
[32] *Ibid.*, 3:487.

for the trial of New York militia delinquents. His correspondence with members of that court was heavy indeed. Involved in the problem was an essentially inefficient system that enmeshed officials of New York State and of the United States in delicate, irritating relationships. Because many militiamen did not answer calls to military service during the War of 1812, courts-martial put them to trial under a statute enacted in 1792 that had not been designed to deal with draft dodgers on a wholesale scale. These courts levied fines totaling roughly half a million dollars against perhaps 10,000 delinquents. In New York State approximately 4,000 men were assessed about $200,000 in fines.

As the system dictated, the members of the New York court-martial were officers of that State's militia. Maj. Gen. Gerard A. Steddiford was its President. The court had first begun its distasteful business in 1814, long before Calhoun became the Secretary of War. It fell to Calhoun's lot to reactivate the court in December, 1817.[33] As following pages reveal, there was hope that the court might complete its labors as early as about October, 1818. Then additional returns of delinquents were received; the court was reduced in size; and efforts to complete the administration of justice under an unpopular law were still proceeding at the end of March, 1819.

To collect a fine was difficult. The court's assessment of it had to be approved by President James Monroe. Then, although it had been imposed by State officials, it had to be collected by a United States Marshal, Thomas Morris. Confusion resulted from many causes. The names of the accused and fined militiamen were often reported incompletely or erroneously, both to and by Calhoun and the President. Some of the accused had names identical with those of other militiamen and took full advantage of that coincidence in efforts to escape punishment. Some fines that Morris had already collected were remitted, and refunds were made by Morris to wrong individuals.

The travel expenses of the several State militia officers who comprised the court-martial and moved with it from place to place were payable only from the proceeds of fines. But Morris and other United States Marshals could muster little enthusiasm for tracking down thousands of widely-scattered citizens for the purpose of getting perhaps $50 from each if they had it or could raise it, which often they did not and could not. Morris collected

[33] *The Papers of John C. Calhoun*, 2:35.

smaller sums in fines than the amounts that were due in payment of the court's expenses. Naturally, its members, having invested hundreds of out-of-pocket dollars in performing a public service that was obviously unappreciated, hounded both Morris and Calhoun impatiently for refunds. Such men could hardly be expected to be at ease while their claims cleared the hurdles of red tape; and they surely should not be expected to be happy when an approved, but perhaps reduced, refund was postponed indefinitely because Morris had no cash in hand. All told, such unsatisfactory court-martial proceedings, supposedly self-sustaining or even profit-making, ended with a net deficit that cost the United States approximately an extra $25,000.[34]

In the following pages you will also be able to discover occasional bits of evidence that Calhoun could not reform promptly the militia's dual system of support and control. States often did not bother to submit annual returns of the strength of their respective militias. Calhoun, and particularly the Army's Ordnance officers, had responsibilities in relation to State militias but were almost wholly unable to gain any official knowledge of the extent of those responsibilities.[35]

Improved Administration

Calhoun's passion for systematic, efficient management of the War Department's business met many challenges and opportunities toward the end of his first year as its top executive and during the first months of his second. He can hardly be said to have worked miracles overnight; progress was piecemeal, but it was also cumulative. In time, the total results became impressive indeed.

His reorganization of the Army's general staff in April, 1818, had been a first, major step forward. It made possible many later steps. The new Quartermaster General, Thomas S. Jesup, began to function actively before August, 1818. So did the new Surgeon General, Dr. Joseph Lovell. The communications of each to Calhoun that appear within these covers indicate that each was becoming increasingly effective.

[34] White, *The Jeffersonians*, pp. 536–539.

[35] For some relevant data antedating 1818 aud postdating 1819, see *ibid.*, pp. 532–533.

The new Commissary General of Subsistence, Col. George Gibson, spent the summer and early autumn of 1818 in the South attempting to straighten out the tangled, knotty problems of accounting and supply that were left in the wake of the Seminole war of 1817–1818. Contractor Benjamin G. Orr had failed miserably to deliver enough rations for the Army and militia units that had engaged in those campaigns. Even after the militiamen were discharged, his deliveries continued to fall short of the Army's requirements. Army officers bought food at exorbitant prices wherever they could; their accounts were often defective, their vouchers inadequate. Funds dispatched from Washington to Quartermaster officers like Maj. Milo Mason—remittances that seemed to Calhoun to be more than sufficient—did not always arrive in the right hands at the right time. Col. Gibson must certainly have received a rough baptism under the fire of such failures in the South. Calhoun's papers do not record exactly when Gibson returned to Washington and assumed personal management there of the subsistence bureau of the Army; he began, however, to write Calhoun from that office late in November, 1818. Surely he must have given to his boss oral reports about the breakdown of the food-supply system in the South that confirmed one of Calhoun's earlier convictions—his conclusion that being totally dependent upon private contractors for occasional deliveries of rations wherever the troops might be moved was no way to feed the Army.

Hope was in the making as early as August, 1818, even before Col. Gibson could get to his desk. The annual contracts for subsistence of the Army were due to expire on May 31, 1819. It was planned that they would not be renewed in the old way. Instead, the Commissary General would buy rations directly from sellers and would have increased responsibility and control over both the supply and distribution of the food. Calhoun had his Chief Clerk, Christopher Vandeventer, advertise invitations to bid on the new contracts. Successful bidders would deliver rations to Army officers at strategically located depots in quarterly installments, well in advance of all foreseeable needs; and these officers would not accept the deliveries unless they met the Army's specifications. The process of transition to the new system would require considerable time. That is why the first step was taken so far in advance of June, 1819. Also well in advance, the suppliers under the contracts for 1818–1819 were given early notification of the quantities that they were to stockpile to meet the Army's needs until deliveries under the new contracts could begin.

In an over-all sense, improved discipline and management in the Army were initiated by other steps that date from September, 1818. Bvt. Maj. Gen. Winfield Scott offered then to prepare a book-length compilation of regulations or standards that would serve for the guidance or government of the entire Army. Calhoun responded promptly and favorably. He made special arrangements to relieve Gen. Scott of other duties, because this one alone was a major project. The comprehensive result could not be completed within the time limits of the present volume, of course; but the task was finished later and was formally reported to Congress about two years after its beginning.[36]

The Missouri Expedition

The eight months comprehended within these covers were a period of preparation for the most glamorous venture that was undertaken by the Army while Calhoun was Secretary of War. Nothing else that he attempted so captivated the public imagination or appealed equally to the popular fancy. People were intrigued that the Army should dare to establish an outpost high up the Missouri River, far beyond the existing frontier and deep in Indian country. British influence within the northern portion of the Louisiana Purchase area would be reduced; profits from the fur trade would flow into the eastern United States, not into Canada; farmers would follow the soldiers and would till cheap but rich lands.

The methods as well as the objectives of the Missouri Expedition captured public attention. The push up the Missouri would be accompanied by a coördinated movement to establish an Army post where the St. Peters River (now known as the Minnesota) empties into the upper Mississippi, at the site of the present-day city of Minneapolis. Thus the chain reaction of Army advance and public land sales and profits and national expansion would be set in motion on another front as well.

[36] *American State Papers: Documents, Legislative and Executive, of the Congress* . . . (37 vols. Washington: various printers, 1832–1861), *Military Affairs,* 2:199–274.

In addition, one of the Army's Topographical Engineers, Bvt. Maj. Stephen H. Long, was simultaneously to lead a party of soldiers and scientists in explorations of the rivers and lands west of the Mississippi as far southward as the Arkansas. Much information would be gained about vast areas that were almost totally unknown, except that some of the findings of the Lewis and Clark Expedition about 15 years earlier had been published. Moreover, it became known that steamboats were to be introduced on the distant Western streams—and this barely more than a decade after the initial voyage of Robert Fulton's *Clermont* up the Hudson and even fewer years after the first steam-powered keel had experimentally produced a wake in the upper Ohio.

This marvelous progress of 1818 was being initiated, too, at a time when some citizens of Louisiana were the only ones in the Union who could enjoy the benefits of State government west of the Mississippi, when Alabama and Illinois to the east of that stream were still Territories and the Michigan–Wisconsin area had not even attained fully the status of a Territory, and when Missouri was the only organized Territory west of the Mississippi.

The grand concept of Army penetration to the upper reaches of the Missouri had been first announced by Calhoun on March 16, 1818.[37] Throughout the next 12 months and especially, as this book often reveals, during the eight months that began with August, 1818, many preparations were made for troop movements on a large scale to begin at about the opening of the spring of 1819. For example, the correspondence in 1819 of Col. Henry Atkinson reveals that a major push was in the making.

Despite the careful preparations of 1818–1819, the Missouri Expedition accomplished less than Calhoun and others optimistically hoped that it would achieve. It never succeeded in justifying its overambitious name as a Yellowstone Expedition. Some of its phases were fiascos. Calhoun relied upon Col. James Johnson of Kentucky, a hero of the War of 1812 and a veteran supplier of rations since then, to provide both food and transportation for the soldiers who were to push up the Missouri. Johnson's efforts would be supported by his several brothers, who included another war hero, Col. Richard M. Johnson, chairman of the House Committee on Military Affairs. The story of James Johnson's failures to fulfill the terms of his contracts will be documented by future volumes of the Calhoun *Papers*. But if Calhoun ever read again late in

[37] *The Papers of John C. Calhoun,* 2:194–195.

1819 or afterward the letters he received in 1818 recommending Johnson, their honeyed tributes to Johnson's alleged financial resources and proved reliability must have turned quite sour in Calhoun's mouth.

Henry Clay, for example, wrote on September 16, 1818, in praise of the ability and "perfect integrity" of Johnson, whose qualifications Clay respected so highly that he urged Calhoun to award contracts to Johnson even if rival businessmen should submit lower bids. About five and a half years later Clay assured the President of the Bank of the United States that "I have believed for several years" that Richard M. Johnson and his brothers "are hopelessly insolvent." [38] The contrast is a wry one. It deepens the poignancy with which we see within these covers Calhoun and others moving toward unforeseen disappointments.

The Seminole War Refought

Whether Andrew Jackson had acted justifiably during the spring of 1818 was a question that was debated long after the summer of that year had ended. In the autumn President James Monroe's message on the state of the Union took pains to portray the General's actions in the best possible light. Authorized to make war against the savage Seminoles within Spanish borders, Jackson had simply found it necessary, Monroe explained, to make war also against the Spanish, because their weak government in the Floridas not only did not control the Indians but also actually connived to support the Seminoles and other enemies.[39] In accordance with a promise made by Monroe, Calhoun had the War Department's Clerks copy for submission to Congress substantiating evidence to this effect—so much of it, indeed, that they could not possibly complete the copying of the voluminous documents in time for them all to be relayed to Congress when they were expected. They grew to book length.[40]

[38] See Clay's letter of September 16, 1818, herein, p. 133. For his letter of January 3, [1824,] to Nicholas Biddle, see James F. Hopkins and Mary W.M. Hargreaves, eds., *The Papers of Henry Clay* (3 vols. to date. [Lexington:] University of Kentucky Press, c. 1959, 1961, 1963), 3:558–560.

[39] Richardson, *Messages and Papers of the Presidents,* 2:39–43.

[40] One large-scale printing of such evidence can be found in the *American State Papers: Military Affairs,* 1:681–769. One large collection of manuscript copies of such materials, probably assembled for publication, constitutes a

Congressmen debated Jackson's conduct throughout most of the session. Partisan motives can be detected in the proceedings. Henry Clay and friends of William H. Crawford attacked both Jackson and the administration by proposing that Congress should censure Jackson for having disobeyed orders that he had received from Calhoun and for having fought a war that had not been declared by Congress in accordance with the federal constitution. The condemnations of Jackson that they urged upon the House of Representatives were defeated by votes taken in that body before mid-February, 1819. Similar denunciations offered by a Senate committee fell short of reaching any formal decision before Congress adjourned on March 3. Some of Jackson's biographers seem to believe that he would not have emerged unscathed if he had not hastened to Washington in January and behaved himself so discreetly and impressively as to win public favor.

However that may be, both the bitter contest in Congress and Jackson's appearance on the scene could not fail to have given many moments of concern to John C. Calhoun. Written records afford to us almost no information about the first known meeting between these two men who were destined to be official friends for years and then open enemies for years. Partial insights are afforded by a letter from Calhoun's wife to one of her relatives. It was dated February 4, 1819. Mrs. Calhoun had sat in the gallery of the House of Representatives to hear at least three major speeches on the proposed censure of Jackson. These addresses had been delivered by Clay, by Richard M. Johnson, and by John Holmes of Massachusetts. Mrs. Calhoun was looking forward to the pleasure of seeing Jackson for the first time soon, when he would dine in the Calhoun home. The General would also be among her honored guests at a ball. "I am sorry Congress have abused him so much, respecting the Seminole War," she confided, "as I am confident he acted to the best of his knowledge, and further, in censuring him, they must my husband, as he directed him in one of his letters to act to the best of his knowledge." [41]

series known as Correspondence Relating to West Florida, 1813–1818, in the National Archives, Record Group 59 (Records of the Department of State).

[41] Mrs. John C. Calhoun to Mrs. Patrick Noble, February 4, 1819, ALS in ScCleA. (Explanations of such symbols as "ALS" and "ScCleA" are appended to the text of this volume.) A printed copy of this letter can be found in Alice Noble Waring, ed., "Letters of John C. Calhoun to Patrick Noble, 1812–1837," *The Journal of Southern History,* vol. XVI, no. 1 (February, 1950), pp. 67–68.

The bitter tensions that were evoked by the controversial General and by his operations south of Georgia and Alabama were eased by a prospect that the United States might acquire the Floridas permanently. Revived negotiations of the long-pending issues with Spain crystallized on February 22, 1819, in a treaty that was acceptable to both Secretary of State John Quincy Adams and Don Luis de Onís. On March 3 it was ratified by the Senate. If Spain should also ratify it, the Floridas would become United States property, and various provisions for the occupation and government of them would become operative.[42] Calhoun's correspondence began promptly to reflect effects that this pending probability imposed upon the Army. Public opinion at the time rather overlooked the fact that, in the same treaty, Spain had obtained a relinquishment of all claims by the United States to an enormous area of which Texas is only a part.

[42] Peters, ed., *The Statutes at Large,* 3:523–524.

THE PAPERS
of
JOHN C. CALHOUN

Volume III

AUGUST 1818

Spain, Florida, the Seminoles, and Andrew Jackson were much in Calhoun's mind throughout this month. From its opening to its close President James Monroe was away from the capital; every member of the Cabinet other than Calhoun was also out of the city during all or part of August; Calhoun handled critical business for the War Department and the State Department as well. Indeed, while war hung in the balance, he served virtually as Acting President of the United States. About mid-month he issued orders for the restoration to Spanish control of posts in the two Floridas that Jackson had conquered, and he countermanded an order for the conquest of St. Augustine. Amid the welter of executive routine, Calhoun watched with alertness the crystallization of public opinion in regard to the administration's policy toward the captured posts and the partial repudiation of their captor.

From former Capt. Francis D. Cummins, Baltimore, 8/1. Applies for a reappointment as an Army officer. ALS in DNA, 11, 12081. (This application was apparently not successful. Heitman, *Historical Register,* 1:344.)

Capt. James Gadsden, Nashville, to Maj. Gen. Andrew Jackson, [Nashville,] 8/1. Gadsden submits a report recommending a plan for defense of the Floridas [if they should be acquired by the U.S.—a report that probably came to Calhoun's attention]. FC in DNA, 22, pp. 337–340.

From Charles F. Grimké, [no place stated,] 8/1. This South Carolinian "received yesterday" and accepts his appointment as a Cadet, dated 7/21. ALS in DNA, 15, 1818, 90.

From [Brig. Gen. Thomas S. Jesup, Quartermaster General,] 8/1. Asks that $4,000 be sent to Capt. A[rchibald] W. Hamilton,

Asst. Deputy Quartermaster General at Boston, and that $1,700 be sent to Lt. Col. [Ninian] Pinkney, commanding officer at Niagara. FC in DNA, 42, 1:28.

From John McKee, [Agent to the Choctaws,] Choctaw Agency, 8/1. Reports that he has issued two drafts totaling $2,181.64 to cover his disbursements "for the last quarter." LS in DNA, 1, M-281.

To Joseph McMinn, Murfreesboro, Tenn., 8/1. Calhoun asks if McMinn called into service a guard unit for the Cherokee Agency, as a muster roll of a Tenn. militia unit alleges. Advises McMinn to apply in the future to [Andrew] Jackson for a guard from the recruits in the area. Encloses an estimate of pay due to the militia guard and suggests that payment be made out of the fund for carrying the Cherokee treaty into effect, in order to relieve the militia and Army appropriations, "which have been nearly exhausted by the late campaign [against the Seminoles and the Spanish]." FC in DNA, 72, D:198–199.

To [James Monroe, Albemarle County, Va.]

War Dep[artmen]t, 1st August 1818

Mr. [William] Wirt returned last evening from Baltimore; and I this morning put into his hands your letter to him, and the other papers in the case [of the court-martial] of Maj. [Nathaniel Nye] Hall. Mr. Wirt will return to Baltimore in a few days, and, it is probable, as he wishes to take pains in forming his opinion, that he will not report for some time. His first impression is much against the opinion of the Judge Advocate.

Nothing important has occur[r]ed since your departure [from Washington]. The publick, I think, will approve of the course which you have persued [*sic*] in relation to Pansacola [*sic*]. The more I reflect on it, the more thoroughly am I persuaded, that it is the most prudent and correct, which the circumstances of the case admitted. Should any event, claiming your attention take place, I will furnish you with the earliest information. It affords me pleasure to learn that Mrs. Monroe's health is better, and I hope, that the fine country air of Albemarle, will completely reinstate her health.

ALS in NN, James Monroe Papers. NOTE: Earlier documents concerning the trial by court-martial of Maj. Hall can be found by using the index to *The Papers of John C. Calhoun,* Volume II.

From THORNTON [F.] JOHNSON

Barboursville, [Va.,] August 2, [18]18

I have the honour to acknowledge the receipt of my provisional warrant of commission to the Academy of West Point and hereby signify my willingness to accept it. I permit myself to hope that on examination I shall not be substantially deficient in the qualifications necessary to admittance. I avail myself of this opportunity of presenting my sincere thanks for the kindness shown me in conferring the opportunity.

ALS in DNA, 15, 1817, 18.

From Capt. Thomas F. Hunt, Asst. Deputy Quartermaster General, New Orleans, 8/3. Encloses a report of his receipts and expenditures during June and July for normal operations in the 8th Military Department. Since his report as to charges for rations and transportation for prosecution of the Seminole War as of 6/3 (Abs in *The Papers of John C. Calhoun,* 2:326), large additional bills have been received; but he has received neither the $42,000 requested for normal use nor the $32,000 requested on 6/3 for the war costs. CC, with an AEI by Calhoun referring it to [Thomas S. Jesup], in DNA, 43, no. 28.

To THOMAS R. PETERS, Philadelphia

Dept. of War, P[ension] Office, August 3, 1818

I have rec[eive]d yours of 30 of last mo[nth] relative to the claims under the Act granting pensions for Revolutionary services. It is certainly a subject of much regret to me, that a Person for whom I have so much respect, as Judge Peters [probably Richard Peters (1744–1828), Judge of the U.S. District Court of Pa., 1792–1828], should conceive, that the construction, which has been given to the act in question by the War Dept. is illegal & unconstitutional, & it is equally my misfortune, after giving the most deliberate attention to the extract from his opinion, which you put under cover to me, that I see no reason to change my original opinion in relation to the Act. The Act was during the Session of Congress, submitted to the opinion of the Attorney General [William Wirt], who decided, that the reduced circumstances contemplated by the 1st section ought to be proved, & that the oath of the Applicant was the proper proof, in analogy to the proof required in the 2nd Sec[tion] of the Act. This opinion was the foundation of the 1st Regulation; & as many of the Judges did not certify as to the reduced circumstances, the 2nd Regulation of the 27th of May was issued, to express the sense of the Dept. on that point. It was considered in no other light than as explanatory of the first. It would seem reasonable, that if the applicant ought to swear to his reduced circumstances, it was equally proper that the Judge should Certify his belief in the oath, or how is the Sec[retar]y of War to be satisfied that he comes within the provision of the Act as required by the law, before the applicant can be placed on the pension list? To be reduced in circumstances is one of the Provisions of the Act, & which was thought to be so important as to require proof, by the oath of the party, to which, I conceive, that the Judge[']s certificate ought to extend, as well as to the other provisions. Such at least is the view which I take of it & in this construction, I can have no motive, but a faithful discharge of what I conceive to be my duty, which would be much diminished, if the Applicants were permitted to receive their pensions upon the Oath alone prescribed by the 2nd Sec[tion] of the Act. If indeed this was the only requisite, I apprehend the door would be opened wide to fraud. Even with all the Guards & caution which can be exercised, numerous impositions will be committed. I daily receive Letters to that effect. It is estimated that from fifteen to twenty thousand applications are already rec[eive]d, & they are coming in, without much abatement. It was estimated in debate [in Congress], that $200,000 annually would be more than sufficient to meet the disbursements under the Act; but if those ideas were permitted to govern me, which some supposed ought [to govern] (exempting me, it is certain, from much trouble & responsibility), $200,000 annually would not meet the demand. In this state of things, caution is certainly my duty. If my construction has been too rigid, Congress can correct it, but an unguarded construction once admitted, it is placed beyond even its power to control. I do trust that Judge Peters, for whom I have a great respect, will, upon farther [*sic*] consideration, certify his belief to the reduced circumstances of the applicants. If he is satisfied with their oath in that particular, no farther [*sic*] proof is necessary; if not, such proof as is calculated to satisfy him, ought to be produced by the applicants. To prescribe poverty as one of the conditions to obtain the Pension, was no act of mine, & it can afford me no pleasure to enforce that which may be deemed odious. But I acted according to the best of my Judgement, & was not afraid to do what, I thought to be my duty.

The rule laid down by Mr. [George] Boyd in my absence, that, when the name of the Applicant is not found on the [muster] Rolls proof of his service ought to be established by two witnesses, attracted my attention as soon as I returned [from my trip of May–July, 1818], & I directed him to require additional proof only when there was reason to apprehend, that the application was not well founded. His zeal to guard against abuses, was no doubt the cause of the rule, which gave him so much additional trouble, & I think you must see, that, when there is no record or means of checking impositions, the fear of its being extensively practiced is not without probable foundation. The Judge [Peters] objects that the seal of the court should be required, but how was the handwriting of so many persons, scattered over this extensive Country, to be known at the [War] Department? It would be very far from my wish to give any additional trouble to those, for whose benefit the Act was intended; but I am sure that the patriot Revolutionary Soldier, would be the last to desire to see fraud & imposition practiced on the Government. The Judge considers the regulations as prescribing the manner in which he ought to perform his duty. I certainly do not consider it in that light. The regulations were prescribed for the applicants, & for the satisfaction of the Sec[retar]y of War as directed by the Act, & it was not anticipated, that it would give the Judges much additional trouble. If he is satisfied with the oath of the party, he merely certifies with the other facts, to his reduced circumstances. As to the cases which you have deposited, if the Judge still continues to refuse to furnish the certificate required by the regulations, other satisfactory proof must be furnished by them, to be Judged of when it is received by the Dept. The rule conceived to be the most convenient to the applicants, and satisfactory to the Dept., was prescribed, but if that cannot be complied with, the applicants ought not to suffer by it. In such cases, the best proof which can be furnished, will be received. Except in this instance, I believe the regulations have been universally complied with. I enclose a Letter of Mr. [James L.] Edwards of the Pens[io]n Office in relation to the six [?] cases mentioned by you. It is impossible to reply to the numerous enquiries made to the Office by applicants. The time of the Office would be totally spent in correspondence, if attempted.

FC in DNA, 91, 5:292–297.

From Ezra Younglove, Detroit, 8/3. Seeks redress for the disabling wounds inflicted upon him, a citizen then in the Indian service, at Green Bay on 10/2/1816 by Col. Talbot Chambers and Capt. [John] O'Fallon, both of the Rifle Regiment, because Younglove protected a Negro employee from punishment by Chambers in a dispute over a pig. Speaks of the assault as "so wanton and signal an outrage on the rights of the citizen, and so daring a violation of the laws." Encloses his sworn deposition dated 8/4 to substantiate his allegations. ALS with En in MiD; ALS with En in DNA, 1, W-211.

From Bvt. Maj. Gen. Edmund P. Gaines, Pensacola, [West Fla.,] 8/4. "Having learned that my brother George S. Gaines is about to resign the office of Agent to the Choctaw trading house, and that Mr. Edward B. Randolph (late paymaster of the fourth Regiment)" and a native of Culpeper County, Va., "recommended for the Creek Factory in 1815, was promised by Mr. [William H.] Crawford, then Secretary of War, the first Agency of the kind that should become vacant," Gaines recommends Randolph. ALS in DNA, 11, 12699.

To Charles J. Ingersoll, [Philadelphia]

War Dep[artmen]t, 4th August 1818

I understood from the President previous to his leaving this [city], he had written to you on the subject of our Florida affairs. The operations of General [Andrew] Jackson, in that quarter, presented some very complicated and delicate questions. It, however, affords much pleasure to observe the acquiescence of publick opinion, in that course, which the Administration thought it its duty to persue [*sic*]. My opinion has been that an open, manly, and honest attachment to truth and justice is the safest basis, on which any administration can place even its popularity. It is delightful to reflect, how, among a people enlightened and experienced upon political subjects, the strait and devoted line of duty becomes to the public functionary that of interest also. When I began, I intended to say nothing but in relation to some private business, but was insensibly drawn away to subjects which were calculated to excite much publick interest.

I am necessitated to give you some trouble on my private account. During my late absence [from this city on a trip to South Carolina], one of my domesticks without any just provocation left me; and as I have not been able to hear of him since, I am inclined to think, that under the seduction and aid of some free blacks near me, he has made for Philadelphia. I have been advised, that the best mode to obtain him is not to advertise, but to employ some active constable, or agent accustomed to that business. As I am unacquainted with any suitable character, the object of this communication, is to ask your aid to obtain one to make an active and diligent search for him. I will make any compensation, which you may deem reasonable. My domestick's Name is Hector, but it is probable he will assume the name of Johnson by which he sometimes calls himself or some other name for concealment. (He left home on the 9th of July last.) He is about 25 years of age, very black, under the middle size, compactly formed; he speaks slow[ly] with a feeble voice, and his upper eye lids hanging very much over his eyes give him a dull and sleepy appearance. Should he be discovered, I do not know the process by which I can secure him, and will expect your instruction in relation to it. I regret to give you this trouble. Accept the assurance of my esteem.

PC in Jameson, ed., *Correspondence*, pp. 136–137. NOTE: Monroe's letter to Ingersoll (to which Calhoun referred in this letter) had been written on 7/24. A PEx of it appears in Bassett, ed., *Correspondence of Andrew Jackson*, 2:383.

To Wilson Lumpkin, [former Representative from Ga., Madison,] Ga., 8/4. Appoints him commissioner to survey the boundaries of the land ceded by the Creeks to the United States by the treaty signed on 1/22. Encloses a copy of the treaty and "a plat of the tract taken from the best map in the possession of the [War] Department." Offers him $8 per day for his service; authorizes him to employ a surveyor @ $5 per day and a marker and the necessary number of chainmen @ $2 each per day. FC in DNA, 72, D:199.

To [Judge JESSE] MOORE, Meadville, Pa.

War Department, Pension Office, August 4, 1818

This day I rec[eive]d your Letter of the 17th July relative to the claim of certain persons for [Revolutionary] pensions under the late Act of Congress. The "pension office," during my absence [of May–July, 1818], prescribed it as a rule that the applicant when he was not to be found on the [muster] rolls, should establish his services by two witnesses. I have directed the rule to be dispensed with, as a general one, & directed that where there is reason to apprehend, that the claim is not well founded, farther [*sic*] & satisfactory proof to be prescribed in each case be required. As you appear to have taken sufficient care, in the cases which have been returned to you by the "pension office," as to the services, no farther [*sic*] proof will be required at that point. As to the reduced circumstances under the Act, it does not extend to indigence, but I conceive no general rule can be satisfactorily prescribed. The conscience of the applicant & the sound discretion of the Judge, can best determine in each case. It is expected in all cases, that the Judge will certify to the reduced circumstances, as well as to the facts, directed to be sworn to, by the Act. You will be so good as to extend, in the cases returned to you, your Certificate to the reduced circumstances. If you deem the oath of the applicant in each case satisfactory as to his reduced circumstances, you will certify on the oath alone, but if not you will of course require other proof.

FC in DNA, 91, 5:307–308; FC in DNA, 3, 10:110.

From David A. Ogden, [Representative from N.Y.,] Madrid, [N.Y.,] 8/4. Acknowledges Calhoun's letter to him of 5/14 (PC in *The Papers of John C. Calhoun,* 2:293). Reports that the Iroquois are opposed, probably unalterably, to emigration to the Arkansas River area but might accept an offer of a chance to emigrate to the Fox River area, west of Lake Michigan. LS in DNA, 1, O-13.

From Col. Decius Wadsworth, [Ordnance Office, Washington,] 8/4. [David] Bussard has presented satisfactory security worth $20,000 [under his contract for the production of gunpowder] and should receive the contractual advance of $10,000. ALS with En in DNA, 1, W-157; FC in DNA, 32, 2:86.

To Benjamin Darlington, W[illiam] B. Foster, William Hill, William McCandless, James [W.] Riddle, Dr. Hanson Catlett, and James Gibson, Pittsburgh, 8/5. Transmits to each of these merchants and government employees an extract from a letter "received from a respectable source [Abner Lacock]" and asks each to state all that he knows about the charges thus brought against Maj. [Abram R.] Woolley. "The character of an officer of the Army, as well as the interest of the public, demands [*sic*] an investigation into such allegations." FC in DNA, 3, 10:111.

To Rufus King, [Senator from N.Y.,] Jamaica (Long Island), N.Y.

War Dep[artmen]t, 5 Aug[us]t 1818

I have decided to purchase the Maps and Charts which you have offered to the Department of War.

Gen[era]l [Joseph G.] Swift will communicate to you the arrangements to be made for the payment and delivery.

LS in NHi; FC in DNA, 3, 10:111. Note: For further information about these maps and a recommendation that they be purchased, see the letter of 4/15 from Joseph G. Swift (Abs in *The Papers of John C. Calhoun,* 2:248). The surname in the second paragraph of the LS of this letter appears clearly to be "Smith," but in the FC this surname was quite plainly written "Swift," which is undoubtedly correct.

From D[ecius] Wadsworth, 8/5. Mistaken figures were written into the contract of Wirt & Clark for the production of cannon and shot. Deviation from it is justified in the name of equity, and Wadsworth itemizes fair prices for eight articles. He approves their claim for $772 in damages because of changes in specifications dictated by the Ordnance Office since their contract was signed. FC in DNA, 32, 2:86–87.

To [Benjamin W. Crowninshield, Secretary of the Navy,] 8/6. "The Secretary of War submits to the Secretary of the Navy, the report of Brig. Gen. [Joseph G.] Swift, recommending the mode to be adopted to accomplish the survey of the coast." CC in DLC, Gideon Welles Papers, 18820.

From Capt. James Gadsden, Aide-de-Camp, Headquarters, Southern Division, Nashville, 8/6. "By comparing the abstracts of letters received by the War Dept. since February last from Major Gen. A[ndrew] Jackson, with his letter book, I find that some of his most important communications have miscarried. Among which is his detailed report of operations up to the 5th of May, containing his correspondence with the Governor of St. Marks & accompanied with the original proceedings of the Court[-martial] against [Alexander] A[r]buthnot & [Robert C.] Armbrister [*sic*], as well as the most important papers captured on board of the Schooner Chance. Copies of all these papers are now preparing & will be forwarded you as early as practicable." ALS in DNA, 1, G-89.

From B[enjamin] Parke, [former Delegate from Ind. Territory,] Vincennes, [Ind.,] 8/6. Negotiations with the Indians for the purchase of the White River country are to begin on 9/10. But $15,000 or $20,000 in specie should be available, not merely the $6,000 authorized; either larger amount would be cheap, since four or five million acres of land "superior to any north west of the River Ohio" are at stake. Parke hopes that Calhoun will write to him at Piqua, O., promptly, so that the reply can be received when Parke will be traveling to St. Marys for the treaty negotiations. He has expected in vain answers to his letters of 6/25 and 7/1 (see *The Papers of John C. Calhoun*, 2:355–356, 429) and still has the same, unfavorable opinion of [Caleb] Lowndes: "The mischief he will do the Indian Department is incalculable." ALS in DNA, 1, P-151.

From [Bvt. Brig. Gen.] J[oseph] G. Swift, [Chief Engineer,] 8/6. As ordered, he reports that the fishery at Billingsport on the Delaware River has produced a gross income of $1,000 to $5,000 per year and that it might rent for as much as $1,000 annually. LS in DNA, 1, S-169.

From Robert Taylor, Norfolk, 8/6. As owner of some land adjacent to Fort Norfolk that was fortified by [Moses] Porter during the War of 1812, Taylor asks Calhoun to order men at that fort to discontinue using that land and to restore it to its former condition, lest Taylor's indulgence in accommodating the Army should establish in it a right to ownership of the land. ALS in DNA, 1, T-95.

From Joseph Wheaton, Washington, 8/6. Reviews the complications of his service as a Quartermaster officer in field operations in Va. and in the Northwest about 1813 that have left his accounts unsettled, although he thinks they are now nearly settled, partly because he has through a couple of years "devoted my whole time to the settlement of my public accounts." Asks that his pay and emoluments be extended to 10/31/1817 and that he be given an advance, in order that he may repay a debt. ALS in DNA, 1, W-183.

To John M. McCalla, Lexington, Ky., 8/7. Answering his letter of 7/26 (Abs in *The Papers of John C. Calhoun,* 2:427), states that, in accordance with Army regulations governing Infantry field exercises and maneuvers, the "Battalion companies will take precedence according to the rank of the Captains." FC in DNA, 3, 10:111.

From Brig. Gen. James Miller, Temple, N.H., 8/7. Acknowledges Calhoun's letter of 7/23 (Abs in *The Papers of John C. Calhoun,* 2:419) and appreciates the approbation. Expects to owe and to pay an indebtedness to the U.S., even after allowance shall have been made for his recent services in his mission to New Brunswick. Explains that [1st] Lt. [Charles Spencer] Merchant is to reach an agreement as to the rental of the magazine at Eastport. ALS in DNA, 1, M-274.

To James Monroe, [Albemarle County, Va.]

War Dep[artmen]t, 7th August 1818

I enclose the proceedings of the court martial in the case of Joseph [*surname illegible*]; and feeling, that you would not feel disposed in time of peace to inflict capital punishment for disertion [*sic*], I have directed the Adjutant & Insp[ecto]r General [Daniel Parker] to inclose the form of the sentence of approval and remission of the punishment [for your signature].

Disertions [*sic*] have increased so much of late, that I have judge[d] it proper to increase the reward for apprehending a deserter from $10 to $30. I hope it will have some effect in checking it; but am inclined to think that nothing very effectual can be done without the aid of Congress.

The Gov[erno]r of Georgia [William Rabun] has expressed his anxiety to have the line under the late Creek treaty run, and I have sent a commission to Mr. [Wilson] Lumpkin, formerly a member of Congress from Georgia, for that purpose.

The Spanish Minister [in Washington, Don Onís,] has, as yet, given no answer to Mr. [John Quincy] Adam[s]'s letter to him; and I have concluded, that if none is received by Monday next, to issue the orders [to Edmund P. Gaines and Andrew Jackson for the return of Pensacola and St. Marks to the Spanish] without waiting any longer.

There is every reason to believe that the course persued [*sic*] by the Administration will meet with the full approbation of the country. Even [newspaper editor William] Duane appears to be at a loss how to object to it.

Cap[tain James] Gadsden has not yet arrived [with the news expected from Andrew Jackson]; and I am at a loss how to account for his delay. I will direct him, when he arrives, to take [the route via] your residence on his return.

My family have been unwell, but [is] now much better. I trust Mrs. Monroe's health is perfectly restored. Accept the assurance of my respect & esteem.

ALS in NN, James Monroe Papers.

To Bvt. Brig. Gen. Moses Porter, Boston, 8/7. Answering his letter of 7/30 (Abs in *The Papers of John C. Calhoun,* 2:443), encloses a copy of an instruction given to Robert Brent governing the pay of brevet officers. "This instruction was framed under the most mature examination of the law" by President [James Monroe] and Calhoun. If Porter's command equals a brigade, then he is entitled to his brevet pay. Calhoun's predecessor had decided that, when a reduction in the command of a Bvt. Brig. Gen. reduces him to lineal rank, he is entitled to neither brevet pay nor an aide-de-camp. FC in DNA, 3, 10:111.

From C[AESAR] A[UGUSTUS] RODNEY, [former Representative from Del.]

Wilmington, [Del.,] Aug. 7th 1818

Permit me to solicit the favor of a Cadet's warrant for a nephew of Mrs. Rodney's, the son of Major Sam[ue]l S. Voorhees lately of Philad[elphi]a who went last fall to the Alabama [Territory]. Major Voorhees had resided in Philad[elphi]a for a number [of] years before his departure for the Territory of Alabama. His son Sillsby Voorhees is now of the proper age for the military school. He is at present with his father.

I had no opportunity of expressing to you the favorable opinion I had formed of Midshipman [James Edward] Calhoun [*or* Colhoun] from his gentlemanly deportment & exemplary conduct on board the *Congress*. I have no doubt, but that he will make a distinguished officer.

ALS in DNA, 15, 1818, 98. NOTE: Rodney had been one of the three commissioners who were sent by President James Monroe to South America to investigate whether or not the U.S. should give formal recognition to the Latin-American republics. The commissioners had begun their journey on 12/4/1817 aboard the *Congress,* with James Edward Colhoun, one of John C. Calhoun's cousins and brothers-in-law, as a member of her crew. *The Papers of John C. Calhoun,* 1:12 and 433; 2:38.

C[HRISTOPHER] VANDEVENTER to J[OSEPH] G. SWIFT

Georgetown, [D.C.,] Aug[us]t 7th 1818

Captain Elijah Mix request[s] me to state that he is prepared to enter upon the execution of the contract which he has made with the Engineer Department to deliver stone at Old Point Comfort, and wishes an advance of ten Thousand dollars for that purpose.

ALS in DNA, 1, V-13. NOTE: An AES by Swift dated 8/8 certifies that the advance was "Approved."

From Lt. Col. W[illiam] A. Trimble, Washington, 8/7. Encloses and explains an estimate, compiled by him in 1817, of the population of about 45 bands of Indians, representing half as many distinct tribes, residing along the Red River and in the country between it and the Rio del Norte; his estimate totals about 13,500 warriors and 46,500 people, of whom Comanches constitute a majority; other tribes represented include the Apalaches, Pascagoulas, Choctaws, Chickasaws, Cherokees, and Caddos. Proposes drawing a line from the Red River to the Gulf of Mexico, perhaps at the mouth of the Sabine River, beyond which the Indians' game ranges should be protected from white settlements. Smallpox has decreased the Indian population in the Southwest severely; the Comanches think they lost 4,000 persons "in 1816 from this horrible disease." "The vaccine inoculation might be introduced among them at a trifling expense. Such a course is dictated by humanity." LS with En in DNA, 1, T-93; PC in Morse, *A Report . . . on Indian Affairs,* pp. 256–260.

From Decius Wadsworth, 8/7. Alexander McRae is under contract to produce 2,000 stands of small arms annually for five years, has already received an advance of $10,000, and asks another $30,000 before delivering a single gun. Wadsworth fears that granting this request would be taken as a precedent by rival contractors, considers himself not authorized to grant an advance beyond the contractual terms, and refers the issue to Calhoun for decision. ALS in DNA, 1, W-48; FC in DNA, 32, 2:87–88.

To William H. Crawford, Secretary of the Treasury

War Dep[artmen]t, 8 Aug[us]t 1818

Be pleased to place in the hands of the Treasurer of the United States, [Thomas Tudor Tucker,] the sum of thirteen hundred and fifty thousand, two hundred and fifty-one dollars and thirty-three cents, on account of the following appropriations, namely,

Pay of the Army	250,000.00
Subsistence	300,000.00
Clothing	250,000.00
Ordnance	74,200.00
Cannon & Shot	70,300.00
Arsenal at Watertown [Mass.]	39,000.00
Arsenal near Augusta [Ga.]	40,000.00
Armories	150,000.00
Contingencies	60,000.00
Q[uarte]r Mas[te]r[']s Department	116,751.33
D[olla]rs	1,350,251.33

FC in DNA, 171, 1:302–303.

From Bvt. Maj. Gen. Edmund P. Gaines, Pensacola, 8/8. He reports possibilities for the defense of that area. LS in DNA, 1, G-103; draft in DNA, 11, 12560.

To John L. Kerr, Easton, Md., 8/8. "Upon our examination of the appropriation to pay the States such balances as may be found due them from the U[nited] States on settlement [of their claims for federal aid to their militias], I find I cannot advance to you more than $40,000 on account of the claim of the State of Maryland. That amount will be paid to any person properly authorized to receive it." FC in DNA, 3, 10:112.

From Pleasant M. Miller

Knoxville, August 8th 1818

My son [Albert S. Miller] rec[eive]d your letter of appointment [as a Cadet] yesterday for which I thank you. Inclosed is his acceptance. It will not be in my power to give him a conveyance [toward West Point] untill William [G.] Blount [of Knoxville, Representative from Tenn.,] comes on this fall [that is, travels to Washington to attend the session of Congress that will open on 11/16]. My son is just fifteen years old, too young I think, to be sent so far without a friend or relative; from Washington the conveyance will be more convenient. If these reasons should be considered insufficient [for his reporting at the Military Academy later than the stipulated date], I would be glad to be informed. Otherwise no answer will be necessary.

ALS in DNA, 15, 1818, 28. NOTE: Albert S. Miller's enclosed ALS of acceptance dated 8/15 and an ALS of recommendation dated 4/14 from W[illiam] G. Blount, each addressed to Calhoun, are both in the same file.

To Thomas Morris, Marshal of N.Y., [New York City,] 8/8. "I have received your letter of the 4th instant [ALS in DNA, 1, M-271, in reply to Calhoun's of 7/27 (Abs in *The Papers of John C. Calhoun*, 2:429)]. The advance which you request from the Treasury cannot be made. I therefore advise that the fines [imposed by the court-martial for N.Y. militia delinquents] be collected as rapidly as practicable, and payment be made to the officers out of the first monies collected. The Judge Advocates have been directed to prepare the warrants for you. Under the peculiar circumstances of Anthony Clemson's case, I consent, in this instance only, and with [some] degree of reluctance, that he be released, and you will release him accordingly." FC in DNA, 3, 10:112.

From Decius Wadsworth, 8/8. Urges strongly, on several grounds, against granting Alexander McRae's request for an excessive advance under his contract for the manufacture of small arms; feels that McRae should attempt only to produce bayonets, ramrods, and musket barrels "in aid of the Armory" at Harpers Ferry, which would enable the government to get something for funds already advanced. ALS in DNA, 1, W-165; FC in DNA, 32, 2:90–91.

From Maj. Gen. Andrew Jackson, Nashville, 8/9. Encloses copies of "my detailed report of operations in the Seminole nation up to the 5th of May," of his correspondence to that date with Spanish officials in Pensacola and St. Marks, and of the proceedings of the court-martial against [Alexander] Arbuthnot and [Robert Christy] Ambrister. "These documents, carefully envelloped [*sic*], were confided to the care of Major [John M.] Davis, Assist[ant] Inspector General, to be deposited in some post office in Georgia for conveyance to Washington. How a package of that size endorsed public service &c. should have miscarried is to me mysterious. I have written to Major Davis on the subject, requesting an investigation into the affair." Recommends Col. George Gibson and Dr. J[ames] C. Bronaugh for appointment as Quartermaster General and Surgeon General, respectively, "as contemplated under the new arrangement of that part of the General Staff" enacted in 4/1818, this recommendation being a reiteration of one that was lost with the package of dispatches entrusted to Maj. Davis. LS in DNA, 1, J-228.

From Robert Smith, Pittsburgh, 8/9. Describes and submits a drawing of his design for cannon carriages. ALS with Ens in DNA, 35, In-2-2, with an AES by Calhoun: "Referred to the Ordnance Dept."

From [Col.] John E. Wool, Inspector General of the Northern Division, Brownville, [N.Y.,] 8/9. Recommends [1st] Lt. Walter Bicker, [Jr.,] and [1st] Lt. Thomas Hunt for appointments as "Assistant Commissary of Provisions [Subsistence]." ALS in DNA, 11, 11904.

From John E. Wool, Brownville, [N.Y.,] 8/9. For two and a half months he has been inspecting the troops in the 5th Military Department; tomorrow he will begin an inspection tour of the 1st, 2nd, and 3rd. [Samuel A.] Storrow has some qualifications for other positions but lacks sufficient military knowledge to serve acceptably as Adjutant General in the Northern Division; Wool cannot explain why [Jacob] Brown recommended Storrow. ALS in DNA, 1, W-231.

To Maj. Loring Austin, Boston, 8/10. "Your letter of the 29th ult[im]o is received. I have received from the plaintiffs in the action against you, certain propositions for a compromise under the act of Congress of the last session, which I shall accept. If adhered to on their part, the compromise will be effected, and you will be released under the act, from all demands for costs and damages." FC in DNA, 3, 10:112.

From James Gadsden, Nashville, 8/10. "I am directed by General [Andrew] Jackson to enclose you a copy of his letter to Major General [Edmund P.] Gaines of the 7th August [CCEx in DNA, 1,

J-116, instructing Gaines how to capture St. Augustine from the Spanish if that should prove to be necessary], accompanied with copies" of two relevant letters written in 6/1818, one being to Jackson on 6/16 and the other from Maj. [David Emanuel] Twiggs to Gaines on 6/25. ALS in NN, James Monroe Papers.

From Andrew Jackson, Nashville, 8/10. His aide-de-camp, Capt. [James] Gadsden, will deliver in person this letter and others, including copies of important letters and documents of 5/5 that have been lost in the mails. Jackson recommends Gadsden to succeed, as Inspector Gen. in the Southern Division, Col. A[rthur] P. Hayne, who has gone to Washington to settle his accounts and to resign. Jackson fears a revival of the Seminoles' attacks upon the Southern frontier, urges consideration of plans for effective border fortifications, and pleads for never surrendering the posts [within Spanish Fla.] that his forces conquered. If these posts are improperly surrendered, he argues, "our frontier will be exposed to all the scenes of blood & massacre heretofore experienced & to regain them will cost us much blood & treasure in the event of war." LS in DNA, 1, J-233; PEx in *American State Papers: Military Affairs,* 1:744–745. (Compare Jackson's letter of 8/10 to James Monroe: PC in Bassett, ed., *Correspondence,* 2:385–387. See also, herein, Calhoun's reply to Jackson on 9/8.)

From John McKee, Choctaw Agency, 8/10. Encloses his bond, executed as required [because of his reappointment on 4/22 as an Indian Agent (see *The Papers of John C. Calhoun,* 2:255)]. ALS in DNA, 1, M-47.

From Return J. Meigs, Cherokee Agency, 8/10. Announces that he has issued drafts payable to John & Lewis Ross & Co. for $2,137 to cover the ordinary expenses of the Cherokee Agency and for $1,055 for the expenses of Cherokee emigration to the Arkansas, each during the April–June quarter. FC with En in DNA, 75 (M-208:7).

To DAVID A. OGDEN, [Representative from N.Y.,] Madrid, N.Y.

Department of War, 10th August, 1818

I have been so much engaged since my return from the South, that I have not been able 'till to day [*sic*] to take up the cases which were referred to this department by an act of the last session of Congress, for a compromise and settlement of the cases referred to in it. I have concluded to accept of the offer which you have made for a compromise, with the exception of the costs in the suits against William Mead and General [Zebulon M.] Pike. As there has been no recovery in the suits against them, I do not think it would be correct to comprehend them in the adjustment. The compromise then will be on the following terms, if acceded to by you. The U[nited] States to pay $4,500 and the taxes costs, in the cases of Austin, Wells, and Richards—amounting in the first to $1,323.30, in the next to $772.92, and in the last to $1,797.30. The plaintiffs on their part to give receipts in full in the above cases, and a relinquishment of all right of action growing out of the original transaction.

Mr. [George ?] Graham has left the City, and will not return for some months, which renders it necessary for me to address this letter to you.

FC in DNA, 3, 10:113.

Regulations Governing Allowances to Officers

Department of War, 10th August, 1818

The Quarter Master General [Thomas S. Jesup] will be allowed quarters and fuel agreeably to his rank, and he will, on requisition, furnish the same to the Commissary General [of Subsistence, George Gibson], and the Chief of the Ordnance Department, [Decius Wadsworth,] at Washington, agreeably to their respective ranks, and to the Surgeon General, [Dr. Joseph Lovell,] the same that was allowed to the Physician and Surgeon General, under former regulations.

The reason for the allowance to the Chief of the Engineers [Joseph G. Swift] and the Adjutant and Inspector General, [Daniel Parker,] in lieu of quarters, no longer existing, since the establishment of the Quarter Master's department, at the termination of the present quarter such allowance will cease, and the Q[uarte]r M[aste]r Gen[era]l will, on requisition, furnish them with fuel and quarters, agreeably to their respective rank.

Officers detailed to perform duties in the office of Chief Engineer, Q[uarte]r M[aste]r Gen[era]l, Adj[utan]t and Insp[ecto]r

Gen[era]l, or the Chief of the Ordnance, will be allowed, while performing such duties, at the rate of $1.25 per diem, in addition to their usual pay and emoluments. The Q[uarte]r M[aste]r General will allow officers so detailed, fuel and quarters agreeably to their respective ranks.

If the Q[uarte]r M[aste]r Gen[era]l cannot furnish the above officers with public quarters, he will allow them at the rate of $12 per month for each room to which they are entitled.

FC in DNA, 3, 10:113–114; CC and CCEx in DNA, 111, 134–135; PEx in House Report No. 61, 16th Cong., 1st Sess.; PEx's in *American State Papers: Military Affairs,* 2:304, 4:380, 6:92. NOTE: A marginal note beside the FC indicates that copies of this regulation were sent to [George Gibson, Thomas S. Jesup, Daniel Parker, Joseph G. Swift, Decius Wadsworth,] and "to officers detailed to do duty in these offices."

From [Bvt. Maj. Gen.] Winfield Scott, Elizabethtown, N.J., 8/10. Recommends [Charles J.] Nourse, the Asst. Adjutant Gen. and senior Maj. in staff service in the Northern Division, to succeed [Thomas S.] Jesup as Adjutant Gen. in that Division. ALS in DNA, 11, 12617.

From [Joseph G. Swift,] 8/10. "Upon enquiry I find that the duties of Major [Samuel] Cooper, the Agent of Fortifications in New York Harbour, require that he should have a Clerk to assist him in the discharge of those duties. I therefore recommend that he be permitted to employ one. I also recommend that $20,000 be remitted to Major Cooper on account of Fortifications in New York Harbour." FC in DNA, 21, 1:33.

J[oseph] G. Swift to Lt. W[illiam] G[ibbs] McNeill, Newark, N.J., 8/10. "Your application & the recommendation of Major [John J.] Abert, for your transfer [from the Artillery] to the Topographical Eng[ineers] were rec[eive]d too late to be of any immediate benefit to you; the vacancy in the [Engineers] Corps was about being filled when your letter arr[ive]d. It is now filled." LS in DNA, 25, no. 97.

From Decius Wadsworth, 8/10. Reviews the history since 1815 of Peter Townsend's contracts for the production of cannon, advances made to him totaling $45,000, and his small, tardy deliveries of principally the most profitable items only. Urges that his request for further advances be denied, his contract considered cancelled because he violated it, and his obligation of about $24,500 or $30,000 recovered promptly. ALS in DNA, 1, W-166; FC in DNA, 32, 2:91–93.

From D[ecius] Wadsworth, 8/10. As Calhoun has suggested, Wadsworth submits observations to be considered by the Board of Officers that is to "deliberate on the Patterns of Cannon &c."; reviews specifications as to most ordnance items and their use. FC in DNA, 32, 2:93–97.

From William Clark, St. Louis, 8/11. By a letter from Lord Selkirk, [the British official,] "which has fallen into my hands," it has been learned that John Tanner, an American, is a prisoner with the Indians of Upper Canada. Tanner's brother "leaves this place in a few days in pursuit of him" and wants the protection and aid of the government in effecting his release. Toward this end Clark has written to both the commanding officer and the Indian Agent at Mackinac, [Mich. Territory,] to solicit their aid. ALS in DNA, 1, C-220.

From George Warren Cross, Providence, R.I., 8/11. Asks "your friendly interference" in behalf of [Peter] Trezevant's application for the appointment of his son, Peter [Dunlop] Trezevant, as a Cadet. Explains: "I am among those who are partially exiled from Charleston [S.C.,] by the scourge of the last summer, and have brought my family to this place to spend their summer and fall—pleasantly—but I find the heat infinitely greater here than it is with us and nothing but the cool nights make[s] the climate at this time tolerable." Adds: "Accept my best wishes for your health and prosperity." Signs himself: "Y[ou]r friend." ALS in DNA, 15, 1818, 100.

To Andrew Jackson, [Nashville]

Department of War, 11th August 1818

By a resolution of the House of Representatives of the 4th of April, 1818, I am directed among other things to report to them at the next session a statement of the roads which have been commenced under the orders or direction of the War Department, the progress which has been made, and the means and prospect of their completion.

In order that I may comply with the resolution, you will report to this department before the meeting of Congress in November next, what progress has been made in opening the road from Tennessee river to New Orleans and Mobile, under the order of the 8th March, 1818, and what are the prospects of completing it.

I send enclosed an act of Congress of the 27th April, 1806, and a copy of the 2d section of an act of the 27th March, 1818. Congress has by the two acts appropriated the sum of $10,000 towards the road from Columbia to Madisonville. On examination, I do not find that any expenditure has been made towards this road; and it appears to me that the military road will, in part, supersede the road contemplated by the act. You will, as early as practicable, take such steps as you may judge most expedient to apply the sum to the object for which it was intended. It is impossible for me to give any precise instruction in relation to the subject. If, however, the sum should not be sufficient, which from the length of the road contemplated, even should it fall into the military road, appears probable, I should think that as far as the sum will go the road ought to be rendered good. It will be better to do a little well than to diffuse the sum, without much effect, over the whole extent. These points, however, I submit to your judgment.

FC in DNA, 3, 10:114–115, with notations that letters similar to the first two paragraphs were sent to D[avid] B. Mitchell as to the road from Fort Hawkins to Fort Stoddert, with an additional inquiry whether or not the appropriation of $10,000 would be adequate and, if not, how much more would be needed; to [Alexander] Macomb as to progress in opening the roads from Detroit to St. Marys and to the Connecticut Reserve and as to the road from the [Indian] reservation on the Sandusky [River] to the settled parts of Ohio south of that point under the order of the 24th of May, 1818; and to [Jacob] Brown as to the road from Sackets Harbor through Chateaugay County, [N.Y.,] under the order of 1817. A CC of the letter to Brown is in MHi.

From D[avid] B. Mitchell, Creek Agency, 8/11. To counterbalance exaggerations and misrepresentations embodied in [Andrew] Jackson's accusations concerning the purchase by Mitchell's son of cattle that Jackson had intended to become a gift to the friendly Creeks, Mitchell encloses copies of Jackson's letter of 7/8 to him and of his reply of 8/10. The latter alleges that Creek warriors returning from the Seminole campaign "became so Impatient that they would rather abandon the Cattle than be detained to drive them into the[ir] nation." LS with Ens in DNA, 1, M-280.

From Decius Wadsworth, 8/11. Reports that Peter Townsend of N.Y. has proved to be unreliable in fulfilling his contract for the manufacture of cannon. Praises the firm of Wirt & Clark for having delivered promptly 300 tons of cannon and shells of superior quality; to counterbalance shortages in deliveries made by Townsend, proposes to order another 300 tons from Wirt & Clark; recommends an advance of $15,000 to that firm. Additional ordnance will be needed for the large fortifications beside the Chesapeake Bay; Wadsworth suggests that it be produced by Bellona Foundry near Richmond, which has the advantages of proximity and of the proprietors' proved willingness to make every effort to give satisfaction. ALS in DNA, 1, W-167; FC in DNA, 32, 2:97–98; PC in *American State Papers: Military Affairs,* 7:514.

From D[ecius] Wadsworth, 8/11. Because a further advance of $15,000 to Alexander McRae has been approved to assist him toward fulfillment of his contract for manufacturing small arms, Wadsworth requests that a warrant for that amount shall be issued to McRae. FC in DNA, 32, 2:98.

From G[EORGE] BOYD

Washington, Aug[us]t 12th 1818

I am sorry that any inconvenience has arisen to your Dep[artmen]t in consequence of the delay in appointing a Chief to the Bureau of Pensions, during my absence. But from the ["definitive" *canceled*] conversation which took place between us on the 24th ultimo, it was believed that a more formal resignation would neither be expected or required. I now Sir, have the honor to tender to you my resignation of the office in question, and to remain with great consideration & respect, Your most obedient & very Humble Servant, G: Boyd.

ALS in WHi, George Boyd Papers.

From Jacob Brown, Plattsburg, [N.Y.,] 8/12. Acknowledges Calhoun's letter of 7/29 (PC in *The Papers of John C. Calhoun*, 2:435–436) concerning deserters. They usually live in remote places within the U.S., hoping thus to prevent capture. By withholding pay and by granting increased rewards for captures, the War Department can reduce desertions more effectively than legislation can. "Laxity of discipline & idleness . . . are most productive of desertion"; daily tasks, "discretely [*sic*] allot[t]ed, are as productive of content as of health & efficiency." Brown plans to transfer the troops from Rouses Point, [N.Y.]. He regrets that the 2nd Regiment cannot complete construction of its barracks because funds are unavailable for lumber and to pay "a few directing Tradesmen." He offers to obtain enough ($2,000) if Calhoun will assure him of reimbursement. LS in DNA, 1, B-278; FC in DLC, Jacob Brown Papers, Letterbooks, 2:114–116; CCEx in DNA, 152, 16A-E6; PEx in Senate Document No. 112, 16th Cong., 2nd Sess.

To Lt. Col. William MacRea, Norfolk, 8/12. "Enclosed I transmit you a copy of a letter from Mr. Robert Taylor of Norfolk. You will give the orders to discontinue the use of the burying ground, and report to this department what will be necessary to be done to place the ground referred to, in its former condition, as requested to be done by Mr. Taylor." FC in DNA, 3, 10:115.

To James B. Reynolds, Clarksville, Tenn., "12th July [8/12]." "On the 4th of February last a commission was enclosed to you [Abs in *The Papers of John C. Calhoun*, 2:120], for Col. [John] Holland, Major [Francis] Murray, and Mr. [Jacob] Thompson, appointing them commissioners to examine the road lately made under the contract with Mr. [Dawsey P.] Hudson, and report the facts concerning the manner of cutting and making the road and the actual state of it. You were also authorized, should those gentlemen decline acting, to name such others as you might think would make a correct report. I will thank you to take the necessary measures to have the report of the commissioners immediately transmitted to the Dept." FC in DNA, 3, 10:114.

From Henry Sherburne, Chickasaw Agency, 8/12. Acknowledges Calhoun's letter of 7/16 (Abs in *The Papers of John C. Calhoun*, 2:389). Will proceed with the repairs to the Agency's buildings when materials arrive from Nashville. "The reduction of my Salary is very unexpected, & the increase thereof I am well convinced is beyond your controul, but such has been & still must be the high rate of the necessaries & comforts of life at this place that nothing will be left me at the end of the year, nay the probability is I shall be in debt; thus circumstanced, I presume no blame will attach to me for the course I have suggested must be pursued, notwithstanding which I consider myself bound in honor & gratitude to remain at my post until Government can make such arrangements as to them may be proper. The annuities for the [Chickasaw] nation that are now on their way I hope will soon arrive, that I may have the aid of Mr. [David Godfrey] Cook's services in the distribution of them, which will be extremely useful to me from his great capability, indefatigable Industry, strict Integrity, & respectable standing among the leading men of the nation who have had an acquaintance with him." ALS in DNA, 1, S-183.

From Decius Wadsworth, 8/12. [2nd] Lt. [John] Hills, recently stationed at Bellona Arsenal, has told Wadsworth this morning that the magazine there will be filled when it receives soon an incoming shipment of about 300 barrels of gunpowder from "the Powder Magazine at Westham," [near Richmond]. It cannot store, therefore, the intended delivery of gunpowder made by Randolph Ross. Hills reports, "contrary to what I had imagined," that all the powder at Bellona is of good quality. ALS in DNA, 1, W-169; FC in DNA, 32, 2:99.

To Maj. A[bram] R. Wo[o]lley, Pittsburg[h], 8/12. "In compliance with the request in your letter of the 3d instant, I enclose you a copy of the contract with Mr. Charles Hegins [*or* Higgins] for supplying with rations the U.S. troops in the State of Pennsylvania from the 1st June 1818 until the 31st May, 1819, inclusive." FC in DNA, 3, 10:115.

To George Boyd, Washington

Department of War, 13th August 1818

You are hereby informed, that you have been, with the approbation of the President of the United States, [James Monroe,] appointed Indian Agent, at Michilimackinac. Should the Senate, at their next session, advise and consent thereto, you will be commissioned accordingly.

Previous to entering upon the duties of your office, it is necessary that you should execute the enclosed bond, with two good and sufficient sureties.

Major William H. Puthuff, the late Agent, will be directed to deliver over to you, on your arrival at Mackinac, all the public property, books and papers belonging to the Agency; together with the instructions which were given to him for his direction in the discharge of the duties of his office, and which you will take for your government.

As your Agency is within the superintendency of His Excell[enc]y Lewis Cass, you will report yourself to him at Detroit, and all your communications must be made thro[ugh] him to this Department.

Your compensation is fixed by law at fourteen hundred dollars per annum.

LS in ICHi; FC in DNA, 72, D:200. NOTE: A marginal note beside the FC reads: "Pay to commence from 1st March, 1819."

From [Thomas S. Jesup], 8/13. Having considered the proposal by E[leazer] W. Ripley that a transport be provided for the use of troops stationed on the coast of the Gulf of Mexico, Jesup approves this suggestion, recommends that the ship be built at New Orleans rather than New York [City], and requests authority to build or to purchase a suitable ship. FC in DNA, 42, 1:33, with a note that Calhoun endorsed and returned the recipient's copy, granting the requested authority.

To JOSEPH KENT, [former Representative from Md.,] near Bladensburg, [Md.]

Department of War, 13th August 1818

I received yesterday your letter relative to the claim of Mr. Henry Yost. I can give no opinion on his claim as it refers itself to the

Navy Department. I have transmitted your letter to that Department.

Accept of the assurance of my Esteem.

FC in DNA, 3, 10:115.

To Caesar A[ugustus] Rodney, [former Representative from Del.,] Wilmington, Del., 8/13. "Your letter of the 9th instant is received. Sillsby Voorhees was appointed a Cadet on the 20th of May last, and a letter of appointment was transmitted to him, in [due] course, of which I now enclose you a duplicate." FC in DNA, 3, 10:115.

From John Jacob Astor, New York [City], 8/14. He recommends the appointment as a Cadet of [William] Whetten, son of John Whetten of that city. LS in DNA, 15, 1818, 105.

To [Edmund P.] Gaines, St. Stephens, Ala. Territory

War Dep[artmen]t, 14 Aug[us]t 1818

The President [James Monroe] having determined to restore St. Marks and Pensacola, with the Bar[r]ancas, to the Spanish authority, I am directed to issue orders to carry this determination into effect.

You will accordingly give the necessary orders to the Commandant at Pensacola to surrender that place with the Bar[r]ancas to any Spanish officer properly authorized to receive them. Authority from the Governor General at the Havannah [Havana, Cuba,] or the Spanish Minister, Don Onís, is considered sufficient; or, in case the Governor, late in possession of West Florida, Don José Masot, should himself appear to receive possession, it will be restored to him on his own authority.

St. Marks will be restored to the late Spanish Commandant, should he appear to receive it, or to any officer having similar authority, as in the case of Pensacola, provided he is accompanied with a Sufficient force to garrison it, so as to prevent the post from being seized by the hostile Indians. Its situation in the midst of the hostile Indians renders this precaution necessary. You, who have an accurate knowledge of the strength of the Indians and of the post, will be able to give precise instructions on this point. It is sufficient that the Spanish force be as considerable as will probably prevent any attempt by the Indians to occupy it.

Publick property will be restored in the condition, (as far as practicable,) in which it was taken possession of.

On evacuating these posts, you will make such arrangements as will be the best calculated to hold the Indians still remaining hostile in check, and to cover our frontier. To effect these objects, it is thought that it will not be necessary to take post to the West of the Apalachicola, within the Florida line, as the Indians in that quarter are said to be very inconsiderable. You will, accordingly, station the troops which may be thought to be necessary for the protection of that portion of the frontier, on our side of the line, unless your impression should be decidedly different from that I have stated, in which event you will take post at any point which you may judge proper within the country possessed by the Indians. On the East of the Apalachicola you may station the troops on either side of the line, as you may judge proper. Fort Gadsden, besides admitting of great facility for supplies, appears to me to be a very commanding position, and ought not to be evacuated. Should you think so, you will retain it and garrison it with a sufficient force.

I trust you will be able to make such a distribution of your command as to afford, with vigilance, effectual protection to the frontier, without resorting to the Militia. It is of great importance, if the Militia can be dispensed with, not to call them out into actual service, as it is harassing to them and exhausting to the Treasury. Protection is the first object, and the second is protection by the regular force.

LS and CC in DNA, 11, 12923; FC in DNA, 3, 10:116; CC in DNA, 202, 15A-E1; 3 CC's in DLC, Andrew Jackson Papers, 7961–7966; PC in House Document No. 14, 15th Cong., 2nd Sess.; PC in *American State Papers: Military Affairs,* 1:696.

To A[NDREW] JACKSON, Nashville

War Dep[artmen]t, 14 Aug[us]t, 1818

I enclose for your information a copy of the orders [that I have written today] to Gen[era]l [Edmund P.] Gaines, growing out of the late decision of the President [James Monroe], relative to St. Marks and Pensacola.

I was directed by the President to wait the reply of the Spanish Minister [Don Onís] to Mr. [John Quincy] Adams's letter to him, which, not being received until the day before yesterday, has caused so great a delay, as to render it necessary to send the orders direct to Gen[era]l Gaines without passing through you.

LS and CC in DLC, Andrew Jackson Papers, 7959; FC in DNA, 3, 10:117; CC in DNA, 202, 15A-E1; PC in House Document No. 14, 15th Cong., 2nd Sess.; PC in *American State Papers: Military Affairs,* 1:734–735.

To [former] Maj. William H. Puthuff, "Late Agent at Mackinac," [Mich. Territory]

Department of War, 14th Aug[us]t 1818

Mr. [Jacob] Tipton, who was appointed to succeed you, on the 22d April last, as Indian Agent at Michilimackinac, having declined, George Boyd, Esq[ui]r[e] of the City of Washington, has received and accepted said appointment. You are, therefore, requested, to deliver to him on his arrival at Mackinac, all the public property, books and papers in your possession, and to give him all the information in your power, in relation to the business of the Agency, as will facilitate the performance of his duties.

FC in DNA, 72, D:200.

From Decius Wadsworth, 8/14. George Boyd owes the U.S. $25,496.61. He should receive a commission on about $17,500 worth of flints and articles for the U.S. armories that he purchased abroad; and he ought to be credited with $2,500 more, half of his anticipated profit, in compensation "for his Time, Expences and Disappointment," from the 10,000 stands of French arms that he did not procure. ALS in DNA, 1, W-177, with an ADS dated 5/15 by Boyd as to his account; FC in DNA, 32, 2:100–101.

To [1st Lt.] Lewis G. De Russy

Department of War, 15th August, 1818

Your letter of the 10th instant, in relation to certain extra charges, has been received. In my letter on the 28th July, I recited the regulation relative to claims for extra services, and tho' it is in the power of the Secretary to depart from regulations established by his own authority, yet it ought to be rarely done. The rule applies to those extra services which require the special sanction of the Secretary; if you can bring yours within any of the established rules (of which I send you a copy) making additional allowance to Engineer officers, it will, on your certificate, be allowed. In fact, if you were not barred by time for extra services of a different character, I cannot think that the bare circumstance of your being detailed to perform duties as Engineer, would entitle you to an extra allowance, unless the duties performed were such, as would also entitle an Engineer officer to receive extra allowance.

FC in DNA, 3, 10:118. NOTE: An Abs of Calhoun's letter of 7/28 to De Russy is in *The Papers of John C. Calhoun,* 2:432.

From Callender Irvine, Commissary General of Purchases, Philadelphia, 8/15. Requests $7,756.23 for payments due to the carpenter, slater, and coppersmith who have reroofed "the Stores at the United States Arsenal" [at Frankford Creek near Philadelphia ?]. "The materials are of the best quality and the work is well done." FC in DNA, 45, 387:127.

From John Melish, Philadelphia, 8/15. Announces that on 8/10 he shipped to Calhoun by water one case containing 10 maps, including six of Ga. and some ordered by William H. Crawford as Secretary of War and by the Engineers and Ordnance Corps. "I trust the different maps will give satisfaction." ALS with Ens in DNA, 1, M-302.

To James Monroe, [Albemarle County, Va.]

War Dept., 15th Aug[us]t 1818

I have received your letter of the 10th Inst.

On Monday last Mr. [John Quincy] Adams received the reply of Don Onís to his letter; and the orders were issued immediately to return the Posts of St. Marks and Pansacola [*sic*], agreeably to your direction. As a very considerable delay had taken place, I did not think it prudent to incur the farther [*sic*] delay of transmitting them through General [Andrew] Jackson but forwarded them directly to General [Edmund P.] Gain[e]s. A copy was furnished General Jackson; and the reason assigned to him, why they were forwarded by the shortest rout[e].

Gov[erno]r [William] Clark and Mr. [Auguste] Chouteau, under the orders issued before I came to the Department, have concluded a treaty of peace and friendship with the several tribes of the Pawnee Indians residing at the head of the La Plat[t]e near the Spaniards. They are a very powerful nation; and their friendship will be of importance to the fur trade of the Missouri and its waters.

Cap[tain James] Gadsden has not arrived [with the expected news from Gen. Jackson]. I cannot account for his delay. The Quartermaster Gen[era]l[']s and the Surgeon General's Departments are now in complete organization; and both officers promise to add greatly to the method & economy of their Departments.

With best wishes for your health & happiness I am . . . .

ALS in NN, James Monroe Papers.

To Thomas Morris, [New York City,] 8/15. "I received your letter of the 11th instant [ALS in DNA, 1, M-275] by this day's mail. It is the wish of the President that the sentences of the court-martial [for N.Y. militia delinquents] should be enforced in all cases, except in those of very great hardship. Should any such occur, and only in such, will you make a report to this department, stating the facts in detail, and your opinion whether they ought to be relieved." FC in DNA, 3, 10:117.

To Randolph Ross, Richmond

Department of War, 15th Aug[us]t 1818

I enclose for your signature the within duplicates [of your contract for the manufacture of gunpowder]; the one you will retain, and the other you will return to the Ordnance Department. [2nd] Lieut[enant John] Hill[s] of the Ordnance [Corps] will be ordered, forthwith, to inspect and receive the powder. I regret, exceedingly, that I cannot make even a small payment. The appropriation for the [purchase of] ordnance will be barely sufficient to meet the expenditures of the year.

It will not be in my power to spare and [*sic*] Ordnance officer in whom full confidence for that purpose could be placed, to inspect and report on your Tennessee Salt Cave. After bestowing further reflection on the subject, I am induced to decline the idea of purchasing, at least, for the present.

FC in DNA, 3, 10:117.

To Henry Sherburne, Chickasaw Agent

Department of War, 15th August, 1818

Your letter of the 27th ultimo, enclosing James Perry's accounts, is received. These accounts have been referred to the 5th Auditor of the Treasury [Stephen Pleasonton], and your draft for the amount will be paid when presented.

The amount of annuities due to the several tribes of Indians in the present year, was placed in the hands of the Superintendent of Indian Trade [Thomas L. McKenney], on 27th Feb[ruar]y last, without any specific instructions, as to their being paid in cash or in goods, and, I presume, in transmitting the Chickasaw annuity of $12,200 in goods, he has pursued the usual course. It is hoped, that the Chiefs of the Chickasaw nation will not be averse to receiving it in that mode, as it was adopted, no doubt, from an impression, that it would be most agreeable to them, and the changing of it now might be attended with some difficulty. All future payments of this annuity, will be made in cash, unless they should expressly wish the contrary.

You will observe from the extract of the treaty herewith enclosed, that of the amount transmitted, $12,000 are to be paid to the Chickasaw nation, and $100 to Gen[era]l William Colbert, and the remaining $100 are to pay the annuity allowed to Chenubbee Mingo, a Chickasaw Chief, by an act of Congress of the 3d of March, 1807.

The annuity due under this treaty for 1817 was remitted to you on the 30th ultimo, together with the amount necessary to carry into effect certain other stipulations contained in said treaty.

FC in DNA, 72, D:201.

From [Bvt. Brig. Gen.] T[homas] A. Smith, Bellefontaine, M[o.] T[erritory], 8/15. Recommends that Capts. [James Simmons] McIntosh of the Rifle Regiment and [Matthew J.] Magee of the Ordnance Corps shall be allowed, as they wish, to exchange positions. LS in DNA, 11, 12914; FC in MoHi, Thomas A. Smith Collection, Letterbooks, 6:55–56.

To JOHN VAUGHAN, Librarian, American Philosophical Society, Philadelphia

War Dept., 15th Aug[us]t 1818

I received your note of the 11th instant, accompanied by the two Military Works, entitled, Considerations sur l'Art de la Guerre, &c.; and Histoire de l'État et des Progres de la Chirurgie Militaire, &c., transmitted by the American Philos[ophical] Society to the War Department. The works are considered a valuable acquisition to the Military Library, attached to the Department.

Should the Department, hereafter, need the assistance which the Society and yourself, individually, have so liberally proffered, it will avail itself of it.

Accept, Sir, the assurance of my respect and regard.

LS in PPAmP; FC in DNA, 3, 10:118. NOTE: Vaughan's letter of transmittal of 8/11 (ALS in DNA, 1, V-14) suggested that these two French treatises, published in 1815 and 1816, might be either retained by the War Department or given to the Library of Congress.

From Dr. Hanson Catlett, Post Surgeon, U.S. Arsenal near Pittsburgh, 8/16, "private." Answering Calhoun's inquiry of 8/5, testifies that he believes that Maj. [Abram R.] Woolley may have profited by receiving government funds at par and paying soldiers and workmen in current money having depreciated value. ALS in DNA, 1, W-200.

From Thomas A. Digges, "Strothers Hotel," Washington, 8/16. Reviews and reasserts his claim for damages done to his fishery adjacent to Fort Warburton. ALS in DNA, 1, D-65.

From Maj. S[tephen] H. Long, Topographical Engineer, Washington, 8/16. "Agreeably to your request I have the honor to lay before you the following estimate of the extent of the U[nited] States Frontier, hastily compiled from the most accurate Maps of the country, and from other sources of intelligence that have come under my observation." He tabulates the mileage of the coastline, including "the meanders of rivers" and the curvatures of bays, etc.; and he also itemizes direct "distances from point to point throughout the whole extent of our Maritime and Inland Frontiers." Some cross-country distances are also reported. "The extent of a line circumscribing the whole of the U[nited] States Territory, not regarding the indentation of Coasts, &c., may be estimated at about 8,000 miles." CC in DNA, 201, 15A-F3; PC in House Document No. 36, 15th Cong., 2nd Sess.; PC in *American State Papers: Military Affairs,* 1:791–792. (Calhoun embodied some of this information in his report to Henry Clay, Speaker of the House of Representatives, dated 12/11, which can be seen herein under that date.)

From [Brig. Gen.] E[dward] Pasteur, Newbern, [N.C.,] 8/16. Retracts his recommendation of James Scott for appointment as a Cadet, because Scott allegedly swore falsely as to his residence in order that he might vote in an election on 8/13 "for a man who has ever been among the most strenuous opposers of our republican government, or at least the late measures of government." Any "man who will pay private favors at the enormous expense of violating his oath in a public capacity, is unfit to be entrusted with a commission in the Army of the United States." ALS in DNA, 15, 1818, 64. (Other documents in this file include letters of application by Scott and of recommendation in 6/1818 and his acceptance on 7/31 of his appointment as a Cadet.)

From J[oseph] A[nderson, First Comptroller,] Treasury Department, 8/17. "The balance of the appropriation for the Survey of the coast of the United States having been paid to the Treasurer of the United States [Thomas Tudor Tucker] as Agent for the War Department, previous to the Settlement of the account of F[erdinand] R[udolf] Hassler, Late Surveyor, of which the enclosed is a Copy, the amount found due to him can now be paid only by that Department & with that view it is respectfully suggested, that a credit be entered in the books of the 3d Auditor of the Treasury, [Peter Hagner,] after which you will have the goodness to issue your warrant in favour of Mr. Hassler for the amount so entered to his credit, and direct that a draft for the same be remitted to him at New Ark [*sic*], New Jersey." FC in DNA, 59, 18:277.

To William Clark, St. Louis

Department of War, 17th August 1818

Your letter to the President [James Monroe] of the 19th April, enclosing the resolution of the Board of Trustees for superintending public schools in St. Louis, has been referred to this Department with instructions, to cause to be designated the public lots in St. Louis, which may be required for military purposes. Major S[tephen] H. Long, of the Topographical Engineers, will be charged with this duty upon his return to Missouri.

FC in DNA, 3, 10:118.

William H. Crawford, Milledgeville, [Ga.,] to James Monroe, [Washington,] 8/17. Crawford arrived at Milledgeville yesterday and will leave today. Is much mortified to learn from the Governor of Ga., [William Rabun,] that he has received no information about a surveying of the boundary between Ga. and East Fla., from the Chattahoochee River to the head of the St. Marys, which the State Department was supposed last fall to authorize Ga. to have run; Crawford still thinks the federal government should make the survey instead, partly because a military force may be needed to protect the surveyors from the Indians. The administration's decision to return the Spanish posts captured in [East and West] Fla. "has, as far as I have been able to understand public opinion from the city [Washington] to this place, been universally approved. The course which has been resolved upon in relation to the general [Andrew Jackson] has not been so universally approbated. The few disputants which have been met with in the former case are either ignorant or passionate. In the latter, they form the mass of intelligence and respectability. It is believed, however, that the course of the Executive will be supported by the great body of the people." ALS in DNA, 1, P-208.

From Benjamin Darlington, Pittsburgh, 8/17. Answering Calhoun's inquiry of 8/5, testifies that he received from Maj. [Abram

R.] Woolley several payments in depreciated money in payment for goods purchased for the Ordnance Department and that general opinion thinks that Woolley has pocketed differentials amounting to "a verry [*sic*] handsome sum." ALS in DNA, 1, W-200.

From William B. Foster, Pittsburgh, 8/17. Answering Calhoun's inquiry of 8/5, testifies at length that he has never known Maj. [Abram R.] Woolley to make private profit from his government position. ALS in DNA, 1, W-200.

To THOMAS L. MCKENNEY, Sup[erintenden]t [of] Ind[ian] Trade, [Georgetown, D.C.]

Department of War, 17 Aug[us]t 1818

I am directed by a resolution of the House of Representatives, to report to them at the next session "a system providing for the abolition of the existing Indian trading establishments of the U[nited] States, and providing for the opening of the trade with the Indians to individuals, under suitable regulations."

To enable me to comply with this resolution, you will report to this Department your opinion of the best mode of bringing to a termination, the existing Indian trading establishment, and such facts and ideas as you may think important, in relation to opening the trade with the Indians to individuals, under suitable regulations.

FC in DNA, 72, D:201–202.

To HENRY SHERBURNE, Chickasaw Agent

Department of War. 17 Aug[us]t 1818

Your letter of the 22d ult[im]o enclosing an account and receipt of David G[odfrey] Cook, and a receipt of Chenubbee Mingo, [a Chickasaw Chief,] has been received.

The arrangements which you have made with Mr. [James] Perry, in relation to the Blacksmith's work for the Agency, are approved.

It is all important to the issue of the negotiation to be entered into with the Chickasaw nation, that the Chiefs should be prepared to give the Commissioners a friendly reception and listen favorably to the propositions which they are instructed to make to them; and, for this purpose, you are requested, on all proper occasions, to use every effort to impress on their minds the great advantages that would mutually result to their nation and the United States, from the proposed exchange of territory.

FC in DNA, 72, D:202.

To Maj. Gen. G[erard] Steddiford, Columbia County, N.Y., 8/17. "Your letter of the 12th instant [ALS in DNA, 1, S-175] is received. It affords me satisfaction to learn, that the Court-martial [for N.Y. militia delinquents, of which you are President,] has so far progressed in the prosecution of its duties, as to authorize the expectation of a speedy termination of its sittings." FC in DNA, 3, 10:119.

From D[ecius] Wadsworth, 8/17. "The Contract with Mess[rs.] Wirt & Clarke [*sic*] requiring an advance of Fifteen thousand dollars, I have to request that a Warrant for that sum may be issued." FC in DNA, 32, 2:101.

From James Gibson, Military Storekeeper, Arsenal near Pittsburgh, 8/18. Answering Calhoun's inquiry of 8/5, testifies that Maj. A[bram R.] Woolley was first accused in 1816 of having "paid the soldiers with depreciated paper" but that Gibson believes Woolley to be innocent. ALS in DNA, 1, W-200.

From Samuel Hodges, Jr., Stoughton, Mass., 8/18. This former 1st Lt. declines reappointment as a 2nd Lt. because he has accepted appointment as U.S. Consul in the Cape Verde Islands, but he discusses two arrangements under which he would be willing to return to the Army. ALS in DNA, 11, 12311.

To Andrew Jackson

War Dep[artmen]t, 18 Aug[us]t 1818

I have received your letter of the 31st of July relative to Quarter Master's funds, the inequality of the present regulation in relation to Forage, and the Treaty proposed to be held with the Chickasaw Indians.

As soon as I was informed of the deficiency in the Quarter Master's funds, immediate steps were taken to remedy it. Through the Quar[te]r Mas[te]r Gen[era]l, [Thomas S. Jesup,] $40,000 has been transmitted to you, and $25,000 to Gen[era]l [Eleazer W.] Ripley, which I trust, with the funds turned over by Major [Milo] Mason to Capt. [Richard J.] Easter will be sufficient. I regret that Col. [George] Gibson did not receive the letter of this Department, informing him of the arrangements which had been made for Quar[te]r Mas[te]r's funds in relation to the Seminole War. It would have avoided much inconvenience and delay.

I am aware that the present regulation in relation to forage falls very unequally on a portion of your [Southern] division, and the subject has occupied my attention, previous to the receipt of your letter. The law itself fixes the price at $8 per month, when it is not drawn in kind, otherwise, there would be no difficulty, as the price would be fixed, (as in justice it ought,) to the places where the officers are stationed. I will endeavour, if possible, to make such a change in the existing regulations as will produce the desired equality.

On the subject of the Chickasaw Annuity I wrote you full[y] under the date of the 30th of July last.

The Agent for the Chickasaws [Henry Sherburne] fears that the last Annuity, being remitted in goods, may not be acceptable to the Indians. I understand from Col. [Thomas L.] McKenney, that he remitted in goods from an assurance that it would be agreeable to them, and as the goods are said to be selected with great care and to be of a good quality, it is probable they will not be unacceptable. Should they not be, however, I have directed the Agent to draw the amount and pay it in money.

LS in PHC; FC in DNA, 72, D:203–204. NOTE: For a PC of Jackson's letter of 7/31 see *The Papers of John C. Calhoun*, 2:446–447; for an Abs of Calhoun's of 7/30 to Jackson see *ibid.*, 2:442.

From William McCandless, Pittsburgh, 8/18. Answering Calhoun's inquiry of 8/5, exonerates Maj. [Abram R.] Woolley of profiteering on any exchange of funds. ALS in DNA, 1, W-200.

From Thomas L. McKenney, Georgetown, [D.C.,] 8/18. "The enclosed letter from Mr. [William] Cocke [to McKenney of 9/29/1817] will not only afford evidence that the Chickasaws wanted merchandize and not money, but also the particular articles which they most needed. An express desire is contained in this letter at the bottom of the third page, to have a very considerable part of the annuity of 1817 & 1818 in articles of a particular kind, which are previously specified. This request on the part of the Indians I took great care to comply with." LS with En in DNA, 1, M-278; FC in DNA, 73, E:112.

To R[ETURN] J. MEIGS, JR., Postmaster General, [Washington]

Department of War, 18 Aug[us]t 1818

By the enclosed copy of a letter from Lieut[enant James] Gadsden, Aid[e] de Camp to Major General Andrew Jackson, you will perceive that important despatches were forwarded by him to this department on the 5th of May last. As they have not been received, I will thank you to take such measures as may lead to the discovery of them, or to the cause of their miscarriage.

FC in DNA, 3, 10:119.

To HENRY SHERBURNE, Chickasaw Agent

Department of War, 18 Aug[us]t 1818

Upon further consideration, I am induced to direct that, should the Chickasaw nation manifest dissatisfaction and an unwillingness to receive the goods which have been sent on by the Superintendent of Indian Trade, for their annuity for the present year, you will give this department immediate information thereof, and you are, in that event, authorized to draw on the Department for the amount of the annuity to be paid in cash.

Mr. [Thomas L.] McKenney, the Superintendent of Indian Trade, will be directed to give instructions as to the manner in which the goods are to be disposed of.

FC in DNA, 72, D:203.

From John Sterrett, Carlisle, [Pa.,] 8/18. Protests that he was informed in 2/1817 that he would be continued as Barrackmaster there, that he served until 10/1817, but that he and his Congressmen have not been able to get more than a pittance of the pay due to him. Begs Calhoun to have his account paid. Otherwise, Sterrett will petition Congress. ALS in DNA, 1, S-182.

To Decius Wadsworth, 8/18. "The Chief of the Ordnance Department will make such communications to be laid before the Board of Officers to be assembled at the seat of government, for the purpose of establishing a system of uniformity in relation to the service of the Artillery, as may serve to explain the views and plans of the Ordnance Department, together with such other observations as may be deemed pertinent to the subject of their deliberations." FC in DNA, 3, 10:119.

From Ab[raha]m Bradley, Jr., [Assistant Postmaster General,] "General Post Office," [Washington,] 8/19. "In the absence of the Postmaster General [Return J. Meigs, Jr.,] I have received your letter to him of yesterday relative to Dispatches sent by Gen. [Andrew] Jackson for your office on the 5th of May last which have not been received. Lieut[enant James] Gadsden has omitted to state by whom and by what route the dispatches were sent. I have directed the postmaster at Nashville to ascertain and make such enquiries as the information he obtains may suggest." ALS in DNA, 1, B-274.

To Paymaster General Robert Brent, 8/19. Notifies Brent that Calhoun approves an arrangement proposed by a Col. Smith and some other officers on 7/13 and 7/18. However, Calhoun insists that [former] Capt. [John] O'Fallon, a proposed substitute Paymaster, cannot be recognized as such by the government and that the regular Paymaster will be held responsible for the substitute's actions. Brent is instructed to notify Smith and the Paymaster to make the necessary arrangements. FC in DNA, 3, 10:120.

To Lewis Cass, Detroit, 8/19. Orders him to ascertain whether any Indians inhabiting the Fox River area or Mich. Territory are willing to grant lands to the Iroquois and to "permit them to reside among them." FC in DNA, 72, D:206; PC in *American State*

Papers: Indian Affairs, 2:176; PC in Carter, ed., *Territorial Papers,* 17:598–599.

To E[dmund] P. Gaines, St. Stephens, Ala. Territory, 8/19. Encloses an extract from the letter written by Secretary of State [John Quincy Adams] to the Spanish Minister [Don Luis de Onís] concerning St. Marks and Pensacola; thus Gaines will "be in possession of the precise ideas communicated to the Spanish Minister in case any difficulty should occur." LS in DNA, 11, 12824; FC in DNA, 3, 10:120; CC in DNA, 202, 15A-E1; PC in *American State Papers: Military Affairs,* 1:696; PC in House Document No. 14, 15th Cong., 2nd Sess.

From Benjamin Homans, [Chief Clerk]

Navy Department, Aug[us]t 19th 1818

On the subject of the letter from Walter R. Kiblee Esq. submitted by you to this Department, I have the honor to state, that the situation of the Naval Service does not at the present time, afford a hope that the young Gentleman to whom Mr. Kiblee alludes could for one or two years obtain the appointment to which he aspires. The Candidates for Warrants as Midshipmen are numerous, exceeding considerably fifteen hundred; many of whom have had the advantage of a Nautical education, and are recommended by the first characters in the Country. Should Mr. Kiblee under these circumstances think proper to forward recommendatory letters, stating the name, age & qualifications of the Applicant, he shall be regularly placed on the List of Candidates and when the service shall require an additional number of Midshipmen, the recommendations of the young Gentleman shall be referred to and receive respectful consideration.

FC in DNA, Record Group 45 (National Historical Publications Commission, special microfilm, Navy Records, Roll 10).

Andrew Jackson, Nashville, to [James] Monroe, "Confidential," 8/19. Answering Monroe's letter to him of 7/19 (PC in *The Papers of John C. Calhoun,* 2:400–405), Jackson argues that he did not transcend his orders and did not act on his own responsibility when he captured Pensacola and other Spanish posts in the two

Floridas. PC in Bassett, ed., *Correspondence,* 2:389–391; PC in *Correspondence between Gen. Andrew Jackson and John C. Calhoun . . . on the Occurrences in the Seminole War,* pp. 39–41.

To Cadet Joseph D. Lauck, Philadelphia

DEPARTMENT OF WAR, 19 Aug[us]t, 1818

SIR, YOU are appointed a CADET in the service of the United States.—You will immediately notify this Department of your acceptance or non-acceptance: In case of the former, you will repair to West Point, in the state of New-York, in the month of September next, and report yourself to the Superintendent of the Military Academy [Bvt. Maj. Sylvanus Thayer] for examination. If you are admitted, you will receive your Warrant, and your pay will commence from that date.

Unless you punctually obey this order, or render satisfactory reasons for delay, your appointment will be recalled.

[Signature] J. C. Calhoun
Secretary of War.

Qualifications necessary for admission.

Each cadet, previous to his being admitted a member of the Military Academy, must be able to read distinctly and pronounce correctly; to write a fair legible hand, and to perform, with facility and accuracy, the various operations of the ground rules of arithmetic, both simple and compound; of the rules of reduction; of single and compound proportion; and also of vulgar and decimal fractions.

PLS (with the name and address of the appointee, the date, and Calhoun's autograph inserted in manuscript) in DNA, 15, 1818, 29. Note: This printed form is typical of hundreds that were issued in Calhoun's name. Lauck's reply appears herein under the date 9/23. This certificate of appointment was issued pursuant to letters of application that had been sent by Lauck to Calhoun on 4/15 and 5/14, one of which contained two postscripts of recommendation signed by 14 persons (2 ALS's in DNA, 15, 1818, 29).

From Thomas L. McKenney

Office of Indian Trade, Georgetown, 19th August 1818

I have the honor to acknowledge the receipt of your letter of the 17th Inst[ant], containing a transcript of the resolution of the House of Representatives "directing you to report to them at the next session, a system providing for the abolition of the existing Indian Trading Establishment of the United States; and providing for the opening of the trade with the Indians to individuals under suitable regulations"—also your direction to me to "report to the Department of War, my opinion of the best mode of bringing to a termination the existing Indian Trading establishment; and such facts, and ideas as I may think important in relation to opening the trade with the Indians to Individuals, under suitable regulations."

In reply, I have the honor to state, that the existing Indian Trading establishment might be terminated by withholding every description of supplies from the Factories, and directing the Factors to close their business, by a sale of the Merchandize and effects on hand—or, by an order, immediately to suspend all intercourse with the Indians, and transport the stocks on hand, to the nearest and most favorable points, and dispose of them at public auction upon such terms as could be commanded—or, by authorizing each Factor to sell the entire stock & furniture, of the establishment entrusted to him upon the best terms he could realize, due notice of such intention being first given—or, by an exhibition at this office, of Inventories of the stocks of all the Factories for the quarter immediately preceding, when the same might be inspected, under a public notice, given to that effect, accompanied by offer of the whole stock in trade, either by Public auction, or upon stipulated terms. Of the several modes referred to, my opinion is, the last mentioned, embracing a stipulation as to cost, and the time, or times of payment, is "the best." It is the best, because, First—It is summary in its process, and involves no consideration, either of loss, or delay. Second—The details of the sale could be so made as to provide for the continuance of the system until it should change hands, without the interruptions to which any other mode would make it liable; and thus keep within reach of the Indians, without any suspension of the means, those articles of necessity, for which they depend, mainly, upon the United States Trading houses. The proceeds of the sale, when completed, would, of course, be paid over to the Treasury, to reimburse its issues under the several apropriations for carrying on trade with the Indians.

But *whatever* mode may be adopted for abolishing the United States trading Houses, there will remain a reconcilement to be brought about, in the stipulations of an existing treaty, made and concluded on the 10th November 1808, between the United States and the Great and Little Osage tribes of Indians, and that new order of things. By the second article of that treaty the United States "engage to establish at Fort Clark, and *permanently to continue* at all seasons of the year, a well assorted store of goods, for the purpose of bartering with the Great and Little Osage, on *moderate terms,* for their Peltries and Furs." It is true, the Government, in any disposition which it may think proper to make of the Factories, and of its present system of intercourse with those Indians, could stipulate the purchasers to make good so much of the obligation as relates to the perpetual continuance of the store, but it would not be so easy, it is presumed, to provide for the continuance of the "*moderate terms*" on which it has engaged the goods shall be furnished. Or, if both could be provided for, it does not require even so much as the experiment of a trial, to ascertain the sense in which the Cheifs [*sic*] and head Men of the Osage Indians, understand this article—that having been expressed by them in the year 1813. (See paper marked A.) If a change in the existing relations be made, therefore, at all, it is already ascertained that it must involve, in relation to the Osage Indians, a violation of the 2d article of the Treaty referred to, so far at least as their opinion of its intention applies. And how far a compulsory change, in the existing relations with those Indians, may accord with the importance which certainly attaches to a preservation of the public faith, will be a matter for the decision of Congress.

How far the other Tribes, who, altho' not entrenched behind the provisions of a treaty, may be inclined to conceive well of a change which involves, necessarily, the overthrow of the existing benevolent system, to the value of which they are by no means insensible, and an abandonment of their commercial intercourse into hands whose sole inducement to undertake its prosecution is *gain,* it is no very difficult matter to foresee, especially as the principal tribes have in one way or another, either by direct communications made on the subject, or in person, during their visits to the Government, expressed their most earnest desire for the continuance of the Factories, and begged to be saved from the consequences which seldom fail of following in the train of private adventurers.

Judging of the future by the past, there are abundant reasons to justify the conclusion that a withdrawal of the existing Government system would be attended with consequences serious in their application as well to the Indians as to our frontier Citizens—and but little doubt can be entertained that the whole system of reform, which has not ceased to command the respect and attention of our Government from its earliest history; and which now, in relation to several tribes, has advanced far beyond any former attainments, would tumble into ruins, and blast, at once, the happiness of thousands of Indians who now enjoy its benefits, and the hopes of those generous Citizens who are so resolutely bent on its enlargement.

The existing Government system has its foundation in *benevolence,* and *reform.* Those are the two pillars, on which it rests. The Factors employed by the United States do not go to supply the more helpless parts of our Family with articles necessary for their support and security against the elements, and upon terms that embrace no more than a preservation of the capital employed, only, but also with implements of husbandry; with suitable instructions how to use them; and with invitations to seek their support from the Earth, and exchange, for her certain compensation, the uncertain products of the chase. The instructions to the Factors also, direct them to cultivate among the Indians a regard for, and attachment to our Government and Country. (See page marked B.)

However inefficient much of this may have proved in its application to some of the more excluded and remote tribes, yet evidences exist, in abundance, to shew that all this good design is not lost; and that but for its workings, savagism would characterize, and deform; and desolation would brood over minds, over which civilization and social life, and the principles of improvement, have a fixed and permanent controul.

I am at a loss to conceive what regulations could be adopted, in a provision for the opening of the trade with the Indians to Individuals, which should preserve both, or either of the two features which so prominently distinguish the Government system. Whatever restrictions might be attempted to force private enterprize within the demands of benevolence, I apprehend they would all prove of no avail. The object of private enterprize is proclaimed in the undertaking. A trader no sooner resolves on a commencement of his career than he fixes his eye upon the object in view; and that object is *gain,* and so far as my information extends I have never detected any evidence going to shew the least unwillingness on the part of the private adventurer to adopt any resort that should promise to favor his scheme of profit. All methods appear to be alike convenient; and are adopted, or rejected, as they may seem most likely to favor, or oppose, his hopes.

It is well known that to the introduction of spirituous liquors amongst the Indians may be attributed a vast majority of those excitements which so often break out into acts of hostility, sometimes involving the almost total extinction of the tribes arrayed against each other; not unfrequently blasting the hopes of our frontier Citizens, and Deluging their distant and otherwise peacefull [*sic*] homes with blood. But this comes not of the Government policy. The distribution of this article is not permitted.

Experience has demonstrated how inefficient are the most promising regulations, when they are intended to govern Men bent upon such enterprises; and especially when the means of evading the agents whose duty it is made to enforce them, are so numerous; and when the opportunities of escape and security are rendered so certain by the unsearchable intricacies of the surrounding Forests.

Of the article of whiskey, to prevent the introduction of which into the Indian Country, and its distribution amongst the Indians, so much labor has been so unsuccessfully bestowed, no less than forty Barrels have been traced in one season, to an entrance at Green Bay; and as many as five thousand pounds of Lead are known to have been secured from the Sac and Fox Indians, in one interview, by those who use this article as a means of traffic, without the Indians receiving for their toils a *solitary remuneration beside.*

So far, therefore, as private, or individual intercourse is concerned, and such is its history from the beginning, there can be perceived in it no one trait which distinguishes it on account of its benevolence. And as to reform, it would be useless to illustrate the consequences which result from the sort of intercourse referred to: any thing, and every thing, but reform must attend upon it.

But the Indian Tribes are not only worried and excited by the conflicting interests of Men whose sole object is gain, and whose chief instrument of competition is that very article which is most pernicious; and which by its inflaming tendency disturbs the tranquility of the forests, and rouses into action the worst passions of their inhabitants, and of which unfortunately the Indians are too fond, but exactions of the most extravagant character are practised by Individuals wherever the means do not exist to make the Indians independent of their supplies. This fact is proved from a variety of sources, in a general way, and has been particularly specified by an intelligent Gentleman now in the north, whose letter dated December 1816 after stating the pleasure manifested by the Indians, at the opening of the Green Bay Factory, and their gratification at the cheapness of the goods, added, on their own authority, that "they had been obliged to pay, in skins, *Fifteen Dollars for a pound of Tobacco; and one Dollar and an half for a thimble*"!

I know it has been assumed that a destruction of the existing Government system would open the way to the enterprising Citizens of our Country, to participate in the benefits of a trade which could be made generally valuable to them, whilst it is of no particular advantage to the Government; but who are excluded from the benefits which their enterprise would secure to them by the overgrown capacity of the United States Trading establishment.

So far as the admission of Individuals into the Indian Country is concerned, it would be impossible, even under an abandonment of the Government system, (unless indeed all legal provisions were dispensed with,) to make a more ready way for them into the Indian Country than is secured to them by the existing law, and so generally do they seem to have availed themselves of its latitude that from every quarter their numbers are represented as beyond all former example. The whole Country from Michilimackinac, to Prairie du Chien, and thence on to the Missouri, is said literally "to swarm" with them. In fact those whose duty it is to licence applicants are left, by the loosseness [*sic*] of the law, without option, even in the most important point of *fitness of character*—hence all description of persons, applying, and conforming to the required regulations, which are within reach of any body, find an unobstructed way into the Indian Country.

It should seem, therefore, that so far as the admission of Individuals, into the privilege to trade with the Indians, is concerned, they can turn their enterprize into that channel, at pleasure. The only difficulty appears, then, to be, the alledged [*sic*] capacity of the United States Trading Establishment, (which difficulty may be found more readily in the *Principles that govern it,* than in its capacity which has always been too limited) to serve the Indians upon terms more advantageous than those who enter into the competition appear willing, to adopt. It is very certain, therefore, that an overthrow of the existing Government system would prove favorable to the individual enterprize; but, it is not less certain, that it would be, in the same proportion, unfavourable to the Indians.

It is submitted, under this view of the subject, whether, before the abolition of the United States trading establishment be determined upon, it is not incumbent on those who seek an enjoyment of this covetted [*sic*] privilege, to demonstrate, that none of the consequences which have been referred to as arising exclusively out of individual intercourse, would ensue? Whether it ought not to be made to appear beyond the possibility of doubt, that their trade and intercourse would be, at least, equally favorable, and equally beneficial to the Indians, and in every particular; and to the full as safe in their relation to our frontier inhabitants, as are the trade, and intercourse carried on with them, by the United States? In a word, whether it would not be proper, that no change in our existing relations should be sanctioned by the Government, that could tend in any one particular, to render the condition of the Indians more distressing than it is? Unless this could be insured, and its certainty made more undoubted than any experience hitherto had upon the subject can, in my opinion, warrant the Government in admitting, would not an abandonment of the present United States policy seem to carry along with it, not only an indifference to the condition of our Indians, bad as it is admitted to be, and loudly as it calls for help, but also, a willingness that it should be made worse, even, than it is? And if this helpless and less improved portion of our great American family, who are, it should seem, specially placed under the protecting care of our Government, within whose boundaries they range; and to which they are held accountable for their misdoings, be thrown beyond the limits of its *special agency*, and benevolent attentions, where shall they find a protector, or guide?

It is argued, again, that if Individuals were permitted to enter freely into the Indian Country, and the present capital employed by the Government were withdrawn, so many agencies would take the place of it, as to create a competition, favorable to the Indians.

Competition is certainly an engine of protection to the consumer; and without it, in relation to almost any other sort of intercourse, than that under consideration, it ought to be promoted. But an exception may be fairly taken to its application to the present question, because no competition, it is presumed, however active, could insure to the Indians, their supplies upon terms even *as good* as those on which they are furnished by the United States, whose policy is prescribed by a law which directs that the profits on the original cost of the articles, shall be no more than to preserve from diminution the capital employed. Nor would the competition in this great wilderness-market, it is presumed, be willing to receive as much, in addition to this, as the United States law *ought* to authorize, say six or Eight per Cent, with a view to cover the losses, and damage to which an intercourse so distant, and so difficult is liable.

Even, however, if Individuals should agree to receive no more than such an advance, taking into the estimate the chance of profit on the Furs and Peltries received in barter, and which is the only source on which the United States can count on *any* profit, yet it will scarcely admit of doubt that the idea of competition, and general participation, would be soon *swallowed* up in *one vast engine of monopoly,* which, in its workings, would defy, and soon force the Individual and smaller capatalists [*sic*] to seek employment for their capital where there were fewer chances of its being so completely useless.

If the entire capital of the South West company be not now in operation in this Country, there is good reason for believing that an amount, more than double that employed by the Government, is; and it is rendered almost certain that the present Capital employed by the United States, if withdrawn, would be immediately supplied, and vastly augmented, not, however, by individuals, on their own personal footing, but by a junction of a few, whose ability, it is as little to be doubted, would, very soon after the overthrow of the Government system, (should it be abolished,) have embodied, a sum, exceeding a million of Dollars, the employment of which would secure to the parties interested, one great union of security and interests, to the exclusion of all others. It is believed that upwards of half a million of Dollars are invested in one stock already.

If, therefore, the object of the resolution of the House of Representatives, be, to make amongst the Citizens of the United States a distribution of trading privileges; and if a system could be devised, and such regulations adopted as should infallibly secure to the Indians a continuance of their existing privileges, and means of improvement, and to our border population an equal protection, there are too many reasons to believe that it would fail of its accomplishment. And if that should be the result, the idea of a privileged monopoly could not fail of having birth given to it, to get rid of which, might be more difficult, than it now is to maintain the existing limited and shackled system; or to enlarge and disembarrass it from the pressure brought in upon it by the loosseness [*sic*] of the law under which private traders are admitted, against which system, whatever other exceptions may be taken, there can be none brought that can apply against, either its benevolence, or its tendency to reform the Indians.

But whilst the resolution of the House of Representatives looks to an admission into the Indian Country, of those individuals who might be disposed to enter it, as traders, are there not many, who, although they might not be induced to hold intercourse with the Indians, in *that* way, yet, are much interested in a participation of the result of their hunting expeditions? I refer to the Mechanical parts of our Country who deal and work in Furs. By the provisions of the 13th Section of the "act for establishing Trading houses with the Indian Tribes," approved 2d March 1811, it is provided, that "the Superintendent of Indian Trade shall cause the Furs and Peltries, and other articles acquired in Trade with the Indian nations, to be sold at public auction, in different parts of the United States, or otherwise disposed of as may be deemed most advantageous to the United States." Altho' by the terms "*otherwise disposed of*" an authority is given to sell at *different places* in the United States; or at *one place;* or to *export* the articles acquired in Trade with the Indians, to foreign markets, yet, it having been considered so important to those who work in Furs and Peltries in our own Country and to our Citizens generally who are the consumers, to provide a market for those articles, *at home,* that in no instance except *one* (and that occurred twelve years ago) have they been exported.

But if the United States system be abolished, can there be any security provided against the exportation of those articles, except that which shall imply a price, at home, corresponding to the price abroad? And if so, is it not to be apprehended, especially under the idea of a large union of capital, and of interests, that the cheif [*sic*] manager, or managers of this great traffic, will take care to realize those prices, and introduce, upon the one hand, a scarcity;

or bring upon our whole population, upon the other, an advance on the price of all such articles as are made of Fur and Peltries?

From what has been advanced may be gathered "my opinion of the best mode of bringing to a termination the existing Indian Trading house establishment." Also, that the change cannot be consistently made as it applies to the Great and Little Osage tribes of Indians. That so far as the remaining Tribes are concerned, and also our frontier Citizens, their condition would not be bettered, but, jud[g]ing from the experience already had, must be rendered worse by its adoption. That the hopes which are entertained, as well by several tribes, as by those who are so generously engaged in promoting a social and moral improvement amongst them, derive considerable aid from the influence and councils emanating from the Government policy, and that those hopes at the moment of their highest promise would be endangered by its abandonment. That however beneficial such a change might prove to individuals who might enter upon the prosecution of Indian trade, in a pecuniary sense, there can be no reasons found, to justify its recognition, if it involve an enlargement of the range of poverty, and disease, and want, amongst the Indians, which would result, naturally, from excess, licentiousness, and undue exactions, or if their tranquility be involved in it, or their lives, or a waste of any portion of the public treasure to allay excitements, and wars. That the idea of Individuals being admitted under this change to a general participation of trade, is fallacious, for the whole would, without doubt, resolve itself into one great system of monopoly, out of which would arise *a tax* upon our entire population. To all which might have been added, the involvement of the humanity and honor of the Country, which, (in the language of an intelligent Gentleman, conversant with Indian affairs, and intimately acquainted with the methods resorted to by individuals in their intercourse with the Indians) "the Traders care not to barter for a single skin."

I am aware that the resolution of the House of Representatives calls for a system, providing for the opening of the trade to Individuals under "*suitable* regulation." But I am aware also of the impractability [*sic*], in my opinion, of framing *any* system, that shall be so "suitable" as to overrule the consequences to which I have referred.

The best system, in my opinion, that can be adopted, is the one which has been once tried and abandoned. And if the "existing

Indian Trading establishments be abolished," I believe a revival of that system (with some variations & additions) will be found to contain as good a substitute as any other. I refer to the regulations of 1786 which continued, I believe, until they were superceded [*sic*] by the existing arrangements.

The system referred to provided for a division of the Country into two Districts, northern and southern. To each District was attached a Superintendent. The Superintendent of the northern division was allowed two deputies, or assistants. The whole of the Indian relations was placed in their hand.

The regulations adopted were the following. "No person, Citizen or other, under the penalty of Five hundred Dollars, was permitted to reside among, or trade with any Indian, or Indian nation within the territories of the United States without a licence for that purpose, first obtained from the Superintendent of the District, or one of the Deputies, who were directed to give such licence to *every person,* who should produce from the Supreme executive of any State, a certificate, under the seal of the State, that he is of good character, and suitably qualified and provided for that employment. For which licence he was to pay the sum of Fifty Dollars for the use of the United States. No licence to trade with the Indians was permitted to be in force for a longer term than one year. Previous to any Person or Persons obtaining a licence to trade as aforesaid, he or they were compelled to give bond in the sum of three thousand Dollars, to the Superintendent of the District for the use of the United States, for his or their strict adhereance [*sic*] to, and observance of, such regulations and rules as the Congress might from time to time establish for the Government of the Indian Trade."

It was provided also that the Superintendents should bond, each in the sum of Six thousand dollars; and the Deputies, or assistants, in the sum of three thousand Dollars.

My opinion is the system would be improved by placeing [*sic*] the Indian concerns in the hands of one Superintendent, instead of two. That he should be obliged before he entered upon the duties of his office, to bond to the United States with approved sureties in the sum of Ten Thousand Dollars—and take an oath of office. He should have an agent settled in each Tribe, unless it should be where the contiguity of Tribes would make one agent answer for more. Each agent should be required to bond to the

United States with approved sureties in a similar sum with the Superintendent, and take an oath of office. It should be made the duty of the agents, in addition to the ordinary routine of holding treaties, and paying annuities, and dispensing Presents, to keep the Superintendent regularly, and constantly, and truely [*sic*] informed, of the state and disposition of the tribe, or tribes, within their respective agencies, and specially so, (and their oath of office ought to embrace this object,) in whatever should relate to any infringement of the law regulating trade with the Indian Tribes; and by whom. The penalty of a violation should involve the forfeiture of the traders' bond which should be given on his receiving his licence, in the sum of Five thousand Dollars; and a forfeiture of his licence, without the privilege of renewal. Licences to traders now employed in the Indian Country to be cancelled; and all interlopers, or peddling traders, should be driven out, wherever they could be found. Any Person found trading six months from the passage of the law under the proposed system, without a licence, obtained under it, to forfeit his effects. No person to be licenced after the passage of the law who should not present to the Superintendent (whose duty it might be made to issue licences, and approve bonds) a certificate from the Cheif [*sic*] Executive of any State under the seal of the State, that he is of good character and suitably qualified and provided for that employment, his bond and sureties also to be presented and approved. For his licence one hundred dollars should be required; the licence and the price of it to be renewed annually. The proceeds of which to be applied to reimburse the Treasury for the compensation paid out of it to the Sup[erintenden]t and the agents. Any trader neglecting to renew his licence to forfeit $500 for the first year, and a thousand for the second, and in the same proportion each year till the fifth year, when his bond shall be considered forfeited. No trader should be allowed the privilege to trade under any circumstances, who would not select his spot, build his factory, & locate himself. No licence to any Individual or Company to embrace more than one factory. The name of the Factor of each to be inserted in each licence. The vending of spirituous liquors to be prohibited under the severest penalties of the law.

Those are the outlines of a system which appear to me to be more suitable than any that have occurred to me, and as being more likely than any other to provide against the abuses which are to be dreaded, even under its adoption. The Indians would still be the victims of a policy the foundation of which could only be sustained by gain, and the difference to them would be vast indeed, between its workings and the milder and more humane system whose principle [*sic*] features are benevolence and reformation.

All which is respectfully submitted.

FC in DNA, 77 (M-271:2, frames 674–699); FC in DNA, 73, E:130–144.

To David A. Ogden, Madrid, N.Y.

Department of War, 19 Aug[us]t 1818

It is certainly much to be regretted, that the Six Nations should, by the acts of officious and designing men, be induced to hesitate in changing their present residence, for one more congenial to their habits, and better calculated, by its remoteness from the settlements of the whites, permanently to secure their interest and happiness. The country on the Arkansaw [*sic*] was designated, as combining every advantage most likely to render the change agreeable to them and to produce these results; while it would, at the same time, promote the views of the government, with which it is a desirable object to induce as many of the tribes of Indians as may be disposed to change their residence, to emigrate to the west of the Mississippi. The objection to the Arkansaw on account of unhealthiness, is an erroneous one. It is believed that no section of the country is more healthy. However, should they adhere to the determination not to remove to that country, Gov[erno]r [Lewis] Cass will be requested to consult with the Indians on Fox river and its vicinity, or with the tribes inhabiting the country lying north of the State of Indiana and the Illinois territory, and ascertain whether they are willing to make a cession of land to the Six Nations and receive them among them; and, in the event of any of them assenting to the proposition, he will be instructed to make the arrangements necessary for their reception and to facilitate their removal: provided, the portion of country so selected for their new residence, receives their approbation.

It is hoped, that the disposition manifested, on all occasions, by this department, to attend to the wishes of the Six Nations, will have the effect of convincing them, that the individuals who endeavor to influence them on this subject and persuade them to act in opposition to their best interests, by whatever motives they may be actuated, are certainly their worst enemies, and that they should not listen to them, but to the government of the U.S., which is their best friend.

FC in DNA, 72, D:204–205.

To Abraham Bradley, [Jr., Washington,] 8/20. From Gen. [Andrew] Jackson's location last May, Calhoun assumes that the lost dispatches mailed at that time were probably put in the post office either at Fort Hawkins or Milledgeville, [Ga.]. FC in DNA, 3, 10:121.

From [former 2nd Lt.] W[illiam] Y[oung] Hansell, Augusta, Ga., 8/20. Seeks payments for rations furnished to Army men, militiamen, and Indians at Fort Hawkins during June and July by O[tho] W. Callis; for rations furnished by Callis at Forts Gaines and Scott by special contract under an order issued by Col. David Brearl[e]y in 1817; and for a debt owed to Callis by Benjamin G. Orr. "I feel a diffidence in asking these favours, as a part of them do not come properly within the sphere of the War Department, but as neither Mr. Callis [n]or myself have [*sic*] an agent at Washington City, it would be received as a special accommodation if the business could be closed through your Department." ALS in DNA, 1, H-252. (Calhoun answered on 8/29.)

From [Thomas S. Jesup], 8/20. Points out that the forage allowances permissible under present regulations work a hardship on Army officers and decrease their effectiveness; urges improvements in the regulations. FC in DNA, 42, 1:37–39.

To Josiah Meigs, [Commissioner, General Land Office,] 8/20. Calhoun asks that certain land surrounding Fort Gratiot, [Mich. Territory,] shall be reserved [for public use], not sold; he also asks if, pursuant to a request of 1817, a similar reservation was ever created beside the Miami River. FC in DNA, 3, 10:121. Meigs replied on 8/21 that he was ordering the land between the Denude and St. Clair Rivers to be reserved and gave assurance that four tracts beside the Miami had been reserved. LS in DNA, 1, M-285; FC in DNA, 82, 8:215.

To JAMES MONROE, [Albemarle County, Va.]

War Dep[artmen]t, 20th August 1818

I have received your letter of the 17th Inst[ant], inclosing a letter from Gen[era]l [Jacob] Brown and one from Mr. [Rufus] King to you.

I had previously received a letter from General Brown, and had in consequence sent a letter of appointment [as Adjutant General of the Northern Division from 8/10] to Col. [Roger] Jones. By my former letter [of 8/15], I informed you, that I had given instructions to Gen[era]l [Edmund P.] Gain[e]s relative to St. Marks and Pansacola [*sic*]; and that Gen[era]l [Andrew] Jackson had been furnished with a copy of the instructions with the reasons why they were transmitted by the shortest rout[e].

Mr. King takes very strong grounds in relation to the Floridas. I cannot but think, that those on which you acted, are not only much more safe, but much more consistent with the letter and sperit [*sic*] of our constitution. They are such as will stand the severest test; and will, I doubt not meet with the approbation of Congress and the country. The ideas which Mr. King has suggested in relation to the observation of Mr. [William] Wilberforce, appear to me to be entirely correct. The right [of] search under any pretence ought, if admitted at all, to be admitted with the greatest caution.

Mr. [William] Wirt returned from Baltimore a few days since; and I expect he will report his opinion in relation to the court-martial [of Nathaniel Nye Hall] in a few days.

A copy of Mr. [John Quincy] Adam[s]'s letter to Don Onís was transmitted shortly after you left this [city]. Capt. [James] Gadsden left Nashville, or expected to do so the 1st instant, so that he may be daily expected. Gen[era]l Jackson it seems had [on 5/5] sent on the proceedings of the court-martial, with the original correspondence, in the case of [Alexander] Arbuthnot & [Robert Christy] Ambrister in May, which from some neglect of the post offices have [*sic*] not been received. I infer from the General's letter [of 8/10] that he took a copy of the proceedings and letters, and that he will send them on by Capt. Gadsden. I have written to the Post M[aster] General [Return J. Meigs, Jr.,] to have a diligent search for the originals [made].

Nothing has occurred since my last requiring your particular attention. I hope your health continues good and that Mrs. Monroe's has improved with the mountain air. Accept the assurance of my sincere respect & esteem.

[P.S.] I return Gen[era]l Brown's & Mr. King's letters.

ALS in NN, James Monroe Papers.

From [Lt. Col.] G[eorge] E. Mitchell, Commanding the 4th Military Department, Baltimore, 8/20. W[illiam] Turner, who wishes to enter the Army, has been so highly commended to Mitchell that he takes pleasure in introducing Turner to Calhoun with a hope that Turner's application will be successful. LS in DNA, 11, 12895. (Turner was appointed a 2nd Lt., 9/17.)

From Robert A. Thruston

Washington, [Ky.,] 20th of August 1818

I accept the appointment of a Cadet in the service of the United States, conferred on me by letter from the [Acting] Secretary of War [George Graham], of the date of the 19th of November last; I beg to be excused, for not having sooner made this communication; the delay arose from inadvertency, in overlooking the requisition in my said letter of appointment, that I should *"immediately advise the department"* of my acceptance.

ALS in DNA, 15, 1818, 118.

From Samuel Gedney, New York [City], 8/21. His Congressman assured him months ago that the $75 fine imposed upon him by the court-martial for N.Y. militia delinquents would be remitted by order of the War Department. [Gerard] Steddiford tells him that no such order has been received. "I fear Sir that unless you enforce your orders I may look in vain for my commission or money either." ALS in DNA, 1, G-91.

From Thomas L. McKenney, Georgetown, [D.C.,] 8/21. Having received with Calhoun's letter of 8/20 (FC in DNA, 72, D:206) a copy of a letter from [Talbot] Chambers to [Thomas A.] Smith, McKenney defends vigorously [John] Johnston, the Factor at Prairie du Chien, against Chambers' charges that Johnston sells goods to improper recipients. McKenney concludes that Chambers has listened with too much gullibility to false reports alleging dissatisfaction on the part of the Indians with the Factories and encloses merchants' letters in proof that the prices at which the Factories sell blankets and other items are cheap. LS with Ens in DNA, 2, M-1818; PC in Carter, ed., *Territorial Papers,* 17:599–600.

From Samuel Hodges, Jr., Stoughton, Mass., 8/22. Asks for an answer to his letter of 8/18; states that he had accepted his diplomatic appointment to Rio de Janeiro before he was offered an Army commission; affirms that he prefers the Army appointment and will accept it if Rio de Janeiro does not recognize his diplomatic position. ALS in DNA, 11, 12311.

From Andrew Jackson, Nashville, 8/22. Defends vigorously the claim of one Gen. Coffee that the officers of Coffee's unit of volunteer cavalry or mounted gunmen, [who were doubtless militiamen,] are entitled to the 40 cents per day provided by a statute of 4/20/1818 as an allowance for the use of their personal horses among Jackson's forces in operations around Pensacola and New Orleans during the War of 1812. "Really, without a quibble on the word 'cavalry' . . . I cannot imagine how a doubt has arisen upon this subject." ALS offered for sale in 1963 by Parke-Bernet Galleries, Inc., New York [City], and described in the catalog for Parke-Bernet Sale Number 2235, item 125, p. 36.

To ANDREW JACKSON, Nashville

War Department, 22d August 1818

From the frequent failure of packages to and from Fort Hawkins the last winter and spring, it is possible that you may not have received a copy of the instruction [of 3/16] to General [Thomas A.] Smith in relation to the contemplated post at the mouth of the Yellow Stone River. I now enclose a copy to you. From information since received, I am inclined to think the principal post ought to be at the Mandan Village. It is the point on the Missouri nearest to the British post on the Red River, and the best calculated to counteract their hostilities against us or influence with the Indians. It appears to be very important that a strong post should be taken at the mouth of the St. Peters [the Minnesota River] on the Mississippi. It is the great thoroughfare of the British trade with the Indians within our limits. That and Fort Armstrong [at Rock Island in Ill. Territory] are said to be the two most commanding posts on the Upper Mississippi. The Michigan Territory has been extended to the Mississippi. The Northern Division [of the Army] has received a similar extension. In order to relieve the Southern Division which by the extension of the posts up the Missouri has so long a line of the frontier to protect I am inclined to think the Mississippi with its waters above the mouth of Rocky River ought to be annexed to the Northern Division. It would not even then have equal duties to perform with that of the South. Should no substantial objection occur to you, that arrangement of the divisions will be made. I am very desirous by taking strong and judicious posts to break the British control over the Northern Indians, and for this purpose it appears proper that a much larger proportion of our Military Establishment should be posted on the Mississippi and its waters, which the arrangement proposed would admit of without any derangement of your command.

LS in DLC, Andrew Jackson Papers, 7992–7993; FC in DNA, 3, 10:122; PC in Jameson, ed., *Correspondence,* p. 138. NOTE: A PC of Calhoun's letter of 3/16 to Thomas A. Smith is in *The Papers of John C. Calhoun,* 2:194–195.

From Dr. JOSEPH LOVELL

Washington, August 22, 1818

The most important points in determining the component parts of the Soldiers' ration (as far as relates to "a due regard to the health and comfort of the Army") are that they be of such a nature as to be furnished of a good quality and not liable to become easily damaged; that there be a due mixture of animal and vegetable food, and as great a variety of each as "oeconomy" will permit; and that they admit of as great a variety as possible in the mode of cooking, for habit has rendered this mixture and change essential to health.

The principle [*sic*] *addition* required is of some vegetable that can be furnished at a cheap rate and be easily transported and preserved; and it is believed none will answer these purposes in this country as dried pease [*sic*] or beans and rice, more especially as a supply of these articles would induce the Soldier to prepare his food much oftener in the form of *soups*, the importance of which has been frequently and justly insisted on by the Surgeons of the Army, as the majority of our camp diseases arise from disordered bowels. Perhaps no part of the ration has caused more disease within the last 5 or 6 years than the flour. Whenever it is deposited in large quantities, it becomes more or less damaged before it is issued, and in that state its effects are extremely unpleasant; and it is so easily injured, that this cannot perhaps be even generally prevented. This may be remedied by furnishing [*one word illegible;* kiln ?] dried corn meal at the South, but its price [*one word illegible;* precludes ?] it in the Northern Division. Might not this difficulty be much lessened, at least, by allowing what is termed "Pilot Bread," which can be more easily preserved, and is more palatable and less injurious when damaged, than flour? Bakers will, I believe, give the same weight of *Bread* they receive of *flour,* so that the only additional expence would arise from the transportation of a greater bulk; but perhaps a less quantity of this Bread would suffice than is given of flour, and the "health and comfort of the Army" would most certainly pay for the remaining difference. I have no doubt the supply of pease and hard Bread to the British troops in Canada during the late War was the great cause of the difference between their sick reports and ours. Hard Bread in all cases is more easy of digestion than soft and for this reason Physicians prescribe it in diseases of the stomach and bowels, or soft Bread sliced and toasted, i.e., better cooked. Bread of corn meal is also preferable to that generally made from wheat flour in complaints of this nature, especially when the risk that the latter may be damaged is taken into consideration.

With regard to Bacon at the South instead of Pork, there can be no doubt from the information I have obtained on the subject of the great advantage to be expected from the change. Whiskey &c. ought most certainly to be omitted, but if prejudice will retain it, but one half the quantity should be allowed, and for the other half vinegar, Beer or Molasses might be added. Vinegar and water is the principle [*sic*] drink of the French Soldier, and would answer equally well for ours, at the South all the year, and at the North in the summer at least. Molasses and water is a very common, convenient and healthy drink. Perhaps there would be too much waste and difficulty in preparing and issuing the necessary quantity of beer, even if the ingredients could be purchased at a cheap rate.

The allowance of soap, candles, and salt is probably sufficient. From these considerations the following ration is proposed:

Present Ration	*Proposed Ration*
Flour (Wheat)	Flour (Wheat)
	or
	Corn Meal
	or
	Pilot Bread
Beef	Beef
Pork	Pork
	or
	Bacon
Whiskey	Whiskey
	Vinegar
	or
	Molasses
	or
	Beer
Soap	Soap
Candles	Candles
Salt	Salt
Vinegar	

As to the quantities to be allowed or the mode of issuing, I am scarcely able to judge. 20 oz. of corn meal or 16 oz. Pilot Bread would probably be equal to the flour now allowed. 10 oz. of Bacon for 12 oz. of Pork, and one gill Vinegar or Molasses or 1 qt. Beer in lieu of half the Whiskey, omitting of course the present allowance of Vinegar when it is issued as a drink. The chief object for health is variety in the *articles* [and] the *mode of cooking;* perhaps therefore the best way would be to issue a regular ration 4 days in the week and on the three others, a supply of pease, Beans or Rice, reducing the Bread stuff and meat in proportion. It is intended that *all* the articles enumerated (except Beer perhaps) be furnished and that, when practicable, the issue of those of the same kind be occasionally varied.

LS in DNA, 1, L-105.

To James Monroe, [Albemarle County, Va.]

War Dep[artmen]t, 22d August 1818

I enclose the proceedings of the court-martial in the case of Dr. [Samuel B.] Hugo. As the charges are few and simple, and the proof not complicated, I do not think it necessary to offer any opinion. The Doctor has recently been promoted to a Post Surgeon; but from information recently received, I doubt whether he deserved it.

Col. [George] Gibson the Commissary General [of Subsistence] has not yet arrived; and as I cannot postpone any longer the proposals for supplying the troops the next year, they will be issued immediately. The law authorises you to make, if you should judge proper, changes in the ration; and I have ventured on the supposition of your approbation, to make some changes. To the South, Bacon and killed [kiln] dried corn meal is substituted to a certain extent in the place of Pork and flour. Twice a week fresh meat, (Beef) and pease [*sic*] or beans, or rice is substituted in lieu of the regular ration. There will be in the whole a saving to the gov[ernmen]t; and an addition to the health and comfort of the Army.

ALS in DLC, James Monroe Papers, 4827; PEx in Jameson, ed., *Correspondence*, p. 137.

From H[enry] Sherburne, Chickasaw Agency, 8/22. Acknowledges Calhoun's letter of 7/30 (Abs in *The Papers of John C. Calhoun*, 2:444); what additional evidence as to the account of Godfrey Jones is required? A Chickasaw has deposited with Sherburne some blankets, butcher knives, etc., taken from a Negro who was selling them for a white man to the Chickasaws without a license; Sherburne will sell these goods at auction on 9/8; but, since treaties contradict each other on this point, shall he give half the proceeds to the informer or to the Chickasaw nation? He has received a draft for $19,350 on the Bank of the United States at New Orleans to cover the Chickasaw annuity for 1817; asks advice as to how to bring so large a sum in small bills safely from New Orleans and whether, if [Isaac] Shelby or [Andrew] Jackson should request it, he shall delay until after the forthcoming treaty negotiations distributing that annuity and the goods for the 1818 annuity, which have not yet arrived. The building materials for the repair of the

Agency house have arrived, one carpenter has been employed, and another is expected soon; but the materials and other costs, required to "make the house comfortable & save it from total ruin," promise to be higher than was estimated. "As many little debts will arise in the course of the repairs & those due to needy people," asks for an advance of $200 "in small bills of the United States Bank, as no other Bank paper has any currency here." LS in DNA, 1, S-194.

John Quincy Adams to President [James Monroe], 8/23. In discussing several subjects, Adams reports: "Mr. Calhoun concurs in the opinion that the additional allowance of 3,000 dollars each should be made to Messrs. [Caesar A.] Rodney and [John] Graham on account of their late mission [as commissioners to ascertain the condition of the Latin-American republics]. I shall consult the Attorney General [William Wirt] upon it to-morrow; and if he assents, shall leave directions for the payment to be made them. Mr. Calhoun doubts the expediency of issuing a Proclamation offering a reward for the apprehension of Captain [Obed] Wright. I shall write further on this subject after consulting with Mr. Wirt." ALS in DLC, James Monroe Papers, 4829–4830.

To Lewis G. De Russy, New York [City], 8/24. "Your letter of the 20th instant is received. You certify that you were engaged in 'exploring the country, making topographical surveys and erecting public fortifications' &c. The rule allows $1.50 a day only for reconnoitering and making topographical surveys, with a view to selecting sites for fortifications, and to superintending the erection of fortifications. Under this rule, you must certify that you were actually engaged the whole of the time stated on your account, upon those duties. There is an extension of the rule to those officers who may have been employed in disbursing public money in erecting fortifications. If you disbursed public money in building fortifications, you must certify the time you were so engaged." FC in DNA, 3, 10:123.

From William B. Foster, Pittsburgh, 8/24. Since writing on 8/17, Foster has lost his rough copy of that letter; he asks for a copy of it, so that it can be transcribed into his letterbook. He reports that Maj. [Abram R.] Woolley's account in the Bank of Pittsburgh from 4/20/1816 to 10/2/1817 amounted to $116,888. ALS in DNA, 1, W-200.

From Cam[illus] Griffith, Thompson's Creek, La., 8/24. Because 150,000 rations have been requisitioned from him by the commisioners to treat with the Choctaws, he has issued a draft for $25,000 and asks that it be honored. ALS in DNA, 1, G-98.

From Sam Lane, [Commissioner of Public Buildings,] "Capitol," [Washington,] 8/24. Recommends Samuel Shannon for an Army appointment. ALS in DNA, 11, 14724, with an EI by Calhoun reading "To be specially attended to" and an EI by Christopher Vandeventer reading "Let Mr. Shannon be appointed." [He became a 2nd Lt., 9/10.]

To Lt. W[illiam] G. McNeill, [Newark, N.J.,] 8/24. Answering McNeill's letter of 8/20 (ALS in DNA, 1, M-279), Calhoun states that McNeill will be allowed $1.50 [per diem] only for time actually employed in the field, not for time employed in quarters. The accounts cannot be paid in New York, because the allowances are not chargeable to the Quartermaster Department or the fortifications fund. McNeill is ordered, therefore, to submit his accounts, stating the orders under which he has been employed, to the Engineer Department for settlement. FC in DNA, 3, 10:124.

To Andrew C. Mitchell, 8/24. "You are appointed a Clerk in this department. Your compensation will be at the rate of $1,400 per annum. You will report yourself immediately to Mr. [James L.] Edwards, of the Pension office, for duty." FC in DNA, 3, 10:123.

To David B. Mitchell, 8/24. "Enclosed you will find a Copy of a letter from J[ohn] Darrington, Esq. You will enquire into the facts referred to in the letter and report the result to this Department. I have frequent enquiries as to the Road from Fort Hawkins to Fort Stoddert. It is my wish that you cause the money appropriated, to be applied as soon as practicable to the repairs of the road." LS in GU; FC in DNA, 3, 10:123; PC in Carter, ed., *Territorial Papers,* 18:406.

From Ferris Pell, New York [City], 8/24. As Agent for N.Y. State, he asks that Army men who are engaged in the survey of the coast shall be ordered to evaluate the fortifications built by the State in N.Y. Harbor, in order that the value of the works as well as of the sites may be considered when the State negotiates the proposed sale of these fortifications to the U.S. LS in DNA, 23, no. 145, with an AEI by Calhoun directing [Joseph G.] Swift to issue the orders necessary "to effect the object proposed."

To Maj. Gen. E[leazer] W. Ripley, Bay of St. Louis via New Orleans, 8/24. Although Calhoun has received several communications from Baton Rouge relative to available sites for barracks in that vicinity, he has not received Ripley's report. Ripley is ordered to forward this report, so that the War Department will be advised of his preference before making a decision. FC in DNA, 3, 10:124.

From H[enry] Sherburne, Chickasaw Agency, 8/24. He asks Calhoun to honor his draft of today for $225 payable to "Malcom McGee, at whose house I am still at Board with my Family & must there continue until the Agency house is repaired." LS in DNA, 1, S-193.

From Maj. James Bankhead, Charleston, [S.C.,] 8/25. Fears that the reduction in the salary of Capt. Robert Wilson, Military Storekeeper there, will compel him to resign; outlines his other services; hopes for some arrangement that will enable him to continue in his position. ALS in DNA, 1, B-288.

Capt. W[illiam] A. Barron, New York [City], to [Christopher] Vandeventer, 8/25. Using pronouns in the Quaker manner, Barron asks Vandeventer to ascertain slyly from Calhoun and Robert Brent whether or not Barron is entitled to extra compensation on two counts. ALS in DNA, 1, B-282.

To Capt. William Bradford, Rifle Regiment, Belle Point, "Arkansaw river," 8/25. "Your letter of the 8th ult[im]o [PC in *The Papers of John C. Calhoun,* 2:366–367] is received. I am pleased that your efforts to reconcile the Cherokees and Osages have so happily terminated. Gov[erno]r [William] Clark and Colo[nel Auguste] Chouteau have been instructed to take the proper measures to induce these tribes to return to peace. Should your operations for that object continue to be successful, their interference will be unnecessary. You will report to Gov[erno]r Clark as well as to this department the final result of your measures for pacifying these two tribes of Indians." FC in DNA, 72, D:207.

To Jacob Brown, New York [City], 8/25. Answering his letter of 8/12, states that the reward for deserters has been increased to $30 and that retention of the deserter's pay is now a regulation of the War Department. Calhoun realizes the importance of completing the barracks [at Rouses Point, N.Y.,] but thinks "the correct course" will be to ask Congress for a specific appropriation. Meanwhile, Thomas S. Jesup has been directed to determine the exact amount of arrearages and the funds necessary for completing the barracks. LS in MHi; FC in DNA, 3, 10:124; FC in DLC, Jacob Brown Papers, Letterbooks, 2:116; CCEx in DNA, 152, 16A-E6; PEx in Senate Document No. 112, 16th Cong., 2nd Sess.

From R[ichard] Graham, St. Louis, 8/25. Explains that he received on 8/23 Calhoun's letter of 3/25, because Graham left St. Louis about 5/15 for business with his brother, George Graham, and "only returned a few days since." Discusses practical problems arising from the treaty with the Ottawas, Chippewas, and Potawatomies to the west and southwest of Lake Michigan as to distributions of their annuities in specie rather than in merchandise and of their rations. ALS in DNA, 1, G-87.

From J.F. Grimké, "Belmont," Cross Keys (Union District), [S.C.,] 8/25. Thanks Calhoun for the appointment of Grimké's youngest son, [Charles F.,] as a Cadet; asks that the son "may be indulged with a small procrastination" or furlough if he cannot report to the Military Academy in September; discusses his own painful illness with boils through the past three months and submission to the War Department of certificates for old soldiers other than himself; states that an older son, Thomas S. Grimké in Charleston, [S.C.,] can be informed about the requested furlough. ALS in DNA, 1, G-94.

From Samuel K. Jennings, President

Asbury College, [Baltimore,] August 25th 1818

The bearer, John C. Taylor, has been a student at this Institution the last twelve months; and during all that period has conducted himself in a manner reputable to himself, and in every respect satisfactory to me and to the professors and teachers of the College.

His attention to his studies has been uncommonly great, of which his very remarkable progress is the most unequivocal testimony. He has made considerable attainments in the French Language. He has studied Geometry plane and solid, Trigonometry plane and spherical. He has been taught the application of Algebra to Geometry, & Algebra up to quadratic equations inclusive, & Mensuration and astronomical calculations to a considerable extent. All of which he understands well.

With much pleasure, therefore, I would recommend him to the Hon. Secretary of the War Department, as a very promising candidate for a place in the Military Academy of the United States.

LS in DNA, 11, 12866.

From Wilson Lumpkin, Madison, Ga., 8/25. Acknowledges Calhoun's letter of 8/4 to him. Accepts the "entirely unexpected" appointment as commissioner to survey the boundary lines called for by the recent Creek treaty, although "I was not desireous [*sic*] of this, or any other appointment." Will begin the work soon. "My friendship & esteem for yourself is unabating." ALS in DNA, 1, L-107.

From Thomas L. McKenney, Georgetown, [D.C.,] 8/25. "My transportation agent [Jere W. Bronaugh] having made an estimate of the disbursements made out of the trade fund, on account of the transportation of the merchandize intended as Presents to be distributed at the treaties to be held at St. Marys, Ohio; and in the Chickasaw and Choctaw Nations, I have to ask that, of the three thousand two hundred Dollars as per estimate which I enclose [ALS from Jere W. Bronaugh to Thomas L. McKenney, 8/24], you will direct a warrant to be made out for $2,500 to reimburse, in part, the trade fund. The accounts will be regularly adjusted on receipt of all the vouchers." LS with En in DNA, 1, M-286; FC in DNA, 73, E:118.

To [Lt. Col.] Talbot Chambers, Bellefontaine, Mo. Territory, 8/26. Answers his letter of 7/25 (ALS with En in DNA, 1, C-213; CC in DNA, 66; Abs in *The Papers of John C. Calhoun*, 2:424) transmitting a draft for $2,412 spent because contractor Hugh Glenn failed last spring to supply the "liquor part of the Ration," which led Chambers to "fear that the privation would affect the health of the Troops . . . when the sickly season was about to commence." In reply, Calhoun states that payment will be made but that the outlay will be charged to Chambers' account "until the proper evidence" of Glenn's failure "be furnished agreeably to the regulations of this Department." FC in DNA, 3, 10:125; CC in DNA, 66.

To A[bner] Lacock, [Senator from Pa., 8]/26. Pursuant to Lacock's report of 7/25 (ALS in DNA, 1, W-200; PC in *The Papers of John C. Calhoun,* 2:425) that the financial dealings of Maj. [Abram R.] Woolley were suspect, Calhoun wrote confidential inquiries to the Pittsburgh merchants and others whom Lacock had suggested. [Military Storekeeper James] Gibson and two others [William B. Foster and William McCandless] have written replies exonerating Woolley; some of the inquiries have not been answered; and Dr. [Hanson] Catlett and [Benjamin] Darlington have replied unfavorably to Woolley. But no accusation specific enough to justify further investigation and prosecution has been received. "I have been taking the most effectual measures to take it out of the power of the officers, to commit a fraud on the government by pocketing the exchange. Prevention is better than punishment. I do hope and believe that the new arrangement of the staff will enable me another year, to bring the Disbursements of the Army into very exact method. The publick has a right to expect it, and if my health and abilities will permit, it shall be done." FC in DNA, 5, 1:94–95.

From Thomas Lloyd, [formerly a shorthand reporter for the 1st Congress,] Philadelphia, 8/26. "On the suggestion of Mr. G[eorge] Boyd, I have again appeared before [Chief] Judge [William] Tilghman [of the Third U.S. Circuit Court] and (instead of getting a *duplicate* of my papers) I have got the *original,* to which I have now added the blank form filled up &c. which was transmitted from the Pension Office thro' him to me. The *original* discharge given me by Lt. Col. Sam[uel] Smith was forwar[d]ed in a note, I think, of 22nd June last." ALS in DNA, 93, W-4672, with a CC of the discharge certificate given by Smith to Lloyd on 2/1/1779 and a DS by Calhoun on 9/25/1818 certifying that Lloyd, as a former Pvt., was granted a Revolutionary pension of $8 per month from 3/28/1818.

From Thomas L. McKenney

Office of Indian Trade, Geo. Town, [D.C.,] August 26 1818
A deputation of the Society of friends, two from Baltimore, viz. Philip E. Thomas and James Elli[c]ott, and two direct from the neighbourhood of Waupagkanetta, where the labors of this society have been in operation for twenty years, the fruits of which are now becoming perfect, have visited this place with a view to represent to the President the consequences of arresting the progress of their labours, which they think will be effectually, and fatally done, by any treaty which the Government may make with those Indians [Shawnees, Wyandots, and Delawares], that shall embrace an abandonment, on their part, of the reservations embraced in a late treaty entered into with them, which was not ratified by the Senate of the United States.

The whole of their views are set forth in a memorial to the President of the United States, which I have the honor herewith to enclose, to you, unsealed, and which is intended for your perusal; and I am requested, by the memorialists, to solicit the favor of you to transmit it to the President with as little delay as possible.

LS with En in DNA, 1, M-270; FC in DNA, 73, E:119.

From Ballard Smith, [Representative from Va.,] Lewisburg, [Va. (later W. Va.),] 8/26. Recommends William Lynn Lewis, who "leaves the Sweet Springs in a few days" on a trip to Washington seeking an appointment as a Cadet; he is "of much intelligence." ALS in DNA, 15, 1819, 123, with an EU showing that an appointment was made on 3/24/1819.

To [former] Col. William Duane

Department of War, 27th Aug[us]t 1818
Shortly after the receipt of your letter of the 9th Jan[uar]y last, the 3d Auditor [Peter Hagner] was directed to proceed in the adjustment of your account, which I understand from him has been done, and the result transmitted to you.

One of the items admitted to your credit, is the charge for a military bureau allowed by Mr. [James] Monroe, while acting as

Secretary at War; and which I presume is referred to in your letter. You will be held liable to account for the bureau.

I have caused a careful examination to be made of the correspondence between you and the Department, but can obtain no information in relation to the various claims which you have submitted, against the government. Without additional evidence, it will be impossible for me to form an opinion whether your claims have a legal or an equitable foundation.

FC in DNA, 3, 10:126.

To Sam[uel] Hodges, Jr., Stoughton, Mass., 8/27. "I have received your letter of the 18th instant. It is necessary for you to make an election between your civil and military appointments, as it is incompatible with the rules of this Department, that you should enter the military, while you exercise the functions of the civil." FC in DNA, 3, 10:126; an LS of identical content but dated at the War Department on 8/28 was offered in Catalogue No. 3 ([June, 1962]) of Kingston Galleries, Inc., 62 Bristol Road, Somerville 44, Mass., and again in 1964 as Item 21 in Catalogue No. 12 of the same firm.

From B[enjamin] Parke, Vincennes, [Ind.,] 8/27. Acknowledges Calhoun's letter to him of 7/27 (Abs in *The Papers of John C. Calhoun,* 2:429) and reiterates his accusations against [Caleb] Lowndes, who moved here from Philadelphia about four years ago and soon earned the reputation of being "totally regardless of truth and callous to all sense of shame." ALS in DNA, 1, P-155.

From T[UNSTALL] QUARLES, [Representative from Ky.]

Somerset [Ky.] August 27th 1818

I have been informed that probably Colo[nel] James Johnson of Kentucky would wish the Contract for supplying the Southern division of the Army of the United States or a part thereof so much as he formerly was bound to furnish and which he has been deprived of by some late arrangement. If not incompatible with other Contracts existing at this time with some other person, I should be highly gratified at his getting the Contract I have stated above. I have no hesitation in saying from my personal acquaintance with Colo[nel] Johnson he would honestly and faithfully comply with any engagement with the Govt. of the United States or any person. His indefatigable industry combined with his abundant resources and his acquaintance in the Western Country would enable him at all times to fulfill any engagements. I am confident no person could get the Contract in the United States who would make use of greater exertions or whose Confidence in the Country at large would be superiour to Colo[nel] James Johnson. Accept assurances of my high respect & consideration.

ALS in DNA, 44.

S[ylvanus] Thayer to Joseph G. Swift

Mil[itary] Academy, West Point, 27th Aug[us]t 1818

I am desirous of obtaining Cadets['] appointments for two young gentlemen who have been recommended to me in a way which leaves no doubt of their being properly qualified for admittance into the Mil[itary] Academy.

The one is George Green, son of Captain Green of Warwick, R[hode] Isl[an]d. He is seventeen years of age, has been fitted for College & is represented to be a lad of uncommon promise.

The other is George Washington Waters of Sutton, Mass[achuset]ts.

ALS in DNA, 15, 1817, 30.

To David Trimble, [Representative from Ky.,] Mount Sterling, Ky., 8/27. Answers his letter of 8/9 (ALS in DNA, 1, T-99) reporting that his brother, Cadet Isaac Trimble, was too ill to report to the Military Academy by 9/1 but might get there by mid-October and requesting that Isaac be granted a furlough. If Isaac cannot reach West Point before October, because of his health, "a suitable indulgence will be granted him. If he does not join [within a few months at most], it may retard him in the progress of his studies a year." FC in DNA, 3, 10:126–127.

To Robert Wright, [former Representative from Md., "Blakeford,"] Queenstown, Md., 8/27. Answers his letter of 8/15 (ALS in DNA, 1, W-186) seeking to recover the property of his son, the late Maj. Clinton Wright, which was reputed to have "been improperly managed." Sends a letter from Col. D[avid] Brearley of the 7th Infantry [Regiment], "which will acquaint you with all that has been done respecting the estate" of the son. "Should you deem any further steps necessary to be taken on the part of the War Department, it will afford me pleasure to give effect to your wishes." FC in DNA, 3, 10:126.

From Maj. John J. Abert, New York [City], 8/28. Encloses and approves an ALS of 8/28 from Lt. Isaac A. Adams to Calhoun, dated at Newark, seeking payment for the time spent by Adams "in drawing and making the necessary calculations" attendant upon his topographical duty—his claim being on the ground that "while on this duty I have no permanent residence and that I am consequently obliged to reside at Taverns." ALS with En in DNA, 1, A-70, with an AEI by Calhoun stating that a rule established in a similar case will apply here, which will mean that Adams can receive no extra pay for time not actually spent in surveying but that he can apply to appropriate Quartermaster officers for quarters.

[2nd] Lt. George Blaney, "Engineer Department," [Washington,] to [Stephen H. Long], 8/28. In behalf of [Joseph G.] Swift, Blaney orders [Long], when he returns to St. Louis, to survey the lots there that "have been reserved for the use of schools by an act of Congress passed the 13 June 1813." CC in DNA, 2, B-1818.

To J[ACOB] BROWN, New York [City], and A[NDREW] JACKSON, Nashville

War Dep[artmen]t, 28 Aug[us]t 1818

At the last Session of Congress, the Secretary of War was directed "to report to the House of Representatives, at an early period of the next Session of Congress, whether any and if any what change ou[gh]t to be made in the ration established by law, and in the mode of issuing the same, and also report a system for the establishment of a Commissariat for the Army."

I have to request your opinion upon all the points of this resolution, in reference to a system adapted to peace or war, as early as practicable.

LS in DLC, Andrew Jackson Papers, 8003; LS (Brown's copy) in MHi; FC in DNA, 3, 10:127; CC in DLC, Jacob Brown Papers, Letterbooks, 2:117.

C[hristopher] Vandeventer to [Jacob] Brown and [Andrew] Jackson, 8/28. In the absence of the Commissary General of Subsistence, [George Gibson,] Vandeventer has been directed to advertise for bidders to supply rations, to be delivered in bulk at the most convenient depots, [for one year to begin in the spring of 1819]. He asks the two Generals to check the enclosed advertisement and to make any suggestions concerning the quantity and components of the rations, the locations of the depots, and the organization of the Commissary Department. FC in DNA, 3, 10:128.

From [former 1st Lt.] Samuel Hodges, Jr., Stoughton, Mass., 8/28. Following up his letter of 8/18, he offers to accept the proffered commission in the Artillery Corps, report to the Army's commanding officer at Portsmouth, N.H., for duty, await there the news whether or not "the Court of Rio De Janeiro" will recognize him as Consul to the Cape Verde Islands, and, if so, to serve as Consul without Army pay for two years, but, if not, to remain in the Army. ALS in DNA, 1, H-256.

To Gates Hoyt, Plattsburg, N.Y., 8/28. "Your letter of the 15th of August, relative to the claims of yourself and Mr. Hatch, for secret service, during the late war, has been received. Claims of this kind require, by an act of Congress, the special sanction of the President, and as he is absent your claims cannot be acted on 'till his return. To me your evidence seems still very defective, and tho' I am aware that transactions of the kind which you performed, cannot receive the usual formalities of ordinary accounts, there is no good reason, but what they ought to have the explicit sanction of the officers under whose agreement they were performed, both as to the nature of the service and the amount of compensation which ought to be made." FC in DNA, 3, 10:127.

From Joseph McMinn

Murfreesboro, Tennessee, 28th August 1818

I was honored with the receipt of your several dispatches by [the] last mail under date [of the] 29th July, viz., one on the subject of [obtaining emigration under] the Cherokee Treaty [of 1817], the other covering Capt. Byrd[']s Pay Roll, having previously received a letter from Mr. C[hristopher] Vandeventer dated 25th June written in your absence which came to hand on the 18th July.

I beg you to be assured that it is with no common degree of pleasure I find in them the most ample grounds of Justification for the manner in which I have executed the trust reposed in me, more particularly as the greater part was conducted under circumstances of the most embarrassing nature and which the Justice and honor of the U[nited] States require should be met with a degree of energy which our Cherokee neighbours from a long course of humane policy practised with them by the U[nited] States did not expect from it. To myself it has always been a source of the highest pleasure ever to receive Justification for any public acts, but how much more acceptable must it be, to receive in the very flattering terms which you are pleased to manifest, the approbation of the President and yourself.

I believe I have not stated to you (though as none of the copies of my letters are here, I cannot be certain) that my life has been threatened in a variety of instances, particularly at Ostannilly at our last meeting. There I was notified before I had time to dismount from my horse, that if I introduced the subject of an Exchange of Countries, the Council had determined to put me to death. Threats had been made long before I set out for the talk, and numbers of my friends were very unwilling that I should proceed without a Guard. I discharged Byrd and his company the day I set out, and myself and boy travelled alone, and the only injury I sustained was the loss of my horses which I have previously communicated. I hope it will not be found that I have troubled you with the history of my personal danger in any former letter; my impression is that I avoided doing so lest it might be supposed that I acted from personal feeling.

I will carefully avoid (as you have suggested) a disclosure of the Plan as coming from the Government; in fact, I had anticipated the propriety of the utmost precaution and did not even surrender my written plan, but delivered it verbally, and stated distinctly, that I had not received your instructions. Having, however, received the most honorable sanction, it shall receive my best efforts for its final accomplishment.

I am using every exertion to leave here about the 1st Sep[tembe]r next for the Agency, from whence I shall write you on my arrival; in the mean time beg you to address your letter to Washington, Rhea Court House [Tenn.]. With sentiments of Grateful respect I am . . . .

ALS in DNA, 1, M-301; FC in DNA, 75 (M-208:14). NOTE: PC's of the two letters from Calhoun to McMinn dated 7/29 appear in *The Papers of John C. Calhoun,* 2:436–439; an Abs of Vandeventer's dated 6/25 is in *ibid.,* 2:349.

C[hristopher] Vandeventer to [Alexander] Macomb, [Eleazer W.] Ripley, and [Thomas A.] Smith, 8/28. In the absence of the Commissary General of Subsistence, [George Gibson,] Vandeventer is seeking bids for bulk rations, to be delivered at convenient depots. He refers to the *National Intelligencer* for 8/28, [an advertisement in] which gives the details of the arrangements he has made. He requests suggestions concerning the quantity and components of the rations, the locations of the depots, and the organization of the Commissary Department. FC in DNA, 3, 10:128.

From [Lt. Col.] GEORGE E. MITCHELL

Baltimore, [*ca.* Aug. 28, 1818]

John Boyle McCoy (the adopted Son of Major [James H.] Boyle of the U.S. Army & who was a most valuable officer) who was appointed a Cadet last September has been prevented by frequent indispositions from completing the preparatory studies necessary for admittance at West Point. If, Sir, you would authorize him to remain with me until the perfect recovery of his health, & he is *prepared for examination,* you would much oblige me, & benefit a promising youth. Major Boyle had nothing to leave this Orphan but a good name, as will appear by the enclosed letter written just before his death. Please to return this letter with your answer.

ALS in DNA, 11, 12512. NOTE: An EU is dated 8/29/1818.

To David A. Ogden, Madrid, N.Y.

Department of War, 28 Aug[us]t 1818

In my letter of the 19th instant, I stated that Gov[erno]r [Lewis] Cass would be requested to consult with the Indians on Fox river and its vicinity, as to the settlement of the Senecas among them. This direction, as you will see by a reference to the letter itself, was given on a supposition that the river referred to, was to the North of the territory of Illinois; but by referring to a fuller and more recent map I find that a river of that name is within the territory, and Gov[erno]r Cass has been instructed not to attempt any arrangement with the Indians in the [State of] Illinois for any cession, for the purpose of accommodating the Senecas, as the Government has already taken steps to extinguish the Indian title within the Illinois territory.

FC in DNA, 72, D:208; LS in NN, Indians (Box)—Iroquois.

From S[amuel] Smith, [Representative from Md.]

Baltimore, 28 Aug[us]t 1818

The present [letter] will be handed [to you] by [Bvt. Lt.] Col. [Nathan] Towson. He informs me that he contemplates leaving the [Army's] service. His pay as a Captain will not support a family. His gallant services during the late War [of 1812] give him as great a Claim on his Country as that of any Citizen of the U.S. He will explain to you his wishes. I have known the Colonel from his infancy. He is Capable of any Office that he will accept. His Character in private life is unblemished. His honor & integrity may safely be relied upon. You will render an essential to a Gentleman who highly merits it, if you will use your best Endeavours to promote his Views and will Confer a great favour on d[ea]r sir your friend & servant, S. Smith.

ALS in DNA, 11, 12883.

Th[omas] T[udor] Tucker, Treasurer of the U.S., Washington, to Christopher Vandeventer, 8/28. As requested by Vandeventer in behalf of Calhoun on 8/27, Tucker lists all bills drawn by the

Treasury to Maj. A[bram] R. Woolley in payment of warrants issued by the War Department, 1/1813–6/1818. "It is not for me to say what paper has depreciated and what not." LS with En in DNA, 1, W-200.

From JOHN WILLIAMS, [Senator from Tenn.]

Knoxville, Aug[us]t 28th 1818

You will herewith recieve [*sic*] a Nashville paper containing the first bullatin [*sic*] from [Andrew Jackson's Southern Division] *Head Quarters* [there], on the President[']s order to restore Pensacola. Great efforts have been made to forestal[l] public opinion on this subject. But with little effect. The dissatisfaction which exists in this State in relation to the President[']s decision is (as far as I can learn) confined to *Head Quarters*, the speculators in Florida property, and a swarm of sycophants who act upon the English principle that the General can do no wrong.

ALS in NN, James Monroe Papers.

From William O. Winston, New York [City], 8/28. Reviews his services as a Judge Advocate under Gens. [William Henry] Harrison and [Andrew] Jackson, *ca.* 1812–1815 and 1816–1818, and his discharge last spring; acting upon a suggestion by [Thomas S.] Jesup, applies for reappointment as successor to [Rider Henry] Winder, who has resigned. ALS in DNA, 11, 12995.

To Paymaster General Robert Brent, Commissary General of Purchases C[allender] Irvine, Surgeon General [Joseph] Lovell, Quartermaster General [Thomas S.] Jesup, Chief Engineer [Joseph G.] Swift, and Chief of Ordnance D[ecius] Wadsworth, 8/29. Calhoun requests their budget estimates for their respective offices for 1819, with each item of appropriation itemized and an estimate of what will be due for arrearages. FC in DNA, 3, 10:129; LS (Brent's copy) in ScU-SC, John C. Calhoun Papers; LS (Lovell's copy) in DNA, 245, 1:27; CC (Lovell's copy) in DNA, 244, A:4; LS (Swift's copy) in DNA, 23, 45.

To [William H. Crawford], 8/29. Asks him "to place in the hands of the Treasurer of the U[nited] States," [Thomas Tudor

Tucker,] $692,204.98, "being the balance of appropriations for Pensions for the years 1817 and 1818." FC in DNA, 171, 1:303.

To the Rev. JOHN D. GARDINER, Sag Harbor (Long Island), [N.Y.]

War Dep[artmen]t, 29th August 1818

I have received your letter of the 17th Inst[ant] in relation to the unoccupied room in the U[nited] States arsenal at Sag Harbour. I have directed the Col. of the Ordnance Department [Decius Wadsworth] to give orders to the Military Storekeeper, to gra[n]t the permission under the conditions on which it has been requested, to make use of the room for religious purposes, till further orders are received. Orders had been given to make sales of the arsenal a few weeks since, and the permission cannot continue longer than till the sale.

I am happy to hear from you and will be at any time happy to render you any service consistent with my duty to the Publick. I hope that your health is good and that you have been p[r]osperous and happy since we parted.

ALS in NcD.

To W[illiam] Y[oung] Hansell, Augusta, Ga., 8/29. Calhoun returns the papers sent to him in Hansell's letter of 8/20, commenting that Calhoun cannot become involved in a matter of private business "between yourself, Mr. [Otho W.] Callis and Mr. [Benjamin G.] Orr." FC in DNA, 3, 10:129.

JOSEPH LOVELL to GEORGE E. MITCHELL

Surgeon Gen[era]l's Office, Washington, August 29, 1818

Doct[o]r [Sylvester] Day resigned his commission as Surgeon of 5th Inf[antr]y on condition of being Post Surgeon at Fort Mifflin, where the Secretary [of War] believed Dr. [Joseph] Wallace to be; who was therefore promoted to that Regiment. On my appointment I found Dr. [Samuel B.] Smith was stationed at Fort Mifflin. Of course under these circumstances it became necessary for him to leave it. When I became acquainted with the Dr.'s situation, I represented it to the Secretary, who being desirous to accommodate both gentlemen as far as possible, directed a Post Surgeon to be stationed at Philadelphia, & that they should be allowed to arrange the matter between themselves. I stated this to Dr. Smith when [he was] here a few weeks since, & he *appeared* to be perfectly satisfied, as he made no objection whatever. In consequence of this Doct[o]r Day was ordered by the Adj[utan]t & Insp[ecto]r Gen[era]l [Daniel Parker] to repair to Philadelphia & await orders, & to communicate to this office the result of their determination, that the necessary instructions may be given on the subject from the Adj[utan]t & Insp[ecto]r Gen[era]l[']s office. Had Dr. Smith objected at first perhaps some other arrangement might have been thought of, but after what has been done, it appears unreasonable for him to require more.

LS in DNA, 11, 12460.

To James Monroe, [Albemarle County, Va.]

War Dep[artmen]t, 29th August 1818

Mr. [John Quincy] Adams left here yesterday; and requested me to open and read the dispa[t]ches from abroad; and to forward to you such as might have any interest. Yesterday's mail brought the enclosed from Mr. [Richard] Rush [in London] and Mr. Irvin [George W. Erving, Minister to Spain]; and they are forwarded agreeably to Mr. Adam[s]'s request.

Cap[tain James] Gadsden arrived yesterday and has brought the copies of the dispa[t]ches from Gen[era]l [Andrew] Jackson [sent on 5/5], the originals of which miscarried. He also brought letters [of 8/10] from Gen[era]l Jackson, of which one is addressed to you and the other to the [War] Department. I enclose both, with a request that the one to me may be returned after you have perused it, as I have not yet answered it. The copies of the proceedings of the court martial in the case of [Alexander] Arbuthnot and [Robert Christy] Ambrister, ["with" *canceled*] & the other dispa[t]ches, I will transmit to you as soon as I have perused them. Capt. Gadsden is under the necessity of going on to New Haven; and cannot go on, at least till after his return, to Albema[r]le [to confer with you], as you wished when you left here.

You will see by Gen[era]l Jackson's letter to me that Col. [Arthur P.] Hayne is about to resign; and that he [Jackson] is anxious for Capt. Gadsden to be appointed in his place. He is a valuable officer and I would be sorry to loose [*sic*] him from the Engineer Corps; but as it is his wish and as he no doubt would be well qualified for the place held by Col. Hayne, I think it would be proper to confer the appointment when the vacancy occurs.

P.S. The act relative to the flag (of the last session) has not been acted on by the War and Navy Departments. I send for your selection two patterns. The only difference is in the distribution of the stars. The one distributed in the form of a square is the most simple, but the other is more emblematical of our Union. As it is necessary to act in relation to this subject soon, I will thank you for the determination as soon as it is made.

ALS in DLC, James Monroe Papers, 4839–4840; PC in Jameson, ed., *Correspondence*, p. 139, where an editorial note errs in assuming that the lost dispatches were not of 5/5 but included a Jackson letter of 1/6. NOTE: An Abs of Jackson's letter of 5/5 to Calhoun appears in *The Papers of John C. Calhoun*, 2:280, with references to several PC's of it. An Abs of Jackson's letter of 8/10 to Calhoun appears herein under that date, with references to two sources in which its text can be found and with references also to Jackson's letter of 8/10 to Monroe.

To Benjamin Parke, 8/29. Answering his letter of 8/16, Calhoun says: "I hope, most sincerely, that your negotiation may prove successful. The funds which have been put under your orders, both in goods and money, were not intended to limit the stipulation which may be made for the lands in negotiation; but as the means of bringing about the treaty. If the sum in specie should not be found sufficient, the Commissioners may draw (in addition to the six for which you now have power) the further sum of ten thousand dollars. In relation to Mr. [Caleb] Lowndes, I wrote to you under date of the 27th of last month [FC in DNA, 72, D:189–190; Abs in *The Papers of John C. Calhoun*, 2:429], which I expect you have received ere now." FC in DNA, 72, D:209.

From Carlos Monefon, Baltimore, 8/30. Since [John Quincy Adams] is reported to be away from his office, Monefon asks Calhoun, because of "the nobleness of your character," to obtain, open, and answer immediately the appeal that Monefon sent on 8/28 to

[Adams, William H. Crawford, Calhoun, and Benjamin W. Crowninshield] in the care of the first. "Translated copy" in DNA, 1, M-291.

From Beaufort T[aylor] Watts, Cambridge, S.C., 8/30. His brother, John Watts, accepts appointment as a Cadet and will report as ordered. ALS in DNA, 15, 1818, 126.

To Maj. John J. Abert, New York [City], 8/31. "I have received your letter of the 21st instant. The rule established in the case of Lieut[enant William G.] McNeil[l], will apply to that of Lieut[enant Isaac A.] Adams. The difficulties of residing in Taverns, as you state there, may be obviated by making a requisition for quarters on the Q[uarter] Master's Dep[artmen]t." FC in DNA, 3, 10:129.

To N[icholas] Boilvin, Indian Agent, Prairie du Chien, [Mich. Territory,] 8/31. "Your letter of the 3d ult[im]o [PC in *The Papers of John C. Calhoun,* 2:357–358] is received. You are authorized to engage a blacksmith for the benefit of the Indian tribes of your Agency, upon the best possible terms. You will report these terms to this Department." FC in DNA, 72, D:208.

From Thomas S. Jesup, 8/31. "Mr. Willson [that is, Robert Wilson, Military Storekeeper at Charleston, S.C.,] has been required under the late order of the War Dep[artmen]t in relation to Storekeepers & Battalion & Regimental Q[uarte]r Masters to perform the duties of Quarter Master" there. LS in DNA, 1, J-198; FC in DNA, 42, 1:46.

From William Prince, Vincennes, [Ind.,] 8/31. He will begin today his trip to St. Marys for the Indian treaty negotiations. [Caleb] Lowndes has tried in vain to get the Indians to sign a paper deeding their land to the French people here. Prince is confident that the Wea Indians will be willing to sell their lands. He will meet the Kickapoos at Fort Harrison on 9/2 to ascertain whether they will accept their annuity and proceed to the treaty. He has incurred unusual expenses in preparing the way for the negotiations. LS in DNA, 1, P-159.

From Maj. M[oses] Swett, New York [City], 8/31. Acknowledges Calhoun's letter of 8/24 ruling that Swett's claim for double rations as commandant of Fort Lewis, [N.Y.,] 11/1/1816–4/30/1817, could not be approved. Protests that the fort was considered a separate post the commander of which was entitled to such rations and that his experience justified this allowance, because "strangers and passing officers were daily visitors." Encloses a deposition supporting this view signed by Winfield Scott as commanding officer of the 1st and 3rd Military Departments at New York [City], 8/28. LS with ADS by Scott in DNA, 1, S-188.

From J[OSEPH] G. SWIFT

Engineer Department, 31 Aug. 1818

Major [Stephen H.] Long has submitted to my examination a List of Astronomical & other Philosophical Instruments which he proposes to use in the geographical survey about to be undertaken by him in a Steam Boat. In my opinion every Instrument which he has mentioned will be necessary to satisfy the enquiries which he will make in those Territories as yet very imperfectly known to us.

LS in DNA, 2, S-1818.

From Joseph Wheaton, Washington, 8/——. In an effort to make his appeal of 8/6 more persuasive, reviews at length his services from 1812 through 1817. LS in DNA, 1, W-197.

SEPTEMBER 1818

Continuing to serve, in effect, as the Acting President of the United States during part of September, Calhoun maintained his unusual correspondence with the absent President, James Monroe. Andrew Jackson's reaction to the restoration of the Spanish posts in the Floridas was still a matter of concern to Monroe and Calhoun. Threats of renewed hostilities by the Seminoles loomed larger in the minds of Generals Jackson and Edmund P. Gaines than in Calhoun's. Indian treaties were negotiated in the Northwest, and Calhoun initiated the surveying of Indian boundary lines in the South. He began more pointedly than before to obtain information that he would report to the next session of Congress. And he began to receive letters recommending the award of contracts for rations and transportation in the West to James Johnson of Kentucky, whose operations were destined to give Calhoun concern for years.

To [Lt. Col.] Talbot Chambers, St. Louis, 9/1. "Ever willing to support commandants against contractors," Calhoun confirms what he wrote to Chambers on [8/26] but urges Chambers to submit as soon as possible evidence of the failure of contractor [Hugh Glenn]. CC in DNA, 66. Chambers answered from Bellefontaine, [Mo. Territory,] on 10/11. ALS in DNA, 1, C-34; CC in DNA, 66.

To Edmund P. Gaines, Fort Hawkins, Ga.

War Dept., 1 Sep[tembe]r 1818

Gen[era]l [Andrew] Jackson has transmitted to this Department a copy of his letter to you of the 7th instant. It is to be presumed that his orders in relation to St. Augustine were given before he was apprized of the decision of the President [James Monroe] in relation to St. Marks and Pensacola; as the principle on which that decision was made, would equally extend to the case of St. Augustine. You will, accordingly, not carry that part of Gen[era]l Jackson's order into execution, except to collect with care the evidence of such facts as go to prove any countenance or assistance from the Spanish Authorities, in St. Augustine, to the hostile Indians; and should you ascertain that they have afforded any, you will report the facts properly supported by evidence to this Department.

You will also report the facts upon which you ordered the issue of rations to the Indians, and the extent of the issue. I refer to the issue which is alluded to in Gen[era]l Jackson's letter to you of the 7th instant, as the Department has not, as yet, received any information on that subject.

LS in DNA, 11, 12215; FC in DNA, 3, 10:130; CC in DNA, 77 (M-271:2, frames 0960–0965); CC in DLC, Andrew Jackson Papers, 8018; PC in *American State Papers: Military Affairs,* 1:745. NOTE: In reply on 9/23 (LS with 2 Ens in DNA, 1, G-125; LS in DNA, 11, 12215), Gaines admitted that there was little evidence (comprising merely oral testimony given by Indians and "blacks") that the Spanish at St. Augustine had afforded ammunition or any other aid to enemies of the U.S.

From Jos[eph] Kent, "Rose Mount," [near Bladensburg, Md.,] 9/1. Recommends Dr. Benjamin King of Md., who graduated in medicine from the University of Md. "last spring," for an appointment as a Post Surgeon. Appended is an AES dated 9/11 by Jos[eph] Lovell observing that "Doct[or] King having so *recently graduated,* does not appear to be qualified for a Post Surgeon." ALS in DNA, 11, 12407.

To Col. William King, Pensacola, 9/1. "I have received your letter of the 20th July last [Abs in *The Papers of John C. Calhoun,* 2:407], and have examined Mr. [Camillus] Griffith's contract. There can be no doubt, as the contract is express, that he is liable to furnish the troops at Pensacola, or any other place in Florida in the vicinity of the States of Louisiana, Mississippi or Territory of Alabama." FC in DNA, 3, 10:131.

From Pierre Menard, Kaskaskia, [Ill. Territory,] 9/1. Submits his claim for carrying to the Piankashaw Indians in 1816 their annuity. LS in DLC, United States: Finance, "Unarranged Box 6."

To JAMES MONROE, [Albemarle County, Va.]

War Dept., 1st Sep[tembe]r 1818

I mentioned in my last [on 8/29] that Captain [James] Gadsden had arrived and that he had brought a copy of the proceedings of the court martial, in the case of [Alexander] Arbuthnot and [Robert C.] Ambrister; and a copy of those dispatches [sent by Andrew Jackson on 5/5] which miscarried, with some other papers of minor importance, which I ["would" *canceled*] will transmit to you as soon as I have perused them. On examination, I found that some of the papers had not been translated, which prevented me from sending the papers yesterday. The papers are important and interesting, and it is to be regretted that they had not been received at an earlier period. I think, however, that they contain nothing which ought or would have changed the decision to restore St. Marks or Pansacola [*sic*].

Among the papers transmitted herewith is a copy of a letter from Gen[era]l Jackson to Gen[era]l [Edmund P.] Gain[e]s, ordering the latter, in a certain event, to take possession of St. Augustine. I have countermanded the order; and enclosed you will find a copy of the letter to Gen[era]l Gain[e]s containing the countermanding order. Gen[era]l Jackson seems in fact to anticipate that his order would be countermanded.

Mr. [Sir Charles] Bagot, [British representative in Washington,] called on me yesterday to obtain a copy of the proceedings of the court martial to send by a messenger, whom he was about to dispatch, to London. I informed him that they would be transmitted to you, and would be subject to such orders as you might give. He expressed much anxiety, in consequence of the delay, which had taken place from the miscarriage, & desires to obtain a copy as soon as possible to transmit to his government. He stated that he would call again to know the result, as soon as I should hear from you.

Mr. [George] Boyd has already received the appointment of Indian agent, which was vacant. I treated him, in consequence of his connexions, with much more kindness than he deserved.

The sentence of the court will be carried into effect in Dr. [Samuel B.] Hugo's case.

I send herewith this morning's Inte[lligence]r. It contains English news of a very late date; and among other things a very exag[g]erated rumour in relation to Pansacola.

Letters have been received from Mr. [Albert] Gallatin, as late as the 6th of July. They are unimportant. I transmit to you a letter from the King of Wurtemburg, enclosed by Mr. Gallatin.

I am happy to hear of the good effect of your fine mountain air and exercise on your health. I hope that Mrs. Monroe's health is also much improved. Myself and family are well.

ALS in NN, James Monroe Papers.

To PATRICK NOBLE, [Abbeville, S.C.]

War Dept., 1st Sept. 1818

I was very glad to hear by your letter of the 17th of August that you were all well, and hope, that, if you have suffered much by the dry weather, it will, as is usual, be compensated by a proportionate share of health. The land warrant has been issued and lodged in the land office, in the case of the heirs of Young; and the patent, when it issues, will be transmitted to you agreeably to your request. They have not commenced drawing yet in the Missouri Territory.

I am glad to hear, that there is not much doubt of your's and [Eldred] Simkins' election [to the S.C. and U.S. Houses of Representatives, respectively]. I felt some fears for yours, while in Carolina, from a strong disposition, which I understood existed to change the old members. I trust however that the people of Abbeville have too much good sense and justice to permit such feelings of indiscriminate opposition to influence them.

In regard to the Floridas not much can be said with certainty. If Spain had any just knowledge of her own interest the cession would certainly take place immediately; but she regulates her conduct in this, as I believe [in] any other particular, upon principles irreconcilable with the dictates of wisdom. It may be relied on that our govt. will omit no fair opportunity to acquire them. As valuable as they are to us, they would cost too much, if acquired by war with Spain (the consequences of which can not be estimated with any certainty) or by any means, which the high moral sense of the country would not fully approbate.

The papers will give you the latest European news. The capture of Pansacola [*sic*] seems, by the English papers, to constitute war between this country and Spain. I do not my self [*sic*] apprehend that consequence unless England will urge Spain to that determination; and I think the fears of the consequences to herself will prevent her from attempting that course.

My best respects to all of my friends of the Village, to Mr. [George] Bowie & family & Dr. [John Henry] Miller & family. Floride joins her love to you & Elizabeth. We are all well; the child [Anna Maria Calhoun] has been very puny but is now pretty well.

[P.S.] I left the copy of the will of Mr. [Andrew] Pickens [Sr.] with Mr. [George] McDuffie, with direction to bring suit, if it cannot be otherwise adjusted. The cure is really so clear, that it is to be regretted that Gov[erno]r [Andrew] Pickens [Jr.] should not view it in its proper light. McDuffie thinks that there is not a shadow of a doubt.

ALS in ScCleA; PC in *The Journal of Southern History,* vol. XVI, no. 1 (February, 1950), pp. 66–67.

From J[oseph] G. Swift, 9/1. Recommends that Col. "Pinckney [Ninian Pinkney ?] may be ordered to receive the Public Property which Lieut[enant William Henry] Chase of the Engineers may deliver to him." ALS in DNA, 11, 610 (M-566:5).

To J[oseph] G. Swift, 9/1. Calhoun approves [Stephen H.] Long's plan to use a steamboat for explorations to be made in the West and Southwest. Swift is instructed to assign Long to this duty. Long can contract for such a boat but should spend "the least sum practicable." The bill is to be paid, so far as possible, from next year's appropriation. LS in DNA, 23, 46 (151); FC in DNA, 3, 10:130.

From Ho[well] Tatum, Nashville, 9/1. Encloses a statement for August showing that he has $8,342.70 for which he is to account in the future. Intends to make as of 9/30 a comprehensive financial report of his services as agent to settle Quartermaster claims in West Tenn.; then he can be given compensation for his "tedious" work; he hopes it will be "liberal." LS with En in DNA, 1, T-102.

From D[ecius] Wadsworth, 9/1. "I have concluded an agreement with Mr. Peter Townsend, rectifying the mistake in his Contract relative to the price" of the medium, 18-pounder cannon. An advance of $15,000 will complete the $60,000 of advances called for by the contract; and he has agreed to receive half now and the remainder next December. Asks that $7,500 be advanced to Townsend now. FC in DNA, 32, 2:102.

To Lewis Cass, Detroit, 9/2. Encloses a copy of Calhoun's letter [of 8/28] to David A. Ogden; "I wish it understood that the [Iroquois] Indians are not to receive lands in exchange for those they have in New York, within the State of Indiana or Illinois." FC in DNA, 72, D:208.

To [John Chew, Washington,] 9/2. Calhoun answers affirmatively his request of 9/2 (ALS in DNA, 1, C-217), made in behalf of the Commonwealth of Va., that it be permitted to retain 100,000 musket carriages and 50,000 pistol cartridges "out of the fixed ammunition now about being turned over by the State to the United States. Capt. [Jeremiah D.] Ha[y]den will be instructed accordingly by the Col. of Ordnance," [Decius Wadsworth]. FC in DNA, 3, 10:131.

To Joel Crawford, [Representative from Ga.]

Department of War, 2d September 1818

I have received your letter of the 19th of July. To obtain satisfactory information [about what payment may be claimed by a Ga. Regiment which did not receive all rations due to it during the War of 1812], it will be necessary to furnish the names of the commanding officers of the respective Companies, because, in some cases, the rations were issued complete, and in others the provisions were delivered in bulk and issued by the Q[uarte]r Masters.

FC in DNA, 3, 10:132; PC in Miller, *The Bench and Bar of Georgia: Memoirs and Sketches . . .*, 1:467. Note: An Abs of Crawford's letter of 7/19 appears in *The Papers of John C. Calhoun*, 2:399–400. Miller's book, at the page cited, contains also a PC of a letter of 9/15 from Crawford to Gen. [David] Blackshear showing that Crawford was acting in this matter for Blackshear and that Crawford considered Calhoun's letter of 9/2 to be bureaucratically evasive.

From Third Auditor Peter Hagner, 9/2. Explains that he cannot approve, without Calhoun's authorization, the claim for a refund of outlays made for food, labor, etc., under direction of the Commissioners of Fortifications at Charleston, S.C., because copies of contracts and proper vouchers have not been submitted. LS owned in 1954 by E.F. Slater of New York City, who has since died; FC (initialed "R[ichard] B[urgess]") in DNA, 53, 5:192. (The LS bears an AES and an AEI by Calhoun, each undated. One directs Hagner, as a prerequisite to Calhoun's authorization for payment, to obtain from the Commissioners "the additional vouchers if in their possession and if not such explination [*sic*] as they may be able to furnish." The other indicates that John Horlbeck wrote on 9/30 satisfactorily to Hagner and that Calhoun then approved the claim.)

From Andrew Jackson, Nashville, 9/2. Encloses his answer dated 9/2 to the letter from Lt. Col. Mathew Arbuckle to himself dated 7/16 (Abs in *The Papers of John C. Calhoun,* 2:388); in Jackson's opinion, Arbuckle has been largely exonerated, but Calhoun will make the ultimate decision. ALS with Ens in DNA, 11, 11823.

To Andrew Jackson, Nashville

War Dept., 2 Sep[tembe]r 1818

The accounts of Mr. [Benjamin G.] Orr being under examination, it is desirable, that all charges which ought to be placed to his account should be made known to the Department.

Col. [George] Gibson has furnished the Department with no information in relation to his late disbursements, at New Orleans, and as it is probable that a part at least of those disbursements were on account of the contractor, it is important that the necessary information should be had in relation to them, and you will, accordingly, order Col. Gibson and all other Quarter Masters, as well as all officers acting in the Quarter Master's Department of your division, who made purchases of provisions, to render a statement of the same to the Department. In all cases where purchases were made upon the failure of the contractor, the evidence of such failure as well as of the distribution of the supply, should accompany these statements. Major [Milo] Mason has already rendered the statement required by the regulations.

I have seen it stated, that the Editor of the Savannah Republican had in his possession, or had read a copy of the proceedings of the Court which tried [Alexander] Arbuthnot and [Robert C.] Ambrister. I make this remark as it is probable by proper enquiry some information may be obtained which will lead to the discovery of the original proceedings, which were directed to this Department.

LS in DLC, Andrew Jackson Papers, 8027; FC in DNA, 3, 10:132.

To Col. William King, Pensacola, 9/2. "You will report, as early as practicable, a copy of the special contract made by Col. [George Mercer] Brooke with Mr. [Benjamin G.] Orr's agent. If it were verbal, a certified statement from Colonel Brooke is required." FC in DNA, 3, 10:132.

To R[eturn] J. Meigs, [Jr.,] 9/2. "It has been reported to me that the Editor of the Savannah Republican has stated that he possessed or had seen a copy of the proceedings of the general court martial which tried [Alexander] Arbuthnot and [Robert C.] Ambrister. It is probable this intimation, if pursued by instructing the post master there, may lead to the discovery of the original documents, and the cause of their miscarriage." FC in DNA, 3, 10:131.

To James Monroe, [Albemarle County, Va.]

War Dept., 2d Sep[tembe]r 1818

I enclose the translation of letter No. 2 from the Commandant of St. Marks to the Gov[erno]r of Pansacola [*sic*], which was not translated in time for yesterday's mail.

ALS in NN, James Monroe Papers.

From J[ames] B. Reynolds, Clarksville, Tenn., 9/2. Acknowledges Calhoun's letter of 8/12. The new commissioners chosen to inspect the road being built [from Reynoldsburg] under a contract by [Dawsey P.] Hudson have told Reynolds that they will report directly to the War Department. ALS in DNA, 2, R-1818.

From Winfield Scott, Elizabethtown, N.J., 9/2. Encloses an "analysis of a work long since projected by me"—a compilation of rules and regulations for the War Department. The preparation of this work has involved much study of all English and French treatises on the subject; and Scott has been helped by his 10 years of experience in the line and staff, in the Infantry and Artillery. Proposes how the publication of a book expanding this "analysis" might be procured, his own compensation while compiling the book, and how he might gain the benefit of corrective opinions from other Army officers. The book would give its author no literary fame; but, because of its potential usefulness, "I should not deem the essay as unworthy of any talents or rank which the country possesses." PC with En in *American State Papers: Military Affairs,* 2:199–267; PC with En in House Document No. 45, 16th Cong., 2nd Sess.; PEx in G. Norman Lieber, *Remarks on the Army Regulations and Executive Regulations in General* (War Department Document No. 93. Washington: U.S. Government Printing Office, 1898), p. 53.

From H[ENRY] SHERBURNE

Chickasaw Agency, September 2d 1818

Inclosed is Perry Cohea's account for articles furnished this Agency amounting to Three hundred & ninety-nine dollars & five cents, with Mr. Malcom [*sic*] McGee his Attorney's receipt thereon, which amount I have this day drawn on you for at sight. The articles have generally cost more than I contemplated[,] particularly the paint & saddles. The first of these articles I consider necessary for the preservation of the outside of the [Agency] House; had it been painted when built the greater part of the Expence that now must accrue for repairing and covering might [have] been saved. The saddles are frequently wanted (& none to be bought or borrowed here,) particularly at this time as a Journey of One hundred & Twenty miles must soon be made to the Chickasaw Bluffs to deliver the nation their Annuity in Goods for this year & for other necessary purposes they are often wanted; the Bar Iron & Steel Mr. Cohea brought the Agency was so indifferent that I would not receive it, but being now intirely [*sic*] without those articles must immediately purchase them in the best way I can.

A few days since I received a letter from General [Andrew] Jackson acquainting me that the proposed Treaty with this nation was to be held the first of October next & that the place & period met the approbation of the Commissioners, & requested that I would use my exertions in promoting a general meeting, which I shall cheerfully do, or anything further that is in my power to promote the object of his mission.

LS in U.S. General Accounting Office, Indian Tribal Branch, Fifth Auditor Accounts, no. 582, account of Henry Sherburne.

To Lt. Col. Nathan Towson, [Greenleafs Point, D.C.,] 9/2. Answers his letter of 9/1 (ALS in DNA, 1, T-100) announcing that the "Board of officers for the amelioration of the Artillery" had "met this day" and was "ready to receive any communication from the War office"; replies that [Decius Wadsworth] "will be instructed to make to the Board such communications as may be deemed necessary to acquaint it with the objects for its deliberations." FC in DNA, 3, 10:131.

From Ab[raha]m Bradley, Jr., [Washington,] 9/3. "In compliance with your note of yesterday [addressed to Return J. Meigs, Jr.,] the postmaster at Savannah has been instructed to obtain information from the Editor of the Savan[na]h Republican, & if he finds any clue to pursue it [until] he obtains or discovers what has become of the dispatches of Gen. [Andrew] Jackson. The postmaster at Milledgeville was previously directed to ascertain from the officers of the Army in his neighbourhood or at Fort Hawkins who was intrusted [*sic*] with the dispatches, what route the person took, & to spare no pains in ascertaining what has become of them." ALS in DNA, 1, B-286.

From Robert Butler, Adjutant General of the Southern Division, Nashville, 9/3. Answers Calhoun's inquiry addressed to [Andrew] Jackson on 8/12; states that nothing has been done toward repair of an existing road between Columbia, Tenn., and Madisonville, La., but that the issuance of contracts has been initiated toward construction of the military road between those places, which Jackson believes that Congress will find acceptable. Butler promises a further report as soon as possible, [which apparently was made on 9/19]. LS with En in DNA, 1, B-148.

To [Dr.] Thomas Cooper, Philadelphia

Department of War, 3d Septem[be]r 1818

I am directed by the President [James Monroe] to communicate with you in relation to the application of Mr. [Thomas] Say and Mr. [Thomas] Nuttall, to go out in the Macedonian, the one as a Zoölogist, the other as a Botanist. I have consulted with the Navy Department on their application; and I find, that the Macedonian is under sailing orders, and will probably sail in a few days, so that the wishes of the young gentlemen cannot be complied with for the present.

It would have been a source of pleasure to me, to contribute in any degree to afford so good an opportunity to persons, so eminently qualified as Mr. Say and Mr. Nuttall appear to be, to add to the stock of science, and their own and their country's reputation. It is not improbable that a similar opportunity may shortly again present itself.

FC in DNA, 3, 10:136.

To Edmund P. Gaines, or Officer Commanding, Pensacola

War Dept., 3 Sept., 1818

The Honble. Wilson Lumpkin has been appointed a Commissioner to run the line, provisionally, between the United States and Florida, from the Appalachicola to the head of St. Marys.

You will furnish him, upon his requisition, with such a Military Force as he may deem necessary for his protection.

LS in DNA, 11, 12215; FC in DNA, 3, 10:135.

To Walter Jones, Esq., Washington

War Dep[artmen]t, 3d Sep[tembe]r 1818

Col. [Josiah] Snelling's report, (which I enclose for your perusal) furnishes conclusive proof, as to the guilt of Pease; and I trust such measures will be taken, as will enable the government to avail itself of it on his trial. The testimony of Col. Snelling and the production of the original papers, I presume will be necessary, and as he is subject to the orders of this Department, if you should deem it necessary and will state the time at which the trial will come on, I will issue an order to him to come to Washington and to bring the necessary papers with him. As the honor and interest of the country require that so great an offender should be brought to condign punishment, I must solicit your early attention to it; and would suggest the propriety of consulting with the Attorney General [William Wirt] as his opinion was originally taken in this case. I am very respectfully yours &c. &c.

ALS in NN, Montague Collection; FC in DNA, 3, 10:134. NOTE: The ALS lacks the name and address of the addressee.

TO WILSON LUMPKIN, [Madison, Ga.]

Department of War, 3d September 1818

I send enclosed a Commission from the President, authorizing you to run out, provisionally, the line between the U[nited] States and East Florida, from the Appalachicola to the head of the St. Marys. Gen. [Edmund P.] Gaines has been ordered to afford you, on your giving notice of the time and place of your commencing this duty, an adequate guard to protect you against the hostilities of the Indians. It will be proper that you should give the Gen[era]l sufficient notice, in order to enable him to make his arrangements. I have stated to Governor [William] Rabun, that I should prefer to postpone the Florida line, 'till after you had ascertained those of the late Creek cessions, as it is probable, that the Seminole Indians may assume a pacific relation in a short time. You will consult with the Governor on this subject, and unless he should advise an opposite course, you will take the one, which I have suggested.

Your pay will be the same as under the Commission to run the line of the Creek cessions, and you are authorized to employ, on the best terms you can, a skilful surveyor, with a sufficient number of chain axemen to mark the line plainly and distinctly. You will, from time to time, advise this department of your arrangements and proceedings.

I enclose an extract from the treaty with Spain, in relation to this subject.

[Enclosure]

James Monroe, President of the U[nited] States of America, to all who shall see these presents, Greeting:

Know ye, That reposing special Trust and Confidence, in the Integrity, Ability and Diligence of Wilson Lumpkin, of the State of Georgia, I do appoint him Commissioner to run the line, provisionally, between the U[nited] States and Spain, from the Appalachicola river to the head of the St. Marys and do vest him with full power and authority to execute the duties of that office. To have and to hold the said office of Commissioner, and to exercise all the rights and privileges appertaining thereto, during the pleasure of the President of the United States, for the time being.

Given under my hand at the City of Washington, this 3d day of September, A. D. 1818, and of the Independence of the U[nited] States, the 43d.

(Signed) James Monroe

By the President,
J. C. Calhoun,
Secretary of War.

FC with En in DNA, 3, 10:133–134; CCEx in DNA, 11, 12215.

From Henry Middleton (1770–1846), [Representative from S.C.,] Washington, 9/3. Recommends the appointment of [Peter Dunlop Trezevant] as a Cadet, "if there should be vacancies . . . at present." ALS in DNA, 15, 1818, 100.

To [James Monroe, Albemarle County, Va.]

[War Department, September 3, 1818]

I have received your letters of the 31st of August and 1st of Sept. Agreeably to your suggestion, I will direct the Commissioner appointed to run out the lines under the late treaty with the Creeks (Mr. [Wilson] Lumpkin) to run provisionally the line from the Appalachicola to the head of the St. Marys. Would it not be proper for Mr. [John Quincy] Adams to inform the Spanish Minister of the object of the government in running out of the line? I have directed Mr. [John] Bail[e]y of the State Department, to furnish the widow of General [Richard ?] Montgomery with a copy of the correspondence which she requested.

Nicholas P. Trist would have been appointed a Cadet as you requested but there is no vacancy at present.

I called on Mr. [William] Wirt this morning, after receiving your letter, and he expects to be able to report in two or three days in the case of Maj. [Nathaniel Nye] Hall.

Letters of a late date have been received from Mr. [Albert] Gallatin and Irvin [George W. Erving], which you will find enclosed. They are more important than those previously sent. I would not be surprised, if Spain should agree to the proposals lately made to Don Onís. It is so obviously her interest; and the fear, which France seems to have of the recognition of the Independence of the Spanish provinces, if our differences with Spain should remain unadjusted will have I hope its weight.

I transmit the proceedings of courts martial in the cases of Lieut[enant]s [Robert M.] Forsyth, [Collin] McLeod and [David Charles] Nicholls. They have all been ordered to be cashiered. The former is very young about 20 years of age, and is a near relation of Mr. [John] Forsyth of Georgia. He wishes him to have leave to resign; which I think under all of the circumstances of the case ["it" *canceled*] is the correct course, and would therefore respectfully suggest it to you. In the case of Lieut. Nicholls I think the sentence of the court ought to be carried into effect, as his conduct appears very improper. In the case of McLeod the enclosed statement expresses my opinion, which, if you should approve may assist you in forming your decision. Besides the objections contained in the statement, I consider the order of Maj. [Zachary] Taylor as unauthorized by law, or regulation. The ration, at that time, was fixed by law, and if the contractor had failed to supply the whisky part, it was the duty of the Commanding officer to purchase it on his risk at any price. He had no right to command the Soldiers to take money in lieu of it. It puts the Soldiers at the mercy of the contractor or his agents, as I fear was the case here.

ALS in DLC, James Monroe Papers, 4849, with the enclosed DU dated 9/3 and entitled "Statement in the case of Lieut[enant] McLeod" as no. 4841 (FC in DNA, 3, 10:135); PEx in Jameson, ed., *Correspondence*, p. 141. NOTE: 2nd Lt. Forsyth was dismissed on 12/1; 2nd Lt. McLeod resigned on 12/31; and 2nd Lt. Nicholls was dismissed on 10/16. Heitman, *Historical Register*, 1:430, 676, and 746. Monroe's letter of 8/31 to Calhoun is an ALS in DNA, 1, P-208.

To William Rabun, Milledgeville, Ga.

Department of War, 3d September 1818

By direction of the President [James Monroe,] I have sent a commission to the Hon. Wilson Lumpkin, to run, provisionally, the line between the U[nited] States and Florida, from the Appalachicola to the head of the St. Marys. Gen[era]l [Edmund P.] Gaines will be ordered, on the requisition of Mr. Lumpkin, to furnish a sufficient force to guard against an attack from the Indians; but it appears to me, as the Indian hostilities will probably cease in a short time, and as much expense would be avoided by dispensing with so large a guard as would now be necessary, that the running of the line ought to be postponed, unless the interest of your State should render it improper, 'til after those of the late cession from the Creek nation, be ascertained. Mr. Lumpkin will, accordingly, be instructed to ascertain those first, unless your Excellency should suggest the opposite course. He will be instructed to consult you in relation to it. As Mr. Lumpkin's post office is not known to the Department, the letter to him has been put under cover to you, with a request, that you will have it properly directed and forwarded.

FC in DNA, 3, 10:134–135; PC in Jameson, ed., *Correspondence,* p. 140.

To Jacob Brown, New York [City], 9/4. Orders him to investigate and report upon the incident [of fighting between U.S. and Canadian soldiers] cited in letters enclosed from the Governor General of Canada and the British Minister in Washington. "The honor and peace of the country are equally concerned in preventing such acts. I have, therefore, to request, that you will take such measures as will prevent their repetition." FC in DNA, 3, 10:136; CC (dated 9/5) in DLC, Jacob Brown Papers, Letterbooks, 2:117. In reply on 9/16 (LS in DNA, 1, B-79; FC in DLC, Jacob Brown Papers, Letterbooks, 2:118, with an FC of his letter of 9/16 to Col. [Henry] Atkinson), Brown reported that he had ordered the commanding officer at Plattsburg, [N.Y.,] to investigate and "to prevent a similar outrage in future."

From Samuel Hodges, Jr., Stoughton, Mass., 9/4. Answering Calhoun's letter of 8/28, Hodges asks that he be allowed to retain his Army appointment until his civil, diplomatic office is recognized by Rio de Janeiro. ALS in DNA, 11, 12311.

From Bvt. Maj. M[orrill] Marston

Detroit, Sept. 4, 1818

I enclose herewith three orders dated at the Head Quarters of the 5th Military Department. You will perceive by the order marked No. 1, that I am placed in arrest & charged with contravening the orders of the Commandant of the Department [Alexander Macomb], in ordering two men from the service of his Excellency Governor [Lewis] Cass. In March last, as will appear by the order marked No. 2, one of the men in question, Bacon, was ordered into the service of the Governor under sanction of the Department of War; the other man, *Copeland,* has been in the service of the Governor for about three years, and as I am informed, has never shouldered a musket or appeared in the ranks of the Regiment during that time, till within the short time that I have commanded the Regiment.

These two men have been constantly employed, to the best of my knowledge & belief solely for the private emolument & advantage of Gov[ernor] Cass; & have been by him placed on the most laborious & fatigueing [*sic*] duties, such as working out his road tax, procuring timber & pickets, cultivating his farm &c. &c.

In consequence of the absence of the commanding General on a visit to the upper posts, the command of this post & its dependencies was assigned to me; I did not hesitate for a moment to order these men to their respective Companies: I did so because I then believed, & do now believe, that I was fully authorised to take this course; & that in so doing I did not contravene any order of the commandant of the Department, for no order had to my knowledge ever been promulgated to entitle the Governor to the services of Copeland. The other soldier, Bacon, I knew had been ordered into his service, but an after order, marked No. 3, ordered the Company to which he belonged to Grosse Isle without making any exception whatever; & I considered that this soldier was placed on the same footing with the other men of the Company, & indeed the Major General himself informed me at the same time that *every man* belonging to the Company was ordered to march.

The many abuses that exist at this post in consequence of the misapplication of the services of the soldiers have long been a subject of general complaint; when I took command of the Regiment in June last I endeavored to correct the evils complained of as far as was in my power to do, in a legal & regular manner; by so doing, I have incur[r]ed the displeasure of the Major General commanding & consequently have been placed in arrest.

My principal object in making this communication is to inquire, whether the Governor of the Territory, the Commanding General of the Department, or any other person, either civil or military, is author[ised] except by the laws of Congress, & the *published* Regulations of the Department of War, to employ for his own private use & emolument any soldier of the U.S. Army. If there is any such authority I request a *certified copy* of the order, letter, or other document containing the same; if none such exists, an *official certificate* that such authority is not contained in the orderly books, nor among the files or documents of the War Department, as such evidence may be of much importance to me in making my defence before the court which may be ordered for my trial.

ALS in DNA, 11, 12491.

To JAMES MONROE, [Albemarle County, Va.]

War Dept., 4d [*sic*] Sep[tembe]r 1818

I received your letter of the 2d Inst[ant] this morning; and have, as you requested, forwarded your letters to Mr. [John Quincy] Adams and Mr. Cooper [that is, Dr. Thomas Cooper].

I had previously directed the settlement to be made with Mr. [George] Boyd on the most liberal terms; much more so in fact, than what he merits.

I regret, on conversing with Mr. [Benjamin] Homans [Chief Clerk in the Navy Department] to find, that the wishes of Mr. Cooper in relation to Mr. [Thomas] Say & [Thomas] Nuttall can not be effected; as the Macedonian is under sailing orders and will probably sail in a few days; I have communicated to him the fact; and suggested that a similar opportunity may again before long present itself. A young gentleman goes out in the Macedonian from the University at Cambridge in the capacity of Surgeon's

Mate, for scientifick purposes. Accept the assurance of my sincere regard and friendship.

[P.S.] I return Mr. Cooper's letter.

ALS in DLC, James Monroe Papers, 4845. NOTE: Compare Calhoun's letter of 9/3 to Thomas Cooper, a transcription of which appears herein.

To [Bvt. Maj.] Gen. E[leazer] W. Ripley, 9/4. Orders have been issued for immediate construction of permanent barracks at Baton Rouge. Ripley is instructed to give full coöperation to this important project. FC in DNA, 3, 10:136.

From P[eter] D[unlop] Trezevant, Charleston, [S.C.,] 9/4. "I this day received my letter of appointment as a Cadet" and shall arrive at West Point "for examination by the middle of October." ALS in DNA, 15, 1818, 100.

From [Mrs.] Catherine Wager, Charles Town (Jefferson County), [Va. (now W. Va.),] 9/4. Claims that the U.S. purchased land at Harpers Ferry from her husband under a promise that it would be used only for the manufacture of arms; argues, therefore, that the U.S. cannot permit the selling of goods at the armory there in competition with her store. ALS with Ens in DNA, 1, W-199.

To Joseph Bellinger, [Representative from S.C.,] Greeneville, Tenn., 9/5. Answers his letter of 8/25 (ALS with En in DNA, 1, B-285) seeking suspension of a mistaken lawsuit against Jennings O'Bannon of Barnwell District, S.C., under O'Bannon's bond as a Paymaster; assures Bellinger that the suit originated in a mistake and will be discontinued. FC in DNA, 3, 10:137.

To [Lewis] Cass, [William] Clark, [Ninian] Edwards, John Jamison, Reuben Lewis, John McKee, Return J. Meigs, David B. Mitchell, and Henry Sherburne, 9/5. Calhoun directs them, as Superintendents and Agents of Indian Affairs, to observe strictly the provisions of the Indian trade act of 3/30/1802 and of existing Indian treaties in respect to claims for reparations for injuries inflicted by Indians upon U.S. citizens or by citizens upon Indians; Calhoun explains what proofs must be submitted to make possible payment of such claims. LS (to Edwards) in ICHi; LS (to Meigs) in InHi, Mitten Collection; FC in DNA, 72, D:210; CC in WHi, Draper Collection, Thomas Forsyth Papers, 5:1–2; CC in DNA, 201, 17A-E4; PC in House Document No. 24, 17th Cong., 1st Sess.; PC in *American State Papers: Indian Affairs*, 2:268–269; PC in Carter, ed., *Territorial Papers*, 15:431–432. To the three first-named addressees, who were the Superintendents of Indian Affairs, there was sent also on this day a letter of transmittal directing them to communicate this "letter of instruction" to the Indian Agents in their respective areas. LS (to Edwards) in ICHi; FC in DNA, 72, D:211.

To David G[odfrey] Cook, Sub-Agent, Chickasaw Agency, 9/5. His resignation of 8/17 (ALS in DNA, 2, C-1818), because his pay is "quite inadequate to my Support," is accepted as of 11/1. FC in DNA, 72 D:209.

From William Florance

Philad[elphi]a, Sep[tember] 5th 1818

Having a great solicitude to obtain a Cadetcy at the Military Academy at West Point, I beg permission to address you on the subject. I deem it proper to remark that I am in my fourteenth year of age, of South Carolina and educated at York Town College in this State. It has been my most ardent and constant wish for several years past, to effect so desireable [*sic*] an object, and which is now my sole pride and conviction; for studiousness of character, and integrity of conduct, I beg leave to refer you to the annexed recommendation.

LS with En in DNA, 15, 1819, 69. Note: The "annexed recommendation" was dated at Philadelphia on 9/7 and was signed by nine men, including H. Solomon, J.N. Barker, Edward D. Coxe, M.M. Russell, and T.P. Cambridge, M.D. Its entire text reads: "The Subscribers respectfully recommend Mr. William Florance to his Excellency the Secretary at War." An EU indicates that Florance was appointed on 3/24/1819 to a Cadetship.

To C[allender] Irvine, 9/5. It "is contemplated to charge the Apothecary Gen[era]l [Francis Le Baron] under the Surgeon General [Joseph Lovell] with the purchase of the medical and hospital

Stores for the use of the Army. You will therefore close the accounts of the purchasing department for the purchase of such items on the 30th instant." FC in DNA, 3, 10:137.

To Thomas L. McKenney, 9/5. "You will deposite [*sic*] the amount of the funds in your hands, on account of purchases made of Mr. George Boyd, in the office of Discount and Deposite, to the credit of the Treasurer of the U[nited] States [Thomas Tudor Tucker]." FC in DNA, 72, D:209. Answered on 9/7 by McKenney, who reported that he had "this day placed in the office of Discount & Deposit of the Branch Bank of the U.S. in Washington . . . $2,239.17." FC in DNA, 73, E:125–126.

To James Monroe, [Albemarle County, Va.]

War Dept., 5th Sep[tembe]r 1818

I transmit to you a letter [of 9/2] rec[eive]d by yesterday's mail from Gen[era]l [Winfield] Scott. A work of the kind, I am informed, is very much needed; and it is said, that none of our officers are [*sic*] better calculated to execute it, than the General. If you should approve of his project, I think it would be advisable to order him to this place, in order to agree upon the details, and the conditions on which it is to be undertaken. Will you be so good as to return me the letter and favour me with your wishes in relation to it[?] Accept of the assurance of my sincere respect & esteem.

ALS in DLC, James Monroe Papers, 5104; PC in Jameson, ed., *Correspondence*, p. 140.

"Regulation requiring reports, &c., from the several offices of the Dep[artmen]t of War," 9/5. Each bureau or branch of the Department is ordered to submit quarterly reports, beginning 11/1, about its respective area of Army administration. FC in DNA, 3, 10:137–138. Recipients were Paymaster General Robert Brent; Nathaniel Cutting in the Bounty Lands Office; James L. Edwards in the Pension Office; Commissary General of Subsistence George Gibson; Quartermaster General Thomas S. Jesup; Surgeon General Joseph Lovell, whose copy is a CC in DNA, 244, A:4; Adjutant and

Inspector General Daniel Parker, whose copy is a CCEx in DNA, 11, 12923; Chief Engineer Joseph G. Swift; and Decius Wadsworth as Chief of Ordnance, whose copy is a CCEx in DNA, 31, 1818, War Department.

From H[enry] Sherburne, Chickasaw Agency, 9/5. He has received Calhoun's letters of 8/15, 8/17, and 8/18. He reports that the Chickasaws refuse to accept their annuities in the form of goods instead of cash, because they have never asked for payment to be made in goods. LS in DNA, 1, S-211.

To CHARLES TAIT, Cook's Law Office, Elbert County, Ga.

War Dept., 5th Sept. 1818

By some delay in the mail your very interesting letter of the 18th of last month did not come to hand till a few days since. Since the commencement of my publick life, it has been my good fortune to have been associated with many, who are justly the pride and ornament of their country. Among these distinguished citizens, I know of none, whose opinions and acts have more invariably pointed to the prosperity and the honor of our country than yours. I know of not one article in your political creed, nor a vote, or act of yours, which ought to give the least regret. Whatever may have been the delusion, for a time, in your State, I know, you must possess, that reward, which no publick man, but the good and independent can enjoy. It is a high reward. I think, I know something of it from experience. I have, on some occasions, felt a conscious pleasure, of doing my duty in oposition [*sic*] to mere momentary popularity, which I would not exchange for scarcely any other moment of my life.

Your train of reflection in relation [to Andrew] Jackson and Pensacola is such as I expected. It is indispensible [*sic*] that the military should on all occasions be held subordinate to orders; and, I know of no excuse except necessity, that ought to ["excuse" *canceled*] exempt from punishment disobedience to orders. It is natural to ask why not apply this principle, so indisputable, to Gen[era]l Jackson? The answer is that there was a diversity of opinion, as to the character of his conduct. Some thought, that tho' he had no orders directing him to do what was done, yet the prohibition, contained in his orders, did not extend to the circumstances under which he acted; and that, altho he may have mistaken the power of an American general, placed as he was, yet he honestly and fairly thought he had, the right to do what he did. By those who took this view, it was not considered as a case of acknowledged disobedience, in which [case,] from the popularity of the General, it was inexpedient to punish. When to this was added, the misconduct of the Spanish Authority in Florida and the relation of this country with Spain, it was thought it would be highly improper, to order any proceedings against the General. Such was the diversity of view taken of this subject. The existence of this different mode of viewing the subject, would itself render it, perhaps, improper, to take the high toned course, as that ought not to be resorted to, but in a case free from doubt. I have spoken to you freely on this interesting subject. You will consider it between ourselves.

I wrote to General [David B.] Mitchel[l] several weeks ago *very urgently* in relation to the road to the Alabama Territory. Shortly after the passage of the bill, I wrote to Gen[era]l [Edmund P.] Gaines to render all of the assistance he could; but the state of things in his command, has prevented him from furnishing any. The road is important & I hope the agent will do his duty.

ALS in A-Ar; PC in Thomas M. Owen, ed., "Letters from John C. Calhoun to Charles Tait," *The Gulf States Historical Magazine,* vol. I, no. 2 (September, 1902), pp. 94–95.

From Joseph Anderson, [First Comptroller, Treasury Department,] Washington, 9/6. Asks if John Cox of Tenn. has been or will be appointed as a Cadet, in accordance with the recommendation of him "last winter" by Capt. Francis Jones, Representative from Tenn.; the Cox family is respectable, and Anderson requests an immediate answer because a Tennesseean visiting Washington will return to Anderson's office for the answer. Anderson adds that Hillary Rhodes cannot "disengage himself from his arrangements and engagements made since he was recommended" and will therefore soon resign his warrant as a Cadet. ALS in DNA, 15, 1818, 138, with an EU that Cox was appointed on 3/24/1819 to be a Cadet.

From Robert Butler, Nashville, 9/6. Encloses a topographical "memoir" of East Fla. and West Fla. that has been prepared by Capt. Hugh Young, who intends to submit during next winter a topographical map of the Floridas. LS in DNA, 1, B-307.

From William Clark and Auguste Chouteau, St. Louis, 9/6. They report their negotiation [on 8/24] of the intended treaty with the Quapaws ceding "a large tract of valuable country." If it is not soon assigned to the Cherokees and other Indians, it will be occupied by "white settlers, thinly scattered in every direction." The Quapaws want an Indian Agent; Clark and Chouteau recommend Charles de Villemont. PC in *American State Papers: Indian Affairs,* 2:177.

From Nath[anie]l Frye, [Jr.,] Chief Clerk, Paymaster General's Office, 9/7. Pursuant to Paymaster General [Robert Brent's] letter of 8/26 to Calhoun, Frye asks for $100,000 to enable him to meet six itemized needs for funds—for examples, purchases of clothing and half-pay pensions to widows and orphans. ALS in DNA, 1, F-46.

To Thomas S. Grimké, Charleston, S.C., 9/7. "Your letter of the 31st ultimo [ALS in DNA, 1, G-94] has been received. It is very desirable that the Cadets should join the Academy in this month; but if it is impracticable in the case of your brother [Charles], the time of joining may be extend[ed] to the 15th of October next." FC in DNA, 3, 10:139.

From Brig. Gen. Alexander Macomb

Detroit, September 7th 1818

I have the honor to report my return from a tour through the upper Lakes, having visited all the posts in this [5th Military] Department, besides went to the Sau[l]t of St. Mary.

It affords me much gratification in being able to say that the troops and posts are in excellent order, presenting an appearance highly creditable to the Army and the government.

I examined the American side of the Strait between Lake Superior and the waters below it and find a site well calculated for a Military post and from what I observed, am induced to believe that a garrison at the falls would have an excellent effect both as it regards our Indian relations & the revenue laws.

The Indians on these Lakes are generally unfriendly to the American government, and in my tour I did not see a man who was pleased with our visiting their country. It would require but little persuasion to induce them to commit hostilities. The cause of this dissatisfaction is uncertain; some attribute it to the losses they sustained during the late war, and others to the treatment they receive from the Indian Agents.

I shall endeavour in my next report to set forth their condition more at length and also to lay before you a sketch of the tour I made in form of a map, having ascertained with good instruments the situation of the most important points.

I had the honor to receive by the last mail your instructions concerning the roads; the troops are employed in cutting and a faithful report will be forwarded in due season. A considerable detachment is now employed between Fort Meigs and the river Raisin, which will complete the road from this to the Miami before the meeting of Congress, not having more than twelve miles unfinished at this moment.

LS in DNA, 1, M-353.

To James Monroe, [Albemarle County, Va.]

War Dept., 7th Sep[tembe]r 1818

I enclose an important dispatch from Mr. [Richard] Rush of the 3d of August. No. 30 to which Mr. Rush refers in this dispatch has not been yet received.

Your letter of the 4th Inst[ant] was received this morning. I have directed a copy of the proceedings of the court martial in the case of [Alexander] Arbuthnot and [Robert C.] Ambrister to be made out for Mr. [Charles] Bagot. I think, on the whole, a copy for the other ministers ought not to be made and delivered till Mr. [John Quincy] Adams['s] return, which I understand will be but a few weeks, as he would be able to accompany it with suitable explination [*sic*] of the whole of our proceedings in that Quarter.

The State Department will transmit to you a translation of the King of Wurtemburg's letter, and the usual answer to the King of Sweden's. Accept the assurance of my sincere respect and esteem.

ALS in NN, James Monroe Papers.

From George Read, Jr., U.S. Attorney for the Del. District, Newcastle, [Del.,] 9/7. Pursuant to a request made by Capt. [Samuel] Babcock of the Engineers, Read delivers his opinion that any claim to the Pea Patch Island that is "not derived from the State of Delaware is entirely groundless"; he traces that State's claim back to a grant given to William Penn in 1682. ADS in DNA, 111, 199; PC in *American State Papers: Military Affairs*, 5:484.

Regulation governing forage allowances, 9/7. Specifies the amount of forage to be allowed to horses in Army service and states the maximum number of forage allowances that Army officers may receive under various conditions. FC in DNA, 3, 10:139; CC in DNA, 25, 101 sub 57.

From J[oseph] G. Swift, New York [City], 9/7. He arrived there last Saturday, met Col. [William] McRee, "& was much pleased to find that the Board of Engineers had not been materially delayed in their operations." All members of it are present; Swift hopes it will proceed "with alacrity" in its business. LS in DNA, 1, S-190.

From H[enry] Clay, Lexington, [Ky.,] 9/8. Recommends Nathan B. Stout, a "resident and native of this place," for appointment as a Cadet. ALS in DNA, 15, 1818, 96.

To ANDREW JACKSON, [Nashville]

Department of War, 8th September, 1818

I received by Captain [James] Gadsden your letter of the 10th of August, accompanied with his report relative to the defence of the Floridas, and a copy of the proceedings of the Court martial in the case of [Alexander] Arbuthnot and [Robert C.] Ambrister, and the despatches which unfortunately miscarried. These documents are very important and interesting, and they have been communicated to the President, who is now absent from the City. I regret very much that they were not regularly received. There has been great neglect some where; and I have furnished the Post Master Gen[era]l [Return J. Meigs, Jr.,] with a list of the lost despatches, with a request that a diligent search should be made. It is stated that there is a copy of the proceedings of the Court martial in New York and Savannah. How were these copies obtained? I trust that the originals will yet be had.

I have stated to the President [James Monroe] your request in relation to Captain Gadsden, and he directs me to say to you, that when the vacancy occurs he [Gadsden] will receive the appointment which he desires. It will be to me a subject of much regret, to lose the aid of his talents and fidelity as an Engineer at this time. The confidence reposed in him caused his selection to superintend the extensive and important fortifications about to be commenced on our Southern frontier. It is a portion of our country, that required in the Superintendent, the greatest skill, activity and fidelity. I was aware of the inadequacy of his pay and rank, and hoped that some opportunity would have occurred to render them more proportionate to his talents and service.

The Colo[nel] of the Ordnance Department [Decius Wadsworth] has been directed to take immediate measures in relation to the points stated in your letter. The Cannon now at Mobile will be withdrawn, as they are not of proper calibre, or pattern, and their place will be supplied from Pittsburg[h], with proper carriages.

I enclose a copy of my orders of the 14th ulto. to Gen[era]l [Edmund P.] Gaines, for your information.

I concur in the view which you have taken in relation to the importance of Florida to the effectual peace and security of our Southern frontier, and such, I believe, is the opinion of every member of the administration. In fact, the grounds assumed are very far from being feeble. St. Marks will be retained till Spain shall be ready to garrison it with a sufficient force, and Fort Gadsden and any other position in East or West Florida within the Indian Country, which may be deemed eligible, will be retained so long as there is any danger; which, it is hoped, will afford the desired security. We ought, it is true, never to resort to timid measures to avoid war; but it appears to me, that a certain degree of caution (not from the fear of the Holy Alliance) ought, at this time, to mark our policy. A war with Spain, were it to continue with her alone, and were there no great neutral powers to avail themselves of the opportunity of embarrassing us, would be nothing; but such a war would not continue long without involving other parties, and it certainly would, in a few years, be an English war. In such a war, I would not fear for the fate of our country, but, certainly, if it can be prudently and honorably avoided for the present, it ought to be. We want time; time to grow, to perfect our forti[fi]cations, to enlarge our Navy, to replenish our depots, and to pay our debts. I speak to you frankly, knowing your zeal for our country, with whose glory yours is now identified. No one who has examined my political course, will, I am sure, think that these opinions are influenced by timid council.

Congress at the last session made a very considerable appropriation for a military depot and barracks at Baton Rouge, and I have given directions to the Ordnance and Quarter master's Departments to make the necessary arrangements by obtaining materials &c. to commence the work with activity. An officer of the Q[uarte]r Master's and another of the Ordnance Department, will be directed to take the special superintendence of those buildings, and Gen[era]l [Eleazer W.] Ripley has been ordered to furnish all of the aid, in their construction, which the state of his command will admit.

As Baton Rouge will be a fortified post, an Engineer will be charged with laying off the positions of these works.

FC in DNA, 3, 10:140–141; 3 CCEx's in DLC, Andrew Jackson Papers, 245–246, 8040–8041, 8046–8047; PEx in *American State Papers: Military Affairs,* 1:745; PEx in Bassett, ed., *Correspondence,* 2:393.

To Alexander Macomb, [Detroit,] and the Indian Agent at Mackinac, [George Boyd,] 9/8. "Herewith you will receive a copy of a letter addressed to this Department by Governor [William] Clark. You will give to Mr. Tanner every facility in your power to recover his brother from the Indians." FC in DNA, 3, 10:140.

To A[rmistead] T[homson] Mason, [former Senator from Va., "Selma," Loudoun County, Va.,] 9/8. Answers his letter of 9/3

(ALS in DNA, 15, 1818, 135). States that a rule prohibits permitting Cadets who have resigned, as William Janners [did on 12/10/1816] upon his father's insistence, to return to the Military Academy; after examining a report about Janners from Sylvanus Thayer, Calhoun sees no reason to make an exception in Janners' case. Promises to attend to the application for promotion of [1st Lt.] Henry Sa[u]nders, "now in the medical staff," whom Mason had recommended. FC in DNA, 3, 10:139–140.

From P. Raymond, Georgetown, [D.C.,] 9/8. He has seen the invitation issued by Commissary [General of Subsistence George Gibson] to bidders to submit by 11/20 proposals for the furnishing of rations for the troops. But he argues that an earlier deadline and award of a contract for the large supply to be delivered at New Orleans will be desirable, explaining that pork should be purchased, packed, delivered, and repacked under a different schedule in order to permit it to be cured and preserved "in a pure state." "I would contract to furnish the supplies for the . . . depot [at New Orleans] providing that I could close the Contract soon. With permission will wait upon you at your Office tomorrow morning at 11 o[']clock. I presume sir on reflection that you will in some measure approbate the above observations." ALS in DNA, 1, R-109.

William Wirt to President [James Monroe], 9/8. "Mr. Calhoun has called on me, at the desire of the Secretary of State [John Quincy Adams], now absent [from Washington], for the purpose of enquiring whether I would advise a proclamation [to be issued by you] against Obed Wright, of Georgia, or private instructions to the marshals of the several districts and territories for the apprehension of the fugitive." Wirt proceeds to advise Monroe not to adopt either course, because each is of dubious constitutionality and is without precedent; and Wirt states that Calhoun agrees with him as to the constitutional questions involved. LS in DNA, 114.

To Capt. William Bradford, Belle Point, Ark.

Department of War, 9th Septem[be]r 1818

Mr. [Reuben] Lewis, Indian Agent on the Arkansaw [*sic*], has been appointed Commissioner to run and mark the line of the land given by the U[nited] States to the Cherokee nation, in exchange for land ceded to them by the treaty of the 8th July, 1817, as designated by the 5th Article of said treaty; and which article stipulates that all citizens of the U[nited] States, except Mrs. P[ersis (Mrs. William L.)] Lovely, who is to remain where she is during life, shall be removed from within said bounds.

You are therefore instructed, so soon as the line is completed, to order all persons, except Mrs. Lovely, who may have settled within said line on the land thus exchanged with the Indians to remove therefrom without delay; and, in the event of their refusing to do so peaceably, you are authorized to remove them by military force.

The enclosed pamphlet contains the treaty with the Cherokee nation above referred to.

FC in DNA, 72, D:211; CC in DLC, Andrew Jackson Papers, 8050.

Certificate given to Nathaniel Cudworth, 9/9. Certifies that Maj. Nathaniel Cudworth appeared personally before Calhoun and stated that he was the same person of that name to whom a Revolutionary pension was granted on 5/4, payable from 4/9 through the S.C. agency. CC in ScHi.

To Reuben Lewis, Indian Agent, Ark. [Mo. Territory], 9/9. Appoints him commissioner and encloses his commission to survey the boundary line of the land ceded to the U.S. by the Cherokees under the treaty of 7/8/1817. Authorizes him to be paid $8 per day and to employ an assistant at $5 and chainmen and axemen at $2. Instructs him to send a plat when the work is finished. FC with En in DNA, 72, D:211–212; PC with En in Carter, ed., *Territorial Papers,* 15:433–434.

From JAMES MONROE

"Highland," [Albemarle County, Va.,] Sept. 9th 1818

I have received General [Andrew] Jackson's reply [of 8/19] to my letter of July 19, from Washington, respecting his taking possession of St. Marks and Pensacola. He contends strenuously, that his orders, left him free, to adopt that course, ["and" *canceled*] if he found it necessary, to terminate the Seminole war; that orders to Gen[era]l [Edmund P.] Gaines, an inferior officer, not refer[r]ed to in the orders to him, of subsequent date, were inapplicable, and not obligatory, on him, especially as his enlarged the sphere of his duties. This letter is, on the whole, is [*sic*] conciliatory, and friendly. He promises to write another. Our view, of his powers, is ["not" *canceled*] decidedly different, from his, on which too we acted, without entertaining any suspicion, that he wou[l]d misunderstand it. I am inclined to think, that I had better answer, this letter, immediately. He may expect that his conception of his orders, should appear, by documents in the [War] department; and it seems it is proper, that the sense in which they were given, & understood by the department, after what has passed, should be recorded there. A communication between you, on this head, and in this stage, seems to be the more necessary, from the presumption, that it may be my duty, to state to Congress, that he transcended his orders, on his own responsibility, or at least to state, the sense, in which they were understood by us. At present, nothing, to this effect exists, in your correspondence with him. It is in mine only which is private. A communication on this point, may commence either with you or him; I will suggest it, to him, thinking, as I do, that it had best begin with him. The affair, may, I hope, be terminated, to the satisfaction of all parties. I will send you in a few days his letter (with a former one) with the answer, which I propose giving to it, which, if you see no objection to it, be so good as to forward to him. But if you do, return it with your objections to it. By coming from him, it [that is, Jackson's expected statement of his interpretation of his orders] will put you more at ease in your answer, & afford a better opportunity for the exercise of kindness & liberality. I shall attach no particular importance to the affair, in my letter, leaving the argument to you & him, so far as it becomes necessary [for you] to enter into it.

Nicholas P. Trist is the name of the young man, I should be glad, to place at W[est] Point from Louisiana. He is now at a grammar school in this neighbourhood, & has made respectable acquir[e]ments. There is a youth, of the name of Wm. Taliaferro of Caroline County in this State, who will probably not attend this year. Could young Trist, in that case, take his place to supply the first vacancy, leaving Mr Taliaferro's open to him afterwards, or is there any unoccupied place, which he might take, on that principle?

[AES by Andrew J. Donelson, signed also by Samuel Houston:] The foregoing is an exact copy from the original letter, in the hand writing of James Monroe Esquire, late President of the United States, having strict regard to its punctuation, and orthography. Compared by us, at the Hermitage this 26th day of May 1828.

CC by Andrew J[ackson] Donelson in DLC, Andrew Jackson Papers, 247–248. NOTE: PC's of the exchange of letters between Monroe and Jackson dated 7/19 and 8/19 appear in Bassett, ed., *Correspondence*, 2:382–383 and 2:389–391.

To JAMES MONROE, [Albemarle County, Va.]

War Dept., 9th Sept. 1818

I received your letter of the 6th Inst[ant] yesterday.

By the last report of the Commissioners for the survey of the coast, they were at New York; but I am in hopes, that they have by this time finished there; and have progressed farther North. They have been repeatedly urged to every expedition consistent with a complete and satisfactory discharge of the duties assigned to them; and to expedite the business 5 topegraphical [*sic*] engineers with two assistants and as many surveyors as they might think proper to employ, were put under their direction and authority. It is a subject on which I feel much solicitude; and I hope the commissioners will be prepared to report during the next session of Congress.

The fortifications have been commenced on an extensive scale. The two at Mobile and those at Lake Pon[t]chartrain have been contracted for, and will be commenced immediately. Materials are collecting at the Pea Patch on the Deleware [*sic*] and old point Comfort. The arrangements made will absorb the whole of the current appropriation.

Dispatch No. 30 from Mr. [Richard] Rush, which I mentioned had not been received, came to hand yesterday; and I send it enclosed. The conte[n]ts are very important. Accept the assurance of my sincere respect and esteem.

ALS in OFH, James Monroe Papers. NOTE: Calhoun evidently started to date this letter the 10th and then imperfectly tried to obliterate the "1" and to make the date read "9th." When Monroe dated this letter in his AEU on it, however, possibly some weeks or years later, he recorded that it was written on 9/19. Nevertheless, there are several indications that Calhoun wrote this letter on 9/9. Among these are: (1) the fact that Calhoun mentions rather casually, as if only two days had elapsed since his previous reference to it in his letter of 9/7, the "very important" Dispatch No. 30; (2) the fact that Calhoun acknowledges routinely his receipt on "yesterday" of Monroe's letter of 9/6 but would probably have made some more elaborate and questioning acknowledgment if this "yesterday" were 9/18, since some other extant letters between Calhoun in Washington and Monroe in Virginia during August and September, 1818, were being delivered in as little as two days; and (3) the fact that Calhoun wrote to Monroe on 9/19 a letter that appears herein and acknowledges his receipt "this morning" of Monroe's letter of 9/17.

From J[ames] A. B[uchanan, President, Branch Bank of the United States, Baltimore,] 9/10. The list of additional pensioners to be added to Buchanan's rolls for Md., sent to him recently by Calhoun, includes three names already on those rolls. Buchanan assumes that these are pensioners whose stipends were increased by a statute of 3/18. FC in DNA, 142, p. 18.

From Robert Butler, Nashville, 9/10. Writing for [Andrew] Jackson, Butler acknowledges Calhoun's letter of 8/22 to Jackson and gives assurance that Jackson has received both the early and the recent copy of Calhoun's instructions of 3/16 to Thomas A. Smith (*The Papers of John C. Calhoun,* 2:194–195). Jackson has given "no orders or instructions whatever" to Smith "to counteract" Calhoun's plans for the Yellowstone Expedition. Jackson agrees to the proposed enlargement of the Northern Division and reduction of the Southern. Jackson has been informed that $30,000 of Quartermaster funds have now become available in New Orleans. Jackson hopes that Calhoun "will see with him the justice" of claims by two Regiments of militia for provisions and will order them paid. LS in DNA, 1, B-299.

To Andrew Jackson, 9/10. "In my letter of the 18th August, I stated in reply to your letter of the 31st July, in relation to the subject of Forage, that I had had the subject under consideration. Enclosed you will find a copy of the regulations on that subject, which I omitted to enclose in my letter to you of the 8th instant." LS in DLC, Andrew Jackson Papers, 8056; FC in DNA, 3, 10:142.

From ELISHA JENKINS

Albany, [N.Y.,] Septem[be]r 10, 1818

My friend Francis Bloodgood Esq. of this City, is about making an application to you, for a Cadet[']s warrant for his son William. I am very desirous that he may be a successful applicant, as well on the score of our intimate friendship, as for the gratification of the young man, who has a *penchant* for the profession of arms. He is of the junior class in Union College & wishes to qualify himself for military life, rather than the profession, which his father designed him for. I ought to apologize to you for intruding upon you. Our acquaintance, limited as it has been, has however, made impressions which lead me to hope, that you would willingly do me such a favor, as I now solicit, if it does not interfere with the arrangements of the School at West Point. At all events, the policy of the government, can only be carried into effect, by appointing the entire number of Cadets, authorized by Law & should there be a vacancy it will be gratifying to me to see young Mr. Bloodgood appointed.

ALS in DNA, 15, 1818, 145.

From John McKee, Choctaw Agency, 9/10. Reports that he has employed William Sugg as Sub-Agent since 8/1, as authorized on 7/13. ALS in DNA, 1, M-310; PC in Carter, ed., *Territorial Papers,* 18:412.

To Joseph McMinn, Knoxville, 9/10. Informs him that a bill drawn by R[eturn] J. Meigs, Cherokee Agent on the Tennessee River, for $1,045 covering expenses of the Arkansas emigration during the second quarter has been paid from funds appropriated for fulfilling the treaty with the Cherokees. FC in DNA, 72, D:213.

To HENRY SHERBURNE, Chickasaw Agent

Department of War, 10th Septem[be]r 1818

Your letter of the 22d ultimo has been received.

The objections to Godfrey Jones' account cannot now be distinc[t]ly recollected. If you will return it to the Dept., it will be examined again, and the grounds of its rejection, and the evidence necessary to support it, stated at large.

The goods stated by you to have been illegally introduced into the Indian Country, and which have been seized, you are authorized to sell at public sale, and the amount of the proceeds thereof to be distributed, one half to the Indians and the other half to the U[nited] States.

In negotiating the draft for $19,350 on the Branch Bank at New Orleans, you will exercise your discretion; and if it cannot be done advantageously without sending to New Orleans, you will not be held responsible for any loss which may be sustained by adopting that course.

I have directed two hundred dollars to be transmitted to you in small post notes; which, it is hoped, will enable you to pay with convenience any demands against you for the repairs of the mansion house at the Agency.

FC in DNA, 72, D:213. NOTE: An Abs of Sherburne's letter of 8/22 appears herein under that date.

From Beaufort T[aylor] Watts, Laurens Courthouse, [S.C.,] 9/10. Recommends Lydall Saxon [of Laurens], who has been prepared for college, for a Cadet's warrant. ALS in DNA, 15, 1818, 142½.

From G[eorge] Boyd, Washington, 9/11. "Finding it impossible to remove my family to Mackinac at this advanced season, I set out to day in order to locate them in a cheaper part of the U.S. than Washington, where they will await my return next summer, in case you Sir, shall still be of opinion that my presence at that post will be of service to the U[nited] States this winter"—an opinion reputedly not true. Before beginning so long a journey, he wants to adjust his accounts, because shipments of arms are arriving for delivery to the Ordnance Corps and to the Office of Indian Trade, which will mean credits against what Boyd owes to the U.S. What he would like best, however, would be to be granted permission to remain in the East until next spring. ALS in DNA, 1, B-47.

CIRCULAR to the Commissioners to Hold Treaties with Indian Tribes

Department of War, 11th Septem[be]r 1818

Gentlemen, The number and importance of the treaties to be held this year, and the great amount of rations which must necessarily be issued to the Indians while attending at the treaties, render it necessary that some system should be adopted to govern such large disbursements. I have therefore to request that you will designate the Indian Agent, if he should be present, or in case he is not, some suitable person, who shall ascertain the number and component parts of rations daily issued. The manner of issuing and certifying, to conform, as near as may be, to the mode which prevails in issuing the rations to soldiers, and at the conclusion of the treaty, to be presented to you for your approval. Where the rations have not been issued by the contractor for the district, the contract or the condition on which the rations were furnished, must be certified to this Department for settlement.

FC in DNA, 72, D:214; CC in DNA, 201, 17A-E4; CC in DNA, 153, 17B-C3; CC in DLC, Andrew Jackson Papers, 8064; CC in DLC, Thomas Flournoy Papers; PC in House Document No. 24, 17th Cong., 1st Sess.; PC's in *American State Papers: Indian Affairs,* 2:269 and 431. NOTE: Marginal notations beside the FC show that copies of this letter were sent to: John McKee, William Carroll, and Daniel Burnet, Commissioners for a Choctaw treaty; Isaac Shelby and Andrew Jackson, Commissioners for a Chickasaw treaty; William Clark and Auguste Chouteau, Commissioners for a Quapaw treaty; Jonathan Jennings, Lewis Cass, and Benjamin Parke, Commissioners for a treaty with the Indians in Ind.; and to Lewis Cass and Duncan McArthur, Commissioners for a treaty with the Wyandot, Seneca, Shawnee, Delaware, Potawatomi, Ottawa, and Chippewa tribes.

Regulations governing transportation allowances, 9/11. Calhoun specifies the baggage allowances that are to be pavable to Army officers. FC in DNA, 3, 10:142–143.

From J[oseph] A[nderson, First Comptroller of the Treasury Department,] 9/12. He has computed that $25,767.50 is owed by the U.S. to the contracting firm of Brown, Cox & Allison for rations supplied during the year that ended on 5/31 to the Cherokee Indians. But the firm owes almost that much to the War Department.

Anderson proposes a method of settling the account by paying the difference. FC in DNA, 59, 18:312.

From WILLIAM F. DOWNS

Laurens Court House, [S.C.,] Sept. 12th 1818

I take the liberty of addressing you for the purpose of procuring an appointment in the Military Academy at West Point for Lydall Saxon, the son of your deceased friend Lewis Saxon, for whom I am guardian.

He is a Youth between 14 & 15 Years of age who has been qualified to enter the South Carolina College but he and his friends are lately inclined to believe that a Diploma from the Military Academy would be of more service to him than to graduate in that institution.

From my intimate acquaintance with him I can venture to recommend him as a youth of excellent moral character and industrious habits possessed of a genius above mediocrity together with advantages of person that challenge respect.

Should he be so fortunate as to obtain the appointment, I have no doubt but that he would do credit to himself and the institution.

Will you be so good as to notify me as soon as convenient of the probability of his success, and a word from you as to the *propriety* of his entering that institution is solicited and will be gratefully received by one who has the honor to be Yours &c., William F. Downs.

ALS in DNA, 15, 1818, 142½. NOTE: The South Carolina College is now the University of South Carolina. Calhoun answered on 9/21 (FC in DNA, 3, 10:148) that no new Cadet appointments could be made before 1819.

From John Garlington and William Dunlap, "Laurensville," [S.C.,] 9/12. They recommend Lydall Saxon for an appointment as a Cadet. LS in DNA, 15, 1818, 142½.

To [Callender Irvine and Thomas S. Jesup, 9/12]. Until otherwise ordered, they are to allow to Military Storekeepers who receive the pay and emoluments of a Capt. of Infantry the same allowances of fuel and quarters that are authorized for a Capt. in the line of the Army. FC (not dated) in DNA, 3, 10:142; CC (dated 9/12) in DNA, 45, 387:149.

To James Monroe, [Albemarle County, Va.]

War Dept., 12th Sep[tembe]r 1818

I have received your two letters of the 6th and 9th Instant. The notice, which you suggest in relation to the [land] grants made in Florida by the King of Spain, under which it is said some of our citizens have been purchasing, has been already substantially made in the Georgia Journal.

I am surprised, I confess, at the ground, which Gen[era]l [Andrew] Jackson has assumed. If I am not greatly mistaken, there is no military principle better established, than that the orders in this case to Gen[era]l [Edmund P.] Gain[e]s, are obligatory on Gen[era]l Jackson. It is a principle of daily occurrence. Besides, if the orders to Gen[era]l Gain[e]s must be set aside, on what principle could the war be carried on within the Spanish limits at all, without the authority of the executive? I will not however continue the argument, as it would be useless at this time. Should the Gen[era]l express a desire, that his views of his orders, should appear on the records of this Dep[artmen]t, it would undoubtedly be proper, that the view taken by the Gov[ernmen]t should also appear; but, I think for the present, we ought to wait to see what course he may choose to take. I hope he will have the good sense and moderation to choose, that which his own character as well as the interest of the country requires of him. I have answered his letter to me by Capt. [James] Gadsden, in the most friendly manner and informed him that Capt. Gadsden, would be appointed to the place of Col. [Arthur P.] Hayne when the latter resigns. I enclose you a letter [dated 8/28] and a Nashville paper, which I received from Col. [John] Williams this morning. Some allowance is to be made for the sentiments, which he expresses, as he is not friendly towards the General.

I also enclose a letter of appointment [as a Cadet] to Nicolus [*sic*] P. Trist, which you will be so good as to transmit to him. Accept the assurance of my sincere respect & esteem.

ALS in NN, James Monroe Papers.

D[aniel] Parker to [Callender Irvine], Philadelphia, 9/12. Parker encloses a drawing, bearing an AES by Calhoun of his approval, of the standard flag (not to exceed 40′ x 20′) that is to be flown at all military posts and arsenals and a list of the requisite materials for use in manufacturing the flag. LS with Ens in DNA, 43, Flag of the U.S.

From B[enjamin] F. Stickney, Fort Wayne, 9/12. Accepts his appointment as an Indian Sub-Agent temporarily, because "the compensation [of $500 annually] is so small, that the sacrifice would be too great as a matter of perminance [*sic*]." ALS in DNA, 1, S-99.

From [Mrs.] Catherine Wager, Washington, 9/12. Asks for an appointment to discuss with Calhoun a matter of importance. ALS in DNA, 1, W-199.

To Maj. Joseph Woodruff, Charleston, S.C., 9/12. [Answering his letter of 8/26 to Christopher Vandeventer (ALS in DNA, 1, W-191),] Calhoun approves the five-year lease under which Woodruff will rent at $1 per acre per year some of the land at Point Peter, Ga. The rent must be paid each January. FC in DNA, 3, 10:143.

From W[ILLIAM] T[AYLOR] BARRY, [former Representative and Senator from Ky.]

Lexington (K[y].), 14th Sept[embe]r 1818

Colo[nel] J[ames] Johnson of this State intends proposeing [*sic*] for a contract with the war department for the supply of the Army. It is probable you are acquainted with his character. He possesses and is entitled to public confidence. No man in our State is more justly esteemed for his integrity[,] patriotism & capacity. His brother Colo[nel] R[ichard] M. Johnson is well known; they were associated in the late war in the field, the former was seacond [*sic*] in command to the latter and not at all inferior to him in patriotic devotion to the service of his country. Colo[nel] J[ames] Johnson has been distinguished in our State counsels and was always found with the most zealous and prominent of the republican party. I presume his terms will be reasonable, and the government may confide in him with safety.

I beg you will accept assurances of my personal regard & believe me very truely [*sic*] & respectfully your ob[e]d[ien]t ser[van]t, W.T. Barry.

ALS in DNA, 43, file of James Johnson, 7.

From Ab[raha]m Bradley, Jr., General Postoffice, [Washington,] 9/14. Encloses letters from the Postmasters at Fort Hawkins and Milledgeville, Ga., concerning the disappearance of dispatches sent by [Andrew] Jackson to Calhoun last May. Each of these Postmasters disclaims any blame; each accuses Maj. [John B.] Hogan. ALS with Ens in DNA, 2, B-1818.

To A[dam] Carruth, Greenville, S.C., 9/14. Answering his letter of 9/5 (ALS in DNA, 1, C-225), Calhoun refuses to grant him an advance beyond that stipulated in his contract to manufacture arms for the government. FC in DNA, 3, 10:144.

From Lewis Cass

St. Marys, [O.,] Sept. 14, 1818

With a view to obtain correct information upon the subject of your letter of the 25th of May last and of the accompanying resolution of the House of Representatives, and to compare my own opinions with those of persons qualified by their situation and experience to judge correctly, I have delayed my answer till this time.

The resolution of the House of Representatives appears to contemplate the abolition of the present trading establishments of the United States among the Indians. My own experience and observation and the opinions of all with whom I have conversed upon the subject are decidedly in favour of this abolition.

This system must have been originally introduced in consequence of our peculiar relations with the Indians, and from an impression that American Capital and enterprize could not supply the demands of this trade, or that the Indians from the nature of it would be liable to imposition. I presume the public trading houses were never established with any view to pecuniary profit, nor that such a result would enter into an estimate of the advantages to be derived from them.

I know not what at the introduction of this system may have been the state of the American Capital employed in the Indian trade, or of the enterprize of those in whom this Capital was vested. Nor do I know anything of the wants of the Western or Southern Indians or the probable means of supplying them. My own experience and information extend to the Indians in this section of the Union only, and to them I shall confine my observations upon this subject.

I have no hesitation in saying that it is now as unnecessary for the Government of the United States to continue their trading houses upon this frontier as to embark in any merchantile [*sic*] speculation whatever. A great abundance of American Capital has been diverted into this channel, and it would be a reflection upon our national character to suppose that enterprize could not be found to distribute this capital or skill to employ it. This trade requires no other impulse than a fair return of profits and, like all other branches of commerce, if left without legal regulation, will regulate itself by the competition of those employed in it. The United States are satisfied to conduct their portion of it without loss, and so far as they supply the demand, the system operates to the injury of the private trade and has a tendency to continue the present state of things.

The individual must look to the profits of his trade for the reward of his industry and enterprize and for the use of the capital vested in it. It must be obvious therefore that the goods at the public trading establishments can be afforded cheaper than they can be sold by private traders and cheaper than, by any fair view of the trade, they could be expected. Were the United States to enter into competition with individuals in any branch of foreign trade and to be satisfied with conducting that without loss, it would not be difficult to foresee the sensation which would be excited nor the individual injury which would be the result.

The capital employed by Government in this quarter is so small, compared with the general amount of the trade, as to produce little effect. There are but three public trading houses upon this frontier, one at Chicago, one at Green Bay, and one at Prairie du Chien. I have no means of ascertaining the quantity of goods which they annually sell, but I am certain it constitutes a very small portion of the amount which enters and is sold in this extensive Country. Since the regulations which have been adopted by the President excluding foreign traders from entering the Indian Country [were put into effect], many enterprizing American Citizens have directed their capital and attention to this business. The island of Michillimackinac is the great entrepôt for all goods destined to this part of the Indian Country. In the months of June and July, the Merchants embark in this trade and, owning the Capital, arrive upon that Island to make arrangements with those whom they supply with goods to receive their outfits for the ensuing year and to deliver their returns for that which has past. It is a fact within my own knowledge that a much larger quantity of goods than were required for this trade were this season taken to that place and have since been withdrawn. This fact I consider decisive as to the supply of this trade keeping pace with the demand. But such an occurrence was not necessary to produce this conviction upon my mind. Since my first acquaintance with Indian affairs I have made this a subject of enquiry, and I have never doubted the result which is thus practically established.

Of the system upon which this trade is conducted, I know nothing. My knowledge of the amiable & intelligent Officer at the head of this branch of the public service [Thomas L. McKenney] and of the Factors employed in this quarter justifies the opinion that all is done for the publick interest which zeal, intelligence and integrity can effect. But believing, as I do, that the system itself is radically incorrect, I cannot but recommend its abolition.

I leave untouched the general question with respect to the propriety under any circumstances of converting the funds of the United States into a commercial capital and its Government into mercantile adventurers. It is the practical operation only of these establishments upon our Citizens and upon the minds of the Indians which I am to consider.

These trading houses are known to belong to the United States, and the Factors are known to be public agents. The reasons & motives which led to their introduction are not understood nor appreciated. The Indians universally attribute them to a speculating disposition on the part of the Government. They believe that goods are thus sent among them for the same reason which induces individuals to embark in the trade. Invidious comparisons are introduced between our Government and the British Government, by whom such a system has never been adopted. It requires but little reflection to perceive the effect which such ideas must have upon a rude, savage, unlettered people. They are not in the habit of abstraction, and objects affect them as they correspond with their own habits and prejudices.

All barter with them is for gain, and it is not to be expected that their ideas upon the subject can be easily changed, nor that they should assign a different motive to the public & private trader while their pursuits & objects are the same.

As I have no disposition to enter too much into detail upon this subject, I shall conclude this branch of it by observing that there is an ample stock of American Capital, skill and enterprize for all the demands of this trade, that the public trading establishments injure the private traders by bringing into competition with them in the Indian market a capital for the use & management of which no advance is required, and that they render the Government obnoxious & contemptible to the Indians.

The laws no[w] in force upon the subject of Indian trade require that every person entering the Indian Country for the purpose of trading should receive a license & give bond, conditioned for a faithful observance of the laws and such regulations as may be required by the officer granting the license. This requisition appears to be effectual, so far as respects the entrance of traders into the Indian Country. Their remote stations, however, render it difficult to procure the necessary evidence to collect the penalty of the bond in those cases where there has been a breach of its conditions.

I believe no statutory provision is necessary to protect the Indians from the impositions of traders, where no whiskey is introduced into the Indian Country.

While the Indians are sober, they are fully competent to manage their own concerns. They understand the value of their peltries and of the goods which are offered for them. It is only while in a state of intoxication, or while labouring under the effects of that craving appetite for spirits which habits of intoxication produce, that they are liable to the impositions.

They are habitually shrewd, cautious, and suspicious. The capital embarked in this trade causes a competition among the persons connected in it, which leaves to the seller but a moderate profit and ensures to the purchaser his goods at a reasonable rate. There are too many traders concerned in this business to permit any combination among them or to allow any impositions to be practised without the danger of detection and punishment.

The entire exclusion of sp[i]rit[u]ous liquors from the Indian Country is therefore the only measure which it is necessary for the Government to adopt with a view to secure the Indians from the frauds of trade. It is also highly important to the success of any rational plan for gradually meliorating their condition and ultimately extending to them the full benefit of civilization. The exclusion, if ever effected, can only be effected by a change in the present laws and by a rigid police upon the subject. However important this measure to [*sic*; may] be to the Indians, yet we are not to expect their participation in any plan for its accomplishment. Their attachment to ardent spirits is a moral phenomenon, and to it they sacrifice every consideration, public or private.

It appears to me that, if more discretion were vested in the Officer granting the license with respect to whom licenses should be granted or refused, and if authority were given to the Officers of the Indian Department to arrest and bring in for trial any person found introducing spirits into the Indian Country and to destroy the spirits thus found, the beneficial results of this change would be soon experienced. The special employment of some persons to enforce these statutory provisions would be necessary. In fact, I have long been convinced that if six or eight men were appointed within the limits of this Superintendency to travel through the Indian Country and to enforce the laws & regulations upon this subject, our prospect of an improvement in the moral & physical condition of the Indians would be much more promising than it now is. I think this the most efficient measure which could be adopted, the most economical & practicable in itself, and the most certain and salutary in its effects.

FC in DNA, 76 (M-1:4, pp. 30–35). NOTE: A PC of Calhoun's letter of 5/25 is in *The Papers of John C. Calhoun,* 2:309.

To William Clark, St. Louis, 9/14. His letter of 6/29 [Abs in *The Papers of John C. Calhoun,* 2:351] has been received; the purchase of the boat @ $690 for the use of James Kennerly, Indian [Sub-]Agent on the Missouri, is approved; but Kennerly should report annually on 10/1 to Clark, and Clark to the War Department, the condition of the boat and her rigging. FC in DNA, 72, D:214.

From [Bvt. Col.] JOHN R. FENWICK

Boston, Sep[tember] 14, 1818

Mr. Manners the English Consul in this Town has made a demand for the release of several of my Men, who he claims as British subjects. I not only object to his right of claim, but have refused to give them up. The enlistment of all of them was voluntary on their part & strictly conformable to the Regulations for the recruiting service. If the wish of the Consul is acceded to, in the above cases, a third of the Garrison will present themselves to him as British Subjects & discontent & insubordination will pervade the remainder. It has already created some Excitement. I think in all the cases now alluded to the Men are under Sentence for Crimes committed, or in confinement for desertion.

May I hope to receive Instructions from you, for the Government of my Conduct, on similar occasions for the present, as well as the future.

ALS owned in 1960 by Harvey S. Teal of West Columbia, S.C.

From John King, Jr., New York [City], to James Monroe, 9/14. Having failed to present his business in person while enroute on a business trip, because Monroe was not in Washington, King, a resident of Mobile, encloses depositions and other complaints from citizens of Mobile against the "outrage" committed against their city on 7/14 by Lt. [Robert] Beall, who ordered Mobile's jail to be demolished. ALS with Ens in DNA, 2, K-1818.

To E[leazer] W. Ripley, 9/14. Calhoun is pleased that Ripley's letter of 8/15 (LS in DNA, 1, R-111) agreed with [Thomas S.] Jesup and [James] Gadsden as to the location of the new barracks [near Baton Rouge]. Calhoun had already decided upon the site preferred by Ripley before receiving Ripley's report and on 9/4 had written to Ripley that Jesup had been ordered to make preparations for the construction. FC in DNA, 3, 10:143–144.

From Decius Wadsworth, 9/14. He has considered and views unfavorably the appeal of Mrs. Catherine Wager. Whatever agreement was made originally with John Wager, Sr., at Harpers Ferry was merely oral and should be considered temporary, not perpetual.

Between 200 and 300 workmen are paid about $8,000 monthly in the Armory there and spend most of their income there; but the location and lack of competition make prices high, and that in turn necessitates wages so high that an average stand of arms manufactured there costs about $1 more than its counterpart produced at the Springfield, [Mass.,] Armory. The U.S. should build at Harpers Ferry a store to be leased to a merchant who would offer ample goods at fair prices and thus prevent "the Impositions of the petty Dealers now established there." To yield to Mrs. Wager's claim would create "an odious Monopoly . . . extremely injurious to the public Interest." ALS in DNA, 1, W-198; FC in DNA, 32, 2:103–105.

From ROBERT WICKLIFFE

Lexington [Ky.,] September 14th 1818

I am informed that Colo[nel] James Johnson of this State is, or will be an applicant for the Contract to supply the Troops in Missouri and perhaps of Alabama also; my acquaintance with Colo[nel] Johnson both as a man and a publick agent, induces me to trouble you with this letter.

Colo[nel] Johnson has long been distinguished as well for his private virtues as for his publick spirit, and has executed every contract with the public, with so much punctuality, that I think the War Department should weigh well the pretensions of another, before it rejects the proposals of Colo[nel] Johnson. He has provided ample means and will no doubt, (as he has heretofore) faithfully apply the funds placed in his hands to accomplish the objects of the Government. He is a man of large Fortune, of extensive family connexions, and an unblemished publick character; these assure the Government of a better result, upon the contract, than famished soldiers, and a contract wound up with a tedious law suit, which have been the issues of most of [the] western contracts. Should the contract, pass to another, I think it would be viewed a publick misfortune by the Friends of the Government, and by none more so, than your obedient Humble Servant, Robert Wickliffe.

LS in DNA, 44.

To Indian Agents Nicholas Boilvin, John Bowyer, Thomas Forsyth, Richard Graham, John Jamison, John Johnston, Charles Jouett, Reuben Lewis, John McKee, R[eturn] J. Meigs, David B. Mitchell, William Prince, Henry Sherburne, and Alexander Wolcott, Jr., 9/15. "The disbursements on account of rations issued to the Indians have become so great as to require the most rigid rules and economy. If consistent with your other duties, you will in all cases attend treaties to be held with the Indians among whom you are Agent and will cause an exact enumeration to be made of those present [who are] to be furnished with rations and will make a daily requisition, accompanied with a certificate of the number to be furnished with rations. The contractor, or the Deputy [Assistant] Commissary [General of Subsistence], as the case may be, can obtain a credit at the office of the 5th Auditor [Stephen Pleasonton] on such requisition and certificate only." Calhoun instructs the Agents to avoid causing all unnecessary assemblages of Indians at which the issuance of rations will be involved; advises them to distribute annuities in assemblages with all possible dispatch; and warns them that they will be held responsible personally for any rations issued improperly. "Indiscriminate issues of rations to straggling Indians who may visit the Agency having the most pernicious effect on them, by encouraging Idleness, no allowance for such will be made." FC in DNA, 72, D:215–216; CC in DNA, 201, 17A-E4; CC in DNA, 76 (M-1:6, pp. 326–327); CC (misdated 9/15/1819) in DNA, 76 (M-1:7, pp. 193–196); CC in DNA, 75 (M-208:7); PC in House Document No. 24, 17th Cong., 1st Sess.; PC in *American State Papers: Indian Affairs*, 2:269.

To Thomas A. Digges, [Washington,] 9/15. Calhoun returns the copy of his deed conveying in 1814 the lot on which Fort Washington stands—the document submitted by Digges on 9/15 (ALU in DNA, 1, D-70) in further support of his claim. Calhoun concedes the government's liability, under the terms of this deed, for any damages done by its personnel to Digges's fisheries adjacent to the fort. But Calhoun reminds Digges that Col. [Walker K.] Armistead and Digges "are at issue on the fact of such injury being done." FC in DNA, 3, 10:144.

To C[allender] Irvine, [Philadelphia,] 9/15. Encloses a letter from [Lt.] Col. [George E.] Mitchell covering a report by Capt. [Julius Frederick] Heileman on shoes issued at Sackets Harbor, N.Y. Orders Irvine to examine the complaint and report upon it. FC in DNA, 3, 10:145. Timothy Banger answered this request for Irvine on 9/26, enclosing four documents in regard to the shoes. FC in DNA, 45, 387:148.

From Hugh McCall

Savannah, Sep[tember] 15th 1818

Mr. Philip Bose, Post Master in this City, called on me yesterday evening and showed me a letter from the Deputy Post Master General, upon the subject of Gen[era]l [Andrew] Jackson[']s despatches from Pensacola to you; which appear to have been purloined from one of the post offices or mails, between Fort Hawkins and the City of Washington. It is to be inferred from the letter, that the fraud may probably be traced from a copy of the trials of Arbithnot & Ambrista [Alexander Arbuthnot and Robert C. Ambrister], mentioned by Mr. [Frederick S.] Fell, Editor of the Republican news paper in this City. The copy to which Mr. Fell had al[l]usion, is now in my possession, and was taken by an officer from the original notes, while the court was in session. A long acquaintance with Capt. Melvin [*sic*; George Washington Melven], from whom I obtained it, warrants me in assuring you, that he would have been amongst the first to detect and punish a fraudulent practice, either against his country, or an individual. The reason why Mr. Fell did not give publicity to the trial, or any part of it, was, that its first appearance in the papers of the U[nited] States, ought to come from headquarters. An injunction to this effect, was laid upon Mr. Fell, by Capt. Melvin, who loaned him the copy of the trial for perusal.

If I thought it would answer you any purpose to send you a copy of the trial, I would do so; and your wishes to this effect, being made known to me hereafter, shall receive prompt attention.

ALS in DNA, 1, M-298.

From Thomas L. McKenney

Indian Trade Office, Geo: Town, September 15th 1818

I had the honor yesterday to receive under cover from the War Dep[artmen]t Mr. [Henry] Sherburne[']s letter, which is returned herewith.

There appears to be no difficulty in the way. Every thing, no doubt, arrived in time. It is as impossible to move the supplies in a body *from* this office, as it is for them to *arrive* together.

The first parcels of the Chickasaws' annuity left this office on the 1st April, and the last on the 29th May. The first parcels of the presents left here the 20th May, the last 13th June.

The amount of the Chickasaws' annuity required to be furnished by the War Department was $12,000 and two items of $100 each for Gen[era]l [William] Colbert & Chinubbee Mingo's annuity, making $12,200.

The amount forwarded to the Bluffs in conformity with said requisition, including articles purchased in Philad[elphi]a, Pittsburg[h], and Shipping-port, was $12,200. The packages from Geo: Town were numbered 1 to 53 inclusive. The packages from the other places were marked "*U.S. Chickasaws' annuity.*" Numbers were not necessary, nor could they be regularly marked without concert. The articles sent without numbers consisted of Guns, Powder, Axes & Cow Bells, which are very distinguishable.

The whole of the goods for C[hickasaw] Bluffs except those forwarded from this office on the 17th June went off on the 20th June from Pittsburg[h]. Those which left here in the 17th June left Pittsburg[h] the 12th July. The whole ought to have (& no doubt did) reach the Bluffs on or about the 15th of August, between which and the 26th, the date of the Agent[']s letter, he might not have received the tidings of their arrival at the Agency house, which is 60 or 70 miles, in the interior, distant from the Factory at the Bluffs.

The Invoice for the Presents was sent to the Commissioners [who are seeking to negotiate a treaty with the Chickasaws].

I have the honor to enclose a letter [of 8/17 to me] from Major Daniel Hughes resisting the charges of the Agent [David B. Mitchell]. The result, also, shall be communicated to the War Department.

LS with En in DNA, 1, M-295; FC in DNA, 73, E:128–129.

To John McLean, [former Representative from O., Ridgeville, near Lebanon, O.,] 9/15. Answering his letter of 9/5 (ALS in DNA, 11, 12849) recommending [James R.] Stubbs of Newport, Ky., for a post in the Topographical Engineers or as a surveyor to run the line between the U.S. and the Western Cherokees, Calhoun regrets there is no vacancy in the Topographical Department. But he is impressed with the recommendations he received from McLean and [Stephen H.] Long and will consider Stubbs when a vacancy occurs. The line to be run between the U.S. and the Cherokees on the Arkansas is so short that Calhoun selected a local man for the job. FC in DNA, 3, 10:144–145.

To G[erard] Steddiford, [New York City,] 9/15. Acknowledges his letter of 9/10 (ALS in DNA, 1, S-201) and approves the decision to adjourn his court-martial "*sine die,* provided the returns [of indictments from several militia regiments] be not made in a reasonable time." Orders him to have [Henry B.] Hagerman and [Hugh] Maxwell complete the court proceedings. He is to report to Calhoun all details relating to extra compensation for the members of the court. FC in DNA, 3, 10:145–146.

From Jacob Brown, New York [City], 9/16. Acknowledges Calhoun's letter of 8/28 and promises to devote his attention soon to suggestions concerning the ration and what Calhoun should report to Congress about its components and distribution. LS in DNA, 1, B-250; FC in DLC, Jacob Brown Papers, Letterbooks, 2:119.

From H[enry] Clay, Lexington, [Ky.,] 9/16. Recommends Col. James Johnson as "an applicant for some contract with your department"; urges that the award be made on the basis of considerations other than the lowest bid; describes Johnson as "a gentleman of great merit, of bold and unceasing enterprize, and of the most perfect integrity" in whose welfare "every one takes a deep and lively interest." ALS in DNA, 44; PC in Hopkins and Hargreaves, eds., *The Papers of Henry Clay,* 2:598–599, with notes identifying the contract sought as one signed on 12/2 for supplying steamboats for Army movements on the Mississippi and Missouri Rivers.

Nathaniel Frye, Jr., Chief Clerk, Paymaster General's Office, Washington, to Daniel Parker, 9/16. States, upon request, "for the information of the Secretary of War" that Maj. John Hall, Paymaster of the Regiment of Riflemen, left Washington before 6/2 for St. Louis, that on 7/30 he was in Louisville, Ky., and expected to reach St. Louis in 10 days, and that $160,000 have been carried by or sent to him. ALS in DNA, 2, B-1818.

To Henry Sherburne, 9/16. Acknowledges his letter of 8/26 (LS in DNA, 1, M-295); because the Chickasaws' annuity for 1818 has been delivered in goods that they do not want, that letter was referred to Thomas L. McKenney, whose reply is enclosed; in reply to Sherburne's inquiry as to what quantity of rations and liquors he will be expected to provide, and when, for the forthcoming treaty negotiations with the Chickasaws, Calhoun tells him to be governed by the enclosed circular [of 9/15] "in the issuing of rations to the Indians who may be assembled at the time of the distribution of the annuities." FC in DNA, 72, D:216.

To J[ohn] Vaughan, Librarian, [American Philosophical Society,] Philadelphia, 9/16. Answering his letter of 9/14 (ALS in DNA, 1, V-17), Calhoun regrets that the U.S. cannot underwrite a translation of the French pamphlet about diseases in horses. It would be of no use to an Army that has no cavalry. Calhoun hopes there "will be no want of patronage, from an enlightened public to a work so valuable, and which from its size must come at a small expense to the purchaser." FC in DNA, 3, 10:146.

From D[ecius] Wadsworth, 9/16. Submits his estimate of Ordnance expenses for 1819 totaling $1,038,200. FC in DNA, 32, 2:105.

To [John Quincy Adams, Boston]

War Dept., 17th Sept. 1818

I received a letter from the President [James Monroe] to day from which the enclosed is an extract. I have directed the letter of Mr. [Joel R.] Poinsett, to which the President refers, to be transmitted to Raleigh N[orth] Carolina. As he may have left there, before your letter can reach him, it, perhaps, would be proper to direct the post master at Raleigh, in that event, to forward it to Charleston So[uth] Carolina.

Accept the assurance of my sincere respect & esteem.

[Enclosure]

Extract of a letter from the President of the U[nited] States to the Secretary of War, dated 15: Sept[embe]r 1818.

"Mr. Poinsett was lately with me. He possesses very extensive information concerning South American affairs, with a sound judgment, of the prospect, which they afford. I informed him that it was probable that his letters &c. in the Department of State would be communicated with the report of our Commissioners, [Theodorick Bland, John Graham, and Caesar A. Rodney, who made a trip to South America during 1817–1818,] to Congress at the approaching session. He said that it would be more agreeable to him, to make a communication at this time, founded on those documents, and other information received since he returned to the United States, as he had maintained a correspondence with South America, uninterrupted since his return, than to suffer, his letters which were written without the expectation of such a purpose, to be laid before Congress. I promised to have his letters sent to him, to enable him to make out such a communication, which I have to request you will be so good as to have done for me. As the ground of such a statement at this time, or rather report, he suggested the propriety of the Secretary of State writing him a letter, intimating the intention of laying his correspondence before Congress, and requesting such further information as he might possess on the subject. Perhaps it will be better, in the letter of the Secretary [of State], to say nothing about laying his correspondence before Congress, but simply to ask the information for the advantage of the Executive, grounding the application on his long residence in South America, and extensive knowledge of their affairs. I wish you to have both purposes carried into effect—that is, to have his letters forwarded to him, as desired in the enclosed letter, immediately, and to request Mr. Adams to write him a letter, in the spirit suggested."

ALS with CCEx in DNA, 101 (M-179:42). NOTE: An AEU by Adams on Calhoun's letter of 9/17 indicates that Adams received that letter in Boston. Calhoun's statement that "I have directed the letter of Mr. Poinsett, to which the President refers, to be transmitted [to Poinsett] at Raleigh" is not clear. Probably Calhoun meant that, as Monroe had asked, Calhoun sent to Poinsett in Raleigh the letters from Poinsett to the Department of State; but no covering letter from Calhoun to Poinsett has been discovered. Nor has any longer version of Monroe's letter of 9/15 to Calhoun been found. Poinsett had been in South America during all or most of 1809–1816.

From W[illiam] W. Bowen, "Merritts Tavern 12 miles from Baltimore," 9/17. As attorney for the plaintiffs in the suits against A[lexander] Richards, Maj. [Loring] Austin, and others, and with the encouragement of David A. Ogden, Bowen has been traveling to Washington to collect the payments due to his clients. But he has discovered that his trunk is missing from the stagecoach and has interrupted his trip to seek to recover it. He hopes to reach Washington tomorrow; but he warns Calhoun not to receive in the meanwhile any imposter who, with identifications that were in the trunk, may impersonate him. ALS in DNA, 1, B-77.

From Aug[uste] Chouteau, St. Louis, 9/17. Transmits his "last account for services rendered as a Commissioner appointed to trade [*sic*] with the Indian nations residing on the western side of the Mississip[p]i and jointly with the Governor William Clark." Announces that he has issued a draft for $720 to cover the balance due to Chouteau. An EU refers to his account "as a Commissioner for treating with the Quapaw Indians." LS in U.S. General Accounting Office, Indian Tribal Branch, Fifth Auditor Accounts, no. 627, "5th Auditor's Certificate on the account of Augustus [*sic*] Chouteau, one of the two commissioners for treating with the Indians."

From [Lt.] Col. H[enry] Leavenworth, Detroit, 9/17. Having taken command of the 5th Infantry Regiment on 9/6, he finds it "very much reduced in numbers" and presents suggestions concerning several officers: having designated Bvt. Maj. [Sullivan] Burbank to recruit for the Regiment, he requests that sufficient funds be made available to him; since Capt. [George] Bender still holds rank in the Regiment, although appointed recently to the Quartermaster General's Department, he requests that Bender rejoin the line or be replaced; recommends that 1st Lt. [and Bvt. Capt.] J[ohn] W. Holding, who "has been in 'the patriot Service' or on a piratical expidition [*sic*]" since June of 1817, be dismissed from service "as soon as possible"; hopes that 2nd Lt. R[ichard] H. Ashley, absent without leave since 5/31/1818, will be dismissed from the Army if he is not now under orders from the Department of War; and he requests that Maj. [Peter] Mühlenberg, [Jr.,] rejoin the Regiment if he is not on duty under War Department orders. Finally, Leavenworth asks for a copy of the *Army Register* and a book on recent Army regulations. ALS in DNA, 11, 1499 (M-566:12).

From Thomas Lee, Charleston, [S.C.,] 9/17. Asks that his "ambitious" son, Stephen Lee, be appointed as a Cadet. ALS in DNA, 15, 1819, 82.

From D[avid] B. Mitchell, Mount Nebo near Milledgeville, [Ga.,] 9/17. Acknowledges Calhoun's letter of 7/13; agrees that the route of the road from Fort Claiborne to Fort Stoddert can be improved; but suggests much greater improvements and urges Calhoun to write to Mitchell in Ala. his consent to have Mitchell establish this "Main Post road from Georgia to [New] Orleans by the nearest and best route." ALS in DNA, 1, M-351; PC in Carter, ed., *Territorial Papers,* 18:415–416.

From JAMES MONROE

"Highland," Sept. 17, 1818

The work suggested by General [Winfield] Scott [in his letter of 9/2 to you, which you sent to me on 9/5], is I am persuaded much wanted for the use and government of our army. If well executed, I have no doubt, that it will be of great utility, & I think him well qualified for it. The only question is, have we a power to engage his service in that way, and to compensate him for it? I presume we have, indeed what was done, in the case of Capt. [John M.] O'Connor seems to settle the point. Whether it will not be better, in engaging him [Scott] in this work, to have his project sanctioned by the commanding general, with an intimation that while thus employed, the service will not suffer, under the arrangement which may be made, in his absence, and to compensate him for extra service in any mode rather than by brevet pay? By obtaining the first, military etiquette will be observed, & the support of the commander with Congress & the army secured in favor of the measure. By the latter some excitement in Congress and other brevet officers, may be avoided. I merely suggest these ideas for consideration, not feeling any anxiety that they be attended to. In the course decided on, I am willing that you proceed to give effect to the measure without delay.

ALS in DNA, 1, P-209.

To [Bvt.] Maj. Thomas Biddle, [Jr.,] Fort Mifflin, [near Philadelphia,] 9/18. "Your correspondence with Mr. Heggins [Charles Hegins], Army contractor, respecting the storehouse at Fort Mifflin, has been referred to this Department. In order to enable me to have a full view of the case, you will report the dimensions and condition of the public storehouses at Fort Mifflin, and whether the[y] will contain a deposit of three months['] supply for the troops under your command." FC in DNA, 3, 10:147.

From Lewis Cass and Duncan McArthur

St. Marys, [O.,] Sept. 18, 1818

Accompanying this we have the honour to transmit you a treaty yesterday concluded by us with the Wyandot, Shawnese, Seneca & Ottawa tribes of Indians.

The proposition to remove to the West of the Mississippi was made to the three former tribes and enforced as far as we believe it politick to enforce it.

It was received by them with such strong symptoms of disapprobation that we did not think it proper to urge them too far upon the subject. The time has not yet arrived from them voluntarily to abandon the land of their fathers and seek a new residence in a Country with which they are unacquainted and among powerful and hostile Indians. As our settlements gradually surround them, their minds will be better prepared to receive this proposition, and we do not doubt but that a few years will accomplish what could not now be accomplished except at an expense greatly disproportioned to the object.

The treaty now concluded requires few observations from us. We trust all its stipulations will be found in strict conformity with our instructions.

The Chippeways, Potawatomies and Delaware tribes of Indians are not parties to this treaty. None of the provisions in the treaty to which this is supplementary which related to them has now been affected, and their participation was therefore unnecessary and might have been injurious.

We have promised to the tribes parties hereunto that they shall receive a quantity of goods equal in value to twelve thousand dollars. The goods cannot now be distributed, because such distribution would provoke the jealousies of the other tribes who are waiting the result of the treaty to be negociated [*sic*] for a cession of land in Indiana. It is thought politick to make a general distribution to all the tribes at the same time, and it is certainly proper that these tribes should receive as much in proportion to their numbers as any others. At the conclusion therefore of that treaty bills will be drawn upon the War Department for the amount of goods which we think it correct to purchase, payable after the ratification of the treaty, and we trust they will be duly honoured.

We transmit an extract from the Speech of the Ottawas in relation to the grant made by them to Dr. William Brown by the treaty concluded last year at the foot of the Rapids. We cannot but hope that this claim will be confirmed. Dr. Brown's professional services to these Indians have been long continued and gratuitous, equally uncommon in their occurrence and honourable to him.

FC in DNA, 76 (M-1:4, pp. 35–36); PC in *American State Papers: Indian Affairs,* 2:177.

From WILLIAM FLORANCE

Philadelphia, Sept. 18th 1818

I beg leave to address you on the subject of the application [dated 9/5] which I have the honor of making to you and which accompanies this letter. My very great solicitude induces me [to] trouble you with a second communication, to assure you of the very peculiar gratitude I should ever feel to you by confer[r]ing on me the commission of a Cadet. My wishes are more heightened by being informed that there is none of my persuasion at this period attached to that important institution. I have the honor of refer[r]ing you to several of the most respectable gentlemen of this city and Charleston, S[outh] Carolina. Should any further testimonials of my ability and integrity be deemed necessary they can be procured with much facility.

ALS with En in DNA, 15, 1819, 69.

From NICH[OLA]S P. TRIST

Monticello, [Albemarle County, Va.,] 18th September 1818

This is to acknowledge the receipt and [to announce my] acceptance of my appointment as a Cadet in the service of the United

States. According to orders, I shall in October next, proceed to West-point; in the interim, I will prepare myself for examination. Y[ou]rs very respectfully, Nich[ola]s P. Trist.

ALS in DNA, 15, 1818, 143.

To C[atherine] (Mrs. John) Wager, Harpers Ferry, 9/18. After examining the claim presented in behalf of her husband's estate, Calhoun informs her that he can find no evidence of a stipulation that would prevent the U.S. from allowing business establishments to operate on land purchased by the government from Wager. Autograph draft signed in MH; FC in DNA, 3, 10:147.

From Col. Robert Butler

Nashville, September 19th, 1818

On the eve of setting out for the Chickisaw [*sic*] Treaty, I deem it necessary to inform you that no reports have been received as yet, of a *particular character*, in relation to the Military road now opening from Columbia, Tennessee, to Madisonville [La.]; but I am enabled to inform you officially that fifty miles have been completed by the troops on the lower part of the road, making many causeways and bridges of the most durable materials; and the detachment on this end have progressed about forty miles south of Tennessee River, making, in like manner, many bridges and causeways.

It is considered that the most laborious part of the road has been completed; and from every information, it has been done in the best manner. An increase of men has been recently afforded to the detachment south of Tennessee River, which will enable it to progress with much greater facility.

Should I receive minute reports shortly, I shall communicate their contents without delay.

LS in DNA, 1, B-312; CC in DNA, 201, 15A-F3; PC in *American State Papers: Miscellaneous*, 2:537; PC in House Document No. 87, 15th Cong., 2nd Sess.

From Samuel Cooper, Agent for Fortifications, New York [City], 9/19. He and an Army engineer agree that Cooper needs $20,000 per month to pay for materials that are being used in constructing the works at Fort Diamond. He has expended almost all of the $20,000 that he received on 8/14. He asks for a remittance of an equal amount. ALS in DNA, 1, C-229.

James Diven, West Point, to Joseph [G.] Swift, 9/19. As Swift suggested, [Claudius] Crozet has examined Diven's son, [James Diven, Jr.,] and has found him prepared for admission into the Military Academy, as Crozet certifies in an AES; if Swift can get the boy appointed, the father will be grateful. ALS in DNA, 15, 1819, 132.

To James Monroe, [Albemarle County, Va.]

War Dept., 19th Sept. 1818

I enclose for your approval regulations for the Medical Department. They have been drawn up with care; and I believe are as good as can be devised for the commencement of the system. Time and experience may no doubt suggest important alterations. If they meet with your approbation, I will thank you to return them with your approval endorsed on them, as soon as convenient, as it is desirable, that they should be issued to the medical officers at an early date.

Mr. [Joel R.] Poinsett's letter and journal was [*sic*] lent to Mr. [John ?] Forsyth by Mr. [John Quincy] Adams; and as Mr. Forsyth is not in the city at present, it cannot be transmitted to Mr. Poinsett until he returns; which it is understood will be in a few days. It will then be sent immediately. I have written to Mr. Adams in relation to the subject, agreeably to your request.

I read your letter of the 17th Inst[ant] this morning. I cannot doubt the power of employing Gen[era]l [Winfield] Scott in the manner which he proposes. The case of Capt. [John M.] O'Connor (as well as many others) is in point. But I agree with you that his compensation ought not to be in the shape of his brevet pay and emoluments, as it would probably give offence to Congress and the Army. It is usual, for Extra Service to be rewarded by extra compensation; and in this case it may be specifically agreed on by the Dep[artmen]t and the Gen[era]l. The better course it appears to me will be to order the Gen[era]l to this place in order to agree on the plan, the compensation, and whatever other particulars would be necessary. I will write to him and state that after your return to the city an order will be given him to repair to this place, for the purpose which I have stated; and in the mean time, Gen[era]l [Jacob] Brown can be informed, of the wishes and the object of the executive. Accept of the assurance of my sincere respect and esteem.

ALS in DLC, James Monroe Papers, 26:4853–4854; PC in Jameson, ed., *Correspondence*, pp. 141–142.

To Daniel N.C. Payne, Lexington, Ky., 9/19. Replying to his letter of 9/3, Calhoun says the understaffed Pension Office has been swamped with an estimated 20,000 applications. They are being treated in the order of arrival, and Payne in his turn will be notified of the results of his application. FC in DNA, 3, 10:147–148.

H[arrison] G[ray] Otis, [Senator from Mass.,] Boston, to J[oseph] G. Swift, New York [City], 9/19. Otis expects Swift and other commissioners who are estimating the cost of fortifications at New York Harbor to proceed to Newport, [R.I.,] and Boston for similar surveys. Otis inquires when they will reach these two places and emphasizes that the purpose of the Senate resolution will be served if the commissioners determine the cost of fortifications without extensive, additional surveys of the depths of the harbors, etc. ALS in DNA, 23, 132.

To James Turk, Maryville, Tenn., 9/19. Answering his letter of 9/5 (ALS in DNA, 1, T-103), states that, under existing contracts, contractors are obliged to furnish rations to Indians when necessary. After 6/1/1819 Indians will receive rations either from the Commissary Department or by special contract. FC in DNA, 3, 10:148.

From William Carroll, Nashville, 9/20. "It will not be convenient for me to act as a commissioner at the Choctaw treaty. Recent circumstances of a private nature, require my attention at home for some months to come." ALS in DNA, 1, C-241.

From Edmund P. Gaines

Fort Hawkins, Ga., September 20, 1818

I had the honor to receive by the last mail your communication of the 3d of the present month, advising me of the appointment of the Honorable Wilson Lumpkin, Commissioner, to run the Line between the United States and Florida, from the head of the Appalachicola to the head of the St. Marys; and requiring me to furnish him with such Military Force as he may deem necessary for his protection.

By the enclosed Field report you will perceive that my whole effective strength East of the Alabama Territory, including the Harbor of Norfolk and Charleston, from the last reports, amounts only to six hundred & fifty-two officers and men; I therefore apprehend that a Force sufficient to enable the commissioner to accomplish the boundary Line, before the probable approach of the rainy season, cannot be detached without ["leaving" *interlined*] several of the frontier posts destitute of the requisite guards. The prospect of peace with the Seminole Indians being soon restored, I think ought not to be so much relied on, as at this time to risk a small detachment upon the Line, which borders on their principal haunts. The commissioner, however, being authorised to decide upon the number of men proper to accompany him, shall be promptly furnished with the whole, or whatever part of my disposable Force he may request.

I detached an express on the 16th inst[ant] with orders to [Bvt.] Major [Alexander C.W.] Fanning of the Corps of Artillery, commanding at St. Marks, to deliver up that post, pursuant to instructions from the department of war, dated the 14th and 19th of the last month. To which I have added that St. Marks shall be delivered only to an officer duly authorised (as directed) to receive it, *who shall be accompanied with a friendly Spanish force of not less than two hundred and fifty efficient men to garrison the post.*

This precaution appears to me indispensably necessary and proper, to obviate the evil effects that would be likely to result from an immediate renewal of intercourse between the outlaw'd savages, and a feeble garrison, such as they have been accustomed to regard only as their Factors, friend, and confederates. It is true that the number of men required, is something greater than our present number at that post—but it is likewise true that the latter consists of a very different description of force, from that which I have usually seen stationed in Florida, and such as will probably return thither.

LS in DNA, 1, G-105; CC in DLC, Andrew Jackson Papers, 8107–8108.

From Edmund P. Gaines

H[ea]d Q[uarte]rs Fort Hawkins, Ga[.,] September 20, 1818
After closing my letter to you of this date I received information of the truth of which there seems no ground to doubt, that six citizens of this State were, some days ago murdered by Indians, near St. Marys; among the slain was a Mr. Bullock, brother of the Post Master at this place.

In communicating this account, which appears st[r]ongly corroborative of the statement inclosed in my letter of the 8th ins[tan]t, I take the liberty to repeat to you the hope that the President [James Monroe] will be pleased to order one of the U.S. Regiments [of] Inf[an]try, and a Company or detachment of the Corps of Artillery from the Northern Division to Amelia Island, to cooperate with the Troops which I have ordered thither—consisting of about 300 recruits of the 4th and 7th Infantry.

I shall in a few days repair to Amelia Island and endeavor to do what can be done with the force which I may be able to collect, to secure that frontier, and pursue the savages.

I should think it my duty to require a Regiment or two of militia for this service, had I not been taught by painful experience that the *good* to be expected from a force of drafted militia falls too far short of the common calculations, founded upon the *numbers* employed, and bears too inconsiderable a proportion to the waste and expence incurred, to justify a requisition for such a force, whilst there is reason to calculate upon the assemblage of the requisite regular Troops—which I am persuaded may be concentrated at Amelia Island by water, sooner than the tardy process of drafting and moving a sufficient body of Militia to that point, could be accompli[s]hed.

Should the Regular Troops in question be ordered from the Northern Division, I am at present under the impression that a secret and rapid movement should be made upon the principal Force of the Indians on the river St. Johns, and thence to Chukechatta, and the Bay of Tampa; to which place supplies may be ordered by water.

I have already given orders for suitable Vessels, with provisions and ammunition, to be held in readiness at Fort Gadsden for the purpose. Their movement, with the disposable force in that quarter will be ordered, whenever the Troops arrive at Amelia Island; so that the arrival of the Transports at the Bay of Tampa may correspond with the march of the Troops by land to that place.

ALS in DNA, 1, G-106; ALS in DNA, 11, 12215.

From ANDREW JACKSON

Nashville, September 20th 1818

Your letter of date 28th ult. relating to the Commissariat and change of the ration, has been duly received, and met attention.

I herewith enclose you my views on that subject, which I think will meet a state of war, as well as peace, by adding to the number of Assistants. There are very strong objections to the system adopted, as officers cannot be spared from the line; and if they could, those qualified would seldom be disposed to engage in that business. If contractors can make overgrown fortunes let the system recommended be liberally adapted to draw men of reputation and business to engage in it, and a great saving will result to the Government; and the troops be infinitely better supplied.

You will also find my views with regard to the change of ration expressed in the recommendation.

I enclose you Col. [Robert] Butler's report [of 9/19], shewing the progress made in opening the military road.

I set out to day for the treaty with the Chickesaws [*sic*], accompanied by Governor [Isaac] Shelby.

[Enclosure dated September 19, 1818]

The Commissariat Department should consist of,

1st. 1 Commissary General (Brev[et] Brig[adier] Gen[era]l) stationed at Washington City. 1 Deputy Commissary General (Brevet Major) at the head Quarters of each Division. As many assistant Commissaries (Brev[et] Captains) as the President of the United States may deem necessary, either in peace or war; all of which to be appointed as other commissioned officers of the Army.

All purchases to be made under the direction of the Commissary General, by the Deputies and Assistants; and before delivery to pass inspection at the depot where they may be intended to issue; and where there may not be any regular inspection, persons not belonging to the Army shall be called on, unless there should be an officer of the Inspector General's department present. All provisions purchased and condemned shall be the loss of the purchaser.

To each post or place where troops are stationed, there shall be [assigned] an issuing Commissary appointed by the Commissary General, who will receive and receipt for all the supplies destined for the use of their posts respectively; and who will be required by the Commissary General to give bond and approved security for the faithful preservation and issue of the same, and be accountable for deficiencies; and to secure two rations. The whole Department to be subject to the rules and regulations governing the Army. The minute detail should be left with the head of the Department.

In a southern climate the following alteration in the ration is recommended. Give Molasses in lieu of whisky and beer, and add to the ration half a pint of peas, beans, or rice, per day.

LS with En in DNA, 1, J-62.

From Lewis Cass

St. Marys, [O.,] Sept. 21, 1818

I have the honour to transmit you a treaty concluded by me with the Chiefs of the Wyandot tribe of Indians in conformity with instructions from the War Department of May 19, 1817.

The delay in concluding this treaty has arisen from the difficulty of effecting the exchange until the land in the Territory of Michigan was surveyed. It could not be located prior to that time without unnecessarily interrupting the continuity of the surveys, and time which would have been gained was not of sufficient importance to justify this measure. The surveys were not returned until the beginning of last July, and I have embraced the first opportunity, which the meeting of the Wyandot Chiefs afforded since that time, to effect the object.

My letter to the Secretary of War of the 30th of July 1816 contains all the information which it is in my power to give upon this subject and renders it unnecessary for me to trouble you with any of the details connected with it.

FC in DNA, 76 (M-1:4, p. 36); PC in *American State Papers: Indian Affairs*, 2:177–178.

To Peter Hagner, 9/21. Transmits the claims of Elisha Dennison and eight others against Maj. Loring Austin and George R. Mills. In compliance with the act of 4/20 for the relief of Austin and Mills, Hagner is ordered to "adjust the claims agreeably to the terms of the enclosed copy of a letter, addressed by me to the Hon. David A. Ogden." FC in DNA, 3, 10:148.

From Harrison Hall, Philadelphia, 9/21. Transmits a copy of the "Acts of the last session of Congress, published 'by Authority' in the American Law Journal. A few copies have been published in this form & are sold at $1.50 each. Should you wish to purchase any number of copies for the use of your Department, a discount of 25 per cent from the above price will be made." ALS in DNA, 1, H-262.

From Ludwell Lee

Belmont, 21st Sep[tembe]r 1818

It is so long since I have had the pleasure of seeing you, that even my name may have escaped your recollection; presuming however upon that acquaintance, which I once had the honor of having had with you, I have ventured to address you, in favor of a young Gentleman of Virginia, who wishes, if possible, to get into an office, by which he may be able to provide a support.

Mr. John James Howell Lewis, the bearer of this, is the son of John Lewis Esqr. of Fredericksburg, with whom & his family, I believe you were well acquainted. He was once in the Navy, where he served with reputation for two years, with Capt. [Sidney ?] Smith of the Essex. He was induced, partly from the wishes of his father; & partly from his own views of greater advancement elsewhere; to leave the Service. He has failed in realising those views, & his father, being unable to assist him; he finds himself compelled, to be an applicant, for public service; in the Navy, or

Army, or in any other situation, which your goodness may think fit, to afford him an opportunity, of being serviceable in.

I have no doubt, from that uniform benevolence; which I may truly say; has been one of the most prominent features of your character, that what you think, can be done with propriety, you will do, to serve a worthy object.

ALS in DNA, 11, 12441.

From D[avid] B. Mitchell, Mount Nebo near Milledgeville, [Ga.,] 9/21. Acknowledges Calhoun's letters of 7/23 and 7/24 concerning the accounts of John Blount; disclaims any knowledge about these accounts; asserts that, even if Blount's claim is valid, it would not be payable out of the funds that Mitchell is disbursing in compensation for losses sustained prior to the Treaty of Fort Jackson, 9/1814. ALS in DNA, 1, M-348.

To James Monroe, [Albemarle County, Va.]

War Dept., 21st Sep[tembe]r 1818

I have received the enclosed letters from Gen[era]l [Edmund P.] Gain[e]s by the Southern mail of this morning.

The Gen[era]l seems to think that the Seminole war to the South is not terminated. There are so many motives for misrepresentation, at this moment, that I am very incredulous as to most of the reports. It happens unfortunately that a sale of a large and valuable tract of publick lands commences very shortly at Mil[l]edge Ville; and the keen speculator, in order to prevent the lands from being explored by those who may wish to buy, will as the land extends to the Florida line, propagate a thousand stories. I regret that Gen[era]l Gain[e]s has omitted to transmit the name of his informant; but it seems to me, that the letter on the face of it bares [*sic*] strong marks of exag[g]eration, if not misstatements. From every information, which I have received, and I put confidence in the statements, the whole force Indian & Negro can not exceed 1,200 warriors, in both west & east Florida.

I have ordered the recruits for the 8th & 4th Regim[en]ts (stationed in that quarter) about 500 to be sent on immediately from Norfolk & Boston; and have directed the Gen[era]l, if he should receive any information on which he can fully rely, to report immediately to the Department, so that necessary measures may be taken to detach troops from the North. The militia, in any view which can be taken, ought not, unless in case of necessity, to be called out. An Indian force under [Creek Chief William] McIntosh, should it be necessary, would be much more cheap and efficient.

I received a letter from Mr. [William H.] Crawford this morning. He expects to return to the city by the last of the month. The course persued [*sic*] by the Administration [in returning to Spain the Florida posts conquered by Andrew Jackson] is, he states, generally approved.

Accept of the assurance of my sincere respect & esteem.

ALS in NN, James Monroe Papers.

To Dr. E[benezer] Sage, [former Representative from N.Y.,] Sag Harbor, N.Y., 9/21. Thanks him for his letter of 9/8 (ALS in DNA, 1, S-203) opposing the proposed sale of the arsenal there. No immediate sale will be made; the Treasury Department will be offered the building "for the accommodation of the Customs, if that Department will undertake to pay the expense of repairs and preservation." FC in DNA, 3, 10:149.

To G[erard] Steddiford, New York [City], 9/21. Answering his letter of 9/15 (LS with En in DNA, 1, S-202; compare DNA, 182, pp. 1–3), Calhoun orders him, in the instances of [N.Y. militia delinquents'] fines that he recommends for remission, to include with his reports the original papers upon which the reports are based. He is to return papers sent to him from the War Department for the [three such] instances about which he reported on 9/15. FC in DNA, 3, 10:149.

From [Bvt.] Maj. Thomas Biddle, [Jr.,] Fort Mifflin, 9/22. Answering Calhoun's letter [of 9/18], Biddle reports that the contractor's store there is inadequate for the storage of three months' rations for a garrison of the size "usually maintained here." He offers, if provided with materials, to use his unit's artificers to make the building adequate "at a very triffling [*sic*] expense." ALS in DNA, 43, Fort Mifflin, 37, with an AES by C[hristopher] Vandeventer in behalf of Calhoun directing Quartermaster General [Thomas S. Jesup] to supply the materials.

From And[re]w Boden, [Representative from Pa.,] Carlisle, Pa., 9/22. He has recommended John Smith and James Ramsey for appointments as Lieutenants. Boden now reiterates his plea for the former but retracts it as to the latter, because "I have changed my opinion of him very much since I wrote you last." ALS in DNA, 11, 12792.

To [Robert Brent, Thomas S.] Jesup, [Joseph] Lovell, [Joseph G.] Swift, and [Decius] Wadsworth, 9/22. "You will in your quarterly account (or report, as the case may be) furnish to the [War] Department any information which you may have of the rate of exchange between the principal posts of disbursements, and the principal towns at which commerce enters; and a statement of the Bank accounts of the regular disbursing officers." FC in DNA, 3, 10:149; LS (Lovell's copy) in DNA, 245, 1:35; CC (Lovell's copy) in DNA, 244, A:5; LS (Swift's copy) in DNA, 23, 48 (161); LS (Wadsworth's copy) in DNA, 31, War Department.

From Jac[ob] Brown, "Head Quarters, New York," 9/22. "I beg to recommend to the attention of the Government Mr. John P[hilip] Dieterich of this city who is desirous of an appointment in the army with a view to a situation in the commissary's department. Mr. Dieterich is a young gentleman standing high in my consideration and served upon the Niagara frontier with credit. I think him fully competent to the situation he wishes and beg to ask the appointment for him." FC in DLC, Jacob Brown Papers, Letterbooks, 2:120.

Thomas Dougherty, Clerk of the House of Representatives, [Washington,] to C[hristopher] Vandeventer, 9/22. Dougherty responds to Vandeventer's request of 9/17 for copies of any resolutions of the House during the session of 1817–1818 related to the War Department other than those listed by Vandeventer on 9/17. Having examined the House Journal for this purpose, Dougherty sends copies of two other resolutions but insists that copies of these "were certainly sent out before. The one respecting internal improvements has been sent out *twice* before, but must have miscarried." ALS in DNA, 1, D-71.

To J[ames] L. Edwards, "Pension Bureau," 9/22. Requests by 10/1 "an estimate of money required in 1819, to pay the several kinds of pensions granted at your bureau." LS in CSmH; FC in DNA, 3, 10:150.

From former Lt. John M. Neel, Tuscaloosa County, Ala. Territory, 9/22. Reports recent skirmishes with some Indians, probably hostile Creeks. ALS in DNA, 1, N-34; PC in Carter, ed., *Territorial Papers,* 18:419–420.

To W[infield] Scott, New York [City], 9/22. James Monroe approves his being employed in preparing the compilation that he proposed in his letter of 9/2; when Monroe returns to the capital, [Jacob] Brown will be ordered to relieve Scott of his present duties, in order that Scott may report to Washington for discussions of details as to the arrangements for his intended duty as author. FC in DNA, 3, 10:149; CC in MHi.

From J[oseph] G. Swift, New York [City], 9/22. He has issued a draft for $5,000 to B[enjamin] W. Hopkins, the contractor for constructing a fort at Mobile Point. Swift will begin tomorrow his trip to Washington. ALS in DNA, 1, S-209.

S[ylvanus] Thayer, West Point, to [Joseph G.] Swift, 9/22. Recommends for a Cadet's appointment Joseph Rowe Smith, aged 17, whose guardian is his brother, Lt. Henry Smith of the 2nd Infantry Regiment. "I have examined Mr. Smith & have found him well qualified for admittance." ALS in DNA, 15, 1818, 149.

To J[acob] Brown, New York [City] or Brownville, N.Y., 9/23. "I enclose a copy of a letter of the 22d instant [from myself] to Brev[e]t Maj[o]r Gen[era]l W[infield] Scott. The General having devoted much time and attention to the police of the Army, affords to the Government, an opportunity, superior to any which could be had from a Board of Officers, or any other mode, to act on a subject, which greatly needs proper regulation." LS in MHi;

CC in DLC, Jacob Brown Papers, Letterbooks, 2:120; FC (dated 9/24) in DNA, 3, 10:153.

To Edmund P. Gaines, Savannah or Fort Hawkins, with copies to Andrew Jackson and James Monroe, 9/23. In reply to Gaines's two letters of 9/8 (ALS in DNA, 11, 12215, and LS in DNA, 1, G-123; ALS in DNA, 1, G-124, and LS's in DNA, 11, 12560, and in DLC, Andrew Jackson Papers, 8044–8045), Calhoun accepts without comment his explanation of his plans for relinquishment to the Spanish, under Calhoun's order of 8/14 to Gaines, of Pensacola and the Barrancas and, less willingly and promptly, of St. Marks. Calhoun responds to Gaines's having relayed reports from Governor [William W.] Bibb [of Ala. Territory] and from a Georgian, who had been in St. Augustine, that some Seminoles apparently intended to renew their attacks upon the U.S., especially if U.S. troops should evacuate St. Marks. Calhoun advises Gaines not to undertake any new campaign against the Seminoles unless information as to their hostile intentions is quite reliable and not until "we are fully prepared to strike an effectual blow." But Calhoun also gives assurance of adequate reinforcements, supplies, and other needs if Gaines finds it necessary to march into Fla.; and he specifically renews the authority to invade Spanish territory that was given to Gaines on 12/16/1817, without canceling, however, the order of 8/14/1818 commanding the restoration of Pensacola and St. Marks to the Spanish. Calhoun also urges Gaines to use regular Army personnel and friendly Creeks and to avoid, if possible, "the expense and vexation attending militia requisitions." He adds: "Economy and the honor of the Army require that, in the farther [*sic*] prosecution of the war, this should be avoided." LS in DNA, 11, 12215; FC in DNA, 3, 10:151–153; CC in DNA, 77 (M-271:2, frames 0966–0979); CC in DLC, Andrew Jackson Papers, 8118–8121; PC in Jameson, ed., *Correspondence*, pp. 142–144.

From Amos Kendall

Frankfort, Ky., Sept. 23d 1818

Understanding that Col. James Johnson is about applying to your department of the government for a contract, and believing that no man will more faithfully or more punctually discharge its duties, I can offer no other apology for obtruding this letter upon your notice, than an earnest desire that he may attain the object of his application.

During the late war Col. Johnson was well known to the people and the administration, not only for his personal services in the Army of the North west, but for the advances he made as contractor and the risk which he incurred to support the credit of government and advance the interests of the country. In devotion to business, unwearied industry and perseverence to meet his engagements, he has no superior, and if any man in this quarter deserves a *preference,* both on account of public services, and due qualifications to fulfil[l] the duties of a contract, it is Col. Johnson.

Indeed, sir, I know of no man more deserving the confidence of the government or on whom the public patronage could fall with more satisfaction to the people.

ALS in DNA, 43, file of James Johnson, 1.

From Joseph D. Lauck

Philad[elphi]a, Sept. 23d 1818

Your letter of 19th Aug[us]t was not received until yesterday; it remained in the hands of Mr. [William] Jones [who had recommended me] nearly one month, he being ignorant of my address. I would now inform you of my acceptance of the appointment of Cadet and shall repair as soon as possible to West Point to undergo the necessary examination. I am so unfortunate at present as to labour under a slight indisposition which has for a few weeks confined me to my room. I hope however that a few days will sufficiently restore me to health to enable me to discharge the duties of my appointment.

ALS in DNA, 15, 1818, 29.

To Hugh McCall, Savannah, 9/23. "Your letter of the 14th instant [LS with En in DNA, 1, M-297] has been received. If you will recur to your letter of the 15th of August to [former] Colo[nel Constant] Freeman, in which you state, in substance, that Mr. [Charles] Harris had not received any reply to his application to this Dept. for payment of rent &c., you will be enabled to explain to Mr. Harris why the duplicate of my letter of the 4th of February last was sent to him. Presuming that letter had miscarried, a duplicate was sent. On further investigation I find that Mr. Harris' letter of the 10th of Ap[ri]l last, in answer to mine of the 4th of Feby., has been received, and is referred to the 3d Auditor of the Treasury [Peter Hagner] for adjustment." Calhoun does not answer McCall's request of 9/14 for $4,000 to cover his Commissary and Quartermaster needs, his comment on the low state of government credit in the South, and his complaint that he had written seven letters about Harris's claim that were not answered directly. FC in DNA, 3, 10:150.

From Henry Sherburne

Chickasaw Agency, September 23d 1818

Inclosed is George B. Wiggins & Co.'s account & Receipt thereon for Eighty-eight dollars & seventy-five cents for Iron & Steel furnished the Public Blacksmith, which amount I yesterday drew on you for in their favor at sight.

LS in U.S. General Accounting Office, Indian Tribal Branch, Fifth Auditor Accounts, no. 582, account of Henry Sherburne.

To S[amuel] Smith, Uniontown, Pa.

Department of War, 23d Septem[be]r 1818

I received your letter of the 15th instant, with the enclosed extract from the "Genius of Liberty" in relation to Revolutionary pensions. The rule to which it refers as being established by the Department, to require two witnesses in certain cases, has never had the sanction of this Department. The fact is that, while I was absent for a few weeks to the South, the Clerk who was charged with the examination of the cases, [George Boyd,] dreading fraud from the number of the applications (exceeding all of the estimates made by Congress), acted without my approbation on that principle in cases where the applicant was not to be found on the roll of the state. As soon as I returned, I gave him different directions, and in no case will additional proof be required but where there is suspicion of fraud. The difficulty is not in the rigidness of the rule[s] established by this Dept., for they are all easily complied with, but in the number of applications being much greater than can be, with every effort, acted on as they come in. This is the real cause of the delay, which to me is very unpleasant but beyond my control. Congress alone can remedy it, by granting an adequate number of Clerks.

As to the censure contained in the extract, it causes but little pain and of itself would not induce a reply to your letter. The statement which I have made is for your satisfaction and those with whose cases you have been charged. If I can do my duty, I am satisfied. On this maxim, and this alone, I have always acted. The number of Applicants is for Congress and not for me to consider. It is my duty to execute the law faithfully.

FC in DNA, 3, 10:150.

Thirty Chiefs of the Ottawa, Chippewa, and Potawatomi Indians, St. Marys, to [James Monroe], 9/23. These Chiefs testify that Dr. William Brown of Detroit has given to them for many years medical services without compensation; they ask that he be given a piece of their land. An AEU by Monroe refers this letter to Calhoun, and an EU indicates that it was received in the War Department in 2/1819. LS in DNA, 1, S-247.

From Dr. BENJ[AMI]N WATERHOUSE, "a Post Surgeon"

Cambridge, [Mass.,] Sep[tembe]r 23d 1818

The As[sis]t[an]t Dep[ut]y Q[uarte]r Master General has enclosed to me an account of 27 dollars for the printing of certain circulars on the subject of Dysentery written & distributed by me to the Surgeons of the Army, and which he was ordered to pay by the commanding General of this Department; but which has been returned to him with the following remark, by the accountant: "There being no law, nor regulation providing for charges of the within description, this account cannot be admitted *without the sanction of the Secretary of War.*" I beg leave to mention the causes which gave occasion to this particular charge.

This time twelve months [ago] the Dysentery raged in several towns on the sea coast of New England. This town of Cambridge,

2 miles from Boston, and about half that distance from Charlestown, lost as many people by Dysentery in seven weeks, as they had of all other disorders in the preceeding [*sic*] seven years. Had so great a mortality occurred in Boston, probably half the town would have been deserted. The colleges were broken up.

Malignant as was the disorder, that was not my greatest concern. I perceived the practitioners did not know how to treat it. It had not prevailed in this region since the earliest period of our Revolutionary war, and there was hardly one of the Physicians of that day now living. Those now on the ground had scarcely ever occasion to contemplate the nature of the distemper, & the true mode of treatment. Whole families were swept away, & many of our collegians [were] under treatment directly the reverse to what it ought to have been. The disorder and the absurd mode of treating it was spreading fast from town to town, and I was fearful that both would reach our garrisons. I directly waited on the Commander of the Department, and imparted to him my design of writing on the subject. General [James] Miller was impressed with the importance of it; and when I presented him with my manuscript, he encouraged the idea of printing it in a pamphlet form, that the Surgeons might keep it by them with their other medical books: and what he suggested and approved was directly done.

It may not be amiss here to remark that *all* those who were treated from the begin[n]ing, in the mode recommended in my circular address, *recovered*: and I hope I may be excused for remarking also, that during the six months of summer and autumn, which included those months when the Dysentery raged in our towns on this coast, there was but *one death,* in *the thousand & nineteen men,* which composed our garrisons, and this one died of consumption.

Although an Hospital *Surgeon & Director* in a military Department is, *ex officio,* the advisery [*sic*] officer of the commanding General in whatever concerns the health of the troops, in the prevention as well as the curing of diseases, yet I am aware that there is no legal provision for the small charge in question, nor in the regulations; yet I presume there is an implyed [*sic*] one in all such works of supererogation for preserving the life of the soldier. In this light it was viewed by [Bvt. Col. John E. Wool,] the Inspector General of this Northern Division; who in answer to the report made to him at the close of the past year says, in his letter to me dated Brownsville [*sic*], [N.Y.,] Dec[embe]r 30th 1817, "We congratulate you on the beneficial effects produced by your circular letter; and would observe, that he, who by his spontaneous exertions, in disseminating useful information, saves the life of a citizen, or a soldier, is deserving the highest honour."

May I be allowed to add the sentiments of the Secretary of State, being a P.S. to a letter to me dated Oct[obe]r 3d 1817, "Just as I was closing my letter I received yours of the 27th ult[im]o with the three pamphlets (on Dysentery) one of which I shall present to the Acting Secretary at War [George Graham], and another to the Secretary of the Treasury [William H. Crawford]. I presume you have sent one to the President [James Monroe]. I shall read the circular letter with great interest, both as coming from you, and as on a subject so awfully important at this time in your neighbourhood, and at all times to military men and armies." J[ohn] Q[uincy] A[dams].

By this view of the matter, you will be able to judge whether the writer of the circular letter (copies of which were sent into the Southern Division) should pay for the printing of it; or the United States, for the benefit of whose soldiers it was written & circulated.

ALS in DNA, 241, W-1818–1832. NOTE: The pamphlet or "circular address" published by Dr. Waterhouse was doubtless *A Circular Letter, from Dr. Benjamin Waterhouse, to the Surgeons of the Different Posts in the Second Military Department of the United States' Army* ([Cambridge ?]: 1817). For Calhoun's reply to this appeal by Waterhouse for a refund of the $27 (an appeal that was answered negatively), see Calhoun's letter to Waterhouse dated 9/29, a transcription of which appears herein.

From Lt. J[ohn] S[ylvanus] Allanson, Boston, 9/24. He did not receive until 9/5 the appointment of his brother, [Dudley W. Allanson,] as a Cadet, "by reason of my absence from Boston with Gen[era]l [James] Miller." His brother is away "'on a journey" and could not be reached promptly; so Lt. Allanson encloses the acceptance [written on 9/20] by "my father," [Richard Allanson,] and asks "the indulgence of a special permission" for Cadet Allanson to report to the Military Academy by 11/1. ALS with En in DNA, 15, 1818, 148, with an EU indicating an order to report by 10/16.

To A[NDREW] JACKSON, [Nashville]

War Dept., 24th Sep[tembe]r 1818

I enclose for your information a copy of a letter [from myself] to Gen[era]l [Edmund P.] Gain[e]s of the 23d Inst[ant], and also a copy of an order to him of the 1st Inst[ant], which was intended to have been sent in mine to you of the 8th Inst[ant] instead of the copy of the order which was enclosed.

Gen[era]l Gain[e]s' correspondent estimates the hostile Indian force on the St. Johns at from 2,000 to 4,000 warriors, which must be a great exag[g]eration.

If hostilities should be renewed, the presence of the Deputy Q[uarter] M[aster] General [Milo Mason] may be very essential, and I have accordingly given him the orders which are referred to in the letter to Gen[era]l Gain[e]s.

Capt. [Hugh] Young's report [concerning the topography of the Floridas] is very creditable to his industry and capacity. It contains a great deal of valuable information, and will be laid before the President [James Monroe] on his return [to Washington].

ALS in DLC, Andrew Jackson Papers, 8130; FC in DNA, 3, 10:153.

To Thomas S. Jesup, 9/24. Lt. Col. [George] Bomford will be entitled after 9/30 to fuel, quarters, and forage in accordance with his rank. Jesup will order the Quartermaster officer at New Orleans to pay for medicines and medical stores purchased there by "Dr. Bacchus [Christopher Backus]," Assistant Apothecary General. FC in DNA, 3, 10:154.

To WILSON LUMPKIN, Madison, Ga.

Department of War, 24th Septem[be]r 1818

By a reference to the report of Mr. [Andrew] Ellicott, who was the mathematician on the U[nited] States to run the boundary between the U[nited] States and Florida, I find that he establishes the junction of Flint and Chatahouchy [*sic*] at 84:45′ west longitude from Greenwich, and latitude 30:42′—and the head of the St. Marys at Long[itude] 82:15′, and lat[itude] 30:34′—and consequently, from the junction of Flint and Chatahouchy to the head of the St.

Marys, the bearing is S[outh] 87:17′ E[ast] and the distance 155 English miles.

If these calculations are correct, a proper allowance being made for the variation of the needle, any surveyor can run the line on the first attempt, with sufficient accuracy.

FC in DNA, 3, 10:153.

From THOMAS WAIDE, "Agent for the parties"

Washington, Sept. 24, 1818

Permit me to trespass a few moment[s] upon your patience while I narrate the following facts. Early in June last I put into the hands of J[ame]s L. Edwards, a Clerk in the Pension Office, the papers of Epenetus H. Jackson & John Folyard, claiming pensions for disabilities incur[r]ed, in the service of the United States during the late war with Eng[lan]d. These claims now lie entombed in some abyss about that office which seems to be fast devouring it's [*sic*] contents and there Sir they are doomed to sleep by the present incumbent of the office [*one word illegible*] evinces unless your Honor speak them again into life. Mr. Edwards alledges [*sic*] that these claims are lost: but I trust your Honor will excuse me, for beleiving [*sic*] them, not lost but intentionally laid aside, to gratify some secret hostility, lurking in the man's bosom against me. This, Sir, is one of those low devices [*footnote:* "The indirect means by which an illegal purpose is effected"] that characterise [*sic*] the inhabitants of a certain quarter of the Union and are there considered mighty clever things: but *which* have allways [*sic*] been observed to be, the *unerring* marks, of a narrow capacity, and base principles.

In relation to the Packet you ordered to the Post-office some time since Mr. Edwards betrayed the deformity of his character very strongly. He sent it from his office encumbered with a thick, heavy, blue, paper, accompanied with a heavy seal and cord; all of which, were useless appendages; and clearly intend[ed] to force from me, a dollar or two more, than I ought to have paid as postage. This malevolence however, was defeated by the gentlemanly conduct of Mr. Monroe, who deducted the weight of these things from the postage, upon my explaining to him, the *motive* that had attached them to the packet.

This is indeed a trifle: but feathers shew which way the winds blow, and I mention this Sir in proof of my premises, that Mr. E[dwar]d's bosom is pregnant with feelings the most unfriendly to me, and that those feelings, have dictated the shallow artifice he has resorted to in relation to the claims pretended to be lost. [*Footnote:* "It is singular that in Mr. (Peter) Hagner's office, nay in every other branch of the Dep(artmen)t over which your Honor presides from the Adj(utan)t Gen(era)l(')s office down, any papers on file or even the name of an individual soldier is found in a few minutes."] But Sir the injuries resulting to your Honor from these malpractices of Mr. Edwards, are by no means to be disregarded. They generate an unfriendly spirit among the people towards you, while the author of the mischief is too obscure, to be seen or noticed by them. (See the L[etter] from Baily No. 1.) I am aware, may it please your Honor, that it will be said the ill will of a pensioner is to be disregarded: but suppose sir, John Folyard, one of the injured persons in this case (who was also a soldier of the Revolution), sitting surrounded by his half dozen brothers and their descendants, together with the husbands of his two or three sisters and their descendants, who are *bound* by the ties of nature to support him, until he obtain the proffered assistance of his country. He recounts to them his toilsome marches, his privations of clothing, his *hunger* and *thirst*, in the Revolutionary War; he then adverts to his services in the late war upon the northern border, he points to his shattered constitution, his withered, broken, and emaciated limbs, and lastly his *head* grown *grey* in the service of his country and now *bowing* beneath the accumulated pressure of *age, infirmity*, and want. He tells them that his papers have for a long time been before the Sec[re]t[ary] of War; that he has had *no* relief; and is now hopeless. They eagerly inquire *who* is the Sec[re]t[ary] of War, and are told your Honor is. I appeal to *you* Sir, to say, whether two of the most powerful *agents* that controul the antipathies and friendship of man, do not conspire to make the whole of this *circle* your enemies, namely, *self interest* and *kindred affection.*

Upon the enclosed letter and power [of attorney] n[umbere]d 2 & 3 from John Hardehy an application was, the day before yesterday, made by me to Mr. Edwards for Harchie's [*sic for* Hardehy's] discharge. It was refused me. Without moving from his chair, he said it could not be found, his papers were deranged.

Now your Honor will perceive this discharge was transmitted *early* in May and the decisions in the office have passed the middle of that month in the order of time. How then can it be said by Mr. Edwards that derangement reaches back to that period and If it do, where does it cease? Have derangement and confusion, like Maab (Queen of the Fairies), been prancing among the papers of the office for 3 or 4 months while Mr. Edwards in the *drowsy* darkness of his intellect, has all this time been slumbering in his chair? But I have allready [*sic*] trespassed much too long upon the time & patience of your Honor—allways devoted to the public good; I will therefore close, by soliciting from you Sir, an order for the *delivery* of the *discharge* of *John Hardehy* together with the claim of John Folyard & Epenetus H. Jackson.

ALS in DNA, 1, W-210.

To Robert Brent, 9/25. "You will, under each head of appropriation, report the probable balance for or against such appropriation, at the end of the year 1818. You will also, judging from the amount paid, include in your report a statement of the average number of rank and file in the Army, during the three first quarters of the same year." FC in DNA, 3, 10:154.

To [William H. Crawford], 9/25. "Be pleased to place in the hands of the Treasurer of the United States, [Thomas Tudor Tucker,] the sum of Eight thousand dollars, on account of the appropriation for completing the surveys of certain ports and harbours, included in the act making appropriations for the support of government for the year 1818." FC in DNA, 171, 1:303–304.

To [Thomas S.] Jesup, 9/25. "By yesterday's mail, I rec[eive]d the enclosed letter and accounts from Gen[era]l [Jacob] Brown. Were I governed in the discharge of my duty by feelings of humanity only, I would certainly direct the account to be paid, but I deem an adherence to fixed rules and principles indispensible [*sic*]. You will accordingly instruct Capt. [William A.] Barron, to pay only for the usual allowance of quarters, while Capt. [James T.B.] Romayne [who died on 9/17] remained in New York, under the Surgeon's certificate." LS in DNA, 41, S-15; FC in DNA, 3, 10:155; CC in MHi.

To [Joseph] Lovell and J[oseph] G. Swift, 9/25. "You will transmit to the Department an estimate of the expense of your [respective] office[s] for the year 1819, including Clerk hire and contingencies, as rent, fuel, stationery &c. &c." FC in DNA, 3, 10:154; LS (Lovell's copy) in DNA, 245, 1:37; CC (Lovell's copy) in DNA, 244, A:5; LS (Swift's copy) in DNA, 23, 47.

From Thomas L. McKenney, Georgetown, [D.C.,] 9/25. "I have the honor to recommend, in conformity with the Factor's [John Fowler's] suggestions, as contained in the enclosed letter, that a portion of the means hitherto disbursed at Natchitoches for the accommodation of the Indians be applied to the Caddo Factory at Sulphur Fork. As many of his remarks as apply to settlers on Red River, and its vicinity and to the Pedlars [*sic*] who vex the natives, I respectfully submit, for the application of such means, to remedy the evils complained of, as may appear best in the judgment of the War Department." LS with En in DNA, 1, M-352; FC in DNA, 73, E:129.

To Thomas L. McKenney, 9/25. "It appears by a letter from Col. [Henry] Sherburne of the 9th inst[ant] that the Chickasaw Indians persevere in their determination not to receive the goods transmitted for their annuity for this year; in consequence of which, I have directed him to draw on this Department for the amount, to be paid in Cash, and to deliver the goods to your order, which you are requested to receive on account of the Indian Trade Dept. and refund the sum paid for them, as soon as convenient, into the Treasury, to the credit of the Indian Department." FC in DNA, 72, D:217.

To Pierre Menard, Sub-Agent, Kaskaskia, 9/25. Acknowledges his letter of 9/1 (ALS with Ens in DNA, 1, M-300) concerning the annuity for 1812 due to the Piankashaw Indians; regrets "extremely" the delay in paying that annuity, which resulted from lack of correct information; is sending $1,000 to facilitate the payment. FC in DNA, 72, D:216.

To Daniel Parker, 9/25. He is directed to report, on the basis of returns or of a probable average, the number of men in the Army during the first three quarters of 1818; to submit an estimate of the expenses of his office for 1819; to furnish [Robert Brent] with a list of Army officers, noting the lineal ranks of those appointed to the general, Regimental, and Battalion staffs; and to report the number of posts that may require an Assistant Commissary [General of Subsistence] under the statute of 4/14/1818 regulating the staff of the Army. LS in DNA, 11, 12923; FC in DNA, 3, 10:154–155.

From Capt. J[oel] Spencer, Fort Gaines, 9/25. Announces that he has issued a draft for $2,633.12 to John Brockman for cattle under an order given by Lt. Col. [Mathew] Arbuckle because the contractor [Benjamin G. Orr] has failed to deliver rations needed in Southwest Ga. ALS in DNA, 1, S-249.

From S[ylvanus] Thayer, West Point, 9/25. Encloses, upon request of the Academic Staff of the Military Academy, a document for [James Monroe's] attention. ALS in DNA, 11, 11804.

To [Lt. Col.] W[illiam] A. Trimble, Lexington, Ky., 9/25. Answering his proposal of 9/17 (ALS with ADS in DNA, 1, T-132), written after Trimble had talked with Calhoun in Washington and during a stopover at White Sulphur Springs, Va. (now W. Va.), that Trimble might lead an exploration of the Texas area, to which the U.S. should not relinquish claim in return for a rumored Spanish cession of the Floridas, Calhoun writes: "Your observations appear to me, in many points of view, to be very judicious and interesting. On the return of the President to the city, your letter will be laid before him, and the results will be communicated to you. It is very important, that fuller and more accurate information should be had, of so interesting a country; and if the state of affairs should render it proper to cause it to be explored, at this time, the Department will avail itself of your spirit of enterprise and capacity for sound observation. In the meantime, it will be prudent to make no observation, which will lead the Publick to a belief, that such an object is in contemplation." FC in DNA, 5, 1:95–96.

Col. H[enry] Atkinson, Plattsburg, [N.Y.,] to Lt. Col. [Josiah] Snelling, Plattsburg, 9/26. Requests a full report concerning an alleged "outrage . . . committed on the British rights and territory [in Canada] by a party of American soldiers commanded by a subaltern" on 7/28. CC in DNA, 101 (M-179).

From Col. Will[iam] King, Pensacola, 9/26. [Andrew] Jackson on 3/25 appointed Alexander Houston of the Tenn. militia a 2nd Lt. in the 4th [Infantry] Regiment, subject to a confirmation by Calhoun that has never arrived. King recommends the intended confirmation. ALS in DNA, 11, 12323.

To Daniel Parker, 9/26. "You will give the requisite order to extend the limits of the Northern Division of the U[nited] States [Army to make that Division include the Mississippi and its tributaries above Rocky River], conformably to the enclosed extract of a letter of this Dep[artmen]t of the 22d ult[im]o to Major Gen[era]l [Andrew] Jackson." FC in DNA, 3, 10:155.

To Henry Sherburne, 9/26. As a concession to the Chickasaws' unwillingness, which he reported on 9/9, to receive their 1818 annuity in the form of goods, he is authorized to do with the shipment what Thomas L. McKenney will direct and to obtain cash with which to pay the annuity, as Sherburne had been directed on 8/18 to do. "The promptness with which this [reversal of policy] has been done will certainly do away every impression of unfairness in the transaction." Besides, the government has incurred extra expense by having shipped the goods. FC in DNA, 72, D:217.

To Thomas Wa[i]de, Washington, 9/26. Calhoun acknowledges Wa[i]de's letter of 9/24 and informs him that [James L.] Edwards of the Pension Office has been instructed to take up each claim in the order received. Wa[i]de's papers cannot be returned until his claim has been examined. FC in DNA, 3, 10:155.

To Patrick [Noble, Abbeville, S.C.]

War Dept., 27th Sept. 1818

I received your letter of the 14th Inst[ant] this morning.

The conduct of Charles Wilson surprises me much. I refuse to pay the claim of Mr. Wilson wholly; as he had no just claim on me, and gave him no directions to apply to you for the money. The state of the case is this, Calhoun and Wilson were plaintiffs in the action against Godman. I recommended a judgment against the Defen[dan]t and Mr. Glover assumed to settle the judgm[en]t. In the settle[men]t between my brother and Wilson, the latter became the owner of the judgm[en]t, by whom indulgence was afforded to the Def[endan]t or Glover for a long time as will appear by a reference to the execution, which I believe is not yet closed. In my settlement with Wilson, I charged him with the cost of the Plaintiff[']s attorney in the action, as I had a right to do; leaving it to him to look to the Defendant or Glover. You will write to Charles Wilson immediately informing him of his mistake and urging him to return the money paid to you immediately. I care not how the cost is to come, from Glover, or Wilson; but I hope you will take such steps as will not permit me to be shuffled out of it. I hope you will pay no bill in future without letting me know of it, as I may be subjected to similar tricks.

Black acts very much in character. I wrote but a very few letters to any of my friends in favour of Sikes, and I believe they were all received too late, to effect [*sic*] the election. I stated to Sikes, when he requested me to write, that I was affraid [*sic*] that Black would make the use of it, which he has done. You say nothing of your own election. I trust there is no doubt. I have great confidence in the good sense and virture [*sic*] of the people of Abbeville. Should a vacancy occur such as you suppose in the Alabama Territory, I will most cheerfully render our friend [George ?] Bowie all of the aid in my power.

We are all well except Ann[a] Maria. She has the croop [*sic*] and has been dangerously ill. I hope she is out of danger.

We have no news except what you see in the papers. Write me often and tell me about the crops and all of the domestic news. Remember me most affectionately to all of my old village friends as particularly as if I had enumerated them. Floride joins her love to you and Elizabeth.

Typescript in DLC, Carnegie Institution of Washington Transcript Collection.

From Samuel C. Reid, New York [City], 9/27. Introduces John P[hilip] Dieterich, [formerly a Bvt. 1st Lt.,] whose surname suggests his "enterprising" Dutch blood. He will be in Washington on business. "Any attention shall be acknowledged & reciprocated the earliest opportunity." ALS in DNA, 11, 12117. (Dieterich became a 2nd Lt. on 10/31.)

From Paymaster C[harles] B. Tallmadge, Boston, 9/27. Asks Calhoun to sustain him in an issue that has arisen. Under authority given by Calhoun, Tallmadge hired a civilian clerk because no soldier there could do the work well. But a Sgt. whom the civilian replaced has entered a claim for the clerk's pay for the period after Tallmadge dispensed with the services of the Sgt.; and Col. [John R.] Fenwick supports the soldier's claim on the allegation that the soldier could not be removed from the clerk's office without a conviction by court-martial. ALS in DNA, 1, T-111.

To [Col.] H[enry] Atkinson, Plattsburg, N.Y., 9/28. "Your letter [of 9/18 (ALS in DNA, 1, A-81)] on the subject of allowing to non-commissioned officers and Privates the same [reward] as is allowed to citizens for apprehending a deserter has been rec[eive]d. Your opinion appears judicious, and the allowance will be made in future." FC in DNA, 3, 10:156.

To James Barbour, [Senator from Va.,] Barboursville, Va., 9/28. Answers affirmatively his request of 9/16 (ALS in DNA, 1, B-298) for permission for his nephew, Thornton F. Johnson, to report to the Military Academy next month, delays having been encountered in Johnson's travel plans. "Major [Sylvanus] Thayer . . . has been directed to admit the Cadets who are qualified, provided they join by the middle of October. I hope your nephew will be in time. Accept the assurance of my sincere respect and esteem." FC in DNA, 3, 10:156.

To Robert Brent, with extracts to Richard Cutts and to William Lee, 9/28. Pursuant to the inquiry from D[avid] S. Townsend, Battalion Paymaster at Boston, to Brent on 9/23 (ALS in DNA, 1, T-104), which Brent referred to Calhoun, Calhoun authorizes double rations for the commanding officer at Fort Sullivan, [District of Me., Mass.]. Calhoun also authorizes an equal allowance to the Infantry officer to whom the training of Cadets in the Military Academy is assigned; and he encloses a letter and muster roll from [George E.] Mitchell. FC in DNA, 3, 10:158; CCEx in DNA, 17, 1:12; PEx in *American State Papers: Military Affairs,* 4:376.

CIRCULAR to Officers Commanding Regiments and Battalions

Department of War, 28th September 1818

On the 1st June 1819 the present system of supplying the Army with rations will be succeeded by that of supplying it by a Commissariat. Feeling great solicitude, as well from a regard to the interest of the Army as to that of the public, that the new system should commence under the most favourable auspices, and as its success will mainly depend on the fidelity and capacity of the Assistant Commissaries, you will report to me the most suitable subaltern to be appointed Assistant Commissary [of Subsistence] at each of the posts at which your regiment or battalion is stationed.

It too often happens that appointments are conferred on those to whom they are most convenient, and not on such as are best qualified to discharge their duties. It is confidently believed that your recommendation in a point deemed so essential will be governed by more worthy considerations and that you will mainly regard integrity, capacity, method and habits of business. If you cannot select a subaltern with such qualifications for the office as he ought to possess, you will report the fact to the Department.

FC in DNA, 3, 10:158; LS (this copy being addressed to Col. G[eorge] E. Mitchell, Baltimore) in DNA, 11, 12923.

From Lt. Col. D[uncan] L[amont] Clinch, Petersburg, [Va.,] 9/28. Asks for $1,000 with which to pay recruiting bounties and premiums and for $500 to cover recruiting expenses. As [Edmund P.] Gaines has ordered, Clinch is sending all of his recruits to Amelia Island. He will be detained for some time in Norfolk on court-martial service and will make that place the headquarters for the recruiting service during that time. ALS in DNA, 11, 12029.

To C[allender] Irvine, Philadelphia, 9/28. Orders him to include, with the estimate Calhoun requested on 8/29, "a statement of the probable balance for or against each of the appropriations pertaining to your department, at the end of the present year, together with a return of the clothing on hand, stating the quantity required to be distributed the ensuing year, and the surplus, if any, on hand after such distribution." FC in DNA, 3, 10:157.

To William Lee, Second Auditor, and to [Richard Cutts,] Second Comptroller, 9/28. "The general order of the 4th of August 1818, 'to encourage the apprehension of deserters,' will be so construed as to extend the reward offered to the non-commissioned officers and Privates of the Army of the U[nited] States." FC in DNA, 3, 10:157; CC in DNA, 11, 12435.

From Joseph Lovell, 9/28. As Calhoun ordered on 9/25, Dr. Lovell submits an estimate of contingent funds needed for the office of the Surgeon General during 1819; he itemizes anticipated outlays totaling $2,574. FC in DNA, 242, 2:13; FC in DNA, 243, 1:8.

From G[erard] Steddiford, New York City, 9/28. He has received no returns except those that he mentioned in his letter of 9/15. Those have, upon examination, "such a palpable deficiency" of testimony against the alleged [N.Y. militia] delinquents "that I do not feel justifiable in assembling" a court-martial in so distant a county without having "sufficient proof to convict them." He acknowledges Calhoun's letter of 9/21, encloses the requested papers, and encloses also some papers concerning other delinquents. LS in DNA, 1, S-230; compare DNA, 182, pp. 3–7.

From D[ecius] Wadsworth, 9/28. Discusses the national armories at Springfield, [Mass.,] and at Harpers Ferry. The appropriations for these manufacturing establishments have been reduced recently and have proved to be insufficient; to insure the annual production of 25,000 stands of arms, a surplus in the appropriation for arming and equipping the militia has been transferred. Harpers Ferry has seemed more expensive recently than Springfield because arrearages antedating 1817 have been paid, in addition to the current costs at Harpers Ferry. It is advisable to take into consideration such possible claims when estimates for 1819 are computed. FC in DNA, 32, 2:107–108.

To Maj. A[bram] R. Woolley, Pittsburgh, 9/28. "Your letter of the 18th instant is received. The bills [of exchange] drawn by you on the Department, for the purpose of supplying rations upon the failure of the contractor [Charles Hegins ?], will be paid. In this case you will strictly comply with the regulations of the Department. I hope the failure will be of short duration." FC in DNA, 3, 10:157.

To Henry Bateman, Pittsburgh, 9/29. "Your letter in relation to Mr. [Charles] Hegins has been received. The Department will make no advances to him, but what are consistent with the usage in such cases; and which may be necessary to enable him to fulfil[l] his contract. Had the information contained in your communication been received before the last advance, it would have influenced its amount tho' it was made on a state of his contract which renders [an advance] safe to the Gov[ernmen]t." FC in DCA, 3, 10:160.

To [William H. Crawford]

War Dept., 29 Sep[tember] 1818

Col[one]l [Decius] Wadsworth has been ordered, in conformity with our conversation of this morning, to direct Henry Dering, Esq[ui]r[e], the Store Keeper at Sag Harbour, [N.Y.,] to [deliver the public property there to] any person authorized by you to take possession of it.

Mr. Dering has been allowed $100 annually for taking charge of the Building; and is reported to me by the Ordnance Department, as being well calculated for the charge, if you should think proper to continue him.

An indulgence has been extended to a Presbyterian congregation at that place, to make use of one of the rooms of the Arsenal, as a place of worship, which it was informed should be continued until further orders or while the building remained in possession of the [War] Department. If compatible with the use to which your Department may apply it, I would suggest the propriety of continuing this indulgence.

It is probable the building will not be wanted by the War Department during a state of peace.

FC in DNA, 171, 1:304.

To Andrew Jackson, Nashville, 9/29. Answers his letter of 9/11 (ALS in DNA, 1, J-205, with enclosed letters to Jackson from Daniel

Ross, 7/27, and John Ford, 8/13). Regrets Jackson's continued illness. Is pleased by Jackson's report of good prospects for speedy settlement of Quartermaster accounts for the Seminole campaign; hopes that more efficient War Department organization will soon make it possible to close all accounts promptly. Explains why the Chickasaws' annuity was sent in the form of goods and how the goods will be replaced with cash. Ross's letter seeking more land than was allotted to the Ross family by the Cherokee treaty [of 1817] will be submitted to President [James Monroe]. Ford's offer to provide a ferry or bridge and a hospital for sick travelers if the military road from Nashville to Madisonville, [La.,] passes his Pearl River property is apparently an unselfish, humane one; it should be accepted on condition that he receive his expenses for the ferry or bridge and any surplus "applied as he suggests." LS in DLC, Andrew Jackson Papers, 8140; FC in DNA, 3, 10:158–159.

From D[avid] B. Mitchell, Mount Nebo near Milledgeville, [Ga.,] 9/29. Acknowledges Calhoun's letter of 8/24; protests that Mitchell has never employed a certain imposter as his representative to take depositions from claimants to lands in Ala. Territory; feels injured that anyone should imply that he has been derelict in his duty. ALS in DNA, 1, M-356.

To D[avid] B. Mitchell

Department of War, 29th Septem[be]r 1818

Your letter of the 11th instant [ALS with Ens in DNA, 1, M-347] has been received; and I regret to learn that you have been so seriously indisposed.

The steps which you have taken to keep quiet the Chehaws, whom, it was apprehended, might be led, unadvisedly, to the commission of acts of violence, on account of the wanton and unauthorized destruction of their village, are entirely approved; and you have not mistaken the disposition of the Government in advising the Chiefs to rely upon its justice.

As it has ever been a favorite object with the government to wean the Indians from their attachment to their barbarous customs and pursuits, and to turn their attention to the cultivation of the arts of civilized life, and gradually prepare them for a full participation and enjoyment with its citizens of all their most valuable moral and political rights, every thing, therefore, that has a tendency to promote these ends, will have the most decided approbation of this Department; and it is with much pleasure I receive the information, that the Creek Indians have shewn a solicitude for the establishment of schools among them; and the same encouragement that has been given to the School in the Cherokee nation (the extent of which may be seen by the enclosed extract of a letter to the Rev[eren]d Mr. [Cyrus] Kingsbury) will cheerfully be afforded.

As this is a subject in which the Creeks have a deep interest, you will use your endeavors with the Chiefs, particularly Gen[era]l [William] McIntosh, to obtain their consent to the appropriation of a portion of their annuities, which are now very considerable, to this object. A small sum set apart, annually, in addition to the aid given by this government, would hold out inducements to competent teachers to undertake the direction of their schools.

The copy of the laws established by their Chiefs, enclosed by you, I have read with much satisfaction, and view them as another evidence of their progress towards civilization, and an effort to form for themselves something like a regular government. They will be laid before the President so soon as he returns.

Conformably to the stipulation of the treaty of the 22d January last, you are authorized to employ one blacksmith in addition to the one already employed.

You were informed on the 9th April 1817, that the sum of $12,000 was allotted to the support of your Agency and that your expenditures must be limitted [*sic*] accordingly; and as the appropriation for the present is the same as it was for the last year, every economy must be used in your disbursements; but your bills on this Dept. to that amount, should it be necessary, for the expenses of your Agency, will receive due attention. You are referred to that letter for the manner in which your accounts must be rendered for settlement.

FC in DNA, 72, D:218–219.

To Col. G[eorge] E. Mitchell, Baltimore, 9/29. "Enclosed you have a letter from C[allender] Irvine, Comm[issar]y Gen[era]l of Purchases, to the Dept. on the subject of shoes issued at Sackett's [*sic*] Harbour, covering a letter from Major [Darby] Noon to the Comm[issar]y Gen[era]l, one from H[eman] A. Fay, Mil[itar]y Storekeeper, to Major Noon, and the affidavit of Richard Hay, Inspector of Shoes, all relative to the same subject. By referring to these, the stock from which the shoes were issued, of which Capt. [Julius Frederick] Heileman has complained, may be designated. You will communicate the result to the Department and return the enclosed papers." FC in DNA, 3, 10:159.

Pension certificate of Noah Mott, 9/29. Calhoun certifies that Mott, formerly a Pvt. "in the Army of the Revolution," is to be paid through the N.Y. pension agency $8 per month from 4/10/1818. DS in PPL.

To Bvt. Brig. Gen. Moses Porter, Boston, 9/29. Answering his appeal of 9/19 (LS in DNA, 1, P-166) for brevet pay and for an aide-de-camp, states that Porter's command is too small to justify either. "I come to these conclusions in your case, I assure you, with much pain. If it were a matter of feeling or discretion, the decision would be far different; but as the mere interpreter of the acts of Congress, I know not how to come to a different decision." FC in DNA, 3, 10:160.

To Dr. Benjamin Waterhouse, Boston

Department of War, 29th Septem[be]r 1818

Your letter of the 23d Septem[be]r [printed herein under that date] in relation to a charge of $27 for printing 200 pamphlets, and not allowed by the Auditor, has been rec[eive]d.

I regret that I cannot admit of the charge. It is not justified by law or regulation, and a cheaper mode of communicating your opinion ought to have been adopted; or, if it were necessary to reduce them [that is, your opinions] to the form of a pamphlet, the assent of the Department ought to have been had, for the expense of its publication. The amount is small, but the principle is deemed important. The voucher is [being] returned [to you herewith].

FC in DNA, 3, 10:159.

To Edmund P. Gaines, Savannah (with a duplicate sent to him at Fort Hawkins), 9/30. Answers his letter of 9/16 (ALS with Ens in DNA, 1, G-122; CC in DNA, 11, 12560) and gives assurance that Calhoun is "happy to infer from it's [*sic*] contents, that we will probably, have not much trouble from the Seminole Indians, for the present," this prospect being the opposite of that concerning which Calhoun had written to Gaines on 9/23. Discusses how Gaines and his subordinates should deal with claims by U.S. citizens, by subjects of the Spanish in Fla., and by Seminoles to the ownership of certain Negro slaves who have been surrendered to U.S. forces, in order "to prevent speculation and the introduction of Negroes into the United States, contrary to the Act of Congress." LS in DNA, 11, 12215; FC in DNA, 3, 10:161; PC in Jameson, ed., *Correspondence*, pp. 144–145.

To C[allender] Irvine, Philad[elphi]a, 9/30. "You will report to the Department what will be the expense, to the U[nited] States, of the clothing of a Private, for the ensuing five years, assuming, in your estimate, the price of each article of clothing, for the present year, as the price of such article, for each of those years." FC in DNA, 3, 10:161.

From John Jamison, Natchitoches, 9/30. Spaniards are reported to be marching in considerable force against Nacogdoches and to intercept some Comanche traders; "but I cannot believe, they will cross the Sabine. Many of the citizens are now rendezvousing at this place, to aid the citizens" of Nacogdoches "and oppose (should they attempt it) their crossing the Sabine." ALS in DNA, 1, J-24.

From D[AVID] B. MITCHELL

Mount Nebo, 30th Septem[be]r 1818

When I was in the Alabama Territory in June last, I used my best endeavours to procure a Contract for building the Bridges on the road from Fort Bainbridge to line Creek [in Bullock County], and from the latter on to Fort Claiborne, but could get no offer. The people in that quarter are so much engaged in clearing land and making Plantations that they will not for any reasonable compensation detach their hands from that object. Since my return however, I have had a letter from Colonel [William] Barnett who resides on line Creek, in which he proposes to build the Bridges on Persimmon Creek, Caleebee and Keebihatchee. I have written to the Colonel giving him a plan or description of the Bridges I wish built, and requesting him to state on his part what he will build them for per foot, taking the length of the bridge for the measurement. When I hear from the Colonel again, I will be better prepared to give a full answer to your letter of the 11th last month. On the road from Fort Hawkins to Fort Bainbridge, the bridges will all be completed by the 1st of November, as the Undertaker has assured me. They are in number as follows; From Fort Hawkins to the Agency, Three—From the Agency to Fort Mitchell Six—And from Fort Mitchell to Fort Bainbridge Two. Those already completed are said by competent Judges to be excellent, and the rest are to be built of similar materials and on the same plan.

To make a general Contract for repairing the road has always seemed to me to be attended with so many difficulties, that I have rather sought to make a specific Contract for laborers, to be paid by the day. In the one case the extent of the repairs must be previously ascertained and Agreed upon which is almost impossible; whilst in the other, it is only necessary to point out the work and see that the laborers perform their duty. Such is the high price of labor, and of provision at this time, that the lowest offer I have yet had, is two dollars per day for each hand employed, and three for a white man to attend them. I have declined these offers for two reasons, first; because I think the wages demanded too high; and second, because I was desirous in the first instance of ascertaining what amount of the $10,000 would remain after building the bridges before I made any positive engagement for the repair of the road. Without the bridges travellers in the winter season cannot pass, but, if the bridges are good they can proceed, altho' in some places through mud & mire. These are the reasons which have procrastinated the expenditure of the $10,000. The sum is small compared to the object, and I have been desirous of making the most of it, but you may rest assured, that I am as anxious to apply it to the purposes intended as you can possibly wish me to be. The difficulty of making Contracts is much greater than you can imagine.

ALS in DNA, 1, M-136; PC in Carter, ed., *Territorial Papers,* 18:424–425.

A[lden] Partridge, Norwich, Vt., to James Monroe, 9/30. Wishes to know why the charges he preferred against Bvt. Brig. Gen. Joseph G. Swift, Bvt. Maj. Sylvanus Thayer, and Capt. John M[ichael] O'Connor have not been tried. Claims that the nation and he have been done a great injustice by this neglect. ALS in DNA, 2, P-1818.

From S[amuel] Smith, [Representative from Md.,] Baltimore, 9/30. Recommends S[amuel] L. Isett for an Army commission. ALS in DNA, 11, 12360. (Isett was appointed a 2nd Lt. on 10/20: Heitman, *Historical Register,* 1:565.)

From J[oseph] G. Swift, 9/30. Lists 17 sites at which "Permanent Fortifications are to be constructed" in 1819: five in La.; Dauphin Island and Mobile Point [in Ala. Territory]; Old Point Comfort, the Rip Raps Shoal, and the York River in Va.; Sandy Hook, Frogs' Point West, Hendricks' Reef, and Rouses Point in N.Y.; the Pea Patch in the Delaware River; Newport, R.I.; and Boston Harbor. "Unless the Corps of Engineers be enlarged, not more than Twelve of the above mentioned Works can be conducted under the immediate and constant superintendance [*sic*] of an Engineer Officer." LS in DNA, 2, S-1818; FC in DNA, 21, 1:33–34.

Samuel Turner, Jr., Office of the Secretary of the U.S. Senate, to [Christopher] Vandeventer, 9/30. Turner answers Vandeventer's request of 9/15 by sending three copies of the Senate's Journal for the session of 1817–1818. The Senate's resolutions relevant to the War Department can be found therein; but Turner insists that a copy of each such resolution was sent to the War Department promptly after each was adopted. ALS in DNA, 1, T-110.

From Henry Baldwin, [Representative from Pa.,] Pittsburgh, 9/——. The contracting firm of Pentland, Hegins & Heele, now dissolved, will not be able to fulfill its contracts to supply rations to the troops; [Charles] Hegins has arranged his financial affairs in such a way as to compel his sureties to pay his obligations. Baldwin encloses a deposition by David Pride dated 9/5 concerning Hegins and a letter from E[dward ?] Pentland and Will[iam] Heele to Calhoun dated 9/4. ALS with Ens in DNA, 1, B-306.

From Five Militia Officers of Missouri

Howard County, Mis[souri] Territory, September 1818

His Excellency Gov. [William] Clarke [*sic*], having thought it would conduce to a more effectual organization of the militia of this Territory to form a new brigade to include the militia of this county & part of St. Charles County, it will become the duty of the President [James Monroe], should he deem it expedient to sanction the views of our Territorial executive, to appoint a Brigadier General for its command.

Presuming that it will be satisfactory to the President to be acquainted with the wishes and feelings of those more immediately affected by the object of his choice, the undersigned field officers of the different corps of which the contemplated brigade are [*sic*] to be composed, take the liberty of recommending, through your friendly agency to the President of the United States, Col. Duff Green, of Charaton [*sic*], as a person well qualified to fill that rank in our militia. Col. Green has resided some time amongst us—is a gentleman of respectable acquirements, and fair character—has heretofore commanded the tenth regiment of the Territorial militia, with credit to himself, and to the advantage and satisfaction of his subordinates. During the recent war, a second glorious contest for our independence, Col. Green proved himself a patriot both in military & civil life, and we have reason to believe that his appointment would be at once acceptable and advantageous to the brigade.

As none of us we feer [*sic*] have the honour of being personally known to either yourself or the President, we have taken the liberty of affixing to our respective names, what else had been ostentatious, the rank with which we are honoured in the militia of the Territory. We pray you to render acceptable to the President our assurances of high respect both personal & political and we beg leave to add the very high sense we have been taught to entertain for your own person & character.

LS in DNA, 11, 12255. NOTE: This letter was signed by Lt. Col. John Snoddy, Maj. Benjamin Nichols, Lt. Col. Nicholas L. Burckhartt, Col. James Pillard, and Maj. John Harrison, who identified themselves as being "of the 10th Regiment, Militia of the Territory of Mo."

OCTOBER 1818

ON THE FIRST OF THIS MONTH CALHOUN WROTE ONCE MORE to a friend in Philadelphia in an effort to recover a runaway slave named Hector. On the 17th, in a letter to Jacob Brown, the commanding General of the Army's Northern Division, Calhoun committed the Army to undertake expeditions for the establishment of posts far up the Mississippi and Missouri Rivers, partly for the purpose of wresting from the British the lucrative fur trade with Indians in the distant Northwest. On the 21st a pioneer named John Stevens proposed a national system of railroads. Secretary of the Navy Benjamin W. Crowninshield's long absence from Washington continued, and Calhoun began to serve as Acting Secretary of the Navy; he permitted Benjamin Homans, the Chief Clerk of the Navy Department, to manage its most routine business but probably gave more active guidance to this other agency of defense than its correspondence shows.

From LEWIS CASS

St. Marys, [O.,] Oct. 1, 1818

The accompanying letter [presumably that of 9/14 from Cass to Calhoun] was written with a view to transmit it to you officially, but subsequent reflection, although it has not changed my opinion with relation to the subject, has convinced me that my observation has been limited and that my views may be partial & incorrect. I however forward it without alteration, as the enquiry will receive your full consideration and as any crude ideas of mine can have no effect upon the system which you are about to digest.

I beg however that it may be considered as a private letter, written to communicate the opinions of an individual upon an important and doubtful question, a satisfactory solution of which must depend upon a full knowledge of the subject and upon a careful and mature consideration of it.

It is difficult to estimate the direct effect of the publick trading establishments. Their abolition appears to me to be justified by every view which I can take of the subject.

But there may be considerations connected with it of which I am ignorant or whose importance I do not appreciate. I am well aware of the facility with which we seize those points of discussion which accord with our preconceived opinions & neglect those which are adverse to them. It may also be found, should the experiment be made, that consequences which are not now foreseen may follow from this abolition equally injurious to the United States and to the Indians. Important changes in the policy of a nation, particularly in its intercourse with a rude, unlettered people, are to be deprecated.

Practical results do not always accord with previous speculations, and it may sometimes be more expedient to continue a doubtful system rather than hazard effects which can neither be foreseen nor controlled.

For these reasons, which have occurred to me since the accompanying letter was written, I have doubted the correctness of my own views and have thought that my ideas may be found rather [more] speculative than practical.

One branch of the enquiry, however, admits of no doubt. This is the entire exclusion of whiskey from the Indian Country. Until this is effected, we may in vain mature and digest systems for the melioration of the condition of the Indians. Instead of advancing, they will retrograde upon the scale of civilization and will continue a stain upon the national escutcheon. All plans of improvement which are not founded on this basis will be overthrown by the first contact with the Indian character. If our remedies are not administered with a single eye to this object, we shall meet the usual fate of empyricks. Every consideration public or private will be sacrificed by an Indian to the gratification of this propensity, & to its gratification there appears to be a total prostration of every moral & prudential barrier.

My views may possibly aid you in your reflections and enquiries, and I have therefore taken the liberty of transmitting them as an unofficial document.

FC in DNA, 76 (M-1:4, pp. 42–43).

To Maj. James Dorman, Camp Parker, Ala. Territory, 10/1. Answering his report of 9/12 (ALS in DNA, 1, D-78) that he had ordered food to be bought locally for his troops because a contractor, [Benjamin G. Orr,] had failed to provide the needed rations, Calhoun informs Dorman that the direct purchases will be charged to his account until he proves the contractor's failure in accordance with regulations, a copy of which Calhoun sends to Dorman. FC in DNA, 3, 10:161.

To [Charles J. Ingersoll, Philadelphia]

War Dept., 1st Oct. 1818

Mr. [John ?] Forsyth who is now in Philadelphia, if I do not mistake can identify my boy Hector, should it be necessary. Will you be so obliging as to inform me, whether there has been any certain information of him. Accept the assurance of my sinc[er]e respect and esteem.

Typescript in DLC, Carnegie Institution of Washington Transcript Collection.

Midshipman Stephen B. Lassalle, U.S.N., to the "Hon. J.C. Calhoun, Act[in]g Secretary of the Navy"

U.S. Ship Independence, Boston Harbour, Oct. 1st 1818

Having received permission from Commodore William Bainbridge, to apply for a Furlough, I take the liberty, Sir, of making application to you. Sir, should it meet with your approbation to grant the above for Four months, it will be thankfully received.

ALS in DNA, 134 (M-148:21).

Pension certificate of Moses Knight, 10/1. Calhoun certifies that Knight, who served as a Pvt. in the Revolution, will receive through the N.H. agency $8 per month from 4/14/1818 under the law of 3/18/1818. DS in NhHi, Hibbard Collection.

From Thomas L. McKenney, 10/1. He will comply with Calhoun's letter of 9/28 [actually dated 9/25] to him. LS in DNA, 1, M-311; FC (dated 9/30) in DNA, 73, E:157.

From JOHN T. MASON, JR.

Lexington, Ky., Oct[obe]r 1, 1818

The deep interest which the people of this country take in the enterprises of their patriotic fellow citizen, Col. James Johnson, induces me, as one of the community to express to you the solicitude which is felt that Col. Johnson obtain the contracts, for which he makes proposals, to furnish rations at different military posts.

Besides the just, prompt and faithful discharge of the duties of a contractor, for which Col. Johnson has been distinguished, other considerations, embracing his valuable public services, his uniform devotion to the country's good, and the universal confidence reposed in him, strongly urge that he be prefer[r]ed for such a trust. His zeal in the public service has been fully manifested in the late war, when on his individual credit, by a pledge of his estate, he raised supplies for the Southern Army, at a period of difficulty and danger, when the credit and resources of the government were inadequate for the object. As a citizen he has been distinguished in the councils of the State and has given evidence in the field of valour and patriotism. And in the battle of the Thames [he] was second in command, and second only in distinction to his gallant brother Col. Richard M. Johnson. Having settled in the country at an early period, grown up with it and participated in its early conflicts, his personal acquaintance is extensive, the high estimation of his worth universal, and his influence every where commanding. His popularity consequently is considerable, and rests upon a permanent basis, the affection of his friends and the confidence of the people. And as a leader in the republican ranks he stands among the first in the State.

In this representation there is nothing exaggerated, and from it may be learnt, why an interest so general, and unusual as applied to others, is always felt in the success of Col. Johnson's enterprises; and that a wish so universally prevails at this time that he obtain the contracts for which he makes proposals. That another of inferior merit and pretensions should be prefer[r]ed to him, would be truly mortifying to his friends and those of the government. Aware however that the contracts are offered for the lowest bid, it is readily presumed that the disposal of them is principally regulated by the terms proposed. But I am induced to believe that the high claims of Col. Johnson to the confidence of the government would, ceteris paribus, give an assurance of preference for him. His experience as a contractor enables ["him" *interlined*] to offer the fair price at which supplies can be furnished, and his intention of making his proposals at a rate so low as to accomplish little more than a security against loss, has been fully expressed. And his inducements to this are, to give effect to his arrangements long since made, to provide occupation for his agents already established, and to secure employment for his steam boats built for this object. I am thus particular to shew the moderate views of Col. Johnson, and to make it appear the fact, that his object is not so much profit upon the contract, as to bring into action his means already so well prepared; and which enables him to fulfil[l] his engagements with a fidelity, certainty and despatch which no other can at present attain. I shall be pardoned the suggestion whether it be not the interest of the government to secure a faithful and punctual compliance with a contract at a price somewhat higher, than to have partial and uncertain supplies at a cheaper rate; and whether it would not tend to injure the public service and defeat important objects, to take the lowest bid, merely because it is the lowest, with a view to no other consideration, when motives of unfounded speculation or sheer ignorance may have prompted it, and the individual who makes it, alike regardless of his own credit & character and that of the government, for the possession of present means, may be indifferent about ultimate loss and certain failure. In support of the correctness of this view, I refer to the circumstance already mentioned in relation to the war in the South, and adduce the facts connected with the north western campaigns under Gen[era]l [William Henry] Harrison, the enormous expence, and difficulties attendant on which may be mainly traced to faithless and speculating contractors.

To warrant the above communication, I must rely upon considerations of public duty, and doubt not my remarks will be received in the same spirit of candour with which they are written. The slight personal acquaintance (if it may be so called) of one or two introductions in the winter of 1816, while at Washington with my brother Gen[era]l A[rmistead] T. Mason, and relation Gen[era]l John Mason, not authorising me to address you as one of whom you have any knowledge.

ALS in DNA, 43, file of James Johnson, 17.

From Jacob Brown

Brownville, [N.Y.,] 2d October 1818

I beg to call your attention to Mr. Charles Harrisson [*actually* Harrison] of the city of New York, late of the 13th Infantry. I sincerely wish that he may be appointed to the first vacant second Lieutenancy in any regiment of Infantry or battalion of Artillery, where he can receive the commissaryship of such corps, whenever such appointments are recognised according to the provision of the act of the last Congress. It would be [a] favour to me, &, as I think, to the service could Mr. Harrisson receive the grade I solicit for it. I should be the better satisfied could it be in my Division.

LS and CC in DNA, 11, 13383; FC in DLC, Jacob Brown Papers, Letterbooks, 2:121.

From Robert Butler

Treaty Ground, 2d October 1818

The Commissioners [to negotiate a treaty with the Chickasaws, Andrew Jackson and Isaac Shelby,] arrived at this place on the evening of the 29th Ult[im]o where they expected to have either met with or heard from the Agent, Col. [Henry] Sherburne: in this they were disappointed, and in consequence Gen[era]l [Andrew] Jackson proceeded to George Colbert[']s where he expected certainly to hear from him. Again disappointed, the General pushed an express with a letter to him requiring his presence. Several of the Chiefs attended on the 1st Inst[ant] and, the Agent [being] still absent, Capt. [Richard J.] Easter was dispatched to enquire the reason of his delay and if not on his way to bring him. The Capt. met [him] about twenty miles from this place, and returned late last evening with information that he was not prepared to pay the annuities, although [Sherburne has been for] a considerable time in possession of a Check, on the United States B[ranch] Bank at New Orleans which he has not negociated [*sic*].

Gen[era]l Jackson, having been advised that the Nation would not receive the annuity of this year in goods, instructed the Agent to draw bills in favour of the Cashier of the B[ranch] Bank at Nashville for the amount, and on sending him the Bills he would see them negotiated and the money brought out; to which letter no answer has been received. This course was adopted on the information communicated by you that he was authorised to draw.

When the Commissioners arrived they were at a loss to account for the distance of the Chiefs, and the general gloom that pervaded the Indians: this has been developed—they say it is useless to treat or make any more engagements with the U[nited] States—we treated two years ago, and was [*sic*] promised money, we have not received it, nor do we know when we will; when we expected money we are offered goods—we cannot make other engagements untill those already made are fulfilled. Whether this state of things has grew [*sic*] out of the supineness of the Agent or want of knowledge of the duty assigned him and the disposition of Indians the Commissioners cannot say.

The Agent was instructed to suspend the payment of the annuities untill the present time and was duly notified that a contract had been made for the furnishing of supplies to the Indians, during the period of receiving their annuities, and the Commissioners were more than astonished to find him entirely unprepared to pay them, or even to attend the treaty at the time appointed—it remains for him to account for those unexpected circumstances over which he has had control.

The Commissioners have come to a determination to prevent the object of their mission from being jeopardized, to push an express to Nashville, raise the money on the check at New Orleans and the balance on the drafts of the Agent which they are aware can be negociated at Nashville. On his arrival which is momently [*sic*] expected, this plan will be put in execution unless the Agent should refuse to send the Check and draw bills to be negociated at Nashville; in which event, rather than abandon the object of their mission after all the expence that has occurred, the Commissioners will draw on you for the amount, and negociate the draft at Nashville which they hope will meet your entire approbation.

The delay thus occasioned will augment the expence, but it is believed useless to say any thing to the Chiefs *in council* untill we can shew them the sums which are due the Nation are ready to be paid.

In the mean time their minds can be prepared casually for the grand talk; and I have only to say that the Commissioners are fully persuaded that an energetic stand will alone enable them to succeed as the Chiefs wish to evade the subject if possible.

10 [o']Clock A.M. The Agent has just arrived and has acceeded [*sic*] to the drawing of bills.

LS in DNA, 1, B-361.

To [William H. Crawford], 10/2. "It appears that a warrant was issued, on the 12th ultimo, in favour of Brown, Cox, and Allison, Contractors, &c., for $25,767.50, on account of the appropriation for the Indian Department, upon the certificate of the 5th Auditor [Stephen Pleasonton], which sum was properly chargeable to the Appropriation for defraying the expenses of the Treaty with the Cherokees, per act of the 20th April 1818; and it becomes necessary that this amount should be transferred from the latter to the credit of the former appropriation. I have, therefore, to request that you will direct the transfer to be made accordingly on the Books of the Treasury Department." FC in DNA, 171, 1:305.

From Thomas Fitch, Washington, 10/2. His estimate of the number of hostile Indians in the Floridas, reported to Calhoun orally yesterday, is so much larger than [Andrew] Jackson's estimate that Fitch feels compelled to explain "the grounds on which my calculations were made." Not one observer whom he considers reliable believes the number of warriors to be as low as 2,000. Fitch implies that Jackson prematurely announced the success of his campaign of this year against the Seminoles, who have since been joined in a confederacy by two other tribes. He encloses a copy of his letter to [Edmund P.] Gaines dated 8/10. "In about a month I shall be compelled to return to [St.] Augustine, and you will readily perceive that a publication of these communications might cost me my life." ALS with En in DNA, 1, F-51.

To Edmund P. Gaines, [Savannah,] 10/2. Discusses the units of Gaines's troops available for service if the Seminoles should renew their attacks; estimates that his forces "will not fall much short of 1,000 strong" in or near East Fla. If friendly Creeks should be called to Gaines's assistance, they "will render you I hope sufficiently strong should hostilities commence, on that side [of the Fla. peninsula] without calling in the militia." Sends a report that the hostile Seminoles recently numbered only 509—a number "which must by surrender and other causes be considerably reduced since." "I confess I have great distrust as to the report of the great force and universal determination to renew the war on the part of the Indians. There are many, and in some instances, I fear, disgraceful motives for these representations." If Gaines should give assurance that he really needs reinforcements, Calhoun will send to him at least 700 enlisted men from the Northern Division. Calhoun believes, however, that by "foresight and prudence you will be able to prevent an accumulation of expense should hostility be renewed; and at the same time effectually guard the lives of our citizens." Again he urges Gaines not to strike the first blow. "I am solicitous if hostility is to be commenced that it should begin on their part. The country and the world ought to be satisfied that we are not actuated by motives of aggrandizement in waging or carrying on this War. That our object is not Florida, but protection." LS in DNA, 11, 12215; FC in DNA, 3, 10:162–163; CC in DNA, 77 (M-271:2, frames 0980–0988); PC in Jameson, ed., *Correspondence,* pp. 145–147.

From Joseph Lovell, 10/2. The commanding Army officer at Norfolk, [Lt. Col. William MacRea,] has decided that the general order of 8/21 prohibits Dr. Robert Archer from continuing to engage in some private practice there. Lovell thinks that Archer is not "at all affected by that order." He asks, therefore, that Archer shall be authorized to continue his private employment. ALS in DNA, 11, 12460, with an AEI by Calhoun directing [Daniel Parker] to instruct MacRea as Lovell wished.

From Andrew Norris

Walnut Grove, [S.C.,] 2nd October 1818

I here inclose a letter to James E[dward] Calhoun, and Three Hundred Dollars to you at his request, would have sent it on immediately on receipt of his letter; but did not like to risque it by mail. Should James Previous to Sailing need a further Supply please Procure it for him, by Mrs. Calhoun or perhaps some earlier opportunity if any such offers. I will inclose for him to you Five Hundred Dollars. I have nothing new. People generally in this Section of our Country have been healthy. The season uncommonly dry—fine weather for Picking Cotton. I heard a few days ago that your Overseer had 20,000 lb[s.] picked. How Crops are on the River I know not, they are in Calhoun's Settlem[en]t good considering the drought. Electioneering at its height. I understand there are upwards of 20 Candidates for the State Legislature, Jos[eph] Richardson from your neighbourhood is one John Blair & M. Brewer al[l] offer & a number of others very little [Quali]fied. I hope you and fa[mily] enjoy health. Please make my Compliments to Floride & Andrew & believe me Yours truly, Andrew Norris.

N.B. The Bills of $100 each are in James's letter, without opening it, you can get them.

ALS in ScU-SC, John C. Calhoun Collection.

To Abraham L. Sands, 10/2. Appoints him to be a Capt. in the Corps of Artillery as of 9/17, subject to confirmation by the U.S. Senate. DS in CtY.

To William Wirt, 10/2. "The principle involved in the enclosed case appearing to me important, I must request the favor of your opinion, whether it would be advisable to acquiesce in the decision which has already taken place or to bring it before the Supreme Court of the United States for final decision. The amount is small, but perhaps on that account there is a greater danger, if the principle is erroneous, of establishing it." LS in DNA, 111; FC in DNA, 3, 10:162.

From Joseph Lovell, 10/3. Submits his quarterly report as Surgeon General, although returns from the Post Surgeons are few and insufficient; blames the soldiers' routine illnesses, such as colds and intestinal disorders, largely upon neglect by their officers. ALS in DNA, 2, L-1818.

To Wilson Lumpkin, Madison, Ga.

Department of War, 3d Oct[obe]r 1818

By information recently received from Gen[era]l [Edmund P.] Gaines it is presumed, that the hostility of the Indians will render it impracticable to run out the line between the U.S. and Florida, this fall. Perhaps it is scarcely necessary to suggest to you, that under the commission to determine the boundaries of the lands ceded by the treaty of the 22d of January last (a copy of which and a plat of the cession was [*sic*] enclosed in my letter of the 4th of Aug[us]t) the only line required to be run out, is the western one of the lower cession, that is, the line described in the first article of the treaty, beginning at a point on the line of the treaty of Ft. Jackson, and "running the nearest and most direct course, by the bend of a Creek, called by the Indians Alcasalikie, to the Oakmulgee [*sic*] river."

FC in DNA, 72, D:219.

To Maj. James Dalaby, [U.S. Arsenal, Watervliet, N.Y.,] 10/5. Answers his report of 9/23 (ALS in DNA, 1, D-77) that in peacetime he causes his men to attend church services regularly and his request for permission to use public funds to pay the annual rent on two or three pews in the nearby church for their occupancy. "I should be happy to aid your views in facilitating the attendance of the troops under your command on divine service; but I cannot discover any authority, either in law or regulation, to incur the expense." FC in DNA, 3, 10:164.

To Peter Hagner, 10/5. "The accompanying extract of a letter and the proceedings of a general court martial may furnish you with evidence of the failure of B[enjamin] G. Orr, Army contractor, during the late campaign on the frontiers of Georgia." FC in DNA, 3, 10:163.

To Daniel Parker

Department of War, 5th October, 1818

You will make a report to this Department of the strength and organization of the present peace establishment, including the General Staff as now established by law.

You will also report, separately, the posts, inland and maritime, at present occupied. Accompanying this last report, you will exhibit the number and positions of the posts occupied by the U[nited] States troops in 1802.

You will render another report, separately, stating the strength and organization of a Brigade, at the close of the Revolutionary war, in 1783, and the organization of the peace establishment under the law of the 16th of March, 1802.

LS in DNA, 11, 12923; FC in DNA, 3, 10:163. NOTE: For Parker's reply, see 10/21.

To Jasper Parrish, Canandaigua, N.Y., 10/5. Answering his letters of 9/23 and 9/24 (2 LS's in DNA, 1, P-177) announcing an Iroquois decision not to emigrate and urging that six Iroquois should be allowed to visit Washington as a means of gaining belief in the good faith of the U.S. in proposing Iroquois emigration to the West, Calhoun states that the expense of bringing a deputation to Washington is great and cannot be met now because all Indian funds will be needed for treaties that are pending. Closes by saying, "It is astonishing that [a schoolmaster named] Hyde should have the assurance to endeavor to persuade these ignorant people that the [government's] communications to which you refer are forgeries." LS in ICN; FC in DNA, 72, D:220.

To THOMAS SERGEANT, Secretary [of State of Pa.]

Department of War, 5th October 1818

Herewith you will receive a receipt of the principal Clerk in the Pension Bureau of this Department [James L. Edwards] for the transcript of the rolls of the Pennsylvania line of troops &c.

Being possessed of these transcripts, an immediate examination of the Pension applications from Pennsylvania will be made, which has been hitherto delayed by the want of this record.

FC in DNA, 3, 10:163–164.

From Henry Sherburne, Treaty Ground, Chickasaw Nation, 10/5. Reports that a boat bringing packages marked "U.S. Chickasaw Annuity & Presents" has been sunk. Two men have been sent to attempt to save that shipment from total ruin. If any of the goods are salvaged, Sherburne wants to know what to do with them. LS with En in DNA, 1, S-42.

Col. H[enry] Atkinson, Plattsburg, [N.Y.,] to [Jacob] Brown, Brownville, [N.Y.,] 10/6. Atkinson answers Brown's letter of 9/16 by enclosing an ALS from Col. J[osiah] Snelling to Atkinson dated 10/1. Snelling reported how a few U.S. soldiers crossed the Canadian border and captured three American Army deserters on 7/28; the soldiers had been provoked by violence done against them on 7/27 by the deserters. Snelling believes that the British need not complain, because the deserters are natives of the U.S. who had resided in Canada less than one year. Atkinson believes that Snelling's report will be satisfactory. ALS with En in DNA, 101 (M-179:42).

To Robert Brent, 10/6. "You will make a report to me, exhibiting the pay and emoluments of officers and [enlisted] men, at the close of the Revolutionary war and, also, at the close of the late war with England." FC in DNA, 3, 10:164. (In reply on 10/24, Chief Clerk Nathaniel Frye, Jr., of the Paymaster General's office submitted statements of monthly pay and emoluments in 1783 and in 1815; he explained that the figures for 1783 might not be "perfectly correct." LS with Ens in DNA, 201, 15A-F3; PC with Ens in House Document No. 36, 15th Cong., 2nd Sess.; PC with Ens in *American State Papers: Military Affairs,* 1:792–801.)

From Jonathan Jennings, Lewis Cass, and B[enjamin] Parke, St. Marys, 10/6. "We have the honour to forward you treaties concluded at this [place] with the Potawatomies, Delawares, Weas & Miamies for the purchase of lands in the State of Indiana. Owing to peculiar circumstances under which we are placed, a detailed communication is deferred, and which you will receive from Gov[erno]r Jennings together with a statement of the disbursements incident to the negotiation." FC in DNA, 76 (M-1:4, p. 40); PC in *American State Papers: Indian Affairs,* 2:179.

From [Thomas S. Jesup], 10/6. He submits a detailed estimate of the funds needed in 1819 for Quartermaster purposes in general, totaling $487,901. FC in DNA, 42, 1:74–76.

From Thomas S. Jesup, 10/6. Estimates that $64,000 will be needed by the Quartermaster Department [in 1819], of which $14,000 will be for arrearages due for labor and materials for the barracks at Sackets Harbor, [N.Y.,] and the rest for "the purpose of erecting works of a permanent nature." LS in DNA, 203, 15A-D15.2; FC in DNA, 42, 1:76.

To T[homas] S. Jesup, 10/6. "You will make a report to me, exhibiting the allowances of every description to officers and men, at the close of the Revolution[ary] war; and, also, at the close of the late war with England." FC in DNA, 3, 10:164. (See Jesup's reply herein under date of 10/19.)

From [former 2nd Lt.] DANIEL D. SMITH

Washington City, Oct. 6th 1818

I am on my return to Illinois. I have it in contemplation to make a survey of the distance & elevation of the ground between the waters of Illinois River & Chicago. Would this be of importance to the public interest? Should you deem it necessary all I would require would be the assistance of some men from Fort Clark. When the Rivers are bridg'd by Ice, is the time I contemplate to effect the object. I put up at Mr. O'Neils [*sic*], [where I] will be happy to receive your answer.

ALS in DNA, 11, 12785.

To Robert Brent, 10/7. Orders him to make the following changes in the estimate for pay and subsistence of the Army for 1819: officers entitled to keep more than two horses are entitled to draw forage in kind for only two horses; Brent will estimate forage allowances accordingly. In the staff, Brent is to estimate only the difference in compensation between lineal and staff ranks. No estimate will be made for arrearages or for brevet rank. FC in DNA, 3, 10:164–165.

From A[lden] Partridge, Norwich, [Vt.,] 10/7. This is a two-page "Note" addressed to Calhoun and appended to a copy of his six-page letter of 9/28/1817 to an unknown person. The letter protests his treatment by Sylvanus Thayer, Joseph G. Swift, and others during 7–9/1817; the "Note" protests alleged illegalities in the court-martial proceedings under which Partridge was cashiered, [11/27/1817]. ADS in DNA, 2, P-1818.

To [William H. Crawford], 10/8. "I enclose for your perusal a letter from Gen[era]l [Eleazer W.] Ripley. The disbursements will be very considerable, the next year, at Baton Rouge; and it would seem proper that the Deposites [*sic*] should be made, at that place, or what would be preferable, that the Branch [Bank of the United States] at New Orleans should be instructed by the Mother Bank to remit to Baton Rouge, free of expenses, the sums which might be required for disbursement there." FC in DNA, 171, 1:305.

From Edmund P. Gaines

Fort Hawkins, Ga., October 8th 1818

I have the honor to acknowledge the receipt of your communication of the 23rd of last month.

I beg you to excuse my omission, in respect to the name of my Savannah correspondent Mr. T[homas] Fitch. I by no means designed to withhold from you his name, which I had intended to attach to the copy of his letter sent to you, desiring that you might disclose the name only to the President [James Monroe], for the reasons assigned by the writer. Apprehending I had made the omission, I mentioned his name in a subsequent letter.

Having seen Mr. Franks, the Agent of the contractor, lately from St. Marys, whence the reported murders mentioned in my letter of the 20th of last month, were not known, late in the month; and the commanding officer at Fernandina being silent upon the subject, I cannot but doubt the truth of the report, and have declined visiting the Island until the latter end of this month.

Refer[r]ing to my letters of the 16th, 20th and 23rd of last month, with their enclosures, I have only to add that, the instruction, and suggestions, contained in your communications shall receive my most particular attention.

I enclose herewith a communication which I have received from the Pay Master of the 7th Regiment, Mr. [Thomas R.] Broom. I think it but just to say that I have neither seen nor heard of any conduct on the part of Broom, since he joined me, in June last, affording any ground for the accusations contained in the letter of Mr. Frye, refer[r]ed to. The Paymaster[']s mode of living appears to me very plain and moderate, and within the limits of his pay.

I have never until now heard of his having played at cards, or other game, even for amusement—nor have I till now heard of it surmised that he had any pecuniary concerns with a suttler [*sic*].

He has not been absent, to my knowledge without leave, since he first joined me, at Fort Scott, in June 1818. His previous movement was indeed attended with improper delay, but from his explanation I considered his conduct excusable, as his delay appeared to have occur[r]ed from a misconception of duty. I have at his request ordered Major [James M.] Glassell to count his money and enclose herewith the Major's report No. 2.

A confidential report which has been forwarded to the Adj[utan]t & Inspector General's Office, states a neglect of duty in making the Payment at Fort Gadsden, by Mr. Brown, in paying money due to some absent Soldiers, into the hands of their officers. The amount is not considerable, say 80 to 100 Dollars—I have ordered the Paymaster to pay the amount to the men, individually, and in future to guard against a similar irregularity.

ALS with 4 Ens in DNA, 1, G-129; LS in DNA, 11, 12215. NOTE: The enclosures include certain accounts of Thomas R. Broom, a letter of 10/7 from him to Gaines, and a letter of 10/7 from J[ames] M. Glassell at Fort Hawkins to Gaines.

A[quila] Giles, New York, to [James Monroe], 10/8. Giles encloses an ALS to himself from S[ylvanus] Thayer dated 9/30 stating that Giles's son, George Giles, cannot be given the entrance examination until a reappointment of George has been made. Giles asks Monroe for such a new appointment, reminding Monroe that illness prevented the normal course of developments after a prior appointment was given about two years ago. ALS with En in DNA, 1, G-71, with an AEI by Monroe referring this matter to the War Department and stating that, since Aquila Giles was a Revolutionary "officer of merit" and is "in indigent circumstances, I wish the accom[m]odation to be afforded him [if] the circumstances will admit."

From Joseph Lovell, 10/8. Submits an estimate of funds needed for the Medical Department during 1819; the Apothecary General [Francis Le Baron] will need $37,382.80. FC in DNA, 242, 2:13; FC with En in DNA, 243, 1:8–11.

To Alexander Macomb, Detroit, 10/8. Answering his letter of 9/19 (LS with Ens in DNA, 1, M-312; PC with Ens in Carter, ed., *Territorial Papers,* 10:782–783), approves his having taken steps to reserve the site of Fort Gratiot in the approaching sales of public lands; Calhoun took action for the same purpose last August. FC in DNA, 3, 10:165; PC in Carter, ed., *Territorial Papers,* 10:784.

To D[avid] B. Mitchell, Creek Agent

Department of War, 8th Oct[obe]r 1818

Your letter of the 25th of Septem[be]r [LS with En in DNA, 1, M-316] enclosing a letter [of 8/31] from Colo[nel Mathew] Arbuckle to you, in relation to the Indians who have surrendered, was received this morning.

You will furnish the Indians referred to, or those which may hereafter be in a similar situation, such assistance as their situation may render necessary.

The Creeks, it is stated, have agreed to receive them into their nation; and you will see that no violence or injustice be done them in person or property. The provisions which you may find it necessary to afford them, will, it is expected, be supplied on the best terms.

I hope Colo[nel] Arbuckle will retain the [29] Negroes [owned by whites and Indians] at Fort Gadsden, as it might open a door to speculation, if they were permitted to be brought across the line. Should, however, any of them be brought with the Indians, you will conform to the instructions to Gen[era]l [Edmund P.] Gaines, of which I enclose a copy.

The case on which you ask my opinion, of a judgment against a white man resident in the Indian nation, I do not think within the intercourse law; but if the judgment was fairly obtained, on personal summons served on the defendent [*sic*], he ought to be made to pay the judgment. The amount, however, cannot, without the assent of the nation, be deducted out of their annuity.

LS in ScHi; FC in DNA, 72, D:220–221.

From [Daniel Parker], 10/8. Answers Calhoun's inquiry of 9/25; estimates that on 12/31 the Army will have 6,000 enlisted men, of whom 2,600 will be entitled to discharges during 1819; that $92,400 will be required in 1819 for enlistment payments to replacements, $1,100 for stationery and printing, and $2,400 for two Clerks. FC in DNA, 12, 5:96.

To Eleazer W. Ripley, Bay of St. Louis, 10/8. Answering his letter of 9/9 (ALS in DNA, 1, R-30), reports resultant actions in respect to both of its subjects. A lawsuit has been ordered for recovery from the sureties of Paymaster [William] Gibb[e]s of the money lost to the U.S. by Gibb[e]s's defalcation; and Gibb[e]s should report to Washington or his accounts should be sent. In response to Ripley's report that the New Orleans Branch of the Bank of the United States is most unaccommodating in handling Army funds even at a profit, Calhoun has asked Secretary of the Treasury [William H. Crawford] to order that Branch to deliver Army funds to Baton Rouge free of charge or to authorize the War Department to make deposits of funds in a state bank at Baton Rouge. FC in DNA, 3, 10:165.

To G[erard] Steddiford, New York [City], 10/8. Answering his report of 10/6 (LS in DNA, 1, S-229) that he has received new returns of N.Y. militia delinquents in Green, Saratoga, and Schenectady Counties and that he will reconvene his general court-martial as promptly as possible, urges him to complete the business before Congress reconvenes. FC in DNA, 3, 10:165–166.

From Ho[well] Tatum, Nashville, 10/8. Submits, with a long explanation, his accounts as Quartermaster agent in the District of West Tenn. from 5/1/1816 through 9/30/1818. LS in DNA, 1, T-138.

From William Turner, St. Marys, [O.,] 10/8. As secretary to the commissioners who negotiated the treaty of 9/29/1817 with the Wyandots, Shawnees, Chippewas, Potawatomies, and Ottawas, he reports that nothing worthy of being communicated to Calhoun developed in a recent council held by the commissioners with those tribes. What happened in recent negotiations with the Delawares, Potawatomies, Weas, and Miamis will be reported by another secretary. ALS in DNA, 1, T-19.

From William Wirt, 10/8. Relays a recommendation from Judge Alex[ander] Stuart, chief judge of Mo. Territory, dated 9/13 that urges the appointment of Maj. William Christie as the Quartermaster officer there. ALS in DNA, 11, 12019½; FC in DLC, William Wirt Papers, Letterbook for 1816–1832.

From Col. H[enry] Atkinson, Plattsburg, [N.Y.,] 10/9. Recommends a new Army commission for [Abram C.] Fowler, who formerly served "with distinguished merit" but resigned because of "pecuniary embarrassment." ALS in DNA, 11, 12206.

David Folsom to James Monroe and John C. Calhoun

Pigeon Roost, Choctaw Nation, Oct. 9th 1818

Honorable and dearly beloved Sirs, having learned by a letter from the Rev[eren]d [Elias] Cornelius the kind treatment you gave my Brother McKee while on his way to the North to receive an education in the Forreign [*sic*] Missionary School [at Cornwall, Conn.,] and the assistance you are pleased to give him [for] that purpose I hereby present you my warmest thankes [*sic*] for such tokens of Friendship not only to my Brother but to my Red Brethern [*sic*] in jeneral [*sic*].

With anxious desire I look forward to the day when School will be established in my Nation, and our Childern [*sic*] be taught to reade [*sic*] and write the talk of our white Brethern.

I am desirous that the Friendship which has long continued between the United States and my Nation may be cherished.

I enterpreted [*sic*] Mr. Cornelius['s] letter of your good intention, to the head man and warriors in the Nation and they were more than pleased, and beli[e]ve your friendship is pure. At the request of Mr. Cornelius my Brother Israel is going to enter the school with McKee, and is now on his way with Mr. Kanouse, who will probibly [*sic*] hand you this letter. I would recommend him to your notice as a Boy apt to lern [*sic*] and who I hope will make a good man.

A desire to do good to my Nation is my highest pride, and I beli[e]ve the surest way to gain my wish is to promote learning among them[;] it gives me much pleasure to be aided by my Father the President and [by the] Secretary [of War]. I do not write to flatter[;] this is not the true spirit of Red men but to assure you of my good wish and that of my Nation. I subscribe myself Your cenecere [*sic*] Friend, David Folsom.

ALS in DNA, 1, F-20.

Maj. C[harles] Gratiot, Washington, to J[oseph] G. Swift, Washington, 10/9. Explains at length that U.S. Army Engineers are underpaid; they receive less than they can earn in civilian employment in the U.S. and less than their counterparts in the armies of Europe receive; their remuneration offers no security to their families and none to the Engineer himself for his old age. ALS in DNA, 2, G-1818.

From Thomas L. McKenney, Georgetown, [D.C.,] 10/9. "I remember something of a conversation had with you in the War Department some time ago respecting the provision of means at Belle Fontaine, [Mo. Territory,] which resulted in your stating that you would direct the officer to draw on me for the amount. But of this I have only an indistinct recollection." McKenney has now received such a draft, sends it by the bearer of this letter to Calhoun for confirmation of Calhoun's desire that it should be paid, and suggests that payment can be made in either of two ways. LS in DNA, 1, M-317; FC in DNA, 73, E:145–146.

From Samuel Annin, Georgetown, [D.C.,] 10/10. Complains that a lawsuit against him instituted by the U.S. is for a sum much greater than is just; contends that the U.S. owes him pay for extra services rendered by him at Harpers Ferry during 1800–1815. ALS in DNA, 1, A-95.

From Col. John R. Fenwick, Boston, 10/10. In accordance with Calhoun's letters of 9/26 and 10/3, Fenwick has discontinued the services of a Sgt. as a Paymaster's clerk. Fenwick is looking for another noncommissioned officer as a replacement but dreads the consequences; to divert such an officer may affect discipline adversely, and the man chosen should himself be required to live under discipline. LS in DNA, 1, F-63.

From Joseph D. Lauck, Philadelphia, 10/10. He has received his appointment as a Cadet but is ill, as an enclosed medical certificate attests, and requests permission to report when he shall have recovered; he seeks this permission from Calhoun in accordance with enclosed advice written on 9/29 by order of [Sylvanus Thayer]. ALS with Ens in DNA, 1, L-125.

From Return J. Meigs

Cherokee Agency, 10th October 1818

Your letter of the 15th September, Circular, came to hand on the 2nd Instant. I shall endeavor to conform to your directions in the issues of provisions to Indians. No idle assemblage of Indians have [*sic*] ever been countenanced here. I have frequently sent them away displeased, because they think the United States can do everything and that the Agent ought not to refuse them rations. When they come more than 100 miles, which is often the case, to receive ploughs, hoes, axes, spin[n]ing wheels &c., they have the ancient custom of bringing their wives & children. And, as I have understood, in such cases they have always had provisions to carry them home, which they call path provisions. I have always given such provisions. Since the negotiations for exchange of land [by Cherokee emigrants to the Arkansas under the treaty of 1817], considerable numbers come here on that account, and it has been thought improper to deny such rations.

I hope a general, if not a complete exchange, will take place soon: but the present ruling party will part with their darling, extreme liberty with great reluctance. They dread the change & still wish to live here in the state [of] nature, for it cannot be called government and is incompatible with their safety or [that] of the surrounding population.

LS in DNA, 1, M-368; quite different draft in DNA, 75 (M-208:7).

From Brig. Gen. M[oses] Porter, Headquarters, 2nd Military Department, Boston, 10/10. Acknowledges Calhoun's letter of 9/29. Porter will no longer urge that he be allowed "any personal or General Staff"; but he does now ask for permission to keep an officer on duty in Porter's office, with the usual extra compensation granted to officers doing extra duty away from their posts. LS in DNA, 11, 12675.

From El[eazer] W. Ripley, Shieldsboro, 10/10. Introduces and recommends Dr. G.B. McKnight for an appointment as a Post Surgeon in the 8th Military Department. "We have at this moment 3 Post Surgeons on duty and one under arrest. We at least require 10 in this Dep[artmen]t. At this moment I am employing three Citizens." ALS in DNA, 11, 12532.

Pension certificate of Daniel Foster, 10/12. Calhoun certifies that Foster, formerly a Pvt. "in the Army of the Revolution," is to be paid through the N.Y. pension agency $8 per month from 4/23/1818. DS in PPL.

From Thomas B[olling] Robertson, [former Representative from La.,] Baton Rouge, 10/12. Encloses an ALS to himself dated 9/30 from John Sibley at Natchitoches reporting the encroachment of Spanish forces in the Southwest. Robertson thinks it probable that those forces cannot intend to attack Natchitoches but might seek to repossess Nacogdoches "& other posts in our neighbourhood from which the Spanish authorities were expelled a few years ago." He suggests that it might be wise to strengthen Army forces in "that distant & exposed frontier. My health is better than it was last winter. Make my respects to Mr. [William] Lowndes and accept the assurance of my respect & friendship." ALS with En in DNA, 1, R-29.

From John Scott, [Delegate from Mo. Territory,] Washington, 10/12. Asks whether the soldiers and civilians who settled at Fort Jefferson, at the iron banks, under George Rogers Clark are entitled to those lands. Copy in DNA, 1, S-248. In reply on 10/17, Nat[haniel] Cutting reported that the inquiry had been referred to him and that there was no known authorization for the granting of such a "*Territorial gratuity.*" Copy in DNA, 1, S-248.

From J[oseph] G. Swift, 10/12. As Calhoun ordered on 8/29, 9/5, and 9/25 (FC's in DNA, 3, 10:129, 137, and 154), Swift submits an estimate of funds that should be appropriated for the Army Engineers' use in 1819, totaling $887,570, as follows: for fortifications, $838,000; for the Military Academy, $35,640; for the Chief Engineer's office, $3,990; for arrearages, $3,440; and for a survey of the Western waters [by Stephen H. Long], including the purchase at $5,000 of a steamboat with a draft of 18 inches, $6,500. LS in DNA, 201, 15A-F3; FC in DNA, 21, 1:37–41; PC with En in House Document No. 56, 15th Cong., 2nd Sess.; PC with En in *American State Papers: Military Affairs,* 1:811–813.

From Decius Wadsworth, 10/12. He proposes in detail a plan for prolonging the useful life of small arms and accoutrements and hence of achieving much economy. Some of his suggestions are that Army units should each be assigned an armorer to repair arms locally; that the Ordnance Department should supply the necessary parts for such repairs; that any soldier guilty of any misconduct that necessitates such repairs should be charged with the cost thereof; and that, if responsibility cannot be assigned to an individual, the Regiment should assume such cost. Such reforms might prolong the life of small arms to as much as 14 years. ALS in DNA, 1, W-216; FC in DNA, 32, 2:110–114.

To Joseph Anderson, [First] Comptroller, 10/13. "I will thank you to cause me to be furnished with a statement of the warrants that have been drawn on the appropriation for the Indian Department in the present year." FC in DNA, 72, D:221. Anderson answered on 10/13 that $250,052.42 (including $15,052.42 unexpended in 1817) were available on 1/1/1818 for expenditure during 1818; that outlays through 10/12 totaled $210,620.21; and that the balance remaining available in 1818 was $39,432.21. LS with En in DNA, 2, A-1818.

From John Gardiner, Chief Clerk, General Land Office, 10/13. As Calhoun requested in his letter of 8/20 [to Josiah Meigs], "orders were sent . . . to rescue from sale certain lands" near the St. Clair River; but the orders reached Detroit after the sales had been completed. Upon request of [Alexander] Macomb, however, "the fraction upon which Fort Gratiot is erected was reserved, & contains 472 acres. The remaining four fractions were sold." ALS in DNA, 1, G-127; FC in DNA, 82, 8:289.

From John Johnston, St. Marys, [O.,] 10/13. He has issued a draft for $13,650 to William Oliver, Cashier of the Miami Exporting Company, for itemized purposes. In a postscript Johnston mentions that he dispatched his bond promptly after having been notified of his appointment as Indian Agent at Fort Wayne and Piqua but that he has not received his commission. He encloses an LS of 10/6 to himself from Jonathan Jennings, Lewis Cass, and B[enjamin] Parke authorizing Johnston to draw upon the War Department for a maximum of $10,000 to "pay the various expenses incurred at the treaty this day [that is, on 10/6] concluded [by them as commissioners] with the Indians at this place." ALS with En in DNA, 1, J-250.

To Joseph McMinn

Department of War, 13th Oct. 1818

Your Excellency's letters of the 20th and 28th ultimo have been received.

It affords me pleasure that [Charles R.] Hicks, Brown, and the Going Snake have so far ceased their opposition as to hold a a [*sic*] council. I trust it may be attended with as favorable a result as you can desire.

I am not sufficiently acquainted with the merits of Major Walker's claim to decide upon it. You will report to me the facts in relation to it and your opinion upon them. In the meantime, as the appropriation to carry the treaty into effect will probably be deficient, you will be sparing in your advances to claimants.

As the arrangement to pay the emigrants in money or store goods, if they prefer them to rifles &c., appears advantageous to the U. States, you will adopt it.

Roger's claim does not appear to be sufficiently vouched to be admitted under the intercourse law. I return it to you for your further examination and request you, at your leisure, to report the circumstances of the case, together [with] your opinion in relation to it.

If you should think it advisable, either from equity or policy, you may make an advance to his agent, but I must repeat to you the apprehension that the appropriation to carry the treaty into effect will be too scanty to make any considerable advances out of it upon claims of this nature.

I cannot decide upon Glass' case, until I shall be favored with your Excellency's report respecting it, which was required in my letter of the 16th of March last.

LS in DNA, 75 (M-208:14); FC in DNA, 72, D:221–222. NOTE: McMinn's letter of 9/20 is an LS in DNA, 1, M-238; a draft of it is in DNA, 75 (M-208:14), A draft of his letter of 9/28 is in DNA, 75 (M-208:14); what Calhoun wrote on 10/13 about the claims made by John Rogers and The Glass was given in reply to McMinn's discussion of those claims on 9/28. An Abs of Calhoun's letter of 3/16 to McMinn is in *The Papers of John C. Calhoun,* 2:194.

From Isaac Pavatt, James Craig, and Nathan Nesbitt, [no place stated,] 10/13. As commissioners for the inspection of the 130-mile-long road from Reynoldsburg, Tenn., through the Chickasaw country to an intersection with the old Natchez road at the Chickasaw old fields—the road being constructed by Dawsey P. Hudson—they report that they "deem the road will be opened, Causewayed, and Bridged agreeable to the Bond as far as the situation of the Ground will admit." LS in DNA, 1, P-29.

From S[amuel] Smith, [Representative from Md.,] Baltimore, 10/13. Repeats his recommendation [of 7/23 that James Henry Benson of Easton, Md.,] shall be appointed as a Cadet, on the ground that the father, Gen. [Peregrine] Benson, served in the Revolution, the "Whiskey Insurrection," and throughout the War of 1812. Encloses a letter from Gen. Benson to Smith dated 10/13. ALS with En in DNA, 15, 1818, 174, with an EU that an answer was dated 10/18 and that the boy would be appointed when 14.

From DECIUS WADSWORTH

Ordnance Office, 13th October 1818

Mr. Asa Waters of Millbury, Massachusetts, was a Contractor for fabricating Arms for the Government before the late War and has an Establishment very advantageously situated for carrying on that Business. Since the War a new Contract has been entered into with him for 5,000 Stands of Arms at 14 Dollars. About one-half have been delivered, and the Remainder in a State of rapid Execution, and he now finds himself in a Situation to make it important for him to have a Decision whether he is to continue the business in future. He is desirous of contracting to supply ten Thousand Stands more at the rate of Two Thousand Stands a Year commencing on the 1st April next. As the Decision of this Question involves an important Point of national Policy, I shall proceed to lay before you my own Views of the subject.

The Arms made by Contract have not in general been of so good a Quality as those made at the National Armouries. By employing some of the Assistant Armourers from the national Armouries to make the Proofs and Inspections we hope and expect in a great measure to remove this objection. It may be presumed however and is a Thing it is impossible entirely to prevent, that Arms made by Contract though the price be nominally about the same, do in Fact cost the Government higher (owing to the Extra Expenses attending their Proof & Inspection, the cases for packing them and the Transportation to the Arsenals) than those made at Springfield and Harpers Ferry.

Nothwithstanding these Objections, the rapid Increase of our Population & the prodigious Consumption of Fire Arms in our Service in Time of War particularly by the Militia render it highly necessary to employ all the Means in our Power to augment the Supplies. Judging by past experience we ought to expect our Resources to fail, in Time of War soonest in this particular. The case is not the Same in this Country as it is in France, or England. In those Countries the manufacturing of Fire Arms for foreign Nations is a great Branch of Business. Their Government can on particular Emergencies call into the Public Service as many Workmen as they may Want. In this Country the Government is almost the Sole Customer, and if Manufactories of Fire Arms do not receive sufficient support & Encouragement from the Government, the Business must be given up. Two or three Years are necessary to put an Armory in Operation, and in Case the national Armouries should not be found adequate, as they cannot be in Time of War, the Government can by no Exertions or Means obtain a supply in Season, if the private Establishments now in Activity should be suffered to decay for Want of Support from the Government.

Two powerful Reasons exist to induce the Government to keep up the private Armouries by due Encouragement. The first is they prove excellent Nurseries to breed up Workmen for the national Armouries. Foreign Mechanics particularly the English and Irish are generally much addicted to the use of spirituous Liquors, and are consequently turbulent and disorderly. The Workmen bred in this Country particularly those who have first served in private Armouries, are generally temperate, industrious and provident. This gives Springfield one advantage over Harpers Ferry, a greater proportion of Foreigners being employed at the latter Place.

The second Reason is in Relation to the Invention of useful Machines for abridging manual Labour, the high Price of which in this Country operates as a Stimulus to the Invention of Such Machines. The better Policy is to let these Machines be invented by Individuals and be corrected, improved and tested by Experience, before we attempt to introduce them into the national Armouries upon a large Scale. It is better to pay a handsome Premium for an Invention the Merit of which is established than to be concerned in plausible Schemes and Contrivances of this Nature which not unfrequently end in Abortion accompanied by great Expences.

Whatever may be the Decision on the general question relative to the Encouragement the private Armouries are entitled to receive from the Government there is a particular Reason, urging us to enter into a new Contract with Mr. Waters. Some years ago he put in Operation a Method of welding Barrels by the Aid of a Tilt-hammer moved by Water. For this Invention he has taken a Patent securing to him an exclusive Privilege for using the Invention. As the same Method has since been adopted at Springfield and one or more Water wheels and a good deal of Machinery erected for the Purpose, and the Process is in full Operation there and answers admirably well, & as it is contemplated to introduce the same Method at Harpers Ferry on a large scale, we should prefer to pay a large sum, say 20 or 30,000 Dollars, rather than abandon the Method, in the using of which we must have the Consent of Mr. Waters. He consents on Condition of his obtaining a Contract on the Terms above Stated, to permit his Invention to be used *gratis* not only at the National Armouries, but at all Places where Arms are made for the Use of the United States, with a verbal Understanding that if at the Conclusion of the Contract he proposes to execute, the Government should continue to purchase Arms on Contract, he will be entitled to a Contract on as favourable Terms as others, allowing the use of his Invention during the Continuance of such other Contract. In other Words the United States will be permitted to use his Invention gratis and all persons employed in fabricating Arms for the Government, so long as he himself shall be a Contractor for furnishing Arms to the United States.

The great advantages attending Mr. Waters' Invention of welding Barrels by the Tilt-hammer moved by Water, consists in the Dispatch; there is consequently a Saving of Iron and Coals; and the Barrels so welded are found to stand the Proof better. He calculates the whole saving at both the national Armouries would Amount to Several Thousand Dollars a Year. Without entering into the Calculations he makes it is sufficient to know that this Method is acknowledged to be of great Utility and Advantage.

The Samples of Arms and of Work exhibited at this Office by Mr. Waters will bear a fair Competition with those executed at the National Armouries, and by the report of the Inspector we may be satisfied the Arms made at his Works are in general of unexceptional quality.

LS in DNA, 1, W-258; FC in DNA, 32, 2:114–118.

From William H. Crawford, 10/14. Reports [to Calhoun as Acting Secretary of the Navy] the number of seamen accommodated in the Marine hospitals, where, and at what expense during 1811–1817. PC with Ens in House Document No. 90, 15th Congress, 2nd Session; PC with Ens in *American State Papers: Naval Affairs*, 1:615.

From Thomas P. McMahon, Philadelphia, 10/14. He wishes to be permitted to supply Army posts with seeds and tools for the proposed gardens. He names Nicholas Biddle and others as his references. He recommends the book by his father, Bernard McMahon, *The American Gardener's Calendar* . . . (11 eds., Philadelphia, 1806 and later). ALS in DNA, 1, M-354.

From [Lt.] George Pearce, U.S. Naval Station, Erie, Pa., 10/14. Reports the death of the post commander, Capt. Daniel S. Dexter; "after a long and painful illness, he expired at ½ past 1 P.M., on the 10th ins[tan]t. He was buried, with military honors, on the 11th. And I have issued an order, that the officers of this station, wear crape upon the left arm, for thirty days from that date." ALS in DNA, 134 (M-148:21).

From J[oseph] G. Swift, Engineer Department, 10/14. Lists 60 fortifications of the U.S., where they are located, and the number of cannon at each. Lists also the new works that have been begun or planned. DS in DNA, 2, B-1818.

From Decius Wadsworth, 10/14. Explains that the deficit in the Ordnance Department will not be considerable at the close of the present year. FC in DNA, 32, 2:118–119.

From Edmund P. Gaines

Fort Hawkins, Ga., October 15, 1818

The hope of receiving by an expected arrival from Fort Gadsden, some information touching our red neighbors in that quarter, had induced me to defer writing in reply to yours of the 23rd ultimo, until the hour of closing the mail. My reply was therefore hasty and incomplete. I am still without the communications due from Fort Gadsden.

Upon the subject of the number of Indians and blacks in East Florida, I have been greatly perplexed with the vague and contradictory accounts given me from time to time. After weighing all that the country, and my opportunity upon the expedition, as well as before and after it, afforded me, I am totally unable, as I think every other officer must be, to offer an opinion, other than such as has for its basis, much vague conjecture, as to the actual number of Indians or blacks. From the number of habitations at and in the vicinity of Mickasuckee I believe little or no doubt exists, that the report previously obtained of the number at those towns, was near the truth—about 450 warriors; yet I doubt whether that number was seen by the whole army during the campaign. Indian Warriors seldom fail to choose their *time* and *place* of shewing themselves.

The army traversed but a small part of East Florida, as will be seen by Captain [Hugh] Young's topographical sketch. Of this tract of country our best guides knew but little. Of the remaining part they knew much less. One of the most intelligent and apparently correct Indian countrymen I have ever known, and the only white man with us who had been among the Indians towards St. Augustine, stated, that he had not been through that part of the

Indian Country since he was a small boy, and then travelled along the common path-way, without knowing what number of Indians were settled at a distance from the route. Mr. [William] Hambly, the person to whom I allude, has estimated the warriors at a lower number than any other person whose information seemed to be creditable. But if I am not much mistaken Mr. Hambly has been somewhat biased by self-interest. He lost a considerable amount of property destroyed by the Indians upon the Appalachicola in the month of December last, for which he will endeavor to obtain remuneration. I wish he may succeed; but not upon the ground I have reason to believe he will resort to, in supporting his claim. He had endeavored to prevail upon Lt. Colonel [Mathew] Arbuckle to move down below the Florida line, with the force then at Fort Scott, and take a position at his residence. If he cannot establish his claim by reducing the supposed strength of the enemy, and showing the practicability, and probable success, of such a movement, he may at least excite more the ordinary sympathy, particularly among those who do not take into view the *authority* and the *means* within Colonel Arbuckle's controul at the time. He was under orders to act with vigilance, but with great caution, until reinforced. Most of the accounts then received, as the strength of the Indians upon the Appalachicola river, under Hillis Hajo, and other Chiefs, estimated the number, at near double that of Lt. Col. Arbuckle's command. The agent, [Alexander] Arbuthnot, himself stated in a letter to a person in England which has been published, and a copy of which I think was among his papers, that Hillis Hajo was, a short time before the date of the letter, at the head of twelve hundred warriors, principally Red Sticks, upon the Appalachicola.

But whatever may be the number now remaining in East Florida, I do not think it at all likely that the whole, or any considerable part will be able to imbody [*sic*] and act together during a month, against one thousand regular troops. Should they (the Indians) be apprised of the approach of a small force, they may be thus tempted to uncover themselves from the bush, and be brought to action.

I am therefore decidedly in favor of making the experiment—as I am convinced they cannot be brought to action in any other way, than by being approached with an efficient force, possessing more the strength of discipline than of mere numbers without discipline. I shall indeed be much gratified to find that the information recently received and communicated to you, of the continued hostility of the Indians may prove to be incorrect. It is however a fact not to be lost sight of, that the Mickasukeans, and all of what are called Seminolians, with some blacks and Red Sticks, are still within the country between Suwanney [*sic*], St. Augustine and the Bay of Tampa, without having evinced any positive or certain disposition to be peaceable.

I am therefore of opinion that they should be visited by a force sufficient to beat them if they are disposed to fight, or to give them peace should they desire it.

Six hundred men in addition to my present command will enable me to visit St. John's, Chuckochatta and the Bay of Tampa.

The 4th & 7th Infantry are ordered to be held in readiness for a movement along the coast from Fort Gadsden to the Bay of Tampa. 600 men added to the recruits ordered to Amelia Island, will enable me to penetrate the country to the Bay of Tampa, and I doubt not, put an end to this most perplexing of all earthly things—Indian War.

ALS in DNA, 1, G-137; LS in DNA, 11, 12215.

To Edmund P. Gaines, Ft. Hawkins, Ga., 10/15. "I have received your letter of the 29th ultimo [LS in DNA, 11, 12215]. I have examined the treaties with the Creek Indians, and do not discover any impediment to leasing such portion of the military reserve about Fort Hawkins as may be deemed useless for military purposes, and not contravening any of the advantages promised to the Indians in the terms of reservation. You may, therefore, if you think it advisable, lease to Mr. Bowen, or to any other person, such ground as may be requested upon the most advantageous terms, and for such periods, and in such manner as you may deem proper." FC in DNA, 3, 10:167.

From Callender Irvine, Philadelphia, 10/15. Acknowledges Calhoun's letters of 8/29, 9/28, 9/30, and 10/13 requesting budget estimates for 1819. On 7/11 and 7/16 all Military Storekeepers and Issuing Commissaries were ordered to submit to Irvine inventories of all clothing, camp equipage, etc., in stock as of 11/1. But Calhoun seems to want estimates so soon that Irvine will not be able to profit by such reports. Is he to estimate clothing needs on the basis of the authorized manpower of the Army and then add 20% for contingencies and for the recruiting service? Or is he to be governed by the second article of the War Department's regulations? If the latter, Calhoun should first obey the fourth article and inform Irvine how much and what kinds of clothing he will be ordered to buy for next year. LS in DNA, 1, I-232; FC in DNA, 45, 387:158.

From JACOB BROWN, "Private"

Brownville, [N.Y.,] 16th October 1818

Your private letter of the 25th of July, relative to the proceedings of the court martial in the case of Major [Nathaniel Nye] Hall, was received by me in New York [City] as I was returning to this place. No one can regret more than I do the aspect this subject has assumed; but I do not perceive that my regrets can be alleviated by any opinion I can give on the question between the court & the President [James Monroe]. Being disposed to assist worth and talent wherever found; and discovering in Major [Samuel A.] Storrow [the Judge Advocate General in the Northern Division] these qualities in an eminent degree, I have set my heart upon being useful to him; this sentiment for him I shall always feel, and feeling it, lament the *character* of the argument addressed to the court at Plattsburgh [*sic*], [N.Y.]. I am not ignorant that this address was heard with pleasure by the members of the court, not that they were influenced by it, but because it breathed their feelings and sentiments, and expressed the opinion they had previously formed. It flattered their self love.

I do not find that I can offer any ideas on the subject of the commissariat but what must be familiar to you: and the proper change to be made in the ration Dr. [Joseph] Lovell can point out perhaps better than a chief of Division.

The Staff of the Army has caused me much thought and to you in confidence I am bound to say that in my judgment a considerable saving may be made in this department, and the duties better performed than they ever will be under the present system. If it was possible for any administration of our country to select from the whole field the best men that offer for the staff, I should prefer the existing law to any other, it being so important to give to the staff all the talent and character possible. But as I have ceased to hope that selections will be made, by the President and Senate, with a single eye to come at the best men for the duties we wish them to perform, I would provide by Law, in a very simple way, a different mode of assigning gentlemen to staff duties.

Every officer now provided for in the staff are [*sic*] nescessary [*sic*], therefore retain them in your system and give to the Secretary of War, Generals of Divisions and Generals of Brigade, the power of selecting from *the Line* of the Army the staff the Law gives them respectively, without reference to President and Senate, and the proper talents will be found when they are most required. The Secretary of War, under such a system, will always have it in his power to select an efficient Adjutant and Inspector General, one that knows the Army and enjoys its confidence. Generals of Divisions and Brigades can then call to their assistance the first officers of the Army and, as the talent at Head Quarters is always presumed to be the property of the chief, he must be a mad man who would not select the best he could find.

FC in DLC, Jacob Brown Papers, Letterbooks, 2:121–122. NOTE: A PC of Calhoun's letter of 7/25 to Brown can be found in *The Papers of John C. Calhoun,* 2:423–424.

From [Lewis Cass ?], Detroit, 10/16, "Private." Under the recent regulation prohibiting Army physicians from engaging in private practice without permission from the Secretary of War, requests such permission for Dr. [Benjamin] Delavan, the Post Surgeon there, whose services are needed by civilians and can be given without harming his official duties. The fact that he will not be paid by civilians "will prevent any improper extension of this branch of his business." LU in DLC, Henry R. Schoolcraft Papers, 1:190–191.

From Ninian Edwards and Aug[uste] Chouteau, St. Louis, 10/16. In accordance with their instructions dated 11/1/1817, they, as commissioners to obtain a cession from several Indian tribes of a large tract of land in Ill. Territory, have negotiated and now enclose a treaty of cession with the tribes having the best claim—[including the Peorias, Kaskaskias, and Cahokias]. LS in DNA, 1, E-5; PC in Carter, ed., *Territorial Papers,* 17:607–608.

From CALLENDER IRVINE

Phila[delphia,] Oct[obe]r 16, 1818

On the receipt of a Copy of the Adjutant & Inspector General[']s [Daniel Parker's] letter of the 26 of June last, addressed to Brigadier Gen[era]l T[homas] A. Smith, Comm[andin]g the 9th [Military] Department, which communicated the decision of the President [James Monroe] in the case of Colo[nel] E[li] B. Clemson, Asst. Commissary of this Department, and on the authority of your letter to me of the 31st of July, Colo[nel] Clemson was ordered by me to resume his duties as Asst. Comm[issar]y at St. Louis, & to concentrate the Stores of this Department at the latter place. Accompanying this you will receive Copies of Colo[nel] Clemson[']s letter to me of the 20th of September, of his letter to Colo[nel] T[albot] Chambers of the Rifle Reg[imen]t, dated the 18th of September, of two letters of the latter to the former bearing date the 18th & 19th of September 1818, by which you will perceive, Sir, that Colo[nel] Clemson has been resisted in the execution of orders which were authorized by the highest authority, & that his functions have been suspended contrary to the clearly expressed wishes & decision of the President. The division Order, to which Colo[nel] Chambers has alluded in his letter to Colo[nel] Clemson, was, I am of opinion, issued whilst Colo[nel] Clemson was absent, from St. Louis, and no doubt without any knowledge of the President[']s decision & order in the case. Your early instructions directing me how I am to act in this unpleasant business, will be very acceptable. There has been no clashing or unpleasant occur[r]ence between the officers of the line of the Army & those of this Department at any other Point, & I sincerely regret that which has occur[r]ed at St. Louis, & the trouble which it has already occasioned to the President & to the Department of War.

FC in DNA, 45, 387:159–160; CC in DLC, Andrew Jackson Papers, 8184–8185. NOTE: An Abs of Calhoun's letter of 7/31 to Irvine appears in *The Papers of John C. Calhoun*, 2:445–446.

From Joseph Lovell, 10/16. Asks that $1,234 be sent to Dr. James Cutbush, [Assistant] Apothecary General, in Philadelphia, to cover purchases this month of medicines, furniture, etc. FC in DNA, 242, 2:16.

To DAVID B. MITCHELL, Creek Agency, Ga.

War Dept., 16th Oct., 1818

I have received your letter of the 1st instant [LS in DNA, 1, M-350, itemizing four annuity obligations totaling $35,500 annually under treaties with the Creeks and acknowledging his receipt of $31,000].

After a full examination into the appropriations of the current year, (the estimates for which were formed before I came into the office,) I cannot find any provision made for the payment of the $3,000 promised to the Creeks, by the treaty of Fort Wilkinson, in 1802. This sum will be remitted with the annuity of next year.

A warrant for one thousand five hundred dollars has been issued in your favour to pay the annuity, agreeably to the treaty of 1790.

The thirty-one thousand dollars already transmitted is intended to satisfy the annuities under the treaties of 1805 and 1818 and will be applied accordingly.

LS in GU; FC in DNA, 72, D:222.

From [Daniel Parker], 10/16. Submits a memorandum about the trial by court-martial of [2nd] Lt. [Collin] McLeod of the 5th Infantry, whose offences originated in his "questioning the propriety or expediency of Major [Zachary] Taylor's order stop[p]ing the whiskey part of the soldiers['] ration." Despite a few objectionable elements, the court's proceedings appear to have been fair and McLeod's course blameworthy, "notwithstanding his motives may have been honest." FC in DNA, 12, 5:106.

From [Daniel Parker], 10/16. Col. [Jacob] Hindman has submitted a report by a subordinate officer at Fort McHenry "that the fire happened about midnight & that" the subordinate "had only a small boat & that the fire raged so violently that any aid he could have afforded would have been too late; that he did not know to whom the property destroyed belonged & that as it was no way connected with the military service he did not attempt an interference which he was convinced could not have saved the property." FC in DNA, 12, 5:105.

From D[aniel] Parker, 10/16. Recommends that a court of inquiry should be held to determine whether or not Lt. Robert

Beall was justified in "pulling down the jail" that was under construction on Army land at Mobile. LS in DNA, 1, P-212; FC in DNA, 12, 5:105–106.

From Richard Rush

London, October 16, 1818

I meet with very many persons in this country who suppose themselves to be the inventors of useful improvements in matters connected with war, and who are often urgent with me, probably finding themselves neglected here, to make known their pretensions to our government. To this class of applicants, not in the military only, but in other lines, it is my general practice to turn a deaf ear. For, first, I have no authority to listen to them; next, the expectations with which in most instances the individuals approach me, are very unreasonable; but, more than all, I entertain an entire conviction, that in all the departments of active ingenuity and skill, where the American is called upon to exert himself in common with the European, and where real utility is the object, the former is superior. Yet, I believe his superiority to be in part derived from the candid examination which he is ever disposed to give to the plans of other times and countries, profiting of what is good in them and rejecting their errors, whilst in a great majority of instances, the European inclines to a tenacious adherence to the same mode of doing things which has been practiced by those who have gone before him. This is one of the causes which must go to account for the inferiority of Great Britain to the United States upon the ocean, and will at some future day, as I firmly believe, lead to the certain destruction of her fleets. Our upland cotton commands a higher price here, and all over the world, not because it is intrinsically better than the cotton of India, the Mediterrenean [*sic*] or the Brazils; but because it is better cleaned, and prepared. There is little danger of these countries ever adopting our machinery, though they should a thousand times be told of it. Had the gin been invented in Sumatra, or Rio Janiero [*sic*], how soon would it have been used in Carolina and Georgia?

I have said thus much as a kind of apology, for sending to you the enclosed paper, which has been transmitted to me in a letter from a person of the name of Mountford, living near Worcester, in this kingdom. It relates, chiefly, to some supposed improvements in making rockets. The officers of our ordnance, and especially the ingenious gentleman who is at the head of it, may possibly discover something in it worth attention, though I neither know, nor have heard, any thing of its merits. In promising the author, who is alike unknown to me, that I would become the mere medium of forwarding his paper to your hands, I knew that it would at all events afford the opportunity, which I with pleasure embrace, of saying with what entire respect I have the honor to be . . . .

ALS with En in DNA, 35, In-4&5-9.

From Henry Sherburne, Treaty Grounds, Chickasaw Nation, 10/16. Acknowledges Calhoun's letter of 9/16 with its instructions about issuing rations to Indians. Reports that the treaty negotiations are proceeding well, because everything due to the Chickasaws has been received. Encloses a disavowal by the captain and crew of the flatboat *Good Hope* of any liability for damage done to U.S. goods when that boat sank. ALS with En in DNA, 1, S-44.

To W[ILLIAM] A. TRIMBLE, Lexington, Ky.

War Dept., 16 Oct., 1818

I have laid your letter of the 17th of September [which Calhoun had already answered on 9/25] offering your service, to explore the country between the Sabine and Red river, on the East, and the Rio del Norte, on the West, before the President [James Monroe]. He duly appreciates the spirit of enterprise, and the laudable zeal, to enlarge our knowledge of a country so little known, and desires me to say to you, that if the state of our relations, at this time, would have justified it, it would have afforded him pleasure to confide so important an undertaking to one, on whose perseverance and capacity for sound observation, he reposes so much confidence. Although in the opinion of the President, it is not proper, at this time, to explore the country in question; yet it is very important that you permit no opportunity to escape you, to enlarge your knowledge of it. Should more accurate or fuller information be had of it, you will communicate the results to this Department. It is a matter of considerable importance to prevent the encroachment of our citizens on lands belonging to the Indians on our South Western Frontier, and to prevent our people from passing into the Buffalo Country, either for the destruction of game or to traffick with the Indians without license. You will report your opinion on the best mode of arresting these evils which may ultimately lead to unpleasant consequences, and in the mean time you will to the utmost of your power, prevent its further growth.

FC in DNA, 5, 1:96; PC in Jameson, ed., *Correspondence*, p. 147.

From William Wirt, 10/16. Explains that, in order to give a satisfactory opinion of the case of the Commonwealth of Pa. vs. Young, "fined for having sold at auction certain lots of the U.S. at Pittsburg[h], it will be necessary for me to have the whole record of the case." FC's in DNA, 112, A1:42–43 and A2:38. (These volumes show also that on 10/20, upon Calhoun's suggestion, Wirt wrote to Henry Baldwin and asked Baldwin to have a copy of the record made and sent to Wirt.)

From [William Woodbridge, Secretary of Mich. Territory, Detroit, *ca.* 10/16]. Begs that Dr. Benjamin Delavan shall be granted permission "to pursue his profession among us" for the benefit of civilians who need "his superior professional talents." Unsigned draft in MiD.

To J[ACOB] BROWN, Brownville, N.Y.

War Dept., 17th Oct. 1818

The complete protection of our North-Western Frontier, and the protection and enlargement of our Trade with the Indians, in that quarter, have rendered it necessary, to take measures, to advance our posts on the Mississippi and the Missouri, to points much more remote than those where they now are.

To effect this object, completely, your [Northern] Division, as you have already been informed by the Adjutant and Inspector Gen[era]l, [Daniel Parker,] has been extended to the Mississippi, above Fort Armstrong, inclusive.

The two principal positions, on the Mississippi, will be, at the junction of the St. Peters [the Minnesota River], and Fort Armstrong. The latter position is an Island, in the river, and is said to be, by nature, very strong. The former, from its remoteness from our settlements; its propinquity to Lord Selkirk's establishment, at Red River of Lake Win[n]ipeg; and from its neighbourhood to the powerful Nations of the Sioux; ought to be made very strong. The Force sent, in the first instance, ought to be as imposing as it can be rendered. With this view, it is thought advisable, to occupy the post on the Mississippi, with an entire Regiment; the whole of which, with the exception of what will be necessary to garrison Fort Armstrong, and Fort Crawford, at Prairie de Chien, ought to be moved up to the St. Peters. The occupation of the last mentioned place, will render Fort Crawford of minor importance. After the post at the St. Peters is fully established, it is in contemplation, to establish a post, at the head of navigation, on that river, so as to form a communication, overland, with the projected Fort, at the Mandan Village; and, another, at the head of navigation, on the St. Croix, which empties into the Mississippi, on the east side, a little below the St. Peters.

I transmit to you a sketch of the country, according to the best information in the Department; by a reference to which, it will be seen, that these positions will completely command the country, and prevent the introduction of foreign traders; and, with those, at Green Bay, Chicago, & Sault of the St. Marys [Sault Sainte Marie], will render your command, in that quarter, imposing.

It appears to me, that you will be able to effect the occupation of the posts on the Mississippi, with greatest facility and least expense, by marching the third Regiment across to Prairie de Chien, as soon, in the spring, as the season will admit of it, with no other supply than will be necessary for them, to reach that post; to which place, the supplies, in the Quarter Master's, the Ordnance, and the Commissary's Departments, necessary for the establishment and the maintenance of the Posts, may be transported from St. Louis.

You will communicate to me your ideas, on this point, so that correspondent and early arrangements may be made, through the respective Departments.

It is contemplated, that an Engineer, and an Assistant Topographical Engineer, will accompany the Regiment.

No effort must be spared to conciliate the Indians, particularly the powerful bands of the Sioux; and to afford every extension and protection to our trade with the Indians.

The Post at the St. Peters, will be made the seat of [an] Indian Agency.

I trust that your arrangements will be made, to effect these important objects, as early, next summer, as may be practicable.

By the direction of the President [James Monroe,] I transmit a copy of the opinion of the Attorney Gen[era]l, [William Wirt,] in the case of Major [Nathaniel Nye] Hall.

LS in MHi; FC in DNA, 3, 10:168–169; CC in DLC, Jacob Brown Papers, Letterbooks, 2:123–124; PC in Jameson, ed., *Correspondence,* pp. 147–149.

From Thomas L. McKenney, Georgetown, [D.C.,] 10/17. "When I had the honor of a conversation with you the other day, you mentioned your purposes of throwing a portion of the military on the western boundaries of Louisiana. Your object if I recollect was to keep down the adventurous & warlike spirit of the natives in that quarter. I have the honor to enclose you a letter from Capt. [John] Fowler, U.S. Factor, whose position is at or near the North West corner of Louisiana, and whose means of gathering information is very good, and in whose representations the most implicit reliance may be placed. I am assured from another quarter that there will be a division in the Sac Nation. War of course will be the result between the contending parties. But it will be a war among the natives only. The other looks to an attack upon our white population; and your own views to which I have referred are those which will most effectually arrest the meditated stroke. I conceive it proper to possess you of this direct information, although you may have it more in detail; and especially so, because of the force & number of the Indians in that quarter. Be so good as to return me Capt. Fowler's letter." LS in DNA, 1, M-357; FC in DNA, 73, E:151.

From Alex[ander] Macomb, Detroit, 10/18. A "difficulty has occurred in ascertaining the bounds" of the Army post there; so he asks for copies of the land plat for it. LS in DNA, 1, M-216. (This letter is dated 1817; but EU's date it as having been written on 10/18/1818 and received in 11/1818.)

To Commodore D[ANIEL] T. PATTERSON, U.S.N., Comm[andin]g Naval Officer, New Orleans

Navy Department, October 17th 1818

The U.S. Vessels of War will be permitted to touch occasionally at the Ports of Kingston & Port Royal in Jamaica and at Nassau in New Providence; and if permitted by the Government at those places, may receive on board such sums in Specie as shall properly belong to the Merchants of the U.S. and be due to them in the course of commercial transactions heretofore existing; this permission is however positively limited to this specific object. No article of merchandise of any description must be put on board any public Vessel of the U[nited] States; and any officer offending in this instance, in contravention of the laws and regulations for the government of the Navy, will incur the severest penalty for such offence, of which you will give due notice, in such orders as you may issue with the permission aforesaid. I am very respectfully &c., J.C. Calhoun, A[cting] S[ecretary of the] N[avy].

FC in DNA, 121, 13:269–270; FC in DNA, 130, 2:558; PC in *American State Papers: Naval Affairs,* 1:674.

To S[AMUEL] SMITH, [Representative from Md.,] Baltimore

War Dept., 17th Oct. 1818

Your letter of the 13th instant, enclosing one from Gen[era]l [Peregrine] Benson, on the subject of the appointing of his son, [James Henry Benson,] a Cadet, has been received.

So soon as he shall be fourteen, the age prescribed for admission, by the regulations of the Military Academy, he will be appointed.

LS in DNA, 15, 1818, 174; FC in DNA, 3, 10:169. NOTE: As to the boy's age, see in the same file the letter of 3/20 from the father. The boy was appointed as a Cadet on 3/24/1819.

From Col. D[avid] Brearley, Philadelphia, 10/18. Submits "interrogations propounded to me" by Edmund P. Gaines and the answers given by Brearley [concerning developments of 1817–1818 involving Indian Agent David B. Mitchell; Gaines; the friendly Creeks and their Chief, William McIntosh; and the alleged smuggling of slaves into the U.S.]. ALS with En in DNA, 77 (M-271:2, frames 528–558).

From JACOB BROWN

Brownville, [N.Y.,] Octob[e]r 18th 1818

I have the honor to enclose the explanation of the officers of my command, [Henry Atkinson and Josiah Snelling,] who are responsible for the aggression, alleged to have been committed within his Britannic Majesty's Dominion in Lower Canada, in July last. I hope that it may prove satisfactory.

ALS in DNA, 101 (M-179:42); FC in DLC, Jacob Brown Papers, Letterbooks, 2:122.

From [1st] Lt. J[ohn] S. Allanson, Fort Constitution, Portsmouth, [N.H.,] 10/19. Requests an order to join the alleged "expedition to the Rocky Mountains [the Yellowstone Expedition]," not because he is unwilling to obey [Daniel Parker's] recent order continuing Allanson as aide-de-camp to Bvt. Brig. Gen. [James] Miller, "but from a wish for more active employment, one that would carry with it an opportunity of acquiring information, and would require enterprise to effect." ALS in DNA, 11, 11805.

From Richard Cutts, Second Comptroller, Treasury Department, 10/19. Encloses statements as to appropriations and expenditures of various pension funds as of 1/1 and 8/31, showing that on 8/31 there was an unexpended balance of only $11,861.02 to cover half-pay pensions to widows and orphans. ALS with Ens in DNA, 1, C-282.

From John Gardiner, 10/19. Secretary of the Treasury [William H. Crawford] has ordered that the public land in Mobile shall be laid off in streets and lots. If any copy of "the original plan of the town" can be found in the War Department, Gardiner asks for permission to have it copied. ALS in DNA, 1, G-128; FC in DNA, 82, 8:295; PC in Carter, ed., *Territorial Papers*, 18:442.

To Callender Irvine, Philadelphia, 10/19. Orders him to forward an estimate for Army clothing and camp equipage for 1819, "predicated upon the number of troops authorized by law, as early as practicable. You will omit the 20 p[e]r cent heretofore called for to meet casualties." FC in DNA, 3, 10:169.

From TH[OMAS] S. JESUP

Quarter Master Gen[era]l[']s Office, 19th October 1818

I have the honor to submit a report exhibiting the allowances to officers at different periods as far as I have been able to ascertain them. This report I am well aware, is extremely defective, but it contains all the information I have been able to collect from the documents in the Public offices here, as well as from other sources.

The allowance for Clothing has undergone but little alteration since the Revolution. That for Fuel is rather better now than it was then—to Troops in camp or quarters the allowance is a valuable one, but to officers whose duties require them to move frequently, it is of trifling advantage. Many officers, and those too the most actively employed are from their situation deprived of the allowance. They as well as the service would in my opinion be benefited if an allowance in money, could be made, in lieu of Fuel.

The allowance for Transportation at the close of the Revolution was estimated in Waggons [*sic*] and Horses, the expence of which I have not the means of ascertaining. To officers travelling on duty and to those employed on the recruiting service, the sum of Three dollars per day was allowed for their expences, and it appears that in many cases of extraordinary duties the actual expenses of the officers employed were paid by Resolution of Congress.

I have not been able to find any regulation in relation to the allowance to officers for Transportation, or for Travelling expences, between 1783 and 1801; but in the appropriation made by Congress for the support of the military establishment, the travelling expences of officers were some times enumerated. The late regulation which reduces the Transportation of General Officers and raises that of others is a fair and liberal allowance and requires no alteration.

The allowance of quarters is ample but such is the operation of the present regulation, that the active officer is the greater part of his time deprived of it, whilst the officer in Garrison is able to avail himself of all its advantages. I think the service would be benefited if an allowance in money were made in lieu of quarters to all officers on duty who are not stationed at permanent Posts, Camps, or Cantonments.

At the close of the Revolutionary War officers either received Forage in Kind, or the actual cost of it in money at the Posts where they were respectively stationed. The present allowance is as liberal as ought to be expected—it should not however be subject to Contingencies, but be made permanent, and paid whether the number of Horses required be kept or not.

From 1783 to the commencement of the late War the allowance for servants was better than at present—it is now however sufficient but the observations made in relation to Forage, apply equally to it.

Straw is an allowance to the soldier, and should only be furnished in Kind.

Stationary [*sic*] and Camp equipage though mentioned in the report are not properly allowances. They are furnished merely to enable officers and soldiers to perform their public duties.

For 1801 the sum of one Hundred and sixty-five Thousand dollars was appropriated for the service of the Quarter Master[']s department.

For 1811 the sum of Two hundred and seventy-Thousand dollars was appropriated and for 1818 the sum of Four Hundred and Sixty Thousand dollars was found necessary. This increase is to be ascribed rather to the extension of our Frontier, to the increased price of supplies and to the situation of our Military Posts, than to the increase of the Army. The supplies for the Troops stationed on the Mississippi and its tributaries are transported at much greater expence than formerly—the increase of population is so rapid in the new States and Territories as to consume the greater part of their surplus produce. Supplies for the Army are, therefore, necessarily drawn from a distance, and those intended for the Posts on the line extending from the Lakes to the Gulph [of] Mexico have to encounter the rapid currents of the Mississippi, the Missouri, the Arkansas and Red River; and as our Posts are every year extending in that direction, the expences of the department must necessarily increase.

ALS with 8 Ens in DNA, 201, 15A-F3; FC in DNA, 42, 1:83–85; PC with Ens in House Document No. 36, 15th Cong., 2nd Sess.; PC with Ens in *American State Papers: Military Affairs,* 1:801–804. NOTE: This report was submitted in response to Calhoun's order to Jesup of 10/6, which appears herein under that date.

To David B. Mitchell, Creek Agency, Ga., 10/19. Approves Mitchell's proposed route for a new road between Forts Bainbridge and Claiborne. Authorizes him to use the appropriation for new construction, not for repairing the old road. FC in DNA, 3, 10:170; PC in Carter, ed., *Territorial Papers,* 18:442.

To James Monroe, 10/19. Reports that the appropriation for the payment of half-pay pensions to widows and orphans is inadequate; requests that $33,138.98 be transferred to that account from the appropriation for pensions to Revolutionary veterans. LS in DNA, 1, P-210, with an AES by Monroe that he approved the transfer on 10/19; FC in DNA, 6, 1:337.

[Lt.] J[ohn] Percival and 10 other wardroom officers of the U.S.S. *Macedonian* to Benjamin Homans, 10/19. During the recent cruise of their ship these men lost personal possessions in a storm because they had relinquished their rooms for the storage of extra public supplies; they apply for reimbursement. An AES by Homans recommends that they be paid an indemnity of $500; an AES by Calhoun as "Act[in]g Sec[retar]y of the Navy" directs that this sum should be "Allowed." LS in DNA, 134.

To John Scott, "now in Washington," 10/19. Answers his letter of 10/19 (ALS with Ens in DNA, 1, S-248), in which Scott reported that he did not fully understand [Nathaniel] Cutting's answer to his inquiry of 10/12 and repeated the question raised on 10/12. Calhoun replies that no one in the War Department knows of any donation or allowance in land that was ever made to the soldiers or civilians who settled at Fort Jefferson under George Rogers Clark. "If a donation was ever made, you will be able to ascertain the fact by application to the Commissioner of the General Land Office," [Josiah Meigs]. FC in DNA, 3, 10:170.

From Nicholas Boilvin, Prairie du Chien, 10/20. He has sent 20 gallons of whisky and 100 pounds of tobacco to the Sioux, White Rock, and Great Swamp Indians in answer to their invitation to him to confer with them; he encloses the invitation in English and in French. ALS with Ens in DNA, 1, B-158.

From John Bowyer, Green Bay, 10/20. He received on 9/1 the letter of 5/16 from Calhoun (Abs in *The Papers of John C. Calhoun,* 2:296). Bowyer answers that the Menominees have an exclusive claim to the land around Green Bay—a claim disputed neither by other Indians nor by the French or British. The Menominees could cede 25 square miles without injuring their wild rice crops or their fishing. "I will assemble them and forward you their talk on this subject." ALS in DNA, 1, B-90; PC in Carter, ed., *Territorial Papers,* 17:608–609.

From Lewis Cass, Detroit, 10/20. Encloses depositions obtained by Maj. [William Henry] Puthuff relating to eight charges made against Puthuff's conduct about 1816 as Indian Agent by representatives of the Southwest Fur Company and relayed by [Ramsay] Crooks and [Robert] Stuart through [John Jacob] Astor to Calhoun. Defends Puthuff vigorously; thinks him maligned unfairly. Discusses problems involved in the licensing of foreigners to trade with the Indians. LS with Ens in DNA, 1, C-31; FC in DNA, 76 (M-1:4, pp. 44–51).

To Commodore I[SAAC] CHAUNCEY, U.S.N., Commanding Naval Officer, New York [City]

Navy Department, Oct[obe]r 20th 1818

The proceedings of the Court Martial convened for the trial of Matthew Rodgers, a Gunner in the U.S. Navy, are received. The sentence of the Court is approved and you are hereby directed to have the same forthwith carried into effect. I am very respectfully, &c., J.C. Calhoun, A[cting] S[ecretary of the] N[avy].

FC in DNA, 121, 13:270. NOTE: The accused Gunner, whose name appears in government archives also as Mathew Rodger, was found guilty of drunkenness and of ungentlemanly conduct and was therefore sentenced by the court-martial to dismissal from the Navy. This confirmation of that sentence is recorded also in an ES by Calhoun on the record of the trial, which can be found in DNA, 251, file 321 (M-273:11, frame 908). Chauncey had served as the president of the court-martial; its other members and officials had included Samuel Angus, Samuel Evans, James A. Hamilton, James Renshaw, and E[dward] Trenchard.

From William Irving, [brother of Washington Irving and Representative from N.Y.,] New York [City], 10/20. Recommends Peter F. Dietrich, who served as a [militia ?] officer during the War of 1812, for whatever position he seeks and Calhoun may award. ALS in DNA, 11, 12118.

From R[euben] Lewis, St. Louis, 10/20. He has issued a bill of exchange for funds to send Talontuskey, Chief of the Western Cherokees, and other Chiefs to Washington and for the hire of a horse for Lewis's Interpreter, who will accompany them. ALS in DNA, 1, L-9.

James Monroe, Washington, to Andrew Jackson, 10/20. "I was sorry to find [by means of your letter of 8/19] that you understood your instructions relative to operations in Florida differently from what we [that is, Calhoun and I] intended." "By supposing that you understood them as we did, I concluded that you proceeded on your own responsibility alone, in which, knowing the purity of your motives, I have done all I could to justify the measure [of your having taken possession of the Spanish posts]." "Finding that you had a different view of your power, it remains only to do justice to you on that ground. Nothing can be further from my intention than to expose you to a responsibility, in any sense, which you did not contemplate. The best course to be pursued seems to me for you to write a letter to the [War] Department, in which you will state that, having reason to think that a difference of opinion existed between you and the Executive, relative to the extent of your powers, you thought it due to yourself to state your view of them, and on which you acted. This will be answered, so as to explain ours, in a friendly manner by Mr. Calhoun, who has very just and liberal sentiments on the subject. This will be necessary in the case of a call for papers by Congress, as may be. Thus we shall all stand on the ground of honor, each doing justice to the other, which is the ground on which we wish to place each other." (Jackson replied on 11/15.) PC in *Correspondence between Gen. Andrew Jackson and John C. Calhoun . . . on the Occurrences in the Seminole War*, pp. 41–42; PC in Hamilton, ed., *Writings of James Monroe*, 6:74–75; PEx in Bassett, ed., *Correspondence*, 2:398.

From J[ohn] Pope, [former Senator from Ky.,] Frankfort, [Ky.,] 10/20. Recommends Dr. William [S.] Madison, an Army Surgeon, who will soon visit Calhoun, for appointment as the Indian Agent at Chicago. ALS in DNA, 11, 13630.

To Eleazer W. Ripley, New Orleans, 10/20. Encloses an extract of a letter from the U.S. Factor at Sulphur Fork on the Red River [John Fowler, disclosing rumors of an impending Indian attack]. Orders Ripley to take whatever steps he considers necessary and to furnish all available information about the danger. Ripley's frontier posts should always be prepared to repel Indian "excursions." Calhoun wants detailed information about the Indians in the Red River area and about possible white encroachments upon their lands. FC in DNA, 3, 10:170.

From Lt. Col. W[illiam] A. Trimble

Lexington, Kentucky, 20th October 1818

I had the pleasure on my arrival here to day to recieve [*sic*] yours of the 25th ultimo in answer to mine of the 17th of the same month.

I have not nor shall I give any hint or intimation in relation to the proposed tour of discovery.

I am persuaded that such an expedition could be so conducted that the Spanish authorities could have no knowledge or suspicion of the object. They will not in any probable event have it in their power to obstruct or defeat such an expedition.

Should the people of Natchitoches have any intimation of the object the intel[l]igence would soon be conveyed to St. [*sic*] Antonio. But the expedition could be fitted out & get entirely clear of the settlements for the ostensable [*sic*] object of establishing a military post high up the Red River. Such a measure was some time since proposed and is generally expected.

Should it be determined to hold a treaty with the south western Indians, inhabiting the country in possession of the United States, the latter part of the winter or early part of the Spring would be the most proper time & some place on Red River near the mouth of Kiamisha would be the most eligible place.

The rainy season ["in that country" *interlined*] usually commences about the middle of April.

Bowling Robinson, Esq[ui]r[e] of Louis[i]ana is very competent & well calculated for a commissioner. Should I be thought qualified I would like to be associated with him in the commission. After the conclusion of the treaty the exploring party could leave there early in May which would be a good time.

It might be desirable for a small party to ascend the Red River in a skiff or small boat. They could form a junction with the party going by land near the sources of the River. In this event the party should be larger than first proposed.

As soon as the water rises sufficiently I will embark in a Steam Boat at Louisville for New Orleans. I shall probably stop for a short time at Natches [*sic*].

ALS in DNA, 1, T-20.

From John Gardiner, 10/21. "I have the honor to return herewith the Plan of the Town of Mobile, & the Papers which accompanied it." FC in DNA, 82, 8:298; PC in Carter, ed., *Territorial Papers,* 18:443.

From Peter H. Green, Bath, [District of Me., Mass.,] 10/21. "From the tenor of your letter of the 10th inst[ant] I am led to believe that an incorrect statement of my account has been exhibited to you, which has been the fact in a former instance." So he provides additional evidence of his need for his pending request for a further advance of funds to him as a contractor supplying rations to the troops in New England and in the two Carolinas. ALS in DNA, 1, G-19.

From Dr. John Locke, U.S. Frigate *Macedonian,* Norfolk, 10/21. With the permission of Capt. [John] Downes, Dr. Locke requests a furlough for six or nine months because of his ill health. He cites two other reasons why he should not sail in the *Macedonian* as "Acting Surgeon[']s Mate . . . for botanical researches in the Pacific": he is "destitute of the means of making excursions at any distance from the ship," and the ship will be there too briefly to enable him "to explore the natural history of an unknown region to any advantage." ALS in DNA, 134.

From Thomas L. McKenney

Office of Indian Trade, October 21st 1818

Tha preparation of Indian medals has been delayed because of a desire to have (as is usual) a perfect likeness of the President [James Monroe]. The artist who takes it is in waiting, and will come from Philadelphia at any moment when it may suit the President's convenience to give him a very few hours of his time. The object of this [letter] is to ask the favour of you (when you shall next see the President) to ascertain when Mr. [Mority] Fürst may attend.

I also ask the further favour of you to procure the President's signature to the enclosed accounts, on which money was advanced to me during his absence.

I will do myself the pleasure to see you soon, and will receive the accounts and give them their proper direction; and know the time to request Mr. Fürst[']s attendance.

LS in DNA, 1, M-369; FC in DNA, 73, E:153.

From D[aniel] Parker, 10/21. In compliance with Calhoun's order of 10/5 (which appears herein under that date), Parker submits four reports that are as complete as possible. LS with Ens in DNA, 201, 15A-F3; FC in DNA, 12, 5:110; PC with Ens in House Document No. 36, 15th Cong., 2nd Sess.; PC with Ens in *American State Papers: Military Affairs,* 1:782–790.

John Stevens, Hoboken, [N.J.,] to James Monroe, 10/21. Stevens has heard that Secretary of War [Calhoun] and Secretary of the Treasury [William H. Crawford] "have been instructed by Congress to report on the subject of internal improvements." Stevens encloses for their attention a long document contrasting the limitations of canals and turnpikes with the advantages of railroads.

It cites, for example, Albert Gallatin's report of 1807 to the Senate and his own *Documents Tending to Prove the Superior Advantages of Rail-ways and Steam-carriages over Canal Navigation* (1812). He offers "to attend personally, at any time," if Calhoun and Crawford should wish to confer with him. Specifically, he proposes to build a railroad from Trenton to New Brunswick, N.J.; yet he evaluates a transportation system of much broader compass: "The necessity of effecting direct communication, between the Atlantic and Western States is so apparent and urgent as to require the immediate attention of the General Government. But the interposition of the Allegany [*sic*] Mountains, forming an uninterrupted chain, extending from the Mississip[p]i nearly to Lake Erie, precludes every idea of effecting this important object by means of canals. Turnpike roads, however well executed, cannot be resorted to for the transportation of bulky articles beyond a very limited distance. Should then rail-roads, on an improved construction, be found, upon trial, to be preferable even to canals, it becomes the imperious duty of the General Government to adopt and to carry into immediate effect a mode of conveyance so facile, cheap, expeditious, and, at the same time, of so universal application." ALS with En in DNA, 2, S-1818.

From [Joseph G. Swift], 10/21. Recommends a payment of $300 to David W. Randolph, in order that Randolph may build a furnace with which to ascertain the amount of lime that exists in stone found beside the York River. This stone is to be used in building the intended fortifications beside Hampton Roads. FC in DNA, 21, 1:42.

To Sylvanus Thayer "& the Gentlemen composing the Academic staff" of the Military Academy, West Point, 10/21. On James Monroe's orders, Calhoun returns the "representation of the Academic staff" that was sent directly to Monroe, not through proper War Department channels. "I am directed by the President to state, that however great his respect for the Academic staff, he cannot, in this instance, depart from an established rule of so much importance." FC in DNA, 3, 10:171.

From Decius Wadsworth, 10/21. "Mr. Tatham [that is, Howell Tatum]," who is acting as Military Storekeeper at Nashville, has never been appointed or recognized as such, has made no returns to the Ordnance Office, has received payments from Ordnance funds, but is not even known to be actually in charge of any Ordnance stores. FC in DNA, 32, 2:121–122.

Joseph Leavitt, Joseph Treat, Samuel Call, William D. Williamson, and John Wilkins, [Committee Representing Penobscot County (District of Me.), Mass.,] Bangor, to William H. Crawford, 10/22. Inspired by the House resolution of 3/30 about roads and canals, they propose the building of a road from Bangor on the Penobscot to the St. Croix, "on the Eastern margin of the American States." An AEI by Crawford refers this proposal "to the War Department as the road seems to be more of a military than commercial character." DS in DNA, 1, H-31.

From Dr. Samuel L[atham] Mitchill, New York [City], 10/22. Recommends Dr. Oliver B. Baldwin as being "qualified to take charge of the sick and disabled soldiers"; makes this affirmation on the basis of personal knowledge. ALS in DNA, 1, B-68.

From D[aniel] Parker, 10/22. On the basis of the most recent militia return received from each State and Territory (ranging from 1811 to 1818, inclusive), and with two unreported, Parker tabulates a total of 832,105 militia officers and men. DS in DNA, 2, P-1818.

From El[eazer] W. Ripley

Head Quarters, New Orleans, Oct. 22d 1818

I take the liberty to recommend to you Bradford Bradley for an appointment in the 1[st] Inf[antry Regiment]. He is now a contractor[']s agent and is a young man of character & merit. In the event of his being appointed I should request that he should be selected as the Commissary of the Reg[imen]t.

The Spaniards have made a movement upon Nacogdoches in the Province of Texas. There [*sic*] number is from 3 to 500 strong. I have ordered the 1[st] Reg[imen]t from B[aton] Rouge to march upon the Sabine & erect a fortification. What the object of the

Dons is I know not—but I suspect to take possession of Galveston & keep the possession de facto of the Province of Texas.

We have 690 effectives in this Department. 2 Comp[anie]s of Artillery and one of Infantry are in Florida and it will require months to concentrate my Recruits. There is no organized militia scarcely in Loui[sian]a.

ALS in DNA, 11, 11932.

From Andrew Jackson, Florence, [Ala. Territory,] 10/23. Transmits the depositions of "many of the most respectable Citizens of Pensacola relative to the conduct [of] the Spanish Government and the Inhabitance [*sic*] of Pensacola towards the hostile [Seminole] Indians who fled to the Spanish Flag for protection during the late Campaign." These make it "evident that those Indians were not only furnished with the necessary Arms, Ammunition and Provision, to enable them to carry [on] their Sanguinary Depredations . . . [and] that whenever they were pursued by Our Troops, they had only to recross the Boundary of the United States and they found an asylum under the Spanish Flag." LS with 2 Ens in DNA, 2, J-1818.

To Joseph G. Swift, 10/23. "Mr. [Dean ?] Weymouth will be continued as a Clerk in your department at the rate of $300 a year from the time he commenced duty until further orders." LS in DNA, 25, 49 (167); FC in DNA, 3, 10:172.

To Howell Tatum, Nashville, 10/23. Answers his letter of 10/1 (LS in DNA, 1, T-134) reporting that the government property in his care as Acting Military Storekeeper has recently been increased and asking for increased pay, equal at least to that of a Capt. Calhoun says that War Department records reveal no evidence that Tatum has ever been appointed a Military Storekeeper and directs Tatum to report the date of his appointment and the quantity of stores in his possession. FC in DNA, 3, 10:172.

From Lewis Cass

Detroit, Oct. 24, 1818

It is due to Mess[rs. Ramsay] Crooks & Steuart [that is, Robert Stuart] to state that my report in relation to the circumstances of

Major [William Henry] Puthuff's affair transmitted by this mail [but dated 10/20] was prepared without any communication with them. They were not here and have had neither time nor opportunity by evidence or argument to support their original statement.

In justice to the respect which I entertain for them, I thought this explanation proper. I am convinced it never was their object to injure Major Puthuff, but to procure the correction of abuses which existed, or which they thought existed. They are too correct & highminded to seek the attainment of any purposes, which are not honourable in themselves and honourably to be attained.

ALS in DNA, 1, C-40; FC in DNA, 76 (M-1:4, pp. 55–56).

From NATHANIEL FRYE, JR., Chief Clerk, Paymaster General's Office

City of Washington, October the 24th 1818

Conformably to your letter of the 6th instant I have the honour to transmit you statements showing the monthly pay and emoluments of the troops of the United States; 1st at the close of the Revolutionary war in the year 1783, and 2nd at the close of the late war with the English in the year 1815.

The first I have elicited exclusively from the thirteen volumes of Journals of the old [Continental] Congress, from the 5th of September 1774 onward; and as the subject is involved in some considerable obscurity, from the frequent repeals and reorganizations which took place respecting the Army, sometimes partial and sometimes total, I can not be answerable that it is perfectly correct; it is the best, however, that the materials afforded, the time allowed, and my other duties have permitted me to make; and I hope may not prove unacceptable.

ALS with Ens in DNA, 201, 15A-F3; PC with Ens in House Document No. 36, 15th Cong., 2nd Sess.; PC with Ens in *American State Papers: Military Affairs,* 1:792–801.

To Edmund P. Gaines, Fort Hawkins, Ga., 10/24. Answers his letter of 10/7 (LS in DNA, 1, G-146; CC in DNA, 11, 12409). Explains a delay in paying the 4th [Infantry] Regiment. Agrees with Gaines's exposition of four causes for desertions; some of the four will soon be corrected by Army regulations, and the others will be submitted to Congress for corrective action. "I concur with you, that the liquor ought not to be a part of the daily issue [of rations], but should be put in depot, subject to the order of the commanding officer." LS in DNA, 11, 12923; FC in DNA, 3, 10:174.

From Callender Irvine, Philadelphia, 10/24. "Agreeably to your instruction of the 19th instant I enclose you my Estimates for Clothing & Camp Equipage for the Army for the year 1819." For clothing, $572,937.75; for [camp equipage], $17,120.00; total, $590,-057.75. FC in DNA, 45, 387:170.

Thomas L. McKenney to C[hristopher] Vandeventer

Office of Indian Trade, October 24, 1818

The last payment made to the Chickasaws, through this office, under the Treaty of 1794, was in 1816. The amount was 3,000 D[o]l-[la]rs and it was paid in merchandize.

On the 5th Jan[uar]y 1815 there were sixty-odd thousand Dollars worth of presents sent to G[enera]l [Andrew] Jackson, some of which, on account of the state of the times, was paid over in Annuities, but in what manner, or to whom, or to what tribes of Indians, is not known at this office.

ALS in DNA, 1, M-376; FC in DNA, 73, E:155.

To all Military Storekeepers of the Ordnance Department, 10/24. Gives them regulations and instructions governing their duties, stipulating their responsibilities, how they are to submit quarterly reports, how they are to make purchases and under what conditions they are to issue materials requisitioned, how their arrangements of materials are to be inspected, what assistance they are to receive from other Army officers, etc. These regulations are issued upon recommendation of the Colonel of Ordnance, [Decius Wadsworth]. DI, with an EI by Calhoun certifying his approval, in DNA, 31, War Department; FC in DNA, 3, 10:173–174.

From S[ILAS] STOW, [former Representative from N.Y.]

Lowville, [N.Y.,] Oct. 24, 1818

Permit me to recommend to your patronage Dr. James H. Bradford, as a skilful [*sic*] physician, tender and careful of human life.

And allow me, dear Sir, to say, my friendship, and esteem for you remain the same—increase they could not.

ALS in DNA, 11, 11931. NOTE: One AES by J[oseph] Lovell states that Bradford "has been appointed [on 10/28]" a [2nd] Lt. in the Corps of Light Artillery. AEU's apparently added by Calhoun indicate that this appointment was made with the intention of assigning Bradford to the duties of an Assistant Commissary [of Subsistence] and refer this letter to [George] Gibson.

From Maj. A[BRAM] R. WOOLLEY

U.S. Arsenal near Pittsburgh, 24 Oct. 1818

Your letter of the 17th Ins[tan]t has been duly rec[eive]d. I refer you to my letter of the 15th for an explanation of my conduct in causing the Bill to be drawn on you by the Quarter Master for Rations furnished at Pittsburgh.

It would have been better in my opinion for the contractor to have stated in his letter to you the am[oun]t of funds he had forwarded to me; he could not expect me to carry on his contract with Two Hundred Doll[ar]s (the sum he sent me per mail).

At the time the Bill was drawn the $200 was absorbed in the issues at this post and I had advanced beyond it $26.64; the Bill did not embrace a Shilling for any Rations furnished the men under my command. In this case I trust I have furnished a satisfactory explanation and it would afford me pleasure to furnish explanations to your Excellency in every case in which I have been misrepresented to the War Dep[artmen]t by persons in all grades of society from Hon[ora]ble Senators down to the meanest of mankind. I can make them equally satisfactory in every case as I have done in this—and you would find that every Draft of mine and every act has been based in good faith and has tended to the public benefit.

ALS in DNA, 1, W-51.

From Armistead T[homson] Mason, [former Senator from Va.]

Selma [Loudoun County, Va. ?] 25th Oct. 1818

I have recently rec[eive]d several letters from Kentucky informing me that Colo[nel] James Johnson of that State intends to make proposals for the Army contracts above St. Louis & near New Orleans. I do not flatter myself that any thing I can say can be of service to a man whose conspicuous merit as a patriot & soldier place him far above common praise. But feeling with all the acquaintances of Col. Johnson, and with his fellow citizens of the West particularly, a deep interest in whatever concerns him, I beg leave to offer my feeble testimony in his favor & to express the great gratification I should feel to see him obtain those contracts, which are at present very important to him in consequence of extensive arrangements which he has made in the confident expectation of obtaining them since it is as it always has been his intention to bid for them as low as possible without exposing himself to actual loss. His zealous & uniform support of the Republican Administration of our Country—and the distinguished bravery with which he signalized himself during the late war added to the great sacrifices of health & property which he has made in the public service entitle him to the gratitude & favor of his Country. His enterprise, and the fidelity & integrity with which I am informed he has always discharged his duty as a Public officer & as a contractor particularly are considerations which cannot be overlooked on the present occasion, & they cannot fail to ensure to him your entire confidence & that of the public at large. All that the friends of Col. Johnson ask is that he may have those contracts at a fair price. They conceive that it is better for the Government to give such contracts to honourable men who will faithfully fulfil[l] them, even at a higher rate, than to speculators at a lower one, whose only object is to get the use of the public money, and who depend upon neglecting their engagements & defrauding the Government to make up for any loss they may sustain by taking such contracts below a fair price. It is apprehended by the friends of Col. Johnson that some such man may bid against him (for any body can give security) and that he may be [*one word illegible, but it looks somewhat like* "chorused"] out of these contracts by a competitor against whom it is impossible for an honest man to enter the lists.

It is to direct your attention to this view of the subject that the friends of Col. Johnson beg leave to address you. They solicit of you to protect the honest bidder against men who bid from such motives & ["w(it)h such" *interlined*] intentions as have been discribed [*sic*] and ["thereby" *interlined*] exclude from a competition with them all those who intend to deal honestly both with the Army & the Government. To you the friends of such men as Col. Johnson look with perfect confidence, and they are well convinced that you will prefer to give those Contracts ["at a fair and reasonable price" *interlined*] to respectable & responsible men whose integrity of character is well established, rather than to speculators at a lower rate, for whose good conduct there can be no certain assurance.

I hope you will excuse this intrusion on your time, and believe me to be most respectfully your very sincere friend, Armistead T. Mason.

ALS in DNA, 43, file of James Johnson, 18.

To Maj. Henry Austin, Boston, 10/26. "The act of the last session of Congress which was passed for your relief, on account of nine judgements against you, provides for the settlement of your claims for expenses in defending those suits. You will therefore render your account for such expenses as early as practicable." FC in DNA, 3, 10:175.

From Quintin Campbell, Cashier of the Philad[elphi]a Bank, 10/26. Encloses a draft written by Henry Sherburne for $18,200 that were paid to Sherburne by a Nashville bank; it understood his need for the cash, since the treaty negotiations with the Chickasaws could have no possibility of being successful unless the Chickasaws first received everything due to them from the U.S. To avoid a loss to the Nashville or the Philadelphia bank if the draft should be discounted under usual rates of exchange between Washington and these distant places, Campbell asks Calhoun to redeem the draft at face value. ALS in DNA, 1, C-38.

To E[dmund] P. Gaines, 10/26. Answering his letter of 10/5, Calhoun cites his letters of 9/3, 9/23, and 10/2 to Gaines for the latter's "general instruction." James Monroe "particularly desires that you should not commence hostility, unless it should be forced on you. You will make such distribution of your forces as will enable you, effectually, to protect the frontier; and, in case of hostility, to act with effect and promptitude." LS in DNA, 11, 12215; FC in DNA, 3, 10:175.

To WILSON LUMPKIN, Madison, Ga.

Department of War, 26th Oct. 1818

I have rec[eive]d your letters of the 9th instant [2 LS's, one with 4 Ens, in DNA, 1, L-134 and L-135]. From the last map of Georgia in this Department, it was supposed, by the description of the boundaries in the treaty, that the U. States would acquire about 1,340,000 acres. I regret to find that the number of acres ceded will be much less and that the lands generally are poor.

I entirely approbate the measures which you have adopted to accomplish the objects of your commission. You are at liberty to draw on this department, should you find it necessary, for such sums as you may want to meet the expenses of the persons employed to assist you: for which you will be held accountable.

In surveying the lower tract, if a guard should be necessary as you now apprehend, you are authorized to call on General [Edmund P.] Gaines for an escort; or, if you should find it more convenient or economical, on Gen. [William] McIntosh.

FC in DNA, 72, D:224.

Thomas L. McKenney to C[hristopher] Vandeventer, 10/26. McKenney thanks Vandeventer for having obtained [James Monroe's] signature on [the accounts about which McKenney wrote to Calhoun on 10/21] and for "the information as to the time when Mr. [Mority] Fürst may come down [from Philadelphia] to take" Monroe's likeness. McKenney reports that the goods that have been reported to have been sunk in the Ohio River were those intended for the Chickasaw annuity and for presents to certain Chickasaw Chiefs. McKenney doubts that the loss is total: he had the goods well packed in water-tight tierces; he hopes that the shipment can be largely salvaged. He tells Vandeventer what instructions McKenney has sent to [Paul] Ballio and to [Henry]

Sherburne concerning an appraisal of the loss, the use of any part of the shipment that may reach the Chickasaw Bluffs in satisfactory condition, and the accounts that will cover this shipment. LS with En in DNA, 1, M-371; FC in DNA, 73, E:159–160.

To DAVID B. MITCHELL, Creek Agent

Department of War, 26 Oct. 1818

I am perfectly aware of the truth of the opinion which you have stated, in your letter of the 7th instant [LS in DNA, 1, M-367], that it is better to make payment to the Indians for their annuity or other sums which may be due to them in goods than in money; but it ought always to be done by a previous request to this department, so that the goods may be purchased thro' the Superintendent of Indian Trade, whose duty it is by law. Every other mode, however fair, gives occasion for suspicion, alike injurious to the government and the agent. It will be necessary in the transactions alluded to that the greatest caution should be used, and, to avoid such suspicions, the transaction should be as advantageous to the nation, and as little so to the agents employed (I mean the Chiefs), as possible. Your payment ought, by all means, to be in money, and as far as possible to each claimant. The remittance will hereafter be made in goods thro' the Superintendent at this place, unless the nation should dissent to it. You will bring the subject, on the first suitable occasion, before it. In the regular manner, the goods will come cheaper and of a better quality than thro' any other channel. You will correspond with the Superintendent as to the kind and quality.

I have submitted that part of your letter relative to the terms on which peace ought to be made with the Seminoles to the President [James Monroe]. He directs that, should they offer to treat for peace, it will be given them on condition that they should remove to the Upper Creeks, with the consent of the latter, whenever the President may direct such removal. The President entertains no doubt of the policy of removing them from Florida, but it might be improper, at this moment, to cause such removal. The more dangerous among them, however, should be removed immediately.

The Upper Creeks must not be permitted to put their supposed law of nations in force against small parties who may surrender.

They are not the only party to the war. The war was between us and the Seminoles, and the Creeks were called in by us and paid for their service. Our law and custom and not theirs must, therefore, prevail in relation to it. You will make an arrangement, on the most economical plan, for the support of those who may surrender and be moved up, which you will report to this department.

It is conceived to be contrary to the laws of the U.S. to bring in Negroes from Florida into the Creek Country. Those belonging to the Seminoles who may surrender and be moved up must be left at one of our posts in Florida, to abide the decision of Congress. If there should be any in that condition, they must be reported to this Department.

FC in DNA, 72, D:222–224; CCEx in DNA, 11, 12576.

To Thomas Morris, New York [City], 10/26. Transmits copies of orders for reconvening the general court-martial for N.Y. militia delinquents. Approves refunds by Morris to seven persons whose fines have been remitted. [Gerard] Steddiford has been directed to put into Morris's hands without delay certificates of other fines levied by the court, and Morris should collect those fines "with all practicable dispatch." FC in DNA, 3, 10:175.

From Lemuel Whitman, Farmington, Conn., 10/26. Asks for information about Caleb Welton, who enlisted during the War of 1812 for five years and whose father does not know whether he is dead or alive. "Do you ever turn your attention to Connecticut? You must know that your friends here almost claim you for a Connecticut man. A mighty political revolution has lately taken place here. We hope soon to render our claim not disgraceful to you." ALS in DNA, 11, 12946.

From Burwell Bassett, [Representative from Va.,] Williamsburg, Va., 10/27. Recommends Dr. Cary Barraud to succeed Dr. [George W.] Maupin, who "is in the last state of Pulmonary Disease," as Post Surgeon at Portsmouth, Va. ALS in DNA, 11, 11868.

To William H. Crawford, 10/27. As Acting Secretary of the Navy, Calhoun requests $10,000 of the appropriation for completion of the ports and harbors survey. FC in DNA, 124.

To F[erdinand] R[udolph] Hassler, 10/27. "I am informed by your letter of the 16th instant, to Gen[era]l [Joseph G.] Swift, that it is almost certain that the line of 45° N. latitude, now running by the Commissioners under the treaty of Ghent [of 1815], will pass South of Rouse's point [N.Y.]." Directs Hassler to keep [Joseph G.] Totten well informed as to the "proceedings in relation to the line at that important point." Calhoun has ordered the instruments needed by Hassler. FC in DNA, 3, 10:175.

To [former] Capt. Alden Partridge, [Norwich, Vt.,] 10/27. Answering several of his letters—among them, those dated 10/6, 10/8, 10/11, and 10/20 (ALS's, two with Ens, in DNA, 2, P-1818) —preferring charges against [Joseph G.] Swift, [Sylvanus] Thayer, [Jared] Mansfield, and others in relationship to the dismissal of Partridge from the Superintendency of the Military Academy and his court-martial in 1817, Calhoun answers particularly Partridge's letter of 9/2 (ALS in DNA, 1, P-152), written in reply to Calhoun's of 3/7 to Partridge, which Partridge received five months later. Calhoun believes that Partridge misunderstands the 77th Article of War, which concerns the arrest of officers. All of the crimes attributed by Partridge to others are outgrowths of the dismissal and trial of Partridge, "and many of them are the counterpart of the charges against yourself, which were then investigated. Further proceedings in relation to them, it is conceived, would be not only useless, but pernicious." FC in DNA, 3, 10:176–177.

To Henry Sherburne, Chickasaw Agent

Department of War, 27 Oct. 1818

Since writing the letter of the 23d in answer to yours of the 2d instant [LS in DNA, 1, S-268, concerning annuity payments to the Chickasaws and treaty negotiations with them], I find that the Treasurer of the U.S. was directed on the 14th inst[ant] in pursuance of your letter of the 21st ult[im]o to remit you $6,000 for the payment of the annuity stated to be due for the years 1817 & '18 to the Chickasaw nation, per act 25th Feb[ruar]y 1799. You will, therefore, should the Treasurer's draft for that sum be rec[eive]d by you previous to drawing for the $18,200 as mentioned in your letter of the 2nd instant, draw only for $12,200; or, should your drafts have been made out for the whole sum and sent on for payment, you will then place the amount of the Treasurer's draft ($6,-000) in the Nashville Bank to the credit of T[homas] T[udor] Tucker, Esq., Treasurer U.S., and your drafts will be paid here when presented. In the event of the latter course being adopted, you will transmit to this Dept. the certificate of the Cashier of such Deposite [*sic*] having been made. It is necessary [that] the Department should have the earliest information on this subject.

I have this moment been informed by a letter from Col. [Thomas L.] McKenney, Superintendent of Indian Trade, that the goods which were intended for the Chickasaw annuity of this year and for presents to be distributed at the approaching treaty, were sunk in the Ohio, on their passage to the [Chickasaw] Bluffs, and he apprehends they have suffered some damage from this circumstance.

You rec[eive]d instructions on the 28th ult[im]o that the goods for the annuity, in consequence of the unwillingness of the Indians to receive them, were to be turned over to the Superintendent of Indian Trade; all the packages, therefore, marked "annuity" are to be placed under his direction, and he has instructed the Factor at the Bluffs in relation to them. Those for the presents remain subject to the original order and, it is hoped, have sustained no material injury.

Col. McKenney states that he has written to you himself on the subject of the transfer of the goods which were intended for the annuity.

FC in DNA, 72, D:225–226.

To [Bvt. Lt.] Col. J[oseph] G. Totten, 10/27. "Enclosed is an extract from Mr. [Ferdinand Rudolph] Hassler's letter to Gen[era]l [Joseph G.] Swift. You are directed to call on the parties named therein for the instruments and to deliver them to Mr. Hassler. You will advise the department regularly of the operations of the astronomers and communicate the result of your reconnaisance. Should you fix on any site, you will report its value, and you will also state the amount of materials collected at Rouse's point." FC in DNA, 3, 10:175–176.

From Samuel Hodges, Jr., Stoughton, Mass., 10/28. He has received Calhoun's letter of 8/28 and bows to the verdict that he cannot hold civil and military offices simultaneously. But he proposes that his name be carried on the Army's rolls without pay while he serves for about two years as consul in the Cape Verde Islands. His pay could then begin when he reports for duty. ALS in DNA, 11, 12311.

From Callender Irvine, Philadelphia, 10/28. Pursuant to Calhoun's order of 9/28, submits a statement of funds received by Irvine for 1818 and another of the probable balances at the end of the present year. A statement of the prices of clothing is being prepared and will be sent when it is ready. LS with En in DNA, 2, I-1818; FC in DNA, 45, 387:177.

From Jonathan Jennings, Charleston, Ind[ian]a, 10/28. Reports that the recent negotiations at St. Marys [in O.] for the extinction of the Indian title to lands in Ind. were as favorable to the U.S. as possible. Attributes the high price the Indians placed on their land to the large number of white persons living near and trading with these Indians. Individual ownership of some tracts was granted, mainly to the Miamis, headed by John Baptiste Richardville, "who is a half breed Indian, sagacious, and possessing as much knowledge of the value of property, as many of our own citizens." The land ceded exceeds 7,000,000 acres, "including a body not equaled [in quality] by any in the State." The annuities to the Miamis appear disproportionate, but their claims were extensive. No Chief refused to sign the treaty. ALS in DNA, 1, J-161.

From George Jones, W.B. Bullock, Joseph Cummins, William Davies, Robert Habersham, Hazen Kimball, J. Bond Read, William Scarbrough, James Wallace, James M. Wayne, John P. Williamson, and seven others, Savannah, 10/28. They petition for removal of the gunpowder that is stored in the magazine at Fort Wayne, within their city "and in the immediate vicinity of a numerous population." The "Fort is without a guard of any kind, and exposed to the mercy of Incendiaries, and the works have already twice taken fire within a short time past from a large wooden building adjoining in which a steam machine is constantly employed." An AEI by Calhoun reads: "Col. [Decius] Wadsworth will give this his immediate attention." DS in DNA, 31, 1818-War Department.

To Col. William King, 10/28. "I enclose herewith a copy of your requisition of the 18th June 1818. You will report to this department without delay to which contract of Mr. [Benjamin G.] Orr's you referred by the expression of Mr. Orr's contract ending on the 30th May"—in 1818 or 1819. FC in DNA, 3, 10:176.

Thomas L. McKenney to Christopher Vandeventer, 10/28. As Calhoun ordered on 3/5 (PC in *The Papers of John C. Calhoun,* 2:175), McKenney has paid the annuities due to various Indian tribes, including the Wyandots, in the form of goods unless otherwise stipulated. He now pays the $1,430 in cash that was then ordered to be withheld from the annuity of the Cherokees. LS with En in DNA, 1, M-370. (The enclosure lists goods that were part of the Chickasaws' annuity that were damaged or lost when the flatboat *Good Hope* sank.)

To [James Monroe], 10/28. Because the appropriation for the [Army's] Medical and Hospital Department is inadequate, Calhoun requests that $20,000 be transferred to that account from the appropriation for Forage. LS in DNA, 1, P-224; FC in DNA, 6, 1:337.

From [Capt.] John Rodgers, President, Board of Naval Commissioners, Naval Commissioners' Office, [Washington,] 10/28. Transmits "all the bound copies, of the [Navy] rules . . . received from the Printers" and some copies "of detached [that is, unbound] rules, agreeably to your request." Delivery of the edition will be complete soon. LS in DNA, 128, 6:92.

From John Rodgers, 10/28. Lends, for Calhoun's information, "an exhibit showing the present state & condition of the public vessels at the Navy Yard at Charlestown," Mass. LS in DNA, 128, 6:93.

To Howell Tatum, [Nashville,] 10/28. Calhoun acknowledges Tatum's letter of 10/5 and allows him $1,566.20 per year for the time Tatum acted as an Assistant Deputy Quartermaster General. His salary as Military Storekeeper during the same time is to be deducted. FC in DNA, 3, 10:176.

From D[ecius] Wadsworth, 10/28. Estimates that $20,000 will be needed in 1819 to permit completion of the arsenal at Watertown, Mass., and that $5,000 will be sufficient for the same purpose at Pittsburgh. Maj. [Abram R.] Woolley has been negligent in sending reports from Pittsburgh, and Wadsworth is taking pains to correct that evil. FC in DNA, 32, 2:122–123.

From ALEXANDER HAMILTON

New York [City], Oct[ober] 29th 1818

I take the liberty to observe that my mother (the widow of the late General Alex[ander] Hamilton) some time since made application for a Midshipman[']s warrant for her adopted son Mr. John Hamilton. Your attention to his promotion will bestow a great favour & much oblige Sir Your Obed[ient] Ser[van]t Alexander Hamilton.

ALS in DNA, 128, 6:94.

ALEXANDER HAMILTON to BENJAMIN HOMANS

New York [City], Oct[ober] 29th 1818

Among the list of applicants for Midshipman's warrants, the name of John Hamilton will be found; this young Gentleman is an adopted son of my mother, for whose advancement we are deeply interested and you would confer upon me a particular obligation, if you will exercise your influence to strengthen & forward his promotion. Mr. [James] Monroe previous to his present elevation, as I understand had my mother[']s application recorded. I should be much gratified with a few lines on this subject & have the honor to remain [with] much respect . . . .

ALS in DNA, 128, 6:95.

From [Isaac Shelby], Nashville, 10/29. Col. [Robert] Butler, who served as Secretary to Shelby and [Andrew] Jackson while they were Commissioners to negotiate the recent Chickasaw treaty, lost his "very valuable horse while on that duty, supposed[ly] from eating green corn." Butler should be remunerated for that loss. Draft, unsigned, in DLC, Shelby Family Papers, 5:1978.

John Forsyth, [Representative from Ga.,] Washington, to [James Monroe], 10/30. Forsyth recommends Maj. [Samuel] Miller for appointment as Commandant of the Marine Corps. "I have no personal acquaintance with Major Miller and this letter is founded solely on his reputation as a Gallant officer and accomplished Gentleman." ALS in DNA, 128, 6:99.

From Maj. Arch[ibald] Henderson, U.S. Marine Corps Headquarters, Washington, 10/30. Submits estimates of appropriations needed in 1819 for the Paymaster's and Quartermaster's services of the Marine Corps; suggests an addition to the contingent fund to cover contractual expenditures for building barracks at Norfolk. ALS in DNA, 128, 6:98.

From Callender Irvine, Philadelphia, 10/30. As ordered on 9/30 to do, Irvine encloses a statement showing the cost of clothing a Private, a Musician, and a Sergeant for the next five years, assuming the continuance of present prices. FC in DNA, 45, 387:179.

Pooshemullaha and Mishulatubbe to President [James Monroe]

In Council at the Chaktaw [*sic*] Trading House
Oct[obe]r 30th 1818

Our Father, You have sent a talk to us; but our land is small and we do not wish to part with any of it, and therefore have not complied with your wishes. We do not wish to leave our country. We have received your Commissioners [Andrew Jackson and Isaac Shelby] & took them by the hand & treated them kindly, but our land is so small we could not spare any.

Father, if you are willing that we should go on [to Washington] & see you we will go, and we wish that you would signify to us your pleasure on this subject; and if you permit us to visit you that you will please to order arrangements to be made for our accommodation on the road.

Father, we thank you for the kind assistance you are affording the foreign mission society in establishing schools among us.

LS (signed with their marks) in DNA, 77 (M-271:2, frames 0671-0672).

John H. Robinson to James Monroe

Philadelphia, 30th Oct[obe]r 1818
I arrived in this City a few days since. My object is to publish my map of Mexico &c. and also Notes, taken during my several tours in that country.

I have brought with me my oldest son [Hamilton Edward V. Robinson] with intention to Educate him for the profession of arms; the object therefore of this note is to solicit thro the kindness of your Excellency, a place for him at the Military Accademy [*sic*] at West Point.

LS in DNA, 15, 1818, 158.

To Capt. John Rodgers, U.S.N., President of the Board of Navy Commissioners

Navy Department, Oct[obe]r 30th 1818
I have the honour to transmit, herewith, for the information of the Commissioners of the Navy, a pamphlet, describing a new system of Naval Architecture, invented by William Annesley, a Citizen of the United States; also a copy of a letter [addressed to the Secretary of the Navy and dated at London on 8/25] accompanying the same, recently received from the Hon[ora]ble Richard Rush, our Minister at the Court of St. James.

LS with a CC of the En in DNA, 135, vol. 10.

John Scott, [Delegate from Mo. Territory,] Washington, to [James Monroe], 10/30. Scott recommends Maj. S[amuel] Miller to succeed the late Col. [Franklin] Wharton as the Commandant of the Marine Corps. ALS in DNA, 128, 6:100.

From Isaac Shelby and Andrew Jackson, Nashville, 10/30. As commissioners for the negotiation, they report that on 10/19 they concluded a treaty with the Chickasaws for the cession to the U.S. of all lands claimed by the Chickasaws in Ky. and Tenn. LS with Ens in DNA, 77 (M-271:2, frames 0817–0821); CC in DLC, Andrew Jackson Papers, 8207–8209; CC in NHi; PC in Bassett, ed., *Correspondence*, 2:399–401.

From Isaac Shelby and Andrew Jackson, Nashville, 10/30. As commissioners to negotiate with the [Chickasaws], they report that they have issued drafts for $2,303.1525 in payment of "expenditures in travelling to and from the Treaty ground, and disbursements while there"; to attest these outlays, they enclose a financial report by Robert Butler, who served as their secretary. LS in DNA, 77 (M-271:2, frames 0826–0827).

To Thomas Aspinwall, U.S. Consul, London, 10/31. Answers his letter of 8/27 (LS with Ens in DNA, 1, A-107, including an LS to Calhoun from James L. Edwards, Chief Clerk of the Pension Office, dated 10/28, of which an FC is in DNA, 91, 5:425). Calhoun states that ample evidence of the "services and circumstances" of Capt. [Joseph] Beaulieu exists to entitle him to an increase in his Revolutionary pension under the new pension act of 3/18 if he had been a resident citizen of the U.S. at the time of that service; but a special act of Congress will be required to increase the pension. FC in DNA, 3, 10:177.

From R[ICHARD] GRAHAM

St. Louis, Oct. 31st 1818

When I had the honor of seeing you last winter, I received your verbal instructions to remove my Agency from Peoria to Rock River, and to endeavour to withdraw the Indians from the Illinois to that point. I have not as yet made any establishment at that point for the following reasons. Gov[ernor Ninian] Edwards & Gov[ernor William] Clark had made some arraingements [*sic*] respecting the Fox & Sac tribe of Indians who reside on the Mississippi immediately at Rock River. Under a belief that all of those Indians would remove to the Missouri side of the Mississippi, Gov. Edwards exercised no superintendance [*sic*] over them. Gov. Clark rec[eive]d their annuities & presents & through the Agent for this territory distributed them. With these circumstances I thought it would only produce confusion among them to interfere in any way, more particularly as Mr. [Thomas] Forsyth had been assigned to those Nations, & [a] great part of them being on the Illinois side must necessa[ri]ly extend his agency over the whole, to secure to all a part of the annuities & presents; consequently my attentions have been confined solely to the Indians of the Illinois.

I would suggest the propriety of the Tribes of Indians being designated to each Agency. The same Tribe of Indians divided in different Agencies produce[s] considerable confusion.

The Wenebagoes [*sic*] of Rock River claim some share of the attention of Government. They are a proud & spirited nation, whose friendship it would be our policy to secure. They have as heretofore not been noticed by any of the Agents for want of presents. I would recommend that presents to the amount of $1,500 be sent to them.

It may not be improper for me to observe that it would be highly desirable for me to remain where I could give some attention to my private affairs & attend to the duties assigned me as Indian Ag[en]t & do the same justice as if I were stationed with any one of the tribes. My reduced salary renders it indispensibly [*sic*] necessary to make a request of this kind.

ALS in DNA, 1, G-31.

From William Hill, Pittsburgh, 10/31. Answering Calhoun's inquiry of 8/15, Hill defends the conduct of Maj. Abram R. Woolley as Ordnance officer there. ALS in DNA, 1, H-33.

From Eben[ezer] Huntington, [Representative from Conn.,] Norwich, [Conn.,] 10/31. Encloses "the returns of the Connecticut Militia for the year 1818." ALS in DNA, 11, 12048.

From Joseph Lovell, 10/31. Points out that the allowances received by the Post Surgeon at Philadelphia, Dr. [Samuel B.] Smith, are unjustly low. Urges revisions but admits that some other officers deserve increases too. ALS in DNA, 1, L-36.

To Thomas L. McKenney, 10/31. "Col. [Henry] Sherburne's draft for the Chickasaw annuity of 1817, which was forwarded in goods but which have since been transferred to the Indian Trade Dept., has been presented and paid at this Department; and as the appropriation for the Indian Dept. is nearly exhausted, it becomes necessary that the $12,200 placed in your hands for the purchase of these goods should be refunded into the Treasury, as soon as practicable, to the credit of that appropriation." FC in DNA, 72, D:226.

From William Wirt

[Washington, *ca.* October 31, 1818]

In relation to the case of the Pittsburg[h] auctioneer, [John Young, who sold some U.S. property at Fort Fayette in behalf of commissioners who were ordered not to pay a duty levied by Pa.,] I am not furnished with the act of assembly of Pennsylvania, of the 28th March 1814, laying a duty on sales at auction, referred to in Mr. [Richard] Rush's opinion. As this, I presume, was the foundation of the judgment in the case of the Comm[onwea]lth ag[ains]t Young, it is necessary that I sh[oul]d see it before I can make up my opinion. Will you have the goodness to cause it to be furnished to me[?]

LS in PPL, Carson Collection. Note: In connection with this lawsuit, see in PPL the letter of Henry Baldwin to William H. Crawford, 9/21, and that of Wirt to Baldwin, 10/20. Relevant letters within this book include those of Calhoun to Wirt, 10/2, and from Wirt to Calhoun, 10/16.

From William Clark, St. Louis, 10/——. He has succeeded, pursuant to Calhoun's letter of 5/8 (Abs in *The Papers of John C. Calhoun,* 2:285), in obtaining a treaty of peace between the Osages and the Western Cherokees; now the Indians want the boundaries of their reservations surveyed and intruders evicted. The Osages request and Clark recommends that Peter Chouteau be reappointed as their Agent. Clark has informed [Lewis] Cass of the recent cession of nearly 30,000,000 acres by the Quapaws, so that other Indians may perhaps be persuaded to settle on part of that land. The Shawnees and Delawares who live within U.S. settlements near the Mississippi are willing to emigrate. LS in DNA, 77 (M-271:2, frames 592–595); LS in MoSHi; PC in Carter, ed., *Territorial Papers,* 15:454–456; PC in *American State Papers: Indian Affairs,* 2:179.

NOVEMBER 1818

ON NOVEMBER 2 CALHOUN SENT TO SECRETARY OF THE Treasury William H. Crawford estimates that the War Department would need in 1819 more than eight and a quarter million dollars. On the 5th, reported James L. Edwards, the Pension Office Clerk, that bureau was swamped with almost 12,500 pending applications from Revolutionary veterans. The next day Calhoun wrote, with matter-of-fact simplicity, that Mrs. Calhoun had suffered the loss, by miscarriage, of an unborn child. Congress convened on the 16th for a session that would end on March 3, 1819. The Army's Chief Engineer, Joseph G. Swift, resigned to become Surveyor of the Port of New York City. Army rations, Indian treaties, the Military Academy—these were some others among Calhoun's concerns as Secretary of War. As Acting Secretary of the Navy, he dispatched three men to the Gulf Coast to search for timbers suitable for the building of new ships for the Navy.

From Joseph Lovell, 11/1. "The reports of sick and returns of Medicines and Stores received at this office [for the quarter that ended on 6/30] have been so few [about half of those that should be submitted] as to render a correct report of the state of 'the health of the Army and the condition of the Medical supplies' impracticable at present, nor had they all been forwarded would the difficulty have been much less, because the Surgeons are with a few exceptions in the habit of sending a mere statement of numbers without comment or observation, not even noticing the causes of death, when it occurred or the number of men present, much less the nature, symptoms and treatment of the prevailing diseases. The form also of the report now in use precludes the possibility of approximating to accuracy, for it requires but a very few diseases to be specified, while by far the greater part and sometimes the whole are included under the indefinite denomination of 'all other contingencies'; these inconveniences it is expected will be remidied [*sic*] by the new regulations of the Medical Department, but in the mean time no report founded upon such imperfect documents can either afford correct information, or admit of comments either practical or usefull." Discusses the causes of illness and death among the troops: excessive intoxication, inflammatory fever, rheumatism, venereal diseases, wounds, diarrhea, dysentery, typhus fever, intermittent and remittent fevers. Verbally chastises Army officers for not taking better care of the soldiers. "In fact there is probably no service in which officers appear to pay so little respect to the character of the soldier as in ours, or in which so little attention is given to their comfort[,] convenience and health. They are not only put upon menial and fatiguing duties for the accommodation of officers but even loaned like so many Negroes, to the citizens." Although not all bills for last month have yet cleared the auditors, the unexpended balance of the medical appropriation for 1818 is apparently $17,898.31 as of today. FC in DNA, 243, 1:1–7.

From 2nd Lt. D[avid] C[harles] Nicholls

Fort Johnson, Charleston, [S.C.,] Nov. 1st 1818

I have the honor to inform you, that I have been, for *three months* past, in *close* confinement at this post by the *Special* order of Major James Bankhead, awaiting the promulgation of the proceedings of the General Court Martial by which I was tried, and which, as yet, have not been heard of. I therefore respectfully request, that I be liberated from confinement, or, that the proceedings, in my case, be ordered to be published as soon as may be.

ALS in DNA, 11, 12612.

[Dr.] William Baldwin, Wilmington, Del., to James Monroe, 11/2. Applies for appointment as surgeon to the Western expedition now being planned, "to enable me to attend to the *botany* of the territory to be explored. Thus situated, every exertion would be made on my part to fulfil[l] the expectations of the Government." LS in DNA, 11, 11855.

To [William H. Crawford], 11/2. "I have the honor to transmit, herewith, an estimate of the expenses of the Army of the United

States, for the year 1819; an estimate of the probable amount necessary for the payment of Military Pensions in the year 1819; and, also, an estimate of the Salaries and Expenses requisite for the offices of the War Department for the same period." These estimates total $8,368,427.85. FC in DNA, 171, 1:306–317.

From C. Hammond, Belmont County, O., 11/2. Representative [Samuel] Herrick of O. has charged a fee equal to one year's pension for his services as a lawyer in preparing the pension applications of at least three invalid veterans. Dr. John Hamm, recently U.S. Pension Agent in O., has served as the examining physician and has charged for his services after each pension was granted. Hammond encloses newspaper clippings publishing certificates by Robert Cue, George Cullens, and William Morrow that they made such payments voluntarily and were content with having done so. "I cannot but regard it as a matter of surprise, that invalids fairly entitled to pensions should be so well satisfied at paying public men such large proportions of a public charity for obtaining them their rights. Gen. Herrick and Doctor Hamm are very particular friends, and it cannot escape your reflection how very easy it is for men of their standing, if unrestrained by principle, to impose upon the public in matters of this kind." ALS with Ens in DNA, 1, H-32.

From Alexander Macomb

Detroit, November 2nd 1818

I have the honour to report that the military way directed to be opened from this place to the Rapids of the Miami has progressed as far as the Eight mile creek that is within eight miles of the rapids making in all a distance of seventy miles. The road is truly a magnificent one, being eighty feet wide, cleared of all the logs and under brush, every low place causewayed and all the creeks and rivers requiring it bridged in a substantial manner. The number of causeway[s] exceed[s] sixty and the bridges are of considerable length. The one on which the troops are now employed is four hundred & fifty feet in length constructed of strong oak framed work. It was found impossible to complete the road to the rapids this season, on account of the time and labour required in throwing bridges over the larger streams—it was also deemed more essential to complete the bridges than to cut the road this season to the rapids as the road would be useless without the means of crossing the large streams.

The officers and soldiers who have been employed in this service deserve much credit for the zeal & perseverance they have displayed on the occasion. The work they have performed has proved highly beneficial both to the people of the country and to the government. Besides greatly adding to the defence and strength of this frontier, the road has been the means of developing the nighness of the publick lands in this territory and greatly augmenting their value.

As soon as Major [John] Anderson, topographical Engineer, can complete the survey of the road a more minute & particular discription [*sic*] of the work will be forwarded.

ALS in DNA, 1, M-166; CC in MiD; PC in *American State Papers: Miscellaneous,* 2:537; PC in House Document No. 87, 15th Cong., 2nd Sess.; PC in Carter, ed., *Territorial Papers,* 10:785.

From William Reed, [former Representative from Mass.,] Marblehead, [Mass.,] 10/2. Pleads apologetically that a discharge shall be granted to Jonathan P. Miller of Randolph, Vt., in order that Miller may study for the ministry. "I hope it will enter into the policy of the Executive & Congress at the ensuing Session, to add to both the Naval & Military establishments of our favoured Country, a liberal provision for the support of Chaplains." ALS in DNA, 11, 12572.

From D[ecius] Wadsworth, 11/2. As ordered by Calhoun's letter of 9/5, Wadsworth submits a quarterly report of the Ordnance Department's business; transmits papers "containing such information as it is conceived the spirit of your order requires." A return of ordnance and of ordnance stores is being prepared for submission in two or three days; it will "include all the stations from which returns have been received," but, to prevent it from becoming too voluminous, it will "omit the articles of minor inspection." FC in DNA, 32, 2:126–127.

To William H. Crawford, 11/3. As Acting Secretary of the Navy, Calhoun submits estimates of money needed for the Navy and Marine Corps during 1819. FC with Ens in DNA, 124.

From [Bvt. Col.] John R. Fenwick, Boston, 11/3. In accordance with a new regulation, of which he has just learned, he submits an estimate of clothing needed by the Regiment of Light Artillery; he asks that the Commissary General [of Purchases, Callender Irvine,] shall send the clothing as soon as possible. ALS in DNA, 11, 1124 (M-566:9).

To E[dmund] P. Gaines, Fort Hawkins, Ga., 11/3. Acknowledges his letter of 10/22 (LS with Ens in DNA, 1, G-18; LS in DNA, 11, 12215) reporting that Gaines believes the strength of the Seminoles to be greater than Calhoun does. Answers Gaines's letter of 10/20 (LS in DNA, 1, G-17; incomplete draft in DNA, 11, 12923) asking whether, for purposes of determining that a Bvt. Maj. Gen. in command of a Division is entitled to pay at his brevet rank, a Division is defined in terms of its territorial size or of the Army units of which it consists. Calhoun replies that two Brigades comprise a Division and should be commanded by a Maj. Gen. LS and CC in DNA, 11, 12923; FC in DNA, 3, 10:178.

To G[erard] Steddiford, New York [City], 11/3. Announces that President [James Monroe] has approved the proceedings of the court-martial for the trial of N.Y. militia delinquents during 5/4–7/18, which were sent to Calhoun on 10/28 (ALS in DNA, 1, J-23) by Lemuel Jenkins, special Judge Advocate of the court. Returns these proceedings. FC in DNA, 3, 10:177.

Pension certificate of James Dailey, 11/4. Calhoun certifies that Dailey, formerly a Pvt. "in the Army of the Revolution," is to be paid through the N.Y. pension agency $8 per month from 5/7/1818. DS in PPL.

From Thomas L. McKenney, 11/4. Acknowledges Calhoun's letter of 10/31 and states that the $12,200 Chickasaw annuity cannot be refunded to the Treasury so soon as Calhoun may wish. McKenney must await the receipt of funds from his sale of furs and peltries on 11/23. He adds that the goods sunk in the Ohio River were only "very partially" damaged. LS in DNA, 1, M-46.

To Archibald Thweatt, Chesterfield Courthouse, Va., 11/4. Pursuant to his letter of 10/21 (ALS in DNA, 11, 11937) to James Monroe, reminding Monroe of "our old acquaintance in difficult times" and recommending for an Army commission Richard H[ayes] Branch, a veteran of the Company of volunteers who marched from Petersburg, Va., to Canada and served under William Henry Harrison during the War of 1812, Calhoun explains that no Captaincy in the Army is vacant but that Branch will be appointed a 2nd Lt. if he wishes. FC in DNA, 3, 10:178. An AEU on the letter of 10/21 shows that Branch was "appointed."

From [James L. Edwards, *ca.* 11/5]. "Report of the state of the business in the Pension Bureau on the 31st of October, 1818, made in conformity with the order of the Secretary of War" of 9/5, "to be continued quarterly." Tabulates 20,247 applications received for pensions under six laws, of which 19,973 were from Revolutionary veterans under the statute of 3/18; reports that 4,295 applications had been approved, 3,539 had been denied, and 12,406 were pending. DU, with an AES by Edwards certifying his approval, in DNA, 2, E-1818.

From John Rodgers, 11/5. Acknowledges Calhoun's letter of 11/4; Rodgers will prepare promptly the necessary instructions [for the guidance of the three men who will be appointed to search the Gulf Coast in the Miss.–La. area for timbers suitable for Naval use]. Rodgers suggests salaries for the three men: $2,500 per year for [James Leander] Cathcart and $2,000 each per year for John Landreth and [James] Hutton. LS in DNA, 128, 6:115.

From William H. Crawford, 11/6. Answers a letter from Calhoun enclosing one from [Eleazer W.] Ripley suggesting that Paymasters of troops at Baton Rouge be compelled to keep their funds in one of the State banks there and not, as heretofore, in New Orleans. If the plan is to be adopted, Crawford wants to know how much to make available at Baton Rouge for use in 1819. ALS in DNA, 1, C-43.

To C[allender] Irvine, Philadelphia, 11/6. Encloses several letters revealing a complaint about Army shoes; asks for an investigation. Calhoun has reduced Irvine's estimate of the appropriation needed for clothing purchases in 1819 to $430,000; experience shows that the Army's manpower cannot be maintained at the maximum authorized strength and that clothing is perishable; Irvine's figures as to clothing in stock indicate that his estimated needs can be reduced about one-fourth, and he will contract for 1819 purchases accordingly. FC in DNA, 3, 10:179.

From Nathaniel Frye, Jr., Paymaster General's Office, 11/7. In answer to the questions of [William H. Crawford] of 11/6 to Calhoun, Frye answers that expenditures at Baton Rouge for 1819 will depend on the number of troops stationed there. The pay for a full Regiment of Infantry is $74,000.60 per year; a Company costs $7,400.67 per year. ALS in DNA, 1, F-17.

From Edmund P. Gaines

Fernandina, E[ast] F[la.], November 7th 1818

I arrived at this place on the 3rd Instant. The recruits of the 4th Infantry under [Bvt.] Major [John A.] Burd had landed but a few days before. They had suffered some injury from a want of room on board the transports: they are however generally in good health, and the state of their discipline proves that the Officers have been attentive to their duty.

Reports here state that no Indians have been for three months past, near the frontier settlements on St. Marys river. The report of six men having been killed near this river in September last, must have originated from an affair which took place on the Alochaway path, some time before, in which six white men fell, and among them a Mr. Bullock, brother of the Post-Master at Fort Hawkins. The Post-Master, it appears received an account of the affair, not untill the 20th of September, without any mention of the date of the occurrence; he therefore believed it to have been very recent.

A Mr. Clarke, an inhabitant of Florida near the river St. Johns, who arrived at this place yesterday, direct from St. Augustine, informs me that there are many small parties of Indians and blacks, daily passing to and from the town; but he discovered among them no positive evidence of hostility or preparation for war. Mr. Clarke's statements correspond with information received by the commanding Officer here, from other persons lately from St. Augustine.

Having learned, previous to my departure from Fort Hawkins, that the Seminole Indians were deterred from going into the upper part of the nation, from Fort Gadsden, by the threats of some of the friendly Chiefs, that they would take their property and make slaves of them, I gave the order of which I enclose a copy, with a view that it should be communicated to such as might be disposed to surrender.

The last reports received from the commandants of Pensacola and St. Mark's, dated the 2d and 7th of last month are silent upon the subject of the return to those posts of the Spanish authorities.

LS in DNA, 1, G-16; LS in DNA, 11, 12560.

From DAVID A. OGDEN, [Representative from N.Y.]

New York [City,] Nov[embe]r 7th 1818

Upon my arrival at this place I was astonished to find that Hyde (the School Master,) had procured a copy of the Letter you addressed to me, on the subject of giving to the Six Nations of Indians a seat to the Westward, and had published the same in the News Papers.

I did not attend the Council held by these Indians in Sept[embe]r last, but with the view of Removing the False Impressions made on their Minds, as to the Unhealthiness of the Climate on the Arkansaw [*sic*] River, I transmitted to Mr. [Jasper] Par[r]ish, the Sub-Agent of the U[nited] States, a Copy of your Letter. He has since Informed me that he Read this Letter to the Indians assembled in Council, and that Hyde being Informed of its contents, had Insisted it was a Forgery. Mr. Par[r]ish further stated that the Indians afterwards requested the Letter, and that he gave it to them, that they might procure some Indifferent Person to Read and explain it, and that whilst in their Hands, Hyde availed himself of the opportunity of Copying it.

I have thought it proper to give this explanation, by way of Apology for the Undue & unexpected Use which has been made of your communication to me. I am some what perplexed as to the course I ought to pursue with respect to Hyde. He is so Insignificant, that I dislike prosecuting him; at the same time I can scarcely reconcile it to my feelings to suffer the Fellow to Interfere with my Interests and the views of the Government.

ALS in DNA, 1, 0-2.

To Commodore John Shaw, u.s.n., "Present"

Navy Department, November 7th, 1818

Proceed to St. Marys, (Georgia) and there await the further orders of this Department.

LS in DLC, Naval History Foundation Collections, Shaw Collection, no. 14.

From Lewis Toncray, Jailor, Abingdon, Va., 11/7. Last July two men, James Lawless and Hiram Adkins, were committed to Toncray's care as being deserters from Capt. James McGavock's recruiting unit in Lynchburg. McGavock has moved on to Petersburg, Norfolk, and Amelia Island, before Toncray could employ "a trusty man" to return the prisoners to McGavock. Therefore, Toncray asks Calhoun for instructions as to the prisoners, who "are much in need of clothing and blanketts [*sic*]." ALS in DNA, 11, 11800.

From Decius Wadsworth, 11/7. He has examined the monthly returns of Maj. [Abram R.] Woolley at Pittsburgh; it appears to Wadsworth that the wages paid are not justified by the amount of work completed. "There is strong Reason to believe the public Interest suffers much at that Establishment, either through Negligence or Mismanagement." ALS in DNA, 1, W-46; FC in DNA, 32, 2:128–129.

To Col. John E[wing] Colhoun, Pendleton, S.C.

War Dept., 8th Nov. 1818

I have received your letter of the 15th Oct[obe]r; and on examination I find that there was due from the U[nited] States to Ashabel James at the time of his death $167.37. If you can pay that amount to his administrator or heir at law on my account and take a receit [*sic*] in the usual form in my name which you will transmit to me, I can draw the money at the treasury without further voucher. If it should be convenient to you, you can debit me with the sum paid; but if not, by calling on my brother William, he will pay you the amount. The hazards of remittance will thus be avoided. His heirs can obtain a patent for his land bounty, by obtaining a certificate from the Ordinary of their being his heirs. The Ordinary knows the forms I expect. They will state in the letter where they wish the land to be located; and to whom they wish the patent to be transmitted.

I regret to hear that your crop has again failed on Cooper river. You have really been unfortunate there. You had a fair prospect I understand in the spring.

Your sister [Floride Colhoun (Mrs. John C.) Calhoun] has been dangerously ill; but is now quite recovered. She had the misfortune to miscarry. The children [Andrew Pickens Calhoun and Anna Maria Calhoun] are both well, and Andrew often speaks of you.

I hope you will be successful in your collection in the lower country. I have bought a house here and am in great need of money. If you make my collection I hope you will transmit [it] to me without delay. You can obtain a bill on N[ew] York Philadelphia Baltimore this place or Richmond.

[P.S.] Your sister joins her love to you and her mother, if she has not left Pendleton. My respects to the Gov[erno]r [Andrew Pickens, Jr.].

ALS in ScCleA.

General Order by [2nd] Lt. George Blaney, Engineer Department, by order of the Secretary of War, 11/9. The resignation of Cadet George K. Gibbs is accepted, as of 11/15. FC in DNA, 18, 1:8.

To Jacob Brown, Brownville, N.Y., 11/9. Answers his letter of 11/1 (LS in DNA, 1, B-44; FC in DLC, Jacob Brown Papers, Letterbooks, 2:124–125), in which Brown agrees heartily with Calhoun's objective as to garrisoning new posts in the Northwest but disapproves Calhoun's designation of the 3rd Infantry Regiment as the one for the task. Calhoun replies, "I merely suggested that Reg[imen]t for your consideration," and gives assurance that he has no desire to dictate the means by which Brown will execute orders. LS in MHi; FC in DNA, 3, 10:180; CC in DLC, Jacob Brown Papers, Letterbooks, 2:127.

To Maj. Gen. John Floyd, St. Marys, Ga., 11/9. As Acting Secretary of the Navy, Calhoun acnowledges his letter of 10/22 and states that a court of inquiry will be created to investigate soon Lt. James B. Taylor, U.S.N. FC in DNA, 122, 13:237.

A[quil]a Giles, New York [City], to J[oseph] G. Swift, 11/9. "You had the goodness to say that you would get my son George [Washington Giles] reappointed as a Cadet. I must entreat you to pay attention to this subject, as soon as you conveniently can, as I am anxious to get him located at the Point, before the cold weather sets in. You will oblige me by mentioning to the President [James Monroe], that my Finances will not admit of sending George to College again." ALS in DNA, 15, 1818, 184.

From [Dr.] Henry Huntt

Washington, Nov[embe]r 9th 1818

The regulations under which I have been doing duty for some time, only provide, for my attendance at the Garrison, Greenleafs Point. I have also to attend a detachment of eight or ten men in the City, and all the officers on duty here amounting to nearly twenty, besides others who occasionally require medical attendance while visiting this place. I am willing to attend this duty, not embraced in the regulations, for a reasonable compensation, which I estimate at three hundred & sixty dollars, excluding attendance on the Indians, who may visit this place.

ALS in DNA, 11, 12348. Note: A postscript to this letter dated 11/17 is signed by Surgeon General Joseph Lovell and states: "Dr. Huntt agrees to attend the post at Greenleafs Point & all officers & others entitled to attendance & medicines from the United States Army Surgeon at $40 per month. The United States to furnish medicines &c. for the Post & he to supply medicines to all others."

To Maj. Milo Mason, Deputy Quartermaster General, Nashville, 11/9. Answering his letter of 10/24 (ALS in DNA, 1, M-50), informs him that [David B.] Mitchell has been directed to pay for the 5,000 rations of flour that Mason furnished last June to the distressed survivors of the Chehaw tribe and that Lt. [Christopher] Keiser is being ordered to furnish for Mason's information a copy of the [abstracts of his vouchers submitted to Peter Hagner and

William Lee for settlement of Keiser's accounts]. FC in DNA, 3, 10:180.

To David B. Mitchell, 11/9. Maj. [Milo] Mason has deposited 5,000 rations of flour and corn meal at the Creek Agency for the relief of the distressed survivors of the attack upon the Chehaw village; Mitchell is to pay for these rations from the fund for the relief of those Indians. FC in DNA, 72, D:227.

From D[aniel] Parker, 11/9. Reports that the 8th Military Department now has assigned to it the 1st and 8th Infantry Regiments and the 3rd and 4th Battalions of Artillery; that these units should have, if they were at full strength, 2,632 men, including officers; and that, judging from "the number of officers on the recruiting service & the success now attending their exertions," these units, "now very much reduced, may be nearly filled by next summer." LS in DNA, 1, P-36; FC in DNA, 12, 5:125.

To Lt. James B. Taylor, U.S.N., St. Marys, Ga., 11/9. Encloses a copy of charges against him that were received recently from Maj. Gen. John Floyd of Ga.; informs Taylor that a court of enquiry has been ordered to convene at St. Marys as soon as practicable, with Capt. John Shaw, U.S.N., as its President; orders Taylor to report to Shaw "immediately upon his arrival" at St. Marys. FC in DNA, 121, 13:285.

From Decius Wadsworth, 11/9. The claim against the [Bellona] Arsenal at Richmond of $520 for slating has been paid and receipted by Capt. [Jeremiah D.] Hayden. There are no funds to cover such expenses at arsenals this year, and Wadsworth suggests transferring funds accumulated from the sale of land at Pittsburgh for that purpose until funds can be appropriated by Congress. ALS in DNA, 1, W-45; FC in DNA, 32, 2:129.

From James Leander Cathcart, Washington, 11/10. Writes to Calhoun as Acting Secretary of the Navy, [quite possibly after a personal conference]. Estimates that Cathcart's proposed search for Naval timbers [in the Gulf Coast area] will certainly require more than one season. Enumerates five needs of the proposed expedition for maps, funds, medicines, arms, personnel, and transportation. ALS in DNA, 128, 6:118; CC in DNA, 85, Appendix, p. 1 (M-8:1).

To W[illiam H.] Crawford, 11/10. "In reply to your letter of the 6th instant, I have to state that the probable expenditure at Baton Rouge during the year 1819 will be about $100,000. The [War] Department will be equally benefited whether the disbursing officers make deposits in the Bank at Baton Rouge or the United States Bank make[s] arrangements for transporting the funds to that place free of Exchange. Will you notify this Department of the Course the Bank adopts[?]" FC in DNA, 171, 1:318.

To Edmund P. Gaines, Fort Hawkins or Amelia Island, 11/10. It has been decided that [Camillus] Griffith is obligated by his contract to supply rations to all posts adjacent to the Gulf of Mexico, to St. Marks, and to Fort Gadsden; at the last two places, [Benjamin G.] Orr's agents will receive requisitions upon Griffith. LS in DNA, 11, 12123; FC in DNA, 3, 10:181.

From R[ichard] Graham and Joseph Philips, St. Louis, 11/10. They relate what advice and instructions they have received from Governor [Ninian] Edwards of Ill. concerning the task of surveying Indian boundary lines in that State under a treaty of 8/1816, explain why they are reluctantly proceeding to attempt the work during the winter season, and estimate that total costs may reach $15,000. LS in DNA, 1, G-53; PC in Carter, ed., *Territorial Papers,* 17:610–611.

From THOMAS S. JESUP

City of New York, Nov[embe]r 10th 1818

I have this moment arrived from Boston. I examined the accounts of Capt. [Archibald W.] Hamilton & Lieut[enant Samuel] Washburn, and found the outstanding debts of the [Quartermaster ?] Department to amount nearly to fifteen thousand dollars. There appears to have been as little system in that [2nd Military ?] Department as in any other.

I have to request that the sum of ten thousand and ten dollars be transmitted to Lieutenant Sam[ue]l Washburn[,] Quarter Master of the Reg[imen]t of Light Artillery at Boston, to enable him to close his accounts, and that he be order[ed] to ["proceed to" *interlined*] Washington, to settle them, before the end of the present month.

I hope to reach Washington by Sunday next.

ALS in DNA, 1, J-16; FC in DNA, 42, 1:105.

From Wilson Lumpkin, Madison, [Ga.,] 11/10. He has completed his survey of the upper boundary under the treaty of 1/22/1818 with the Creek Indians. He will forward the report when the survey of the southern line is completed. He acknowledges Calhoun's letter of 10/3 and agrees "that the only line necessary to be run out in the lower cession, is the line run[n]ing the nearest and most direct course, by the head of a Creek called by the Indians Alcasilukie to the Oakmulgee [*sic*] River." "I not only deem it impracticable on account of Indian hostility, to run out the line between the U[nited] States & Florida, this fall: But, should the winter be as wet as usual in that section of the Country, the local situation of the Country would greatly retard the progress, if not utterly prevent the business from being performed." ALS in DNA, 1, L-24.

To Capt. Alexander S. Wadsworth, U.S.N., U.S.S. *John Adams,* New York [City]

Navy Department, Nov. 10, 1818

Your letter[s] of the 29th Ult[im]o and of the 1st instant were duly received. The Lieutenants whom you have designated are all ordered. The particular Service for which the Ship under your command is intended will require a Marine Officer, and one is accordingly directed to report to you. You will please to engage for the Service such persons to act as Gunner, Carpenter, &c. as may appear to you to be properly qualified, with an assurance that Warrants will be granted to them on their return, if their conduct & qualifications shall prove satisfactory.

FC in DNA, 121, 13:285.

Pension certificate of William Allen, 11/11. Calhoun certifies that Allen, who served as a Pvt. during the Revolution, is to receive through the S.C. pension agency $8 per month from 11/11. Copy owned in 1960 by Harvey S. Teal, West Columbia, S.C.

From Callender Irvine

Philad[elphi]a, Novem[be]r 11th 1818

It frequently happens that Clothing which has been issued for the Recruiting Service, after it has been tossed about, and sometimes much abused and defaced, perhaps in consequence of inattention to it on the part of the Officers, is turned over to a Military Storekeeper or Assistant Commissary, often too unaccompanied by letter, Statement or Invoice; and if such Clothing should be offered to an Officer of the same Regiment from which it has been received, it would be rejected, or if received its condition would be made the foundation of complaint against this Department. Clothing of the above description accumulates annually to a considerable amount, & it has to be sold at a heavy loss to the public. The cause of the evil is, that too much clothing is drawn by officers on the Recruiting Service at a time. It is done no doubt with an expectation that men will be readily recruited, but when disappointed in obtaining recruits, the clothing becomes an encumbrance, and from the circumstance of not having convenient & safe storehouses, it receives damage. The only remedy for the evil which presents itself to my mind is, that all surplus clothing drawn for the recruiting service shall be turned over to the respective Regiments, and that recruiting officers shall be held responsible for its safe keeping.

ALS in DNA, 11, 12356; FC in DNA, 45, 387:194.

Chiefs and Warriors of the Oneida Indians, Oneida Castle, to [James Monroe], 11/11. These Oneidas (33 of them) feel that they have made notable advances towards civilization where they now reside and see their proposed removal as a threat to their continued progress. They have agreed to relinquish their lands whenever they may emigrate but have not agreed to any specific date for their removal. They "entreat that you will not permit any steps to be taken for our immediate removal without our full and explicit assent to that effect. And also that no persons be authorized to disturb the peace & tranquility of your children by importuning us on that subject." LS (signed with their marks) in DNA, 1, O-18.

Gabriel E. DeSaussure to B[enjamin] W. Crowninshield

Columbia, So[uth] Ca[rolina,] Nov[embe]r 12th 1818

I hope you will excuse the liberty I take in thus addressing you, for I am anxious to be informed on the following subject.

I rec[eive]d a warrant as a Midshipman in the United States Navy on the 30th Jan[uar]y 1818. But from ill health, produced from the rupture of a Blood vessel, I was against my inclination forced to decline the acceptation of it. But having now completely regained my health[,] I am still very desirous of entering the Navy of my Country, & I wish to know if it is too late now to accept of it. I have still the warrant in my possession. A line or two from you as soon as convenient on this subject, will greatly oblige, Sir, your most obed[ien]t, Humble Serv[an]t, Gabriel E. DeSaussure.

ALS in DNA, 134.

From George Huntington, Wheeler Barnes, Benjamin Wright, James Lynch, William Wright, Joel Hayes, and one other person, Rome (Oneida County), N.Y., 11/12. Responding to a public invitation encouraging citizens to write to Calhoun about roads that should be built or maintained for their military value, these men argue the importance of keeping in repair the 65-mile-long road from Rome to Sackets Harbor. LS in DNA, 1, H-31.

Armistead T[homson] Mason, [former Senator from Va.,] "Selma," to James Monroe, 11/12. Persuasively recommends Maj. [Samuel] Miller for appointment as the Commandant of the Marine Corps. ALS in DNA, 128, 6:120.

To Josiah Meigs, Commissioner, General Land Office, 11/12. As Acting Secretary of the Navy, Calhoun asks Meigs to direct the Surveyor General "of the Southern section of the Union," [Thomas Freeman at St. Stephens, Miss.,] to give all possible information and assistance to James Leander Cathcart and James Hutton in their effort [to reserve public lands near the Gulf Coast that will supply Naval timbers]. FC in DNA, 122, 13:239; CC (not dated) in DNA, 85, Appendix, pp. 1–2 (M-8:1).

From C[aesar] A[ugustus] Rodney, [former Representative from Del.,] 11/12. Introduces the bearer, Navy Capt. [James] Renshaw, who "wishes some appointment on Lake Erie" and whom Rodney has known since his infancy. ALS in DNA, 128, 6:122.

To Henry Sherburne, 11/12. Acknowledges his letter of 10/24; "it affords me much pleasure to learn that the treaty with the Chickasaws has been successful." The bills sent by Sherburne will be paid, and $300 are being sent to him for Agency expenses. FC in DNA, 72, D:227.

From Decius Wadsworth, 11/12. Gen. [Joseph G.] Swift has told Wadsworth that the Ordnance Department is to pay for 165 swords and belts for the Cadets at the Military Academy. If Calhoun approves, Wadsworth requests that $1,980 be advanced to Swift for this purpose. FC in DNA, 32, 2:131.

To James L[eander] Cathcart, Esq., "Present," 11/13. As Acting Secretary of the Navy, Calhoun appoints him an Agent for examining such vacant and unappropriated lands of the U.S. as produce live oak and red cedar timbers suitable for Naval use, under a law enacted on 3/1/1817; directs him to go to New Orleans and gives him instructions. CC in DNA, 201, 15A-F4.

To Lt. Commandant Alexander Claxton, U.S.N., Norfolk, 11/13. Orders him to convey aboard the U.S. Schooner *Nonsuch* to New Orleans three men—James L[eander] Cathcart, John Landreth, and Dr. Elnathan Judson—and there to perform such service as Commodore Daniel T. Patterson, U.S.N., may assign to Claxton. FC in DNA, 121, 13:286.

To [William H. Crawford], 11/13. "Be pleased to issue your warrant in favour of the Treasurer of the United States" for the following sums from the following accounts: pay of the Army, $219,000; subsistence, $300,000; clothing, $250,000; ordnance, $80,-000; arsenal at Baton Rouge, $15,000; arsenal at Detroit, $10,000; arsenal at Watervliet, $10,000; arsenal at Pittsburgh, $5,000; armories, $150,000; Quartermaster Department, $100,000. (The total shown at the bottom of an itemized column is $1,139,000, which is correct; but the total requested in words in the body of the letter is $739,000.) FC in DNA, 171, 1:318.

Pension certificate of Jared Dixon, 11/13. Calhoun certifies that Dixon, a Pvt. in Revolutionary service, has been granted a pension of $8 per month, payable in Vt. from 4/21. DS in DNA, 204, 17A-F15.1.

From Bvt. Maj. Arch[ibal]d Henderson, Commandant of the U.S. Marine Corps, Washington, 11/13. "Your order of the 11th Inst[ant] places the whole Marine Corps, with the single exception of the Command at Head quarters, under the Rules and Regulations for the Government of the Navy." The estimate for the Marines' rations should be raised, therefore, from $.20 to $.25 [per man per day]. ALS in DNA, 128, 7:2.

From Callender Irvine, Philadelphia, 11/13. Points out that the "compensation of some of the Military Storekeepers has been considerably reduced in consequence of the abolition of the additional appointments of Assistant Barrackmasters" that were given to some for the purpose "of giving them reasonable allowances for their services"; that the flat salary of $840 annually established by Congress is adequate compensation for those Military Storekeepers whose duties are lightest but quite unjust to those who have heavier responsibilities; and that the Military Storekeepers near Philadelphia and at Boston receive too little. ALS in DNA, 1, I-21; FC in DNA, 45, 387:199.

To Andrew Jackson, Nashville, 11/13. Col. John McKee has been directed to make the payment to the Choctaws; Maj. [John B. ?] Hogan, whose duties "are already laborious," can be relieved of that task. Calhoun expresses satisfaction that, by the Choctaw treaty [of 10/19], "a cession has been obtained, upon terms so favourable." LS in DLC, Andrew Jackson Papers, 8281; FC in DNA, 72, D:227–228; PC in Carter, ed., *Territorial Papers,* 18:466.

From Joseph McMinn, Cherokee Agency, 11/13. Acknowledges Calhoun's letters of 9/10 and 10/13. Discusses adjustments made in McMinn's accounts with [Return J.] Meigs, as Calhoun authorized, and drafts issued by McMinn totaling more than $20,000 to obtain cash with which to make payments to Cherokees for their improvements and to pay other necessary expenses. "Altho I only intended this letter to exemplify in some degree the causes which led to these late demands on the Treasury, I will nevertheless state that the most numerous and respectable council that has been assembled for many years in this nation is now sitting, with the King at their head, and on yesterday I occupied their attention by reading sundry extracts from your letters, the object of which was to exhibit the powers with which I am vested, as well as to shew that you had approved of the measures I had adopted and in conclusion read the new plan for carrying the treaty into effect, which had been previously copied except the clause which you added fixing the sum to be given on the part of the U[nited] States—which will be kept entirely out of view untill they agree to enter into the arrangement. What its fate will be God only knows. At present it excites great interest on both sides, and is warmly supported, by our friends [John] Walker, [Richard] Taylor, and Adair, who are amongst the most Prominent Chiefs in the Nation." A postscript reads: "So soon as the result is known I will give you the earliest information." Draft in DNA, 75 (M-208:14); PEx in *American State Papers: Indian Affairs,* 2:481.

To Commodore D[ANIEL] T. PATTERSON, U.S.N., Commanding Naval Officer, New Orleans

Navy Department, Nov. 13th 1818

James Leander Cathcart and James Hutton, Esquires, together with John Landreth, Esq[uir]e, Surveyor, have been appointed by the President of the United States [James Monroe], to carry into effect the objects contemplated by the Act of Congress, passed on the 1st day of March 1817, entitled, an "Act making reservation of certain public lands to supply timber for Naval purposes," and you are required to afford to these Gentlemen every facility in your power, to enable them to discharge the important duties assigned to them by the Government. They proceed from Norfolk in the U.S. Schooner Nonsuch, Lieu[tenan]t Comm[an]d[an]t Alexander Claxton, who, with the Vessel under his command, will be subject to your orders, and employed in such manner as the Service on the Station shall require. In the Spring, when the said Agents and Surveyor shall desire to return, you will have them conveyed in a Public Vessel to some port in the Chesapeake.

FC in DNA, 121, 13:287.

Pension Certificate of Amos Pearson, 11/13. Certifies that Amos Pearson, "late an Ensign in the Army of the Revolution," is to receive in Mass. a pension of $20 per month from 3/30/1818. DS in ScU-SC, John C. Calhoun Papers.

From Dr. Joseph P. Russell, Michilimackinac, [Mich. Territory,] 11/13. He has received today his appointment as a Post Surgeon but cannot report promptly, as ordered, to [Andrew] Jackson in Nashville because there is no one to relieve him where he has been stationed by [Alexander] Macomb. "The last vessels for the season have arrived from Detroit, and as I cannot be relieved until the opening of the navigation in the spring, if then relieved I shall obey the order with alacrity." ALS in DNA, 11, 12743.

To Commodore John Shaw, U.S.N., "Present," 11/13. Orders him to convene a court of enquiry upon his arrival at St. Marys, Ga., with himself as President; with Capt. Charles Morris and Lt. John Porter as members; and with Robert Kearney as Judge Advocate. This court is to consider the charges preferred by John Floyd against Lt. James [B.] Taylor and others; it is to report facts relevant to the complaint and its opinion, in order that "such ulterior measures, may be adopted as justice & the nature of the case shall appear to require." FC in DNA, 121, 13:286–287. A similar letter from Calhoun to Shaw dated 11/9 appointed Master Commandant William Carter, Jr., U.S.N., to serve as a member of the court; but on 11/10 a request was made to Shaw by B[enjamin] H[omans] that the letter of 11/9 should be returned, in order that Morris might be assigned to this duty in lieu of Carter. FC's in DNA, 121, 13:284–285; Calhoun's LS of 11/9 is in DNA, 133 (M-125:60). Homans' request of 11/10 was answered by Shaw from Baltimore on 11/14, the eve of Shaw's scheduled sailing for Charleston, S.C. ALS in DNA, 133 (M-125:60).

From Lt. Col. W[ILLIAM] A. TRIMBLE

Lexington, Kentucky, 13th Nov[embe]r 1818

I received, to day on my return to this place, your communication of the 16 ultimo.

Notwithstanding, it would have given me great pleasure, to have exerted my feeble powers, to perform a service which I have concieved [*sic*] to be of much importance; yet I most cheerfully acquiesce in the decision of the President [James Monroe]; because I am satisfied, that it has been the result of a clear & comprehensive view of our foreign relations, in regard to the peculiar situation of the country between the Red River & Rio del Norte.

If at any time, in the opinion of the President, it should be deemed expedient to adopt the measure proposed, it would be gratifying to me to be employed on such a service. In the mean time, I will avail myself of every available source of information, to which I can have access, & loose [*sic*] no time in communicating the result.

I will report my opinion on the best mode of protecting the Indians, on the south western frontier, from the encroachments & depredations of the white people, as soon as I can obtain my papers, which, with part of my baggage, were sent by water, & have not yet been received.

The Ohio River is very low. Steam Boats cannot pass. If the dry weather continues I will set out by land for New Orleans.

ALS in DNA, 1, T-26.

From Decius Wadsworth, 11/13. Expresses his belief that there "can be no great difficulty" in enforcing a rigid system of accountability to the Treasury Department for all articles of Army property that are in the arsenals, storehouses, and magazines. But he believes that the Treasury's concern should cease when the stores have been issued for actual use and that an entirely different system of control by the Army should then begin to prevent waste or loss. "Every person connected with the Army, has more, or less, to do with public property, in some shape or other." It "is totally impossible to trace distinctly the various articles, to their ultimate destination, and Consumption." To demand a receipt from each receiver of public property would produce so prodigious an accumulation of Accounts "as to defeat the End in View." Wadsworth approves the possibility that Artillery, and even Infantry and other, officers might be designated as Conductors of Stores; and he explains how such officers might be held accountable for the public property they would handle. If subaltern officers were paid $10 per month for assuming the extra duties of Conductor of Stores, this compensation would operate as a stimulus and reward to men "whose Pay is now hardly adequate to their decent, and comfortable support"; and yet the additional expense "would be quite trifling." LS in DNA, 1, W-37; FC in DNA, 32, 2:133–136.

To James A. Buchanan, President, Baltimore Branch of the Bank of the United States, 11/14. Answering his request of 11/12 (LS in DNA, 1, B-42; FC in DNA, 142, p. 21) for a list of Marylanders added since 9/4 to the Revolutionary pension rolls, so that he can answer "daily and importunate demands," Calhoun says that the Pension Office "is so pressed with business" that such lists can be prepared only twice a year. Calhoun hopes that newspaper announcements that pensions will be paid only twice a year will forestall applications for payments before the semiannual dates arrive. FC in DNA, 3, 10:181.

From four Chickasaw Indian Chiefs (Chinnumbee Mingo, Levi Colbert, George Pettygrove, and Samuel Seeley), Chickasaw Agency, 11/14. Having been assured by Commissioners [Isaac] Shelby and [Andrew] Jackson, with whom the Chickasaws "made a Treaty for the Sale of Land last Month," that all of the Chickasaws' remaining land is free from rival claims by any State or individual and is "to be enjoyed by them forever, to hunt upon or cultivate as they see fit," these Chiefs respectfully ask that all of this land "may be Guaranteed unto them by Congress or in such other way as may be proper so as to secure the Nation all the rights & advantages they are Intitled [*sic*] to in Virtue of the promise made by the said Commissioners." LS (signed with their marks) in DNA, 1, C-79.

W[illiam] Eustis, Washington, to Maj. [Samuel] Miller, U.S. Marine Corps, 11/14. Eustis certifies that Miller is well qualified to command the Marine Corps. ALS in DNA, 128, 7:4.

From [Bvt. Maj.] Samuel Miller, U.S.M.C., Washington, 11/14. "Some indispensible [*sic*] private concerns requiring my attention, I will ask the indulgence of a continuation of my present leave of absence for a few weeks." ALS in DNA, 128, 7:3.

J[oseph] G. Swift to W[illiam] H. Crawford, "Private"

Baltimore, 14th Nov. 1818

On my arrival in this place I find that my Kinsman Mr. William R. Swift, a Merchant, can have sent to him from the Island of Jamaica from 300 to 500,000 Dollars *in specie*, provided he could have a safe conveyance. He has asked me if any of our Public Brigs or Schooners of War could transport this cash. I am unable to give him any reply. Recollecting the conversation which I had with you yesterday in relation to the failures of our principal Merchants, & believing as I do that this evil is in a great degree attributable to our Indian trade & the consequent drain which the commercial cities have sustained, it has occurred to me that it would be proper to mention the subject to you, as possibly some advantage might thereby derive to the community. I learn that from 1 to 2 Millions may be brought into the U.S. by the above mentioned aid. A line from you on this subject, whether proper to be pursued or not, will find me in New York.

ALS in DNA, 128, 7:5. Note: An AEI by Crawford referred this letter to the Navy Department.

[Andrew] Jackson to [James] Monroe, 11/15. Jackson answers Monroe's letter of 10/20, "from an attentive perusal of which, I have concluded that you have not yet seen my despatches from Fort Gadsden, of the 5th of May last, which it is reported reached the Department of War by due course of mail, and owing to the negligence of the Clerks was thrown aside as a bundle of Revolutionary and pension claims. This I sincerely regret, as it would have brought to your view the light in which I viewed my orders" and would "make manifest the difference of opinion that exists. Indeed, there are no data at present upon which such a letter as you wish written to the Secretary of War can be bottomed. I have no ground that a difference of opinion exists between the Government and myself, relative to the powers given me in my orders, unless I advert either to your private and confidential letters, or the public prints, neither of which can be made the basis of an official communication to the Secretary of War. Had I ever, or were I now to receive an official letter from the Secretary of War, explanatory of the light in which it was intended by the Government that my orders should be viewed, I would with pleasure give my understanding of them." PEx in *Correspondence between Gen. Andrew Jackson and John C. Calhoun . . . on the Occurrences in the Seminole War,* p. 42.

To Thomas S. Jesup, 11/15. "You will cause to be issued at New Orleans to James L[eander] Cathcart, John [*sic*; actually James] Hutton & John Land[reth] or either of them, such Tents, Tent poles, and Camp Kettles, as they or either of them may require, holding them responsible for the preservation & return of the same to the proper officer of [the] U[nited] States at New Orleans." FC in DNA, 3, 10:181–182.

From James Leander Cathcart, Washington, 11/16. Requests that $500 be deducted from his salary quarterly during his absence and paid to John Woodside of the Treasury Department for the use of Mrs. Cathcart. ALS in DNA, 128, 7:7.

From Nat[haniel] Cutting, Section of Bounty Lands, War Department, 11/16. Reports the claims filed and the claims approved since the close of the last session of Congress on 4/20. ALS in DNA, 1, C-36.

From Nathaniel Frye, Jr., [Clerk, Paymaster General's Office,] 11/16. As ordered on 9/5, Frye submits a "view of the affairs of the Pay Department." ALS with 21 Ens in DNA, 2, B-1818.

To the Rev. A[RD] HOYT, [Brainerd, Cherokee Nation]

Department of War, November 16th 1820

Your letter of the 1st ultimo containing a report of the state of the missionary establishment in the Cherokee Nation of which you are the Superintendent has been received.

The report is very satisfactory, and upon a view of the whole ground, as therein presented, I have agreed to pay the expense of erecting the new building at Brainerd for a female school, provided it does not exceed $1,000, and the Agent [Return J. Meigs] has been so informed.

LS in DNA, 71 (M-234:772, frame 256); FC in DNA, 72, E:31.

From Callender Irvine, Philadelphia, 11/16. "I will thank you to cause a Statement to be furnished me which will exhibit the several Military Posts & Cantonments and their positions to the Southward & Westward of Charleston, S.C., and Saint Louis, designating also the nearest Post Office & the most eligible route of transmitting supplies to each Post & Cantonment. This information is indispensibly necessary for me. Without it, I cannot determine at all times correctly from what depot supplies should be drawn, & with the information much expence & time may be saved in the forwarding [of] supplies to some of these Posts & Cantonments." ALS in DNA, 11, 13518; FC in DNA, 45, 387:543.

To ANDREW JACKSON, Nashville

Department of War, 16th Nov. 1818

Under the late treaty with the Quapaws and Osages, very extensive tracts of land have been acquired, a considerable portion of which is not intended to be brought immediately into the market, and which may hereafter become the means of exchanging for lands held by the Southern Indians on this side of the Mississippi.

The President [James Monroe] has directed me to issue orders to prevent the extension of the settlements on the Red river above the Northern boundary line of the state of Louisiana, and on the Arkansaw above the point where the Eastern boundary line of the tract assigned to the Cherokees of the Arkansaw intersects that line;

and that no settlements be permitted to be formed West of a line drawn from the points on Red river and Arkansaw already mentioned. Those persons settled to the West of the line specified, or at points higher up the Red river & the Arkansaw than those mentioned, will be removed.

You will give the necessary orders to carry the views of the President into effect. It will be advisable to take the necessary measures at an early period, so as to give to such families as may be removed an opportunity to make arrangements for planting next Spring.

FC in DNA, 72, D:228.

From Surgeon General Joseph Lovell, 11/16. As ordered by Calhoun, Lovell discusses at length possible changes in the component parts of the ration. He views the matter medically, in terms of the health of the soldiers, and recommends several improvements. He questions the continuance of whisky in the ration; recognizes the value of flexibility in respect to alternative components like beef or pork; discusses sanitary means of preserving such foods as flour; and indicates his approval of having the soldiers grow some of their own vegetables near their respective posts. In his final paragraph he considers such questions from a viewpoint beyond that of the regular Army alone: "If from these considerations it should appear that the health of the Army requires alterations in the ration, they will be of still greater weight when we remember that from the nature of our public institutions the greater part of our force in actual service does, and will for many years, consist of Militia; of men who must necessarily in all cases be suddenly taken from their customary habits and comforts and exposed to all the hardships and privations of the soldier, without any of his advantages; the effects of this have been too lately and too severely felt to be soon forgotten. And it is suggested whether this circumstance be not of sufficient importance to have a very considerable influence in deciding not only the nature of the ration, but of all those supplies upon which militia when on duty are equally as dependant [*sic*] as the regular soldiers; and as every able bodied citizen is liable at a moment[']s warning to feel the necessity of having these supplies as good as practicable, he will have less objection to furnish his portion of any additional expense that may be necessary to insure their provision." LS in DNA, 201, 15A-F3; FC in DNA, 243, 1:12–25; PC in House Document No. 36, 15th Cong., 2nd Sess.; PC in *American State Papers: Military Affairs,* 1:804–807. (Evidence of the fact that this report influenced directly the content of Calhoun's report to the House of Representatives dated 12/11, addressed to Speaker Henry Clay, can be seen therein within this volume.)

From John Rodgers, Office of the Commissioners of the Navy, 11/16. Encloses an estimate of his Office's expenses during 1819; explains his need for three more Clerks and for one draftsman. LS with En in DNA, 128, 7:9.

From D[ecius] Wadsworth, 11/16. Answers the complaint made in John H. Hall's letter of 11/12 to Calhoun that Wadsworth has treated Hall's patented firearms "with coldness and neglect." About two years ago Wadsworth contracted with Hall for 100 rifles at Hall's offered price of $25 each, in order that a Company of the Rifle Regiment might "ascertain their Merits by Experiment in Actual Service." A 12-month test is now in progress in the Missouri Expedition, and a report at the end of the year has been ordered. The arms more recently produced with extraordinary care under Hall's inspection at Harpers Ferry have cost almost $200 each. Hall's demand that they be tested, and particularly his suggestion that they be fired 25,000 times, are unreasonable; such experiments "can hardly lead to any practical result, because we can never afford to introduce such [expensive] Arms into the Service." Even if all other considerations were favorable, Wadsworth questions whether it is wise to equip only certain Army units, instead of all, with distinctive arms, whether "the facility of firing will not occasion an extravagant rise and waste of Ammunition," and whether enough transportation could be supplied to provide sufficient ammunition for practical service. FC in DNA, 32, 2:132–133.

From [John Quincy Adams], 11/17. "The Secretary of State presents his compliments to the Secretary of War and begs the loan from his office of the original of the proceedings of the Court Martial at Fort St. Marks in the cases of [Alexander] Arbuthnott [*sic*] and [Robert C.] Ambrister, and of the certificates received last week from General [Andrew] Jackson, together with that of Col. [James] Gadsden." FC in DNA, 102 (M-40:15).

To John W. Davis, Clerk of the U.S. District Court, Boston

Navy Department, November 17, 1818

Your letter of the 5th instant, together with its enclosures, was duly received; and it is to be regretted that you have not rendered an account of the Sales of the Brig Atlantic and [her] Cargo, as that is a case, respecting which the [Navy] Department was particularly desirous of obtaining information; as the Costs and charges amounted to nearly one third of the proceeds. I am, very respectfully, &c., J.C. Calhoun, Act[in]g Secretary of the Navy.

CC in DNA, 201, 15A-F4; PC in House Document No. 6, 15th Cong., 2nd Sess.; PC in *American State Papers: Naval Affairs,* 1:558.

To James Monroe, 11/17. Transmits the correspondence with [Andrew] Jackson, [Edmund P.] Gaines, and [William W.] Bibb concerning the Seminole War that was not included in Calhoun's similar communication of 3/24 and a copy of the court-martial proceedings against A[lexander] Arbuthnot and R[obert] C. Ambrister. LS in DNA, 2, C-1818; FC in DNA, 6, 1:338; PC in Carter, ed., *Territorial Papers,* 18:471.

To Patrick Noble, [Abbeville, S.C.]

War Dept., 17th Nov. 1818

I sold a tract of land to Mr. Wideman last fall and agreed to make him tittles [*sic*] on a final payment on the 1st Jan[uar]y next; and have sent my name in blank to my brother William for that purpose. I must request you to draw up the deed of conveyance for me. The tittles are in the draw[er] up stairs of which Elizabeth has the key. Mrs. Calhoun will make her renunciation of dower, when we return next spring. Mr. Wideman is very punctual and I hope he will not be disappointed.

You will learn the state of our affairs by the President[']s [James Monroe's] message [to Congress]. Our prosperity certainly never was greater. In fact there is but one draw back, the state of our paper currency which in many parts of the country is much disordered. I fear it will give much trouble. Give my respects to your Colleagues, to [George] McDuffie & the Gov[erno]r [Andrew Pickens, Jr.].

[P.S.] Mrs. Calhoun has been dangerously ill, but is now quite recovered.

ALS in ScCleA.

From A[lden] Partridge, Norwich, Vt., 11/17. Acknowledges Calhoun's letter of 10/[27] but defers a detailed answer to the letter as he is "on the verge of leaving this place for New York." Continues the argument as to the proper interpretation of the 77th Article of War and its application to his own dismissal as Superintendent of the Military Academy. ALS in DNA, 1, P-44.

From [the Rev.] THOMAS PICTON, [Chaplain and Professor of Ethics]

U.S. Military Academy, West-Point, Nov. 17th 1818

You would confer a great favour on me, by giving my son, John M.W. Picton, an appointment as Cadet in the Military Academy. He is fourteen years old, *this day*. He has studied common Arithmetick throughout; and paid some attention to Algebra and Mensuration: besides having read several books of Latin and Greek.

ALS in DNA, 15, 1818, 162, with an EU indicating that the son was appointed "in fact" on 9/7/1819 as of 9/1/1819.

To John Rhea, [Representative from Tenn.,] 11/17. "I have received your letter of the 13th instant. In order to effect the arrangement you propose, it will be necessary to obtain the consent of the Bank of Knoxville. If you will procure that consent, orders will be given to prepare the Roll of the pensioners in East Tennessee, so that they may be paid at Knoxville after the 3d of March next." FC in DNA, 3, 10:182.

To J[OSEPH] G. SWIFT

War Dept., 17th Nov. 1818

I was not aware how much I had identified my feelings with those of the officers of the Army till I received your letter of resignation of the 12th inst[ant]. I felt very much, as if I had bid a final farewell to an old friend.

I have no doubt, but that in the discharge of your new duties, that your attention, impartiality and gentlemanly deportment, will render you as agreeable to the citizens of New York as they have done to the officers of the Army. I most sincerely wish you prosperity.

ALS in NWM.

William D. Bates, New York [City], to James Monroe, 11/18. Bates, an immigrant from England who wants to obtain "means to send for my Brother and two Sisters," offers to sell a weapon invented by Bates's father, who is now deceased—apparently a weapon designed for strengthening fortifications against invasion and something in the nature of an incendiary projectile having the range of a cannon ball. ALS in DNA, 128, 7:21.

To Jacob Brown, Brownville, N.Y., 11/18. Concurs with his contention, in his letter of 11/8 (LS in DNA, 1, B-43; FC in DLC, Jacob Brown Papers, Letterbooks, 2:125–126), that it will be most economical to use durable materials like stone in constructing the Army's permanent buildings and other works, especially in the new posts to be established in the Northwest. For this reason an Engineer was ordered last summer to select the site for the new construction at St. Marys [in O.]; he has not yet reported. An Engineer will accompany the troops to recently designated posts in the Northwest. Quartermaster General [Thomas S. Jesup] will decide whether to retain or abandon the wooden barracks of Greenbush [Cantonment, N.Y.]. LS in MHi; FC in DNA, 3, 10:182; CC in DLC, Jacob Brown Papers, Letterbooks, 2:129.

To Speaker [Henry Clay], 11/18. Complying with a House resolution of 4/20 seeking a report as to the number and ranks of Army officers, where they are stationed, the numbers on duty and on furloughs, and the lengths of the furloughs, Calhoun transmits a report submitted to him with D[aniel] Parker's letter of 11/17 (FC in DNA, 12, 5:129). LS with Ens in DNA, 201, 15A-F3; FC in DNA, 4, 2:1; PC with Ens in House Document No. 3, 15th Cong., 2nd Sess.

From Nathaniel Frye, Jr., 11/18. Pursuant to an order of 9/22, Frye transmits reports from Battalion and Regimental Paymasters concerning rates of money exchange and their bank accounts. ALS with Ens in DNA, 2, B-1818.

From [Bvt. Maj.] Archibald Henderson, U.S.M.C., Washington, 11/18. In support of his application to be appointed the Commandant of the Marine Corps, he submits information to be brought to the attention of President [James Monroe]. ALS in DNA, 128, 7:16.

[Bvt. Maj.] Archibald Henderson, Washington, to [James Monroe], 11/18. Henderson discusses his claims to the appointment as Commandant of the Marine Corps; he brands the only man who outranks him, [Bvt. Maj. Anthony Gale,] as incompetent. ALS in DNA, 128, 7:13.

J[ohn] D. Henley, Gosport, [Va.,] to [Bvt. Maj.] Richard Smith, New York [City], 11/18. Henley would be gratified by the success of Smith's application for appointment as the Commandant of the Marine Corps. LS in DNA, 128, 7:15.

From Callender Irvine, Philadelphia, 11/18. Answering Calhoun's letter of 11/6, Irvine confesses, "I am apprehensive that in some cases there is too much foundation for complaint" about the quality of shoes bought by him for the Army. Some manufacturers have used excellent leather but have done inferior work in the inseam, "where the deception cannot be . . . readily detected." He has had Army shoes examined by impartial men who have pronounced them to be satisfactory. "Yet I am satisfied from my own examination of shoes, a part of those which were made in the State of New York, & forwarded to this city by my directions, that they are not precisely what they ought to be. I will endeavour to correct the evil by having the shoes made upon a different construction,

& most of them more immediately under my own eye, for it is impossible to be more particular & precise in my instructions, relative to shoes, to purchasing officers, than I have already been. Some officers, however, will complain without just cause." ALS in DNA, 1, I-32; FC in DNA, 45, 387:203–204.

To Reuben Lewis, Indian Agent on the Arkansas River

Department of War, Nov. 18: 1818

I have rec[eive]d your letter of the 11th ultimo.

You are authorized to erect a small and plain house on the new site which you have selected for the Agency. On the subject of the boundary line, you will find yourself fully instructed by my letter of the 9th of Septem[be]r. When you have determined the line, you will unite your efforts with those of Capt. [William] Bradford, to prevent white settlements extending beyond it, so as to encroach upon the Indian Country. As regards the presents of Cotton Cards and blacksmith's work, I would prefer making them a compensation for the articles specified by you, rather than furnish them. You will make the usual presents of spinning wheels, Looms, &c.

FC in DNA, 72, D:229; CC in DLC, Andrew Jackson Papers, 8297. Note: Lewis's letter of 10/11 is an LS in DNA, 1, L-10, accompanied by an unrelated, two-page DU designated L-10 and undated that is headed "Memorandum," in which the unknown writer asks many questions about salaries, allowances, personnel, provisions, etc., for what appears to have been the Missouri Expedition.

From Jasper Parrish, Canandaigua, [N.Y.,] 11/18. Acknowledges Calhoun's letter of 10/5, which Parrish has explained to the Chiefs of the Six Nations. The Chiefs have decided to let their business remain as it is until some further word is heard from Calhoun about their requests made on 9/24. Parrish intends to set out for Washington on 1/1/1819 to settle his Indian accounts for the last two years unless he is otherwise instructed by Calhoun. ALS in DNA, 1, P-45.

Capt. Daniel T. Patterson, U.S.N., to [Acting] Secretary of the Navy [John C. Calhoun]

New Orleans, November 18th 1818

I have the honor to report to you the capture by the U.S. Ketch *Surprise,* Lt. Com[man]d[an]t [Isaac] McKeever, of a small schooner in ballast under Mexican colours coming from Galveston & bound to this place, having on board the ex-French General [Jean Joseph Amable] Humbert, who had for many months been exercising the office of Governor of that place & its dependencies, and as such issuing commissions to eleven Privateers, a list of which I herein enclose; the above mentioned vessel was also sailing under his commission. On board of her were a number of French emigrants from the French settlement of Camp D'Asile, which has been abandoned & the inhabitants dispersed in consequence of the orders of our Government as communicated to them by Mr. [George ?] Graham. From every thing I can learn a total abandonment of Galveston by the piratical association will immediately take place if it has not already, in consequence of the frequent capture of their cruisers by U.S. vessels, the great difficulty & loss they experience in introducing their captured goods into the United States & the seductive invitation of [Luis] Aury at Old Providence, whither they will repair & under his commissions infest the West Indies. The *Fire Brand* is on our western coast & will I hope bring in for trial some of the vessels stated in the within list. The schooner captured by her & reported by my letter of 10th ultimo is the last mentioned one on that list.

ALS with En in DNA, 133 (M-125:60).

From Henry Sherburne

Chickasaw Agency, Nov[embe]r 18th 1818

On the 16th inst[ant] I rec'd your letter of the 28th Sept. last by the mail from the Choctaw Agency; where this letter has been for fifty-one days since it was written, it is to me a mystery. I presume it was mismailed at Washington, but had it been of the greatest importance to the United States the injury by the delay must have taken place, and of course requires a remedy. The [Chickasaw] Nation appears to be satisfied with the late Treaty, & all former impressions of unfairness in paying them in goods for the Annuity of $12,000 wholly done away by the payment of every cent due them being made in cash. The only favour the Nation now ask (as by their address to you of the 15th inst[ant]) is that the Land they now possess may be made secure to them from the claim of any State or individual.

A few evenings since the woods & cane patches were set on fire by the Hunters, & nut gatherers, about two miles from the Agency House. Such was the violence of the Wind at the southward, & the extreme dryness of the grass &c. (being no rain for nine weeks) that the fire extended itself near the Agency House both to the east & west, & placed us in such eminent [*sic*] danger, from the extreme rapidity of the flames that it became necessary to move our baggage & papers. But happily by our own exertions, with a few neighbours that came to our assistance, we changed its course about 3 o'clock in the morning & saved all the buildings, but with the loss of about Twenty-five hundred rails, that were round the Inclosed lotts [*sic*].

LS in DNA, 77 (M-271:2, frames 0830–0832).

To Thomas Waide, Washington, 11/18. "I return herewith the papers which you transmitted me on the 10th instant. The remarks of Mr. [Nathaniel] Cutting will explain to you the difficulties of the case." FC in DNA, 3, 10:183.

To Seth Wheaton, Providence, R.I., 11/18. Answering the letter of 11/9 from this agent for payments to Revolutionary pensioners, Calhoun says that the War Department's duties "will not allow the pension rolls to be made & transmitted oftener than twice a year; and it is considered unsafe to pay on the [discharge] certificates alone. The Acting Secretary of War, Mr. [George] Graham, relaxed the rule and allowed payments to be made on the certificates alone; but a little practice soon exposed numerous attempts at fraud, and I was obliged to discontinue" that exception to the rule. FC in DNA, 3, 10:182.

To P[hilip] P[endleton] Barbour, [Representative from Va.,] 11/19. Answering his letter of 11/18, explains that consideration of applications for pensions from Revolutionary veterans in Va. was delayed "in order to procure from the Governor a transcript of the records of the line of that State during the Revolutionary War. It has not yet been obtained." In order to avoid further delay, consideration of those applications without the requested information was recently ordered. FC in DNA, 3, 10:183–184.

To Samuel R. Betts, Newburgh, N.Y., 11/19. Calhoun agrees with Betts's statement in his letter of 11/14 (ALS in DNA, 1, B-46) respecting the remission of [N.Y. militia delinquents'] fines. Great caution is being exercised in granting remissions. [Gerard] Steddiford misconstrued Calhoun's order [of 9/21], and Betts is to retain the original papers of the court[-martial] until further orders from the [War] Department. FC in DNA, 3, 10:184.

To Robert Brent, 11/19. "Instead of the Quarterly reports required of you by the regulation of the 5th September last, you will render a report every four months, to this Dep[art]m[en]t," beginning on 12/1. FC in DNA, 3, 10:184.

To William H[enry] Harrison, [Representative from O.,] 11/19. Asks him to bring before Congress the War Department's need for 10 extra Clerks, in order that it may be enabled to proceed with the 16,000 remaining applications for Revolutionary pensions. FC in DNA, 3, 10:184–185.

From John Johnston, Piqua, [O.,] 11/19. The Miami Chiefs have delivered a speech requesting that [Benjamin F.] Stickney be removed from Fort Wayne. Johnston could discharge the duties of his Agency better if Stickney could be stationed elsewhere, and Johnston suggests the Agency for the Wyandots at Sandusky. Stickney would then be subject to the control of [Lewis] Cass. Johnston would like to appoint his own assistant at Fort Wayne. Praises the aid of Sub-Agent John Kinzie during the recent negotiations at St. Marys. ALS in DNA, 1, J-64.

To [James Monroe]

[Navy Department, *ca.* November 19, 1818]

Maj. [Archibald] Henderson of the Marine Corps has requested me to lay before you the enclosed letter. I do it with pleasure, as I believe he is a deserving officer. Yours truly, J.C. Calhoun.

ALS in DNA, 128, 1818, 2:88. NOTE: The "enclosed letter" to which Calhoun referred was probably that of 11/18 from Henderson applying for appointment as the Commandant of the Marine Corps and specifically asking Calhoun to bring that letter to Monroe's attention.

From John Rhea, [Representative from Tenn.,] 11/19. In reply to Calhoun's letter of 11/17, Rhea reports that Senator John Williams says that the Bank of Knoxville will gladly serve as Agent for Paying U.S. Pensioners in East Tenn. if the Bank is supplied with the necessary funds. ALS in DNA, 1, R-28.

From Capt. J[oel] Spencer, [Assistant Deputy Quartermaster General,] Fort Gadsden, [Ala. Territory,] 11/19. He defends himself against charges of misconduct and asks Calhoun not to accept the unfavorable opinion that those charges were intended to create "until I have a trial before a Court Martial, or a correct course of conduct convinces you of the improper motives of the person wishing to disgrace me." ALS in DNA, 1, S-185.

To G[erard] Steddiford, N[ew] York [City], 11/19. A letter from S[amuel] R. Betts shows that Steddiford apparently misconstrued Calhoun's order of 9/21. The original papers referred to in that order were the applications [of N.Y. militia delinquents] for remission of fines, not the minutes of the court[-martial]. Calhoun encloses Allen Wilmot's application for a remission. FC in DNA, 3, 10:184.

J[oseph] G. Swift, New York [City], to Ch[ristopher] Vandeventer, 11/19. Asks that a new warrant be given to George [Washington] Giles, son of Gen. [Aquila] Giles, because the son was permitted by [James Monroe] to remain at his school beyond the deadline for his former appointment. "We are all well, myself very busy taking the 'Properties' of my new office." ALS in DNA, 15, 1816, 62.

From Decius Wadsworth, 11/19. Because the appropriation for the national armories in 1818 is insufficient and because Paymaster William McGuire at Harpers Ferry needs about $20,000 now to cover his payrolls for last month and this month, Wadsworth requests that $34,000 of the $34,639.98 added to the fund for arsenals from the sale of lots in Pittsburgh that constituted Fort Fayette be transferred to the fund for armories. A computation filed with the ALS shows, however, that the amount available for transfer, plus the present balance in the fund for armories, total only $17,097.95 and concludes that a supplementary appropriation by Congress will be necessary. ALS with En in DNA, 1, W-61; FC in DNA, 32, 2:136–137.

To Jacob Brown, Brownville, N.Y., 11/20. "No answer having been received to the letter addressed to you from this Department on the 11th of August last; it is, therefore, presumed, that it never reached you; and I now enclose a copy, with the request, that you will prepare and forward the statement required, as early as practicable." LS in MHi; FC in DNA, 3, 10:186; FC in DLC, Jacob Brown Papers, Letterbooks, 2:129.

From James Leander Cathcart, Norfolk, 11/20. He has arrived there and has been informed that the U.S.S. *Nonsuch* will sail in a few days. As instructed on 11/13, he will embark on her for New Orleans. He will proceed with minimum possible delay to accomplish his mission. ALS in DNA, 128, 7:26; CC in DNA, 85, Appendix, pp. 2–3 (M-8:1).

From I[saac] Chauncey, U.S.S. *Washington,* New York [City], 11/20. Answers Calhoun's letter of 11/16: "The Court Martial ordered for the trial of David Moore shall be convened immediately." ALS in DNA, 133 (M-125:60).

J[ames] L. Edwards, Pension Office, to [Christopher] Vandeventer, 11/20. Encloses copies of all published regulations governing [Revolutionary] pensions. "The Regulation respecting the certificates of the Judges as to the [reduced financial] circumstances of the claimants was not *printed* except in the Newspapers." ALS in DNA, 1, E-16.

From John Hanes, St. Stephens, A[la.] T[erritory], 11/20. Acknowledges Calhoun's letter of 10/23 and replies that he has forwarded all the pension records to [LeRoy] Pope. Regrets the delay; "the unfrequent conveyance and the importance of safety in the conveyance, produced it." ALS in DNA, 1, H-78.

To Capt. John D. Henley, U.S. Frigate *Congress,* Norfolk, 11/20. "Be pleased to report from time to time the number of men who may have joined the U.S. Ship *Congress* under your command, in order that the Rendezvous [that is, the recruiting station] may be directed to enter a crew for the" *John Adams* when the *Congress* has a full complement. FC in DNA, 121, 13:289.

From [William Lee], 11/20. Returns by Ordnance officers, at various posts, of the ordnance and military equipment for which they were responsible have not been received from every officer, "though they have been much more generally made to this office than heretofore." Lee submits statements reporting all ordnance and clothing (including Quartermaster stores in the care of Military Storekeepers and Assistant Commissaries [of Issues]) as of 6/30 and 9/30. FC in DNA, 52, 2:504.

From J[oseph] G. Swift, New York [City], 11/20. Urges a remittance of $500 in payment for a survey of about 24 square miles including New York Harbor that was made during last month under Swift's direction. ALS in DNA, 23, 159 (170).

S[ylvanus] Thayer, West Point, to Joseph G. Swift, 11/20. Thayer encloses an ALS of 11/4 to himself from Dr. Samuel A. Walsh arguing that it is necessary to allow the civilian who is employed as Steward and Wardmaster in the hospital at West Point at least the recent compensation of $16 and two rations per day, not the $10 and one ration stipulated by a new regulation. Thayer thinks that Walsh is correct and asks that Walsh's request be granted. ALS with En in DNA, 241, W-1818–1832, with an AEI by Calhoun referring these letters to Surgeon General [Joseph Lovell].

To SYLVANUS THAYER and the Academic Staff, [United States Military Academy,] West Point

Dep[art]m[en]t of War, 20th Novemb[e]r 1818

I have laid the representation of the Academick Staff of the first of November before the President [James Monroe] and I am directed by him to state that the rules proposed by the Staff as far as they apply to the Army meet his approbation, and they will accordingly be inserted among the other rules and regulations for the government of the Military Academy. When the [newly appointed] Secretary of the Navy [Smith Thompson] arrives, so much of the regulations as apply to the Marine Corps and the Navy will be laid before him for his consideration & the result will be communicated to the Staff. The appointment of Capt. Balche [Nathaniel Balch or Samuel Y. Balch ?] & of Lieut[enant] [Edward] Polk, [Wilson Cary Nicholas] Armistead, [Robert or William ?] Wright, Jamaison [Titus T. Jamison], and [Edward Henry] Alexander cannot be revoked or suspended. It would be an act of injustice to apply to them rules which were not in existence at the time of their appointment and no officer ought to be deprived of his rank or suspended in the exercise of his functions without having committed any military offense. In communicating the decision of the President I avail myself of the opportunity to assure the Academick Staff that it will at all times afford me much pleasure to support them with the weight of the Dep[art]m[en]t in the discharge of their very arduous & important duties; and that it is with great satisfaction that I perceive the zeal and devotion with which they are performed.

It is thus & thus only that the Academy will become the nursery of officers who, while they reflect glory on their Country, will add new lustre to the institution to which they are indebted for their education.

FC in DNA, 3, 10:186.

To Col. W[alker] K[eith] Armistead, "Present," 11/21. "You will assume the command of the Engineer Corps and the direction of the Engineer Dep[art]m[en]t at this place until further orders." FC in DNA, 3, 10:187.

To Speaker [Henry Clay], 11/21. Obeying a House resolution of 4/8, Calhoun, as Acting Secretary of the Navy, reports on the Navy Pension Fund, its sources, its amount, how its revenue is collected, and its annual receipts from each State since 6/20/1812; he submits about 75 enclosures. LS with Ens in DNA, 201, 15A-F4; FC in DNA, 125, 3:8–11; PC with Ens in House Document No. 6, 15th Cong., 2nd Sess.; PC with Ens in *American State Papers: Naval Affairs,* 1:535–562.

From Th[omas] S. Jesup, 11/21. Expenditures at Detroit have "exceeded any reasonable expectation," and Jesup requests that Otis Fisher, the Quartermaster there, shall be ordered to Washington promptly to settle his accounts. LS in DNA, 11, 13190; FC in DNA, 42, 1:112.

To John Landreth, "Present," 11/21. James Leander Cathcart has received instructions [dated 11/13], from Calhoun as Acting Secretary of the Navy, concerning the quest that Cathcart, Landreth, and James Hutton are to make jointly for live oak and red cedar timbers. Landreth "will therefore proceed to Baltimore for the purpose of procuring the [surveying] instruments which shall be necessary for the performance of the trust confided in you"; and then Landreth is to join Cathcart at Norfolk for their trip by water. CC in DNA, 201, 15A-F4.

From Joseph Lovell, 11/21. Discusses several needs for improvements, at increased cost, in the Medical staff since the reorganization of the Army's general staff last April. LS and DS in DNA, 203, 15A-D8.2; FC in DNA, 243, 1:26–28.

To [William] McRee, "Present," 11/21. Asks for the information about possible additional military academies that has been requested by the House Committee on Military Affairs. FC in DNA, 3, 10:187.

To John Rhea, 11/21. "A Roll of the pensioners of East Tennessee will be prepared and transmitted together with Funds to the President of the Bank at Knoxville, upon the supposition that the bank agrees to the arrangement, before the 4th of March next and payments will be made in future at Knoxville. I have no objections to the Bank at Knoxville making payments to the Pensioners in East Tennessee through any other Bank that it may deem safe and proper." FC in DNA, 3, 10:187, with a draft of 11/20 on p. 185 that "was not sent."

From Henry Sherburne, Chickasaw Agency, 11/21. Calhoun's letter of 10/27 has been received, but not the $6,000. All goods shipped to Chickasaw Bluffs were delivered to Paul Ballio, and the invoices were sent to [Thomas L.] McKenney on 11/11. Sherburne refutes a news announcement in the Nashville *Whig* and other newspapers that Sherburne's alleged neglect in paying the Chickasaws' annuity compelled [Andrew] Jackson to issue special drafts and to make the payment; Sherburne has written to Jackson about this matter. ALS in DNA, 1, S-129.

From Ho[well] Tatum, Nashville, 11/21. Acknowledges Calhoun's letter of 10/23 and is surprised "that no evidence of my appointment as Acting Military Store Keeper appears in the War Office. I will endeavour to give you as perfect a history of that business as I can." His salary has been $500 per year, which he considers insufficient for the necessary duties. His Quartermaster funds are nearly exhausted. LS in DNA, 2, T-1818.

To Decius Wadsworth

Department of War, 21st Novem[be]r 1818

I transmit herewith a copy of a letter [dated 11/20 (ALS in DNA, 1, J-39)] received from the Chairman of the Military Committee of the House of Representatives, [Richard M. Johnson,] and have to call your attention to so much of his enquiry as relates to the Ordnance Department; and will thank you to favour me with your ideas on the subject, as early as practicable.

LS in ScU-SC, John C. Calhoun Papers; FC in DNA, 3, 10:187. Note: Wadsworth answered on 12/2 this inquiry about the quantity of arms produced by the U.S. armories at Harpers Ferry and at Springfield, Mass., and the estimated cost of establishing a new armory in the West. Calhoun relayed the information on 12/3 to Johnson and recommended that a new armory should be established somewhere in the West.

From [Simon] Bernard and W[illiam] McRee, Washington, 11/22. They report, as instructed, concerning defense sites and fortifications on the right bank of the "narrows" in New York Harbor; although they are not yet prepared to give an opinion as to the extent to which the existing works can be used advantageously in a general system of harbor defenses, they are certain that the position must be occupied and fortified. LS in DNA, 1, B-70.

From Lt. C[harles] R. Broom, Marine Barracks, Philadelphia, 11/22. Recommends former Maj. John Hall of the Marine Corps for appointment as its Commandant; cites Hall's long and valued service, until he was mustered out in the recent reduction of the Corps, as a recommendation. ALS in DNA, 128, 7:28.

[Lt.] ALEXANDER CLAXTON, [U.S.N.,] to "JOHN C. CALHOUN, Secretary at War, Private"

U.S. Schooner *Nonsuch,* Norfolk, Nov. 22d 1818

I understand from one of the Gentlemen [surveyors in the party of three headed by James Leander Cathcart whom] I am about to convey to New Orleans, that orders have been forwarded to Commodore [Daniel T.] Patterson to provide a public vessel to return with them in the Spring. I know not that I may be selected for that purpose, but as it very deeply concerns my future happiness, I most urgently solicit of you Sir, that Com[modore] Patterson may be desired to allow me to return on that duty.

I am very sensible of your kindnesses to me, and assure you that I would not intrude this suggestion, had not circumstances of infinite importance to me demanded it.

ALS in DNA, 134.

To [John Gaillard], President [Pro Tempore] of the Senate, 11/23. Pursuant to a Senate resolution of 3/17 (DS in DNA, 1, S-68), Calhoun submits a return showing the organization and strength of the militias of the States and Territories, so far as these have been reported, together with copies of all State and Territorial militia laws that have been received. (This return was submitted to the Senate on 11/26.) LS with Ens in DNA, 154, 15A-F4; FC in DNA, 4, 2:2; PC with Ens in Senate Document No. 11, 15th Cong., 2nd Sess.; PC with Ens in *American State Papers: Military Affairs,* 1:769–772.

From CALLENDER IRVINE

Philad[elphi]a, Nov. 23d 1818

In your letter of the 6th instant I have been informed that my estimate for 1819 has been reduced in the proportion of 9,000 to 12,127 in the aggregate. Am I to understand, Sir, that a reduction in the above ratio is to take place as to all the Corps? Perhaps some of the Corps are more nearly complete than others. From a letter lately received from Col. [John R.] Fenwick, I find that an estimate has been made for the clothing for the Light Artillery, as tho' the Regiment was complete to the [maximum limit defined by the law governing the size of the military] establishment.

Very few Army Returns have been received at this office, and I am quite in the dark as well as to the strength of the Reg[i]m[en]ts, as to the present stations of some of them. I fear, Sir, that if clothing shall be provided only for the men actually serving annually that it will be impracticable to get it to the distant Posts in due season. The surplus clothing of 1818 will prevent any embarrassments for want of clothing for 1819.

ALS in DNA, 1, I-30; FC in DNA, 45, 387:207.

RICHARD M. JOHNSON, [Representative from Ky.,] to President [JAMES MONROE]

House of Rep[resentatives,] 23d Nov. 1818

I have just been informed that a selection will soon be made from the Marine Corps to fill the vacancy [in the office of the Commandant] occasioned by the death of Col. [Franklin] Wharton. Permit me to bring to your consideration the merits & claims of Maj. [Samuel] Miller. If seniority should not be absolute on this occasion, I take pleasure in stating that in my humble opinion no officer can have higher claims to promotion. Maj. Miller is an officer who has distinguished himself in the zeal & ability which he has manifested on several occasions. Independent of these considerations of service, his correct deportment, his political principles & his devotion to his country entitle him to consideration.

ALS in DNA, 128, 7:30.

To [James Monroe], 11/23. Complying with a Senate resolution of 4/17, Acting Secretary of the Navy Calhoun sends two reports concerning the Navy Pension Fund since 6/1812. LS with Ens in DNA, 155, 15A-E6; FC in DNA, 123, 1:341; PC with Ens in Senate Document No. 14, 15th Congress, 2nd Session.

Marcus Morton, [Representative from Mass.,] to [James Monroe], 11/23. Morton urges that Maj. Samuel Miller be appointed Commandant of the Marines. ALS in DNA, 128, 7:29.

To Capt. Daniel T. Patterson, u.s.n., New Orleans

Navy Department, Nov. 23d 1818

Under the general instructions of the 17th October last, you will be pleased to direct Lieut. Commandant William B. Finch, to proceed with the U.S. Brig Prometheus under his command to the Island of Bermuda, where arrangements are made for transporting a considerable amount in Specie and Bullion to the United States.

Lt. Comm[an]d[an]t Finch will, upon arrival, call upon Mr. May Humphreys at Messrs. Michael Cavan & Co., Bermuda, and when Mr. Humphreys shall be ready to embark he will take him on board, and proceed to Port Royal, Jamaica, and after accomplishing the object at Jamaica, he will proceed to the Chesapeake [Bay], or New York, according to circumstances and the weather he may meet with upon the coast.

Your orders and instructions to Lt. Comm[an]d[an]t Finch are to be considered by him strictly confidential, and no third person is to have any knowledge of the object of the cruise.

LS in DNA, 133 (M-125:60). Note: Compare, herein, the order to Patterson of 11/26.

From Decius Wadsworth, 11/23. Defends his own actions and condemns those of Maj. [Abram R.] Woolley concerning the purchase of a four-acre site at Waterford, Pa., for a proposed arsenal at a price of $1,200, which seems suspiciously high. But in a postscript added on 12/8 to both copies of this letter Wadsworth retracts his suspicions and exonerates Woolley, on the basis of a report made by Capt. [William] Wade. ALS in DNA, 2, W-1818; FC in DNA, 32, 2:138–140, 155.

From Col. H[enry] Atkinson

Plattsburgh [N.Y.] Novem[be]r 24, 1818

I have the honor to enclose herewith an abstract of the labor performed by the troops under my command on the fortifications at

Rouse's Point and the military way through the Chateauguay [*sic*] woods. The nature of the labor on the fortifications can be best explained to you by the superintending officers of Engineers. That bestowed on the road has been heavy & labourious; six miles of the road has [*sic*] been completed this season, most of the distance through a heavy forest. The road is excellent, having twenty four feet base and made in the very best manner. Perhaps so good a road has not been made, as the thirteen miles now completed, in any part of the United States. All the brooks and ravines that cross it have stone walls to conduct away the waters, and in passing through swampy lands, stone walls have been made and the road raised and formed between them. I will take occasion at a subsequent time, by your permission, to give you a detailed view of the importance of completing this road to the St. Lawrence, the distance yet to be made, the amount of labour, the number of men & the time necessary to finish it.

ALS with DS in DNA, 1, A-26, the enclosure tabulating 25,942 man-days of labor by the 6th Infantry Regiment during 4/1–11/20; FC in DNA, 181, pp. 48–49.

Lt. George Blaney, "Engineer Department," to Thomas Grimbrede, 11/24. "Your letter to the Secretary of War has been referred to this Department. A Mr. Milbert has applied for the situation of Drawing master at West Point and will be appointed to that station provided Major [Sylvanus] Thayer reports favourably of his talents and acquirements. If, however, a vacancy should occur, your name will be considered as the first on the list of applicants. By order." FC in DNA, 13 (M-91:1, p. 68). (The *Army Register* issued 1/1/1820 and several later issues listed Grimbrede as "teacher of drawing" in the Academy.)

Lt. George Blaney, "Engineer Department," to "Dr. S.L. Mitchell [probably Samuel Latham Mitchill]," 11/24. "Your letter to the Secretary of War recommending Mr. Grimbridge [Thomas Grimbrede] for the situation of Drawing master at West Point has been received and referred to this Department. A Mr. Milbert applied for the place some time since and has conditionally received the appointment. If a vacancy should occur, Mr. Grimbridge will be borne in mind. By order." FC in DNA, 13 (M-91:1, p. 68).

To Jacob Brown, Brownville, N.Y., 11/24. Regrets "that I cannot comply with your request" of 11/15 (LS in DNA, 1, B-67; FC dated 11/—— in DLC, Jacob Brown Papers, Letterbooks, 2:127) that [1st] Lt. [Horace C.] Story of the Corps of Engineers be assigned to serve as Brown's aide-de-camp. "The Corps of Engineers is small, and the duties of its officers arduous and so multiplied, that they are found inadequate to perform all that is required of their Corps." LS in MHi; FC in DNA, 3, 10:188; CC in DLC, Jacob Brown Papers, Letterbooks, 2:130.

From James L. Edwards, Pension Office, 11/24. Encloses a list of about 4,430 Revolutionary pensions granted through 11/10 under the law of 3/18—the list relayed to Henry Clay by Calhoun on 11/26. ALS in DNA, 1, E-12; FC in DNA, 91, 6:30, with an appended recapitulation of the numbers and amounts of the pensions by States and Territories and with a marginal note about later revisions made in the list.

Wilson M. C. Fairfax, Charles R. Holmes, Nathaniel H. Loring, Thomas Ragland, and Charles R. Vining, West Point, to S[ylvanus] Thayer, [West Point,] 11/24. As a "Committee of Cadets" allegedly representing "a large majority" of the student body, they submit a statement of grievances and ask for redress. Specifically, they charge the Commandant of Cadets, Capt. [John] Bliss, with having on 11/22 violently seized, shaken, and publicly damned Cadet [Edward L.] Nicholson for a quite minor offense during drill and with having then unjustly confined that victim. They protest that such an indignity and wrong is, in their opinion, a violation of "the contract between the government and ourselves." A postscript signed by Fairfax and Ragland at Washington on 1/10/1819 corrects their former statement that Bliss charged Nicholson with mutiny by stating that, instead, Nicholson was confined under "the charge of disobedience of orders." CC in DLC, Andrew Jackson Papers, 8323–8324; PC in House Document No. 14, 16th Cong., 1st Sess.; PC in *American State Papers: Military Affairs*, 2:12–13. (This document is the first major item in a series that soon began to trouble Calhoun for more than a year and constituted one of the most serious crises concerning student discipline in the Military Academy during the years 1817–1825. PC's of many of the relevant documents can be found in *American State Papers: Military Affairs*, 2:1–30.)

From Edmund P. Gaines

Fernandina, E[ast] F[lorida], Nov[embe]r 24th 1818

I had the honor to receive on the 21st Instant your letter of the 24th Ultimo, by the way of Fort Hawkins.

Your attention being turned towards the subject of desertion, I take the liberty to observe that no mode of punishment, ["other than capital," *canceled*] heretofore resorted to, has been sufficient to avert the evil, or even to strike the minds of the Soldiery with a due sense of the enormity of the crime. After all that can be said upon the subject, it will, I think, be found that well-timed examples of capital punishment furnish the only means, yet tried, capable of giving a visible check to this great and growing evil. Capital punishment however in a land of liberty, in an enlightened age, where every rational head and heart must strongly incline towards humanity, is truly a very awfull [*sic*] alternative. Humanity demands that every effort on the part of the national government and the Army should be made use of to cure the evil—to eradicate the offence without taking away the life of the offender; particularly during a period of peace. The State penitentiaries offer a mode of punishment heretofore untried, or but partially tried in the Army. I think most officers of experience will concur with me in the opinion that a deserter should not for several years at least, after conviction of the crime, be permitted to bear arms, or in any way to serve or associate with the troops who have witnessed his disgrace. This would be likely to produce (what exists at this time but in a very small degree) that keen sense of shame which the extent and turpitude of the offence ought to excite, in the ranks of the Army. Under present circumstances but few, comparatively, of the many who desert are apprehended, and these are, in part, soon restored to the ranks, and to the enjoyment of every priviledge [*sic*] and comfort allowed the meritorious soldier. They speak familiarly to their associates of the offence of which they have been guilty, not indeed by the name of *desertion*, but they "decamped," "got tipsey and walked off," or "run away." Their associates listen, and the crime or vice which they had perhaps viewed with abhorrence as a 'monster' they "first endure, then pity, then embrace." I think we should try the effect of the Penitentiaries, for ten or twenty years, or during life:—the life of a deserter is forfeited and at the disposal of the law—hence the right to confine during life. In time of War the option of shooting or confinement during life, should rest with the court and the General; because there are cases not unfrequently occurring, when before, or near to an enemy, in which not only *justice* but the tenderest *mercy* calls aloud for prompt and exemplary capital punishment. He whose desertion clearly exposes his associates to the inevitable peril of being defeated, in consequence of such desertion, he should if apprehended be allowed no hope of escaping immediate trial and execution; otherwise his corps would be still more weakened and exposed by losing the services of the Guard placed over him. The army lost by desertion, in the two first years of the War [of 1812], probably 1,000 men. A corps of reserve amounting to this number of efficient regulars, with the army on the Niagara, or at Fort Erie, or at New-Orleans, I have no doubt would have effected the entire capture of the British army at either of those places—such a force at Washington must have saved the Capital of our beloved country; and I think I am warranted by the proceedings of courts and the frequent pardons granted in the early part of the War, in saying that the evil was greatly increased by ill-timed or mistaken lenity.

ALS in DNA, 1, G-41; LS in DNA, 2, G-1818; 2 LS's in DLC, Andrew Jackson Papers, 8330–8333; draft in DNA, 11, 12215.

From George Gibson, 11/24. Encloses a list of "efficient bids" for supplying rations, totaling $473,752.805. "To those of Mr. [James] Johnson I have added one dollar per barrel on corn meal and I have taken Robeson & Wallace[']s bid for Arkansas." LS with En in DNA, 2, G-1818.

From David A. Ogden, [Representative from N.Y.]

Washington, Nov[embe]r 24, 1818

I now transmit you agreeably to your request, the Two News Papers, which contain the publications of Hyde Numbered 3 & 4.

Altho these publications have unquestionably been made, with the View to lessen the Influence, and Aleenate [*sic*] the Confidence of the Indians, as well as that of the White Population from the measures of the Government and their Agents, still the Insignificance of Hyde, would scarcely make it worth the trouble to prosecute him for a Libel.

I however avail myself of the present opportunity to state, That Hyde now is and for some years past, has been resident upon the Buffaloe [*sic*] Reservation, that he has endeavored & under various pretences has succeeded in control[l]ing the measures of the Six Nations of Indians, that these proceedings have a Tendency to Weaken the Influence of the Government, and that of Its Agents, and that his Residing upon these Lands is in direct contravention of the Act of the 30th March 1802—See 3 Vol. S[tatutes of the] U[nited] St[ates] fol. 462 Sect. 5.

Under these circumstances I take the Liberty of suggesting for your consideration—Whether the Unwarrantable measures of this Man, does [*sic*] not render him a fit subject for Prosecution under the Act above Reffered [*sic*] to—And also whether the true Policy of the Government and a Just Regard to the Rights of the Individuals possessing the Right of Pre-emption to these Lands, does not dictate, that the Agent of the United States shall be Instructed to adopt measures for the Removal of all other Intruders from the same.

ALS in DNA, 1, O-8.

To Col. Ferris Pell of New York [City], "Present"

Dep[art]m[en]t of War, November 24th 1818

Your letter of the 19th inst[ant] offering to dispose of, on the part of the State of New York, the fortification owned by it in the harbour of New York, has been received. In conversation on the same subject last winter I stated to you that the opinion of the Officers of the Corps of Engineers who were charged with the survey of the coast with a view to its effectual and permanent fortification would be taken in relation to the work in question and that until their opinion was known, a definitive answer could not be given. I enclose a copy of a report from General [Simon] Bernard & [Lt.] Col. [William] McRee, by which you will perceive that they will not be able to furnish the information required till the survey and plan for the defence of the City of New York are completed. In the mean time, I can only repeat what has already been stated in conversation. It is conceived that from sound policy and a just regard to the principles of the Constitution, the General Government ought to assume the burden of the general defence of the Country; and that in conformity with these views should the report of the Officers be favorable, the government ought to purchase the fortification at a fair price. This however cannot be effected by applying a part of the annual appropriation of $830,000 for fortifications, but an application to Congress for a specifick appropriation for the purpose would be necessary. Should the report be favorable the Dep[art]m[en]t would unhesitatingly make the necessary recommendation to Congress for the appropriation.

FC in DNA, 3, 10:189; PC in Jameson, ed., *Correspondence,* pp. 149–150. NOTE: Pell's letter of 11/19, written in Washington, is an ALS in DNA, 1, P-54.

To E[leazer] W. Ripley, New Orleans, 11/24. "Preparatory to commencing the building of the Barracks at Baton-rouge, I will thank you to transmit to me a plan for the same. The appropriation of last year is $40,000; the estimate for 1819 is $25,000. The plan therefore ought to be adjusted, to be within these sums, and at the same time commensurate with the wants of that section of Country." FC in DNA, 3, 10:187.

From Decius Wadsworth, 11/24. Answers the inquiries of the House Committee on Military Affairs dated 11/20. The two national armories—at Springfield, Mass., and Harpers Ferry—could increase their annual production of 25,000 stands of arms to 30,000 by subletting some work at an increased cost of about $6,000. Wadsworth favors the proposal to establish in the West a new armory, which should grow in time to equal the output of either of the other two. He argues, too, the need for a school of practice for the Artillery and cites the French military experience for schools to be imitated. FC in DNA, 32, 2:141–143.

To Lt. Col. T[albot] Chambers, Bellefontaine, [Mo. Territory,] 11/25. Demands of him a report concerning the "most violent outrage" inflicted upon a civilian boatman of the Yellowstone Expedition, a Mr. Boadwin, who was tried by a court-martial and received 50 lashes "for an offence entirely accidental." "The great responsibility attatched [*sic*] to so distant and important a Command requires the greatest degree of firmness and prudence on the part of the commander. Without these qualities the great object of affording additional security to our frontiers and extending our fur trade, will be entirely defeated," much to the dishonor of the commanding officer and of "the Executive by whom it was planned." Calhoun hopes to supply to the expedition by early next spring a steamboat "for ascending the [Missouri] river" and additional troops. FC in DNA, 3, 10:189–190; PC in Carter, ed., *Territorial Papers,* 15:462.

From H[enry] Clay, Wash[ingto]n, 11/25. He believes that William Ward, John T. Johnson, Joel Johnson, and Henry Johnson afford ample sureties for James Johnson, [their brother-in-law and brother,] in respect to his [proposed steamboat] contract involving $200,000. ALS in DNA, 44; PC in Hopkins and Hargreaves, eds., *The Papers of Henry Clay,* 2:605.

To Speaker [Henry Clay], 11/25. In accordance with requirements of a statute of 4/10/1806, Calhoun reports the names of five applicants for pensions and of three applicants for increased pensions, each since 4/20, under laws awarding benefits to wounded and disabled soldiers of the Revolution and later years. LS and DS in DNA, 201, 15A-F3; FC in DNA, 4, 2:1; FC with En (both dated 11/26) in DNA, 91, 6:36–37.

From James L. Edwards

War Department, Pension Office, Nov[embe]r 25, 1818

In the case of Amos Strong, I have remarked that "Teamsters are not provided for by the [pension] law of March 18, 1818"; and I am still of the opinion that he is not entitled to a pension for services in the waggon [*sic*] department, he having been neither a commissioned officer, a non-commissioned officer, nor a private soldier. Waggon-masters, or, in other words, conductors of teams, were, during the Revolutionary war, appointed as they now are, by the Quarter Master General, or any of his Deputies, and received the pay and rations of Captains. The only persons appointed in the same manner as waggon-masters, and [who] are provided for by the law in question, are Surgeon's Mates (who were appointed by the Surgeons), and I think the law maxim may apply here: *"Inclusio unius, est exclusio alterius."*

ALS in DNA, 1, E-13; FC in DNA, 91, 6:32.

To Fourth Auditor Constant Freeman, 11/25. As Acting Secretary of the Navy, Calhoun encloses the claim of Samuel F. Hooker of Sackets Harbor, [N.Y.,] for damages sustained because Commodore Isaac Chauncey allegedly failed to receive goods at the times specified in Hooker's contract; Calhoun asks what sum, in equity, Hooker should receive. FC in DNA, 122, 13:240.

To Edmund P. Gaines, Amelia Island, 11/25. Answering his letter of 11/10 (LS in DNA, 1, G-32; LS in DNA, 11, 12203), authorizes him to "exercise a sound discretion in fixing" the duration of the leases to public lands at Fort Hawkins; Gaines had recommended leases for as many as 20 years, because shorter terms would not encourage lessees to build improvements that would enhance the value of surrounding lands. In answer to Gaines's letter of 11/14 (LS in DNA, 1, G-33; unsigned draft in DNA, 11, 12560) reporting that some of the Seminoles were destitute and had discussed surrendering, Calhoun orders Gaines to provide rations to all who may surrender "until arrangements for their support among the Upper Creeks can be made." These rations should be obtained from contractor [Camillus] Griffith. As a supplement to Calhoun's letters of 9/30 and 10/8 to Gaines, Calhoun encloses an extract from a letter to [David B.] Mitchell, because that extract "exhibits the views of this department in relation to a peace with the Seminoles." "Until the President [James Monroe] shall order the removal of the Seminoles, you will make such arrangements for their residence in Florida, as you may deem proper." LS in DNA, 11, 12352; FC in DNA, 3, 10:190.

J[ohn] D. Henley, Gosport, [Va.,] to [Acting] Secretary of the Navy [Calhoun], 11/25. The *Congress* must be coppered anew and must be given new rigging, etc., which will require "some time." In reply to the inquiry of 10/20, Henley reports that the *Congress* now has 120 seamen (88 recruited there and 32 at Baltimore), that about 100 have probably enlisted in New York [City], and that Henley hopes that Capt. [Samuel] Angus will be permitted to recruit about 75 more, because those gotten at New York are better." LS in DNA, 133 (M-125:60).

B[enjamin] H[omans] to George S. Wise, Purser, U.S. Navy [Yard, New York City], "Present," 11/25. Pursuant to his report of 11/21 (LS in DNA, 134) that he had settled his account with a balance in his favor and was ready to resume his duties, Homans informs him that [Acting] Secretary of the Navy [Calhoun] "expresses his satisfaction, at your having so honorably adjusted accounts of so long standing and to so large an amount" and encloses an order to Wise assigning him to his duty as Purser at New York [City]. FC in DNA, 121, 13:289.

One of James Johnson's subsistence contracts, 11/25. By these "Articles of Agreement" between himself and George Gibson, Johnson obligates himself to deliver at St. Louis [for the Missouri and Mississippi Expeditions] on 6/1/1819 one-half of specified quantities of the components of rations and to deliver to the same place the other half on 10/1/1819. Such quantities as 102,500 pounds of bacon and 689 barrels of prime pork are stipulated. By giving 60 days' prior notice, the U.S. can change the quantities and the place of delivery. How these rations in bulk are to be packed and inspected is stipulated; Johnson is to be "liable for the expenses of inspection, and for all other expenses, until the articles are safely delivered at such store house as may be designated." The price to be paid for each individual component of these rations is specified. If Johnson should fail to deliver all of the quantities requisitioned, the government "shall have power to supply the deficiency, and the said James Johnson agrees to forfeit to the United States" one-third of the specified costs. Johnson is to render accounts of all funds that may be advanced to him; any surplus advanced is to be "repaid to the United States immediately after the expiration of this contract, together with an interest of six per centum per annum." Whatever the government may owe to Johnson at the expiration of the contract will be paid promptly to him or his estate, but no "member of Congress shall be admitted to any share or part of this contract, or any benefit to arise therefrom." No date of expiration is explicit in this agreement. In behalf of the contractor, this document was signed by Richard M. Johnson, acting under a power of attorney. PC in House Document No. 110, 16th Cong., 2nd Sess.

To [James Monroe], 11/25. Pursuant to a Senate resolution of 3/17, transmits a return of the organization and strength of the militia of the States and Territories and copies of their militia laws, each as completely as they have been obtainable. FC in DNA, 6, 1:339.

Robert Troup, Geneva, N.Y., to Smith Thompson, "Secretary of the Navy," Washington, 11/25. Recommends Sub-Agent Jasper Parrish to succeed Erastus Granger as Agent for the Six Nations, because Parrish has had 26 years of service with those tribes. LS in DNA, 128, 7:33.

Order by W[alker] K. Armistead, by order of the Secretary of War, 11/26. The resignation of Cadet Jacques Ruden is accepted to take effect on 11/30. FC in DNA, 18, 1:8.

To Commodore H[ugh] G. Campbell, Commanding Naval Officer, Charleston, S.C., 11/26. Informs him about the forthcoming trial of James B. Taylor and others under charges preferred by John Floyd of Ga. FC in DNA, 121, 13:291.

To Speaker Henry Clay, 11/26. Pursuant to a House resolution of 4/20 (DS in DNA, 1, H-189), Calhoun encloses a very long list of Revolutionary pensioners under the law enacted on 3/18, reporting their names, addresses, annuities, terms and units of service, and the ranks of officers. LS with En in DNA, 201, 15A-F3; FC in DNA, 4, 2:2. (Compare Calhoun's report of 1/2/1819 to Clay about pensioners.)

From Joseph Lovell, 11/26. Dr. [Richard] Randall, whom Lovell had ordered to duty at Amelia Island, has been detained at Baltimore, where his services are not equally needed, by orders issued by officers outside the Medical Department and without the knowledge or approval of the Adjutant General, [Daniel Parker]. Lovell protests that such interference should not be permitted to occur or to recur. ALS with En in DNA, 1, L-25; FC in DNA, 242, 2:21.

To [James Monroe], 11/26. "The Secretary of War has the honor to represent to the President of the United States that the appropriation for the National Armouries is inadequate to the accomplishment of its object; and that it has become necessary for the Public Service, that $10,000 standing on the books of the Treasury to the Credit of Arsenals be transferred to the appropriation above named." FC in DNA, 6, 1:338.

To [James Monroe], 11/26. "I have the honor to submit for your approbation, the appointment of George Boyd, of the District of Columbia, as Indian Agent at Michilimackinac, vice Jacob Tipton, who has declined the acceptance of said appointment." FC in DNA, 6, 1:339.

Thomas Newton, [Jr., Representative from Va.,] to [James Monroe], 11/26. Recommends Samuel Miller for the position of Commandant of the Marine Corps. ALS in DNA, 128, 7:35.

To Commodore D[aniel] T. Patterson, New Orleans, 11/26. Because repairs to the U.S. Brig *Prometheus* have not been completed as soon as was expected, Calhoun asks Patterson to return the order issued on 11/23 that assigned that ship, under the command of Lt. Commandant William B. Finch, to a special duty; the order will be canceled. FC in DNA, 121, 13:291.

To Commodore D[aniel] T. Patterson, New Orleans, 11/26. If Lt. James B. Taylor and an Acting Midshipman named Brant are within Patterson's command, he is to order them to report to Capt. John Shaw at St. Marys, Ga. FC in DNA, 121, 13:290.

From Thomas Thorpe, Washington, 11/26. Applies for an appointment as a Clerk in the War Department, where, it is reported, new Clerkships are to be created. ALS in DNA, 103. (Letters recommending Thorpe to Calhoun that are in the same file were written on 11/25 from Richard Parrott, on [11]/28 from J[ohn] Mason, on 11/30 from Henry Foxall, on 12/2 from D. English, and on 12/3 from George Peter, [Representative from Md.].

To William A. Trimble, Lexington, Ky., 11/26. Pursuant to his conference with Calhoun and before Calhoun received his letter of 11/14 (ALS in DNA, 1, T-27) demanding a copy of the court-martial proceedings against [Edmund P.] Gaines "as a *right*" and threatening to resign if the copy is not made, Calhoun had ordered a copy made and sent. But he informs Trimble that "you are not strictly entitled to a copy, and that it is furnished from the peculiar circumstances of the case, and as a document which you deem important to be preserved among your papers." FC in DNA, 5, 1:97.

From D[ecius] Wadsworth, 11/26. Recommends that $7,000 be paid to Adam Carruth, who has delivered 250 stands of arms that have been approved and 500 stands that are now being inspected. FC in DNA, 32, 2:144.

To Capt. MEL[ANCTHON] T. WOOLSEY, U.S.N., Commanding Naval Officer, Sackets Harbor, [N.Y.]

Navy Department, Nov. 26th 1818

In reply to your letter of the 18th Ult[im]o relative to Mr. James Brooks, Acting Chaplain in the Navy, I have to inform you that the President of the United States [James Monroe] has decided that no unnecessary Courts Martial shall be held, and that the respective Commanding Naval Officers, shall dismiss all such complaints and charges as shall appear frivolous and vexatious, exercising their judgment & discretion; and in case of reference to this Department, their decisions would be confirmed, unless the good of the service should appear to require further measures.

You will cause Mr. Brooks to be released from arrest and order him to resume his duties.

FC in DNA, 131, 13:291–292. NOTE: Woolsey's letter of 10/18 is an LS with En in DNA, 133 (M-125:60). It reported that Midshipman Robert H. Nichols had provoked Brooks into comparing Nichols with a common sailor who deserved a severe whipping—words which led Nichols to demand the arrest and trial of Brooks. It enclosed a complaint by eight Navy officers against Marine Capt. William Strong.

To [John Quincy Adams], 11/27. Calhoun submits to Adams an ALS from Nat[haniel] Cutting, Chief Clerk in the War Department's Section of Bounty Lands, to Adams dated 11/26. Cutting has examined the claim of the heirs of the Chevalier Thomas de Mandiet du Plessis; has searched the extant records; has concluded that de Mandiet, "like many other gallant Foreign Officers" during the Revolution, "only took *temporary service* in the Army of the United States as a Voluntier [*sic*]" but "did not remain in it until the termination of the Contest"; and implies that the claim should be rejected. LU with En in DNA, 101 (M-179:42).

P[hilip] P[endleton] Barbour, [Representative from Va.,] to James Monroe, 11/27. Barbour recommends Maj. [Samuel] Miller for appointment as Commandant of the Marine Corps. ALS in DNA, 128, 7:37.

From Robert Butler, Washington, 11/27. Answers Calhoun's inquiry of "this date" concerning the distribution of the Chickasaws' goods: no part of the annuity or presents has been received or distributed by the treaty commissioners, [Andrew Jackson and Isaac Shelby]. ALS in DNA, 1, B-91.

From [Capt.] I[saac] Chauncey, New York [City], 11/27. Introduces and recommends Maj. Richard Smith as a worthy Marine who served with great distinction under Chauncey's command in the War of 1812 and as an applicant [for appointment as the Commandant of the Marine Corps]. LS in DNA, 128, 7:38.

To Commodore Isaac Chauncey, U.S.N., Commanding Naval Officer, New York [City]

Navy Department, Nov. 27th 1818

That the crew of the U.S. Brig Saranac may have an opportunity of re-entering [the Navy] at the Rendezvous [that is, recruiting station] for the U.S. Ship John Adams, now preparing for a cruise, you will please to issue orders directing the crew aforesaid to be paid off and discharged; and direct the officers attached to the Saranac to report to this Department.

FC in DNA, 121, 13:292.

From John W. Davis, Boston, 11/27. Forwards to Calhoun, in response to his request of 11/17 as Acting Secretary of the Navy, a report of the sale of the brigantine *Atlantic* and her cargo, [the proceeds of which will benefit the Navy Pension Fund]. CC with Ens in DNA, 201, 15A-F4; PC with Ens in House Document No. 6, 15th Cong., 2nd Sess.; PC with Ens in *American State Papers: Naval Affairs*, 1:558–562.

To M[AHLON] DICKERSON, [Senator from N.J.]

Friday, 27 Nov[embe]r 1818

J.C. Calhoun requests the favor of Hon. Mr. Dickerson's company to dinner on Tuesday next at half past 4 o'clock.

CC in NjHi, Mahlon Dickerson Papers.

To Constant Freeman, 11/27. Encloses for his information two copies of "the Regulations and Instructions for the Naval Service" that have recently been approved and ordered to be promulgated by James Monroe. They are to become effective for Navy officers within the U.S. on 12/1, for those in foreign service on 1/1/1819. FC in DNA, 122, 13:241.

Resolution by the House of Representatives, 11/27. In addition to the report of Revolutionary pensioners "made to this House in pursuance of a resolution of the last session," this resolution instructs Calhoun "to designate on the list thereof, the line, Corps, or vessel to which the pensioner belonged, the time of his service, and, if an Officer, his rank in the Army or Navy." Attested by Th[omas] Dougherty as the Clerk of the House. DS in DNA, 1, H-47.

To C[allender] Irvine, Philadelphia, 11/27. Discusses what surplus Army clothing will be available for distribution during 1819; estimates that 3,000 suits will be in stock on 12/31. FC in DNA, 3, 10:191. In reply on 12/3, Irvine confirmed this estimate. ALS in DNA, 1, I-42; FC in DNA, 45, 387:220.

To John Jamison, Natchitoches, La., 11/27. His letter of 10/28 (ALS in DNA, 1, J-29, discussing his policy as to rations, his failure to obtain a land cession from the Pascagoula and Apalache Indians, a new Spanish post 200 miles away, and a destructive tornado at Galveston) has been received. He is to continue to issue rations to such "Indians as may visit your post, by invitation, or to get their guns or other utensils mended. The offer of the government to the Pascagoula and Apalache Indians was made at their suggestion, as being advantageous to them, and no regret is experienced at the failure." FC in DNA, 72, D:230; FC in DNA, 3, 10:190–191.

From Thomas Jefferson

Monticello, Nov. 27, [18]18

Th[omas] Jefferson with great reluctance trespasses on the labors of the Secretary at war, merely to remind him of the case of M[onsieur] Poirey, aid[e] de camp and Secretary to Gen[era]l la Fayette; lest in the overwhelming mass of his duties it might escape his notice. He salutes him with assurance of his great personal esteem and high respect.

ALU in DLC, Thomas Jefferson Papers, vol. 214, 38160.

From Joseph Lovell, 11/27. "In conversing with Dr. [Hanson] Catlett a few days since upon the impropriety of punishing soldiers by protracted confinement in dungeons, by which their health is often materially affected, he mentioned several cases at Pittsburgh where he has for some time been stationed; and as I considered it a subject appertaining to the duties of a Medical Officer, he was directed to report the facts, which he has accordingly done in the enclosed letter." FC in DNA, 242, 2:21.

To James Monroe

Dep[art]m[en]t of War, 27 Nov[embe]r 1818

I have the honor to transmit treaties recently made with the Chickasaws, the Quapaws, the Wyandot, Seneca, Delaware, Shawnese, Potawatomies, Ottawas and Chippewas, the Peoria, Kaskaskias, Mitchigania, Cahokia & Tamarois, the Great & little Osages, the Weas, Potawatomies, Delaware and Miami, the Wyandot & the four Pawnees tribes of Indians. These treaties appear to be formed upon advantageous terms. By reference to the Journal of the Commissioners it appears that George & Levi Colbert, have bargained and sold to the United States, the reservations made to them by the treaty of September 1816 and that a deed of trust of the same has been made by them to James Jackson of Nashville. I would therefore suggest the propriety, in case the Chickasaw treaty be confirmed by the Senate, of providing by law for the payment of the sum stipulated to be given to them for their reservations.

FC in DNA, 6, 1:340.

To [James Monroe], 11/27. "I have the honor to lay before you a list of promotions & appointments made in the Army since the last session of the Senate." LS with En in DNA, 156, 15B-A2; FC in DNA, 6, 1:340.

From [Daniel Parker], 11/27. Reports that Peter Mossey, who has been on the Vt. pension roll since 8/2/1815, enlisted in the 2nd Infantry [Regiment] on 9/22/1818 and deserted a month later. Reports also that Edward Vickery, who has been on the N.Y. pension roll since 6/8/1815, enlisted in the Rifle Regiment on 2/21/1818 and deserted in 8/1818. Both men were able-bodied. FC in DNA, 12, 5:137.

From John Rodgers, President of the N[avy] Board

Navy Comm[issioners'] Off[ice,] 27 Nov[embe]r 1818

The Board of Navy Commissioners having concluded contracts for all the live oak timber contemplated, under the act for the gradual increase of the Navy, beg leave to state, that the contractors, in procuring this timber, fell many trees which are found not of sufficient dimensions to side & mould for the frames of line of battle ships or frigates, but would be abundantly large for sloops of war, & probably as much as would furnish the frames of twenty sloops, will be cut down—all of which will be lost to the service.

The Board beg leave to inform you that live oak timber has already become very scarce, & they apprehend, from the clearing of the grounds, on which it grows, for the culture of cotton, that it will become much more so. They would therefore respectfully suggest, that great advantage would arise to the service, if authority could be obtained to contract for the frames of Twenty sloops, which they have reason to believe can be done at a reduced price.

LS in DNA, 128, 7:41. NOTE: An AEI by Calhoun reads: "Mr. [Benjamin] Homans will see me upon this subject." An EU seems to constitute a copy of a reply written to Rodgers, saying, in effect, that Calhoun had "no hesitation in approving" the proposed means of procuring timbers for the construction of 20 sloops except that, because the law for the gradual increase of the Navy comprehended no ships smaller than frigates, Congressional approval should also be obtained.

From John Rodgers, 11/27. The U.S. brig *Prometheus* has been found to be unseaworthy and "is considered unworthy of repair, being generally rotten." Rodgers suggests that she be sold at public auction, after her armament shall have been removed first. LS in DNA, 128, 7:40.

From Lt. Col. W[ILLIAM] A. TRIMBLE

Maysville, Kentucky, 27 Nov[embe]r 1818

A prospect of the water rising induced me to abandon the plan of traveling through the wilderness.

I came to this place, with an expectation of obtaining my baggage, which was sent by Pittsburgh.

It has not yet ar[r]ived, but is expected in a few days, when I will proceed to New Orleans.

Herewith inclosed is a report, in relation to trade & intercourse with the Indians, on our south-western frontier, in pursuance of your instructions of the 16 ultimo. It would have been more full, and, to myself, more satisfactory, if I could have obtained my papers; but I was unwilling to delay it longer.

[Enclosure]

In yours of the 16 ultimo, received at Lexington, I am required to "report my opinion on the best mode to prevent the encroachment of our citizens, on lands belonging to the Indians, on our south-western frontier; & to prevent our people from passing into the Buffaloe [*sic*] country, either for the destruction of game, or to traffick with the Indians, without license."

Completely to effect these objects, it is very important that the south-western boundary, between the United States & the Spanish territories, should be definitely settled.

The Indian boundary should be extended from the Arkansaw [*sic*], to intersect the national boundary, at a point which would exclude, or leave to the north west, the principal nations, & tribes of Indians in that country.

And a chain of military posts should be established, on the national and Indian boundaries, to protect the frontiers; to restrain the white people from encroaching, or trespassing, on the Indians; and to prevent an illicit trade with the Spaniards & Indians.

As those posts cannot be placed so near each other, as to guard every point on those lines, it is suggested whether it might not be expedient to authorize the Indians to seize and deliver, to the civil or military authorities of the United States, persons found trespassing on their lands; and to authorize Indians under certain restrictions, to give testimony against persons so offending.

Until the south-western boundary of the United States, is established, the western & northern boundary of the State of Louisiana, to the point where it crosses Red River, thence up that River to its source, might be assumed as a temporary boundary.

I have not, at present, a sufficient knowledge of that country, to indicate the best site for an Indian boundary. Rivers or mountains are preferable to artificial lines.

The Arkansaw, from where the present Indian boundary strikes it, to the mouth of the Canadian; thence with the Canadian to its source; thence to the source of Blue River; thence with Blue River to its confluence with Red River & thence with Red River to the northern boundary of the State of Louisiana, is suggested as an Indian boundary which will probably combine the most advantages.

The Cad[d]o Indians, who I believe, have the only legitimate claim to the country, on the waters of Red River, within those limits, would willingly cede their lands on the left bank of Red River, if the United States would protect them in their possessions, on the right bank against the encroachment of American Citizens & the depredations of the Osage & Towcash or Panis Indians.

Within those limits there are but a few small tribes of Indians, who have recently settled in that country, by the express permission of the Cad[d]o Nation, & who might easily be induced to remove beyond the line.

It would be advisable to hold a treaty with all the Indian tribes on that frontier, for the purpose of set[t]ling their boundaries; and to explain to them the laws of the United States, in relation to Indians; & the determination of the executive to protect them in their rights.

The factory system should be sufficiently extended to supply all the Indians within the territories of the United States, or it should be entirely abolished, & a fair competition permitted, between citizens of the United States, under such regulations as it might be thought proper to prescribe. The present has all the disadvantages of both plans, without the advantages of either.

The trading establishments should be located in the Indian country, & the Indians discouraged, or prohibited from coming into the American settlements, for the purposes of trade: otherwise it will be impracticable to prevent the Indians from obtaining spirituous liquors. The laws in relation to that subject have been vioated with impunity, and to a very great extent, on the south-western frontier. The consequences are ruinous to the Indians, & injurious to the United States. White people should not be suffered to reside near the Indian boundary; & no Indians should be permitted to settle on or near the right bank of Red River, below where the Indian boundary strikes it.

The Indian Agents should reside in the Indian country, & where there is but one Agent for several nations, he should be located in a central & convenient situation.

If the French emigrants are permitted to retain possession of the country, which they occupy, on the Trinity River, it will not be practicable for the United States, to controul the Indian trade on that frontier.

No people have ever had so much influence, over the Indians of North America, as the French. If the French on the Trinity succeed in extending their influence over all the Indians on that frontier, they may become troublesome neighbours; & might, at a favourable crisis, afford a pretext for the interference of the French nation.

It is of some consequence to the United States, that their frontier (particularly such an important section as that occupied by the French) should be settled with American citizens, whose language, principles, habits, manners, & prejudices, are emphatically American.

ALS with En in DNA, 1, T-45.

From D[ECIUS] W[ADSWORTH]

Ordnance Office, Nov. 27, 1818

By examining the Books of the 2d Auditor, [William Lee,] it appears the sum of $7,000 has been charged on account of the Powder Contract with Col. [James] Johnson, & Maj. [Abram R.] Woolley claims to have paid $3,000 on account of the same; which has not yet been finally carried to his Credit, as the Evidence had not been furnished of the Powder having been proved; yet it must doubtless be considered as an advance.

The total amount therefore rec[eive]d on account of the Powder Contract, by Col. Johnson, is already $10,000, which is the sum you calculated to advance, & falls short but $500 of entire payment, for the quantity contracted for.

Besides it does not appear in this office that Major Woolley had any proper authority for concluding such a Contract. It will be proper therefore to charge the Bill of $3,000 drawn by Col. R[ichard] M. Johnson, to the St. Louis Army Contract.

P.S. On further Examination it appears the sum paid by Maj. Woolley is not $3,000 but $3,500 so that the 30,000 lb[s]. of Powder has been already paid for. D.W.

FC in DNA, 32, 2:145. NOTE: For corrective information see, herein, the letter of 12/1 from Wadsworth.

From Decius Wadsworth, 11/27. Returns the letter of 11/6 from Maj. [Abram R.] Woolley, commanding officer of the U.S. arsenal near Pittsburgh, who "appears to think" that "the Regulations respecting the Duties of Military Storekeepers" have a tendency "to abridge the authority of the commanding officer too much." In contrast, Wadsworth believes that, because "it is the Intention of Government to hold the Military Storekeepers accountable for the public Property in the Arsenals & Magazines, they ought to possess a certain Independence of Character in their official Capacity and not be made so far subordinate as to be in Danger of becoming mere Tools to the commanding officer." ALS in DNA, 1, W-78; FC in DNA, 32, 2:144–145.

John Quincy Adams to [John C. Calhoun, Acting] Secretary of the Navy, 11/28. Adams names 49 citizens of the U.S. who are imprisoned in Havana and designates two additional groups who are detained elsewhere [by the Spanish]. He requests [Calhoun] to obtain authorization from [James Monroe] and to dispatch a Navy ship to these three places, with its commanding officer to be ordered "to demand the release of those persons, and of all other Citizens of the United States who may be there imprisoned, unless satisfactory cause for their further detention be shewn [*sic*]." FC in DNA, 102 (M-40:15).

From Edmund P. Gaines, Fernandina, E[ast] F[la.], 11/28. Transmits a corrected copy of his letter of 11/24 [concerning desertions]; says he expects anything found objectionable in that letter, after "a liberal and comprehensive scrutiny," to be "rejected or laid aside without the least ceremony." ALS with En in DNA, 2, G-1818; LS in DNA, 11, 12215.

From Andrew Jackson

Nashville, 28 Nov[embe]r 1818

I enclose you a communication [of 10/31] from General [Eleazer W.] Ripley with my reply [of 11/15], as well as an answer [dated 11/27] of mine to a previous letter of his on the same subject. I cannot but think that the claims of the Louisianians are unfounded. Spain is at present too weak in the Texas [area], to effect any military projects against our territory from that quarter; and it would be the height of imprudence at present, to permit the occupancy of the Rio Hondo [?] with an inconsiderable force, to attract our attention from more important and vulnerable points. The Spanish designs should be unmasked, before counter movements are attempted; in the mean while I shall keep my forces so disposed that they may be concentrated to act with celerity and effect upon any point assailed.

I enclose you a copy of a letter [of 10/15] from Col. [William] King, detailing a conflict between Captain Boyles of the Rangers & a detatchment [*sic*] of Hostile warriors. The conduct of the Captain in this affair was meritorious, and I trust ere this he has recovered from his wound, and disappointed the hopes of the warriors of the Choctawhatchy. A short time since every mail from the South reported the pleasing intelligence of the general submission of the Seminoles; the cause of the reassumption of hostilities is stated in the Colonel[']s communication. The fact that the news of the restoration of Pensacola to Spain had revived their hopes and again excited them to war is an additional evidence of the propriety of my operations in the Floridas, and has confirmed me in my unalterable opinion that the Seminole conflict could not have been terminated by any other means than [were] there adopted. My only apprehensions are that my operations were not sufficiently extensive to ensure permanent tranquility in the South. St. Augustine is still in possession of the Spaniards, and the whole Peninsula is beyond the controul of our Garrisons. The situation of Florida in relation to our country is peculiar and demands the early attention of our government. Bordering almost on the Creek nation, and within the vicinity of the four southern Tribes of Indians, her territory will always prove an assylum [*sic*] to the disaffected and and restless savage as well as to a more dangerous population, unless some energetic government can be established to controul or exclude these Interlopers. The Savages & Negroes who have not submitted to our authority have fled east of the Suwaney [*sic*] river, and whether settled in the Alatchaway plains, near St. Augustine, or more southwardly we have yet to learn. Their force no doubt is too inconsiderable to create any serious disturbances with this country, but if unmolested they may acquire confidence with their strength, and prove a destructive enemy to our Frontier settlers. They should be persued [*sic*], before they recover from the panic of our last operations. I submit to your considerations military operations for the spring connected with the occupancy of the Bay of Tampea [*sic*]. The plan proposed is to embark from Fort Gadsden, or Pensacola 500 Regulars, for the Bay of Tampea, together with a force, say 150 or 200 men adequate to the maintaining of the work to the [*sic*; be] constructed at that point. Simultaneous with this movement, to push a force of 5 or 600 men up the St. Johns, and occupy a position at or near the old Indian Town Pecolota. This force as soon as strongly fortified to be actively employed in scouring the country as far west as Suwaney forcing to, or receiving the, submission of the hostile Indians, who will be sent into the interior of the Creek nation. The Troops detached to the Bay of Tampea, having constructed and garrisoned a suitable work, having reconnoitered the neighbouring country, and destroyed Woodbynes [*sic;* George Woodbine's] Negro establishment, to march directly to the position occupied on the St. Johns, deviating only where Indian villages or settlements (if there are any in the country) invite their attention. From the best information which I can collect, the march from Tampea to the point proposed on the St. Johns, would not exceed 7 days. Each man from my own experience can march with 8 days rations on his back, which with due economy will last twelve, time sufficient to perform the operation intended. The expence of the expedition would be trifling as it is proposed that none but Regulars should be employed, and the advantage to the nation incalculable, as finally crushing savage hostilities in the South, and affording active service to some of our Regiments who have grown sluggish from the inactivity of garrison outlets.

LS with Ens in DNA, 1, J-71; CCEx with En in DNA, 202, 15A-E1; PEx in House Document No. 117, 15th Cong., 2nd Sess.; PEx in *American State Papers: Military Affairs,* 1:752. NOTE: Calhoun's answer to this letter appears herein under the date of 12/28.

Jonathan Roberts, [Senator from Pa.,] New Jersey Ave., [Washington,] to "John C. Calhoun, Secretary of War," 11/28. Explains that Lt. Wolcott Chauncey, U.S.N., has suffered unjustly from opposition by his brother, Commodore Isaac Chauncey, and urges that the Lt. should be given his long-overdue promotion. ALS in DNA, 128, 7:42.

Midshipman CHARLES H. STARR to SMITH THOMPSON, "Sec[reta]ry [of the] Navy," Washington

Wilmington (Del:) 28th Nov[embe]r 1818

Having recently received an appointment as Midshipman in the Navy of the United States (during the period of the acting Secretaryship of Hon. J.C. Calhoun) but having not yet received a confirmation of my appoint[men]t from that Gentleman, from miscarriage ["of my letter" *interlined*] I fear, I have thought proper to inform you of the receipt of my warrant on the 20th inst[ant] & to request an answer from you enclosing orders to repair on board some vessel, as I am anxious to put to practice my theoretical knowledge of navigation which I have obtained. A compliance with my request will much oblige your . . . .

ALS in DNA, 134. NOTE: An EU indicates that orders were sent to Starr on 12/4.

To Maj. A[bram] R. Wool[l]ey, Pittsburgh, 11/28. Informs him that Calhoun has examined the evidence offered in support of certain allegations against Woolley's financial transactions, has found the evidence insufficient to justify a formal inquiry, and intends to have no further investigation of the charges. FC in DNA, 5, 1:97.

From John Bowyer, Green Bay, 11/29. Encloses his bond as Indian Agent. Requests a copy of the laws of the U.S. to enable him "to execute the duties of my appointment correctly." ALS with En in DNA, 1, B-195.

From JACOB BROWN

Brownville, [N.Y.,] November 29th 1818

Major [Samuel A.] Storrow some time since delivered to me the enclosed view of Major [Nathaniel Nye] Hall's case. I have been at a loss to know what to do with it, but, upon reflection supposing that you would be pleased to compare it with the opinion of the Attorney General on the same subject, I have concluded to transmit it to you.

FC in DLC, Jacob Brown Papers, Letterbooks, 2:128.

From Jacob Brown, Brownville, [N.Y.,] 11/29. Col. [Henry] Atkinson reports that six miles of the road from Sackets Harbor to Plattsburg, [N.Y.,] have been completed. LU in DNA, 1, B-87; CC in DLC, Jacob Brown Papers, Letterbooks, 2:127–128.

From I[saac] Chauncey, U.S.S. *Washington,* New York [City], 11/29. Encloses a recent letter from his Purser, written in protest against the requirement, in the new Navy regulations, that fresh meat should be used in rations twice a week; that Purser is serving fresh beef exclusively and getting it for only $.085 per pound. "As the ration of fresh meat is considerably cheaper than salt, I wish to be instructed whether the fresh is to be continued. I am under the impression that the new regulation upon the subject was intended to apply more to foreign stations than in the United States where fresh meat is always cheaper than salt." LS with En in DNA, 133 (M-125:60).

From E[li] B. Clemson, St. Louis, 11/29. Encloses a letter [dated at St. Louis on 11/29 and addressed to Calhoun] from Judge [John B.C.] Lucas defending Clemson against "the foul Statements" of Col. [Talbot] Chambers. Clemson asks Calhoun to decide nothing "till my letters forwarded this day to the Commissary General [of Purchases, Callender Irvine,] are before you." ALS with En in DNA, 1, C-99; PC with En in Carter, ed., *Territorial Papers,* 15:465.

From Joseph McMinn, Cherokee Agency, 11/29. Reports in some detail how his negotiations of this month with the Eastern Cherokees proceeded. They disdained an indemnity offer as high as $200,000; but McMinn put them on the defensive in respect to their opposition to emigration; they are now pledged to discontinue this opposition. McMinn reports that "718 families have been enrolled for emigration" since 12/20/1817 (289 of them since 10/20/1818); 146 other families "have made reservations"; so a total of 864 families have relinquished their claims to land east of the Mississippi. "When we add these to the population settled on the Arkansaw previous to the date of the Treaty, I believe we may safely conclude that we have one half the Cherokee population on our side." He explains that he needs urgently such items as 200 long rifles, 1,000 blankets, 500 brass kettles, and 20,000 flints, to be distributed through four stores, which would help to persuade other Cherokees to emigrate. "For my self I feel very anxious to see the Cherokee title extinguished, and should not in the present case feel otherwise than honor[e]d by being continued, and in that event, I believe I would resign my Executive office [as Governor of Tenn.], or at least decline a reëlection, and devote myself entirely to the duties which would attach to this business." He has received but has not encouraged an application by "a very influencial [*sic*] Chief formerly in the opposition [to emigration], (and not yet fully removed) to sanction the visit of an opposition deputation from here to Washington"; if such men should be allowed to make the proposed trip, "I should feel my self bound to attend at the City with them." LS in DNA, 77 (M-271:2, frames 1296–1303); draft in DNA, 75 (M-208:14); PEx in *American State Papers: Indian Affairs,* 2:481–482.

From Joseph McMinn, Cherokee Agency, 11/29. In response to a call from Andrew Jackson for men, McMinn has detached one Lt. and 30 enlisted men from the detail guarding the public stores there "to remove the intruders from the Cherokee lands." To the Cherokees who oppose U.S. policies McMinn has issued the threat "that they had forf[e]ited their right to protection, from the United States," and that McMinn might "discharge the troops." He suggests that 30 *mounted* militia guardsmen may be sufficient. Now that the boundary between Tenn. and Ga. has been surveyed, he also suggests that it might "be better policy that each State, should remove its own intruders." LS in DNA, 1, M-132; FC in DNA, 75 (M-208:14); PEx in *American State Papers: Indian Affairs,* 2:482.

From Charles R. Vining, Nathaniel H. Loring, Charles R. Holmes, Thomas Ragland, and Wilson M.C. Fairfax, Committee in Behalf of the Corps of Cadets, New York City, 11/29. They relate developments that have produced complaints against Capt. [John] Bliss, commander of the Cadet Corps, and disciplinary measures by [Sylvanus Thayer] against themselves. They ask Calhoun to decide "whether our conduct has been *ill-timed, indelicate,* or *unmilitary.*" CC in DLC, Andrew Jackson Papers, 8434–8435; PC in *American State Papers: Military Affairs,* 2:16–17; PC in House Document No. 14, 16th Cong., 1st Sess.

From P[HILIP] P[ENDLETON] BARBOUR, [Representative from Va.]

[Washington ?], Nov. 30th 1818

Thinking it probable from your letter, that there will be some appointments of Cadets in the next spring, I beg leave to present

William L. Harris, & Uriel Wright, two respectable young men of my District, as candidates for a Cadetcy, whensoever a vacancy shall occur; I am also requested to present George P. French of Fredericksburg, as a candidate for the office of one of the additional Clerks to be appointed to the War Department; altho' I am not personally acquainted with him, I am with his family, & I have no doubt, but that he is a young man of respectability, & abundantly qualified for the office which he solicits.

ALS in DNA, 15, 1819, 93, with an EU indicating that Harris was appointed on 3/24/1819 to be a Cadet.

From GEORGE GIBSON, Commissary General of Subsistence

Office of the Com. Gen. of Subsistence, Nov. 30, 1818

As the movement of the troops destined for Yellow Stone & St. Peters will take place before the commencement of the new contracts [on 6/1/1819], I must request that a requisition be made on Colo[nel] James Johnson, under the contract for Bellefountain [*sic*], for four hundred & thirty thousand Rations to be in deposit at St. Louis or Bellefountain on the 20th of March next.

I have further to request that in addition to the above the several contractors be ordered to leave in deposit at the expiration of their contracts, provisions for two months at all posts where troops may be stationed on the last day of May next on the Missouri & upper Mississipi [*sic*] and at Fort Wayne—at all other posts where troops may be stationed on the last day of May next provisions for one month except at Chicago, Green Bay and Michilimackinac, where the deposits stipulated in the contracts are thought sufficient.

LS in DNA, 1, G-42; FC (dated 11/20) in DNA, 191, 1:3.

From ANDREW JACKSON

Nashville, 30[t]h Nov[.] 1818

I have the honor to acknowledge the receipt of your Letter of the 13th Ins[tan]t advising that Col. [John] McKee, Agent of the Choctaws, has been charged with the payment of the Warriors of that Nation lately in the [military] Service of the United States, of which

I have notified Capt. [John B.] Hogan, Paymaster of the 4th Infantry. It is gratifying to me to find that the late treaty concluded by Governor [Isaac] Shelby and myself with the Chickasaw Nation of Indians meets with your approbation.

CC in DLC, Andrew Jackson Papers.

From ALEX[ANDER] KERR, Cashier

Bank of the Metropolis, [Washington,] 30 Nov. 1818

I have been led into a disagreeable situation in this Institution by Mr. [Benjamin G.] Orr's acceptance, for which he has drawn a draft on you; our Board gave the money for it on my application & they now expect me to return it, which is not convenient: should you think it safe, & w[oul]d order a Warrant to issue for it, it would confer a particular favor on me.

ALS in DNA, 1, K-15, with an EI by L[ewis] E[dwards] that Kerr was informed that no further advances would be allowed to Orr until his accounts were settled.

To John McKee, 11/30. "Your letter of the 27th ult[im]o [LS in DNA, 1, M-88, signed also by his fellow Commissioner, Daniel Burnet, and reporting their failure to persuade even one Choctaw Chief to vote for a cession of any land to the U.S.] has been rec[eive]d, and I regret to learn that the Commissioners have failed in effecting the object for which they were appointed. The goods which were forwarded to be distributed as presents at the treaty you will cause to be delivered to the order of Thos. L. McKenney, Esq., Superintendent of Indian Trade." FC in DNA, 72. D:231.

To Thomas L. McKenney, Georgetown, 11/30. Henry Sherburne and John McKee have been ordered to deliver to McKenney the goods that were to be used as presents at two recent Indian treaties; McKenney is to be held responsible for the goods under the principles of his letter of 11/24 [LS in DNA, 1, M-93, with which McKenney enclosed a confidential journal of the recent Chickasaw treaty negotiations; in which he gave a significant report of businessmen's opinions at the public sale of Indian goods on 11/23, which "was well attended, and profitable beyond all former example"; and in which he proposed to sell the treaty goods in one of the Indian Factories, at a loss if necessary]. FC in DNA, 72, D:231.

To Stephen Pleasonton, 11/30. Discusses the accounts of the commissioners to treat with the Chickasaws, including a payment of more than $12,000 to J.H. Reily and rations to be charged to contractor [Camillus] Griffith. FC in DNA, 72, D:230.

To Tunstall Quarles, [Representative from Ky.,] 11/30. Answers his inquiry of 11/26 (ALS in DNA, 1, Q-1) in behalf of a constiituent, Howard Elliot, whose remote residence would make it inconvenient for him to obtain a discharge certificate and who would like, therefore, to submit a certificate of faithful service with his application for a veteran's benefits. Replies that Elliot is known to have received "a regular discharge" and that he must either produce his discharge certificate or swear that it has been lost. FC in DNA, 3, 10:192.

From El[eazer] W. Ripley

On board The Shield, Nov[ember] 30, 1818

I have recieved [*sic*] your letter enclosing one from the Assistant Agent of Indian Affairs at the Sulphur Forks [John Jamison ?] to T[homas L.] McKenn[e]y Esq. Superintendant [*sic*].

In a short time I will arrange and forward to you all the intelligence which I have on this subject and will renew to you a proposition which I made a year and an half since to the [Acting] Sec[retar]y of War [George Graham] on the subject of exploring thoroughly the Country up Red River.

That the Indians have long felt dis[s]atisfied I have known for some time—but I am in hopes, that no great degree of danger menaces us from that quarter.

The fresh Reg[imen]t will be on the Sabine eer [*sic*] long and this force will have an improving effect along our western frontier.

I wish you to examine Darby['']s map of Lou[i]s[ian]a and you will percieve [*sic*] a sort of road marked from Stark Island in the Mississippi River to Na[t]chitoches. This only exists on paper but it is very practicable over a high ridgy Country. Two Comp[anies] of Infantry would complete it in 1 year. The effect would be to turn a pretty strong current of population towards the Sabine & up Red River and would do more than Posts and fortifications to cover that section of our Country. Shall I undertake it as soon as my force will allow?

ALS in DNA, 1, R-72.

To E[leazer] W. Ripley, New Orleans, 11/30. Answers his two letters of 10/31 (LS's in DNA, 1, R-46 and R-48, with 2 CC's of the latter in DLC, Andrew Jackson Papers, 8215–8217) complaining that he has at his command only about 630 men; protesting that the 8th Regiment, already undermanned, should not have been weakened by detaching some of its men for recruiting duty at Boston; enumerating various units of his troops that have been diverted to duties in the Floridas and elsewhere; and reporting that he has sent some of his troops to the Sabine River because of a menacing approach by Spanish forces. "Every aid" possible "has been furnished to enable you to fill the ranks of the Regiments under your command"; the detachments of the 8th have been ordered to rejoin it. In answer to Ripley's proposal of 11/1 (LS in DNA, 1, R-47; PC in Carter, ed., *Territorial Papers,* 18:451) that he be allowed to employ one "Robinson [William H. Robertson]" to procure at Havana, [Cuba,] documents to prove government ownership of additional land at Mobile, approves any action that Ripley's judgment dictates. FC in DNA, 3, 10:192.

From John Rodgers

Navy Comm[issioners'] Off[ice,] 30 Nov[embe]r 1818

On the 1st July 1818, the Board of Navy Commissioners entered into contract with Col. James Johnson of Great Crossing[s,] Kentuckey [*sic*], for 2,000 barrels of pork, for the use of the Navy, for the year 1819, at seventeen dollars p[e]r barrel, payable on delivery of the pork, & Col. Johnson has given bond with satisfactory sureties, in the sum of seventeen thousand dollars, for the faithful performance of the contract. The contract stipulates that the whole of the pork will be delivered in the course of the ensuing winter & spring.

Under these circumstances Col. Johnson has drawn on the President of this Board, under date 17 Nov[embe]r instant, for $5,000, payable ninety days after date.

This draft is not warranted by the contract; but as it is understood to have arisen from peculiar & unexpected circumstances on the part of Col. Johnson, & as it is probable that by the time it shall become due, Col. Johnson will have delivered pork exceeding its amount, as it operates with him as a great facility in enabling him to execute his contract, as his sureties are, like himself, responsible men, & as moreover, Rich[ar]d M. Johnson esq. has pledged himself, in the event of the Pork not being delivered at maturity of the draft to pay the amount of it, if required, the Board of Navy Commissioners are of opinion that the draft may be accepted without incurring any risk. And, considering that the contract, so far as relates to the price agreed to be given, is a favorable one to the Public, they would, under all the circumstances of the case, respectfully recommend that it be accepted, or that an assurance be given to the holder, that it will at maturity be paid.

The Board have the honor to enclose the draft in question, which has just been presented to them.

LS in DNA, 128, 7:45. NOTE: An EU states that the draft was accepted on 11/30.

To Henry Sherburne, 11/30. "I have received your letter of the 9th instant [LS in DNA, 1, S-101], and the accounts [totaling $37,550 paid to the Chickasaws 'under former Treaties'] are referred to the 5th Auditor of the Treasury [Stephen Pleasonton] for adjustment. You will cause the goods forwarded to the Chickasaws and intended to be presented to them during the late treaty to be delivered over to the order of Thos. L. McKenney, Esq., Superintendent of Indian Trade." Calhoun does not reply to Sherburne's submission of his census of the Chickasaws, his appeal for government employment for himself near Newport, R.I., and his announcement that [David Godfrey] Cook would leave in a few days to seek private employment in the South. FC in DNA, 72, D:231.

S[ylvanus] Thayer, West Point, to W[alker] K. Armistead, 11/30. Thayer reports to the Chief Engineer the "disagreeable" developments in the Military Academy "during the last week," in which friction arose between Capt. John Bliss of the faculty and some of the Cadets. CC in DNA, 203, 16A-D14.1.

From Decius Wadsworth, 11/30. If $10,000 have been transferred from the arsenal fund to the armory fund, as Wadsworth suggested on 11/19, he requests that $12,500 be sent to John Chaffee, Paymaster of the Springfield, Mass., Armory. "The expences at Harpers ferry [*sic*] and Springfield for the month of December will remain to be provided for by subsequent appropriation of about $25,000." FC in DNA, 32, 2:146.

From William P. Zantzinger, Washington, 11/30. Solicits an appointment to one of the 12 positions as Clerk about to be established in the War Department. Encloses a petition in his behalf dated 11/25. ALS with En in DNA, 11, 14889.

Maj. [Samuel] Miller, [Washington,] to [James Monroe], 11/——. Encloses the letter from W[illiam] Eustis dated 11/14 recommending Miller for appointment as the commander of the U.S. Marine Corps. ALU in DNA, 128, 7:4.

DECEMBER 1818

CALHOUN SUBMITTED TO THE HOUSE OF REPRESENTATIVES, through Speaker Henry Clay, two major reports, each quite thoughtfully prepared. One proposed to substitute private enterprise for government operation in the Indian trade. The other suggested improvements in the legal ration for subsistence of the Army. Fateful contracts were awarded to James Johnson for supplying the Mississippi and Missouri Expeditions with rations and with transportation. Orders were given to Topographical Engineer Stephen H. Long on the 15th for explorations in the West that were to become known as "Long's first expedition." The daily pressure of business with Congressmen and Senators concerning applications, recommendations, appointments, promotions, pensions, and the like was incessant, inescapable. Army funds appropriated for more than one activity during 1818 were totally exhausted; creditors had to await next year.

From J[oseph] A[nderson, First Comptroller,] 12/1. Fifth Auditor [Stephen Pleasonton] has decided that Benjamin G. Orr is entitled to receive $707.31 for rations furnished to Indians and interpreters at Fort Claiborne in the year that ended on 5/31/1818. Anderson proposes that this sum be credited against some of Orr's debts under other accounts that have not yet been settled and seeks Calhoun's warrant. FC in DNA, 59, 18:393.

From N[icholas] Boilvin, Prairie du Chien, [Ill. Territory,] 12/1. Expresses his delight that Calhoun succeeded [William H.] Crawford as Secretary of War; appreciates his appointment in the Indian service; discusses British influence among the Indians in the Northwest and three alternative courses to combat it; says, "I am not a little exposed to danger, and . . . I fear for my life." Translation (from the French) in DNA, 1, B-161.

From I[saac] Chauncey, New York [City], 12/1. He has received Calhoun's letter of 11/27 "directing the Crew of the United States Brig *Saranac* to be paid off and discharged, and I have this day issued orders to that effect." LS in DNA, 133 (M-125:60).

To John J. Crittenden, U.S. Senate, 12/1. "I have received your letter of yesterday covering the account of Governor [Isaac] Shelby. The voucher in its present form is not complete: to make it so, it will be necessary for the Gov[erno]r to certify that 'he was actually, for the time charged, engaged in the performance of the duties of his commission, and that he incurred the expences charged.' But if the immediate payment is an object of any importance, I will direct the money to be advanced; and, in the meantime, you may obtain the requisite certificate to be filed with his account." FC in DNA, 72, D:232.

To [James L.] Edwards, Pension Office, 12/1. "I have received your report [of 11/25 (ALS in DNA, 1, E-17)] of the inattention to business of the Clerks in your office. I am pleased to find that you except Messrs. [William] Hickey & Gannt [*sic* for Edward A. Gantt] from the number of those whose conduct deserves reprehension. By the enclosed you will perceive the course I shall pursue in relation to negligence and inattention of Clerks for the future." FC in DNA, 3, 10:193.

From Nathaniel Frye, Jr., 12/1. As ordered by Calhoun on 9/5, Frye reports about half-pay pensioners and the funds available for paying them. LS with En in DNA, 2, B-1818.

To W[ILLIAM] LAMBERT, [Clerk, Pension Office]

Dep[art]m[en]t of War, Dec[embe]r 1, 1818

From the report of Mr. [James L.] Edwards I learn that you have been at the Pension Office but one day for a fortnight past and no cause is assigned for your absence; such negligence will not be tolerated & unless you give strict and punctual attention to your duty within office hours your name shall be stricken from the list of Clerks.

FC in DNA, 3, 10:193. NOTE: Lambert answered on 12/4.

To John McKee, Choctaw Agent

Department of War, 1st Dec[embe]r 1818

I have rec[eive]d your letter [of 10/30] covering a talk of two Chiefs of the Choctaw nation [who want to visit Washington for conferences] to [James Monroe,] the President of the United States [ALS in DNA, 77, 4060 (M-271:2, frames 669–673)].

Under every circumstance the President thinks their [proposed] visit to this place would be attended with no good, and, therefore, directs that you give them no encouragement to undertake it.

FC in DNA, 72, D:232.

Miami Indian Chiefs to James Monroe, 12/1. In a friendly "speech" by Chief Little Eyes, delivered for Jackow and other Chiefs, they request compensation for lands to which they granted hunting rights to the Delawares and other tribes, which sold those lands to the U.S. DS (signed with the marks of the Chiefs) in DNA, 2, S-1818.

To D[avid] B. Mitchell, Milledgeville, 12/1. "I enclose herewith for your information a copy of a letter addressed to this Dep[art]m[en]t by S[amuel] B. Shields, Esq., concerning the Road between Fort Hawkins & Fort Claiborn[e]. Perhaps you will find some valuable hints in it, which, if improved, may be beneficial to the public." FC in DNA, 3, 10:194.

From J[ames] B. Reynolds

Clarksville, [Tenn.,] 1st Dec[embe]r 1818

I am informed the Commissioners have reported favourably on the Reynoldsburgh [*sic*] Road. The Contractor [Dawsey P. Hudson] has therefore been urging me for the Balance of the money, alledging [*sic*] that it was improper to detain it, as the Sureties he gave was [*sic*] sufficient for any failure on his part. Those Commissioners, have also been soliciting me to apply to you in their behalf for Compensation. I can vouch for the integrity of those men.

I am glad this business is disposed of. I have had trouble and anxiety enough about it. But I trust it will afford to the people of this country all the Convenience and Utility I so warmly calculated on, and do now most sincerely wish. This road is found of great advtange to those who are migrating to the late purchase, and I am told there are already numbers in motion.

ALS in DNA, 1, R-63.

To H[enry] Shaw, [Representative from Mass.,] 12/1. Answering his letter of 11/24, assures him that it will not be necessary for Dr. [Samuel] Shaw, [Henry Shaw's father and a former Representative from Vt.,] to be present in Washington for his accounts to be settled [prior to his resignation as a Post Surgeon as of 12/31]. FC in DNA, 3, 10:194.

From Henry Sherburne

Chickasaw Agency, Dec[embe]r 1st 1818

Yesterday I rec[eive]d the enclosed copies of a deposition & letter from Benjamin Fooy Esq[ui]r[e] dated at Hopefield, Nov[embe]r 23d 1818, which I forward that you may be acquainted with the fact, & thereby give such directions as you may think necessary & proper. The party [of Indians] that robbed the boat Noble I suppose went over to the West side of the Mississippi, as nothing has been heard of them since to my knowledge. The robbery took place about ten or twelve miles from Fort Pickering, Chickasaw Bluffs, & I am very apprehensive that further mischief will happen, if some immediate remedy is not provided. I have written Maj. Gen[era]l [Andrew] Jackson on that subject & sent him a copy of the deposition, & letter of Mr. Fooy's.

LS with 2 Ens in DNA, 1, S-133.

To Henry Sherburne, 12/1. His letter of 11/9 to James Monroe [LS in DNA, 1, S-105] pleading for an appointment in government service near Newport, R.I., has been forwarded to the War Department, and Monroe has told Calhoun to inform Sherburne "that there exists no opportunity of which he [Monroe] can avail himself to gratify your wishes." FC in DNA, 72, D:232.

To S[amuel] B. Shie[l]ds, Jackson (Clark County), Ala. Territory, 12/1. Answering his letter of 11/16 (ALS in DNA, 1, S-98;

PC in Carter, ed., *Territorial Papers,* 18:470–471), Calhoun shows him that Calhoun had previously gotten the same idea about the road westward from Fort Hawkins. Because Calhoun thinks that Shields has made "some valuable suggestions," a copy of Shields's letter has been sent to [David B.] Mitchell. Shields can write to Mitchell if he thinks it "advisable." FC in DNA, 3, 10:193; PC in Carter, ed., *Territorial Papers,* 18:485.

To William Stelle, [Pension Office,] 12/1. "Enclosed you have the report of Mr. [James L.] Edwards upon the negligent manner [in which] you have performed your duty in the Pension Office. Strict and punctual attention to duty within office hours is enjoined on all, and unless you give such attention or render a satisfactory excuse, you will be dismissed [from] the service." FC in DNA, 3, 10:193. (The index in the manuscript volume cited indicates that this Clerk's name was William Stelle, which is correct; but p. 193 in the volume indicates that his name was "Laub Stelle," and pp. 339–340 give it as "William Steele.")

J[OSEPH] G. SWIFT to the "Secretary of War"

New York [City], 1 Dec. 1818

Major [Richard] Smith of the Marines will have the honour to present you this line of introduction, which I have taken the liberty to give in favour [of] a much respected & exemplary man whom I have long known to be a good officer. The Brevet which he holds was the reward of his military services on the Lakes during the late War.

ALS in DNA, 128, 7:50.

From D[ECIUS] WADSWORTH

Ordnance Office, 1 Dec. 1818

I find myself to have been mistaken in supposing the sum of $3,500 paid by Maj. [Abram R.] Woolley on account of Powder, to have been rec[eive]d on account of the last Contract [as I reported to you on 11/27]. That sum was paid on account of a previous Contract for Powder. There can be no objection therefore to a further advance of $3,000 if you think best to Sanction it. There will still remain a Balance of $500 due from the U[nited] States after all the Powder shall have been received.

FC in DNA, 32, 2:146.

From Capt. Samuel Evans, Navy Yard, New York [City], 12/2. Recommends that Bvt. Maj. [Richard] Smith of the Marine Corps be promoted. ALS in DNA, 128, 7:52.

Order by the House of Representatives, 12/2. "Ordered, That the petitions of William Lawrence, Luther Gregory, Levi B. Stewart, Thomas Hook and Edward Dean, be severally referred to the Secretary of War." Attested by Th[omas] Dougherty as Clerk of the House. DS in DNA, 1, H-62.

Transportation contract of James Johnson, 12/2. These articles of agreement between Quartermaster General Thomas S. Jesup, as the representative of the U.S. government, and James Johnson of Scott County, Ky., obligate Johnson "to furnish two steam-boats, calculated to navigate the Mississippi and its waters," and to have these craft ready for Jesup's orders by 3/1/1819. These boats are to transport "provisions, munitions of war, detachments and their Baggage," and other articles to the mouth of the St. Peters River on the Mississippi, the mouth of the Yellowstone River on the Missouri, Belle Point on the Arkansas River, "and all other posts whether intermediate or beyond." If "this mode of navigation should succeed" but the two steamboats should prove insufficient, then Johnson shall provide, "on due and reasonable notice," one or more additional steamboats. If "upon experiment it shall be found that any difficulty should exist as to the entire transportation of the provisions, and munitions of war, and other articles aforesaid, in this way, then and in this case, the said James Johnson shall in a reasonable time, say thirty days, provide a sufficient number of Keel boats, and transport the same by them." Jesup promises to furnish "a Corporal's Guard for the protection of each Boat thus employed and the property laden therein." In view of the difficulty of specifying a precise payment to be made for Johnson's service, it is agreed that he "shall be allowed a reasonable compensation . . . equitable and just," based upon "ordinary rates" but with an extra allowance in consideration of "the hazard attending the navigation of waters, at points so distant and heretofore unexplored by such mode of navigation." If Jesup and Johnson should disagree as to the amount of this differential, each should choose one arbiter to settle the matter; if these arbiters should disagree, the arbiters shall appoint one umpire, "whose decision shall be final." Jesup is obligated to make "reasonable" advances "from time to time" to Johnson, when Johnson shall have given "good and sufficient security for the faithful performance of his several obligations herein stipulated." This contract was signed in Washington by Jesup and by Richard M. Johnson as attorney in fact for James Johnson; it was witnessed by 1st Lt. John L. Gardner and by 2nd Lt. Thomas Johnston, Artillery officers. 2 CC's in DLC, United States Army: Quartermaster Department; CC in DLC, John Rodgers Papers, vol. 2; CC in DNA, 1, C-67; PC in House Document No. 110, 16th Cong., 2nd Sess.

Performance bond for James Johnson's transportation contract, 12/2. In view of the fact that advances are to be made under this contract, the signers of this bond bind themselves and their estates to the maximum extent of "the penal sum of 50,000 Dollars" to prevent loss to the U.S. under the contract. This performance bond was signed in Washington by Richard M. Johnson as attorney for his four brothers and one brother-in-law, James Johnson, William Ward, John T. Johnson, Joel Johnson, and Henry Johnson; and it is witnessed by John L. Gardner and Thomas Johnston. Some copies have an EI stating that it was approved by Calhoun. CC in DNA, 1, P-40; 2 CC's in DLC, United States Army: Quartermaster Department; CC in DLC, John Rodgers Papers, vol. 2; CC (not dated) in DNA, 1, C-67; PC in House Document No. 110, 16th Cong., 2nd Sess.

From Joseph Lovell, 12/2. Reports that no quarterly returns have been received from Drs. M[oses] H. Elliot[t], German "Center [Senter]," Jabez W. Heustis, George W. Maupin, Squire Lea, and George C. Clitherall. Orders have been sent to them through their commanding officers demanding explanations of this neglect of duty. ALS in DNA, 11, 12460; FC in DNA, 242, 2:22; FC in DNA, 243, 1:28.

From Thomas L. McKenney, 12/2. Acknowledges Calhoun's letter of 11/30 and agrees to abide by its directions. McKenney has already directed [John] McKee to deliver the $6,500 worth of goods that had been sent to the Southwest to be used as presents to the Choctaws in treaty negotiations to the Choctaw Factory for sale. LS in DNA, 1, M-96; FC in DNA, 73, E:170.

From Samuel R. Marshall, New York [City], 12/2. Attests the admirable qualities of [Bvt.] Maj. [Richard] Smith of the Marine Corps. ALS in DNA, 128, 7:53.

Monsieur —— Milon, Baltimore, to [Benjamin W.] Crowninshield, 12/2. Milon asks Crowninshield to recommend him to [Thomas] Jefferson for appointment as a teacher of design, music, French, or penmanship in Jefferson's proposed college [the University of Virginia]. ALS (in French) in DNA, 134.

To Return J. Meigs, 12/2. Encloses a copy of Calhoun's letter to him of 1/23 (Abs in *The Papers of John C. Calhoun,* 2:91) asking for a report as to the Eastern Cherokees' attitude toward a proposed road through their area. That report has not been received, and Calhoun requests it as soon as practicable. LS with En in DNA, 75 (M-208:7); FC in DNA, 72, D:233.

James Monroe to the House of Representatives, 12/2. Having promised in his message to Congress [of 11/16] that copies of documents relevant to the U.S. Army's invasion of the Floridas in 1818 would be submitted to Congress, Monroe transmits such of these "as have been prepared" since then. "They present a full view, of the operations of our troops, employ[e]d in the Seminole war, who enter[e]d Florida. The residue of the documents, which are very voluminous," will be transmitted as soon as they can be copied. ALS with Ens in DNA, 202, 15A-El; PC in Richardson, *Messages and Papers of the Presidents,* 2:48. (The Ens included 30 letters ranging in date from 10/1817 through 8/1818 and involving, as writers or recipients or both, Calhoun, Edmund P. Gaines, Andrew Jackson, and William W. Bibb. Also enclosed was a copy of the court-martial proceedings in the trials of Alexander Arbuthnot and Robert C. Ambrister.)

Daniel T. Patterson, New Orleans, to [Acting] Secretary of the Navy [Calhoun], 12/2. Encloses a detailed letter to Patterson from Lt. Thomas S. Cunningham, commander of the U.S. schooner *Fire Brand,* reporting continued piracy and smuggling centered upon Galveston, particularly by [Jean] Lafitte. LS with En in DNA, 133 (M-125:60).

To William Rabun, Governor of Ga., Milledgeville, 12/2. Transmits a copy of the opinion of Attorney General [William Wirt] in the case of Midshipman [Enos R. *or* Charles B.] Childs. Requests "that information may be given to this [Navy] Department of the time when it will be necessary for Midshipman Childs to attend the sitting of the Court in Georgia, in order that he may be directed to proceed with such witnesses as he may deem essential to his defence before said Court, and such further measures will be taken as your Excellency shall be pleased to intimate, and a due respect for the Laws shall require." FC in DNA, 122, 13:241.

From George H. Richards, Eben[eze]r Prentis, and Amosa Miller, New London, Conn., 12/2. As a committee of the Republican inhabitants of New London, they submit a memorial adopted by those Republicans unanimously in an effort to get a Naval depot located there. LS with En in DNA, 1, M-119; LS in DNA, 128, 7:55.

From James Turk & Thomas Henderson, Washington, 12/2. This firm offers to deliver rations at the Cherokee Agency or anywhere on "Highwassee [Hiawassee] river" at $.125 per lb. for bacon; $16 per barrel for pork or beef; $8 per barrel for flour; $4 per barrel for corn meal; $.50 per gallon for whisky; and $2.50 per bushel for salt. CC in DNA, 75 (M-208:7).

From J[ames] Turk & T[homas] Henderson, Washington, 12/2. This firm offers to deliver for the use of the Cherokee Indians at the Agency or at any other point on the Hiawassee or Tennessee Rivers the following provisions at the following prices "by the ration": flour or [corn] meal, six cents; beef or pork, six cents; bacon, eight cents; salt, eight mills. It also offers whisky at 50 cents per gallon. "It is probably more necessary to furnish the Indians in this way than the other, as there are rations, more or less, issued every day thro' the year to the Arkansas party [of emigrants]." CC and draft in DNA, 75 (M-208:7).

From Decius Wadsworth, 12/2. In response to an inquiry of 11/20 (ALS in DNA, 1, J-39) addressed to Calhoun by Richard M. Johnson, Chairman, House Committee on Military Affairs, [relayed to Wadsworth on 11/21,] Wadsworth reports that the U.S. armories at Harpers Ferry and Springfield, [Mass.,] are each employing about 230 workers and that they are now capable of producing a total of about 25,000 stands of arms at an annual cost of about $360,000. He estimates that an armory in the West could properly employ about 150 workers to produce about 8,000 stands of arms annually at a cost of about $125,000. ALS in DNA, 1, W-80; FC in DNA, 32, 1:147–149; CC in DNA, 201, 15A-F3; PC in *American State Papers: Military Affairs,* 1:773; PC in House Document No. 17, 15th Cong., 2nd Sess. (Calhoun relayed this information from Wadsworth to Johnson on 12/3.)

From Heman Allen, [former Representative from Vt.,] Washington, 12/3. Recommends Dr. [Charles] McCreedy of Vt. for an appointment in the Medical Department of the Army. ALS in DNA, 11, 12514. (An ES by Calhoun reads: "Entitled to great attention." An EU states that McCreedy was appointed, and Heitman, *Historical Register,* 1:661, reports that the appointment was as a Surgeon's Mate on 2/3/1819.)

From W[alker] K. Armistead, 12/3. Submits a "Roll of the [20] Officers of the Corps of Engineers, their stations and duties." DS in DNA, 2, A-1818.

To Commodore William Bainbridge, Boston; Capt. Samuel Evans, New York [City]; Capt. Charles Morris, Portsmouth, N.H.; Commodore [Alexander] Murray, Philadelphia; and Capt. R[obert] T. Spence, Baltimore, 12/3. Calhoun asks each of these Navy officers to send to the Navy Department a muster roll of the commissioned and warrant officers serving at the station under his command. FC in DNA, 121, 13:293–294.

From W[illiam] G. Blount, [Representative from Tenn.,] Washington, 12/3. Upon request of [James] Turk, Blount testifies: "I believe the price at which Mr. Turk proposes to furnish rations to be very reasonable, as I am convinced Bacon, flour, whiskey &c. cannot be purchased in East Tennessee for less than the price fixed by him, owing in a great degree to the settlement of Alabama and the number of Emigrants to the West." Offers to serve as security for Turk & [Thomas] Henderson "for the performance of any contract they may make with the government." CC in DNA, 75 (M-208:8).

To William H. Crawford, 12/3. Asks him to pay $7,000 out of the not-yet-enacted appropriation for arrearages of expenditures incurred in negotiating Indian treaties this year, when that appropriation shall have been made available, to cover outlays made by [William] Clark. CC in DNA, 77 (M-271:2, frames 0903–0904).

Order by the House of Representatives, 12/3. "Ordered, That the petition of Caleb Brooks, be referred to the Secretary of War." Attested by "Th[omas] Dougherty, C[lerk of the] H[ouse of] R[epresentatives]." DS in DNA, 1, H-61.

To [Charles J.] Ingersoll, [U.S. District Attorney for Pa.,] Philadelphia, 12/3. "Suspicions having been excited by the name of Tho[ma]s Armstrong being written in different hands that the within papers are forgeries, I request you will institute an examination, & if my suspicions be well founded to commence the necessary prosecution." FC in DNA, 3, 10:195.

From [Thomas S. Jesup], 12/3. Encloses a report written to Jesup on 12/3 by Capt. T[rueman] Cross (ALS in DNA, 1, C-96) in favor of the exchange of land at Baton Rouge proposed in 9/1818 by Gen. [Eleazer W.] Ripley. FC with En in DNA, 42, 1:126–127.

From Richard M. Johnson, [*ca.* 12/3.] The House Committee on Military Affairs has directed Johnson to request Calhoun's "opinion on the subject of the with[in] petition of E[dward] Baker & to [have Calhoun] say whether the Gun Lock is of such importance as would induce you to adopt it at this time & of such importance as to make it an object to secure it by patent or otherwise." The Committee also requests reports on two applications for benefits to two individuals that Calhoun probably is empowered to grant without additional legislative authorization. ALS in DNA, 1, J-60. (An EU indicates that this letter was received or filed in 12/1818. It was answered on 12/7.)

To Richard M. Johnson, Chairman, House Committee on Military Affairs

Department of War, 3d Decem[be]r 1818

In reply to so much of your letter of the 20th ult[im]o [ALS in DNA, 1, J-39] as requires my opinion "as to the expediency or necessity of the establishment of a national armory on the Western waters," I have the honor to enclose, for the consideration of the Military Committee, a report of the Ordnance department, [written by Decius Wadsworth on 12/2,] containing a statement of such facts as appear to be connected with the object of your inquiry.

Whether it would be expedient to establish an additional national armory, will depend, in the first place, on the fact, whether those already established are sufficient to fabricate as many arms, as the necessity of the country requires; and if they are not sufficient, whether it would be more advisable, to fabricate them by a national armory, or by contract.

In presenting this view of the subject it is assumed, that the supply of arms ought to be manufactured within the country, and ought not to be imported.

By a reference to the report of the Ordnance department, it will appear, that the national armories can fabricate, annually, about 25,000. This number, it is conceived, is not sufficient, whether we regard the present supply, or, the increased number which the growing population of the country requires.

Our principal reliance for defence, is on the militia, which requires a much more ample supply than regular troops; as experience proves them to be much more wasteful of arms. At the commencement of the late war, our supply amounted to 200,000 stands, and tho' it continued less than three years, our stock at its termination was nearly exhausted.

It is believed that, as arms can be fabricated at least as cheap and of a better quality by a national armory than by contract, it is the perferable mode.

If these observations are correct, it would appear expedient to establish an additional national armory, and that the "place of its location," ought to be on the Western waters. It is probable that arms can be fabricated in that portion of our country, at least as cheap, as at Harper's ferry or Springfield; and a very considerable expense would be annually saved in transportation. As to the particular "place of location," I am not in possession of such information as will enable me to give an opinion, on the subject.

LS with En in DNA, 201, 15A-F3; FC in DNA, 4, 2:3; PC with En in House Document No. 17, 15th Cong., 2nd Sess.; PC with En in *American State Papers: Military Affairs,* 1:773. NOTE: Despite the recommendation by Wadsworth and Calhoun that a third, Western armory should be established, none was initiated promptly as a result of the consideration given during 1818–1819 to the possibility.

To Richard McCall, U.S. Consul, Barcelona, [Spain,] 12/3. The refusal by Charles Stewart, commander of the U.S. Navy squadron in the Mediterranean, to recognize McCall as Naval purchasing agent will be rectified by a letter of today to Stewart, a copy of which is enclosed. McCall is instructed to obtain funds from the Baring Bros. of London and to keep the Navy Department correctly informed as to rates of exchange that prevail between the Mediterranean, London, and the U.S. FC in DNA, 122, 13:242–243.

From Jasper Parrish, Canandaigua, [N.Y.,] 12/3. Itemizes the populations and reservations of the Six Nations, totaling 4,575 persons and 14 reservations scattered over an extent of 250 miles and comprising more than a quarter of a million acres. Comments upon their advancement in civilization. Because every reservation is surrounded by white settlements, endorses Calhoun's proposal of 5/14 that they should emigrate—a proposal that Parrish has "fully explained to them." LS in DNA, 1, P-70; PEx in Morse, *A Report . . . on Indian Affairs,* Appendix, pp. 77–78.

From John Rodgers, 12/3. Acknowledges Calhoun's letter of 12/2 approving the form for a Steward's weekly return. Rodgers will have 5,000 copies printed. ALS in DNA, 128, 7:57.

To Samuel Smith, Chairman, House Committee on Ways and Means, 12/3. Requests an appropriation of $200,000 for subsistence, so that rations contractors can be given advances and can lay in a stock of foods during the winter for rations. The "numerous treaties which have been held during the present year, having been more expensive than was calculated, the appropriation for holding Indian treaties has been exhausted"; Calhoun requests an appropriation of $50,000 to cover the arrearages in this item. LS in DNA, 201, 15A-F3; FC in DNA, 4, 2:2.

From D[ecius] Wadsworth, 12/3. Recommends that a payment made to the State of Ga. by Lt. [Christopher] Keiser for $3,111 worth of ordnance should be approved. "It is not to be presumed the State would have charged a higher price for the Stores than they actually cost, nor does it seem the charges are unreasonable if the time and place are taken into consideration. I understand by an interview with Lt. Keiser that the Stores were originally obtained from Georgia by way of Loan; but it not being found convenient to replace them, it was recommended to Lieut[enant] Keiser by Lt. Col. [George] Bomford to pay for the Stores. It appears therefore that Lieut[enant] Keiser has incurred no censure in transacting this Business." FC in DNA, 32, 2:149.

From John Williams, [Senator from Tenn.,] 12/3. "Mr. [James] Turk has shewn me proposals which he intends making for the supply of the Cherokee Indians and requests that I would state the market price at Knoxville of some of those articles." That price recently was $.125 per lb. for bacon, $.50 per gallon for whisky, $8 per barrel for superfine flour, $2.50 per "50 weight by the barrel" for salt, and about $6 or $7 [per barrel] for pork. "The price of every article of subsistence has risen in East Tennessee, in consequence of the settlements in Alabama and the crowd of emigrants on the roads. Altho' I cannot speak with certainty as to the price of all the articles stated in the proposals, I believe good supplies cannot be furnished for less than is proposed by Mr. Turk." CC in DNA, 75 (M-208:8).

To Lewis Williams, [Representative from N.C. and] C[hairman] of the C[ommittee] on Claims

War Department, December 3rd 1818

In answer to your letter of the 29th ult[im]o referring the Claim of Isaac Clark to this Department, I have the honor to state that there is no rule in this Department by which such claims can be allowed.

FC in DNA, 4, 2:2.

To Thomas Wilson, Philadelphia, 12/3. Acknowledges his reply, addressed to Christopher Vandeventer, of 11/30 (LS in DNA, 1, W-173; CCEx in DNA, 1, W-195) to Vandeventer's inquiry of 11/21 addressed to [N.G.] Dufief. Orders a copy of the Paris edition of 1817 of Boyer's French–English dictionary, to be bound in calf. Neither of the Spanish–English and Spanish–French dictionaries in stock is adequate; Wilson will write to Dufief, who is now in Europe, and authorize him to buy the best such dictionary and to have it bound in calf to match the Boyer. Wilson's inquiry as to bounty land for the widow of Revolutionary veteran William Emerson has been referred to the proper office. FC in DNA, 3, 10:207. (An AES by Nathaniel Cutting that appears on the CCEx states that Mrs. Emerson was not entitled to bounty land.)

To Maj. A[bram] R. Woolley, Pittsburgh, 12/3. "I have received your [undated] letter [ALS in DNA, 1, W-83] requesting a court of inquiry to be held [before your intended resignation] upon your conduct at Pittsburgh. I am ever willing to afford every opportunity to officers to stand well before the public, but before I can decide upon your application it will be necessary to inform me of the points in which you feel yourself aggrieved and which you desire to be investigated." FC in DNA, 3, 10:195.

From John Gaillard, [Senator from S.C.,] 12/4. Encloses a letter from [former 1st Lt. James W.] Rouse. "As this Gentleman was an officer in the late Army his merits & pretensions must be better known to you than they can be to me." ALS in DNA, 11, 12739.

From Edmund P. Gaines

Fort Scott, Ga[.,] December 4th 1818

I had but just closed my letter of the 2d Ins[tan]t when I received yours of the 12th of last month communicating the order of the President [James Monroe] for me to repair to Point Petre.

The order being peremptory, I could not for a moment doubt the propriety of prompt obedience on my part, although I cannot but persuade myself that had the President anticipated the present state and extent of Indian hostility, in this quarter, I should have been permitted to remain here until the only effectual remedy for reducing that hostility should be applied. I have therefore to request that you will communicate to the President my warmest desire that I may be permitted to return, with a suitable force to convince those Indians of our ability and willingness to punish them for every aggression—not that I am by any means partial to this species of war—far from it—I would much more willingly devote my time and humble faculties to the delightful occupation of bringing our savage man to the walks of civil life, wherever this is practicable without force, than to contribute to the destruction of any one of the human race. But every effort towards civilization to be effectual must accord with the immutable principles of Justice.

The Savage must be taught and *compelled* to do that which is right, and to abstain from doing that which is radically wrong. The poisonous cup of barbarism cannot be taken from the lips of the savage by the mild voice of reason alone: the strong mandate of Justice must be resorted to, and enforced.

After all that the wisdom and philanthropy of our Country and government aided by Millions of money have yet been able to effect, it is a melancholy truth that in no nation of Indians within my knowledge (except the Chickasaws) has the scalping knife been laid aside ["for" *interlined*] any considerable length of time until their every hope of using it with impunity had been defeated. Permit me to add that I solicit this service not from any expectation of acquiring in it military fame. I entered the wilderness pursuant to the order of Major General [Andrew] Jackson, earnestly hoping that the appearance of the force with me, and the rumour of additional force comeing [*sic*] from Georgia, would lead to an adjustment of differences without resorting to the Sword. In this hope I was disappointed; I then engaged heartily in making such disposition of the means under my controul as should enable me to make the best possible impression on the Indians, with the least possible loss of blood on either side.

I must now retire from this part of my command if not at the commencement, at least at a very inauspicious stage of my operations. It is on this account I ask permission to return.

I leave Lieut. Col. [Mathew] Arbuckle in command, with orders corresponding with the views of the President as communicated from the War Department under ["date the" *interlined*] 20th Oct. and with the existing state of the service at this place, as communicated in my last of the 2nd Instant which owing to the danger of sending an express, has been delayed and will accompany this; I shall set out tomorrow for Point Petre by the way of Fort Hawkins, that being the only practicable route at this time.

LS in DLC, Andrew Jackson Papers, 8363.

To George Gibson, 12/4. Encloses a bid by Turk & Henderson to supply rations at the Creek Agency and asks for a report as to Gibson's opinion about it. FC in DNA, 3, 10:196.

From William Lambert, 12/4. Acknowledges Calhoun's letter of 12/1. James L. Edwards has been informed that Lambert's absence from the Pension Office was caused by a "severe attack of chronic rheumatism in my neck, shoulders, and arms, which has for some days, been attended with fevers that confined me to my bed." Lambert declares that he has served the U.S. Government with "uniform steadiness" and would never neglect any duty "which my health and capacity will enable me to perform." ALS in DNA, 1, L-27.

To Andrew C. Mitchell, 12/4. "Your resignation [of 12/4 (ALS in DNA, 2, M-1818)] as second Clerk in the Pension Office is accepted." FC in DNA, 3, 10:195.

Jacob Mordecai, Richmond, to [Joseph G. Swift], 12/4. Mordecai's letter [of 10/27] has not been acknowledged; so he asks again for Swift's influence in obtaining a Cadet's warrant for his son, Alfred Mordecai. ALS in DNA, 15, 1818, 177, with an AES by Swift certifying that Mordecai's claims are truthful.

General order issued by D[aniel] Parker, 12/4. Capt. N[athaniel] N[ye] Hall of the Artillery Corps is to be released from arrest and returned to duty; the court-martial for his trial is to be dissolved. ADS in DNA, 2, P-1818.

To Pension Office Appointees, 12/4. Appoints these men Clerks in the Pension Office at $1,000 per annum. Those who accept the appointment are to report to work immediately. FC in DNA, 3, 10:196, with a marginal notation that the addressees were George S. Bulfinch, William S. Colquhoun, William Gordon, John H. Henshaw, R.C. Jones, Ebenezer Stout, —— Scott, Alexander Stewart, John Tucker, Francis Wright, George Wood, and Edwin R. Wallace.

From Decius Wadsworth, 12/4. Maj. [Abram R.] Woolley has not complied with the regulation obligating him to deposit U.S. funds in the Pittsburgh Branch of the Bank of the United States. The Auditors charge him with a large deficit; but his own accounts appear to be juggled to show a balance in his favor. Wadsworth encloses copies of his letters that Woolley has ignored. Wadsworth suggests that Woolley be court-martialed or transferred to another post; Wadsworth prefers the latter alternative. "Such an officer as Major [James] Dallaby [Dalaby] I have no doubt would put things in order there [at Pittsburgh] promptly and take Measures either to diminish the Expence by discharging useless Hands, or by infusing more Energy into the outdoor business render the Expenditure more productive." ALS with En in DNA, 2, W-1818; FC in DNA, 32, 2:150–152.

To John Wilson, 12/4. "You are appointed a Clerk in this department. Your compensation will be at the rate of $1,400 per annum. You will immediately report yourself for duty to Mr. [James L.] Edwards of the Pension Office." FC in DNA, 3, 10:196.

To [John Quincy Adams], 12/5. "The President [James Monroe] handed me the enclosed, for information, with a request, that after I had done with it, I would transmit it to you for the same purpose." LS in DNA, 101 (M-179:42).

To Speaker Henry Clay

Department of War, December 5, 1818

In compliance with a resolution of the House of Representatives of the 4th of April, 1818, [DS in DNA, 1, H-261,] directing the

Secretary of War to prepare and report, at their next session, "a system providing for the abolition of the existing Indian trade establishments of the United States, and providing for the opening of the trade with the Indians to individuals, under suitable regulations," I have the honor to make the following report:

The nations of Indians who inhabit this portion of our continent were, on its first discovery, in a state of the most perfect commercial independence. Their knowledge of the useful arts was, indeed, very limited, but it was commensurate with their wants and desires. With their rude implements of husbandry, their hook and bow, in the construction of which they were well instructed, they drew a scanty but (for them) a sufficient supply from the soil, the water, and the forest. A great change has since taken place, such as appears to be inevitable by a fixed law of nature, in the intercourse between a civilized and savage people. Helplessness has succeeded independence. While their wants have been greatly multiplied and enlarged by their intercourse with their more civilized neighbors, their knowledge even of their former rude arts has been lost, without acquiring those which are necessary in their new condition. The manufacture of the axe and the hoe, by which they now clear and cultivate the soil, and the gun and ammunition, by which they take their game, are far above their skill; and, with the exhaustion of their present stock, without a new supply, they would be reduced to extreme want. On trade, then, with those from whom they can draw these and other supplies, they are wholly dependent. We have the exclusive right to trade with those within our limits; and cut off, as the southern tribes are, by our acquisition in the late war, from intercourse with foreigners on the side of the Gulf of Mexico, we have the means, by a proper extension of our posts on the lakes, the Mississippi, and the Missouri, (to effect which measures have already been taken,) to enforce effectually, without much additional expense, this important right. The period seems, then, to have arrived to give to our control over the Indians, through an exclusive supply of their wants, the greatest efficiency, and to promote their and our interest, by a judicious system of trade fairly and justly directed.

A similar view of this branch of our trade seems to have been taken at an early period by our Government. It directed its attention to this interesting and important subject as early as the year 1775, when a committee was appointed by Congress to devise a plan for carrying on trade with the Indians. In the next year a very considerable purchase of goods was directed to be made for the Indian trade; and trade with them, except under license and bond, was strictly prohibited. The subject was frequently acted on during the Confederation, but no systematic effort was made to regulate it till 1786, when an ordinance was passed dividing the Indian Department into two districts, and appointing a Superintendent [of Indian Affairs] with a deputy to each. It was made their duty to execute such regulations as Congress might establish in relation to Indian affairs; to correspond with the Secretary of War, through whom their communications were directed to be made to Congress; to obey the instructions of the War Department; and to grant licenses to trade with Indians. This ordinance directed that no license should be granted to foreigners, and only to citizens whose good moral character should be certified by the Governor of a State, under the seal of the State; and that bonds should be given to conform to established regulations. Licenses were granted to continue in force for one year only, and upon the payment of $50.00. To trade without license incurred a penalty of $500 and forfeiture of goods. The Superintendents and their deputies were prohibited from engaging in trade.

The change in the form of the government a few years after the passing of this ordinance, and the debility into which public affairs fell about the termination of the Confederation, prevented this judicious system from being carried into effect.

Under the present constitution, the subject of Indian trade attracted the attention of Congress as early as the year 1790. The system of trade by licenses was retained, which were directed to be granted for two years, by persons to be appointed by the President, to applicants of good character, who gave bonds to conform to regulations; and to trade without license was subjected to a forfeiture of merchandise. The act contains no prohibitions of foreigners, and requires nothing to be paid for the licenses. In the years 1793 and 1796, acts were passed very similar in their provisions to the one just recited; and in the year 1802, an act repealing former acts, and which still continues in force, was passed. It inflicts a fine of $100, and imprisonment not exceeding thirty days, in addition to the forfeiture of goods, for trading without license; and directs licenses to be granted on bond, with sufficient security, to conform to law and regulations, without making a good character or citizenship a requisite.

By an act of 1816, (the last passed on this subject,) foreigners are prohibited from trading with the Indians, except permitted by the President, and under such regulations as he should establish. Instructions have been given under this act to prohibit foreigners from passing into the Indian country, except as boatmen, and, under certain conditions, as interpreters.

The system of trade by public Factors, now proposed to be abolished, commenced in the year 1796, but without superseding the original mode of carrying on the trade by license. The President was authorized to establish trading-houses, and to appoint an agent [titled a Factor] to each house, to carry on, as the act states, "a liberal trade with the Indians." The act appropriated $150,000 as the capital of this trade, and the additional sum of $8,000 annually, for the payment of agents and clerks; and directed the trade to be carried on so as not to diminish the capital. It was limited to two years; but was, by a subsequent act, continued in force till 1806. A superintendent of Indians was then appointed, and the capital increased to $260,000, and $13,000 was annually appropriated for the payment of superintendent, agents, and clerks. This act was limited to three years, but afterwards continued in force till 1811. The capital was then increased to $300,000, with an annual appropriation of $19,250 for the payment of superintendent, agents, and clerks. It was limited to three years, but has been extended by subsequent acts to the 1st of March next.

The capital at present is distributed among eight trading-houses, or factories, established at the following places: Fort Mitchell; the Chickasaw Bluffs; Fort Confederation, on the Tombigbee; Fort Osage [also known as Fort Clark or Clarke], on the Missouri [near the western boundary of present-day Mo.]; Prairie du Chien, on the Mississippi; Sulphur Fork, on Red river; Green bay; and Chicago.

Such is the rise, progress, and present condition of our Indian trade. It was commenced, and has been continued, from motives both of prudence and humanity; and though it may not have fully realized the expectations of its friends, it has no doubt produced beneficial effects. If wars have not been entirely prevented by it, they probably, without it, would have been more frequent; and if the Indians have made but little advances in civilization, they probably, without it, would have made less. If greater effects have not resulted, it is to be attributed not to a want of dependence on the part of the Indians on commercial supplies, but to defects in the system itself, or in its administration. Scarcely any attempt has been made till lately to exclude foreigners, and the granting of licenses has not been subject to those checks which are necessary to give to it the most salutary effects.

Should it be thought unadvisable to continue the present trading system by factories, by permitting the act to expire by its limitation on the 1st of March next, it will then, of course, terminate. In winding up its concerns, two points are to be regarded: to sustain as little loss as possible; and to withdraw from the trade gradually, in order that the capital employed may be supplied from other sources. To effect both of these objects, I would suggest that so much of the act of 1811 as authorizes the appointment of a Superintendent [of Indian Trade] and Factors be continued in force for one year; and that they be authorized to make sales, as heretofore, of the goods and effects on hand, and those which may be acquired from the Indians.

The Superintendent of Indian Trade should also be authorized and directed to exhibit at his office, for inspection, an inventory of the stock in trade, with the property attached to the respective factories; and he should be directed to sell the same on the best terms offered, provided the sales can be effected at cost and charges. It would be proper to allow considerable credit, upon approved bonds and security; and the President ought to be empowered to annex, as the condition of the sale, if he should think it advisable, to sell the goods to the Indians at the place at which the factory is established, provided the sales can be effected within the period of one year. The factory at Fort Clarke, being established by a treaty with the Great and Little Osages in the year 1808, must be continued by the Government, or sold out, subject to the condition of being continued so long as the Indians may desire it. It would, perhaps, be advisable to direct a new treaty, rescinding, on suitable compensation, the stipulation referred to.

The establishment would, by these means, terminate gradually, without the hazard of any considerable losses.

To provide for opening the trade to individuals, under suitable regulations, is a task of much greater difficulty. The vast extent of the country inhabited by the Indians, and the numbers and variety of the tribes, render it impossible to apply, with propriety, any one uniform system to the whole. The various tribes, for the purpose of trade, may, however, be comprehended in two classes: those in our immediate neighborhood, surrounded by our settlements and our military posts, and who, from long intercourse with us, have become partially civilized; and those more remote, who still retain their original character and customs. In the former are comprehended the four southern tribes; the Osages, and the small tribes immediately west of the Mississippi; those within the limits of Illinois, Indiana, Ohio, and that part of the Michigan Territory east of Lake Michigan. The latter comprehends all of the tribes without those limits. I propose to consider the system of trade best calculated for each division, beginning with the former.

After giving the subject that full consideration which its importance merits, it appears to me that the provisions of the ordinance of 1786, with a few additions and modifications, particularly in the administrative part, so as to adjust it to our present form of government, are, for this division of our Indian trade, the best that can be devised. The provisions of the acts now in force in relation to licenses are not as well guarded or as efficient as those of the ordinance referred to. The introduction of the factories seems to have relaxed the attention of Government to the system of trade under license. I would then propose to assume the provisions of the ordinance referred to, as the basis of a system to open the trade with the contiguous tribes of Indians to individual enterprise. Instead, however, of appointing two Superintendents, I would propose a Superintendent of Indian Affairs, to be attached to the War Department, with a salary of $3,000 per annum; the Superintendent to be under the control of the Secretary of War, and to be charged, subject to such regulations as the President may prescribe, with the correspondence, superintendence, and general management of Indian affairs; and to be authorized, with the approbation of the Secretary of War, to grant licenses to trade with the Indians. Licenses to be granted to citizens of good moral character, and to continue in force till revoked. A sum not less than $100, nor more than $500, to be determined under regulations to be prescribed by the President, to be paid for the privilege of using it at the time of granting the license, and annually during its continuance; and bonds, with sufficient security, to be taken to conform to law and regulations. Licenses to be revoked by the President whenever he may judge proper. To trade without license, to [be] subject to a fine not exceeding $1,000, and imprisonment not to exceed six months, with a forfeiture of the goods. Licenses to be granted to trade at specified places, to be selected by the applicants, and not to be changed without the consent of the Superintendent. All peddling and sales of spirituous liquors to be strictly prohibited. Each trading-house, or establishment, to require a separate license; and books to be kept at the establishment, in which the prices of the goods sold and the articles purchased should be regularly and fairly entered; and to be subject at all times to the inspection of the Indian Agent, or such persons as the Superintendent may appoint.

The reasons for most of these provisions are so obvious as to require no illustration. They will all be passed over, accordingly, without observation, except the provision which requires the payment of an annual sum for the use of a license, and that which requires the trading establishment to be fixed. The former provision is taken from the ordinance of 1786, which directed licenses to be granted for one year only, and on payment of $50 to the superintendent, for the use of the United States; a sum nearly equal to that now proposed, if the value of money at that time be taken into consideration.

But it will probably be objected that it is our interest, and, as we propose to monopolize their trade, our duty, too, to furnish the Indians with goods on as moderate terms as possible; and that the sum to be paid for a license, by acting as a duty on the goods sold under it, will tend to enhance their price. In answer to which it may be justly observed, that it is not a matter of so much importance that they should obtain their supplies for a few cents more or less, as that the trade should, as far as practicable, be put effectually under the control of the Government, in order that they may be protected against the fraud and the violence to which their ignorance and weakness would, without such protection, expose them. It is this very ignorance and weakness which render it necessary for the Government to interfere; and, if such interference is proper at all, it ought to be rendered effectual. Such will be the tendency of this provision. Its first and obvious effects will be to diminish more certainly, and with less injurious effect than any other provision which can be devised, the number of traders, and to increase the amount of capital which each would employ. The profit of a small capital of a few hundred dollars would scarcely pay for the license; while that on a large one would not be much diminished by it. Both of these effects—the diminution of the number of traders, and the increase of the capital—would add greatly to the control of the Government over the trade. It would be almost impossible to inspect the conduct, and consequently control the actions, of the multitude of traders with small capitals, diffused over the Indian country, and settled at remote and obscure places. The greatest vigilance on the part of the Superintendent and his agents would be unequal to the task. By diminishing the number, and bringing each more permanently before the view of the Government, a due inspection and superintendence becomes practicable. Again: what control can the Government have over the conduct of a trader, with a capital of a few hundred dollars only? Suppose he should violate the express injunctions of law and regulations; what serious loss would he sustain by revoking his license, or by putting his bond in suit? To him it would be nothing to wind up his business, and give his capital another direction; and as to the bond, in such distant and obscure transactions, he might pretty safely calculate on escaping its penalty. Very different would be the case with the trader of a large capital. To revoke his license would be a serious evil, which must subject him to certain loss; and, should he break the conditions of his bond, he would be much more in danger of feeling its penalty. The control of the Government would not only be greater over such traders, but (what is of equal importance) their influence with the Indians would have a more salutary direction. A war between them and us would, in all cases, be injurious, and in many cases would be ruinous, to the trader of a large capital; but not so with one of small capital. A single profitable speculation may be of more importance to him than the continuance of peace. From the effects of war he can as easily escape as from the revocation of his license or the penalty of his bond. Let the character of the former be what it may, he must, from interest, be the advocate of peace and the influence of his own Government; while the latter, unless influenced by virtuous motives, would feel in either but little interest.

From the nature of the trade, the more it can be concentrated, provided there is reasonable competition, the better it will be for the Indians and ourselves. The very opposite, it is true, would be the fact if they had the capacity and intelligence to take care of their own interest without our protection; but, situated as they are, indefinite competition would be no less injurious to them than to our citizens; and such appear to be their sentiments. The Chickasaws, in a late treaty, complained of the injury which they had sustained from peddlers and small traders; and they had a stipulation inserted against the granting of any license to trade with their nation, as the only effectual means which suggested itself to prevent it.

The reasons for fixing the trading establishments are no less strong. By rendering them stationary, and compelling the proprietor to keep books, containing regular entries of all their sales and purchases, important checks will be presented to prevent fraud and exorbitant charges. It will also strongly tend to prevent collision between the traders, and, consequently, the creation of parties among the Indians for or against particular traders—a state of things unfriendly to their interest, and dangerous to the peace of the frontier. Besides, the trading establishments, being fixed, as they will be, in the most advantageous positions, will, in time, become the nucleus of Indian settlements, which, by giving greater density and steadiness to their population, will tend to introduce a division of real property, and thus hasten their ultimate civilization.

Such are the provisions under which the trade with those tribes of Indians in our immediate neighborhood may, with safety and advantage, be opened to individual enterprise. With a vigilant administration, it will produce results equally salutary to the Indians and ourselves. In fact, the knowledge of the use of money, and the prices of most of the ordinary articles of trade, is so far advanced among them, as to guard them, to a considerable extent, against mere fraud and imposition; and, with the control which the Government may exercise over the trade with them, they would generally receive their supplies on fair and moderate terms. The system is not less calculated to secure peace. The regular traders, who have paid for the use of their licenses, will be the most active to prevent vexatious pedding and retailing of spirituous liquors, which are the bane of the frontier. They will, besides, become the most active promoters of industry; for the almost total destruction of game has rendered the amount of peltries and furs of little value in this branch of Indian trade; and their capacity of paying for the goods purchased must consequently, in a great measure, depend on the proceeds of the soil. In fact, the neighboring tribes are becoming daily less warlike, and more helpless and dependent on us, through their numerous wants; and they are rendered still more pacific by the fear of forfeiting their lands and annuities. They have, in a great measure, ceased to be an object of terror, and have become that of commiseration. The time seems to have arrived when our policy towards them should undergo an important change. They neither are, in fact, nor ought to be, considered as independent nations. Our views of their interest, and not their own, ought to govern them. By a proper combination of force and persuasion, of punishments and rewards, they ought to be brought within the pales of law and civilization. Left to themselves, they will never reach that desirable condition. Before the slow operation of reason and experience can convince them of its superior advantages, they must be overwhelmed by the mighty torrent of our population. Such small bodies, with savage customs and character, cannot, and ought not, to be permitted to exist in an independent condition in the midst of civilized society. Our laws and manners ought to supersede their present savage manners and customs. Beginning with those most advanced in civilization, and surrounded by our people, they ought to be made to contract their settlements within reasonable bounds, with a distinct understanding that the United States intend to make no further acquisition of land from them, and that the settlements reserved are intended for their permanent home. The land ought to be divided among families; and the idea of individual property in the soil carefully inculcated. Their annuities would constitute an ample school fund; and education, comprehending as well the common arts of life, as reading, writing, and arithmetic, ought not to be left discretionary with the parents. Those who might not choose to submit, ought to be permitted and aided in forming new settlements at a distance from ours. When sufficiently advanced in civilization, they would be permitted to participate in such civil and political rights as the respective States within whose limits they are situated might safely extend to them. It is only by causing our opinion of their interest to prevail, that they can be civilized and saved from extinction. Under the present policy, they are continually decreasing and degenerating, notwithstanding the Government has, under all of its administrations, been actuated by the most sincere desire to promote their happiness and civilization. The fault has been, not in the want of zeal, but in the mode by which it has been attempted to effect these desirable objects. The Indians are not so situated as to leave it to time and experience to effect their civilization. By selecting prudently the occasion for the change, by establishing a few essential regulations, and by appointing persons to administer them fairly and honestly, our efforts could scarcely fail of success. Nor ought it to be feared that the power would be abused on our part; for, in addition to the dictates of benevolence, we have a strong interest in their civilization. The enmity even of the frontier settlers towards them is caused principally by the imperfection of the present system; and under the one which I have suggested, it will greatly abate, if not entirely subside. The natural humanity and generosity of the American character would no longer be weakened by the disorders and savage cruelty to which our frontiers are now exposed. A deep conviction of the importance of the subject, and a strong desire to arrest the current of events, which, if permitted to flow in their present channel, must end in the annihilation of those who were once the proprietors of this prosperous country, must be my apology for this digression.

It remains to consider in what manner our trade can be the most successfully prosecuted with the numerous Indian tribes who occupy the vast region extending west to the Pacific Ocean. It is obvious that the system proposed for the partially civilized tribes bordering on our settlements would prove altogether inadequate to this branch of our Indian trade. It will require a system of far more energy to effect the great objects which ought to be pursued through it. To establish a decided control over the numerous and savage tribes within these vast limits, and to give to our trade with them its utmost extension, are deemed to be objects of great national importance. It is believed that, within our limits, along the range of the Rocky Mountains, quite to the Mexican frontier is the best region for fur and peltries on this continent. With proper efforts, the whole of this valuable trade, extending quite across to the great western ocean, would, in a few years, be exclusively in our possession. To produce these desirable results, foreign adventurers, whose influence must at all times be hostile to our interest, and dangerous to our peace, must be excluded. With this view, and to protect our own trade, means have been taken to extend our military posts on the Mississippi and Missouri. Whatever character our trade in that quarter may assume, the extension of our posts, as contemplated, will be indispensable to its enlarged and successful prosecution; but it is believed that, with all of the advantages which they will afford, unless the trade be properly and efficiently organized, we shall not be able to compete with entire success with the British companies on the north, nor to acquire that decided control over the Indians which is indispensable to its complete success.

In order to have just ideas on this subject, it is necessary to take into consideration not only the vast extent and remoteness of the region over which it is proposed to extend our trade, but the character of the numerous tribes who inhabit it. They are all more or less migratory; in the summer moving towards the north, and in the winter to the south, in pursuit of the buffalo and other game. They are thus, in the summer, brought into the neighborhood of the British establishments to the north of our limits, where, notwithstanding our military posts and the advantage of our position, much of the trade and influence over these fierce and warlike tribes will centre, unless our means of carrying it on should be as well organized and as efficient as theirs. The difficulty, though of an opposite kind, is no less considerable on the southern frontier of this portion of our country. The line between us and the Spanish possessions in Mexico is, in its whole extent, a subject of discussion; and, even should it be adjusted, will probably, to a considerable extent, be without natural and visible boundaries. To a trade thus situated, extending over so vast a region, inhabited by numerous tribes not less warlike than savage, with the competition of powerful and long established companies on one side, and danger of collision on the other, the unorganized efforts of individuals, always with jarring, and frequently with opposing interests, appear to be wholly inadequate to its successful or safe prosecution. The rivalry of trade, which, in well-regulated communities, gives the greatest prosperity to commerce, would, in these distant regions, beyond the control of law or superior authority, amongst fierce and ignorant savages, lead to the most fatal consequences. Each trader, or association of traders, would endeavor to monopolize the trade within certain limits, and would exert their cunning and influence to render the savages their partisans, and the enemy of their rivals in trade. Among a people at once so fierce and so easily duped, the result may be readily anticipated. A state of disorder and violence would universally prevail, equally unfortunate to the Indians and ourselves; and which would strongly tend to turn the trade, and with it the influence over the Indians, to the well-organized foreign fur companies near our limits.

If these observations are correct; if the uncombined efforts of individuals are inadequate to a successful competition with the British fur companies; if they will endanger our peace with our southern neighbors, and lead to fierce and dangerous rivalry among themselves, it only remains to consider whether a mode can be devised of carrying on this branch of our Indian trade which will obviate these evils, and accomplish the desirable objects of giving the greatest extension to it, accompanied with the most efficient control over the Indians themselves.

The united influence and combined efforts of the fur companies referred to can be met successfully, it is believed, only by an equal concentration of influence and efforts on our part; the jealous rivalry of independent traders, with its fatal consequences, can be obviated only by removing the diversity of interest by which it would be excited, and the danger of collision on our southern limits, by subjecting the trade completely to the will and control of the Government. The mode, then, which I would propose, would be to vest the trade in a company with sufficient capital, to be divided into shares of one hundred dollars each, and to be limited to the term of twenty years; to pay an annual tax on its subscribed capital, for the privilege of exclusive trade; and to be subject, in like manner as private traders, to such rules and regulations as may be prescribed. It is thus that most of the evils to be apprehended, by leaving the trade open to the competition of private adventurers, would, it is believed, be avoided. The efforts of the company, undisturbed by rival interests, would be directed to establish its control over the various tribes of Indians, to exclude foreign adventurers, and to give the greatest degree of profits to its trade. The success of such a company, properly conducted, scarcely admits of a doubt. Our position in regard to this trade, the facility which the navigation of our great and numerous rivers in that quarter would afford, and the protection from our military posts, would speedily destroy all foreign competition, and would in a few years push our trade to the Pacific Ocean. The most profitable fur and and peltry trade in the world would be ours, accompanied with a decided influence over the numerous and warlike tribes inhabiting those extensive regions. The mere objection that it would create a monopoly ought not to outweigh so many advantages. The trade with the Indians has never been opened, without restrictions, to our citizens. Licenses from the Government have at all times been required; and the Government has, itself, through its factories, to a considerable extent, monopolized the trade; and, by an extension of its capital only, might engross the whole of it. All of these provisions, however necessary in the Indian trade, would be absurd in any other branch of our commerce. Besides, the profit of the trade with the Indians has, at all times, been confined to a few individuals; and it is highly probable that a greater portion of the community would participate in it, by carrying it on in the manner proposed, than in any other mode. In fact, absurd as commercial monopoly would be, where law and authority exist to repress the mischievous effects which might spring from unbounded rivalry, and to give to such rivalry salutary consequences, just in the same degree would it be wise and advantageous to carry on the trade under consideration by an incorporated company. A nation discovers its wisdom no less in departing from general maxims, where it is no longer wise to adhere to them, than in its adherence to them in ordinary circumstances. In fact, it evinces a greater effort of reason. The first advance of a nation is marked by the establishment of maxims which are deemed universal, but which further experience and reflection teach to be only general, admitting of occasional modifications and exceptions.

Should the House, however, not adopt these views, but prefer to open the trade to the enterprise of single individuals, or such associations as might be formed for the purpose, I would suggest the provisions already proposed for the trade with the neighboring tribes of Indians as the most advisable, with the exception of the provisions which require the trader to be located, and that regular books of sales and purchases should be kept. In lieu of which provisions, I would propose that the goods intended for this branch of Indian trade, and the articles acquired by purchase from the Indians, should be entered under oath, (the former with a copy of the invoice, and the latter with a statement of prices,) with the Indian Agent at Mackinaw [that is, Mackinac], St. Louis, Belle Point, on the Arkansas River, or Natchitoches on Red River, or such other places as the President may designate.

The entry can be made without much inconvenience to the trader, as the geography of the country is such as to make it necessary for the trade to pass by one or the other of the points proposed, at each of which there is now an Agent.

It is believed that these provisions would be as effectual as any that can be devised, short of a company incorporated for the purpose; but it is proper to observe that they are open to the objections which have already been stated. In fact, they equally apply to any system, so long as the trade is exposed to the effects which must flow from the jealous rivalry of independent traders, where law and authority cannot step in to restrain its consequences within proper bounds. The Indians themselves are not the proper judges of their own interest, and so far from restraining the effects of such rivalry, they would become the instruments of the most cunning and vicious of the traders, to wreak their vengeance on such as might stand in the way of their profits.

All of which is respectfully submitted.

PC in *American State Papers: Indian Affairs,* 2:181–185; LS in DNA, 201, 15A-F3; FC on DNA, 4, 2:4–14; PC in House Document No. 25, 15th Cong., 2nd Sess.; PC in Crallé, ed., *Works,* 5:8–24.

To Commodore Isaac Chauncey, New York [City], 12/5. His letter of 12/1 [LS in DNA, 133 (M-125:60)] and the proceedings of the court-martial that tried [Marine Pvt.] David Moore are acknowledged. The sentence is approved, and Chauncey is to execute it, "mitigating such proportion of the punishment as shall appear to you to be proper, after an impartial examination of the circumstances of the case." It has been customary for all members of Navy courts-martial to sign the record copy of the proceedings, but the signatures of this court's President and Judge Advocate are considered sufficient authentication. FC in DNA, 121, 13:294–295.

To William H. Crawford, 12/5. "The President [James Monroe] handed me the enclosed for information with a request that after I had done with it I would transmit it to you for the same purpose." FC in DNA, 171, 1:319.

From F[erdinand] R[udolf] Hassler, Newark, N.J., 12/5. He has completed the field work for his survey of the northern boundary line and is now ready to deliver the instruments and other items of U.S. property that have been in his care. He discusses in detail where the instruments are located, what care they should be given, and how they may be moved and used in the future. ALS in DNA, 1, A-31, with an AEI by Calhoun referring this and Hassler's other letter of this date to the Chief Engineer: "Col. [Walker K.] Armistead will see me tomorrow in relation to the objects of Mr. Has[s]ler's communications."

From F[erdinand] R[udolf] Hassler, Newark, N.J., 12/5. "Lt. J[ohn] R. Vinton of the Artillery who has, upon Your Orders, been with me last season as Assistant, in the Expedition to the Northern Boundary line, and accompanied me already before in the Survey of the Coast, wishes very much to be transfer[r]ed to the Corps of Engineers." Hassler urges that Vinton's wish be granted, partly because Hassler can give him no more practical experience than Vinton has already gained. Hassler requests that [2nd] Lt. [Andrew] Talcott and [2nd] Lt. Richard Delafield be assigned to assist Hassler in calculating the many observations that remain yet to be made "from the last summer[']s work for the Boundary line." He argues that "if I should go again to the line next year there would be also opportunity to introduce them in the practice of Observations, so necessary to them and particularly to Lt. Delafield, if, as I understand, he is destined for an Expedition in the interior." ALS in DNA, 1, A-31.

To David B. Mitchell, 12/5. "I have received your letters of the 24th & 25th ultimo [the former is an LS in ICN, the latter an LS with En in DNA, 1, M-95, the enclosure being a claim by Edmund Doyle for losses inflicted by the Seminoles] relating to the accounts of Doyle and [William] Hambly, and to provisions issued to the Indians at that place for the last eighteen months; and am pleased with the strict adherence to the prescribed forms in the transaction of the business of your agency. On an examination of the trial of A[lexander] A[r]buthnot, I find mention made of your talk to the Seminole Indians, sent to them in Novem[be]r or Decem[be]r 1817, as well as of a letter of Arbuthnot to you dated the 17th August 1817. Will you cause copies of these documents, and of such others as may relate to Arbuthnot intermeddling in Indian affairs as may be in your possession to be transmitted as early as practicable?" FC in DNA, 72, D:233.

From Decius Wadsworth

Ordnance Office, 5 Dec[embe]r 1818

In Relation to the Petition of Edward Baker which has been presented to the House of Representatives in Congress, and the Consideration of which has been referred from the War office to this Department, I beg leave respectfully to state:

That the Gun Lock in Question undoubtedly possesses the Merits ascribed to it, of being secure against going off at the *half-bent;* and in the Strength and Durability of some of its Parts is rather superior to the common Lock. Whether it would be expedient to introduce this Improvement, in the Arms fabricated for national Purposes, is a question deserving mature Deliberation; and one which I should not venture to decide alone, because every change in the Patterns of Fire Arms, at the national Armouries, produces, by destroying Uniformity, Inconveniences, which are felt for a long Series of Years. Nor does it seem necessary to have an immediate Decision take Place of that question; because, if Mr. Baker should be authorized under the particular Circumstances of the Case, to take out a Patent for the Invention, in the usual Manner (excepting the affidavit of his being the original Inventor) the Agents of the Government will be at Liberty, after consulting the Superintendants [*sic*] of the national Armouries, and other competent Persons, to treat with him for a Transfer of his exclusive Privilege to the United States, for a Compensation mutually satisfactory.

No material objection is perceived to the Course suggested, of permitting Mr. Baker under the peculiar Circumstances of the Case, to take out a Patent, securing to him and his Assigns the exclusive Privilege of using this Invention for a Period of fourteen Years. Should there be any Misrepresentation, relative to the gratuitous Transfer to him, from the original Inventor, living in England (of which however no Suspicion is entertained) the patent would be subject, it is believed, to be revoked under the existing Laws, on Account of its having been improperly obtained.

Leaving, at present, undecided, the question whether it would be expedient to introduce this Improvement into the Arms manufactured for the United States, it would seem quite reasonable to authorise Mr. Baker to receive a Patent, securing to him and his

Assigns the exclusive Privilege of using and profiting by this Invention, for a certain Number of Years.

ALS in DNA, 35, In-6-26; FC in DNA, 32, 2:152–153.

To John Williams, [Senator from Tenn.]

War Department, 5th December 1818

I have received your letter [of 12/4 (ALS in DNA, 1, W-84)] expressing the wish of the Senate "to be informed of the ages of the several Cadets nominated for appointments in the Army" [as commissioned officers], and have the honor to state that no Cadet is admitted into the Academy at West Point under 14 y[ea]rs of age and no one can be nominated for a Commission in the Army untill after he shall have received a diploma, which requires Four Years['] study to obtain—consequently the youngest Cadet on the list of nomination now before the Senate must be more than 18 years old.

I have directed the Superintendent of the Military Academy [Sylvanus Thayer] to report the age of each Cadet if he has the information, but I do not believe that a register of the ages of those before the Senate have [*sic*] been kept at that institution.

FC in DNA, 4, 2:3–4.

From Jacob Brown

Brownville, [N.Y.,] 6th December 1818

Your letter, covering a copy of the one of the 11th of August, calling for a report of the labour performed on the road leading from Sacketts [*sic*] Harbour through the Chataguay [that is, Chateaugay] Country, is before me.

My letter of the 29th of November will inform you what has been done, but I fear will not exhibit the progress of this work to the extent you have expected. It may therefore be proper to state, in this place, that when the President, [James Monroe,] in the autumn of 1817, directed the road in question to be opened and improved, I did not understand, that, the Second Regiment were to be ordered from the duty they were then upon. This Regiment, at the time referred to, were employed enclosing with pickets the public ground at Sacketts Harbour, and that duty occupied them the remainder of the season. Expecting the Troops, at the Harbour, would have been employed in completing the Barracks at that place this year, they were not put upon the road, but allowed to be engaged in improving the public grounds for gardens; and as these grounds were new, it required much labour to put them in good condition.

These causes and the reasons assigned in my letter from this place and Plattsburgh [*sic*] produced the delay that has occurred in putting Col. [Hugh] Brady's command upon the road, and if your letter of the 11th of August had not been received upon my return to this place, I fear that this work would not yet have been commenced.

I pray you to believe that I regret the delay and I beg of you to find good cause for it in the reasons I have endeavored to assign.

It is due to the commands of Col. Brady and of Col. [Henry] Atkinson to say, that they have discovered not only a becoming cheerfulness in obeying the orders received for perfecting the Plattsburgh and Sacketts Harbour road, but much zeal in the performance of this duty, and if these Regiments are continued upon this important work the next season, more than double the length of way will be completed, than has been passed the last and present year.

LS with En in DNA, 1, B-113; FC in DLC, Jacob Brown Papers, Letterbooks, 2:130–131; PC in House Document No. 87, 15th Cong., 2nd Sess.; PC in *American State Papers: Miscellaneous,* 2:537.

To H[enry] Atkinson, Plattsburg, N.Y., 12/7. Answering his letter of 11/24, Calhoun commends the officers and men of the 6th Regiment for the "useful direction" of their extra labor. "By such honourable exertions the Army is recommended to the favourable notice of the country." President [James Monroe] will also be pleased. FC in DNA, 3, 10:197.

From [Lewis Cass ?], Detroit, 12/7. Introduces the bearer of this letter, Dr. [Benjamin] Delavan, an Army surgeon, who "wishes to exchange that situation for some civil appointment"; recommends him as "deserving the patronage of the Government." LU in DLC, Henry R. Schoolcraft Papers, 1:192–193.

From George Gibson, 12/7. "The proposals of Turk & Henderson for supplying subsistence for the Cherokee Indians have been examined. The difference in the price of the Ration proposed to be issued by them, and that to be placed in depot, will be two cents & three mills, and when corn meal is issued the difference will be still more. Should you, however, be of the opinion that the issues will not exceed thirty thousand Rations the proposals [*sic*] for furnishing by the Ration is to be prefer[r]ed; for the expence of an agent and the unavoidable waste will make up the difference in the price when the issues are few & casual." ALS in DNA, 1, G-39; FC in DNA, 191, 1:3.

From W[ILLIAM] H[ENRY] HARRISON, [Representative from O.]

Washington, 7th Dec[embe]r 1818

Permit me to recommend to you Mr. Jacob [R.] Burley of Cincinnati Ohio for the appointment of Cadet at the Military School at West Point. He is a young man of very respectable connections and respectable information.

I must also beg leave to remind you of the reasons which urge the appointment of Colo[nel] P[aul D.] Butler as Indian Agent at Sandusky.

With great Respect & Regard, I am . . . .

ALS in DNA, 15, 1819, 86.

To Callender Irvine, [Philadelphia,] 12/7. "I have ordered a warrent [*sic*] for $30,000 on account of cloathing [*sic*] to be issued, in your favor. By the enclosed statement from the Books of the Comptroller you will perceive that the appropriation is exhausted." FC in DNA, 3, 10:197.

Andrew Jackson, "Hermitage, near Nashville," to James Monroe, 12/7. "I have just received your message to both Houses of Congress, [delivered on 11/16 (Richardson, *Messages and Papers of the Presidents,* 2:39–47),] forwarded by you, and have read it with great attention and satisfaction. The Florida question being now fairly before Congress, I hope that body will take measures to secure our southern frontier from a repetition of massacre and murder." Jackson fears that the return of Pensacola to the Spanish will be followed by "a renewal of all the horrid scenes of massacre on our frontier that existed before the campaign" prosecuted by Jackson in 1818 against the Seminoles. "Col. [Henry] Sherburne, Chickasaw Agent, requested me to name to you, that he was wearied with his situation, of which I have no doubt: his age and former habits of life but little calculated him for happiness amidst a savage nation. But being dependent for the support of himself and sister on the perquisites of his office, he cannot resign; but it would be a great accommodation to him to be transferred to Newport, [R.I.,] should a vacancy in any office occur that he was competent to fill. I have no doubt but he is an amiable old man; and from his Revolutionary services, I sincerely feel for him. He is unacquainted with Indians, and all business that relates to them; but at the treaty [negotiations with the Chickasaws this autumn], as soon as he did understand our wishes and that of the Governement, he aided us with all his might." PC in *Correspondence between Gen. Andrew Jackson and John C. Calhoun . . . on the Occurrences in the Seminole War,* p. 43.

To R[ICHARD] M. JOHNSON

Department of War, 7th Decem[be]r 1818

In returning to you the papers in the case of Henry Wakefield, I have to state that this Department possesses no power to grant relief. And in the case of the application for bounty land, presented by Mr. Walker of N[orth] Carolina, it has been referred to the land office with orders to admit it, provided the fact of his having enlisted for the war, instead of five years, be satisfactorily established.

FC in DNA, 4, 2:14.

To R[ICHARD] M. JOHNSON

Department of War, 7th Decem[be]r 1818

In answer to your note [of *ca.* 12/3] concerning the petition of Edward Baker, I respectfully submit a report from the Ordnance Department [written by Decius Wadsworth on 12/5].

FC in DNA, 4, 2:14.

D[ANIEL] PARKER to the Commanding Officers of Divisions and Military Departments

7th Decem[ber] 1818

The Secr[etar]y of War directs me to advise you that arrangements have been made for provisioning the Army by an organized department of supplies. This arrangement will go into effect on the first of June next, previous to which the Commissary General of Supplies [that is, of Subsistence, George Gibson,] will communicate with all Commandants of Divisions, Departments, Regiments, Corps, Cantonments & Posts. In the mean time the Contractors will continue their supplies according to their contracts and under the orders of the War Department, by which there will be left in deposit on the first of June next, two mo[nths'] supply at Fort Armstrong and Fort Crawford on the Mississippi, and the posts on the Missourie [*sic*]; and the deposit stipulated in the contract at Chicago, Green Bay, and Mackinac. At all other posts and stations there will be left one month[']s supply at the expiration of the contract which will be inspected, receipted for, and issued by the Commissaries of Issues, which will be stationed at the several posts, with proper instructions, by the last of May next.

This information is transmitted, that the requisitions within your department may be made in conformity with the arrangements of the War Depart[men]t.

LS (Andrew Jackson's copy) in DLC, Andrew Jackson Papers, 8371; CC in DNA, 2, P-1818. NOTE: This circular is addressed to the Com[man]d[in]g Gen[era]ls of Divisions & to the com[man]d[in]g officers of [the nine Military] Departments.

Benjamin Romaine, New York [City], to J[oseph] G. Swift, [New York City], 12/7. Because Romaine has met Calhoun only once and casually, he asks Swift's help in getting an appointment as a Cadet for Romaine's son, Washington Romaine, who is now 18 and has been studying for two years in Princeton College. The father cites his own military services during the Revolution and the War of 1812. ALS in DNA, 15, 1818, 169, with an AEU of recommendation by Swift dated 12/8 and an EU that an appointment was sent in Swift's care.

Resolution by the Senate, 12/7. Confirms the appointment as 2nd Lts. in the Army of 23 named graduates of 1818 from the Military Academy; attested by Charles Cutts, Secretary of the Senate. DS in DNA, 1, S-95.

From Eldred Simkins, [Representative from S.C.]

Ho[use of] Rep[resentatives,] 7 Dec[embe]r 1818

I have taken the liberty of enclosing a letter from one of your officers [probably Capt. Joel Spencer] who complains strongly of being misrepresented. Will you read it and communicate to me such information in relation to it, as you may deem compatible with your sense of duty.

ALS in DNA, 2, S-1818. Note: An AEU by Calhoun reads: "Write to Spencer." Compare herein Calhoun's letter to Spencer of 12/9 and Spencer's letter that was then being answered.

To Gerard Steddiford, New York [City], 12/7. "I have received your letter of the 27th ult[im]o [LS in DNA, 1, S-103] and am glad the court has adjourned sine die. Mr. [Samuel R.] Betts will be instructed to transmit to you the original proceedings in order to enable you to comply with my order of the 15th September last. A copy of instructions to Mr. Betts is enclosed." FC in DNA, 3, 10:196–197.

To Commodore Isaac Chauncey, New York [City], 12/8. If no Boatswain is attached to the U.S.S. *John Adams,* Chauncey is to order Boatswain John M. Fate of the U.S. Brig *Saranac* to report to the *John Adams.* FC in DNA, 121, 13:295.

To Lt. Edgar Freeman, U.S.N., New York [City], 12/8. In reply to his letters of 12/4 (2 LS's, one to Calhoun and one to Benjamin Homans, in DNA, 134) requesting assignment to the recruiting station at Boston because his ship, the U.S. Brig *Saranac,* is to be sold this month, Calhoun explains that one Lt. is already attached to that station and that regulations prohibit a second one serving there. FC in DNA, 121, 13:295.

From C[allender] Irvine, Philadelphia, 12/8. "I have the honor to transmit a Statement, of Contracts, made in this Department, for the service of the year 1818, for materials of Domestic manufacture, for Clothing the Army . . . . The duplicate shall be sent in a few days." LS in DNA, 2, I-1819; FC in DNA, 45, 387:227; PC (of 3 Ens only) in *American State Papers: Military Affairs,* 1:856–858.

From Thomas L. McKenney, 12/8. "The inclosed escaped my observation when I forwarded the rest to you the other day," [12/2]. An EU reads: "Enclosing a Statement of Henry Sherburne of the goods that were damaged by their sinking in the Mississippi." ALI in DNA, 1, M-98.

From Joseph McMinn, Cherokee Agency, 12/8. Reports his progress in a recent meeting with the Cherokee council, during which he spent much time and "every energy of my mind in placing their true situation before them." The Cherokees' king has stated that he understands what he should do and that he will persuade his people to send a deputation to see the "father [President James Monroe], who should possess full power to settle everything." McMinn believes that a deputation will actually be sent [to Washington] and that emigration of the Eastern Cherokees to the Arkansas will be accepted on the proposed terms [during the deputation's negotiations]. PC in *American State Papers: Indian Affairs,* 2:482.

To Return J. Meigs, Cherokee Agent

Department of War, 8th Decem[be]r 1818

I enclose proposals made to this Department by Turk and Henderson, of Tennessee, [on 12/2] for the supply of rations to the Cherokee Indians, under the late treaty. As these proposals appear reasonable, will you make a contract with these gentlemen for the supply of such rations as you may require for the Indians at your Agency, as well as for such Indians as may emigrate to the Arkansaw. The object being to furnish the Indians with such parts of the ration as are essential, you will omit in your requisitions the small parts, such as liquor, soap, vinegar, candles, and salt when salted meat is issued. It would also be well to issue corn meal, instead of wheat flour, when it can be done with economy.

The state of the Indian appropriation requires a rigid regard to economy in all the disbursements. You will therefore pay strict attention to the subject.

LS with En in DNA, 75 (M-208:7); FC in DNA, 72, D:234.

To Lewis Cass, Detroit, 12/9. Answers his letter of 11/21, which is an LS in DNA, 1, C-80, with an FC in DNA, 76 (M-1:4, pp. 57–58). Cass had heard that the Wyandot Chiefs have returned to Washington. Cass protested that "this practise of visiting the seat of Government without invitation & communicating directly with the War Department, of which these Chiefs set the first example last winter, will, if continued, introduce an entire change in the mode of conducting our Indian relations." He explained: "If the Indians find that all subjects can be brought directly before the Government, the officers of the Indian Department will become ciphers and their usefulness & respectability destroyed. I need scarcely say that it is only by an examination upon the spot and by information to be there collected [where the tribes live] that questions relating to the local concerns of the Indians can be fully investigated and correctly determined." Cass suspected that two U.S. citizens, Isaac Walker and another Walker, may have prompted this unauthorized trip, partly "to procure the appointment of one of the family as the Agent of the Wyandots, an appointment for which I take the liberty of stating either of them is utterly unfit, and in any effort to obtain which I trust neither of them will succeed." Cass suggested that Isaac Walker be rebuked and that the Chiefs be referred to [John] Johnston, "their proper Agent, an intelligent & faithful officer, for any redress their situation may require or for an answer to any proposition which they may make." In reply, Calhoun reports that Isaac Walker and seven Indians passed through Washington recently while simply making a tour of large cities in the East and that Cass's letter of 11/21 arrived after their departure from Washington. FC in DNA, 72, D:234.

To Midshipman Enos R. Childs, U.S.N., New York [City], 12/9. Encloses affidavits received from the Governor of Ga., [William

Rabun,] containing charges against "your character." If an indictment by the civil authorities in Ga. and a trial should come, what witnesses would Childs consider essential to his defense? FC in DNA, 121, 13:295.

To Speaker [Henry Clay], 12/9. As Acting Secretary of the Navy, Calhoun submits supplementary information as to the Navy Pension Fund that has been received since his report of 11/21, this information comprising his exchange of letters [dated 11/17 and 11/27] with John W. Davis and Davis's enclosures. LS with Ens in DNA, 201, 15A-F4; FC in DNA, 125, 3:11; PC with Ens in House Document No. 6, 15th Cong., 2nd Sess.

To W[illiam] H. Crawford, 12/9. Encloses correspondence explaining the delay in paying the Ga. militia for serving in the War [of 1812], which Crawford is to forward to Gen. [John] Floyd. The payments will be completed promptly. "As regards the Naval officer you are already made acquainted with the steps taken. The Navy Department has notified Gen. Floyd of the course adopted." FC in DNA, 3, 10:198–199.

To Fourth Auditor Constant Freeman, 12/9. Pursuant to a House resolution of 12/7, Calhoun asks Freeman to supply a statement of expenditures from the fund for the gradual increase of the Navy. FC in DNA, 122, 13:244.

To Camillus Griffith, Alexandria, D.C., 12/9. Orders him to deposit on 5/31/1819 two months' rations for the troops along the Mississippi and one month's supply for troops stationed elsewhere within the area of his contract, upon requisition by the commanding officers, whom he is to inform about this order. FC in DNA, 3, 10:199.

From Callender Irvine

Philad[elphi]a, Decemb[er] 9th 1818

I transmitted by yesterday[']s mail a statement of contracts made in this Department for articles & materials of Army clothing &c., of *domestic* manufacture, for the present year[']s service. By this statement you will find, Sir, that the interests of the manufacturers have not been neglected. Yet from the resolution instructing the Military Committee of Congress to enquire into the expediency of making provision by law for clothing the Army of the United States in domestic manufactures, it might be inferred that the manufacturers had just grounds of complaint against this Department. I question whether the contracts of other Departments exhibit so favorable a result to the manufacturers of this Country. Be this as it may, I am decidedly of opinion, & I conceive it to be my duty to repeat to you the conviction, that if it shall be made obligatory on the Department to clothe the Army entirely of articles of domestic origin & manufacture, we must calculate on a very considerable advance in the prices & materials of domestic manufacture & particularly those made of wool; for the manufacturers of wo[o]l[en] goods have already hinted at the necessity of an advance, alleging that British agents have purchased & shipped to England large quantities of wool, & continue to purchase all that is offered in our markets; and they have stated to me that a particular quality of wool which they purchased last year at 35 cents p[e]r pound, cannot be had now for a less sum than 50 c[en]ts p[e]r pound. You will therefore, Sir, perceive the consequences of a law such as is contemplated by the resolution of Congress alluded to. The expences of the military establishment, already made a cause of complaint, will be much increased, and it is to be apprehended, that the quality of the domestic manufacture will gradually deteriorate. I embrace this opportunity of remarking, that since I became a purchasing officer I have given all the encouragement & protection that I could & believed to be consistent with my duty, to domestic manufacturers. Other modes must be devised, than the profits arising from the contracts with this office, divided & subdivided as they are amongst the numerous manufacturers, for their protection, or they will sink.

ALS in DNA, 1, I-122; FC in DNA, 45, 387:228.

To James Johnson, Great Crossings, Ky., 12/9. Directs him to deposit on 3/30 at Bellefontaine, [Mo. Territory,] "430,000 complete rations for two months, for the troops at all the posts on the Missouri; and [you will also deliver enough rations] for one month at all other places where troops are stationed or recruiting within the limits of your contract, on the requisition of the Commanding Officers, to whom you will seasonably communicate this order." FC in DNA, 3, 10:198. (Compare Calhoun's letter of 12/10/1818 to James Johnson.)

To R[ICHARD] M. JOHNSON

Department of War, 9th Decem[be]r 1818

I enclose herewith a report of the 3d Auditor of the Treasury Department [Peter Hagner] upon the petition of C.L. Rockwood. This Department does not possess power to grant the relief prayed for by the petitioner.

FC in DNA, 4, 2:14.

From W[illiam] L[ee, Second Auditor, Treasury Department,] 12/9. Because a law of 4/2/1816 failed to stipulate the salaries to be paid to certain commissioners who were intended to deal with loans and pensions, he asks Calhoun to furnish him with directives concerning the compensations that will be "applicable to the several cases that may occur." FC in DNA, 51, 1:140.

To Lt. Commandant JAMES RAMAGE, U.S.N., "Present"

Navy Department, Dec[embe]r 9th 1818

You will proceed to Norfolk, Va., and have the U.S. Sch[oone]r Hornet, under your command, prepared with as little delay as practicable for a cruise. When the necessary preparations shall have been made, orders will be transmitted to you from this Department.

FC in DNA, 121, 13:296.

To P.H. Rathbone, New York [City], 12/9. Orders him to deposit on 5/31/1819 a two-months' supply of rations for the troops stationed at Michilimackinac, Green Bay, and Chicago and a one-month supply for all other troops within the area of his contract, upon requisitions by the commanding officers, whom he is to inform about this order. FC in DNA, 3, 10:199.

To Capt. GEORGE C. READ, U.S.S. *Hornet,* Boston

Navy Department, Dec[embe]r 9th 1818

Your letter of the 2d instant, announcing your arrival at Boston, has happily relieved the anxiety long felt for your safety. According to your suggestion, you will pay off such part of the crew as you judge will be for the good of the service, and permit your officers to leave the Ship, and to report to this Department accordingly. The Navy Commissioners are requested to order a Survey upon the Ship Hornet and to report her state & condition and the repairs necessary to be made to fit her for service.

FC in DNA, 121, 13:296.

C[hristopher] V[andeventer] to E[ldred] "Simpkins [*actually* Simkins," Representative from S.C.,] 12/9. "At the request of the Secretary of War, I enclose you a copy of a letter addressed by him to Capt. [Arthur] Simkins, [Jr., from S.C.,] which shows the light in which his conduct is viewed at the War Dep[artmen]t." FC in DNA, 3, 10:199.

To Capt. Joel Spencer, Assistant Deputy Quartermaster General, Fort Hawkins, [Ga.,] 12/9. "I have received your letter of the 14th ult[im]o [ALS in DNA, 1, S-102, admitting that he gambled in 8/1818]. The representation made against you is much the same as you have disclosed yourself. I am pleased with the frankness with which you confess your error and have no doubt but you will in future avoid a similar indiscretion." FC in DNA, 3, 10:198.

To Subsistence Contractors, 12/9. [In anticipation of the change to be made about 6/1819 under which rations will be bought and inspected by the Commissary General of Subsistence, George Gibson, and his subordinates,] Calhoun orders each of six contractors to deposit on 5/31/1819, the expiration date of his contract, rations for one month for all troops stationed or being recruited within the area of his respective contract. FC in DNA, 3, 10:199, with marginal notes showing that copies were sent to [James] Turk & [Thomas] Henderson, Charles Hegins, P[eter] H. Green, Robinson & Taylor, Matthew L. Davis, and B[enjamin] G. Orr. (Compare Calhoun's letters of 12/9/1818 to Camillus Griffith, James Johnson, and P.H. Rathbone.)

From Decius Wadsworth

Ordnance Office, 9 Dec. 1818

I have received a letter from Mr. [James] Stubblefield, Superintendant [*sic*] of the Armoury [*sic*] at Harper's [*sic*] Ferry, on the Subject of the improved Gunlock introduced by Mr. [Edward] Baker. It will probably advance the views of the latter to have a Copy of the Letter transmitted to the Military Committee [of the House of Representatives], together with some certificates obtained by him from Harper's Ferry.

ALS in DNA, 36, Ex-6-12; FC in DNA, 32, 2:156. Note: An AES by Richard M. Johnson on the ALS states that the House Committee on Military Affairs "would have no difficulty if the War Department would adopt the Lock" and adds that if the Secretary of War has authority to give the $3,000 or $4,000 involved, that would "make short metre of it."

"Memo" from W[alker] K. Armistead, [Chief Engineer]

[*Ca.* December 10, 1818]

I do not think it proper to transfer Artillery Officers to the Corps of Engineers, [as was proposed for John R. Vinton by Ferdinand Rudolf Hassler on 12/5,] because it will destroy that emulation which now exists among the Cadets of the Military Academy. They have been led to believe that the two most distinguished in the 1st Class are to be commissioned in the Engineers.

Relative to Mr. Has[s]ler[']s papers and instruments, I have to request that a proper room be fitted up for them in Philadelphia, as the danger of removal to instruments of their construction is always attended with risk. They should remain where they were purchased. The Waggon [*sic*] and Horses should be sent to Old Point Comfort as they may be usefully employed there.

The repeating Circle [is] to be deposited with [Bvt.] Col. [Joseph G.] Totten until he can send it to West Point.

From Capt. [René Edward] De Russy[']s letter to the Pilots of New York [Harbor], it is thought that sufficient priviledges [*sic*] are granted to the Pilots. Respectfully submitted, W.K. Armistead.

ALS in DNA, 1, A-31.

To P[hilip] P. Barbour, 12/10. Answers his inquiry of 12/9 (ALS in DNA, 1, B-117) asking whether an otherwise-eligible man who served in the Revolution partly in person and partly "by substitute" can receive a pension. "It has been decided that a substitute cannot claim the benefits of the law of the 18th of March last." FC in DNA, 3, 10:201.

From Jacob Brown, Brownville, [N.Y.,] 12/10. He feels that his letters of 11/29 and 12/6 do not provide sufficient information on the "important subject" of the military road from Sackets Harbor to Plattsburg. So he now discusses at length the route of this road and its value in the defense of the area through which it is to be built, and he suggests some changes in the plans to strengthen the fortifications on that frontier. LU (incomplete but with the last paragraph and some revisions in Brown's hand) in DNA, 1, B-113; FC dated 12/9 in DLC, Jacob Brown Papers, Letterbooks, 2:131–135.

From Lt. R[obert] M. Desha, U.S.M.C. Headquarters, Washington, 12/10. Desha sent on 7/31 to [Bvt.] Maj. [Anthony] Gale at New Orleans a payroll remittance of $4,000; it has never been acknowledged, and Desha fears that Gale has used the money for other purposes. Desha hopes that he will not be held accountable for the money; it was sent in accordance with the regulations of his office. ALS in DNA, 128, 7:69.

From John Gassaway

Annapolis, Dec[embe]r 10th 1818

Having had the honor of being introduced to you this last summer, while the President of the United States [James Monroe] was here, I take the liberty of recommending to your notice Master Lewis Caton, the son of William Caton of this place, who wishes to obtain an appointment in the Military Academy at West Point.

I shou[l]d not attempt to recommend the young Gentleman, if I was not acquainted with his Qualifications, as to his being a steady, correct youth, and who received his Education at this place, and has proved himself to be a bright and lively genius, and no doubt will prove an ornament to his country, when he quits the

Academy, shou[l]d he have the honor to be appointed. It is the first time I have attempted to recommend any person to you, since you have been in the War department, and hope it will meet with your approbation. Be so good as to inform me by Letter whether there will be any probability of his succeeding. Caton is now about 16 years old.

ALS in DNA, 15, 1818, 173.

From A[quila] Giles, New York [City], 12/10. Asks that his son, George [Washington] Giles, shall be given a new appointment as a Cadet, illness having prevented him from accepting that of 1817; argues that, under the new regulations approved by Calhoun on 7/23/1818, George can take the entrance examination in 1/1819 with the class that entered in 9/1818. ALS in DNA, 15, 1816, 62.

To Thomas S. Jesup, 12/10. Answers his letter of 12/9 (LS in DNA, 1, J-44; FC in DNA, 42, 1:134–135); [Bvt.] Capt. [Thomas] Tupper, whose accounts are unpaid and unsettled to the extent of roughly $50,000, has been ordered to Washington to settle them; claimants awaiting payments to which Tupper has obligated the U.S. should be made to understand that the availability of funds for payment depends upon a Congressional appropriation. FC in DNA, 3, 10:200.

To James Johnson, Great Crossings, Ky., 12/10. Orders 420,000 complete rations deposited at Bellefontaine, [Mo. Territory,] by 3/21/1819. FC in DNA, 3, 10:200; PC in House Document No. 110, 16th Cong., 2nd Sess.

To R[ICHARD] M. JOHNSON

Department of War, 10th Decem[be]r 1818

I have the honor to transmit herewith a further report of the Colonel of Ordnance, [Decius Wadsworth,] respecting the improvements of the gun lock introduced by Mr. [Edward] Baker.

LS in DNA, 157, 16A-G8; FC in DNA, 4, 2:14.

From W[illiam] L[ee], 12/10. Upon request made by H[owell] Tatum, Acting Military Storekeeper at Nashville, Lee submits Tatum's statement of property in his hands as of 9/30 and Tatum's letter about it. FC in DNA, 52, 3:3.

D[aniel] Parker to Capt. Thomas Tupper, 12/10. "The Secretary of War directs that you repair forthwith to this place, and report to the Quartermaster General, [Thomas S. Jesup,] prepared to settle your public accounts." PC in House Report No. 69, 17th Cong., 1st Sess.; PC in House Report No. 28, 17th Cong., 2nd Sess.

From Nathan Plumer, Portland, [District of Me., Mass.,] 12/10. Suggests that Army officers who receive captured deserters should be supplied with funds to pay the rewards in cash, because payment by drafts on distant banks can be redeemed only at a great discount or with much inconvenience. ALS in DNA, 1, P-69.

To Moses Porter, Boston, 12/10. Answers his request of 12/5 (LS with En in DNA, 1, P-66) for permission to build the guardhouse at Fort Independence that was recommended to Porter on 12/3 by Abram Eustis as being needed. Asks for a report of the probable cost. "I am in hopes that the late order to remove convicts to Southern stations to labour on public works will so reduce the number of prisoners as not to make an additional guard house necessary." FC in DNA, 3, 10:200.

To James P. Preston, [Governor of Va.,] Richmond, 12/10. All vacant Clerkships in the War Department were filled before his request of 12/8 arrived. FC in DNA, 3, 10:201.

From John Rodgers, 12/10. As Calhoun has ordered today, the U.S.S. *Hornet* and the schooner *Hornet* will be repaired and made fit for active service. ALS in DNA, 128, 7:72.

From John Rodgers, 12/10. Pursuant to Calhoun's request of 12/9, Rodgers lists the 293 petty officers and crewmen who are deemed sufficient to sail the U.S.S. *Congress* to India. ALS in DNA, 128, 7:73. A similar report, with a list of 30 higher officers assigned to the *Congress,* was addressed on 12/10 by Rodgers to Smith Thompson and was sent to Benjamin Homans. CC in DNA, 128, 7:76.

Resolution by the Senate, 12/10. "Resolved, That the President . . . [James Monroe] be requested to communicate to the Senate, the instructions to the Commissioners who negotiated the Indian treaties now before the Senate." DS (attested by Charles Cutts, Secretary of the Senate) in DNA, 1, S-131.

To Talbot Chambers, Bellefontaine, [Mo. Territory,] 12/11. Answers his letter to [Christopher] Vandeventer of 11/1 (ALS in DNA, 1, C-72). James Johnson has been ordered to deliver by 3/20/1819 to Bellefontaine 430,000 rations for the Yellowstone expedition and to transport provisions and troops by steamboats. Calhoun hopes that Chambers will not be compelled to buy any provisions but urges economy if he must. FC in DNA, 3, 10:202–203; PC in Carter, ed., *Territorial Papers,* 15:471–472.

To Speaker HENRY CLAY

Department of War, 11th December 1818

In compliance with a resolution of the House of Representatives, passed the 17th of April last, directing "the Secretary of War to report at an early period of the next session of Congress, whether any, and, if any, what reduction may be made in the military peace establishment of the United States, with safety to the public service, and whether any, and if any, what change ought to be made in the ration established by law, and in the mode of issuing the same; and also report a system for the establishment of a Commissariat for the Army," I have the honor to submit the following Report:

In order to form a correct opinion on a subject involving so many particulars, as the expense of our military establishment, it will be necessary to consider it under distinct and proper heads. To ascertain, then, "whether any, and if any, what reductions may be made in the expenses of our military peace establishment," I propose to consider its number, organization, pay and emoluments, and administration. To the one or the other of these heads, all of its expenses may be traced; and if they are greater than they ought to be, we must search for the cause in the improper extent of the establishment, the excessive number of officers in proportion to the men, the extravagance of the pay and emoluments, or the want of proper responsibility and economy in its administration.

Pursuing the subject in the order in which it has been stated, the first question which offers itself for consideration is, whether our military establishment can be reduced "with safety to the public service," or can its expenditures be, with propriety, reduced, by reducing the Army itself. It is obvious that, viewed in the abstract, few questions present so wide a field for observation, or which are so well calculated to produce a great diversity of sentiment, as the one now proposed. Considered as an original question, it would involve in its discussion, the political institutions of the country, its geographical position and character, the number and distance of our posts, and our relations with the Indian tribes, and the principal European powers. It is conceived, however, that a satisfactory view of it may be taken without discussing topics so extensive and indefinite.

The military establishments of 1802 and 1808, have been admitted, almost universally, to be sufficiently small. The latter, it is true, received an enlargement from the uncertain state of our foreign relations, at that time, but the former was established at a period of profound quiet, (the commencement of Mr. [Thomas] Jefferson's administration) and was professedly reduced, with a view to economy, to the smallest number then supposed to be consistent with the public safety. Assuming these as a standard and comparing the present establishment (taking into the comparison the increase of the country) with them, a satisfactory opinion may be formed on a subject, which, otherwise might admit so great a diversity of opinion.

Our military peace establishment is limited by the act of 1815, passed at the termination of the late war, at ten thousand men. The Corps of Engineers & Ordnance by that, and a subsequent act [of 1816], were retained as they then existed; and the President was directed to constitute the establishment of such portions of Artillery, Infantry and Riflemen as he might judge proper. The general order of the 17th May, 1815, fixes the Artillery at 3,200, the Light Artillery at 660, the Infantry [at] 5,440, and the Rifle [Regiment at] 660 Privates and matrosses. Document A exhibits a statement of the military establishment, including the general staff, as at present organized; and B exhibits a similar view of those of 1802 and 1808, by a reference to which, it will appear, that our military establishments at the respective periods taken in the order of their dates, present an aggregate of 3,323, 9,996, and 12,656. It is obvious, that the establishment of 1808 compared with the then wealth and population of the country, [and] the number and extent of the military posts, is larger in proportion, than the present, but the unsettled state of our relations with France and England at that period, renders the comparison not entirely just. Passing, then, that of 1808, let us compare the establishment of 1802 with the present. To form a correct comparison it will be necessary to compare the capacity and necessities of the country then, with those of the present time. Since that period, our population has nearly doubled, and our wealth more than doubled. We have added [the] Louisiana [Territory] to our possessions, and with it, a great extent of frontier, both maritime and inland. With the extension of our frontier and the increase of our commercial cities, our military posts and fortifications have been greatly multiplied. Document marked C exhibits the number and positions of posts in the year 1802, and document D those of the present time. By a reference to which it will be seen, that at the former period, we had but 27 posts, the most remote of which was, to the North, at Mackinaw, and to the South, at Fort Stoddert, on Mobile river; but now we have 73, which occupy a line of frontier, proportionally extended. On the Lakes, the Mississippi, Missouri, Arkansaw and Red River, our posts are now, or will be shortly, extended, for the protection of our trade and the preservation of the peace of the frontiers, to Green Bay, the mouths of the St. Peters, and the Yellow Stone River, Bellepoint and Natchitoches. Document marked E exhibits a statement of the extent of the line of our frontier, inland and maritime, with the distance of some of the more remote posts from the seat of government, drawn up by Maj[o]r [Stephen H.] Long, of the Topographical Engineers, from the most approved maps.

If, then, the military establishment of 1802 be assumed to be as small, as was then consistent with the safety of the country, our present establishment, when we take into comparison the prodigious increase of wealth, population, extent of territory, number and distance of military posts, cannot be pronounced extravagant; but, on the contrary, after a fair and full comparison, that of the former period must, in proportion to the necessities and capacity of the country, be admitted to be quite as large as the present, and on the assumption, that the establishment of 1802 was as small as the public safety would then admit, a reduction of the expense of our present establishment cannot be made, with safety to the public service, by reducing the Army. In coming to this conclusion, I have not overlooked the maxim, that a large standing army is dangerous to the liberty of the country; and that our ultimate reliance for defense, ought to be on the militia. Its most zealous advocate must, however, acknowledge, that a standing army, to a limitted [*sic*] extent, is necessary; and no good reason can be assigned, why any should exist, but what will equally prove, that the present is not too large. To consider the present Army as dangerous to our liberty, partakes, it is conceived, more of timidity than wisdom. Not to insist on the character of the officers, who, as a body, are high minded and honorable men, attached to the principles of freedom by education and reflection, what well founded apprehension can there be from an establishment distributed on so extended a frontier, with many thousand miles intervening between the extreme points occupied? But the danger, it may be said, is not so much from its numbers, as a spirit hostile to liberty, by which, it is supposed, all regular armies are actuated. This observation is probably true, when applied to standing armies collected into large and powerful masses, but dispersed as our[s] is, over so vast a surface, the danger, I conceive, is of an opposite character, that both officers and soldiers will lose their military habits and feelings, by sliding gradually into those purely civil.

I proceed next to consider whether any reduction can be made with propriety by changing the organization, or by reducing the number of officers of the line, or the staff, in proportion to the men. It is obvious, that as the officers are much more expensive in proportion to their numbers than the soldiers, that the pay of the Army, in relation to its aggregate numbers, must be increased or diminished, with the increase or diminution of the former. It is impossible to fix any absolute proportion between officers and men which will suit every country and every service; and the organization of different countries and of different periods, in the same country, has, accordingly, varied considerably. Our present organization, of which document marked A contains an exhibit, is probably as well or better adapted to the nature of our country and service than any other; as it seems to be the result of experience: for by a reference to document marked B, it will be seen, that it is nearly similar, with the exception of the general staff, in which the present is more extensive, to the organization of the military establishments of 1802 and 1808. It is believed that the proportion of officers of the line to the men, will require no further observations.

The staff as organized by the act of the last session, combines simplicity with efficiency; and is considered to be superior to that of the periods to which I have reference. In estimating the expenses of the Army, and particularly that of the staff, the two most expensive branches of it, the Engineer and Ordnance Departments, ought not fairly to be included. Their duties are connected with the permanent preparation and defense of the country; and have so little reference to the existing military establishment, that, if the Army were reduced to a single Regiment, no reduction could safely be made in either of them. To form a correct estimate of the duties of the other branches of the staff, and consequently the number of officers required, we must take into consideration not only the number of troops, but what is equally essential, the number of posts and extent of country, which they occupy. Were our military establishment reduced one half, it is obvious, that, if the same posts continued to be occupied which now are, the same number of officers, in the Quarter Master's, Commissary'es [*sic*], Paymaster's, Medical, and Adjutant and Inspector General's Department, would be required.

To compare then, as is sometimes done our staff with those of European armies assembled in large bodies is manifestly unfair. The act of the last session, it is believed, has made all the reduction, which ought to be attempted. It has rendered the staff efficient without making it expensive. Such a staff is not only indispensable to the efficiency of the Army but is also necessary to a proper economy in its disbursements; and should an attempt be made, at retrenchment, by reducing the present number, it would, in its consequences, probably prove wasteful and extravagant.

In fact no part of our military organization requires more attention in peace than the general staff. It is in every service invariably the last in attaining perfection; and if neglected in peace, when there is leisure, it will be impossible, in the midst of the hurry and bustle of war, to bring it to perfection. It is in peace, that it should receive a perfect organization, and that the officers should be trained to method and punctuality, so that at the commencement of war, instead of creating anew, nothing more should be necessary, than to give it the necessary enlargement. In this country, particularly, the staff cannot be neglected with impunity. As difficult as its operations are, in actual service, every where, it has here to encounter great and peculiar impediments, from the extent of the country, the badness, and frequently the want of roads, and the sudden and unexpected calls which are often made on the militia. If it could be shewn that the staff, in its present extent, was not necessary in peace, it would, with the view taken, be unwise to lop off on [*sic*] any of its branches, which would be necessary in actual service. With a defective staff, we must carry on our military operations under great disadvantages, and be exposed, particularly at the commencement of a war, to great losses, embarrassments and disasters.

As intimately connected with this part of the subject, it is proper to observe, that so many and such distant small posts as our service requires, not only adds, to the expense of the Army, by rendering a more numerous staff necessary, but it increases the price of almost every article of supply, and the difficulty of enforcing a proper responsibility and economy. To an Army thus situated, the expenses and losses resulting from transportation alone constitutes [*sic*] a considerable sum. Under the best management, our Army must be more expensive, even were our supplies equally cheap, than European armies collected in large bodies, in the midst of populous and wealthy communities. These observations are not made to justify an improper management, or to divert the attention of the House from so important a subject, as the expense of our military establishment. They, in fact, ought to have an opposite effect, for just in the same proportion, that it is liable to be expensive ought the attention and efforts of the government [to] be roused to confine its expenses within the most moderate limits, which may be practicable.

The next question which presents itself for consideration is, can the expenses of our military establishment be reduced, without injury to the public service, by reducing the pay and emoluments of the officers and soldiers? There is no class in the community whose compensation has advanced less since the termination of the war of the Revolution, than that of the officers and soldiers of our Army. While money has depreciated more rapidly than at any other period, and the price of all the necessaries of life has advanced proportionably, their compensation has remained nearly stationary. The effects are severely felt by the subaltern officers. It requires the most rigid economy for them to subsist on their pay and emoluments. Documents marked F and G exhibit the pay and subsistence during the Revolution, and as at present established; and document marked H exhibits the allowance of clothing, fuel, forage, transportation, quarters, waiters, stationery, and straw, at the termination of the Revolutionary war, and in 1802, 1815, and 1818. By a reference to those documents, it will be seen that under most of the heads, the variations of the different periods have been very small; and that on a comparison of the whole, the pay of an officer is not near equal now, if allowance is made for the depreciation of money, to what it was during the Revolution. I will abstain from further remarks, as it must be obvious from these statements, that the expense of our military establishment cannot be materially reduced, without injury to the public service, by reducing the pay and emoluments of the officers and soldiers.

It only remains to consider, in relation to this part of the resolution of the House, whether the expense of our military establishment can be reduced by a proper attention to its administration, or by a more rigid enforcement of responsibility and economy. Our military establishment is doubtless susceptible of great improvement in its administration. The field is extensive, and the attention of the government has not heretofore been so strongly directed towards it, as its importance deserves. Here all savings are real gain, not only in a monied, but a moral & political point of view. An inefficient administration, without economy or responsibility, not only exhausts the public resources, but strongly tends to contaminate the moral and political principles of the officers, who are charged with the disbursements of the Army. To introduce, however, a high state of economy and responsibility in the management of a subject so extensive and complicated as our military establishment, is a task of great difficulty, and requires not only a perfect organization of the department charged with it, but a continued, energetic and judicious enforcement of the laws and regulations established for its government. The organization is the proper sphere of legislation, as the application of the laws and regulations is that of the administration. The former has done all, or nearly all, that can be done. It is believed, that the organization of the War Department, as well as the general staff, is not susceptible of much improvement. The act of the last session regulating the staff, has not only made important savings in the expenses of the Army, but has given both to the department and the staff, a much more efficient organization, than they ever before had. Every department of the Army charged with disbursements, has now a proper head, who under the laws and regulations, is responsible for its administration. The head of the department is thus freed from detail, and has leisure to inspect and control the whole of the disbursements. Much time and reflection will be required to bring the system into complete operation, and to derive from it all the advantages which ought to be expected. The extent of the saving which may result from it, can only be ascertained by time and experience, but with an attentive and vigorous administration, it doubtless will be considerable. In war, it will be much more difficult to enforce economy and responsibility; but, with a system well organized, and with officers trained to method and punctuality, much of the waste and frauds which would otherwise take place in war, will be prevented. In peace, there can be no insuperable difficulty in attaining a high degree of responsibility and economy. The mere monied responsibility, or that of purchases and disbursements, will be easily enforced. The public now sustains much greater losses in the waste and improper use of public property, than in its monied transactions. In our military establishment, responsibility in the latter is well checked, and not badly enforced. The accounts are rendered with considerable punctuality, and are promptly settled; and even neglect or misapplication of public funds, by the disbursing officers, are [*sic*] not often accompanied with ultimate losses, as they are under bonds for the faithful discharge of their duties. Accountability, as it regards the public property, is much more difficult, and has heretofore been much less complete. Returns of property in many cases, particularly in the Medical department, have rarely been required; and even where they have been, they have not been made with punctuality. It cannot be doubted, but what the public has sustained very considerable damage from this want of accountability. Every article of public property, even the smallest, ought, if possible, to be in charge of some person, who should be responsible for it. It will be difficult to attain this degree of perfection; but it is hoped, by making each of the subordinate departments of the War Department liable for the property in its charge, a very considerable improvement and reduction of expenses will be made.

On the quality of the ration, and the system of supplying and issuing it, which I propose next to consider, the health, comfort and efficiency of the Army mainly depend. Too much care cannot be bestowed on these important subjects; for let the military system be ever so perfect in other particulars, any considerable deficiency in these, must, in all great military operations, expose an army to the greatest disasters. All human efforts must, of necessity, be limited by the means [of] sustenance. Food sustains the immense machinery of war, and gives the impulse to all its operations; and if this essential be withdrawn, even but for a few days, the whole must cease to act. No absolute standard can be fixed, as it regards either the quantity or quality of the ration. These must vary, according to the habits and products of different countries. The great objects are, first, and mainly, to sustain the health and spirit of the troops; and the next, to do it with the least possible expense. The system which effects these in the greatest degree, is the most perfect. The ration, as established by the act of the 16th March, 1802, experience proves to be ample in quantity, but not of the quality, best calculated to secure either health or economy. It consists of eighteen ounces of bread, or flour; one pound and a quarter of beef or three-quarters of a pound of pork; one gill of rum, brandy, or whiskey; and at the rate of two quarts of salt, four quarts of vinegar, four pounds of soap, and one pound and a half of candles, to every hundred rations.

The objection to it in relation to the health of the Army, is fully stated in a report of the Surgeon General [Joseph Lovell] to the War Department, [dated 11/16 and] marked I, which [I] would respectfully annex as a part of this report. Under this view of the subject, more need not be added, except to urge its importance, both on the score of humanity and policy.

Our people, even the poorest, being accustomed to a plentiful mode of living, require, to preserve their health, a continuation, in a considerable degree, of the same habits of life, in a camp; and a sudden and great departure from it, subjects them, as is proved by experience, to great mortality. Our losses in the late and Revolutionary wars, from this cause, were probably much greater than from the sword. However well qualified for war in other respects, in the mere capacity of bearing privations, we are inferior to most nations. An American would starve on what a Tartar would live [on] with comfort. In fact, barbarous and oppressed nations have, in this particular, a striking advantage, which, however, ought to be much more than compensated by the skill and resources of a free and civilized people. If, however, such a people want the skill and spirit to direct its resources to its defense, the very wealth, by which it ought to defend itself, becomes the motive for invasion & conquest. Besides, there is something shocking to the feelings, that in a country of plenty beyond all others, in a country which ordinarily, is so careful of the happiness and life of the meanest of its citizens, that its brave defenders, who are not only ready, but anxious to expose their lives for the safety and glory of their country, should, thro' a defective system of supply, be permitted almost to starve, or to perish by the poison of unwholesome food, as has frequently been the case. If it could be supposed that these considerations are not sufficient to excite the most anxious care on this subject, we ought to remember, that nothing adds more to the expense of military operations, or exposes more to its disasters, than the sickness and mortality which result from defective, or unwholesome supplies. Impressed with this view of the subject, considerable changes have been made in the ration, under the authority of the 8th section of the act regulating the staff of the Army, passed at the last session of Congress. The vegetable part of the ration has been much increased. Twice a weak [*sic*], a half allowance of meat, with a suitable quantity of peas or beans, is directed to be issued. Fresh meat has also been substituted twice a week for salted. In the Southern Division, bacon and kiln dried Indian corn meal, has [*sic*] been, to a certain extent, substituted for pork and wheat flour. In addition, orders have been given at all of the permanent posts, where it can be done, to cultivate a sufficient supply of ordinary garden vegetables for the use of the troops; and at the posts remote from the settled parts of the country, the order is extended to the cultivation of corn, and to the supply of the meat part of the ration, both to avoid the expense of distant and expensive transportation, and to secure at all times a supply within the posts themselves.

In addition to these changes, I am of opinion, the spirit part of the ration, as a regular issue, ought to be dispensed with; and such appears to be the opinion of most of the officers of the Army. It both produces, and perpetuates, habits of intemperance, destructive alike to the health and moral and physical energy of the soldiers. The spirits ought to be placed in depot, and be issued occasionally under the discretion of the commander. Thus used, its [*sic*] noxious effects would be avoided, and the troops, when great efforts were necessary, would, by a judicious use, derive important benefits from it. Molasses, beer, and cider, according to circumstances, might be used as substitutes. The substitution of bacon and kiln dried corn meal, in the Southern Division will have, it is believed, the most valuable effects. They are both much more congenial to the habits of the people in that section of our country. Corn meal has another, and in my opinion great and almost decisive advantage; it requires so little art to prepare it for use. It is not easy to make good bread of wheat flour, whilst it is almost impossible to make bad of that of Indian corn. Besides, wheat is much more liable to be damaged than Indian corn; for the latter is better protected against disease and the effects of bad seasons in time of harvest, than any other grain; and when injured, the good is easily separated from the bad. Experience proves it to be not less nutritious than wheat, or any other grain. Parched corn constitutes the principal food of the Indian warrior, and such are its nutritious qualities, that they can support long and fatiguing marches on it alone.

I next proceed to consider the system of supplying the Army with provisions, or the establishment of a Commissariat, and, as they are connected in their nature, I propose to consider that part of the resolution in relation to a commissariat, and the mode of issuing the rations, at the same time.

The system established, at the last session, will, in time of peace, be adequate to the cheap and certain supply of the Army. The act provides for the appointment of a Commissary General, and as many assistants as the service may require, and authorized the President to assign to them their duties in purchasing and issuing rations. It also directs, that the ordinary supplies of the Army should be purchased on contracts to be made by the Commissary General, and to be delivered on inspection, in the bulk, at such places as shall be stipulated in the contract. Document marked J contains the rules and regulations which have been established by the order of the President, and presents the operations of the system in detail. It is believed, that it is as well guarded against fraud, as any other department of our military supplies; and judging from the contracts already formed under it, will, when improved by experience, probably make a very considerable saving. It would improve the system, to authorize the appointment of two deputy commissaries, one for each Division, with the pay, rank, and emoluments, of [a] Major of Infantry, to be taken from the line or from citizens, and so to amend the act of the last session, as to authorize the President to appoint the assistant commissaries, either from the line, or citizens. When the assistant commissary is not taken from the line, to make his pay equal to that of a subaltern appointed from the line, it ought to be fifty dollars per month, with two rations a day. It should be the duty of the deputy commissaries to perform such service as the Commissary General might prescribe, and particularly to inspect the principal depots, and, in cases of necessity, to make the necessary purchases. When a suitable subaltern cannot be had, or when his services are necessary in the line, the power proposed to be vested in the President to select from citizens, would be important. It is not believed that any other alteration would be necessary in peace; but the system would require great enlargement in war, to render it sufficiently energetic to meet the many vicissitures incidental to the operations of war.

It would then be necessary to divide the system into two divisions, one for purchasing, and the other for issuing of rations, with as many deputy commissaries of purchases and issues, as there may be armies and military districts, to whom ought to be added, a suitable number of assistants. The basis of the system ought, in war, to be the same as is now established. The ordinary supplies ought to be by contract on public proposals. By a judicious collection of provisions at proper depots combined with an active and energetic transportation, it would be seldom necessary to resort to any other mode of purchasing. To provide however for contingencies, the purchasing department ought to be efficiently organized, and a branch of it, as already stated, attached to each army, and military department. As it is the means to be resorted to in cases of necessity, it ought to possess those high and discretionary powers, which do not admit of exact control. It is in its nature, liable to many abuses; and to prevent them from being great, more efficient regulations and checks are required, than in any other branch of the general staff.

The defects of the mere contract system, is [*sic*] so universally acknowledged, by those who have experienced its operation in the late war, that it cannot be necessary, to make many observations in relation to it. Nothing can appear more absurd, than that the success of the most important military operations, on which the very fate of the country may depend, should, ultimately rest on men, who are subject to no military responsibility, and on whom there is no other hold, than the penalty of a bond. When we add to this observation, that it is often the interest of a contractor to fail, at the most critical juncture, when the means of supply become the most expensive, it seems strange, that the system should have been continued for a single campaign. It may be said, that when the contractor fails, the commander has a right to purchase at his risk, by which the disasters, which naturally result from a failure, may be avoided. The observation is more specious than solid. If on failure of the contractor, there existed a well organized system for purchasing the supplies there would be some truth in it, but without such a system, without depots of provisions, and with the funds intended for the supply of the Army, perhaps in the hands of the contractor, his failure must generally be fatal to a campaign. It is believed that a well organized commissariat, whose ordinary supplies, are obtained by contract founded on public notice, possesses (besides those peculiar to itself,) all of the advantages fairly attributable to the system of issuing rations by contract. It is equally guarded against fraud, and its purchases can be made on terms more advantageous. A considerable objection, to the system of issuing the ration by contract, is, that the merchants and capitalists, are deterred from bidding, by the hazard of issuing the ration; and thus the sphere of competition is contracted, and the contracts for supplying the Army, often thrown into the hands of adventurers. This objection is avoided, under the present system, by which the ration will be cheaply supplied, and the danger of failure, almost wholly removed.

All of which is respectfully submitted. J.C. Calhoun.

FC with Ens in DNA, 4, 2:14–67; LS with Ens in DNA, 201, 15A-F3; PC with Ens in House Document No. 36, 15th Cong., 2nd Sess.; PC with Ens in *American State Papers: Military Affairs,* 1:779–810; PC in Crallé, ed., *Works,* 5:25–40. NOTE: A DS of the House resolution of 4/17, attested by the Clerk of the House, Thomas Dougherty, is in DNA, 1, H-187.

To De Witt Clinton, Governor of N.Y., 12/11. "I have rec[eive]d your Excellency's letter of the 7th instant [ALS with Ens in DNA, 1, C-94], relative to the interdiction of some priviledges of the pilots of the harbour of New York, by Capt. [René Edward] De Russy. I am aware of the importance of granting every facility to the pilots in performing their duty, but on examining their letter to Capt. De Russy and comparing it with his answer, I am at a loss to know what rights necessary to discharge their duties as pilots are withheld from them." FC in DNA, 3, 10:201.

From J[AMES] L. E[DWARDS]

War Department, Pension Office, Dec[embe]r 11, 1818

The question is respectfully submitted to you, whether an insane man, whose services were sufficiently long, during the Revolutionary war, and whose pecuniary circumstances are such, as to entitle him to the provisions of the Act of the 18th of March last, can on due proof being made of the foregoing facts, be placed on the Pension roll, under that Act? Or in other words, can the declaration [by the veteran], which is a mere form, be in any case dispensed with?

FC in DNA, 91, 6:78.

To F[erdinand] R[udolf] Hassler, Newark, N.J., 12/11. "Your letters of the 5th Inst[ant] have been received. The regulations of the Army will not admit of the transfer you request in favor of Lieut[enant John R.] Vinton. You will deliver such instruments as you have with you to Capt. [René Edward] De R[ussy] at New York, those in Philadelphia to Capt. [Samuel] Babcock at Philadelphia, and the repeating circle to Lt. Col. [Joseph G.] Totten at Plattsburg. These gentlemen will be instructed on the subject. The Horses & Carriage will be delivered to Capt. [William A.] Barron at New York." FC in DNA, 3, 10:202; CCEx in DNA, 23, 50 (173).

To Thomas S. Jesup, 12/11. Encloses an extract of a letter [of 12/11] to F[erdinand] R[udolf] Hassler at Newark ordering him to deliver a wagon and horses to Capt. William A. Barron. Barron is to be ordered to sell them as soon as possible and to deposit the proceeds in the New York City Branch of the Bank of the United States. FC in DNA, 3, 10:201.

To Col. William King, Pensacola, 12/11. "I have a pleasure in introducing to your acquaintance and particular notice Mr. Miller who visits Pensacola for the benefit of his health. Any attentions you may have it in your power to render him will be requited by an acquaintance with an intelligent gentleman & will be esteemed a particular favour done to" me. FC in DNA, 3, 10:201.

To John McKee, 12/11. "Since writing the letter to you of the 30th yours of the 15th ult[im]o, stating the manner in which you have disposed of the goods sent on as presents to the Choctaws at the treaty, has been received; and, as the course you have adopted is approved, you will consider the order contained in that communication as revoked." FC in DNA, 72, D:235; CC in DNA, 77 (M-271:2, frames 0990–0991).

To Thomas L. McKenney, 12/11. "In a letter from Col. [John] McKee received at this Dept. since the one addressed to you on the 30th ult[im]o, he states that he has applied the goods sent for presents to the payment of the Choctaw annuity; and, as that course is approved, you will not act on the part of that letter which relates to this subject." FC in DNA, 72, D:235; LU in DNA, 77 (M-271:2, frames 0992–0993).

R.M. Patterson, Secretary, American Philosophical Society, Philadelphia, to John Sergeant, [Representative from Pa.,] 12/11. The Society's petition of last spring, presented by Sergeant, "praying for the use of certain astronomical instruments, belonging to the United States, and now deposited in Philadelphia," has not been answered. Patterson asks Sergeant to renew the plea, upon the answer to which "depends" the "establishment of an institution, which we hope to be able to make both useful and honourable to our country." ALS in DNA, 1, A-51.

From [Dr.] Samuel Shaw, Albany, 12/11. Resigns as Post Surgeon. ALS in DNA, 11, 12771, with an EU stating that the resignation will take effect on 12/31.

Maj. Z[achary] Taylor, Louisville, Ky., to Callender Irvine, Philadelphia, 12/11. Submits an estimate of clothing, camp equipage, and Quartermaster stores needed by Taylor for the recruiting service. "There is such complaint of the clothing furnished at Newport, Ky., relative to its quality that I would be glad if you would forward the amount from Philadelphia." CC in DNA, 1, I-78.

To Commodore WILLIAM BAINBRIDGE,
Commanding Naval Officer, Boston

Navy Department, Dec[embe]r 12th 1818

Be pleased to direct Lt. [Joseph C.] Hall, Commanding the Guard of Marines on board the U.S. Ship Hornet, Captain George C. Read, to be detached from that Ship, and ordered to report to the Commandant of the Marines at Head Quarters.

FC in DNA, 121, 13:297.

To Capt. Thomas Brown, Naval Recruiting Officer, Philadelphia, 12/12. Directs him to open a recruiting rendezvous there for seamen and ordinary seamen for the U.S.S. *John Adams* and to send the enlistees to New York [City] under competent officers. FC in DNA, 121, 13:298.

From T[homas] Forsyth, St. Louis, 12/12. Recommends John Kinzie, citing Kinzie's qualifications persuasively, for appointment as the Indian Agent at Chicago if, as is reported, C[harles] Jouett resigns. ALS in DNA, 11, 12412.

From Donald Fraser, Secretary of the Boundary Commission, New York [City], 12/12. Requests that the sword honoring the late Midshipman James M. Baldwin's heroism in action on Lake Champlain will be delivered to Baldwin's half-brother, John T. Lacy, Jr., through Lt. [Thomas W.] Freelon, who has offered to bring it with him from Washington. ALS in DNA, 128, 7:79.

Samuel R. Marshall, Surgeon, U.S.N., New York [City], "to the Secretary of the Navy," 12/12. Answering belatedly, because of illness, an inquiry of 5/6, Marshall reports that the number of patients accommodated in the Navy Hospital there averages about 180 to 230, that the allowance of rations is adequate, and that the present building is sufficiently large. CC in DNA, 201, 15A-F4; PC in House Document No. 90, 15th Cong., 2nd Sess.; PC in *American State Papers: Naval Affairs,* 1:614.

To [President JAMES MONROE]

War Department, 12th Dec[embe]r 1818

In compliance with the resolution of the House of Representatives of the 10th instant, the Secretary of War has the honor to transmit to the President of the United States copies of the correspondence between the Governor of the State of Georgia [William Rabun] and Major Gen[era]l [Andrew] Jackson, relative to the arrest of Capt. Obed Wright, transmitted by them to this Department.

LS with Ens in DNA, 202, 15A-E1; FC in DNA, 6, 1:341; PC with Ens in House Document No. 34, 15th Cong., 2nd Sess.; PC with Ens in *American State Papers: Military Affairs,* 1:774–778. NOTE: Three of these sources show that Monroe transmitted this letter from Calhoun and its enclosures to the House of Representatives by means of Monroe's letter of 12/12 to the House, a PC of which appears also in Richardson, *Messages and Papers of the Presidents,* 2:49.

From Thomas Morris, [U.S. Marshal,] New York [City], 12/12. Members of the court-martial [for the trial of N.Y. militia delinquents] have called upon him for payment of their expenses, but he has no funds and no prospect of having any soon. He considers it impractical for the members of the court to be dependent for their pay solely upon his collections of fines levied against the delinquents. ALS in DNA, 2, M-1818.

B[enjamin] H[omans] to Lt. John Porter, U.S.N., Charleston, S.C., 12/12. Answering his letter of 12/6, states that Acting Secretary of the Navy [Calhoun] has decided that it would be inexpedient to make at this time any alteration in the precept and that it is presumed that this decision will not interfere materially with Porter's views, because Lt. [James B.] Taylor will soon arrive at St. Marys, [Ga.,] for the forthcoming investigation of his conduct. FC in DNA, 121, 13:298.

From CHARLES RICH, [Representative from Vt.]

Washington, 12th Dec[embe]r 1818

I have just rec[eive]d from Mr. William Strong, who was here [in the House of Representatives] from Vermont, in the 13th Congress, and is again elected for the 15th [*actually the* 16th, to take office on 3/4/1819,] a letter of which the following is an extract.

"About a year ago, I addressed Mr. [James] Fisk then at Washington [as a Senator from Vt., 11/4/1817–1/8/1818] in behalf of Aven Esterbrooks [Alvin Esterbrook], a young man of this vicinity (Hartford, Vermont), a young man well qualified, and recommended [him] as a Cadet for the national military school at West Point. Mr. Fisk answered my letter on that subject, stating that he applied to the war office, and was informed that the candidate should be placed on the books, and as soon as the vacancies should be filled, he should stand a chance with the rest of the applicants from Vermont, for an appointment.

"I now understand that several appointments have been made from this county [Windsor County, Vt.,] during the last summer, only by the recommendation of [Lieutenant] Gov[erno]r [Paul] Brigham. I wish you to take the trouble to enquire at the office, and inform me what their regulations are respecting appointments of Cadets, and whither [*sic*] there is any prospect for the young man whom I formerly recommended, to obtain [an appointment] at the next filling of vacancies in the school."

I feel it my duty, sir, to ask of you to enable me to answer the above enquiries, and am very respectfully . . . .

ALS in DNA, 15, 1819, 88, with an EU indicating an appointment on 3/24/1819. Note: See herein Calhoun's noncommittal reply of 12/17, which explains nothing but promises that Esterbrook will be considered at the time of the next appointments.

From H[enry] Sherburne, Chickasaw Agency, 12/12. Reports his deposit of $6,000 in a Nashville bank for credit to the account of Thomas T[udor] Tucker and the robbery committed by a party of Indians, apparently because of drunkenness rather than deliberate hostility, against a party of whites traveling by boat. LS in DNA, 1, S-151.

Decius Wadsworth to Ebenezer Huntington, [Representative from Conn.,] 12/12. Wadsworth explains, in answer to Huntington's letter of 12/11, why and how the arms and accountrements distributed recently to the Conn. militia were limited, and particularly that Congressional appropriations for accoutrements have limited the purchase and distribution of them to about 10% of what had been planned. Wadsworth confesses that the formula for division of the available arms and accoutrements has been questioned not only by Conn.; it "has been particularly contested by the State of Virginia." If Huntington agrees with Wadsworth's belief that it would be sound policy for the U.S. to purchase and to distribute to the militias of the States and Territories accoutrements in nearly the same proportion as firearms, Huntington should get the [House] Committee on Ways and Means to increase the appropriation for that object, because the budget request for 1819 will provide for only 2,000 sets of accoutrements. ALS in DNA, 1, W-144.

To Capt. M[ELANCTHON] T. WOOLSEY, U.S.N., Commanding Naval Officer, Sackets Harbor, [N.Y.]

Navy Department, Dec[embe]r 12th 1818

You are hereby authorised to deliver one of the boats belonging to the Navy at Sackett's [*sic*] Harbour to Captain Julius F. Heileman for the use of the Army, taking his receipt for the same, to be accounted for with the War Department.

FC in DNA, 121, 13:297.

From James M. Broom, Philadelphia, 12/13. Recommends former Maj. [John] Hall for appointment as the Commandant of the Marine Corps. ALS in DNA, 128, 7:81.

Lt. George Blaney "for Col. [Walker K.] Armistead, [Chief Engineer,]" to R[ené Edward] De Russy, New York [City], 12/14. [Ferdinand R.] Hassler has been ordered by Calhoun to deliver to De Russy the instruments at New York [City] that have been in Hassler's possession. De Russy is to give to Hassler proper receipts in return and is to send to the War Department an inventory of what De Russy receives. CC in DNA, 2, B-1818.

From Mat[thew] L. Davis, New York [City], 12/14. He will comply with Calhoun's instructions of 12/10 "respecting the provisions to be left on hand, at the expiration [on 5/31/1819] of my Contract [for supplying rations]." ALS in DNA, 1, D-34.

From Mat[thew] L. Davis, New York [City], 12/14. Encloses a draft for $10,000; hopes it will be honored immediately. "Our Banks are much pressed for money; but from all that I can learn, the pressure has diminished. Money, however, is an article in great demand, in our market." ALS in DNA, 1, D-33.

To [Henry] Middleton, [Representative from S.C.,] 12/14. "I have examined the enclosed papers & find after consulting with the proper Auditor that the forms of the Treasury will not permit them to be passed to the credit of the person who took up the discharges without an act of Congress. If I am not mistaken, an act similar to the one suggested has been introduced." FC in DNA, 3, 10:203.

From E[leazer] W. Ripley, Bay of St. Louis, [Miss.,] 12/14. He recommends Jesse Depew for an appointment as a 2nd Lt. in the 8th [Infantry] Regiment, which now has about eight vacancies of that rank; and he recommends again Bradford Bradley for a corresponding appointment in the 1st [Infantry] Regiment, which has nine or ten such vacancies. Ripley encloses "Confidential" lists of the two Regiments' officers as they will be after pending resignations are accepted. ALS with En in DNA, 11, 12723.

To E[leazer] W. Ripley, New Orleans, 12/14. Answers his proposal of 11/3 (ALS in DNA, 1, R-36, with an AEI by Calhoun asking for [Thomas S.] Jesup's opinion) by approving the proposed exchange of five acres of land at Baton Rouge between the U.S. and a Mr. Gracie, preferably on an acre-for-acre basis; but Jesup doubts that the 20-foot-wide strip between the U.S. and Gracie lands is privately owned, and Calhoun directs Ripley to investigate with care the title to that strip before purchasing it. FC in DNA, 3, 10:203–204.

From D[ECIUS] WADSWORTH

Ordnance Office, 14 Dec. 1818

I think it very probable from the favorable report of Mr. [James] Stubblefield, in relation to the improved Gun lock [*sic*] introduced by Mr. [Edward] Baker, that it will be judged expedient to adopt the Improvements it embraces in the Arms made at Springfield [Mass.] & Harper's [*sic*] ferry [*sic*] for the public Service.

Nevertheless I am of opinion the decision should not be made hastily, nor before an opportunity has been had of consulting the Superintendent [Roswell Lee] & Master Armorer at Springfield & learning their opinion.

I learn by Mr. Baker that it is the opinion of Col. [Richard M.] Johnson, Congress will not be induced to grant an exclusive privilege to him for using the improvement, and as the Method is now fully made known, he is not likely to receive any advantage from the Invention unless it should be decided to adopt it in the National Armories.

If it be worth while to adopt the Improvement in the National Armories, I should conceive it would be reasonable to allow Mr. Baker a compensation for the same of from three to five thousand Dollars.

FC in DNA, 32, 2:156–157.

From Maj. W[illiam] J[enkins] Worth, [Greenbush, N.Y.,] 12/14. As commanding officer of the cantonment there, he states three charges and seven specifications against Post Surgeon Samuel Shaw, alleging neglect of duty, etc. DS in DNA, 11, 12771.

From George Washington Giles, New York [City], 12/15. Accepts his appointment as a Cadet; promises to report as soon as he can. ALS in DNA, 15, 1816, 62.

To Andrew Jackson, Nashville, 12/15. Informs him of the extensive tracts of land recently acquired from the Quapaws and Osages. "The President [James Monroe] has directed me to issue orders to prevent, for the present, the extension of the [whites'] settlements on Red River. Those persons settled to the west of the line specified, or at points higher up the Red river and the Arkansaw than those mentioned, will be removed. You will give the necessary orders . . . [to your troops]. It will be advisable to take the necessary measures at an early period, so as to give to such families as may be removed an opportunity to make arrangements for planting the next spring." FC in DNA, 72, D:236; LU in DNA, 77 (M-271:2, frames 0994–0997); PC's in *American State*

Papers: Indian Affairs, 2:704, and *Public Lands,* 4:960; PC in *Niles' Weekly Register,* 45:159.

To Lt. Commandant L[awrence] Kearney, U.S. Brig *Enterprize,* New York [City], 12/15. Acknowledges his two letters of 12/6 (LS's in DNA, 134, one with 2 Ens), addressed to Benjamin W. Crowninshield from Charleston, S.C., while enroute from New Orleans to New York [City] and reporting that he must stand trial in 1/1819 in a damage suit for having detained the merchant brig *General Macomb* at Charleston to examine her papers because she long refused to show her colors. Calhoun approves Kearney's conduct and has directed Thomas Parker, U.S. Attorney for the District of S.C., to appear in Kearney's behalf and, if necessary, to employ counsel for his defense. FC in DNA, 121, 13:299.

To Maj. S[TEPHEN] H. LONG, Topographical Engineer

Department of War, 15th Dec[embe]r 1818

As soon as the appropriation is made, funds will be transmitted to you as may be necessary to meet the expenses of building the steam boat.

In the mean time, should your arrangements render it necessary to cover any expenses which may accrue before the passage of the bill, you will draw on this Department for the sum which may be required.

A steam boat has been engaged to transport the expedition destined for the Yellow Stone. It is expected that she will sail early in April. There would be many advantages if you could be prepared to sail from St. Louis at the same time so as to accompany the expedition. To effect this, it is necessary that the arrangements for your expedition should be fixed as early as possible.

The instructions & powers which you recieved [*sic*] before you left Washington were, I believe, ample as to the boat and such mathematical instruments as might be necessary. It is of importance that your instruments should be good, so that the longitude and latitude of the principal points may be ascertained with precision. You will report what instruments you have obtained or made arrangements to obtain and whether any other will be necessary. Besides the immediate objects of the expedition, I feel much anxiety that it should be rendered as useful to science & general knowledge as possible. This can best be effected by associating with the expedition persons eminent for their zeal & scientifick acquirements. You will report what applications have been made to you from such characters and whether you have entered into any engagements or arrangements with them as well as your views generally in relation to this part.

A Mr. [Joshua] Shaw and [Titian Ramsay Peale] a son of Mr. [Charles Willson] Peale the proprietor of the Museum at Philadelphia have made application to this Department to be of the party. The former is said to be a landscape painter of eminence and the latter young gentleman very fond of natural history. Would you think it advisable to grant their request?

As the immediate object of the expedition under your command is to obtain an accurate geographical knowledge of that portion of our country drained by the Mississippi not heretofore accurately explored, [together] with [a knowledge of] the various Indian tribes who inhabit it, you will report to the Department, in order to effect this important object, which of the rivers & in what order or succession ought to be ascended in the steam boat, with such general observations as may occur to you in regard to the expedition.

FC in DNA, 3, 10:204. NOTE: Long answered on 12/24.

From Hugh McCall, Savannah, 12/15. He has heard that citizens of Savannah have petitioned Calhoun for soldiers to guard the U.S. magazine near the edge of the city. On 12/1 a letter from [Edmund P.] Gaines gave assurance that a detachment from Fernandina will be sent to protect the munitions in the magazine from any who might attempt to appropriate them. No action by Calhoun is needed. ALS in DNA, 1, M-135.

To THOMAS PARKER, U.S. District Attorney, Charleston, S.C.

Navy Department, Dec[embe]r 15th 1818

A suit having been instituted against Lieut[en]a[nt] Commandant Lawrence Kearney, the Commander of the U.S. Brig Enterprise, for the detention of a Merchant Vessel for the purpose of making the necessary examination into her character, as will appear to you on a perusal of the enclosed Copies, which explain the circumstances of the case, I have to request that you will appear on behalf of Lt. Commandant Kearney and defend the cause; and, if requisite, you are hereby authorised to employ Counsel to aid in the defence.

FC in DNA, 122, 13:246.

From William Rabun, Milledgeville, [Ga.,] 12/15. Calhoun's letter of 12/2 is acknowledged; the Midshipman in question will be treated like the others accused. LS in DNA, 128, 7:85.

From John Rodgers, 12/15. Acknowledges Calhoun's letter of 12/14. The regulations concerning fresh foods for Navy personnel are intended to require commanding officers to supply fresh foods at least twice a week for reasons of health; but these foods may be used more frequently for the sake of economy or to promote health. ALS in DNA, 128, 7:86.

From [Lt.] John White, U.S.N.

Salem, [Mass.,] Dec[embe]r 15th 1818

Having been indulged by Mr. [Benjamin W.] Crowninshield with an extension of Furlough on account of severe and dangerous illness in my family which required my constant care and attention, and although the cause is but partially removed, I have been so much longer on Furlough than I had originally contemplated [that] my anxiety to enter again on duty prompts me to request of you, Sir, to give me orders to some ship at the Navy yard in Charlestown, [Mass.]; if not inconsistent with propriety I would ask to be attatched [*sic*] to the Constitution or Java. Commodore [William] Bainbridge under whom I have had the honor & pleasure to serve is aware and approves my motives for making this application.

ALS in DNA, 133 (M-125:60).

From Thomas Wilson for John Laval, Philadelphia, 12/15. Encloses a bill for the two-volume French–English dictionary that has been sent to C[hristopher] Vandeventer for the War Department. Laval expects to obtain a Spanish–English dictionary that will meet Calhoun's specifications. Because of the "wishes of several officers of the U.S. Army," Laval offers an illustrated volume about European military history and uniforms. "The widow's claim has been promptly noticed, and I have forwarded the regulation of this office for her guidance." LS in DNA, 1, W-173.

William Bainbridge, Boston, to "Smith Thompson, Secretary of the Navy, Washington," 12/16. "Lieutenant John White, who has served under my command and who is a good Officer, being desirous of receiving orders from the Navy Department, I enclose to you his application," which is White's letter of 12/15 to Calhoun. LS with En in DNA, 133 (M-125:60).

To S[amuel] R. Betts, Newburgh, [N.Y.,] 12/16. Informs him that Marshal [Thomas Morris] cannot collect the fines imposed by the court-martial for the trial of N.Y. militia delinquents because certificates have not been delivered to Morris; shows Betts that [Gerard] Steddiford has been ordered to procure the certificates without further delay. By Betts's letter of 8/27 "I was led to believe" that Betts would complete the preparation of his certificates within "a few days." FC in DNA, 3, 10:205.

To Speaker [Henry Clay], 12/16. Pursuant to a House resolution of 4/4, Acting Secretary of the Navy Calhoun transmits a report of 11/21 by Fourth Auditor Constant Freeman and five financial accounts as to Navy expenditures in payment of rewards to Navy officers and crew members for the capture of enemy vessels during the War of 1812. LS with Ens in DNA, 201, 15A-F4; FC in DNA, 125, 13:12; PC with Ens in House Document No. 42, 15th Cong., 2nd Sess.; PC with Ens in *American State Papers: Naval Affairs,* 1:562–582.

From N[inian] Edwards, [Senator from Ill.,] 12/16. "I have the honor to transmit herewith to you certain letters which were enclosed to me by Gov[erno]r [William] Clark. As to Colo[nel Duff] Green, he being a very near connection of mine, delicacy forbids any interposition on my part in his favor." ALS with Ens in DNA, 11, 12255, with endorsements indicating that Green was recommended for and received in 12/1818 an appointment in the Mo. militia.

To Lemuel Jenkins, [District Attorney of Sullivan Connty,] Bloomingburg, [N.Y.,] 12/16. Acknowledges his letters of 10/28 (ALS in DNA, 1, J-23) and 11/7; his claim and the claims of other members and officers of the court-martial for N.Y. militia delinquents cannot be considered until that court has been finally closed and its proceedings reported to Calhoun; then these men can be given the "extra compensation" to which they may be entitled. FC in DNA, 3, 10:205.

John Sergeant to "Secretary of the Treasury [William H. Crawford]," 12/16. "As my engagements in the house of representatives may not permit me to call upon you at the office for some days, I take the liberty of inclosing to you a letter from the American Philosophical Society, upon the subject of the instruments about which I had the ho[nor to lay] before you their application during the last s[ession. I] need not say that it will give me great pleasure to learn that their request may be complied with, as I believe the instruments will be very useful in their hands, and will be carefully preserved." ALS in DNA, 1, S-150, with an EU indicating that the enclosure was "a letter from Mr. [R.M.] Patterson, Sec[retar]y" of the Society, "requesting the loan of certain instruments."

To G[erard] Steddiford, New York [City], 12/16. The Marshal of N.Y., [Thomas Morris,] reports that "he has not made any progress in the collection of the fines assessed" by the court-martial for the trial of N.Y. militia delinquents "for the want of the certificates." Calhoun expected that such certificates would have been delivered long ago to Morris, both for the court's sessions before [Samuel R.] Betts resigned as Judge Advocate and for the later sessions in New York [City]. Steddiford is ordered to cause the delivery of the certificates to be completed. "As much inconvenience has already resulted from delays, dispatch in which remains to be done is particularly enjoined." FC in DNA, 3, 10:205.

From D[ECIUS] WADSWORTH

Ordnance Office, 16th Dec[embe]r 1818

The Estimate of Clothing for the Ordnance Department at the several Posts and Stations was made out and transmitted to the Com[missar]y Gen[era]l of Purchases [Callender Irvine] some Time ago, pursuing the Instructions of 1817, the variations in the Regulations of 1818 not having been adverted to at the Time.

It is presumed no serious Inconvenience has been occasioned by this small Informality.

FC in DNA, 32, 2:157.

From Samuel R. Betts, Newburgh, [N.Y.,] 12/17. Answering Calhoun's letter of 12/7, he states that all reports and certificates required of him were delivered to Marshal [Thomas Morris] early in 9/1818 and that Betts has sent the proceedings of the court-martial [for the trial of N.Y. militia delinquents] to [Gerard] Steddiford today. Betts does not understand why the court's life has been so prolonged; he hopes that delays in receiving information from Betts have not been used as an excuse to extend the court's life. ALS in DNA, 1, B-109.

To Commodore Isaac Chauncey, New York [City], 12/17. Encloses a recommendation for modification of the 37th Article of the Navy Regulations, respecting Pursers. Chauncey is to use his discretion in substituting fresh meat for salt meat, "having on all occasions a due regard to economy & the health of those under your command." FC in DNA, 121, 13:299.

To C[allender] Irvine, Philadelphia, 12/17. Tells him that Maj. Howell Tatum of Nashvile has been serving for some years as Miitary Storekeeper there and that Tatum evidently has some clothing in storage there. Asks if Tatum's services are needed and, if so, at what compensation. FC in DNA, 3, 10:206. In reply on 12/22 (LS with En in DNA, 1, I-73; FC in DNA, 45, 387:250), Irvine reported that, under a temporary appointment given by [Andrew] Jackson, Tatum had received some clothing and camp equipage in 12/1815 for preservation, that Irvine had supposed that troops had used these items long ago, and that Tatum "has not rendered a single return to this office. I therefore do not consider him as an officer belonging to this [Purchasing] Dept., nor having any claim, except for storage & perhaps a small consideration for the care he may have taken of the property entrusted to his charge."

From Lts. Thomas ap Catesby Jones and W[illiam] B. Shubrick, [U.S.N.,] Washington, 12/17. In behalf of themselves and fellow officers who sent directly to the Senate from the Mediterranean a memorial impugning the officer who was immediately superior to them, they apologize for any impropriety in not having relayed the memorial through the chain of cammand; they intended no disrespect to anyone in the executive branch of government; they enclose a similar letter from themselves to the Secretary of the Navy [Benjamin W. Crowninshield] dated 8/1/1818. LS with En in DNA, 128, 7:93–94.

To [James Monroe], 12/17. Pursuant to a Senate resolution of 12/10, Calhoun transmits "copies of the instructions to the commissioners who negotiated the Indian treaties now before the Senate." FC in DNA, 4, 2:68.

From Thomas Morris, New York [City], 12/17. "Having informed you a few days since that I was not in possession of Court Martial Certificates on which I could raise funds to pay the officers of that Court [for the trial of N.Y. militia delinquents], I think it right now to notify you" that two members of the court have "just brought to me the Certificates of several Counties. In justice to these gentlemen I must also say that I am persuaded that Circumstances beyond their Controul [*sic*] have prevented my receiving these papers earlier." ALS in DNA, 1, M-121.

From D[aniel] Parker, 12/17. Encloses a complaint written on 11/26 by William Lorman to Calhoun that troops at Fort Covington were damaging Lorman's adjacent property. Encloses also reports by Col. [George E.] Mitchell and Capt. [James H.] Hook and recommends retention of the fort, because it is "so important in case of war, and so convenient at all times, as a depot for recruits." Reports that measures have been taken to prevent trespassing on Lorman's land. LS with Ens in DNA, 1, P-67; FC in DNA, 12, 5:150.

From Adam Seybert, [Representative from Pa.,] 12/17. He forwards an ALS dated 12/17 in Philadelphia from Charles Thomas to Calhoun; an ALS by [Dr.] Thomas Cooper, signed also by Ch[ristopher] Chauncey, to Calhoun, dated in Philadelphia on 12/1 and recommending Thomas for a commission as an Ordnance officer; and an ES by Hor[ace] Binney dated 11/30 recommending Thomas. ALS with Ens in DNA, 11, 12874. (For a summary of the long, distinguished Army career of Charles Thomas, beginning with his appointment as a 3rd Lt. of Ordnance on 8/13/1819, see Heitman, *Historical Register,* 1:953.)

From D[ecius] Wadsworth, 12/17. Pursuant to inquiries from the [House] Committee on Ways and Means and Calhoun's oral suggestions, Wadsworth states motives for renewing the contract with John Clarke & Company for about 300 tons of castings. The reduced appropriation for the national armories has caused much embarrassment; a supplementary appropriation of $25,000 is needed to cover this month's expenses. Funds for the construction of the arsenal at Augusta, [Ga.,] will prove insufficient, because materials and labor have grown more costly since the estimate for it was made. No reductions can be made in outlays by the Ordnance Department without serious damage to "the permanent Plan of providing in Time of Peace for a State of active Hostilities." FC in DNA, 32, 2:158–160.

From I[SAAC] CHAUNCEY

U.S. Ship Washington, New York [City], 18th Dec. 1818

I have been duly honored, with your letter of the 10th Inst[ant] ordering me to report myself to the Navy Department for the purpose of settling my accounts.

The Honorable Chief Justice [Smith] Thompson [of N.Y. State] having requested me to wait and accompany him to Washington, [when he goes to become Secretary of the Navy,] I have taken the liberty to accept of his invitation, and shall leave here on the 26th inst[an]t with that gentleman.

LS in DNA, 133 (M-125:60).

From Nat[haniel] Cutting, 12/18. Reports how much money is due, as arrearages of salary, to three Clerks in the Section of Bounty Lands, William M. Steuart, John Earle Frost, and William T. Washington, because the appropriations for 1817 did not include provision for their services. ALS with Ens in DNA, 1, C-95.

Financial statement by Second Comptroller Richard Cutts, 12/18. Reports that several War Department appropriations, including those for pensions, the militias, contingencies, etc., are overdrawn. DS in DNA, 2, C-1819.

To George Gibson, 12/18. "You will report to this Department as early as practicable after [the] 31st Instant what contracts have been made by you during the present year." FC in DNA, 3, 10:206.

To C[allender] Irvine, Philadelphia

Department of War, 18th Dec[embe]r 1818

Feeling every friendship to domestic manufactures, as my public life will evince, I entertain a preference for them, but until Congress shall direct the clothing of the Army to be entirely of such manufactures, I do not think it advisable to increase the expenditure for clothing to any considerable amount by giving a preference to domestic fabrics. Therefore in your future contracts you will not give the preference to domestic manufactures unless they are offered very nearly as low as foreign fabrics.

FC in DNA, 3, 10:207. Note: Compare Calhoun to Irvine, 12/19.

To Callender Irvine, Philadelphia, 12/18. "You will report to this Department as early as practicable after the 31st instant, what contracts have been made by the Purchasing Dep[artmen]t during the present year." FC in DNA, 3, 10:206.

From Daniel T. Patterson

New Orleans, Dec[embe]r 18th 1818

Enclosed I do myself the honor to transmit a Copy of a deposition of a Spaniard who was detained several months a prisoner at Galveston, & taken in an Open Boat by the U.S. Schooner Fire Brand; from the tenor of which it appears that [Jean] Lafitte and his confederates were making arrangements for their early abandonment of Galveston.

ALS with En in DNA, 133 (M-125:60).

From John Rodgers, 12/18. Answers Calhoun's letter of today by stating that the table of rations as it was printed in the book of Navy regulations is correct. The corresponding table "contained in the separate sheets is by an error of the Printer, incorrect in several items. The Commissioners were not apprized until the receipt of your letter that there was any difference between the two sheets." Rodgers sends 400 copies of the table of rations. ALS in DNA, 128, 7:96.

To John Sergeant, [Representative from Pa.,] 12/18. In reply to his appeal of 12/16 (ALS in DNA, 1, S-132) that Joseph D. Lauck be admitted to the Military Academy despite the fact that illness has prevented him from reporting there and taking the required examination at the usual time this autumn, Calhoun asserts, "Unless the young man can pass the examination required by the regulations of the Military Academy, it will be impossible for him to be admitted this year. It would be better, then, for him to return his appointment to this Department & when the appointment[s] for the next year [shall] be made, a new one will be given to him." FC in DNA, 3, 10:206; copy in DNA, 15, 1818, 29. In reply on 12/30, Sergeant returned the appointment and expressed for Lauck and his friends "their sense of the kind disposition you have manifested towards this young man." ALS in DNA, 15, 1818, 29.

From Archibald Thweatt, Wilkinsville Postoffice (Chesterfield County), Va., 12/18. Richard H. Branch's proffered Army commission [as a 2nd Lt.] is accepted and can be mailed to him at Manchester, Va.; he would prefer an assignment in the South. ALS in DNA, 11, 11937.

From Alexander S. Wadsworth, U.S.S. *John Adams,* New York [City], 12/18. Reiterates his request that Midshipman Samuel

Dusenberry be assigned to duty as Acting Sailing Master of the *John Adams.* No Surgeon's Mate has yet reported for duty. Some of the crewmen are willing to reënlist for two years, provided that they do not have to serve out, in addition, the remaining eight months or thereabouts of their present enlistments. Wadsworth advises yielding this concession as a means of enabling the *John Adams* to sail by 1/10/1819, unless severe weather should delay or prevent sailing. ALS in DNA, 132 (M-147:7).

To Decius Wadsworth, 12/18. "You will report to this Department as early as practicable after the 31st Instant what contracts have been made by the Ordnance Department during the present year." LS in ScU-SC; FC in DNA, 3, 10:206–207.

From J.F. Wingate, Washington, 12/18. Requests that advances to the full amount of [Peter H.] Green's contracts with the War Department be made, because more expensive supplies are required now than heretofore. "A large stock of supplies must necessarily be purchased in advance, and can only be obtained for the cash, on fair terms, at this season of the year . . . ." ALS in DNA, 2, W-1818.

From Sam[uel] S. Conner, [former Representative from Mass.,] Washington, 12/19. Recommends the bearer, [former] Capt. [Edward] Webb, for an appointment. "I never knew a more prompt, honorable, exemplary & indefatigable officer." "His father is a respectable clergyman at Albany." Certainly the son, "if anybody[,] has demands on the sympathy of government." ALS in DNA, 11, 12935. (Webb was commissioned as a 2nd Lt. in the 8th Infantry on 2/3/1819. Heitman, *Historical Register,* 1:1011.)

To Edmund P. Gaines, Fernandina, East Fla., 12/19. Acknowledges his letter of 12/8 (ALS in DNA, 1, G-47; draft in DNA, 11, 12215) reporting that he had not received the copy of the contract promised in Calhoun's letter of 11/10. Calhoun now encloses that copy. LS in DNA, 11, 14021; FC in DNA, 3, 10:208.

To Richard Graham, 12/19. "I have rec[eive]d your several drafts on account of disbursements to be made in [surveying] the Indian boundary line in the State of Illinois. Being much pressed with buisness [*sic*] *at this* [*time*], I cannot examine the subject immediately, but in the course of a few days will do so. In the mean time you will suspend further proceedings as well as all disbursements for that object until further directions. This suspension becomes necessary because your drafts & estimate exceed the sum appropriated, $15,000. You will report in detail the cause of the expenses of running this line." FC in DNA, 3, 10:208.

From John H. Hall, Washington, 12/19. If the proposed armory on the western waters should be established, Hall wants to become its Superintendent; he cites as qualifications his experience with machinery, "mechanical operations," and improvements in small arms. ALS in DNA, 11, 13430.

To Capt. John D. Henley, U.S.S. *Congress,* Norfolk, 12/19. Answering his report as to the repairing and outfitting of his ship as of 12/13 [LS with En in DNA, 133 (M-125:60)], Calhoun clarifies the discrepancy in orders as to the components of rations that was discovered by Purser [Alexander P.] Darragh. LS in DLC, J. Henley-Smith Papers, 2:1718; FC in DNA, 121, 13:300.

To Callender Irvine, Philadelphia

Department of War, 19th Dec[embe]r 1818

Before you act on my letter of the 18th instant you will report what additional expense during the last year you have incurred in consequence of giving a preference to domestic manufactures in purchasing the the [*sic*] clothing of the Army. I should also like to have the report required by my order of the 28th Sept. last before the appropriations for the ensuing year be made.

FC in DNA, 3, 10:208–209.

To Lt. Commandant John R. Madison, Commanding Naval Officer, St. Marys, Ga., 12/19. Encloses a copy of a letter from John B. Fanning, Purser of the U.S. Schooner *Lynx,* discussing the substitution of fresh meat for salt meat in rations; also encloses a recent ruling by the Commissioners of the Navy to the same effect. Madison is to conform with the new ruling insofar as economy and sailors' health will permit. Calhoun also encloses some new Navy regulations approved by President [James Monroe], which contain corrections in the rations required by regulations that were sent to Fanning on 10/26/1818. FC in DNA, 121, 13:300–301.

From Return J. Meigs, Cherokee Agency, 12/19. "The [month-long] conference held here by Governor [Joseph] McMinn with the Cherokees ended on the 29th Ult[imo] without coming to a satisfactory conclusion to either of the parties. Notwithstanding this result, so much has been gained by the Governor as to remove all violent opposition & I believe convince all that a general exchange of lands [and emigration to the Arkansas] cannot long be delayed. I say general exchange because a strong party yet cherish the idea of continuing here in their ancient, savage state." Under leadership of the Pathkiller, a Cherokee council about 12/1, "being anxious to bring the subject of exchange to a satisfactory termination, appointed twelve Chiefs as a delegation to repair to the seat of Government and request their Father the President [James Monroe] to have that business decided more immediately under his direction." Despite the fact that Meigs has told them that prior permission for the trip should be received, they propose to begin the journey within about three weeks, before approval can arrive by mail. McMinn will probably reach Washington shortly after the delegation does. Meigs has been asked to travel with the delegation. Charles Hicks and the Pathkiller jointly head the delegation; some of its other members are George Lowry, James Brown, John Ross, John Martin, John Walker, Richard Taylor, and Gideon Morgan, Jr.; eight of the 12 "can understand & speak the English language." ALS in DNA, 77 (M-271:2, frames 1337–1339); FC, together with a rough, quite different draft dated 12/16, in DNA, 75 (M-208:7). (Only the FC contains the names of the 12 in the delegation and the final phrase quoted above.)

From David Robinson, Bennington, [Vt.,] 12/19. Having lost his office as Marshal of the District of Vt., he explains how he has discharged also the duties of agent for the distribution of pensions for several years; he seeks to be retained in the latter position. ALS in DNA, 1, M-130.

C[aesar] A[ugustus] Rodney, Wilmington, Del., to Smith Thompson, 12/19. Recommends former Maj. [John] Hall for appointment as Commandant of the Marine Corps. ALS in DNA, 128, 7:94.

To Henry Sherburne, Chickasaw Agency, 2/19. Answering his letter of 11/28 (LS in DNA, 1, S-128), in which Sherburne discussed such other matters as financial remittances and the thrice-repeated tardiness of mail sent to Sherburne via Nashville, Calhoun informs Sherburne simply that the treaty of 10/4/1816 with the Chickasaws prohibits the granting of any licenses to trade with them. FC in DNA, 72, D:235–236.

To Samuel Smith, Chairman, House Committee on Ways and Means

Department of War, December 19th, 1818

I have received your three letters of the 16th and 17th instant [2 ALS's in DNA, 2, S-1818, dated 12/16, and an ALS dated 12/17 in DNA, 1, S-130], in relation to the estimates of the War Department for the year 1819; in answer to which I respectfully submit, for the consideration of the committee, the reports and statements upon which the estimates were formed. It is believed that they will afford a much fuller and more satisfactory view of the reasons which governed the Department in determining the amount of the respective appropriations which have been asked for, than could be presented within the ordinary limits of a letter. The documents are so voluminous, that, to avoid the trouble of copying, I have transmitted the originals; and I must request of you to return them, after the committee shall have done with them. Should it be thought advisable to lay any part of them before the House, they can be copied for that purpose.

Under the head of "pay of the Army," it is estimated that there will be a probable balance, at the end of the year, of about $300,000; and, consequently, that sum may be deducted from the appropriation of the ensuing year. Orders have been given to suspend the works at Rouse's [*sic*] Point [N.Y.] until the line between the United States and Lower Canada shall be determined. The sum of $200,000, which was estimated for it, will probably not be required, and may be omitted in the appropriation for fortifications.

Since the estimates were formed, the contracts under the new system for supplying the Army with provisions after the 1st of June next have been completed, and it is ascertained that a reduction may be made under the head of subsistence. The contract system will terminate on the 1st of June next. To complete the deliveries under the present contracts until that time will probably require the sum of $303,441; and it is estimated that the expense of subsistence from the 1st of June, 1819, at which time the system of supplying the Army by Companies will commence, until the 1st of June, 1820, cannot exceed $503,700; but as four-fifths of the rations will be required, by the terms of the contracts, to be delivered between the 1st of June, 1819, and the 1st of January, 1820, the sum of $403,160 will be necessary to meet the deliveries in 1819; and consequently, the whole appropriation required for the next year, under this head, will be $706,601, instead of $858,125, the sum stated in the estimate. On a review of the estimate for clothing, it is believed that the sum of $400,000 will be ample; and, consequently, $30,000 may be subtracted from the estimate. Document marked E, will show on what grounds the sum of $50,000 is asked for the Medical and Hospital Department. On the 1st of January last it was estimated that there was a balance of $15,000, which, added to the sum appropriated for the current year, viz., $15,000, makes $30,000, as applicable to the service of this year; in addition to which, there was transferred to this item, by order of the President [James Monroe], during the present year, the sum of $50,000. The disbursements in the Medical and Hospital Department will probably not fall short of $70,000 during the present year.

By the statement from the Ordnance Department, marked G, it will appear that no new contract has been made during the present year for cannon, except with Wirt & Clark; and, consequently, the estimates under that item are on account of old contracts, and will be necessary to meet the engagements under them. It will also appear that the sum of $70,000 instead of $50,000, will be required for the arsenal at Augusta [Ga.]. The estimate for the arsenal at Frankfort [Ky.] is to complete the works commenced there.

The appropriations already made, of $200,000 on account of subsistence, and $50,000 for arrearages for holding Indian treaties, will of course be deducted from their respective items in the general appropriation.

There will probably be a balance, under the head of bounties and premiums, of near $30,000; which sum will be applicable to the service of the ensuing year, and may be taken from the sum contained in the estimates.

The appropriations made for the current expenses of the Army, for the year 1818, amounted to $3,599,245, which, of course, excludes the disbursements for fortifications and ordnance, which are of a permanent nature. The appropriation asked for the current expenses of the year 1819, excluding the same disbursements, and estimating the expense of subsistence under the new system of supplying the Army, for seven months only (viz., from the 1st of June, 1819, until the 1st of January, 1820), amounts to $3,077,789, making a difference of $521,456.

The estimates have been formed on the supposition of our military establishment being full, which, in that case, would consist of 12,656 officers, non-commissioned officers, musicians, and Privates.

If further information should be required, it will afford me pleasure to give it.

FC in DNA, 4, 2:68–69; LS in DNA, 201, 15A-F3; PC with En in House Document No. 56, 15th Cong., 2nd Sess.; PC with En in *American State Papers: Military Affairs*, 1:810–813; PC in Crallé, ed., *Works*, 5:58–60. NOTE: The one enclosure to which reference is made in some of these references is the letter of 10/12 from J[oseph] G. Swift to Calhoun, which has been summarized herein under that date.

To S[amuel] Smith, 12/19. Requests appropriation of two sums: $3,000 due as an annuity to the Creeks and $2,000 overdue since 1808 to the Choctaws. LS in DNA, 203, 15A-D15.2; FC in DNA, 4, 2:70.

From William H. Sumner, Adjutant General [of Mass.,] Boston, 12/19. He transmits in duplicate the Mass. militia return for 1818. ALS in DNA, 11, 12565; CC in DNA, 11, 12497.

From William Wigton, New York [City], 12/19. As a member of the court-martial [for the trial of N.Y. militia delinquents], he complains of not being compensated sufficiently and promptly for his services. ALS in DNA, 1, W-115.

From Thomas S. Jesup, 12/20. Discusses the needs of the Quartermaster Department as to personnel, funds, etc. LS and DU in DNA, 203, 15A-D8.2.

From Richard M. Johnson, [Representative from Ky.]

City of Washington, 20th Dec[ember] 1818

Knowing that it is the general sentiment that a reasonable preference should be given by you to domestic over foreign cloths &c. for the Army, and knowing the great confidence the nation reposes in you on all subjects connected with a discharge of your many & great duties I think it my duty to bring your attention particularly to this subject, that the original intention of Congress may be carried into effect.

It was expressly understood in the framing & passage of the purchasing Commissareat [*sic*] that a reasonable preference should be given to home fabricks on two grounds, first, incidental encouragement to this branch of our national industry & 2ly & more particularly that in time of war or public calamity our Army should never be dependent on foreign importations for the comfort of cloathing [*sic*] &c.

I enclose a letter [of 12/7 to myself] just rec[eive]d from Col. [John] McKinney of Newport, Kentucky, on the subject; he coincides with me in opinion, 1st that in the *Western Country* contracts should be made for more than one year—the same reason would not apply to other parts where the competition is great & more capital is vested in factories; 2ly that it is necessary that he possess the power of [being] given a price not to exceed that in Phi[ladelphi]a & the transportation to the Western Country. If these matters are within your power & disposition, it is much better to appeal to the administration of the system for the power & remedy than to trouble Congress with it.

ALS with En in DNA, 1, J-58.

From Joseph McMinn

Cherokee Agency, 20th Dec[embe]r 1818

The expectation, I expressed in my last relative to a deputation going on to the City [of Washington], from the Cherokee Council is now realized. Colo[nel Return J.] Meigs has been chosen to conduct them to Washington, for which place they will leave here on the 1st January. They have neither sought nor have they obtained the slightest sanction from me to embark on this expedition, tho I hope if they are found to be sincere in their professions of friendship, that they will meet an appropriate reception from the President [James Monroe] & yourself.

I am told the deputation will possess competent powers to enter into any arrangement for an entire extinguishment of their claim. And nothing short of that has been the subject of controversy between them, and my self for several weeks past which you will discover by correspondance [*sic*] heretofore forwarded you.

Having supposed it to be my duty to attend at the City with them, compells [*sic*] me to leave here in a few minutes for Murfreesboro, [Tenn.,] where I will remain about 15 days before I set out, which may enable the Cherokees to reach the city a few days earlier than my self. If so I hope no decisive steps will be taken with them untill my arrival which I presume ["shall" *canceled and* "will" *interlined*] not be delayed beyond what necessity requires, and in the mean time will do my self the honor to keep you advised of passing events.

FC in DNA, 75 (M-208:14).

From Alexander S. Wadsworth, U.S.S. *John Adams,* New York [City], 12/20. To replace Lt. [William B.] Shubrick, whose health requires him to leave the *John Adams,* Wadsworth asks that Lt. William H. Watson be ordered to serve as her 1st Lt. Wadsworth explains that he wants Midshipman [Samuel] Dusenberry assigned to her as her Sailing Master "for his knowledge of the Spanish language." ALS in DNA, 132 (M-147:7).

To "Herman [*sic* for Heman] Allen," [former Representative from Vt.,] 12/21. Appoints him to serve as Agent for Paying U.S.

Military Pensioners in the District of Vt.; gives him instructions; requires of him a bond for $5,000. FC in DNA, 91, 1:116–117.

To R[ICHARD] M. JOHNSON, Chairman, House Committee on Military Affairs

Department of War, 21 Dec[embe]r, 1818

Agreeably to your request, I have drafted a bill containing provisions, which will embrace the several points suggested in our conversations.

The alterations contemplated will improve our Military Establishment considerably, without incurring much additional expense. The proposed enlargement of the Corps of Engineers, is rendered necessary from the increased duties of that Corps; and no good reason can be assigned, why the pay of the Engineer Officers, should be inferior to that of the officers of the Ordnance [Department].

In the Quarter Master[']s Department, it is thought to be real economy, to secure the service of Officers of adequate talents and experience; which can be effected, only, by adequate pay and rank. The increased expense which will be incurred by increasing the number of Deputy Quarter Masters, or Majors, will ultimately be more than saved by the command of talents and experience, which it will give to the Department. The provisions in relation to Forage and Servants, will be an accom[m]odation to the Officers, and a saving to the Publick.

It is proposed to give to the Commissary Gen[era]l, (whose duty will be very important and responsible,) the same rank and pay as to the Quarter Master Gen[era]l. The reasons for the other alterations proposed in this Department, are stated in a report in relation to it made on the 16th instant, in conformity to a resolution of the House, at the last Session.

In the Medical Department, great inconvenience is experienced from frequent resignations. The present pay is altogether insufficient to secure adequate talents and experience. I cannot doubt but, that the proposed increase of pay to the Surgeons, will prove a substantial saving to the publick.

The Corps of Artillery constitutes nearly a third of our Military Force; but it is, at present, so organized, that there is no officer in the Corps above the grade of a Lieut[enan]t Col[one]l. The evil effects can readily be conceived. The present mode of promotion in it by the line, has many disadvantages. It destroys the Esprit de Corps, and subjects the service to considerable expense for transportation; for, when an officer is promoted, the Battalion to which he becomes attached may be posted quite at the other extremity of the Union.

The other provisions of the proposed bill, will, it is believed, require no explanation.

LS in DNA, 201, 15A-F3; FC in DNA, 4, 2:70–71; PC in House Document No. 54, 15th Cong., 2nd Sess.

To William Lorman, Baltimore, 12/21. "I have given to your application relative to Fort Covington, near Baltimore, all the attention that its importance required. The report of the commanding officer in that quarter will not justify the idea of selling the site or abandoning it as a military station, but I have given a standing order for that post, that the military shall not be allowed to trespass on private property or pass to or from the fort in any other than the proper road. This order will be rigidly enforced [and,] it is believed, will relieve you from all cause of dissatisfaction from the troops who are or may be stationed there." FC in DNA, 3, 10:209.

To James Monroe, 12/21. "I . . . propose Herman [*sic*; Heman] Allen Esquire, Commissioner of Loans for the District of Vermont, to be Agent for paying the Military Pensioners of the United States, within the said District, vice David Robinson Esquire." FC in DNA, 91, 1:116.

To [James Monroe], 12/21. Proposes the appointment of Duff Green as a Brig. Gen. in the militia of Mo. Territory. FC in DNA, 6, 1:341.

To James Pleasants, Jr., [Representative from Va.,] 12/21. Pursuant to Pleasants' request of 12/9 (ALS in DNA, 128, 7:68) as Chairman of the House Committee on Naval Affairs, Acting Secretary of the Navy Calhoun submits a list of Navy agents and their residences, the amount of the bond given by each, the names of their sureties, and a list of former agents with the amount owed by each to the U.S. FC in DNA, 125, 13:12–13; PC with Ens in House Document No. 72, 15th Cong., 2nd Sess.; PC with Ens in *American State Papers: Naval Affairs*, 1:588–589.

To David Robinson, Bennington, Vt., 12/21. Orders him to deliver to Heman Allen, Robinson's successor as Commissioner of Loans and Agent for Paying the U.S. Pensioners in the District of Vt., "all the books, papers and any balance of public funds, relating to or having any connection with the duties of the said Agency; for which you will take duplicate receipts, one of which you will please to transmit to the Treasury Department." FC in DNA, 91, 6:118.

James Rundlet, Portsmouth, [N.H.,] to Callender Irvine, [Philadelphia,] 12/21. Rundlet bids for a contract to produce six kinds of cloth for the Army for 1819 at prices "as low as the goods can possibly be made [for], to leave the Manufacturer a living profit." CC with En in DNA, 2, R-1819.

From Eldred Simkins, [Representative from S.C.,] 12/21. Recommends James W. Paxton for appointment as a surgeon in the Army or the Navy. "Dr. [Moses] Waddel & Mr. William Calhoun recommend him & I should be gratified if he succeeds in his wishes." ALS in DNA, 11, 12641.

To S[amuel] Smith, 12/21. Requests that $100,000 be appropriated under the classification of arrearages to make possible the payment of outstanding claims—this in addition to Calhoun's budget estimates of 12/19. LS with En in DNA, 203, 15A-D15.2, the En being Peter Hagner's ALS of 12/19 to Calhoun suggesting that $100,000 is needed for overdue payments; FC in DNA, 4, 2:70.

From Charles R. Vining, Nathaniel H. Loring, Charles R. Holmes, Thomas Ragland, and Wilson M.C. Fairfax, Committee in Behalf of the Corps of Cadets, [12/21]. These five Cadets, being tried by a court of inquiry, present to Calhoun their case against the officers of the Military Academy. They cite examples of situations in which they believe that Cadets have been mistreated by their superior officers, particularly Capt. John Bliss, and other complaints against the administration of the Academy. They urge the adoption of a code of regulations and ask to have their position clarified. PC in *American State Papers: Military Affairs,* 2:17–19; PC in House Document No. 14, 16th Cong., 1st Sess.

To Capt. Alexander S. Wadsworth, U.S.S. *John Adams,* New York [City], 12/21. Answering his letter of 12/18, Calhoun authorizes him to let Midshipman [Samuel] Dusenberry act as Master of the *John Adams* when and if Wadsworth judges Dusenberry to be capable enough. Calhoun discusses his efforts to obtain a full, 220-man crew for the *John Adams,* in order that she can cruise soon. FC in DNA, 121, 13:301.

From Col. H[enry] Atkinson, Plattsburg, [N.Y.,] 12/22. Encloses a letter [of 12/20] to himself from [Gad] Humphreys asking for permission for Humphreys to travel to Washington to settle his public accounts; Atkinson recommends that the request be granted. ALS with En in DNA, 11, 11838.

From T[albot] Chambers, St. Louis, 12/22. Answers tentatively Calhoun's letter to him of 11/25 and promises a fuller report later about the alleged outrage committed against a Mr. Boardman under an order given by Capt. [Wyly] Martin as the commanding officer of the Yellowstone Expedition. Expresses gratification over the news that steamboats will spare the men of the expedition from "excessive fatigue." Because "the effective force now under orders for the Yellow Stone, will in consequence of discharges, be reduced in the Spring to about one hundred and eighty men, principally recruits," Talbot suggests that the services of many should be extended but without requiring them to reënlist for five years. He expresses eagerness to receive additional information about plans for the expedition and to promote its success. ALS in DNA, 1, C-153.

Col. A[rthur] P. Hayne, Washington, to [Daniel Parker], 12/22. Submits through Parker to Calhoun several suggestions to improve the staff of the Army, particularly in the Adjutant General's bureau. ALS in DNA, 1, H-100.

From C[allender] Irvine, Philadelphia, 12/22. Encloses an extract from a letter written by J[oseph] G. Swift about the uniforms used by the Corps of Engineers at West Point. Irvine considers the proposed change improper; the cost of the coat ($16) is prohibitive. LS with En in DNA, 1, I-72; FC in DNA, 45, 387:251.

From C[allender] Irvine, Philadelphia, 12/22. Answers Calhoun's letters of 12/18 and 12/19. So very little clothing of foreign origin has been purchased this year that no satisfactory report of the kind requested on the latter date can be made. He will delay until about 1/15/1819 the awarding of contracts for next year. He hopes to submit early in 1/1819 the report that Calhoun ordered on 9/28/1818. LS in DNA, 1, I-80; FC in DNA, 45, 387:252.

To Andrew Jackson, [Nashville,] 12/22. Acknowledges his letter of 11/25 (LS with Ens in DNA, 2; FC in DLC, Andrew Jackson Papers, Letters and Orders, L:7–8) concerning the arrest of Col. [Eli B.] Clemson on a charge of desertion preferred by T[homas] A. Smith because Clemson was absent from his post on a furlough authorized by Callender Irvine. The enclosures include testimony by Clemson, Smith, Irvine, Col. T[albot] Chambers, Daniel Parker, and Robert Butler; they also include a CC of an order on 7/31 from Calhoun to Chambers for removal of the Army stores in Mo. Territory from Bellefontaine to St. Louis. Jackson's letter of 11/25 questions the advisability of making St. Louis the Commissary headquarters in that area and insists that, under Jackson's interpretation of an act of Congress and of War Department regulations, all Commissary officers and Military Storekeepers must be under the authority of the commanding officer in the area each serves, not under Irvine. [Thus Jackson takes Smith's side in the controversy.] Calhoun answers to opposite effect, explaining that he has submitted the issue to President [James Monroe], who, as commander-in-chief of the Army, "has the ultimate right of construing the acts of Congress in military questions." General orders [to be issued soon] will disclose Monroe's decision. Monroe sees no "contrarity" between the act of Congress and the War Department regulations cited by Jackson. If Commissary officers "were subjected to the orders of the officers where they happened to be stationed, it would be impossible to enforce either regularity or economy." Keeping military stores at St. Louis, Calhoun explains, will make them convenient for troops to be stationed on both the Mississippi and the Missouri Rivers. Echoing a sentiment expressed in Jackson's letter, Calhoun concludes: "You do me no more than justice in attributing to me a sincere attachment to the Army. I feel the obligation as sensibly I trust as I ought of omitting no exertion to render it useful, efficient and respectable, for on the character of the Army the safety and honor of the Country must greatly depend." FC in DNA, 5, 1:98–101.

To Maj. W[illoughby] Morgan, Fort Crawford at Prairie du Chien, 12/22. In reply to his appeal of 10/12 (ALS in DNA, 1, M-120; PC in Carter, ed., *Territorial Papers,* 15:312–316) for indemnification in a lawsuit against him for having about 10/1/1817 arrested licensed Indian trader [Russel] Farnham and others, assures him that "it is reasonable that the government should indemnify you" because Morgan was obeying orders in making the arrest; declines to express an opinion as to a point of law, which will be decided by the court; directs Morgan to employ counsel for his defense and to keep the War Department advised of all developments. FC in DNA, 3, 10:209.

From Alexander Richards, Georgetown, D.C., 12/22. Warns that many fraudulent claims to benefits are pending from Canadian volunteers, as [Maj. Isaac] Finch, their commander, has testified; suggests, therefore, thorough investigations of all such claims. ALS in DNA, 1, R-106.

From C[aesar] A[ugustus] Rodney, 12/22. Recommends that [former Maj. John] Hall be reinstated in the Marine Corps and appointed as its Commandant. ALS in DNA, 128, 7:101. (This letter was postmarked in Philadelphia on 12/24.)

To G[erard] Steddiford, New York [City], 12/22. "The General Court Martial of which you are president having adjourned sine die, you will report what business now remains unfinished before the Court. It will be dissolved in ten days unless your report induce[s] a different discision [*sic*]." FC in DNA, 3, 10:210.

From J[oseph] G. Swift, New York [City], 12/22. Encloses a letter to himself as Chief Engineer, dated 11/15 and written by contractor B[enjamin] W. Hopkins at Mobile Point, announcing that Hopkins has issued a draft for $3,000 to pay for the following:

400 casks of Thomaston stone lime; 30,000 feet of lumber; and the fares from Boston of 15 carpenters, four blacksmiths, and 23 laborers. Swift states that a letterbook in the office of the Chief Engineer will show that payments "for *Materials* & *Passages*" have been authorized "at Mobile." ALS with En in DNA, 1, S-152.

To John W. Taylor, [Representative from N.Y.,] 12/22. "I have examined the case of the heirs of W. S. Hunt, and think the decision of Mr. [Nathaniel] Cutting correct." LS in NHi.

From Peter Hagner, 12/23. Discusses the War Department's advances to a rations contractor for Pa., Charles Hegins (or Higgins) of Sunbury, made in 1817 under Acting Secretary of War [George Graham]. This report is relevant to Hegins's petition to Congress. Jared Irwin, [a Representative from Pa.,] was involved in Hegins's financial affairs. FC in DNA, 53, 9:58–59; PC in Senate Document No. 55, 15th Cong., 2nd Sess.; PC in *American State Papers: Claims*, pp. 662–663.

Regulations Established by the Secretary of War for Substantiating Claims to Pensions

War Department, Pension Office, December 23, 1818

The following evidence will be required in all militia cases, and in cases of the regular Army, where the discharge and surgeon's certificate have been lost or destroyed, or where they have never been originally granted, to enable the Secretary of War to grant pensions: viz.

In cases where the regular discharge and the surgeon's certificate for disability cannot be had, the applicant for a pension, whether he has been a soldier of the regular Army, or a militiaman, in the service of the United States, must produce the sworn certificate of his Captain, or other officer under whom he served, stating distinctly the time and place of his having been wounded, or otherwise disabled; and that the same wounds or disabilities arose while in the service of the United States, and in the line of his duty; with the affidavit of one or more surgeons or physicians, whether of the Army or citizens, accurately describing the wound and stating the degree of disability to which the soldier may be entitled under it. These documents to be sworn to before a judge of the United States' court, or some State judge, or justice of the peace; and, if a State judge or justice of the peace, then, under the seal of the clerk of the county in which such judge or justice may reside; and the name of the paymaster, who last paid the soldier, as belonging to the service of the United States, to be in every instance furnished by the applicant, in order to determine the date of the commencement of his pension.

PC in MoSHi, Auguste Chouteau Papers.

From Decius Wadsworth, 12/23. Sale of the so-called furnace tract of land near Harpers Ferry has been proposed because the scarcity and high price of wood and charcoal in the vicinity has made its intended purpose impractical. Wadsworth reviews the acquisition of the tract by the U.S. and the leasing of it to Henry Strider. ALS in DNA, 1, W-118; FC in DNA, 32, 2:160–162.

To Speaker Henry Clay, 12/24. As Acting Secretary of the Navy, Calhoun assures him that Dr. Samuel C. Smith will be nominated to become a Surgeon's Mate in the Navy "as soon as may be practicable after the arrival of the [new] Secretary of the Navy [Smith Thompson] at the Seat of Government." FC in DNA, 122, 13:248; PC in Hopkins and Hargreaves, eds., *The Papers of Henry Clay,* 2:620.

Resolution by the House of Representatives, 12/24. Asks President [James Monroe] "to cause to be laid before this House, if in his opinion the same should not be inconsistent with the public interest," copies of any reply from the War Department to Ga. Governor [William Rabun's] letter of 6/1 to Calhoun and to Andrew Jackson's letter to Calhoun of 5/7. ADS, attested by Clerk Thomas Dougherty, in DNA, 1, H-151.

JOHN JOHNSTON to JAMES NOBLE, [Senator from Ind.]

Piqua, [O.,] Dec[embe]r 24, 1818

Should the Treaty with the Delawares be ratified, the following things are to be attended to with a view to their speedy removal out of the country on White River.

The whole of the negotiation with the Delawares was conducted by myself, aided by the two Comm[ission]ers. In order to get the Indians to leave the country entirely, many promises had to be made and several stipulations out of the usual way entered into. In the written terms handed in by myself to the Commissioners it was agreed that the improvements of the Delawares should be estimated by John Johnston and William Conner. The Treaty says that the President [James Monroe] shall appoint persons for the purpose, it not having been considered proper that our names should appear in the Treaty. An appointment to value their improvements should be forwarded.

The money assumed in the Treaty to pay the Debts of the Delaware Nation to be placed at the disposal of the Agent [John Johnston] as early in the spring as practicable, in order to [make possible] a final settlement with their Traders.

Authority to the Agent to procure the 120 Head of Horses stipulated in the Treaty to be furnished the Nation to enable them to move across the Mississippi.

There is a stipulation in the Treaty of Fort Meigs for paying the Indians who adhered to us during the late War about $14,000 for losses sustained by reason of their frequent removal, abandoning their homes, and destruction of their property by the Troops of the United States. The accounts and vouchers in detail for the whole amount were forwarded by me to the Secretary of War on the 11th July 1816 and still remain in the war office. As I have no duplicates of these accounts, if the Treaty of F[ort] Meigs is ratified, they will have to be returned to me before I can pay the Indians off; part of this sum is coming to the Delawares who are to move.

Should all the Treaties concluded at Saint Marys be sanctioned and I have the necessary instructions in time, I purpose setting out for the Indian Towns about the 15th May, to commence with the Shawaneese [*sic*], pass to the Wyandotts [*sic*] and Senecas on Sandusky River, thence accross [*sic*] the country to take in the Miamie [*sic*] villages on the Wabash, returning by the Delaware Towns on White River. This route will occupy the chief part of the summer, and I want while among the Indians to make all the arrangements required by the several Treaties, more especially with the Delawares, that they may have no excuse to delay their removal. This tribe is much scattered, many of them residing within the limits of Ohio. It is wanted to have them all collected on White River by the commencement of the next hunting season (Oct[o-be]r), when it is expected the greater part will move westward not to return again.

The Miamie Chiefs at my last conference with them at Saint Marys requested that Mr. [Benjamin] Stickney might be removed from the Sub-Agency of their Tribe. He has agreed to leave Fort Wayne as early as the navigation opens in the spring. This will releive [*sic*] me from a very serious difficulty in managing the Indians in that quarter. He was among the greatest obstacles I had to encounter in preparing the minds of the ["Miamie" *interlined*] Indians, for the late cession, having carried his hostility so far that he refused to deliver my written speeches to the Indians, declaring that he would deliver no man[']s speech to them, not even that of the President of the U.S. This most improper conduct of his kept the Miamies near 2 weeks too late in attending the Treaty, thereby subjecting us to great expence and uncertainty.

Be pleased to have the necessary communication with the Sec[retar]y of War in relation to the subject matter of this letter.

ALS in DNA, 2, J-1818.

From Maj. S[TEPHEN] H. LONG

Pittsburgh, Decem[ber] 24, 1818

I have had the honor to receive your instructions of the 15th inst-[ant] agreeably to which I am authorised to draw on the War Department for funds to cover any expenses that may accrue in the building of the Steam Boat, previously to the passage of the Bill for the next year[']s contingencies. Agreeably to the arrangements I have already made, about two thousand dollars as nearly as I can judge, will become due for labour & materials for the construction of the Boat, on the first day of January next. I would therefore request that funds to that amount may be placed at my disposal, with the least possible delay.

The Boat I think will be completed by the first of March, so that I may be able to sail in company with the other Steam Boat destined for the Yellowstone, and in all probability preceed [*sic*] it.

In regard to instruments &c. I beg leave to defer my report a few days longer.

Numerous applications have been made by gentlemen of science, to accompany the expedition out of which I have made three selections: viz. one in favour of Dr. [William] Baldwin of the Navy, who agreeably to the best information I can obtain stands unrivalled in this country as to his acquirements in Botany, one in favour of Dr. [Thomas] Say of Philadelphia, who ranks equally as high in Zoölogy, and the other in favour of Dr. John Torrey of New York, who was strongly recommended to me by the Lyceum of Nat[ural] History of that City, as well versed in the science of Mineralogy & Geology.

I am not personally acquainted with any of these gentlemen, except Dr. Say, with whom I became acquainted, after having received the most flat[t]ering accounts of his talents as a gentleman of science, from the most respectable authority.

With Mr. [Joshua] Shaw I had an interview while at Philadelphia, at his request, and have no doubt that he is an artist of the first respectability. The only objection to his being of the party, that presented itself, was that he is a foreigner. Whether this ought to debar him from his wishes, I submit to your decision.

With Mr. [Titian Ramsay] Peal[e] I also became acquainted at Philadelphia; he is a young gentleman of much promise, and in many respects would no doubt be a valuable acquisition to the party; he paints with a good degree of execution, is well skilled in preparing birds and other animals, and collecting specimens of minerals, plants &c.

The order in which I had contemplated to survey the waters of the Mississippi, is firstly to ascend the Missouri to the Platt[e], in which the spring tide will probably be at its greatest flood at the time we reach it, ascend this river, and return with all possible dispa[t]ch, pursue our course up the Missouri, and arrive at the Yellow Stone at or before the arrival of the Troops destined to that place—ascend the Yellow Stone which would then be swollen by the Spring tide, after which our course should be directed up the Missouri to the falls, and up as many of its tributaries below that point as the season would allow us to ascend.

Should my outfit prove not sufficiently complete, after this reconnoisance [*sic*], I would then return late in the season to this place, and supply all deficiencies. Otherwise it would be better for us to descend the Mississippi, & explore during the Winter some of its more southern tributaries. Or should it be found consistent, to venture into the Gulph [*sic*] of Mexico, and spend the Winter on the Sabine, Tayac, Trinity and del Nort[e], or some parts of these rivers. Afterwards the upper Mississippi and its tributaries may be explored, in any convenient order, also the Ohio, White, Arkansas, Red, Yazoo, & their tributaries, all of which I think may be affected [*sic*] in the course of between 2 or 3 years from the date of our first departure.

I have the satisfaction to inform you that the Boat is in such a state of forwardness, as to justify the belief that she will be completed by the time above proposed, also, that she will ex[h]ibit specimens of workmanship throughout, not surpassed, if equalled, by any thing of the kind on the Western Waters. I have only to regret, that I can procure no seasoned oak timber, for the construction of those parts that are contiguous to the Engine. Also that the facilities for building the Boat at the Arsenal, are not so complete as I had reason to anticipate.

ALS in DNA, 1, L-121.

From Return J. Meigs, Cherokee Agency, 12/24. Answering Calhoun's request of 12/2 for a report about the Eastern Cherokees' attitude toward the proposed road from N.C. through their land to Ga., Meigs explains that he and [Joseph] McMinn agreed not to ask the Cherokees about it at all during the two conferences held with them this year. They might accede to the proposal; but, if so, "they would make a merit of doing it and excuse themselves for not complying with the great object of an exchange of land." Besides, if the main object—Cherokee emigration—were attained, the road would be made possible automatically. The principal object was not hazarded. ALS in DNA, 1, M-169; FC in DNA, 75 (M-208:7).

To Lt. Commandant James Ramage, U.S. Schooner *Hornet*, Norfolk, 12/24. Now that the *Hornet* is completely equipped for service, Ramage is to sail her with the least practicable delay to New Orleans and to report for duty to Daniel T. Patterson. FC in DNA, 121, 13:302.

James J[efferson] Wilson, [Senator from N.Y.,] "Senate Chamber," to John C. Calhoun, "Secretary at War, and having charge of the Navy Department," 12/24. "The joint Committee of Congress on the subject of the Public Printing, have directed me to request from you a statement, as much in detail as possible, of all the printing executed, and all the Stationary [*sic*] purchased, for the use of the Departments over which you preside, with the prices thereof, for the year ending 31st October 1818." ALS in DNA, 2, W-1818; CC in DNA, 11, 12987; CC in DNA, 23, 180; CC in DNA, 31; CC in DNA, 44; CC in DNA, 128, vol. 7; CC in DNA, 245, 1:43.

From Capt. JOHN BLISS

West Point, N.Y., 25 Dec[embe]r 1818

The court of inquiry at this Post having closed its session, I take the liberty to inform you that in those parts of its proceedings where my reputation and conduct has been implicated I was by order of the Court debarred the privilege of calling witnesses or of putting questions to those on examination which would have removed any unfavourable impressions, relative to my conduct, from the minds of this Court. Neither was I permitted to make any defence as I was led to expect from the terms of the order.

The enclosed representation drawn up with a view to my defence before the court is respectfully submitted to your consideration as containing the most essential facts which have been excluded from the records of this course of proceedure [*sic*].

CC with En in DNA, 203, 16A-D14.1.

To J[ACOB] BROWN, "Private"

War Dept., 26th Dec[embe]r 1818

I regret exceedingly that my decision in the case of [1st] Lieut. [Horace C.] Story should be regarded by you with so much feeling. It has been my disposition to leave to the Generals an unlimited range in the selection of their Aide de Camps, and I should have been very far from making an exception in this case, unless I had been forced almost by necessity.

The Engineer Corps is altogether too small for its extensive duties. The publick is at this moment much injuried [*sic*] from this defect of numbers; and, if officers should be permitted to be detached out of it for other duties, the evil would be aggrevated [*sic*]. For this reason, it had been determined to remove Capt. [James] Gadsden, before his promotion, from his place as aid[e] to General [Andrew] Jackson; tho he had been long with him and was a great favourite. I have asked, however, for an enlargement of the Corps, which, if Congress should grant, will, hereafter, permit me to remove this restriction on the choice of Aide de Camps.

With this explination [*sic*], which I am happy to afford, I trust the course persued [*sic*], will appear satisfactory. It will ever prove to me a source of real pleasure to conform to your wishes in any military arrangement, where it can be done consistently with what I conceive to be my duty to the publick; and I am sure you would not desire it in any other case. To make the Army useful and popular is my sincere desire; and, as it must be your's [*sic*], I think we cannot disagree much in opinion. With sentiment[s] of great respect & esteem, I am, &c.

ALS in MHi.

From Edmund P. Gaines

Fernandina, E[ast] F[la.], December 26, 1818

I have heard nothing from the Seminola [*sic*] Indians, of their desire to make peace with us, since the date of my communication to you upon that subject, excepting vague reports that they wish to have a peace talk with us at St. Augustine.

I have ascertained that Governor [José] Coppinger was advised about the 20th of last month by a Captain Fleming of the Spanish provincial Militia, near St. Augustine, that the Indians had made a proposition to me, to make peace; and of my reply. This circumstance, added to the fact of my not having heard from them since the date of their proposition, reported in my letter of the 14th of last month, affords grounds to suspect, that they are still misled by their evil disposed neighbours, the Spanish Authorities.

[Bvt.] Major [Alexander C.W.] Fanning reports that four of his men were fired on by a small party of Indians near St. Marks, since the date of his preceding report; they escaped unhurt.

LS in DNA, 1, G-60; draft in DNA, 11, 12560.

From Daniel T. Patterson, New Orleans, 12/26. "Pursuant to your instructions of the 26th ult[im]o I do myself the honor to return herewith the orders of the Department under date of the [23rd of] same month. And [I] regret extremely that the situation of the Prometheus deprives Lt. Com[man]d[an]t [William] Finch of the performance of so desirable a Cruise." ALS in DNA, 133 (M-125:60).

To E[leazer] W. Ripley, New Orleans, 12/26. Answers his letter of 11/27 (LS in DNA, 1, R-Miscellaneous; PC in Carter, ed., *Territorial Papers*, 18:482–484) concerning difficulties and delays in beginning the construction work at Mobile Point and Dauphin Island. Approves remuneration for the contractors who have sustained damages because Capt. [James] Gadsden and his Engineers have not arrived there. Gadsden left Washington in time to reach Mobile, it was expected, before the contractor; Lt. [George] Trescot left with the plans even earlier and should have arrived before either. Calhoun hopes that Gadsden or Trescot has arrived by now and that all difficulties have been removed. FC in DNA, 3, 10:210–211; CC in DNA, 224, C-403.

From Capt. JAMES GADSDEN

Nashville, 27 Dec[embe]r 1818

Major General [Andrew] Jackson has relieved Capt. H[ugh] Young of the Topo[graphical] Engineers, from duty on the military road, with a view that he may be more profitably employed in the low country. Capt. Young will receive orders to report to you, and I have to request that that officer may be associated with me, for the performance of the Topographical duties, within the Engineer Department to which I have been assigned. The construction of the Fortifications in the Gulf of Mexico, will require so much of my personal attention, that I apprehend a necessary neglect of the subjects to which you directed my notice. Capt. Young however may be immediately instructed to examine the bayous St. Johns, and Bienvenue, with a view of the feasibility of connecting either of those streams by canals with the Mississippi. The Inland communication between Mobile Bay & Lakes Borgne & Pontchartrain may be surveyed, and should the Floridas be annexed to our territory, there will be subjects enough demanding the early attention of a Topographer.

I take the liberty of suggesting to you, as connected with your enlarged view of internal improvement, and inland navigation, the possibility of a union being effected, between the Atlantic and Gulf of Mexico, by the rivers St. Marys, and Sahwanne [Suwanee]. I know not whether this idea may not have struck many others; it is original with me, and suggested upon reflecting on the sources of those streams, and the nature of the Okefonoke [*sic*] swamp. The St. Marys and Sahwanne rivers both rise in that swamp. Mr. [Andrew] Ellicott states, ["the principles" *canceled*] that drift wood is the principal obstruction to the navigation, with canoes, of the St.Marys river into the Okefonoke swamp and I have been informed by Mr. Hambley [William Hambly] that many of the Seminole Indians have penetrated into the said swamp by the Sahwanne river. These Indians state that the swamp at certain seasons of the year is so inundated as to admit of the free passage of canoes; it is not improbable therefore that at that period a canoe navigation may be obtained between the two rivers, which navigation must be susceptable [*sic*] of improvement.

To ascertain these facts is well worth an exploring voyage, and as I am disposed for any adventurous expedition, should the Government think proper to impose the duty on me, it shall be executed with cheerfulness and zeal.

Should the proposition be favourably received I will then suggest such plans for the organization of the exploring party, as will afford the greatest probability of a happy result.

ALS in DNA, 1, G-139.

To Joseph McMinn, Knoxville

Department of War, 27th Decem[be]r 1818

I have rec[eive]d your two letters of the 29th of Novem[be]r together with the papers detailing the proceedings at the last council of the [Eastern] Cherokee nation.

The tone of the nation has greatly altered. That high spirit of Independence which they assumed some months since, has subsided into an acknowledgement of their dependence on the government of the United States; and, whatever may have been their former opposition to the fair execution of the [plan for emigration embodied in the] treaty [of 7/8/1817], they appear now disposed to act correctly. I do not now see any sufficient reason to delay the taking of the census for which the treaty provides, and for the taking of which, commissioners have already been appointed on our part. You will therefore, notify the the [*sic*] Cherokees, in order that they may appoint a Commissioner, that the census will be taken in June next, or if you should judge an earlier period practicable, at such time as you may designate. The information must also be given to the Cherokees on the Arkansaw [*sic*], immediately, that they may have their commissioner appointed in time.

The rifles and other articles mentioned in your letters will be forwarded immediately. The state of the Indian fund, and particularly that for carrying the Cherokee treaty into effect, will not permit arrangements so extensive as the establishment of the stores which you suggest. If the President [James Monroe] had acceded to the proposition, he would have availed himself of your zeal and experience to carry it into effect. The means of preserving the public stores and preventing the intrusion of the white people are left to your discretion; which, I doubt not, you will effect in the most judicious and economical manner.

It is to be hoped that the effects of the measures which have been pursued, will, in a few years, accomplish the object of the government. The number of the Cherokees on the Arkansaw will be annually increasing by emigration; and those which remain behind will be compelled from circumstances, to take reservations and become citizens.

I transmit a statement of the state of the appropriation to carry the treaty into effect. The balance that remains is small, but I hope there will be no considerable deficit.

LS in DNA, 75 (M-208:14); FC (dated 12/29) in DNA, 72, D:238–239; CC (dated 12/29) in DNA, 77 (M-271:2, frames 999–1001); PC (dated 12/29) in *American State Papers: Indian Affairs,* 2:480; PC's in Senate Document No. 63 and in House Document No. 127, 18th Cong., 1st Sess.

To [Walker K.] Armistead, [George] Gibson, [Thomas S.] Jesup, [Joseph] Lovell, [Daniel Parker], and [Decius] Wadsworth, 12/28. Calhoun encloses a copy of a letter [of 12/24] from James J[efferson] Wilson, Chairman of the Joint Committee on Public

Printing. "You will report thereon to this department." FC in DNA, 3, 10:211; ALS (Armistead's copy, signed by C[hristopher] Vandeventer) in DNA, 23, 180; ALS (Lovell's copy, signed by Vandeventer) with En in DNA, 245, 1:43 and 47; CC (Lovell's copy, signed by Vandeventer) in DNA, 244, A:5.

From Samuel R. Betts, Newburgh, [N.Y.,] 12/28. Acknowledges Calhoun's letter of 12/16; comments that his own letter [of 12/17] anticipated most of the points of information requested. Gives information about courts-martial to which he has been a party and asserts that "there is no case upon my minutes upon which a warrant is yet required." ALS in DNA, 1, B-128.

The Rev. Ard Hoyt to R[eturn] J. Meigs

Brainerd, [Eastern Cherokee Reservation,] Dec. 28, 1818

Will you please to inform me at some convenient time whether you have instructions to pay, on behalf of the government, all reasonable & necessary charges for the [school] buildings errected [*sic*] at this establishment; & whether the account last sent up by Mr. [Cyrus] Kingsbury has been allowed.

I suppose you are acquainted with the fact that Mr. Kingsbury left the buildings in an unfinished state. He had put forward the work as fast as possible, & was continuing it when the charge of the establishment was committed to me. According to his plans we have proceeded in finishing, except that the Prud[ential] Com[mittee of the American Board of Commissioners for Foreign Missions] have directed some additions in order to accom[m]odate more children than the first plan of the buildings would admit. Not having been informed whether Mr. Kingsbury's last acc[oun]t will be paid, I do not know what is my duty in respect to sending up an account of the expenses which have been incurred since.

If you think proper for this latter account to go up, & will give me information, I can forward it at any time.

The school has been somewhat affected by the emigration, i. e., some of the children have been taken out to go over the [Mississippi] river [to the Arkansas reservation], but it is now filling again fast. We have got a little more work to do on our buildings & we shall then be prepared for 100 scholars.

ALS in DNA, 77.

From C[allender] Irvine, Philadelphia, 12/28. Acknowledges Calhoun's letter of 12/22 and its enclosures. Irvine objects to giving preference to particular establishments in the manufacturing of Army clothing, and he considers it improper to award contracts for terms longer than one year because appropriations are made annually. The "supplies procurable by this [Purchasing] Department can, very generally, be had without making any advances on contracts; and an experience of several years has satisfied me that those manufacturers who have required least advances, or who have not asked any, have invariably executed their contracts most satisfactorily." Irvine does not approve of paying a higher price in Ky. for goods that can be made cheaper and of better quality in Philadelphia and shipped thence at the manufacturer's expense. ALS in DNA, 1, I-78; FC in DNA, 45, 387:259–260.

To [ANDREW] JACKSON, Nashville

Department of War, 28th Dec[embe]r 1818

I have recieved [*sic*] your letter of the 28th of November, with the enclosed papers. Experience has proved, that the opinion which you had formed of the movements of the Spaniards on our South western frontier, is correct. After breaking up the French Settlement on the Trinity, it is stated, that they retired. In fact, a hostile movement in that quarter, on the part of Spain, would at present, be absurd, and the apprehension which is said to have been produced appears quite unaccountable. Should farther Military operations, against the Indians and outlaws in Florida, become necessary, or should Congress authorize the occupation of the Country, the operations which you propose, would, certainly, be the most effectual and prompt mode of putting down all hostilities, and it could be effected with almost no additional expense.

I concur with you in opinion, that the situation of Florida, at this moment, is very peculiar, and that it [will] require, the early attention of Government. Its acquisition, in a Commercial, Military, and Political point of view, would be of great importance to us.

You, no doubt, are aware of the great importance I attach to the expedition to the mouth of the Yellow Stone, and as much of its Success will depend upon the Commander, I have to request, that the ablest and most experienced officer of the Rifle Regiment, be selected for that Command. The remoteness of the position, surrounded by Indians, and in the neighbourhood of the British Fur company, requires the greatest prudence, in the Commander to effect the objects of the expedition. Capt. [Wyly] Martin of that Regiment is now in command of the expedition. As I do not know his merits, I leave it with you to determine whether he combines the requisite qualities for such a command.

FC in DNA, 5, 1:97–98; 2 CC's in DLC, Andrew Jackson Papers, 8425–8430; PC in Jameson, ed., *Correspondence,* pp. 150–151.

To James Johnson, [Representative from Va.,] 12/28. In reply to his protest of 12/20 (ALS in DNA, 1, J-77) against [Nathaniel] Cutting's decision not to grant bounty land to the heirs of Willis Burn (alias Willis Burn Barlow)—a protest made partly on the ground that a Va. law allows illegitimate offspring to inherit and to transmit an inheritance—, Calhoun states that the claim of the heirs "has been referred to Mr. Cutting with directions to issue a land warrant." FC in DNA, 3, 10:211.

From G[erard] Steddiford, New York [City], 12/28. He acknowledges Calhoun's letters of 12/7, 12/16, and 12/22. Warrants totaling a large sum have been sent to Marshal [Thomas Morris] for the collection [of fines imposed by the court-martial for N.Y. militia delinquents]. All cases have been tried, but much paperwork yet remains. LS in DNA, 1, S-149.

From W[alker] K. Armistead, 12/29. Acknowledges Calhoun's letter of 12/28 enclosing an inquiry from James J[efferson] Wilson, [Senator from N.J.,] about the cost of public printing. Gen. [Joseph G.] Swift settled his accounts to the date of his resignation as Chief Engineer. Estimated printing costs for 1819 in the Engineer Department will be $1,254, twice the amount of this year's outlay. Swift will return in a few days to Washington; all accounts and estimates can then be more accurately ascertained and reported. FC in DNA, 21, 1:43.

To Commodore William Bainbridge, Boston, 12/29. Pursuant to his request of 12/25 [LS in DNA, 133 (M-125:60)] addressed to "Smith Thompson, Secretary of the Navy," Acting Secretary Calhoun directs Bainbridge to convene a court-martial for the trial of William Bounds, Carpenter's Mate on the U.S.S. *Independence*, on the charges submitted by Bainbridge and returned to him; Calhoun also designates William C. Aylwin to serve as the Judge Advocate. FC in DNA, 121, 13:303; CC in DNA, 251, case 326 (M-273:11, frame 1002).

From Edmund P. Gaines, Fernandina, East Fla., 12/29. Reports an attack made by an Army deserter, allegedly acting under orders from the Governor of East Fla., [José] Coppinger, against a Sgt. and two civilians from Ga. Gaines believes that "the Spanish authorities want the means to enable them to give us open and unequivocal proofs of their settled hostility, and intimate connection with our red enemies." He encloses evidence, derived from Indian testimony, "that the Spanish at St. Augustine with all their affected purity have lately furnished hostile Indians at the Bay of Tampa with ten horse loads of ammunition, recommending to them united and vigorous operations against us. I shall hold myself in readiness to do what can be done with the limited means under my controul and shall strike at any force that may present itself." He asks that a Quartermaster officer with $20,000 and a Battalion of Infantry shall be ordered to join him. LS with Ens in DNA, 1, G-72; CC with Ens in DNA, 202, 15A-E1; PC in House Document No. 117, 15th Cong., 2nd Sess.; PC in *American State Papers: Military Affairs*, 1:753.

To Richard Graham and Joseph Philips, Commissioners

Department of War, 29th Decem[be]r, 1818

I have examined the subject of the running [of] the lines under the treaty of the 24th Aug[us]t 1816; and as you have not furnished me with a detailed estimate of the expenses, I shall not be able in all probability to procure an increase to the present appropriation for that object. I shall, however, request the Hon[ora]ble N[inian] Edwards to endeavour to increase the appropriation when the bill is called up in the Senate. In the meantime, you will limit your disbursements to the sum appropriated, as the sum you state to be necessary appears absolutely too high. Under these circumstances, you will see the necessity of limiting your disbursements to the sum already appropriated.

FC in DNA, 72, D:237.

From [Thomas S. Jesup], 12/29. As ordered today, he encloses an itemized report by G[eorge] Bender as to the cost of printing and stationery for the Quartermaster Department to 10/31. FC with En in DNA, 42, 1:150–151.

From [Thomas S. Jesup], 12/29. To pay his Quartermaster obligations for 1818, he must receive $68,300 additional. He submits an estimate showing the amount required in each Military Department. FC in DNA, 42, 1:148–149.

To Frank [*actually* Francis] Jones, [Representative from Tenn.,] 12/29. "I have examined the papers submitted by you under date of the 26th Inst[ant (ALS in DNA, 1, J-76)] but do not [find] that there are sufficient reasons to alter the decision of Mr. [Nathaniel] Cutting. The certificate of heirship by the laws of South Carolina ought to be given by the Ordinary. I think it probable if you should transmit the papers to John T. Lewis, Clerk of the Court, he will cause the proper certificate to be taken before an Ordinary, when the claim can be allowed." FC in DNA, 3, 10:311.

Capt. John LeConte, Norfolk, to W[alker] K[eith] Armistead, 12/29. He reports as to the topography and geology of the area around Norfolk. FC in DNA, 22, pp. 340–342.

To Wilson Lumpkin, Madison, Ga., 12/29. Calhoun acknowledges Lumpkin's letter of 12/10 [LS in DNA, 77 (M-271:2, frames 1210–1215)] reporting that he went last month to Fort Hawkins, that his efforts to survey the Creek boundary had been delayed, and that he had incurred some expenses that seemed excessive. Calhoun agrees with Lumpkin's interpretation as to a creek to which reference was made in the treaty and approves his conduct and the economy with which he has operated. A payment will be sent to him, and he should submit his vouchers. FC in DNA, 72, D:237–238; LU in DNA, 77 (M-271:2, frames 1004–1006).

To David B. Mitchell, 12/29. "I enclose an extract of a letter from the Hon[ora]ble B[olling] Hall, which exhibits many complaints against the roads, & exorbitant charges on them, between Fort Hawkins and Fort Jackson. The charges for corn, forage, and ferriage appear exorbitantly high; and I request you will report to me the cause of such high charges. The rate of the ferriage ought, if there is not sufficient reason to the contrary, to be reduced." FC in DNA, 72, D:236–237; LU in DNA, 77 (M-271:2, frames 1002–1003); PC in Carter, ed., *Territorial Papers*, 18:504.

From W[ALKER] K. ARMISTEAD, Chief Engineer

Engineer Department, 30th December 1818

It is believed that by loaning the Astronomical Instruments to the American Philosophical Society they can receive no material injury, as they will be in the hands of Scientific Men. But should any of the Instruments be injured, the Society should be made responsible. Should the Topographical Engineers be required to make a survey of the Coast, the ensuing Spring, the Instruments will be required for their use.

ALS in DNA, 1, A-51.

From W[alker] K. Armistead, 12/30. Requests that the uniform of members of the band at the Military Academy be made in accordance with an order given by [Joseph G.] Swift, because "the extra expense will be inconsiderable." LS in DNA, 2, A-1818; FC in DNA, 13 (M-91:1, p. 70).

To O[liver] C[romwell] Comstock, [Representative from N.Y.,] 12/30. Answers his letter, written jointly with Daniel Cruger, [Representative from N.Y.,] of 12/28 (LS in DNA, 1, C-120) attempting to speed payments to the officers of the court-martial for N.Y. militia delinquents; explains that payments are required, by regulations, to come from the court's fines when they have been collected. Until Calhoun has been informed that no such funds are available, "I cannot decide out of what fund the officers shall be paid." FC in DNA, 3, 10:212.

From Geo[rge] Gibson, 12/30. "I have the honour to enclose a statement of all Stationery purchased and printing executed for the office of the Commissary G[enera]l of Sub[sistence] for the year ending 31st October [1818]." FC in DNA, 191, 1:6.

To Callender Irvine, Philadelphia, 12/30. "You will suspend the execution of the order of Gen[era]l [Joseph G.] Swift of the 27th of July last respecting the uniform proposed to be furnished the Board of the Corps of Engineers, until further orders." FC in DNA, 3, 10:213.

From Andrew Jackson, Nashville, 12/30. Encloses and discusses an address to him from James Pitchlynn, a half-breed Choctaw who served as a commissioner for that tribe in the recent negotiations. Jackson regrets the failure of those negotiations to result in the Choctaws agreeing to exchange their lands for others farther west. Jackson reports what he has told Pitchlynn to tell the Choctaws, tentatively; and Jackson promises to relay to Pitchlynn any more authoritative answer from Calhoun. ALS with En in DNA, 1, J-85; PC with Ex in Bassett, ed., *Correspondence*, 2:405–407.

To R[ichard] M. Johnson, Chairman, House Committee on Military Affairs, 12/30. In response to his request of 12/28, Calhoun encloses a report dated 12/30 [FC in DNA, 13 (M-91:1, p. 70)] by [Walker K.] Armistead about the injury received by [former] Cadet [John] Payne. William Morin's name cannot be found on muster rolls of the 17th and 28th Regiments; more accurate information about his unit and a certificate of heirship must be supplied before his application can be approved. FC in DNA, 3, 10:212–213.

From Maj. S[TEPHEN] H. LONG

Pittsburg[h,] Dec[ember] 30, 1818

In answer to that part of your Instructions, relative to Instruments necessary for the Expedition, I have the honour to report, that the arrangements I have made are not yet sufficiently extensive to embrace all we shall stand in need of. Those most essential and most difficult to obtain I have already contracted for. There are others highly necessary in the accomplishment of the objects you have in view, which I propose to procure in the course of the winter. This, as well as the collection and the safe transportation of the Instruments I have ordered, will render it necessary for me to travel South of the Alleganies [*sic*] before I set out on the Expedition.

I herewith enclose you the Account of Mr. Patten of N[ew] York for various Instruments therein specified, all of which are to be ready for delivery on the 1st of February next. In addition to these I have contracted for several other Instruments, which are probably now in readiness at Philadelphia, viz. 2 Portable Barometers, 1 Dip Needle, 1 Hygrometer, I Cyanometer, 1 Measuring Chain, 1 Microscope, 2 Cases Mathematical Instruments, Drawing Apparatus, and 1 Graphic Telescope, for tracing Landscapes with the greatest expedition.

I have also made the arrangements to purchase the works of a variety of Authors concerning the Western Country. Also, Gregory's Dictionary of Arts & Sciences, Hutton's Mathematical Dictionary, and Tables, [Nathaniel] Bowdi[t]ch's Navigation [*The New American Practical Navigator*], [James] Mackay's Longitude, Garnet[']s Tables, Nautical Ephemires's [?] &c. &c. Blanks for Meteorological Registers, and Blank Vocabularies for the different Indian Languages, are to be printed for our use.

At Mr. Voyt's [*sic*; Henry Voigt] of Philadelphia are two Chronometers, the property of the U[nited] States, the one a Box, and the other a Pocket Chronometer. I have requested Mr. V. to have them adjusted with the utmost precision, for the use of the expedition. There are a few Instruments at Washington which would be of service to us, viz, a Circle of Reflexion [*sic*], a small Sea Sextant and a Box Chronometer, probably some others.

In regard to Instruments, Tests &c. required by the Naturalists to be attached to the expedition, I wish each one may be authorised to procure a small cabinet for himself, not exceeding the weight of 50 pounds.

In addition to the above, various articles of Stationary [*sic*] will be required, which may be specified, should it be deemed necessary.

The Ordnance, Ordnance Stores, and Q[uarte]r Master's Stores to equip the Boat, will probably require an order from the War Department, before they can be drawn.

In the construction of the Boat I have deemed it advisable to deviate a little from the original plan. To the length of the Keel I have added 3 feet, and to that of the Beam, as much more, under the presumption that it would meet your approbation.

ALS in DNA, 1, L-120.

From Joseph Lovell, 12/30. As Calhoun ordered on 12/28, Lovell encloses a report as to all stationery and printing purchased by the office of the Surgeon General from its establishment in the spring of 1818 through 10/31/1818. FC in DNA, 242, 2:24; FC with En in DNA, 243, 1:29.

To Thomas L. McKenney, Georgetown, [D.C.,] 12/30. He is to send, even if he must buy them, as promptly as possible to Joseph McMinn at the [Eastern] Cherokee Agency the following articles for emigrating Cherokees: 100 long rifles, 500 blankets of the best quality, 250 brass kettles of medium size, and 10,000 flnts. LS in DNA, 75 (M-208:14); FC in DNA, 72, D:240.

To Joseph McMinn, Murfreesboro, Tenn.

Department of War, 30th Dec[embe]r 1818

In pursuance of the request contained in your letter of the 29th ultimo, I have directed the Superintendent of Indian Trade [Thomas L. McKenney] to forward to the Cherokee Agency, subject to your order, the following articles, for the use of the Emigrants to the Arkansas, to wit: 100 Rifles of the longest class, 500 best blankets, 250 Brass Kettles, and 10,000 Flints; being half the number of each article required by you.

The state of the Indian appropriation will not admit of a compliance, at this time, with the whole extent of your statement.

FC in DNA, 72, D:239.

To President [James Monroe], 12/30. In compliance with a House resolution of 12/7, Acting Secretary of the Navy Calhoun transmits a report made to him by John Rodgers, President of the

Navy Board of Commissioners, on 12/24 (LS in DNA, 128, 7:97) on the Navy's progress in shipbuilding under the "Act for the gradual increase of the Navy." LS with Ens in DNA, 202, 15A-E1; FC in DNA, 123, 1:342; PC with Ens in House Document No. 70, 15th Cong., 2nd Sess.; PC with Ens in *American State Papers: Naval Affairs,* 1:583–587.

To President [James Monroe], 12/30. Pursuant to a House resolution of 12/24 asking for copies of additional letters concerning [Capt. Obed Wright of the Ga. militia], Calhoun sends an extract of [Christopher] Vandeventer's reply [of 6/2] to Andrew Jackson's letter of 5/7 to Calhoun and states that the War Department never answered William Rabun's letter of 6/1 to Calhoun. LS with CCEx in DNA, 202, 15A-E1; FC in DNA, 6, 1:341–342; PC with En in House Document No. 68, 15th Cong., 2nd Sess.; PC with En in *American State Papers: Military Affairs,* 1:778.

From Henry Sherburne, Chickasaw Agency, 12/30. Reports that a man "returned two days since from the Chickasaw Bluffs, and informed me that the robbery committed on board the boat Noble, which I stated to you in a former communication, is by the best informed men at the Bluffs, much questioned, as nothing had been heard of the robbers, since the event happened, & [because of] the mere trifling articles they carried off. At any rate, the inhabitants at & about the Bluffs appear to be perfectly satisfied with their situation, & not in the least apprehensive of danger." LS in DNA, 1, S-183.

To B[enjamin] Lloyd Beall, Georgetown, [D.C.,] 12/31. Appoints him to be a War Department Clerk in the Pension Office, under a recent act of Congress, at $1,000 per year; he is to report immediately to [James L.] Edwards for duty. FC in DNA, 3, 10:214. Beall accepted on 1/1. ALS in DNA, 2, B-1819.

From N[icholas] Boilvin, Prairie du Chien, 12/31. He submits a census of the Indian tribes that live near there and visit there; it reports the principal Chiefs, the numbers of men, women, and children, and the numbers and locations of villages. ALS with En (both in French) in DNA, 1, B-174.

From William Clark, [Governor of Mo.,] Louisville, [Ky.,] 12/31. States that Benjamin O'Fallon has been employed as Indian Agent to the Missouri tribes since 8/23 without compensation. ALS in DNA, 1, C-200.

From Edmund P. Gaines, Fernandina, E[ast] F[la.], 12/31. When Gaines wrote his letter of 11/24 concerning the right to confine deserters beyond their periods of enlistment, he had not received the general order of 11/12 from the Adjutant and Inspector General, [Daniel Parker,] which reached Gaines on 12/1. ALS in DNA, 1, G-74; ALS in DNA, 11, 12215.

Resolution of the House of Representatives, 12/31. Asks Calhoun for a report as to the arms and military stores distributed to the militias of the States and Territories under a statute of 1808 and as to the principle upon which the distribution has been made. DS in DNA, 1, H-71. (This document, signed by Thomas Dougherty as Clerk of the House, bears a postscript dated 2/19/1818 [*sic* for 1819] stating that a copy of this resolution had been sent on 1/2/[1819] and that this is a duplicate.)

To C[allender] Irvine, Philadelphia, 12/31. Informs him that it has been decided to discontinue the services of the Military Storekeeper at Nashville, [Howell Tatum]. Irvine is to receive the public property there and to dispose of it "as the good of the service requires." FC in DNA, 3, 10:214.

To Thomas S. Jesup, 12/31. [Howell] Tatum, Acting Military Storekeeper at Nashville, "has been directed to turn over to your department such public property in his possession as may belong to it. Enclosed you have an inventory thereof. You will immediately give the necessary instructions relating to it." FC in DNA, 3, 10:213.

From Thomas L. McKenney

Office [of] Indian Trade, 31st Dec[embe]r 1818

The histories of the fur associations, under the various titles of Hudson[']s Bay, North West, Michilimackinac and South West companies, are not within my reach. Such writers as I have been able to glance over, since I saw you yesterday, deal cheifly [*sic*] in the details which make up the expeditions of the traders, the routes, portages, rapids, river courses, &c. &c. without affording much information respecting the amount of capital vested in the several branches; and none at all in relation to the charters, or rules of association.

I am only able to state that the amount of capital employed by the North West company in 1788 was £40,000 Sterling, and that this amount in 1793 trebled, making it about 530,000 Dollars.

In 1798 the N.W. Company divided, one branch continuing to trade under its old title and on the old stock, and the other under the title of the Michilimackinac with a new stock, but what amount constituted this new stock I am unable to ascertain. It is reasonable however to infer that it was not less than the amount employed by the N.W. branch, but it was probably more. For no doubt superior advantages were contemplated by the new party, and these of course must have embraced superior resources. However it is fair to put the whole capital employed by these two branches at one million of Dollars. To this may be reasonably added a quarter of a million more, in the hands of unassociated individuals. I do not conceive however that this addition ought to weigh any thing in this estimate; as there will be two divisions of trade, under the view you have taken of the subject, not less than the 500,000 will be employed in the home trade, which may go to take the place of the 250,000 Dollars supposed to be in the hands of Individuals in 1798.

I think a company suitably organized and vigorously managed could prosecute the outer division of the trade to advantage on a capital of a million of Dollars—that more would be unnecessary because, by the side of it would be ranged another set of operations, with 500,000 Dollars more[;] and a million and a half on reflection I hold to be adequate for the whole trade, or if it should turn out to be the minimum, I conceive that it would be better so, than for the capital to be augmented to an overgrown amount—better as it relates to the Interests of the Company, and better for the maintenance of a fur market which it is so desireable [*sic*] to preserve in our Country, and better for the Indians themselves.

If the capital stock were larger than could be managed with activity, the short interest upon it might discourage the owners, and produce a relaxation of efforts, and ultimate loss. Whereas, if, after trial it should be found too small, it could be enlarged by a law authorising that measure, and if the capital were beyond certain limits which would make it no object for the managers of the trade to turn it over with expedition, it would afford opportunities and leisure to wait for the returns from China, or other foreign markets, or give the Company power to oblige our manufacturers to buy at home under circumstances which might be deemed oppressive at least by the consumers. But if the Capital be at its minimum, it will tend to keep up that activity of intercourse with the natives, with a view to make the best of it, as will serve their wants more effectually, inasmuch as the necessity for quick returns will lead the agents to accom[m]odate their locations to the hunting grounds of the Indians, without waiting for the Indians to march hundreds of miles to them.

I think a million of Dollars, for these reasons, the most suitable capital, for the outer trade, and I think that amount, will be subscribed for, *provided* it will not be found more advantageous for the successors of the present Gov[ernmen]t policy, to oppose and successfully counteract the creation of such a company, with a view to reach out into those distant parts by means of their agencies from within the posts. It strikes me this view of the case will not be lost sight of by those who understand how to make the best of a new state of things. Nor do I see how a provision in the law would prevent them. An invoice upon the horns of a stag would be as easily got at, as would be the Indian adventurers, who might wish, even if the law should *forbid* it, to extend their enterprize into the wilds of the Missouri, & beyond the limits which might be assigned to them. This view of the subject [*one verb illegible*] me and it has this moment occurred to me to apprehend that if the Gov[ernmen]t abandon the home trade, it will not be able to realize the object of a Company beyond the posts, and for the reasons just glanced at.

But the company plan would be more certain to carry if the home trade were continued in the hands of the Government—Inasmuch as the fur mongers and hungry parts of our Citizens who so longingly desire to become traders would then have but the single chance, and their funds would be directed into that channel without delay.

These latter remarks have occur[r]ed to me, as I went along, and I have followed the impulse, and added them to the little light which I have been able to illicit [*sic*] from the records of narratives respecting the Capital of the North West company.

FC in DNA, 73, E:181–184.

From Thomas L. McKenney

Office [of] Indian Trade, 31st Dec[embe]r 1818

I have varied from the terms of your reference to the act of March 1811, and instead of entering "so much of it" (only) "as relates to the appointment of Sup[erintenden]t and Factors," *the whole is recognized.* My reasons are these. First, if [there should be] a suspension of forwarding the supplies usual to take place on the supposition of a sale, which *might* not take place, then the supplies necessary for the next year would be withheld from the Indians, & the firm injured, by the loss of a year[']s business. Second, a purchaser would prefer to take the Factory and its contents, & the goods in transit necessary for the coming season to a bare purchase of the Factory and its contents *alone,* as he would save a year by the continuance of the regular routine of supplies, which would be an additional inducement for him to buy. The second date referring to [*sic*] the terms &c. to the President [James Monroe,] I will be prepared with a proposal for his approval at any time. It is quite easy to make ready.

FC in DNA, 73, E:184–185.

From Nath[anie]l Macon, [Senator from N.C.,] 12/31. Recommends Arthur B. Gloster of N.C. for appointment as a Cadet. "I am aware of the rule of office, which forbids answers to letters of this kind, yet I should be highly gratified with a line, informing me, the day when the applications for admittance will be decided, that I may transmit it, to his friends." ALS in DNA, 15, 1819, 51.

From [Daniel Parker], 12/31. Because [Talbot] Chambers wrote on 11/20 that the portion of the Rifle Regiment that has been ordered to ascend the Missouri River is undermanned, [Parker] points out that no report as to the strength of that part of the Regiment has been submitted since 3/1818. [Parker] suggests various transfers of units to strengthen the Missouri Expedition. FC in DNA, 12, 5:158–159.

[Fifth Auditor Stephen Pleasonton's report on the account of Benjamin F. Stickney as Indian Agent at Fort Wayne, Ind., 1812–1818, *ca.* 12/31.] This fragment of a document bears the following AEI by Calhoun: "From this abstract I should think the vouchers are as regular as ought to be expected; and the 5th Audi[t]or will according[ly] allow them." Fragment in U.S. General Accounting Office, Indian Tribal Branch, Fifth Auditor Accounts.

From C[HARLES] TAIT, Chairman, Senate Committee on Naval Affairs

Senate Chamber, Dec. 31st 1818

"The Act," from the House of Representatives, "making appropriations for the support of the Navy of the United States for the year 1819" has been referred to the Committee of the Senate on Naval Affairs. It appears that the amount of appropriations for the Navy proper, in this act and also of the estimates, for the year eighteen hundred & nineteen, exceeds the appropriations for the same service in the present year, two hundred & twenty-eight thousand, seven hundred & seventy-six dollars: And that the excess for the Marine Corps is $7,505.60. It also appears that the Estimates for the year 1818 were made for the support of five thousand four hundred & ninety-seven *persons* in the Navy, and for the year 1819, for six thousand, five hundred & ten *persons* for the same service; making a difference of 913 *persons,* of which 850 are seamen. I have been directed by the Committee on Naval Affairs of the Senate, to enquire what are the circumstances which make it necessary to provide for this increase of seamen in the Naval service for the year 1819: And also what number of ships & their rates are now in commission; distinguishing those that are in service abroad from those that are employed on our own coasts or in our own waters.

ALS in DNA, 128, 7:114.

To Howell Tatum, Nashville, 12/31. "From the property return of the 2nd Auditor [William Lee] it does not appear necessary to continue a Military Storekeeper at Nashville." Tatum is to deliver to three government officials the stores in his possession, and then "your compensation will cease." FC in DNA, 3, 10:214.

[James Monroe] to Jacob Brown, [12/——]. Discusses at length opinions concerning the ordered retrial by court-martial of Maj. [Nathaniel Nye] Hall. CC in DNA, 1, P-68.

JANUARY 1819

WASHINGTON WAS AGOG WITH EXCITEMENT OVER THE question whether Andrew Jackson exceeded his authority in 1818 by capturing Spanish posts in the two Floridas. Some Congressmen urged that Jackson should be censured; others argued in his defense. The accused put in his personal appearance and accepted an invitation to dine with the Calhouns. Apparent victory eventuated for both the War Department and Jackson, in that neither was condemned officially. Meanwhile, Calhoun submitted to Henry Clay a persuasive appeal for the improvement of roads as a means of promoting both the civilian vitality of the nation and its military capacity for self-defense. To Henry Southard, another Congressman, Calhoun submitted drafts of three bills about Indian policies. Because Smith Thompson became Secretary of the Navy, Calhoun was freer to consider an appeal from the American Philosophical Society.

From J[ames] L. Edwards, 1/1. Pursuant to House resolutions of 4/20/1818 and 11/28/1818, Edwards submits a list of 4,431 men who were granted Revolutionary pensions through 11/16/1818 under the statute of 3/18/1818, their residences, their terms and units of service, their ranks, and the amounts of their pensions. LS in DNA, 1, E-24; FC with En in DNA, 91, 6:143–144.

To [John Gaillard], 1/1. In compliance with a Senate resolution of 12/15/1815, Calhoun transmits "a copy of the Army Register, corrected to this date, for each member of the Senate." LS in DNA, 15A-F4; FC in DNA, 4, 2:71.

From RICHARD M. JOHNSON

City of Washington, 1st Jan[uar]y 1818 [1819]

In reading over the letters of my Brother [James Johnson], I find he thinks it very probable that the Indians will be inclined to oppose the passage of any small force up the Missouri. Letters from that quarter speak of the hostility of certain tribes. My Brother is determined to have his boats fixed in such manner, that he can use several six pounders, & also to have the crew well furnished with small arms. It will be adviseable [*sic*] to have a small detachment [of soldiers] with each boat.

ALS in DNA, 1, J-82.

From Joseph McMinn, Murfreesboro, Tenn., 1/1. Reports that the Eastern Cherokees do not trust their Chiefs, who are suspected of not distributing annuities and other payments from the U.S. to those who should receive them. Some of these Cherokees are enrolling for emigration to the Arkansas but fear that payments for their improvements will never reach them. Some are not happy, therefore, that a delegation will soon be in Washington and may receive funds. McMinn expects to reach Washington late this month for the conferences. LS in DNA, 77 (M-271:2, frames 1304–1307); FC in DNA, 75 (M-208:14).

From Maj. Charles J. Nourse, Assistant Adjutant General, 2nd Military Department, Boston, 1/1. A bill being considered in a House committee prompts him to fear that line officers will suffer losses in rank when they serve as staff officers. Nourse argues that a statute of 3/3/1813 prohibits this kind of discrimination. ALS in DNA, 1, N-23.

From [Daniel Parker], 1/1. Reports from whom and at what cost he purchased printing and stationery during the year that ended on 10/31/1818. "I have made it a rule to apply for the various articles required for the office at those places where they could be obtained on the best terms." FC in DNA, 12, 5:159.

From Jasper Parrish, Canandaigua, [N.Y.,] 1/1. Supplementing his report of 10/5/1818, he states "further for your information the condition and advantages pos[s]essed by the Six Nations of Indians." They want their annuity of $4,500 to be paid in clothing and tools, not in cash. LS in DNA, 1, P-93.

From Maj. Perrin Willis, New Orleans, 1/1. Urges that staff officers be promoted to fill vacancies in the line and that the vacancies thus created be filled by transferring line officers to them. ALS in DNA, 1, W-189.

From Heman Allen, Burlington, [Vt.,] 1/2. Accepts his appointment as Commissioner of Loans and Agent for Paying U.S. Pensioners in the District of Vt.; encloses his bond for the faithful execution of his duties. ALS in DNA, 1, A-53.

Isaac L. Baker, New Orleans, to [George Graham, Washington,] 1/2. "Knowing you well disposed to assist and bring forward young men of the western country," Baker asks for Graham's assistance in getting a Cadetship for 15-year-old Owen Thomas of La. "I feel very anxious to know your determination about making an establishment [of your home] in our country. Emigrants begin to turn more of their attention than they formerly did to our District and now or never is the time to strike." Baker is in New Orleans as a La. legislator. Capt. [Ferdinand L.] Amelung is petitioning Congress for a share of the prizes he captured on the coast "and calculates on your good offices." James Brown "arrived here a few days since from France and will most probably be elected to fill Mr. [Eligius] Fromentin's vacancy [in the U.S. Senate, beginning 3/4]." ALS in DNA, 15, 1819, 63a, with an AEU by Calhoun reading: "If appointed, give to Mr. Graham the certificate."

To Speaker [HENRY CLAY]

Department of War, 2 Jan[uar]y 1819

I have the honor to transmit to you a statement of the names, &c., of the persons who have been placed on the Pension List, to the 16th day of November last, inclusive, under the law of the 18th of March 1818; in compliance with the resolution of the House of Representatives of the 20th of April, and the 28th of November 1818.

LS with an En of 215 pp. in DNA, 201, 15A-F3; FC in DNA, 4, 2:71.

From EDMUND P. GAINES

Fernandina, E[ast] F[la.], January 2, 1819

I have not yet heard from the Governor of St. Augustine [José Coppinger] upon the subject of the outrage reported in my letter of the

29th ultimo. The facts then communicated have been confirmed by the reports of a Mr. Ham of Georgia, and Mr. Kingsly of this province, and others; none of whom however witnessed the act, nor have they seen either of the wounded men: one of whom is reported to be dead.

Some deserters from this place were, a few days ago pursued by a Sergeant and small party near to the St. Johns. The party returned on the 31st with four of the deserters. The Sergeant states that he was informed by the inhabitants living near the place where Sergeant [Augustus] Santee and his companions were fired on, that one of the men was mortally wounded, and the Sergeant and another had been sent under guard to St. Augustine.

The 20,000 Dollars requested in my last, are intended to provide for a movement should it become necessary. The acting Quartermaster at this place being supplied with funds for the present ordinary expenses of that department—about $5,000.

ALS in DNA, 1, G-75.

From Roswell Lee, Springfield, Mass., 1/2. William Sheldon of Springfield has invented a method of manufacturing cannon from wrought iron. The cost of such cannon can be determined only by experience. Lee believes such guns to be preferable to those made from cast iron "in point of strength and on account of the celerity with which they might be exercised or transported." He encloses an undated letter to Calhoun from Sheldon and an undated explanation of the manufacture and advantages of the new product. ALS with Ens in DNA, 1, W-143; FC in DNA, 39, 1818–1821:58.

To Benjamin Parke, Vincennes, [Ind.,] 1/2. "I have received your letter of the 7th ult[im]o. By comparing your remarks concerning the issue of provisions to Indians with my circular [of 9/15] on that subject, I presume the last paragraph, respecting the issue to 'straggling Indians,' occasions the difficulty. The prohibition does not apply to the case of Chiefs or other respectable Indians who may visit the Agency on business or otherwise, but only to those idle and worthless Indians who infest government offices solely to procure supplies. These ought not to be indulged." FC in DNA, 72, D:240.

By William T. Wolfe Tone, 1/2. Twelve pages of "Observations on the Standing Army of the United States," by a veteran of service in the French army. ADS in DNA, 1, T-80.

From RICHARD M. JOHNSON

City of Washington, [*ca.* January 3, 1819]

I have read the letter of Callender Irvine [dated 12/28/1818]. His view is partial & erroneous, & if his bias for Philadelphia, and his original opposition to the law is to be carried into effect by drawing to Ph[iladelphi]a & to his own hands the whole expenditure then Congress legislated in vain. He puts down all hopes of the least patronage to manufacturers in the western country. I understood that you considered it reasonable to allow the additional price of transportation & I consider his impression as to the inferiority of the cloths in the West totally without foundation upon a general principle.

Col. [John] McKinney stands high & see his views of this subject. To have all the funds in Ph[iladelphi]a at this crisis is important but I hope it will not all go there. Respectfully, R[ic]h[ar]d M. Johnson.

ALS in DNA, 1, J-81. NOTE: An EU indicates that this letter was received or filed in 1/1819. This letter may have had some influence upon Calhoun's letter of 1/5 to Irvine.

From John Barron, Jr., Baltimore, 1/4. His bill for wharfage of stone at Fort McHenry has been unpaid ever since 9/1818 because Quartermaster and Engineer officers each think it should be charged to the other's appropriation. Barron begs Calhoun "to have the goodness to order the settlement of the Acc[ount] by the proper officer." ALS in DNA, 221, 3.

To John Crowell, [Delegate from Ala. Territory,] 1/4. Thinks the petition of Capt. [Abraham L.] Sands requires no legislation; War Department regulations can permit a refund to him of the money stolen. LS in CtY; FC in DNA, 3, 10:215. (By inadvertent error, the LS was dated "1818.")

From William Eaton, New York [City], 1/4. Seeks to obtain payment of his claims totaling $9,000 expended for wages and provisions for work on fortifications at Mobile Point and Dauphin Island, beginning in 9/1818. Payment has been halted because there was no resident Engineer to approve his accounts; and on 12/3/1818 his laborers were left idle and stranded at the two sites. [Joseph G.] Swift promised that any government-caused delay will be recompensed by the U.S. Eaton's creditors and his employees' families are distressed. ALS in DNA, 221, 2.

From Peter Hagner, 1/4. He has experienced "great difficulties" in ascertaining from Paymaster records of the War of 1812 "that the same Troops are not twice paid for the same service" and in determining with any assurance whether deceased soldiers, particularly officers, have been paid to the dates of their deaths. He submits, therefore, several "propositions which I presume if adopted may have a tendency to obviate" inadequate records concerning payments made to the "dispersed" Army. LS in DNA, 1, H-162; FC in DNA, 53, 9:112–114.

[Dr.] Samuel L[atham] Mitchill, New York [City], to [James Monroe], 1/4. Introduces Moses Hoyt of New York City, a Revolutionary patriot and admirer of Monroe, who will soon visit Washington and see Monroe. ALS in DNA, 1, M-200.

To Augustus Porter, Niagara Falls, N.Y., 1/4. Acknowledges his letter of 12/21/1818 seeking appointment as Indian Agent to the Six Nations. If such an office were authorized by law, Calhoun would avail himself of Porter's talents; but there is only a Sub-Agency, and it is filled by Jasper Parrish. FC in DNA, 72, D:240.

W[alker] K[eith] Armistead to Thomas Grimbrede, New York [City], 1/5. "Mr. Milbert having declined the appointment of Drawing Master at the Military Academy," Grimbrede is appointed provisionally, is told to report immediately to [Sylvanus] Thayer for examination and to acknowledge promptly this letter, and is informed that, if commissioned, his pay and emoluments will be those of a Capt. of Engineers. FC in DNA, 13 (M-91:1, p. 70).

From W[alker] K. Armistead, 1/5. Recommends that $2,000 be remitted to Maj. S[tephen] H. Long, Topographical Engineer, at Pittsburgh to cover some expenses for his "Survey of Western Waters." FC in DNA, 21, 1:44.

To P[hilip] P[endleton] Barbour, [Representative from Va.,] 1/5. Calhoun refers to his letter of 12/10/1818 to Barbour and says, "I find that through the hum of business there was an omission. I meant to say that a man who served by substitute was not entitled to a pension. But the substitute himself is entitled provided his services in other respects entitle him to a pension." FC in DNA, 3, 10:217.

To P[hilip] P[endleton] Barbour, 1/5. Encloses evidence that the word "honorable" was omitted purposely from the discharge certificates of certain soldiers; their claim, therefore, cannot be allowed. FC in DNA, 3, 10:216.

To George D. "Brewster [*actually* Brewerton]," Newburgh, N.Y., 1/5. Answers his complaining appeal of 12/31/1818 (ALS in DNA, 11, 11944) for a decision as to his application. In that letter Brewerton stated, "When I left Washington, I was certainly to have an answer in two days; more than three months have expired and I have not yet received any communication from the War Department, whatever, on the subject." Brewerton added a reminder that a year of his life had been devoted to seeking an appointment and that he had been kept "in a continued state of suspence." In reply, Calhoun wrote: "By the regulations of the Mil[itary] Academy . . . you cannot be appointed in the Army immediately." FC in DNA, 3, 10:216.

To C[ALLENDER] IRVINE, Philadelphia

Department of War, 5th January 1819

I have received your letter of the 28th Ult[im]o and approve of your views on the subject. It appears, however, but fair that a portion of the clothing should be made west of the mountains provided the material be as good & the clothing can be furnished as cheap as at Philadelphia adding the cost of transportation from that [city] to Newport [Ky.].

FC in DNA, 3, 10:215.

To A[NDREW] JACKSON, Nashville

Department of War, 5 Jan[uar]y 1819

I have received the letter of Col[one]l [Talbot] Chambers addressed to Col[one]l [Robert] Butler, which, by your order, has been transmitted to this Department, for instructions in relation to the subject to which it refers.

By a letter of the 28th Ult[im]o, from this Department, you were apprized of the arrangements which had been formed through the Q[uarte]r Mas[te]r Gen[era]l, [Thomas S. Jesup,] to transport the detachment intended to occupy the Missouri, with its supplies, by steam-boat; and that the arrangements would be completed, early in April. In order to meet Indian hostilities, the boat will be prepared with strong bulwarks, and will mount a few light pieces on her deck. If the Missouri will admit of such navigation, all resistance from the Indians, even if aided and instigated by British traders, will easily be overcome. In the mean time, it appears to me, that it would be imprudent for the detachment, at present, to risk anything. Its further advance, at present, if not already arrested by the ice, would be of no importance; as it would not, in the least, expedite the ultimate object of the expedition. I regret that the Indians have, in this early stage of the movements, evinced a hostile disposition; and I trust that every degree of moderation and firmness will be exercised by Capt[ai]n [Wyly] Martin, to prevent the hostility from extending itself, or becoming settled. The command requires great prudence and skill. Jealousy on the part of the Indians, ought to be expected, and soothed; and the instigation of British traders, from interest and enmity, ought to be counteracted, by seizing on every occasion to gain the confidence of the Indians; but, as I have already, in my letter of the 28th Ultimo, expressed my opinion on these points, I will not extend these observations. Everything will depend on the character of the Commander of the Expedition.

In relation to the strength of the Rifle Regiment, and the means in the power of the Department to fill up the places of the men who will be entitled to discharges, I enclose a report from the Adj[utan]t and Insp[ecto]r Gen[era]l, [Daniel Parker].

I have had several reports of ill and cruel treatment, on the part of the officers of the detachment, to persons attached to, or accompanying the Expedition. The enclosed letter exhibits a case of the kind, and appears to be absolutely prohibited by the 51st Rule of the Rules and Articles of War; and I must requ[est] your early attention to it.

LS in DLC, Andrew Jackson Papers, 8477–8478, with an AEI by Jackson indicating that this letter was received on 3/7 and how it was to be answered; FC in DNA, 5, 1:101–102; PEx in Jameson, *Correspondence*, pp. 151–152. NOTE: The letter acknowledged in Calhoun's first paragraph was written on 11/20/1818 and was relayed to Calhoun from Nashville on 12/14/1818 with a covering letter from Capt. Richard J. Easter under an order from Jackson. Chambers complained about Indian depredations in the Missouri River area and requested instructions as to countermeasures.

From Maj. S[TEPHEN] H. LONG

Pittsburgh, 5th Jan[uar]y 1819

I beg leave to represent that agreeably to Intelligence recently received from Philadelphia the two Chronometers alluded to in my late report which are in the Hands of Mr. Voyt [*sic;* Henry Voigt] of Philadelphia have been called for by Mr. [Ferdinand Rudolf] Has[s]ler, but have been withheld for a short time in consequence of the arrangement I made with Mr. V——. While at N[ew] York I sought an opportunity to see Mr. Has[s]ler, but was disappointed on account of his being absent on a journey; consequently I could make no arrangements with Mr. H. in regard to the Instruments. I have therefore to request, if Mr. H. can dispense with the use of the Chronometers that Mr. V. may be instructed to retain them on hand, 'till I call for them as I know of none else to be had.

LS in DNA, 1, L-85.

To O[rsamus] C[ook] Merrill, [Representative from Vt.,] 1/[5]. Answering his inquiry of 12/25/1818 (ALS in DNA, 1, M-134), relaying reports that some Vermonters question the propriety of permitting a U.S. Marshal to serve also as Pension Agent, Calhoun states: "As the appointment of Pension Agent has hitherto been considered as accompanying that of Marshall [*sic*] I have given it to Mr. [Heman] Allen," [who resigned in 12/1818 from the House of Representatives in order to become Marshal for the District of Vt.]. FC in DNA, 3, 10:216.

To J[OHN] SERGEANT, [Representative from Pa.]

Department of War, 5th Jan[uar]y 1819

Mr. [R.M.] Patterson's letter of the 11th ult[im]o addressed to you relative to the mathematical instruments belonging to the U[nited] States has been submitted to this departmen [by William H. Crawford]. The memorial mentioned by Mr. Patterson has never been rec[eive]d at this office. Previously to deciding upon the application of the faculty [of the American Philosophical Society for the use of some government-owned instruments], I should like to see it.

FC in DNA, 3, 10:217. NOTE: Compare the letter of 12/16/1818 from Sergeant to Crawford, an abstract of which appears herein.

Jona[than] Smith, Cashier, Bank [of the] United States, to William H. Crawford, 1/5. Pursuant to Crawford's letter of 12/23/1818 enclosing Calhoun's request that funds be made available at Baton Rouge, Smith has ordered the Bank's Branch at New Orleans "to make such an arrangement with the Bank at Baton Rouge as will ensure the accommodation required by the Secretary of War." ALS in DNA, 1, S-189.

To Samuel Smith, 1/5. Calhoun has received recently from Second Auditor [William Lee] "a statement of the appropriation of arrearages subsequently to the 1st of July, 1815. It is presumed, that the appropriation of $26,207 will be ample [for 1819 for arrearages]." Calhoun asks that this sum be inserted in the appropriation bill. FC in DNA, 4, 2:71.

To G[erard] Steddiford, New York [City], 1/5. Answers his letter of 12/30/1818 (LS in DNA, 1, S-156), in which he reported that he had just received returns listing more than 100 militia delinquents of the 110th Infantry Regiment who failed to respond to calls to service in 8/1814 and 9/1814 and stated that he was awaiting Calhoun's instructions to reassemble the N.Y. court-martial for the trial of these men. Calhoun replies: "The court has been so long sitting that I do not think it advisable [to] reassemble it to try the delinquents reported by you." FC in DNA, 3, 10:216–217.

From Archibald Thweatt, Chesterfield County, Va., 1/5. "I presume my answer [of 12/18/1818] has miscarried." Repeats that Richard H. Branch will accept a commission as a 2nd Lt., addressed to him at Manchester, Va. ALS in DNA, 11, 11937.

From D[ecius] Wadsworth, 1/5. Adds supplementary information to be reported to the House of Representatives [on 2/24] concerning four additional contracts signed in 1818 by the Ordnance Department for supplies of sabres, swords, and accoutrements for the Infantry. ALS in DNA, 1, W-269; FC with En in DNA, 32, 2:165–166; PC in *American State Papers: Military Affairs,* 1:855.

From Lewis Cass, Detroit, 1/6. He thinks it possible to secure a cession of the Saginaw Bay area from the Chippewas. "Favourable moments must be embraced for this purpose as they occur. The contiguity of these Indians to the British possessions in Canada and the use which might be made of them [by the British] in the event of any future difficulties upon this frontier furnish additional reasons in favour of this attempt." Others are the quality of the land and a desire to gain emigration by Indians who "have always been troublesome and discon[ten]ted." Cass urges also that now is a propitious time for procuring a cession of the land at the Falls of the St. Marys. LS in DNA, 1, C-155; FC in DNA, 76 (M-1:4, pp. 60–61); PC in Carter, ed., *Territorial Papers,* 10:808–809.

From Jer[emia]h Evarts, Boston, 1/6. Seeks a stay of execution for "the unhappy men condemned for Piracy & murder" there. Hopes that at least part of the travel expenses of some Indian youths who are going to the North for education will be reimbursed by the U.S. Asks if the U.S. will pay the whole cost of building a school for the Cherokees. Col. [Return J.] Meigs, if he is authorized, will pay an account for $700. ALS in DNA, 1, E-32, with an AEI by Calhoun reading: "The President [James Monroe]. The writer is a clergyman [*sic*] of great respectability."

From CALLENDER IRVINE

Phila[delphia,] Jan[uar]y 6, 1819

I have the honor to transmit herewith a consolidated return of Clothing on hand, at the several Depots, on the 1st of the present month, which is founded on the returns rec[eive]d at this office up to the 1st of Nov[embe]r 1818, excepting those from the Storekeepers near this City & at New York, whose returns are made to the 1st of the present month; in all other cases, I have deducted twenty p[e]r cent, to cover the issues for the months of Nov[embe]r & Dec[embe]r 1818, which I presume will be found to be an ample allowance. The great body of the Clothing is at the depots in the vicinity of the out Posts, and from whence it can be drawn for service with facility, at [New] Orleans, Detroit, Sacketts [*sic*] Harbor, Plattsburg, &c. The Storekeepers & Asst. Commissaries were directed to transmit to this office returns exhibiting the Clothing in their possession on the 1st of Nov[embe]r 1818, & they were particularly instructed as to the forms of the returns. Some of these returns when rec[eive]d required explanation. This circumstance, with a disposition on my part to make the return to the War Office as correct as possible, have caused a delay in its transmittal which I very much regret. The consolidated return now sent exhibits a large surplus of Clothing on hand on the 1st Jan[uar]y 1819, something larger in some Articles than I had anticipated, & considerably so in others. This I impute in a measure, to the system of issue lately in opperation [*sic*], which was a check upon officers in making requisitions. Many of the articles, however, embraced in the consolidated return are not of the present uniform, such as Cap Plates, Pompons, Artillery & other Caps &c. &c. which cannot be sold, & are therefore borne upon the Returns of the Storekeepers. Upon these articles I have made remarks upon the face of the return. No doubt a considerable portion of the Winter Clothing exhibited in the return will be issued in three months, to the Reg[imen]ts in service, & for the recruiting service, and as Caps, Blankets & Great Coats are issuable to the troops the present year, & several months must necessarily elapse before domestic material for Army Clothing can be procured, made up & forwarded to its respective destinations, I recommend that 9,000 Winter Suits of Clothing complete be provided the present year. I have noted on the return such articles as need not be purchased the present year. However, I am decidedly of opinion there should be, at all times, nearly an annual supply of Clothing on hand in advance, in which case Contracts can be made on more favorable terms for Gov[ernmen]t, the materials will be of better quality & the Clothing can be better made than if the purchases are deferred 'till the period when the Clothing is required for service. In the latter case the Army can never be regularly, properly & cheaply supplied. The experience of years fully justifies this opinion. I am aware, Sir, that Clothing is a perishable article, but it rarely happens that Clothing in depot, under the controul of this office receives damage; most of that exhibited by the return as damaged & unfit for service, is Clothing remaining from the War [of 1812], & Clothing which was abused in the possession of officers on the recruiting service, & then returned to the officers of this Dep[artmen]t. Of the first description, perhaps too much was retained at the close of the War from motives of economy, yet it would not have commanded much money, if it had been sold at public auction. My instructions to the officers of the Dep[artmen]t are, to issue first the Clothing first rec[eive]d by them. Much Clothing is lost & destroyed on the recruiting service. This perhaps cannot be avoided, & a very considerable quantity of Clothing is requisite to meet casualties. These extra issues are no doubt accounted for by deductions from the pay of the men. Still, however, the extra Clothing must be provided. As regards the recruiting service, I presume that fifteen, & perhaps twenty p[e]r cent of Clothing is lost upon it by desertion. Another advantage in having Clothing on hand, in advance, is, that the most favorable seasons for its transportation to distant Posts, & those difficult of access, & when the cost [of] carriage is lowest, can be selected. Clothing forwarded from New York [City] & Albany in August & Sept[embe]r of 1816, for Detroit did not reach it 'till May 1817, & then much of it in a damaged state, having been strewed along the lake shores. Early in the Spring & Summer of 1818, I forwarded the summer supplies for 1819 to Detroit. They all reached [that place] in safety. I repeat, Sir, my entire conviction that by having an annual supply of Clothing in advance, there will [be] economy in it, & in this way only can the Troops be regularly & well supplied. We now have this advantage & for the first time, & I think it ought not to be given up. It has been obtained by having made full Estimates for two or three years past & in consequence of the Regiments not being full. Provided the Regiments cannot be kept complete to the Establishment, deductions may be made in the Estimates, gradually & annually for some time to come.

ALS with DS in DNA, 1, I-95; FC in DNA, 45, 387:270–271.

To R[eturn] J. Meigs, Washington, Tenn.

Department of War, 6th January, 1819

I have received your letter of the 14th Novem[be]r last submitting the Claim of the Headmen of the Cherokees for Indians killed by Americans.

General [Henry] Dearborn's proposition to make pecuniary compensation for murders of this nature would seem to refer to murders which had been previously committed. But as you have extended it to cases subsequent to Gen[era]l Dearborn's letter, it seems proper to apply it in this case, and you will accordingly pay the sum of one hundred and fifty dollars to the widow of the deceased. You will inform the Chiefs that the practice will not be continued in future, as it is repugnant to those principles by which we govern ourselves in such cases.

LS in DNA, 75 (M-208:8).

To O[rsamus] C[ook] Merrill, [Representative from Vt.,] 1/6. Answers his letter of 1/5 (ALS with En in DNA, 1, M-130) enclosing David Robinson's letter of 12/19/1818 to Calhoun and proposing that Robinson be permitted to make the next semiannual pension payments in the District of Vt. Calhoun replies that instructions have already been given to the new Marshal and Pension Agent in Vt., [Heman] Allen, to make the pension payments and that "these instructions cannot be revoked. Mr. Allen is appointed Marshal and [Pension] Agent upon the recommendation of the whole delegation of Vermont except yourself." FC in DNA, 3, 10:217.

From JOHN SERGEANT, [Representative from Pa.]

Washington, Jan. 6, 1819

In reply to your note of the 5th inst[ant], received to day, I have the honor to inform you, that the memorial referred to by Mr. [R.M.] Patterson was presented during the last winter to the Secretary of the Treasury [William H. Crawford], who was then supposed to have the power of granting its request. I have written to Mr. Patterson to send me a copy, which shall be laid before you as soon as received.

ALS in DNA, 1, S-184.

To SAMUEL SMITH, Chairman, House Committee on Ways and Means

Department of War, January 6th 1819

I have received your letters of the 4th [ALS in DNA, 1, S-148] and 5th inst[ant].

I have not received the return of Clothing from the Commissary General [of Purchases, Callender Irvine,] to which you allude, but I presume no change will be necessary in the estimate of $400,000.

The estimate of $706,126 was not intended to include the Subsistence of Officers &c. but both Subsistence to Officers and men were comprehended in the aggregate of the current expences of the Army for 1819 as stated in my letter of the 19th ult[im]o.

The sum estimated for extra pay to soldiers was intended to be applied to the pay of soldiers engaged in labour upon roads as well as upon barracks and other public works. If it be determined to strike out this item ["I presume" *canceled*] about the sum of ten thousand dollars was intended to be applied to that object.

You have enclosed herewith Copies of the regulations on the subject of extra allowance to soldiers detailed for labour—the first dated in 1808, the latter in 1816.

LS with 2 Ens in DNA, 201, 15A-F3; FC in DNA, 4, 2:72; PC in House Document No. 76, 15th Cong., 2nd Sess.

From Brig. Gen. [Simon] Bernard and Maj. W[illiam] McRee, Georgetown, D.C., 1/7. They submit two documents on military education—an essay entitled "Considerations on the course of instruction necessary for the Officers of the different arms of an Army" and a "Table of a course of instruction . . ."—which concern the curriculum of the Military Academy and of the proposed additional military academy in the West but which deal especially with the proposed new school of practice or "application." LS and CC with 2 Ens in DNA, 222, F-42. (A manuscript copy of the 2 Ens is in DNA, 201, 15A-F3; a PC of the 2 Ens is in *American State Papers: Military Affairs*, 1:834–836. For Calhoun's submission of these documents to a Congressional committee, see his letter of 1/15 to Richard M. Johnson.)

Robert Bogardus, Newark, to [Joseph G.] Swift, [New York City,] 1/7. Bogardus urges Swift, when he will be in Washington, to testify that the U.S. should buy for defense purposes the land at Hell's Gate [in New York Harbor]. "The Old Lady" who owns it, [Mrs. Eleanor Lawrance,] "is extremely anxious to have her business closed." ALS in DNA, 1, S-219.

Robert Bogardus, Newark, to C[hristopher] Vandeventer, 1/7. Argues that the U.S. must buy a defense site at Hell's Gate [in New York Harbor] that it first occupied during the War of 1812, at which it has invested heavily for fortifications, but which it has never bought. ALS in DNA, 1, B-24.

From James Burrill, Jr., [Senator from R.I.,] 1/7. Introduces [1st] Lt. [John R.] Vinton, who wants to be transferred from the Artillery to the Engineers. "I have had too many proofs of your friendship to doubt your readiness to oblige on all proper occasions." ALS in DNA, 1, V-10.

To Speaker HENRY CLAY

Department of War, January 7, 1819

In compliance with a resolution of the House of Representatives of the 4th of April, 1818, instructing the Secretary of War to report to that House at their next session "a plan for the application of such means as are within the power of Congress, for the purpose of opening and constructing such roads and canals as may deserve and require the aid of Government, with a view to military operations in time of war; the transportation of munitions of war; and also a statement of the nature of the works above mentioned, which have been commenced, the progress which has been made, and the means and prospect of their completion; together with such information as, in the opinion of the Secretary, shall be material in relation to the objects of the resolution"; I have the honor to make the following report:

A judicious system of roads and canals, constructed for the convenience of commerce, and the transportation of the mail only, without any reference to military operations, is itself among the most efficient means for "the more complete defence of the United States." Without adverting to the fact that the roads and canals which such a system would require are, with few exceptions, precisely those which would be required for the operations of war, such a system, by consolidating our Union, and increasing our wealth and fiscal capacity, would add greatly to our resources in war. It is in a state of war, when a nation is compelled to put all of its resources in men, money, skill, and devotion to country into requisition, that its Government realizes in its security the beneficial effects from a people made prosperous and happy by a wise direction of its resources in peace. But I forbear to pursue this subject, though so interesting, and which, the further it is pursued, will the more clearly establish the intimate connexion between the defence and safety of the country and its improvement and prosperity, as I do not conceive that it constitutes the immediate object of this report.

There is no country to which a good system of military roads and canals is more indispensable than to the United States. As great as our military capacity is, when compared with the number of our people, yet, when considered in relation to the vast extent of our country, it is very small; and if so great an extent of territory renders it very difficult to conquer us, as has frequently been observed, it ought not to be forgotten that it renders it no less difficult for the Government to afford protection to every portion of the community. In the very nature of things, the difficulty of protecting every part, so long as our population bears so small a proportion to the extent of the country, cannot be entirely overcome, but it may be very greatly diminished, by a good system of military roads and canals. The necessity of such a system is still more apparent, if we take into consideration the character of our political maxims and institutions. Opposed in principle to a large standing army, our main reliance for defence must be on the militia, to be called out frequently from a great distance, and under the pressure of an actual invasion. The experience of the late war amply proves, in the present state of our internal improvements, the delay, the uncertainty, the anxiety, and exhausting effects of such calls. The facts are too recent to require details, and the impression too deep to be soon forgotten. As it is the part of wisdom to profit by experience, so it is of the utmost importance to prevent a recurrence of a similar state of things, by the application of a portion of our means to the construction of such roads and canals as are required "with a view to military operations in time of war, the transportation of the munitions of war, and more complete defence of the United States."

In all questions of military preparations, three of our frontiers require special attention: the eastern, or Atlantic frontier; the northern, or Canadian frontier; and the southern, or the frontier of the Gulf of Mexico. On the west and northwest we are secure, except against Indian hostilities; and the only military preparations required in that quarter are such as are necessary to keep the Indian tribes in awe, and to protect the frontier from their ravages. All of our great military efforts growing out of a war with a European Power must for the present be directed towards our eastern, northern, or southern frontiers; and the roads and canals which will enable the Government to concentrate its means for defence, promptly and cheaply, on the vulnerable points of either of those frontiers, are those which, in a military point of view, require the aid of the Government. I propose to consider each of those frontiers separately, beginning with the Atlantic, which, in many respects, is the weakest and most exposed.

From the mouth of the St. Croix to that of the St. Marys, the two extremes of this frontier, is a distance along the line of the coast and principal bays, without following their sinuosities, of about 2,100 miles. On this line, including its navigable rivers and bays, are situated our most populous cities, the great depots of the wealth and commerce of the country. That portion of it which extends to the south of the Chesapeake has, with the exceptions of the cities and their immediate neighborhood, a sparse population, with a low marshy country, extending back from 100 to 150 miles. To the north of the Chesapeake, inclusive, it affords everywhere deep and bold navigable bays and rivers, which readily admit vessels of any size. Against a line so long, so weak, so exposed, and presenting such strong motives for depredations, hostilities the most harassing and exhausting may be carried on by a naval Power; and should the subjugation of the country ever be attempted, it is probable that against this frontier, facing Europe, the seat of the great Powers of the world, the principal efforts would be turned. Thus circumstanced, it is the duty of the Government to render it as secure as possible. For much of this security we ought to look to a navy and a judicious and strong system of fortifications; but not to the neglect of such roads and canals as will enable the Government to concentrate promptly and cheaply, at any point which may be menaced, the necessary force and means for defence.

To resist ordinary hostilities, having for their object the destruction of our towns, and the exhaustion of our means, the force ought to be drawn from the country lying between the coast and the sources of the principal rivers which discharge through it into the ocean; but to resist greater efforts, aiming at conquest, should it ever be attempted, the force and resources of the whole community must be brought into resistance. To concentrate, then, a sufficient force on any point of this frontier which may be invaded, troops must be marched, and munitions of war transported either along the line of the coast, or from the interior of the Atlantic States to the coast; or, should the invading force be of such magnitude as to require it, from the western States; and the roads and canals necessary for the defence of this frontier are those which will render these operations prompt, certain, and economical.

From the coast to the Allegany [*sic*] mountains, and the high land separating the streams which enter into the St. Lawrence from those of the Atlantic, in which the principal Atlantic rivers take their rise, the distance may be averaged at about two hundred and fifty miles; and the whole extent from the St. Marys to the St. Croix is intersected at short intervals by large navigable rivers, and the principal roads of this portion of our country, through which its great commercial operations are carried on. These, aided by the steamboats now introduced on almost all of our great rivers, present great facilities to collect the militia from the interior, and to transport the necessary supplies and munitions of war.

Much undoubtedly remains to be done to perfect the roads and improve the navigation of the rivers; but this, for the most part, may be safely left to the States and the commercial cities particularly interested, as the appropriate objects of their care and exertions. The attention of both has recently been much turned towards these objects, and a few years will probably add much to facilitate the intercourse between the coast and the interior of the Atlantic States. Very different is the case with the great and important line of communication extending along the coast through the Atlantic States. No object of the kind is more important; and there is none to which State or individual capacity is more inadequate. It must be perfected by the General Government, or not be perfected at all, at least for many years. No one or two States have a sufficient interest. It is immediately beneficial to more than half of the States of the Union, and, without the aid of the General Government, would require their coöperation. It is at all times a most important object to the nation, and, in a war with a naval Power, is almost indispensable to our military, commercial, and financial operations. It may, in a single view, be considered the great artery of the country; and when the coasting trade is suspended by war, the vast intercourse between the north and south, which annually requires five hundred thousand tons of shipping, and which is necessary to the commerce, the agriculture, and manufacture of more than half of the Union, seeks this channel of communication. If it were thoroughly opened by land and water; if Louisiana were connected by a durable and well-finished road with Maine, and Boston with Savannah by a well-established line of inland navigation, for which so many facilities are presented, more than half of the pressure of war would be removed. A country so vast in its means, and abounding in its various latitudes with almost all of the products of the globe, is a world of itself; and with the facility of intercourse, to perfect which the disposable means of the country is adequate, would flourish and prosper under the pressure of a war with any Power. But, dropping this more elevated view, and considering the subject only as it regards "military operations in time of war, and the transportation of the munitions of war," what could contribute so much as this communication to the effectual and cheap defence of our Atlantic frontier? Take the line of inland navigation along the coast, the whole of which, it is estimated, could be completed for sea vessels by digging one hundred miles, and at the expence of $3,000,000, the advantage which an enemy with a naval force now has, by rapidly moving along the coast, and harassing and exhausting the country, would be in a great measure lost to him. In fact, the capacity for rapid and prompt movements and concentration would be to the full as much in our power. We would have, in most of the points of attack, a shorter line to move over, in order to concentrate our means; and, aided by steamboats, would have the capacity to pass it in a shorter time and with greater certainty, than an enemy, even with a naval superiority, would have to attack us. Suppose the fleet of such an enemy should appear off the capes of Delaware; before it could possibly approach and attack Philadelphia, information, by telegraphic communication, might be given to Baltimore and New York, and the forces stationed there thrown in for its relief. The same might take place if Baltimore or New York should be invaded; and should an attack be made on any of our cities, the militia and regular forces at a great distance along the coast could in a short time be thrown in for its relief. By this speedy communication, the regular forces, with the militia of the cities and their neighborhood, would be sufficient to repel ordinary invasions, and would either prevent, or greatly diminish, the harassing calls upon the militia of the interior. If to these considerations we add the character of the climate of the southern portion of the Atlantic frontier, so fatal to those whose constitutions are not inured to it, the value of this system of defence, by the regular troops and the militia accustomed to the climate, will be greatly enhanced.

Should this line of inland navigation be constructed, to enjoy its benefits fully it will be necessary to cover it against the naval operations of an enemy. It is thought that this may be easily effected to the south of the Chesapeake, by land and steam batteries. That bay is itself one of the most important links in this line of communication, and its defence against a naval force ought, if practicable, to be rendered complete. It was carefully surveyed the last summer by skil[l]ful officers for this purpose, in part, and it is expected that their report will throw much light upon this important subject. Long Island Sound, another part of the line which is exposed, can be fully defended by a naval force only.

It remains, in relation to the defence of the Atlantic frontier, to consider the means of communication between it and the western States, which require the aid of the Government. Most of the observations made relative to the increased strength and capacity of the country to bear up under the pressure of war, from the coastwise communication, are applicable in a high degree at present, and are daily becoming more so, to those with the western States; and should a war for conquest ever be waged against us, (an event not probable, but not to be laid entirely out of view,) the roads and canals necessary to complete the communication with that portion of our country would be of the utmost importance.

The interest of commerce and the spirit of rivalry between the great Atlantic cities will do much to perfect the means of intercourse with the west. The most important lines of communication appear to be from Albany to the lakes; from Philadelphia, Baltimore, Washington, and Richmond, to the Ohio river; and from Charleston and Augusta to the Tennessee—all of which are now commanding the attention, in a greater or less degree, of the sections of the country immediately interested. But in such great undertakings, so interesting in every point of view to the whole Union, and which may ultimately become necessary to its defence, the expense ought not to fall wholly on the portions of the country more immediately interested. As the Government has a deep stake in them, and as the system of defence will not be perfect without their completion, it ought at least to bear a proportional share of the expense of their construction.

I proceed next to consider the roads and canals connected with the defence of our northern frontier. That portion of it which extends to the east of Lake Champlain has not heretofore been the scene of extensive military operations, and I am not sufficiently acquainted with the nature of the country to venture an opinion whether we may hereafter be called on to make considerable military efforts in that quarter. Without, then, designating any military improvements as connected with this portion of our northern frontier, I would suggest the propriety, should Congress approve of the plan for a military survey of the country, to be hereafter proposed, to make a survey of it the duty of the engineers who may be designated for that purpose.

For the defence of the other part of this line of frontier, the most important objects are, a canal or water communication between

Albany and Lake George and Lake Ontario, and between Pittsburg[h] and Lake Erie. The two former have been commenced by the State of New York, and will, when completed, connected with the great inland navigation along the coast, enable the Government, at a moderate expense and in a short time, to transport munitions of war, and to concentrate its troops from any portion of the Atlantic States, fresh and unexhausted by the fatigue of marching, on the inland frontier of the State of New York. The road, commenced by order of the Executive, from Plattsburg to Sackett's [*sic*] Harbor, is essentially connected with military operations on this portion of the northern frontier. A water communication from Pittsburg[h] to Lake Erie would greatly increase our power on the upper lakes. The Allegany river, by its main branch, is said to be navigable within seven miles of Lake Erie, and by French creek within sixteen miles. Pittsburg[h] is the great military depot of the country to the west of the Alleganies, and, if it were connected by a canal with Lake Erie, would furnish military supplies with facility to the upper lakes, as well as to the country watered by the Mississippi. If to these communications we add a road from Detroit to Ohio, which has already been commenced, and a canal from the Illinois river to Lake Michigan, which the growing population of the State of Illinois renders very important, all the facilities which would be essential "to carry on military operations in time of war, and the transportation of the munitions of war" for the defence of the western portion of our northern frontiers, would be afforded.

It only remains to consider the system of roads and canals connected with the defence of our southern frontier, or that on the Gulf of Mexico. For the defence of this portion of our country, though at present weak of itself, nature has done much. The bay of Mobile, and the entrance into the Mississippi through all its channels, are highly capable of defence. A military survey has been made, and the necessary fortifications have been commenced, and will be in a few years completed. But the real strength of this frontier is the Mississippi, which is no less the cause of its security than that of its commerce and wealth. Its rapid stream, aided by the force of steam, can, in the hour of danger, concentrate at once an irresistible force. Made strong by this noble river, little remains to be done by roads and canals for the defence of our southern frontier. The continuation of the road along the Atlantic coast from Milledgeville to New Orleans, and the completion of the road which has already been commenced from Tennessee river to the same place, with the inland navigation through the canal of Carondelet, Lake Pontchartrain, and the islands along the coast, to Mobile, covered against the operations of a naval force, every facility required for the transportation of munitions of war, and movements and concentration of troops, to protect this distant and important frontier, would be afforded.

Such are the roads and canals which military operations in time of war, the transportation of the munitions of war, and the more complete defence of the United States, require.

Many of the roads and canals which have been suggested are no doubt of the first importance to the commerce, the manufacture, the agriculture, and political prosperity of the country, but are not, for that reason, less useful or necessary for military purposes. It is, in fact, one of the great advantages of our country, enjoying so many others, that, whether we regard its internal improvements in relation to military, civil, or political purposes, very nearly the same system, in all its parts, is required. The road or canal can scarcely be designated, which is highly useful for military operations, which is not equally required for the industry or political prosperity of the community. If those roads or canals had been pointed out which are necessary for military purposes only, the list would have been small indeed. I have, therefore, presented all, without regarding the fact that they might be employed for other uses which, in the event of war, would be necessary to give economy, certainty, and success to our military operations, and which, if they had been completed before the late war, would, by their saving in that single contest in men, money, and reputation, have more than indemnified the country for the expense of their construction. I have not prepared an estimate of expenses, nor pointed out the particular routes for the roads or canals recommended, as I conceive that this can be ascertained with satisfaction only by able and skil[l]ful engineers, after a careful survey and examination.

I would therefore respectfully suggest as the *basis* of the system, and the first measure in the "plan for the application of such means as are in the power of Congress," that Congress should direct such a survey and estimate to be made, and the result to be laid before them as soon as practicable. The expense would be inconsiderable, for, as the army can furnish able military and topographical engineers, it would be principally confined to the employment of one or more skil[l]ful civil engineers to be associated with them. By their combined skill, an efficient system of military roads and canals would be presented in detail, accompanied with such estimates of expenses as may be relied on. Thus, full and satisfactory information would be had; and though some time might be lost in the commencement of the system, it would be more than compensated by its assured efficiency when completed.

For the construction of the roads and canals which Congress may choose to direct, the army, to a certain extent, may be brought in aid of the moneyed resources of the country. The propriety of employing the army on works of public utility cannot be doubted. Labor adds to its usefulness and health. A mere garrison life is equally hostile to its vigor and discipline; both officers and men become the subjects of its deleterious effects. But when the vast extent of our country is compared with the extent of our military establishment, and taking into consideration the necessity of employing the soldiers on fortifications, barracks, and roads, connected with remote frontier posts, we ought not to be sanguine in the expectation of aid to be derived from the army in the construction of permanent military roads and canals at a distance from the frontiers. When our military posts come to be extended up the Mississippi and Missouri as far as is contemplated, the military frontier of the United States, not including sinuosities, and the coasts of navigable bays and lakes opening into our country, as was stated in a former report, will present a line of more than nine thousand miles, and, including them, of more than eleven thousand. Thinly scattered along so extensive a frontier, it will be impossible, I fear, without leaving some points exposed, to collect any considerable bodies in the interior of the country to construct roads and canals.

As connected with this subject, I would respectfully suggest the propriety of making an adequate provision for the soldiers while regularly and continually employed in constructing works of public utility. The present allowance is fifteen cents a day, which is considered sufficient in occasional fatigue duty, such as is now done at most of the posts; but if systematic employ[ment] on permanent works should be made the regular duty of the soldiers who can be spared for that purpose, a compensation (taking into the estimate the obligation of the Government to provide medical attention and pensions to the diseased and disabled soldiers) not much short of the wages of daily labor ought to be granted to them. Without such provision, which is dictated by justice, an increase of desertion and difficulty in obtaining recruits ought to be expected. Among the leading inducements to enlist is the exemption from labor; and if the life of a soldier should be equally subjected to it as that of other citizens in the same grade, he will prefer, if the wages are much inferior, to labor for himself to that of laboring for the public. The pay of a soldier is sixty dollars per annum; and if he were allowed, when employed permanently on fatigue, twenty-five cents a day, and suppose him to be employed two hundred days in the year, his compensation, including his pay, would be one hundred and ten dollars per annum—a sum, it is thought, considerably short of the average wages of labor. If this sum should be allowed, the greater portion of it ought to be paid at the expiration of the term of enlistment. If fifteen cents a day were so reserved, and the soldier should be employed one thousand days in the five years for which he is enlisted, it would constitute a sum of one hundred and fifty dollars, to be paid at the expiration of his term, which ought, in the same manner as the bounty land, to be made to depend on an honorable discharge. This would furnish an important hold on the fidelity of the soldier, and would be a powerful check to the great and growing crime of desertion. An honorable discharge is now worth but little to the soldier, and the consequence is, that desertions are more frequent with those enlisted since the war than those who were then enlisted, and are entitled to the bounty in land on their honorable discharge; the latter patiently waits the expiration of his term of service, while the former frequently seizes the first favorable opportunity for desertion.

Should Congress think proper to commence a system of roads and canals for the "more complete defence of the United States," the disbursement of the sums appropriated for the purpose might be made by the Department of War, under the direction of the President. Where incorporated companies are already formed, or the road or canal commenced under the superintendence of a State, it perhaps would be advisable to direct a subscription on the part of the United States, on such terms and conditions as might be thought proper. In other cases, and where the army cannot be made to execute it, the work ought to be done by contract, under the superintendence and inspection of officers of the engineer corps, to be detailed for that purpose. It is thus the Government will be able, it is thought, to construct on terms at least as favorable as corporate companies. The system of constructing all public works (which admit of it) by contract would be attended with important advantages. It has recently been adopted in the construction of fortifications, and, it is expected, will be attended with beneficial effects. The principal works at Mobile and New Orleans have been contracted for on terms considerably under the estimates of the engineers. Such a system extended to military roads and canals, combined with a careful inspection and superintendence by skil[l]ful engineers, will enable the Government to complete them with economy, durability, and despatch.

In the view which has been taken, I have thought it improper, under the resolution of the House, to discuss the constitutional question, or how far the system of internal improvements which has been presented may be carried into effect on the principles of our Government; and, therefore, the whole of the arguments which are used, and the measures proposed, must be considered as depending on the decision of that question.

The only military roads which have been commenced are, from Plattsburg to Sackett's Harbor, through the Chateaugay country; from the southern boundary of the State of Tennessee, and crossing the Tennessee river, near the Muscle Shoals, to Madisonville, Louisiana; and from Detroit to Fort Meigs, at the foot of the rapids of the Miami of the Lakes. Documents marked A, B, and C show the progress which has been made. These roads have been commenced and thus far completed by the labor of the soldiers, who, while they are so employed, receive fifteen cents per day, with an extra allowance of a gill of whiskey [*sic*]. The labor of the troops is the only means within the reach of the Department of completing these roads; and as the troops are so employed only when they are not engaged in active service, it is impossible to state with accuracy when the roads will be completed.

PC with 3 Ens in *American State Papers: Miscellaneous,* 2:533–537; LS with 3 Ens in DNA, 201, 15A-F3; LI (or rough draft) in NN, James Monroe Papers; FC with 3 Ens in DNA, 4, 2:72–81; PC in Crallé, ed., *Works,* 5:40–54. NOTE: Enclosure A was the letter from Jacob Brown to Calhoun dated 12/6/1818, reporting about the progress of the road from Plattsburg to Sackets Harbor. Enclosure B was the letter from Robert Butler to Calhoun dated 9/19/1818, reporting the progress of the road from Columbia, Tenn., to Madisonville, La. Enclosure C was the letter from Alexander Macomb to

Calhoun dated 11/2/1818, reporting the progress of the road from Detroit to Fort Meigs.

To PATRICK [NOBLE, Abbeville, S.C.]

War Dept., 7th Jan[uar]y 1819

I have received your letter of the 17th Dec[embe]r; and can assure you that your election to the Speaker's chair [of the S.C. House of Representatives], was to me a most gratifying event. I think it fortunate that you did not succeed as [a candidate for the office of] Solicitor, as it has afforded the legislature an opportunity to give a more distinguished proof of the confidence which they have in your talents and judgment. With prudence, the post which you now occupy will enable you to attain any office in the gift of the State which you may desire. You will soon render yourself familiar with the duties of the chair. They are few and not very complicated.

I am delighted with the zeal which the legislature has discovered on the subject of internal improv[e]m[en]ts. They have acted in the sperit [*sic*] of munificence; and if the sums are wisely applied, will add much to the prosperity of the State. The great fear is that instead of directing the fund to a few great objects to be completed in the most durable manner, it will be disapated [*sic*] on a multitude of small objects, which will add not much to the prosperity of the State.

I regret that the amendment to the Constitution proposed by N[orth] Carolina did not succeed. I deem it almost the only amend[men]t of much importance which has been proposed. It would add exceedingly to the solidity of our political insti[tu]tions. The smaller States particularly have a deep stake in it; and I can not see by what argum[en]ts it could be opposed in our State.

We are all well, and we expect to be in Abbeville early in May. We shall go by the way of Charleston. Floride joins her love to you and Eliz[abet]h. Rem[em]ber me affectionat[e]ly to all of my old village friends.

P.S. I hope most sinc[ere]ly that [Langdon] Cheves may be elected Pr[esiden]t of the national bank. The institution has need of his talents and firmness. I think there is considerable expectation of his election. J.C.C.

ALS in ScCleA; variant PC in *The Journal of Southern History,* vol. XVI, no. 1 (February, 1950), pp. 68–69. NOTE: Calhoun's third paragraph presumably refers to a recent vote in the S.C. legislature against ratification of an amendment to the Constitution of the United States that had been proposed in 1813 by N.C.; it would require the elections of members of the U.S. House of Representatives by districts and the choosing of Presidential electors by districts. Ames, *The Proposed Amendments to the Constitution of the United States during the First Century of Its History,* 2:56–57 and 80–83.

From Daniel Parker, 1/7. He reports what allowances in cash, additions to rations, and clothing have been granted, under regulations of 1801, 1812, 1813, and 1816 and under present regulations, to noncommissioned officers and Privates who, as artificers or otherwise, have performed extra labor on such projects as fortifications and roads. He encloses a printed General Order of 9/11/1818, signed by himself, concerning the cultivation of vegetable gardens at all permanent Army posts. LS with En in DNA, 1, P-99; FC in DNA, 12, 5:160.

From [Daniel Parker], 1/7. Complying with orders from Calhoun, [Parker] reports about several things. His most recent general return of the Army, submitted during the present session of Congress, includes all the information that he can now supply about the strength and distribution of the Army. "I have no reports which will enable me to state the number of days of extra labour performed by the troops, during the last year, except that from the 6th Inf[antr]y, stationed at Plattsburg. Colonel [Henry] Atkinson" has reported 25,716 days of extra labor between 4/1/1818 and 10/31/1818 having been devoted by the 6th to repairing muskets, barracks, and fortifications and to the building of roads—and this excludes the hours devoted to the cultivation of a garden for the production of food for the Regiment. The Army's Northern Division having been enlarged to include the area northward of a line drawn from the southern tip of Lake Michigan to the mouth of the Rock River, the 5th Infantry Regiment will be sent from Detroit to Mississippi River posts; it will relieve there the Riflemen, "who are to occupy the posts below & on the Missouri & Arkansas." A new unit will probably be needed to replace the 5th Regiment at Detroit; probably the 2nd Infantry Regiment will be moved from Sackets Harbor or the 6th from Plattsburg. "These changes will necessarily lessen the extra labour of the troops," and Parker cannot anticipate what fatigue duty will be performed this year other than that some fortresses and barracks will be repaired, some new posts constructed on the frontier, and some gardens cultivated in accordance with Calhoun's order of 9/11/1818. LU with En in DNA, 1, P-98; FC in DNA, 12, 5:161.

From Stephen Pleasonton, 1/7. Answers Calhoun's request of 1/6, pursuant to a House resolution, for information concerning the adjustment and payment of claims of the friendly Creek Indians under a treaty of 8/9/1814. Pleasonton says that the claims arose instead under a statute of 3/3/1817, which appropriated $85,000 to indemnify property damages inflicted upon the friendly Creeks by hostile Creeks. Pleasonton submits some accounts and correspondence that he has received from D[avid] B. Mitchell. LS with CCEx's in DNA, 77 (M-271:2, frames 1542–1548); FC in DNA, 58, 1:102–103.

D[ecius] Wadsworth to [Christopher] Vandeventer, 1/7. Wadsworth answers the inquiries of W.H. Sabine, communicated through [James] Tallmadge, [Jr.]. During 1817 or 1818 it was intended to contract with a Judge Forman, who would manufacture cannon shot and shells to supply the posts at Sackets Harbor, at Niagara, and beside the upper Great Lakes. Because Congress appropriated no funds "for new Contracts for Cannon & Shot, the Business was dropped. The Shot and Shells made by Judge Forman during the late War were among the best we have ever had, and I should feel very desirous of giving him further Encouragement should we have any funds to spare during the present Year applicable to that object." FC in DNA, 32, 2:167.

From JOHN WILLIAMS, [Senator from Tenn.]

Senate Chamber, Jan[uar]y 7th 1819

The Senate will probably pass a resolution requesting the President [James Monroe] to institute a negotiation with the Chickasaw tribe of Indians to purchase a reservation reserved to the Indians, including a salt spring. The same if purchased will be for the benefit of the State of Tennessee. Permit me to request that you will cause the Agent to said Tribe [Henry Sherburne], to request of the Indians not to sign any *other* lease until further advised on that subject by the general Government.

ALS in DNA, 1, W-142.

From William Clark, Louisville, [Ky.,] 1/8. Introduces Benjamin O'Fallon, Indian Agent to the tribes on the Missouri River; encloses a memorandum concerning a purchase of Indian lands and bearing the approval both of prominent Indian Chiefs and of U.S. Army men. ALS with En in DNA, 1, C-172.

From Edmund P. Gaines, Fernandina, E[ast] F[la.], 1/8. As Calhoun authorized on 9/23/1818, Gaines wrote on 10/14 an order that Capt. Thomas F. Hunt, Quartermaster officer at New Orleans, should send $6,000 to Col. William King. Hunt has claimed that he has no funds available. Gaines still considers the payment necessary "to defray the current expenses at Pensacola" and "also to afford a moderate advance upon the charter of transports for the troops [of the 4th Infantry Regiment] to Fort Gadsden" if an advance into East Fla. is to be undertaken. ALS in DNA, 1, G-91.

To John Jamison, Natchitoches, La., 1/8. "I have received your letter of the 6th ultimo [ALS in DNA, 1, J-89]. The Indians must be made to yield the exercise of their barbarous custom of retaliation upon murderers, to the milder influence of our laws. You will not, therefore, surrender the Pascagoula Indian & family to the Choctaws nor permit the latter in any way to disturb the peace of the former. Should they persist and commit any outrage upon the persons of the Pascagoulas, it will be considered an offence against the United States, and the offenders must be arraigned and tried under our laws." FC in DNA, 72, D:241.

From C[harles] Jouett, Lexington, Ky., 1/8. [Lewis] Cass has given him permission to move his family from Chicago to Ky., to visit Washington, and to travel to Salem, N.C., in order "to take from school a daughter, I have not seen for three years." The illness of Mrs. Jouett has delayed his trip to Washington; but he will report there as soon as possible and will then tender his bond. ALS in DNA, 1, J-88.

From Joseph McMinn, Murfreesboro, [Tenn.,] 1/8. Explains in much detail three reasons why he has authorized the [Eastern] Cherokee "emigrants to dispose of their possessions previous to their departure" and why he believes that the best interests of both the emigrants and the U.S. are being served by not delaying these purchases. He makes this explanation in writing largely because he fears that he may not be able to join the Eastern Cherokee Delegation in Washington for conferences with Calhoun. FC (dated 7/8/1819) and draft (endorsed 1/15/1819) in DNA, 75 (M-208:14).

From Lt. Col. William MacRea, Fort Nelson, [Norfolk,] 1/8. Pursuant to Calhoun's letter of 8/12/1818, MacRea reports that Robert Taylor wants no more soldiers buried in his land adjacent to Fort Norfolk; MacRea has issued an order to that effect to the commanding officer. ALS in DNA, 1, M-164.

To John Rhea, Chairman, House Committee on Revolutionary Claims, 1/8. Returns the petition of Reuben Colburn, together with a report by P[eter] Hagner [dated 1/7 (FC in DNA, 53, 9:120)] stating that lost records make it impossible to find information relevant to Colburn's claim, that it seems "extraordinary" that such a claim should have remained unpaid during 1775–1783, and that it was voided by the statute of limitations in 1794. FC in DNA, 3, 10:218.

To Henry Sherburne, 1/8. Expects instructions to be issued for a treaty with the Chickasaws to acquire a part of their reservation, including Salt Spring. Tell them to sign no new lease until advised by Calhoun. FC in DNA, 72, D:241.

To H[enry] Shaw, [Representative from Mass.,] 1/8. In reply to his inquiry of 1/6 (ALS in DNA, 1, S-186), expressing his desire to become a bidder if the U.S. plans to discontinue and to sell Greenbush Cantonment [in N.Y.], Calhoun states that no such decision has been reached but that any such sale will be made by public auction. FC in DNA, 3, 10:218.

To Henry Southard, [Representative from N.J.]

Department of War, 8th January, 1819

I have the honor to enclose you copies of three proposed acts in relation to Indian Affairs, prepared in conformity to the report made by the Department on the 5th ultimo, and, with the following exceptions, in accordance with your own suggestions.

It is proposed to limit the duration of the licenses to trade with the Indians to five years, as, in case it should hereafter be found desirable to change or modify the system, the unlimited duration of the licenses might present an obstacle thereto.

So much of an act passed on the 20th of April 1818 as provides for an Indian Agent to the Lakes, is proposed to be repealed, so far as it fixes his Agency to the Lakes, and it is proposed, that the President of the United States should be authorized to employ the said Agent on the Mississippi and its waters, above Prairie du Chien, as the contemplated extension of our posts to the mouth of the St. Peters, will render an Agent necessary at that point.

In consequence of the extension of our military posts to the Yellow Stone river, it is deemed desirable to authorize the appointment of two additional Indian Agents to be employed on the Missouri and its waters; and as these two Agencies are considered very important, it is proposed to fix their compensation at $1,800 p[e]r annum, in order to command the most suitable talents.

There is a blank left in the 2d section of the act incorporating the American Fur Company, to be filled up with the title of the Bank in the Territory of Missouri in which it is proposed that the Commissioners shall deposit the payments received by them on account of subscriptions. The Delegate [from Mo. Territory, John Scott,] will, I presume, be able to inform you of the name of the Bank.

FC in DNA, 4, 2:82.

From 2nd Lt. John R. Vinton, Washington, 1/8. Having completed his work in the survey of the northern boundary of the U.S., he wants to join [Ferdinand R.] Hassler in a survey of harbors. Hassler has complimented Vinton and has requested an assignment of Vinton to his unit. ALS in DNA, 1, V-10.

From Decius Wadsworth, 1/8. Transmits information received since he wrote on 12/23/1818 about the sale of the furnace tract near Harpers Ferry. FC in DNA, 32, 2:167–170.

Pension Certificate of Samuel Baker, 1/9. Certifies that this former Pvt. in the Revolutionary forces is to receive $8 per month in Me. from 12/13/1818. DS in ScU-SC, John C. Calhoun Papers.

From Andrew Bartle, [Alexandria, D.C.,] 1/9. Reviving an old claim, Bartle seeks compensation for work that he did some years ago in connection with Fort Washington. He believes, in particular, that he and the U.S. have been defrauded by Maj. Marsteller [former Capt. Ferdinand Marsteller ?], and he seems to accuse Peter Hagner and others of consciously conniving in a plan of systematic profiteering. LS in DNA, 1, B-149.

To Maj. Gen. JACOB BROWN, Brownville, N.Y.

Department of War, 9th January 1819

I have received your letter of the 13th ult[im]o and submitted it to the President's [James Monroe's] consideration. He approves the connection suggested by you of the St. Lawrence with Lake Champlain, by a road, from Plattsburg to some suitable point on the St. Lawrence, below Sacketts Harbour, at Hamilton, for example, or Ogdensburg, or some other point in that quarter. From the point at which the road from Plattsburg strikes the St. Lawrence, the communication should be along the river, or as near it as may be convenient and proper. He doubts the advantage of opening roads, in different directions, from Plattsburg towards Montreal, or to any point immediately above or below it. In the event of another war with G[reat] Britian [*sic*], should we invade Canada, as may be presumed, we shall probably do it from Lake Champlain or from that quarter, or from some point on the St. Lawrence, either that where the road from Plattsburg strikes the St. Lawrence, or at no great distance from it. Roads therefore from Plattsburg, or from any other point on the communication between Plattsburg and the St. Lawrence, towards Montreal, would be of little use to us, in the event of our invading Canada. In the event, however, of a war of invasion, by G[reat] Britian, which, however improbable, is always to be guarded against, all such improvements would operate in her favor.

The great advantage of a communication from Lake Champlain to the St. Lawrence, in a line from Plattsburg to a proper point on that river and along the river, to the other important posts at Sacketts Harbour, is, that, in case of war, it would operate, exclusively, in our favor. By means of this communication, the intercourse between our troops on the St. Lawrence and Lake Champlain would be perfectly easy, the want of which, in the last war, was so severely felt. To our posts on Lake Champlain and St. Lawrence, from the interior of the country, the roads will of course be sufficiently good, whereas in case of an invasion from Canada, the enemy would cross the road, as soon as he touched it, provided he was in force and had a view to conquest.

These remarks are presented for consideration. You are requested to weigh them and to communicate the result of your reflections on them.

LS in MHi; FC dated 1/10/1819 in DNA, 3, 10:218–219; CC dated 1/9/1819 in DLC, Jacob Brown Papers, Letterbooks, 2:170–171.

From Lewis Cass, Detroit, 1/9. Acknowledges Calhoun's letter of 12/15/1818 with a copy of [John] Johnston's letter. Recommends the appointment as Agent to the Wyandots at Upper Sandusky of [Benjamin] Stickney, whose usefulness as Sub-Agent at Fort Wayne has been diminished by his honorable conduct in an issue involving whisky. Johnston's recommendation as to a successor at Fort Wayne will be so trustworthy that it should be accorded "great weight." If [Charles] Jouett resigns as Agent at Chicago, Cass agrees with Johnston that the Sub-Agent there, John Kinzie, should be appointed Agent. LS in DNA, 1, C-155; FC in DNA, 76 (M-1:4, pp. 61–62).

From Thomas Grimbrede, New York [City], 1/9. "I have had the honour of receiving the letter of appointment requesting me to go to West Point immediately. I feel grateful for your polite attention & am now busily employed settling my affairs in order to leave New York [City] for the Point in the begin[n]ing of the next week." LS in DNA, 15, 1819, 117.

Invoice from George Miller, [*ca.* 1/9]. Bills the U.S. for boarding seven groups of Cherokees a total of 88 man-days at $1 per person per day, without stating the place, [probably Alexandria or Georgetown, D.C.,] between 10/19/1818 and 1/4/1819, inclusive. An undated AEI by Calhoun reads: "Allowed." An AES by Lund Washington, a Clerk in the [First] Comptroller's [Joseph Anderson's] Office, is dated "Jan[uar]y 9th 1818 [probably an inadvertent error for 1819]." DU in U.S. General Accounting Office, Indian Tribal Branch, Fifth Auditor Accounts, no. 595, "Reports of the account of George Miller (Cherokee)."

From Smith Thompson, [Secretary of the Navy, Washington,] 1/9. Upon request of Francis Bloodgood, "who has been many years one of the Clerks of the Supreme Court of New York," Thompson urges that the application for a Cadet's warrant for William Bloodgood be accepted. ALS in DNA, 15, 1818, 145.

From Edward Colston, [Representative from Va., *ca.* 1/10]. Requests apologetically Calhoun's attention anew to the claim of "a poor woman with a large family whose interests are most deeply affected by the decision of the [War] department," [Catherine (Mrs. John) Wager of Harpers Ferry]. Her claim has previously been considered "but perhaps not with so much evidence." Colston submits in evidence one three-year-old deposition. (An EU indicates that this letter was received or filed in 1/1819.) ALS in DNA, 1, C-145.

From [Bvt.] Col. H[enry] Leavenworth, Detroit, 1/10. On 11/7/1818 he recommended Joseph Gleason for the position of Assistant Commissary [of Subsistence] at the Detroit and Grosse Isle posts; but Gleason's health is precarious. Leavenworth believes 1st Lt. Thomas Hunt to be better qualified for the position. ALS in DNA, 11, 13403.

From Andrew Bartle, Alexandria, [D.C.,] 1/11. Supplements his accusations [of 1/9] of fraud against himself and the U.S. practiced more than two years ago by a Maj. Marsteller [former Capt. Ferdinand Marsteller ?] in connection with a construction contract for Fort Washington; implicates Peter Hagner, whose records Bartle has examined and found to include forged and otherwise false documents. Bartle's losses, almost ruinous, appear to have been about $10,000. LS in DNA, 1, B-149.

From [Simon] Bernard, 1/11. Reports the curricula of the Polytechnic School at Paris and of the School of Application at Metz, for the information of a Congressional committee that is studying U.S. military schools. ALS in DNA, 1, B-145.

To Robert Brent, 1/11. Supplementing the order given by Calhoun to Brent on 3/12/1818 [*The Papers of John C. Calhoun,* 2:186] to deposit his public funds in the Bank of the United States, Calhoun directs Brent to instruct the employees in the Paymaster General's office to keep their personal accounts in the same Bank. FC in DNA, 3, 10:219.

To Daniel Burnet, Grindstone Ford, Miss., 1/11. Acknowledges his letter of 12/16/1818 (ALS in DNA, 1, B-131) submitting his claim for $330 for his services as a treaty commissioner in 10/1818 with the Choctaws; informs him that his account cannot be approved until he certifies that he was actually engaged in that business during the time alleged. FC in DNA, 72, D:241.

From J[AMES] L. EDWARDS

War Department, Pension Office, Jan[uar]y 11, 1819

In obedience to your order of Saturday last, requiring me to give my opinion, as to the expediency of an amendment to the act of the 18th of March, last [providing pensions for Revolutionary veterans who are in reduced circumstances], as far as relates to the taking of testimony, in applications for pensions under that act, I have to state to you, that I consider any alteration at this time unnecessary. Almost any attempts at fraud, in relation to service, can be detected by the [muster] rolls and other means of information within the reach of the Department. The only description of persons who will be likely to succeed in obtaining the provisions of that act improperly, is that portion who are in easy circumstances (and of course, are not contemplated by the law) but whose services are not questioned. Requiring other testimony, however, than the claimant's own declaration as to his pecuniary situation, will, in general, be an effectual guard against imposition.

Since the first of November, last, only eighteen hundred applications have been received at this office. For the seven months immediately preceding that period, no less that 20,000 were received. The great mass of claims, therefore, have been already presented, and among the few that remain to come in, there will not be, I presume, so many spurious ones as to require legislative interposition.

LS in DNA, 1, E-31; FC in DNA, 91, 6:174.

Solomon U. Hendrick and other Chiefs of the New Stockbridge Indians, at New Stockbridge, to James Monroe, 1/11. They petition for adjustment of several matters that involve their relationships with the Delaware and Miami Indians. A kind of postcript dated at Washington on 1/22, signed by Hendrick and two other New Stockbridge Chiefs, points out that the Treaty of St. Marys with the Delawares on 10/3/1818 failed to reserve to the New Stockbridge Indians some land granted to them in 1808. LS in DNA, 1, D-93.

To C[allender] Irvine, Philadelphia, 1/11. Acknowledges his letter of 1/6 (ALS with DS in DNA, 1, I-95; FC in DNA, 45, 387: 270–271) enclosing and discussing at length his return of clothing supplies on hand as of 1/1; questions one comment made in the return, to the effect that commanding officers have authority to requisition the 11,276 fatigue frocks and 5,449 fatigue trousers that were on hand: "I have not been able to find such authority on our records. Will you communicate to me a copy of the order to which you allude? The last regulations allow only one fatigue frock and one pair of fatigue trousers annually." FC in DNA, 3, 10:220.

From T[homas] S. Jesup, 1/11. Capt. [Thomas] Tupper was not authorized to draw on Col. [James R.] Mullany for funds. Persons holding Tupper's drafts have no just claim against the U.S., because they failed to investigate Tupper's authority. If the government be held responsible for the unauthorized acts of Tupper, the only logical conclusion would be that the War Department is subject to the control of its subordinate officers. LS in DNA, 201,

17A-E4; FC in DNA, 42, 1:158; PC in House Report No. 69, 17th Cong., 1st Sess.; PC in House Report No. 28, 17th Cong., 2nd Sess.; PC in *American State Papers: Claims,* 1:841.

To Thomas S. Jesup, 1/11. "I enclose for your information a copy of a letter addressed by the Cash[ie]r of the U.S. Bank, to the Secretary of the Treasury. In addition to orders of the 5th of June last [*see* Christopher Vandeventer to Jesup, June 5, 1818, in *The Papers of John C. Calhoun,* 2:330] you will instruct the officers of your Department to keep their private accounts in [the] Bank, seperate [*sic*] and distinct from their public acc[oun]t." FC in DNA, 3, 10:219.

To [James Monroe], 1/11. Complying with a Senate resolution of 1/5 (ADS by Charles Cutts in DNA, 1, S-188; CC in DNA, 31, War Department) requesting information about the strength and distribution of the Army's personnel and ordnance, Calhoun encloses reports to himself by D[aniel] Parker [dated 1/9 (LS in DNA, 152, 15A-E5; FC in DNA, 12, 5:162)] and by Decius Wadsworth [dated 1/11 (LS in DNA, 152, 15A-E5; FC in DNA, 32, 2:170)]. (Monroe submitted to the Senate on 1/11 this report from Calhoun.) LS with Ens in DNA, 152, 15A-E5; FC in DNA, 6, 1:342; PC with Ens in Senate Document No. 58, 15th Cong., 2nd Sess.; PC with Ens in *American State Papers: Military Affairs,* 1:813–821.

To William A[dams] Palmer, [Senator from Vt.,] 1/11. "I have rec[eive]d from Mr. [Heman] Allen his bond for the faithful performance of the duties of Pension Agent and Commissioner of Loans [in the District of Vt.]. The rule of this department requires that the sufficiency of the sureties be certified by the District Attorney, district Judge or a member of Congress. I have sent the bond to you believing that you are acquainted with the parties and may be able to give the certificate." FC in DNA, 3, 10:220.

To E[ldred] "Simpkins [*actually* Simkins]," [Representative from S.C.,] 1/11. Answers the major item discussed in his protest of 1/3 (ALS in DNA, 1, L-68) that a payment due to a Dr. McWhorter at Augusta for about $36 worth of medical services rendered to soldiers there under an authorization given by [Edmund

P.] Gaines should not be withheld because of failure to comply with red-tape requirements; assures Simkins that a certificate certifying that Dr. McWhorter was actually employed by an Army officer and a statement of the prices of the medicines used must be submitted as evidence that the account is "reasonable." FC in DNA, 3, 10:219–220.

From WILLIAM SMITH, [Senator from S.C.]

Senate Chamber, January 11th 1819

If it is possible to grant it, I would entreat you for a warrant for Lydall Saxon as a Cadet at the military academy.

I am influenced to this application from the peculiar worth of this youth.

He is an orphan of fifteen years old, a native of Laurens District, South Carolina. He has all the advantages of a vigorous mind, a fine person, and a literary education, that few of his age have attained; and among his literary acquirements, he is an excellent Latin and Greek scholar.

I have no doubt but that he would do honor to the appointment.

I believe but very few young men from that State have been admitted to this honor.

ALS in DNA, 15, 1818, 142½.

To Gerard Steddiford, New York [City], 1/11. "The Militia Gen[era]l Court Martial whereof Maj. Gen. Gerard Steddiford is President is dissolved. The President of the Court and one of the judge advocates to be selected by the President, will be considered in service for the purpose of completing the records of the Court and of examining & reporting to the Secretary of War upon such cases as may be presented to them." FC in DNA, 3, 10:219.

From GEORGE WATTERSTON, [Librarian of Congress]

Jan[uar]y 11th 1819

Agreeably to my promise, I have examined the different works in the Lib[rar]y which I supposed would contain information on the subject of the fur trade; but my search has been fruitless & unsatisfactory. You will find some facts, not uninteresting in Colqhoun's "Resources of the British Empire," but the best authority I can direct you to, is a pamphlet on the subject written by Lord LeCherk [?] & now, I believe in the possession of Mr. R[ufus] King [Senator from N.Y.]. This, I think, contains every thing you may require.

ALS in DNA, 1, W-142.

From H[enry] Atkinson, Plattsburg, [N.Y.,] 1/12. "Presuming that Brevet Major [Turner] Crooker, under an impression that there would not be a Court ordered for his trial at an early day, has applied for a Court of inquiry to investigate his conduct relative to charges prefer[r]ed against him by Major [Gad] Humphreys, I beg leave to inform you that a General Court Martial has recently been ordered to convene at this Post on the 15th instant, before which he will be arraigned." LS in DNA, 11, 13247; FC in DNA, 181, p. 67.

From Edmund P. Gaines, Fernandina, E[ast] F[la.], 1/12. Encloses copies of letters exchanged between Maj. J[ames] M. Glassell and Don José Coppinger, the Spanish Governor of East Fla., concerning certain U.S. citizens wounded, captured, and held as prisoners by the Spanish. ALS with Ens in DNA, 1, G-81; ALS in DNA, 11, 13377.

From Peter Hagner, 1/12. Reports the payments he has made for labor upon roads and other objects of fatigue duty by U.S. troops from 10/1/1817 to 10/1/1818, to which he adds the probable cost of extra whisky. No extra clothing has been allowed. ALS in DNA, 1, H-122; FC in DNA, 53, 9:136.

To A[bner] Lacock, [Senator from Pa.]

Department of War, 12th January 1819

I have received your letter of the 8th instant [ALS in DNA, 1, L-69] with the resolution enclosed [inquiring whether a certain kind of amendment to the act of 3/18/1818 providing Revolutionary pensions would "prevent frauds on the Government"], and after mature consideration, I respectfully submit, to the committee [on Pensions], my opinion that no amendment to the act of the 18th March 1818 "providing for certain persons engaged in the land and naval service of the United States, in the revolutionary war," is a[d]viseable.

It is most probable that by far the greater part of the claims have been received at the [War] Department; as, since the 1st of November last, only eighteen hundred applications have been made, and this, at a moment when, from the convening of Congress, they would, of course, come in.

It is presumed, that no legislative interposition could affect claims already received, whose proofs have been perfected under the present act; and, it is believed, that those yet to come in are, for the most part, of the poor and ignorant, who are least able to bear the additional expense and trouble [to which] any further legislative interposition would necessarily subject them.

With respect to frauds, there is no reason to believe that any attempts of that nature have been made in relation to service; and if they were, they would most probably be detected by a recurrence [that is, reference] to the rolls and other means of information within the reach of the Department. If any impositions have been attempted, it is supposed that it has been under that part of the act which relates to the ["reduced"] circumstances of the applicant, by persons who are more wealthy than the act was intended to embrace; and this, it is thought, can scarcely be guarded against by any legal provision.

The resolution is returned herewith.

FC in DNA, 3, 10:221.

From William Lee and Peter Hagner, 1/12. They report in duplicate all expenditures made under Calhoun's authority during the year that ended on 9/30/1818. LS in DNA, 1, L-67; FC in DNA, 53, 9:136.

From Joseph McMinn

Murfreesboro, [Tenn.,] 12 Jan[uar]y 1819

The mail of this morning has brought me intelligence, which I am apprehensive will prevent me from visiting the city [of Washington], agreeably to notice given in my last; the business is of an official character and my duty compells [*sic*] me to respect it accordingly.

I will however give you by next mail as comprehensive a view as lies within my power of the Cherokee business, and at the same time give you the character of the most Prominent amongst the Chiefs, and the part they have taken in relation to an exchange of countries [that is, concerning emigration to the Arkansas River area].

I was about ready to leave here as the information above reported, was handed me and had fully intended to have taken on all my papers for settlement, as well as every Document that would have shed light on the expected negociation [*sic*].

LS in DNA, 77 (M-271:2, frames 1308–1309); variant FC in DNA, 75 (M-208:14).

From El[eazer] W. Ripley, New Orleans, 1/12. Recommends sale of the barracks there, because "they are not wanted," and retention of the "present works at Fort St. Charles" until completion of the depot at Baton Rouge. ALS in DNA, 1, R-96.

To John Sergeant

War Dep[artmen]t, 12 Jan[uar]y 1819

Your letter of the 11th ins[tan]t has been received: I shall be happy to see you & the gentlemen whom you mention, at my house tomorrow at 10 O'Clock. And am very respectfully, Y[ou]r Obed[ien]t Serv[an]t, J.C. Calhoun.

CC in DLC, Carnegie Institution of Washington Transcript Collection.

James Taylor, Chillicothe, [O.,] to R[ichard] M. Johnson, 1/12. Taylor informs Johnson how Taylor has cashed two $5,000 drafts given by Johnson and by James Johnson. Taylor discusses several political matters in Ky. of concern to Johnson, approves Johnson's efforts to get a new military academy or armory located in the West, and suggests a site near Newport, Ky. Taylor also protests the dismissal of Dr. Evans Dozier, [a civilian physician] who for years has served the garrison at Newport but has been replaced by Cincinnatians; Taylor believes that Calhoun will correct this unexpected change. An AES by Johnson asks Calhoun to answer whether or not Dozier can be reinstated. An AEI by Calhoun states that Dozier cannot be and that [Daniel Parker] "will state the facts (briefly) which led to the change complained of." ALS in DNA, 1, J-120.

From Solomon Tobias, Charleston, [S.C.,] 1/12. Strengthens his application for a Lieutenancy by sending appended testimonials signed by M.M. Russell, John Geddes, and John D. Heath. ALS in DNA, 11, 13979.

From Decius Wadsworth, 1/12. Reports adversely on the proposal by William Sheldon to use wrought iron in the manufacture of cannon, which is not a brand-new idea anyway. Sheldon is correct in contending that "Guns made of wrought Iron, if perfectly executed, would bear much heavier charges than those in common Use," because wrought iron is "a much stronger Metal than Cast Iron or even the Mixture of Copper and Tin commonly used for Cannon." But there is a fallacy in "all Attempts to give Celerity to the Movements of Artillery much beyond common Practice. Light Guns recoil with more violence and strain their Carriages more than the heavier." Lighter barrels require, therefore, heavier carriages. "The Weight of the Ammunition is another Impediment which defeats the Plan of giving to Field Artillery that Celerity and Facility of Movement, which might be desirable." To enable a cannon to be fired for two hours at a standard pace requires 150 to 200 rounds of ammunition, which will weigh almost twice as much as the cannon itself. "It is believed our Field Pieces are now quite as light as they ought to be." Moreover, wrought-iron cannon would cost more than those made of cast iron and perhaps more than cannon made of brass, and Sheldon's proposed method "for forging them appears to me exceptionable." Because "our present Field Pieces made of cast iron are light enough and strong enough, I see no Reason for recommending a Trial of wrought iron Cannon." ALS in DNA, 1, W-143; FC in DNA, 32, 2:171–172.

To Felix Walker, [Representative from N.C.,] 1/12. Encloses a letter of 12/24/1818 from [Return] J. Meigs about a road wanted by N.C. Representatives through the Eastern Cherokee reservation to Ga. A Cherokee deputation will soon be in Washington, and the matter will be considered. FC in DNA, 72, D:241–242.

To Thomas Wilson, Philadelphia, 1/12. Acknowledges his letter to C[hristopher] Vandeventer of 1/9 (ALS in DNA, 1, W-173) and the safe arrival of Boyer's [French–English] dictionary; payment will be sent as soon as a new appropriation becomes available. Asks Wilson to write to his employer, N.G. Dufief, [who is now in Europe,] and to authorize the purchase of "the most copious & improved Dictionary that can be procured in Spanish and English, or in Spanish and French, which ever may be the best." FC in DNA, 3, 10:221–222.

From W[alker] K. Armistead, 1/13. Reports the expenditures of the Chief Engineer's office for stationery during 12 months ending 10/31/1818. FC in DNA, 21, 1:44–45.

From Lewis Cass, Detroit, 1/13. He explains several reasons which "will render every economical exertion necessary to keep within the sum of $45,000 assigned as the amount of expenditures for Indian affairs by the different Agents upon this frontier." Toward that objective, Cass proposes "that no goods be sent here for distribution as presents to the Indians. It is a branch of the service which, although very useful, yet may be dispensed with more easily than any other." LS in DNA, 1, C-214; FC in DNA, 76 (M-1:4, pp. 62–63).

To [John Gaillard], President of the Senate, and Speaker [Henry Clay], 1/13. Calhoun reports all expenditures made under authority of the War Department during the year that ended on 9/30/1818, both from the appropriations for 1818 and from balances that were unexpended on 10/1/1817. LS (Gaillard's copy) in DNA, 154, 15A-F4; LS with En (Clay's copy) in DNA, 201, 15A-F3; FC in DNA, 4, 2:82; PC with En in House Document No. 88, 15th Cong., 2nd Sess.

From Thomas S. Jesup, 1/13. Estimates the funds, time, and manpower that will be required to make necessary repairs to barracks, other quarters, hospitals, and storehouses at the principal

Army posts along the Atlantic seaboard and on the Canadian and Fla. frontiers. LS with 2 Ens in DNA, 1, J-92; FC in DNA, 42, 1:160.

Jacob Mordecai, Warrenton, [N.C.,] to [Nathaniel Macon, Senator from N.C.,] "13th January 1818 [*actually* 1819]." Knowing "your dislike to solicit appointments from Government," Mordecai reluctantly asks [Macon] to apply for a Cadet's appointment for Mordecai's son, Alfred Mordecai. The father's letter of 12/[4] to [Joseph G.] Swift for this purpose has not been answered. A Dr. Gloster died this morning. ALS in DNA, 15, 1818, 177, with an EU indicating an appointment on 3/24/1819.

To J[ames] P. Preston, Richmond, 1/13. Answering his letter of 1/11 (ALS in DNA, 1, P-100) seeking a payment due to Randolph Ross for the manufacture of [gun]powder, Calhoun assures Preston that the remittance will be sent as soon as a new appropriation becomes available and that the needed bill has already passed the House of Representatives; but Calhoun also asks for evidence that Preston is entitled to receive the money for Ross. FC in DNA, 3, 10:223.

To John Wilson, [Representative from Mass.,] 1/13. As he requested on 12/24/1818, Calhoun submits seven reports as to the stationery and printing used in the War Department in the year that ended on 10/31/1818. FC in DNA, 3, 10:222–223.

R.S. Briscoe, Benjamin Harrison, Thomas Munroe, Benjamin G. Orr, Tench Ringgold, John Woodside, and five others, Washington, to John Quincy Adams, Calhoun, and Smith Thompson, 1/14. They recommend Jacob Hines for appointment to the vacant position of Superintendent of the "public buildings" occupied by the Departments of State, War, and the Navy. LS in DNA, 103.

To [Henry Clay], 1/14. Calhoun responds to House resolutions, transmitted by Clerk Thomas Dougherty, of 1/6 (ADS in DNA, 1, H-123) and 1/7 (ADS in DNA, 1, H-123). He reminds the House that, in compliance with a resolution it adopted on 4/20/1818, he reported on 11/18/1818 "the strength and distribution of the Army." He encloses a report by Third Auditor [Peter

Hagner], which shows "the number and value of the extra days' labour, performed by the several detachments of the Army . . . upon roads and other objects of fatigue duty" during the year that ended on 9/30/1818. He plans during the present year "to employ the soldiers, as far as practicable, upon the road between Plattsburgh [*sic*] and Sackett's [*sic*] Harbour, in the State of New York, upon the road from Detroit to Fort Meigs [at the Rapids of the Miami], in the State of Ohio, upon the road from the Muscle Shoal [*sic*], [near Columbia,] in Tennessee, to Madisonville [La.] &c., and upon fortifications and the repairs of barracks, particularly in constructing the barracks at Baton Rouge. No extra subsistence, except Whiskey, nor extra articles of clothing, are allowed to soldiers while employed on extra labour; when a greater quantity of clothing than what is allowed by fixed regulations is issued, its value is deducted from the pay of the soldier." LS with En in DNA, 201, 15A-F3; FC with En in DNA, 4, 2:83–84; PC with En in *American State Papers: Military Affairs,* 1:822–823; PC in Crallé, ed., *Works,* 5:61–62; PC with Ens in House Document No. 110, 15th Cong., 2nd Sess.

D[ANIEL] PARKER to S[YLVANUS] THAYER, West Point

14 January 1819

The Secretary of War directs that you relieve Captain [John] Bliss of the 6th Infantry [Regiment] from duty within your command and that you order him to repair to Plattsburg [N.Y.] and report to the Commanding officer of his Regiment [Henry Atkinson].

CC in DNA, 203, 16A-D14.1.

Resolution by the Senate, 1/14. Requests "a negotiation with the Chickasaw tribe of Indians for the cession of a tract of land four miles square including a salt spring reserved to said tribe" by the treaty concluded on 10/19/1818 and that the ceded land be given to Tenn. "on said State paying the expense of holding said treaty." ADS by Charles Cutts in DNA, 1, S-256.

To S[amuel] Smith, [Representative from Md.,] 1/14. In reply to his inquiry, as Chairman of the House Committee on Ways and

Means, of 1/13 (ALS in DNA, 1, S-187), Calhoun writes in justification of the War Department's requested appropriation for Clerks in the Engineer, Medical, Ordnance, and Commissary (Subsistence) Departments of the Army's staff. He expects the average annual disbursements of the Engineers to approximate $900,000, those for Subsistence to be about $600,000. He insists that all four units really need the sums requested for Clerks. He explains that the Quartermaster General [Thomas S. Jesup] uses two subaltern officers for such services; and he names four officers who are detached for work in the Engineer and Ordnance offices. FC in DNA, 3, 10:223–224.

[1st] Lt. C[harles] M[ynn] Thruston, Adjutant, 3rd Artillery, Fort McHenry, to C[hristopher] Vandeventer, 1/14. In behalf of [Bvt.] Col. [Jacob] Hindman, Thruston acknowledges the receipt of several pairs of shoes and promises a report about them in approximately a month, "when they will have received a fair trial." ALS in DNA, 1, T-71.

From John Wilson, [Civil Engineer of the State of S.C.]

Charleston, S.C., 14th Jan[uar]y 1819

As the buildings belonging to the United States at Rocky Mount are of no use to the Government in the present state of the Catawba River, I request permission of you to make use of them in the prosecution of the work which I am about commencing on behalf of the State of South Carolina, to render that river navigable. At the same spot there are tools and building materials which are no longer of any use to Government and which I shall be glad to purchase for this State.

ALS in DNA, 1, W-178. Note: See Calhoun's affirmative reply herein under 2/4. The village of Rocky Mount, S.C., and the mill of that name appear in the maps of Chester and Fairfield Districts, at the eastern end of the common boundary between those Districts, in Robert Mills, *Atlas of the State of South Carolina.* No reference to the U.S. barracks or other property at Rocky Mount appears under that name or under the alternative name of Mount Dearborn, S.C., in the list of forts, batteries, named camps, redoubts, reservations, general hospitals, national cemeteries, etc., in Heitman, *Historical Register,* 2:526 and 539. Some plats of the U.S. property at Mount Dearborn, together with relevant correspondence of 1820–1828, appear in *American State Papers: Military Affairs,* 3:656–658.

To Lt. Col. W[alker] K. Armistead, 1/15. "It appears that three hundred dollars a year is insufficient to support Mr. [Dean] Weymouth, at this place; he will therefore be allowed four hundred dollars a year, ["estimating from the time he commenced" *interlined,*] while he acts as Clerk in your department." LS in DNA, 221, 9; FC in DNA, 3, 10:224.

To Capt. [René] Edward De Russy, New York [City]

Department of War, 15 January 1819

I enclose a letter from the Hon. Rufus King in relation to the pilots of New York.

Being desirous to grant to the pilots every privilege consistent with the public interest, you will restore such of them to their former privileges as will enter into written articles not to injure the public property at that port. With this requisition [that is, requirement] they are willing to comply and you will afford every facility to carry the arrangement into effect.

FC in DNA, 3, 10:226–227.

From N[inian] Edwards, [Senator from Ill.]

Senate Chamber, Jan[uar]y 15, 1819

I have the honor herewith to transmit to you, the petition of Tho[ma]s D.L. Weeks for compensation of losses sustained by depredations of certain Indians, with the proofs to support his claim.

This occurrence took place previous to the late war, and satisfaction was demanded of the Indians according to law, by myself, as Superintendent of Indian Affairs within the Illinois Territory, but no satisfaction could be obtained from them, nor were they entitled to any annuity, at that time, which could have been withheld for the purpose of indemnifying Mr. Weeks.

ALS in U.S. General Accounting Office, Indian Tribal Branch, Fifth Auditor Accounts, no. 602, "Fifth Auditor's Certificate on the Account of Thomas D.[L.] Weeks, Claim, 1819." Note: This manuscript bears an AEI by Calhoun that this claim was "Admitted." An EU in another hand reads: "The Hon. Mr. Edwards will call for this claim with whom the 5th Aud[ito]r will adjust it." As to the latter endorsement, compare Calhoun's letter of 1/16/1819 to Stephen Pleasonton.

From Ninian Edwards, [Senator from Ill.,] 1/15. Encloses a letter of 11/30/1818 to himself from Auguste Chouteau in St. Louis; in accordance with its request, Edwards informs Calhoun that Blue Eyes, a Kickapoo Chief, wants the help of the U.S. in establishing peace between the Kickapoos and the neighboring Osages and Cherokees. ALS with En in DNA, 1, E-30.

To Gen. A[quila] Giles, New York [City], 1/15. Answering his appeal of 1/12 (ALS in DNA, 1, G-71) for the immediate admission of his son, George [Washington] Giles, into the Military Academy, Calhoun states simply: "It appears your son arrived too late at West Point to be examined on the 1st of January and of course by the regulations of the Academy could not be admitted before that of June next." FC in DNA, 3, 10:226.

To R[ICHARD] M. JOHNSON, Chairman, House Committee on Military Affairs

Department of War, January 15th, 1819

In reply to that part of your letter of the 20th of November, [1818 (ALS in DNA, 1, J-39),] which requests my opinion on the expediency of establishing one or more additional military academies, and their places of location, and such other information and facts as I may deem proper to communicate on these subjects, with the probable annual expenses of these establishments, I have the honor to make the following statement:

The number of Cadets now authorized by law is two hundred and fifty, who are divided into four classes; the Cadets of one of which every year terminate their studies, and are promoted into the Army. As the academy is now nearly full, it is probable that the number which will annually terminate their studies, and, consequently, will be candidates for promotion, will not be much short of fifty. The number of vacancies in the Army, which have occurred from the 1st of August, 1816, to the 1st of May, 1818, has been one hundred and forty-eight, or about eighty-four per annum; but, as it is probable that the causes which have operated to produce so many vacancies in this time have been accidental, and consequent on the change from active service to the inactivities of a peace establishment, there will not, it is believed, in future be so many; and that the Cadets who will annually terminate their studies at West Point will be equal, or nearly so, to the annual average vacancies. In this view of the subject, an additional military academy would not now be required. But it seems to me that the question ought not to be determined by a reference simply to the wants of our military peace establishment, which, from our geographical position, and the policy of our Government, will always bear a small proportion to the population of the country, and to our military establishment in time of war. So far from graduating the number or extent of our military academies, by the want of the Army in time of peace, the opposite principle would probably be more correct; that, in proportion, as our regular military establishment is small, the Government ought to be careful to disseminate, by education, a knowledge of the art of war.

The Army itself is a practical school of this art, which, except in the higher branches, may, where it bears a large proportion to the population of the country, supersede other modes of perpetuating or disseminating this indispensable art. But in a country situated as ours is, with a small standing Army, and far removed from any power from which we have much to fear, the important knowledge of the art of defending our shores will, in a long peace, without the particular patronage of the Government, be nearly lost.

The establishment of military academies is the cheapest and safest mode of producing and perpetuating this knowledge. The Government ought to furnish the means to those who are willing to bestow their time to acquire it. The Cadets who cannot be provided for in the Army will return to private life; but in the event of war, their knowledge will not be lost to the country. The Government may then avail itself of their military science; and, though they may not be practically acquainted with all of the details of the duty in the Army, they will acquire it in a much shorter time than those who have not had the advantage of a military education. No truth is better supported by history than that, other circumstances being nearly equal, victory will be on the side of those who have the best instructed officers. The duties of a soldier are few and simple, and, with well-instructed officers, they can be acquired in a short time; as our own experience, and that of other countries, has satisfactorily proved. To form competent officers, in the present improved state of the art of war, is much more difficult; as an officer, besides a knowledge of the duties belonging to the soldier, has others of a more difficult nature to acquire, and which can only be acquired by a long experience, or by regular military education.

With these views, I would recommend an additional military academy. It ought to be placed where it would mutually accommodate the Southern and Western portions of our country, which are the most remote from the present institution. Besides an additional academy, I would submit, for the consideration of the Committee, the propriety of establishing a school of practice, to be fixed near the seat of Government. On this important subject, I respectfully annex, as a part of this communication, a report from Gen. [Simon] Bernard and Col. [William] McRee [submitted with their letter of 1/7] to this Department, in which the subject is so fully discussed as to supersede the necessity of any further observations. The expense of erecting the necessary buildings for an additional military academy, on a scale as extensive as that at West Point, would cost about one hundred and thirty thousand dollars, of which sum, however, but a small part would be required for this year. The current expenses of the institution would (excluding the pay of the Cadets, which is sixteen dollars per month, and two rations per day) probably amount to about $22,000 per annum.

For the school of practice there would be but little expense, except the erection of the necessary buildings for the accommodation of the institution. The pay of the superintendent and professors, should they be even taken from citizens, would not exceed eight thousand five hundred dollars, which would constitute nearly the whole of the current expense, as the subalterns of the Artillery and Engineers, while at the institution, will not receive any additional pay or emoluments. The expense of the buildings may be estimated at $80,000, of which, however, but a small part would be required for the present year.

FC in DNA, 3, 10:224–226; LS with 2 Ens in DNA, 201, 15A-F3; PC with 2 Ens in *American State Papers: Military Affairs,* 1:834–836; PC in Crallé, ed., *Works,* 5:54–57; PC with Ens in House Document No. 115, 15th Cong., 2nd Sess. NOTE: A manuscript copy of each of the two above mentioned Ens can also be found with the letter of 1/7/1819 from [Simon] Bernard and W[illiam] McRee in DNA, 222, F-42. The two are entitled "Considerations on the course of instruction necessary for the Officers of the different arms of an Army" and "Table of a course of instruction . . . ."

Capt. WYLY MARTIN to Col. TALBOT CHAMBERS, St. Louis

Cantonment on Missouri, January 15th 1819

You have done me the honor in yours of 25 Dec[embe]r to ask my ideas on the steam boat system. I must confess that I advance my opinions with much hesitation, not being well acquainted with the machinery which propels a steam boat. Should that power be sufficient to stem this current and the boat should set out early in the spring, I know no reason why she should not progress with very little danger. But so soon as the river falls and the water becomes as low as when we ascended, I have no hesitation in saying that any steam boat on this river of 80 tons or upwards will never reach the Yellow Stone, nor do I think she will ever return from whence she came.

The river even this high up becomes much more narrow, the sand bars abound in greater numbers, and indeed there are many places in low water where the sand bars on the one side project so near to the planters and sawyers on the other that it is with some difficulty that large keel boats can wind their way safely through them, and furthermore there are so many hidden planters which conseal [*sic*] their stubborn heads a little below the surface of the water, that a large steam boat must always be in danger of being stove.

Again there are many places where the river expands to an astonishing width, with innumerable intervening sand bars, shallows and quick sands and these so perpetually changing as the water obtrud[e]s upon this or that bar, leaves [*sic*] the river without any determined channel, and baffles the art of the best pilots upon the river. I have not a doubt however that small steam boats of 50 tons and under would do well upon this river, but for my own part give me the Cordell [?] and the sail. The opinions of most of the officers here are against steam boats unless they be verry [*sic*] small.

Should you come up in a steam boat, suffer me to advise you to provide yourself well with anchors, as they will frequently get foul of logs at the bottom of the river and render it necessary to cut the cable.

ALS in DNA, 2, M-1819.

JAMES MONROE'S Talk to the Senecas Residing on the Alleghany River

15th January, 1819

My Red Children:

I am very glad to learn by your friends, Sam[ue]l Bettle, Thomas Wistar, Thomas Stewardson, and John Cook, that you no longer live in that destitute and miserable state which you once did. They say that most of you have become sober and industrious and have got good houses to live in; and that, by cultivating the ground and raising cattle, you have now aplenty to eat. This is to me very good news, as I shall always rejoice to hear of the happiness of my Red Children.

My Red Children:

You cannot become civilized 'till you advance one step farther. You know that, among my white children, each one has his own land separate from all others. You ought to do the same. You ought to divide your lands among families, into lots sufficiently large to maintain a family according to its size. Your good friends, the Quakers, would, no doubt, enable you to make a just and equitable division. By thus dividing your land, each one could then say, this is mine, and he would have inducements to put up good houses on it and improve his land by cultivation.

My Red Children:

I have annexed the seal of the United States to this talk, so that you may know it comes from your father the President.

FC in DNA, 72, D:243–244.

To Caleb Stark, Pembroke, N.H., 1/15. Pursuant to his letter of 1/7 to Secretary of the Treasury [William H. Crawford], Calhoun encloses a copy of the statute granting a pension to Gen. John Stark and informs Caleb Stark that a first payment, covering 8/16/1817–12/28/1818, can be obtained by applying to the Pension Agent at Boston. Future payments will be made there in the regular way semiannually. LS in NhHi, Morris and Stark Papers; FC in DNA, 3, 10:226.

To S[ylvanus] Thayer, West Point

War Department, 15th January 1819

The proceedings & report of the Court of Inquiry which convened at West Point, under the order of this department of the 9th of Decem[be]r last, have been examined by the President [James Monroe], & I have the pleasure to state that your conduct as Superintendent of the Military Academy in the unpleasant occurrences which induced that investigation has been satisfactory & is approved.

As Capt. [John] Bliss does not appear to possess sufficient command of his temper, an order will be transmitted to you relieving him as Instructor of Tactics at the Academy and a copy of the order detaching Capt. [John R.] Bell of the Light Artillery for that duty.

The course pursued by the Cadets is highly reprehensible throughout the whole transaction, and particularly objectionable on the part of the young gentlemen who composed their committee. The redress of military grievances must never be extorted or obtained by combinations which are alike mutinous.

If Capt. Bliss acted unjustifiably or oppressively, his conduct was a proper subject of complaint, to the Superintendent, from the Cadet who was personally aggrieved, and the youth & inexperience of the gentlemen, alone, induce the President to overlook the insubordinate course pursued through their committee. But, however, as that youth & inexperience were probably the cause of their irregular conduct, you will restore the young gentlemen who were sent from the Academy by your order of the 27th of November last whenever, in your opinion, it can be done without injury to the discipline of the instruction.

LS in NWM; FC in DNA, 3, 10:227; FC in DNA, 13 (M-91:26, pp. 16–17); CC in DNA, 203, 16A-D14.1; CC in DNA, 30, no. 1; PC in *American State Papers: Military Affairs,* 2:22; PC in House Document No. 14, 16th Cong., 1st Sess.

From John Williams, [Senator from Tenn.]

Senate Chamber, Jan[uar]y 15th 1819

I send you enclosed a recommendation signed by all the delegation from Tennessee in favour of John Overton, Newton Cannon & Rob[er]t Weakley to treat with the Chic[k]asaws.

ALS in DNA, 11, 13174.

From H[enry] Atkinson, Plattsburg, [N.Y.,] 1/16. "I deem it proper to state to you that there remain in the Magazines at this Post 11,569 lb[s.] of cannon, 3,586 of musket, & 200 of Rifle powder, agreeably to the report of the acting Ordnance officer. The powder has been in depot for several years, say before the close of the War. Loose powder, particularly the quality of common powder, deteriorates by time and ultimately perishes. I beg leave to submit to your consideration, if it will not be advisable to dispose of the greatest part of this article. It would probably sell for but little here; it may, however, be transported to Albany or New York [City] in the Spring at a small expense, where it would find a better sale." FC in DNA, 181, p. 68.

To [Henry Clay], 1/16. Pursuant to the House resolution [of 1/4 (ADS by Thomas Dougherty, Clerk, in DNA, 1, H-125)], Calhoun reports what payments have been made to the Friendly Creek Indians, in accordance with the treaty of 8/9/1814, as indemnity for property destroyed by the hostile Creeks. LS with 3 Ens in DNA, 201, 15A-F3; FC with 3 Ens in DNA, 4, 2:85–86; FC in DNA, 3, 10:227–228; PC with Ens in *American State Papers: Indian Affairs,* 2:186–187; PC with Ens in House Document No. 98, 15th Cong., 2nd Sess. (The enclosures include copies and extracts of a letter of 3/20/1817 from George Graham to David B. Mitchell and of 3/18/1818 from Mitchell to Calhoun.)

From EDMUND P. GAINES

Fernandina, E[ast] F[la.], January 16th 1819

After the departure of the last mail with my letter of the 12th I received from Major [James M.] Glassell a report upon the subject of his visit to St. Augustine, which I have the honor to transmit herewith, accompanied by the enclosures referred to, with the exception of such as I had previously received copies of, and forwarded to you on the 12th instant.

In the hope of being favored with your views upon the subject of my correspondence with Governor [José] Coppinger, and wishing to avoid a controversy in which the want of authority on my part would necessarily restrain and place me under every disadvantage, I have considered it to be proper to remain silent; but should the Governor fail to restore the Sergeant [Augustus Santee] and wounded citizens agre[e]able to promise, I hope that I may be honored with authority to open their prison and liberate them. The force now at this place, is not perhaps entirely sufficient to *ensure success* in this enterprise; but it is very sufficient to authorize the attempt—and in doing so to preserve the honor of our Army and Country.

An additional Battalion with a naval force to Blockade the Harbour, added to the troops here, would be sufficient to effect the reduction of St. Augustine with its present force, although the place possesses many natural advantages, and is strongly fortified. The garrison is supposed to consist of near 300 regular troops, to which may be added from 150 to 200 militia.

My Aid[e]-de-Camp Lieut[enant Daniel E.] Burch who accompanied Major Glassell has nearly completed a sketch of the Harbour and town of St. Augustine, which will accompany my next.

Our troops at this place are unhealthy, having nearly one fourth of the whole number on the sick report. They have been afflicted for the most part with severe dysentery, produced by bad water, intemperance, and the want of wholesome vegetables. Doctors [William Horace] Buckner and [William P.] Marshall are both sick, and permitted to remain at Charleston for the recovery of their health. Doctor [Richard] Weightman is therefore necessarily detained at this place. He is aided by Doctor [Richard] Randall, both of whom appear to be valuable officers. The former will repair to Fort Hawkins as soon as he can be relieved by Doctor Marshall.

A Company of the 7th [Infantry Regiment] (Recruits) under Captain [French Strother] Gray arrived on the 13th from Philadelphia, having been out at Sea but seven days. The Captain is in very bad health—the recruits are tolerably healthy.

LS with En in DNA, 1, G-92. NOTE: The enclosure is Glassell's report about the detention of Santee.

From Callender Irvine, Philadelphia, 1/16. "Your letter of the 11th instant is received. On examination, I find I was in error in stating on the return transmitted to the War Department, that Fatigue Clothing was issued on requisitions of Comm[issar]y officers of [the Military] Dep[artmen]ts without restriction. On referring to the regulations for the purchasing Department dated 1st of Feb[ruar]y 1818, I find that the last section of the General order, of the same date, promulgating them directs that, 'Commanding officers of Corps & Detachments, may be allowed to make requisitions for such quantity of Clothing for fatigue parties, as may be necessary, & not exceeding two fatigue Frocks, & three pair of trousers, & one p[ai]r of Shoes per year. These requisitions shall be approved by the officer Comm[andin]g the Dep[artmen]t or the Post.'" ALS in DNA, 1, I-90; FC in DNA, 45, 387:289.

To Thomas L. McKenney, 1/16. Answering in part his letter of 1/15 (FC in DNA, 73, E:190), directs how outlays amounting to $1,013.09 under the authority of [John] McKee shall be paid for, since the fund from which that sum should be paid is nearly exhausted. FC in DNA, 72, D:243. (The portion of McKenney's letter that was left unacknowledged is his offer of a quarter million pounds of lead, stockpiled at Prairie du Chien and St. Louis, "which I should be glad to get cost for from any Department of the Government wanting the article.")

To Stephen Pleasonton, 1/16. "I enclose a claim of Tho[ma]s D.L. Weeks for property stolen from him by a party of the Potawatamy [*sic*] nation of Indians, which you will adjust & settle with the Hon. N[inian] Edwards, on account of the Indian Department; the amount to be deducted and refunded to the credit of that Department, from the annuity of that nation for the present year, when the same shall be drawn for payment." LS in U.S. General Accounting Office, Indian Tribal Branch, Fifth Auditor Accounts, no. 602, "Fifth Auditor's Certificate on the Account of Thomas D.[L.] Weeks, Claim, 1819"; FC in DNA, 72, D:242.

To Jacob Brown, New York [City], 1/18. "I have received your letter of the 11th instant [FC in DLC, Jacob Brown Papers, Letterbooks, 2:135] and it will afford me pleasure to see you at Washington [about 2/1]." FC in DNA, 3, 10:229; CC in DLC, Jacob Brown Papers, Letterbooks, 2:171.

From Capt. R[ené] E[dward] De Russy, New York [City], 1/18. Reports that [Ferdinand Rudolf] Hassler is willing to deliver the instruments belonging to the survey of the coast to De

Russy in Newark, N.J.; asks for instructions because Calhoun's order to De Russy to receive the instruments specified that he should do so in "New York." ALS in DNA, 1, D-69.

To E[dmund] P. Gaines, Amelia Island, 1/18. "I have received your letter of the 5th instant [(ALS with En in DNA, 1, G-73; draft in DNA, 11, 13213)]. I approve of the issue of provisions made by Lt. Col. [Duncan Lamont] Clinch to the distressed widows and children of Amelia Island. You may continue the issues in cases of necessity and report the amount issued to this Department." LS in DNA, 11, 13213; FC in DNA, 3, 10:230.

From George [Washington] Giles, New York [City], 1/18. On 12/31/1818 he reported to the Military Academy for examination but was denied admission before 6/1819. Giles has since returned to his home and awaits Calhoun's further orders. ALS in DNA, 1, G-71.

To P[eter] H. Green, Boston, 1/18. [Pursuant to his report of 12/29/1818 (ALS in DNA, 1, G-62) that a draft for $5,000 has been unavoidable,] Calhoun explains: "On examining your account there appears due you $5,908.14. So soon, therefore, as the appropriation bill passes, the advance of $20,000 comprehending the draft presented by the Hon. Jon[athan] Mason, [Representative from Mass., who relayed it to me on 1/15 (ALS in DNA, 1, M-160)], will be made. The bill has passed the House of Representatives and is expected to pass the Senate in a few days." FC in DNA, 3, 10:228.

To Lemuel Jenkins, Bloomingsburg, Sullivan County, N.Y., 1/18. Acknowledges his letter of 1/7; informs him that the court-martial for the trial of N.Y. militia delinquents has been dissolved but that [Gerard] Steddiford is continuing to report on petitions for the remission of fines; orders Jenkins to send to Steddiford "the original proceedings of the court which are in your possession." FC in DNA, 3, 10:229.

From Thomas L. McKenney, 1/18. He accepts a proposed way of paying $1,013.09 to the Office of Indian Trade. "If the War Dep[artmen]t have demands for Lead, I will sell to it, at cost, as much as will re-imburse the amount of Merchandize transferred to this Office by the Indian Department. The cost [is] *about* $5 [per hundred pounds] delivered at St. Louis." LS in DNA, 1, M-158; FC (dated 1/17) in DNA, 73, E:190–191.

From Nath[anie]l Macon, [Senator from N.C.,] 1/18. Encloses a letter [dated 1/13 to Macon (Abs herein under 1/13)] from Jacob Mordecai, "the celebrated teacher of females at Warrenton, [N.C., who was seeking an appointment as a Cadet for his son Alfred]." Macon imagines that it "would be very agreeable to Alfred Mordecai and A[rthur] B. Gloster to go to West Point at the same time, provided they should get situations there." ALS in DNA, 15, 1819, 51.

To Jon[athan] Mason, [Representative from Mass.,] 1/18. "The advance required by Mr. [Peter H.] Green will be made so soon as the appropriation bill passes the Senate, and the draft of Mr. Green [for $5,000], which you presented, will be accepted to be paid on the passage of that bill." FC in DNA, 3, 10:229.

From Col. G[eorge] E. Mitchell, Baltimore, 1/18. Approves of the application by Maj. [Thomas] Biddle, [Jr.,] for an assignment "to accompany Major [Stephen H.] Long on his expedition to the Falls of the Missouri River." LS in DNA, 11, 13100.

Contract with [James] Turk & [Thomas] Henderson, Maryville, Tenn., 1/18. By this document, signed in behalf of the U.S. by Return J. Meigs, this firm agrees to supply rations to the Cherokees and gives its bond for $300,000 for the faithful performance of its obligations. DS in DNA, 77, with an AES reading "Approved, J.C. Calhoun"; FC in DNA, 75 (M-208:8).

Lt. Isaac A. Adams, Fort Nelson, [Norfolk Harbor, Va.,] to Joseph G. Swift, [New York City ?], 1/19. Seeks "your influence . . . with the Hon. Secretary at War" in favor of the application of Adams's brother, Edwin Adams, for a Cadetship. ALS in DNA, 15, 1819, 65.

To W[alker] K. Armistead, 1/19. "You will transmit to this Department, as early as practicable, a Statement of the Contracts made, by the Engineer Department, in the year 1818, and, also, a duplicate thereof." LS in DNA, 221, 12; FC in DNA, 3, 10:230.

To JOHN W[AYLES] EPPES, [Senator from Va.,] Chairman, Senate Committee "on Finance &c."

Department of War, 19 January, 1819

By accounts of disbursements of the officers of the Quarter Master's department, which have been recently received, I find that the contingent expenses of the Department have been considerably enhanced, in consequence of operating against the Seminole Indians, and that the sum appropriated for contingencies for 1818, will be deficient about $26,000. I therefore request that that sum be inserted in the appropriation bill, as an arrearage under the head of contingencies for 1818.

FC in DNA, 4, 2:87.

From Col. John R. Fenwick, Washington, 1/19. Submits his suggestions for the instruction of soldiers "in the field Evolutions of Light Artillery." Fenwick has also prepared new regulations for the Artillery, because he considers the present manual "bad and dangerous." He believes the military penal code to be "contradictory in its principles, destructive in its effect and ruinous to the morale of the service." He deplores also the "want of system in the Military Judicial code." ALS with En in DNA, 1, F-55.

To [JOHN GAILLARD] and [HENRY CLAY]

Department of War, 19th January, 1819

In pursuance of the 5th section of the act of the 3d of March, 1809, entitled "An act further to amend the several acts for the establishment and regulation of the Treasury, War, and Navy departments," I have the honor to transmit to Congress a statement, shewing the expenditure of monies appropriated for the contingent expenses of the military establishment, for the year, 1818.

LS with En (Gaillard's copy) in DNA, 154, 15A-F4; LS with En (Clay's copy) in DNA, 201, 15A-F3; FC in DNA, 4, 2:87; PC with En in House

Document No. 102, 15th Cong., 2nd Sess. NOTE: The En preserved with each of the two LS's is a financial statement concerning office expenses, etc., comprising about 14 manuscript pages and dated 1/1; each copy had been prepared for Calhoun and submitted to him by Second Auditor William Lee, who signed each copy. Lee's covering letter transmitting the two copies of this statement to Calhoun is dated 1/1 (LS in DNA, 1, L-66; FC in DNA, 51, 2:447).

To EDMUND P. GAINES, Amelia Island

Department of War, 19th Jan[uar]y, 1819

I have rec[eive]d your letter of the 29th ult[im]o and have submitted it to the President of the United States, who directs that you do not commence hostile operations in that quarter, without being previously ordered to do so by this Department. The Indians, in their present situation, cannot operate with any success against our forces, and, before offensive movements are made against them, their intentions to renew the war should be unequivocally ascertained.

So soon as you are favoured with the reply of the Governor of St. Augustine to your note of the 28th ult[im]o, you will report it to this Department.

Some of the Representatives in Congress from Georgia have manifested a desire that the U[nited] States should obtain from the Creeks a cession of their reservation at Fort Hawkins. You will report to me whether the occupation of that post, by the United States, is necessary in a military point of view, and, if not, whether it would be advisable to abandon it altogether. In the meantime, you will suspend the Execution of my order of the 16th of last October relative to the lease of certain lots on the Oakmulgee until further orders.

LS in DNA, 11, 13511; FC in DNA, 72, D:244.

To George Gibson, 1/19. "You will transmit to this Dept., as early as practicable, a statement of the contracts made by your Dept., in the year 1818, and also, a duplicate thereof." FC in DNA, 3, 10:230–231.

From John H. Hall, Washington, 1/19. Applies for appointment as the Superintendent of the proposed armory on the western waters. ALS in DNA, 11, 13430.

From Callender Irvine, Philadelphia, 1/19. "I instructed Mr. James Ward, who stiles [*sic*] himself Military Storekeeper for North Carolina, to deliver to the order of the Military Storekeeper at Charleston, S[outh] Ca[rolina], [Robert Wilson,] the few articles of Camp Equipage in his possession; & Mr. Wilson has been ordered to take Charge of them without delay. I transmit herewith, a copy of a letter [of 12/30/1818] rec[eive]d at this office, from Mr. Ward, by which it appears that he was appointed Storekeeper for the Ordnance Department." ALS with En in DNA, 1, I-105; FC in DNA, 45, 387:292.

To William "Irwin [*actually* Irving, Representative from N.Y. and brother of Washington Irving]," 1/19. Encloses a report as to the decision of the court-martial for [N.Y.] militia delinquents in respect to Samuel Gedway. FC in DNA, 3, 10:230.

From Thomas S. Jesup, 1/19. Encloses an estimate of Quartermaster expenses "growing out of the capture of the Spanish posts of St. Marks, Pensacola, and Barrancas," totaling $25,365. LS with En in DNA, 1, J-87; FC in DNA, 42, 1:164.

From El[eazer] W. Ripley, New Orleans, 1/19. Reports several personnel matters. Wants Dr. [Clement Alexander] Finley transferred to the line and Theodore Ayer of New Orleans to be appointed a 2nd Lt. Ripley has forwarded to [Andrew] Jackson the resignations of [Ferdinand Louis] Amelung, who has been appointed the sheriff of Baton Rouge, [Capt. Anatole] Peychaud, [Jr.,] and [James] Smith. [Thomas F]. Hunt has been ordered to Pa., and [Thomas S.] Rogers has been assigned to Hunt's duties. Ripley recommends Robert Beall for appointment as an Assistant Deputy Quartermaster General. ALS in DNA, 11, 13292.

From Decius Wadsworth, 1/19. Thomas L. McKenney has at St. Louis and Prairie du Chien some surplus lead that Wadsworth would like to acquire, with some small-caliber rifles as part payment. If the trade is acceptable to McKenney, Wadsworth will arrange. it. ALS in DNA, 1, W-141; FC in DNA, 32, 2:173.

To John Williams, [Senator from Tenn.]

Department of War, 19th January 1819

I have received your letter of this day[']s date [ALS in DNA, 1, W-140] covering a bill for the better organization of the Military Academy and return it with the [requested] estimate of the [additional] expenses [that will result if the bill is enacted,] which you will perceive.

The provisions of the bill are excellent, and if passed, will contribute eminently to the improvement of the institution. As I concur entirely with Gen. [Simon] Bernard and Col. [William] McRae [McRee] in the view which they have taken of the Military Academy, it is not necessary for me to go into a detail of the provisions of the bill which are in conformity with their recommendations.

FC in DNA, 3, 10:231.

To [John Gaillard] and [Henry Clay]

Department of War, 20th January, 1819

In pursuance of the 9th section of the act of Congress passed the 20th April, 1818, I have the honor to transmit herewith, statements marked A, B, C, D, exhibiting the names of the Clerks employed in the Department of War, and the sums given to each, in the last year.

LS with 4 Ens (Gaillard's copy) in DNA, 154, 15A-F4; LS with 4 Ens (Clay's copy) in DNA, 201, 15A-F3; FC with 4 Ens in DNA, 4, 2:87–89; PC with Ens in House Document No. 106, 15th Cong., 2nd Sess. Note: Statement A is dated 1/16; it names 30 Clerks who served in the War Department proper (as opposed to the bureaus mentioned below), states the period of the service during 1818 of each, and lists the compensation paid to each. Statement B, signed by Chief Clerk Nathaniel Frye, Jr., on 1/17, gives similar information about eight employees in the office of the Paymaster General [Robert Brent]. Statement C was signed by Capt. John Morton on 1/19 and gives similar information about three Clerks in the office of the Ordnance Department. Statement D is in the form of a letter from D[aniel] Parker to Calhoun dated 1/18; it reports that the two veteran Clerks in the office of the Adjutant and Inspector General were Brooke Williams and John M. Hepburn and recommends for each the restoration of a recent reduction in his salary. In addition to the four versions of this letter from Parker cited above, there is an FC in DNA, 12, 5:167.

From John Johnston, Piqua, 1/20. Forwards a letter from [Lewis] Cass to Johnston in which Cass represents Dr. [William] Turner as an unsuitable person to replace [Benjamin F.] Stickney as Sub-Agent at Fort Wayne. The Indians are more convinced every day that moving farther westward will not relieve them from the encroachments of the whites. Johnston has urged the Indians to break up their villages and to scatter over their land in detached farms, but the Indians have not the means. For about $2,000 more a year, Johnston thinks that he can do a great deal toward reclaiming the people. "It is impossible for any man associated with them as I am not to feel for their degraded, unhappy situation. I knew them many years ago when the game was plenty [*sic*]; every individual was rich and happy; now the Country is chiefly destitute of wild animals; and no substitute for a livelihood has taken their place." ALS in DNA, 1, J-118.

Resolution by the Senate, 1/20. Calls for submission to the Senate in its next session of a report "shewing how far it may be expedient or not to provide by law for the clothing of the Army with articles manufactured in the United States." ADS by Charles Cutts in DNA, 1, S-213.

To First Comptroller Joseph Anderson, 1/21. Answers his request of 1/14 (LS in DNA, 1, A-47; FC in DNA, 59, 19:16) for the loan of any available copy of the bond of [former Col.] Simeon Knight, [former] Quartermaster General, in order "to bring suit for the Recovery of the balance found due . . . on settlement of his account," by stating that no copy can be found in War Department files. LS in DNA, 141.

From Maj. James Bankhead, Fort Johnson, Charleston Harbor, [S.C.,] 1/21. Reports the "inefficient state of the Fortifications, and the general materials of defence, in this Harbour." Fort Johnson is too dilapidated to be worthy of repair; Fort Moultrie is in better condition, but its palisade is falling down; Castle Pinckney needs a sea wall of stone to protect its basement. Nearly all of the gun carriages are "quite useless." Bankhead encloses "a minute inventory" of all ordnance, implements, and ordnance stores at Charleston. ALS in DNA, 1, B-194; CCEx in DNA, 221, 14.

TO THOMAS JEFFERSON

Washington, 21st Jan[uar]y 1819

I have read with much interest the proceedings and report of the commissioners for the University of Virginia, with a copy of which you have honored me. The view presented by the report is concise and comprehensive; and the system of education, which it proposes, appears to me, to be excellent.

I most sincerely hope, that your effort in the cause of education may be crowned with complete success. Nothing is now wanting to produce this happy result, but the enlightened patronage of your State Legislature; and supported as the report of the Commissioners is, by the names of many of our most enlightened citizens, its favourable reception by the Legislature can scarcely be doubted.

The claim of M. Poirey has passed the House of Representative[s]; and it will probably pass the Senate without difficulty.

That you may long continue to enjoy in the full possession of your health and faculties the gratitude of our country for your illustrious services is my most ardent prayer.

ALS in DLC, Thomas Jefferson Papers, vol. 214, 38241–38242.

From A[braham] A. Massias, Charleston, [S.C.,] 1/21. Applies for an appointment as a Deputy Commissary of Purchases; cites his Army experience and the recommendation of him by John Gaillard, [Senator from S.C.]. ALS in DNA, 11, 13646.

TO JAMES MONROE

Department of War, 21 Jan[uar]y, 1819

The Secretary of War, to whom was referred the Resolution of the House of Representatives of the 18th instant, requesting the President of the United States to cause any information, not already communicated, to be laid before the House, whether Amelia Island, St. Marks, and Pensacola, yet remain in possession of the United States; and, if so, by what Laws the inhabitants thereof are governed; whether articles imported therein from foreign countries are subject to any, and what, duties; and by what laws, and whether the said duties are collected, and how; whether Vessels arriving in the United States, from Pensacola, and Amelia Island, and in Pensacola, and Amelia Island, from the United States, respectively, are considered and treated as Vessels arriving from foreign countries; has the honor to report, so far as the information called for refers to the War Department, that, by the latest reports, the places referred to in the resolution, to wit, Amelia Island, St. Marks, and Pensacola, yet remain in possession of the United States.

He also encloses an extract of a letter from Major [James] Bankhead, dated the 10th of January 1818, marked A, which accompanied the regulations ["(a copy of which is annexed)" *interlined*] for the government of the inhabitants of Amelia Island, and also a copy of a letter from this Department, prohibiting the taking of Bonds, for the payment of duties on goods imported into Amelia Island, marked B.

The Division Order of Major Gen[era]l A[ndrew] Jackson issued at Pensacola, on the 29th of May, 1818, communicated in the Message of the President of the United States to the House of Representatives, on the 2nd Ul[tim]o, shews by what Laws the inhabitants thereof are governed, and the duties which the goods imported are subject to, and the laws by which such importations are regulated.

As St. Marks is a mere military Post, without inhabitants, the commandant[']s authority is confined to the Garrison.

FC in DNA, 6, 1:343; LS with Ens in DNA, 202, 15A-E1; PC with Ens in House Document No. 117, 15th Cong., 2nd Sess. NOTE: As is shown by an LS of 1/30 from James Monroe to the House of Representatives that is preserved in DNA, 202, 15A-E1, Monroe relayed to the House on 1/30 this letter of 1/21 from Calhoun, together with a report [dated 1/25] from Secretary of the Treasury [William H. Crawford].

From Col. H[ENRY] ATKINSON

Plattsburgh [*sic,* N.Y.,] Jan[uar]y 22nd 1819

Agreeably to your instructions of the 9th instant, communicated by the Adj[utan]t & Insp[ecto]r General [Daniel Parker], requiring me to make a report of the number of days of fatigue, or extra labour performed by the troops under my command during the year ending the 31st October last; designating the kind of labour, and number of days of each, and the value of such labour, I have the honor to report that the troops of the 6th Reg[imen]t performed the following amount of labour within the time specified, taken accurately from diaries kept by commandants of Companies and certified upon honor by them to be correct.

To wit: 7,013 days labour on the fortifications at Rouse's Point, 17,238 in constructing a road thro' the Chateaugay woods, 1,465 by artificers in repairing barracks & officers' quarters and 226 in cultivating gardens for the men, amounting in the whole to 25,942 days labour.

As some diversity of opinion may be entertained with respect to the value of the several sorts of labour performed by the troops, it is necessary in order to come to a fair conclusion, to bring into view the value of similar labour when performed by hired hands, or on contract. Taking these data as a just criterion, the 7,013 days labour performed on the fortifications may be estimated at $7,013, or one dollar a day per man, which is the price that was given by the superintending Engineer officer to common labourers. But in order to remove any doubts, and to reduce the price of this labour to the lowest estimate that it should be fixed at, the 7,013 days labour may be put down at seventy-five cents a day per man, which amounts to $5,259.75. Altho' this deduction of twenty-five per cent is made from the ordinary price of labour, it must be admitted, that the troops performed as much work as the same number of hired hands would have done, being required as they were, and performed as they actually did (with the exception of the ordinary time for taking their meals) labour, from Reveillie [*sic*] in the morning 'till retreat beating, and that, too, with a spirit of industry & willingness highly creditable to the most faithful labourer.

In ascertaining the value of the labour bestowed on the road, it is necessary to assume the principle governing the calculations respecting the labour on the fortifications, in as much as the same system was pursued in regard to the hours of labour, and as to assidious [*sic*] industry. Hence, the 17,238 days labour in constructing the road may be put down as $17,238. But following the principle of reduction as laid down above brings the estimate to $12,-928.50. As a further illustration of the correctness of this calculation, it is proper to observe, that it is the opinion of the best informed people in this neighbourhood, that the road could not be made on contract in the superior manner it is constructed for less than $2,000 per mile, and, indeed, I am of opinion it could not be done for that sum.

By correct admeasurement, in addition to the seven & a half miles of road made in the autumn of 1817, six miles was [*sic*] completed the last season in the best and most durable manner, over a rugged and mountainous country, intersected by many brooks & deep ravines. The road has a base of 24 feet, elevated five feet above the bottom of the ditches, and bedded with rock where it passes over wet & swampy ground. The intersecting brooks & ravines are conducted under it by bridges & sewers walled with stone, & its sides are walled in the same manner when passing and winding around the declivity of hills. Upon the whole, it may be regarded as one of the best roads made in any country and much better than any turn pike that I have seen in our own.

In addition to the labour stated as performed on the fortifications & roads, the constant attention of one field officer, six Captains & twelve to fourteen Subalterns was given in superintending the labour of the men & directing the construction of the road, which should be taken into the general estimate. But as it is somewhat difficult to ascertain the value of such attention and superintendence it is left indefinate [*sic*].

The value of the labour in repairing barracks & officers' quarters can be estimated with accuracy. The 1,465 days labour of artificers may be safely put down at $1,465, or one dollar a day p[e]r man as a moderate price.

In ascertaining the value of the labour in cultivating vegetables for the sole use of the troops, the best criterion is, to calculate the amount and worth of the vegetables themselves. 1,500 bushels of potatoes, 60 of Beets, 50 of carrots, 40 of parsnips & 1,500 heads of good cabbages & three times the number of indifferent ones were gathered for winter use; besides various other vegetables for summer use, such as peas, beans, sallads [*sic*] &c. On a moderate calculation, the value of the vegetables may be estimated at $1,000. It is proper to remark in this place, that owing to the impropiciousness [*sic*] of the last season, the crop of vegetables from the same ground was not as great by one half as was gathered from it for the use of the troops the preceeding [*sic*] year.

To elucidate the foregoing statements, it is necessary to recapitulate them respectively. The value of the labour on the fortifications is first estimated at $7,013 & reduced to $5,259.75. That in constructing the road at $17,238, reduced to $12,928.50. The labour of artificers at $1,465 & the value of the products of the soldiers' gardens at $1,000. The estimates without being reduced gives [*sic*] an aggregate value to the labour of $26,716. Take from this sum $3,857.40, the actual amount paid the men for extra labour, there remains a balance in favour of the troops for labour of $22,-858.60. The estimates under the reduction of twenty-five p[e]r cent gives an aggregate value to the labour of $20,652.25. Take from this sum the $3,857.40 paid for extra labour, and there remains a balance in favour of the troops for labour of $16,794.85. Hence, it is seen at a single view, that the troops have during the last season earned over and above the compensation allowed them for extra labour, the sum of $16,794.85, or, upon a more liberal construction, $22,858.60.

In closing this report I should do injustice to the officers & men employed, were I not to express to you the great credit they are entitled to, for the universal industry & willingness they manifested during the discharge of their laborious duties, preserving at the same time, the character and appearance of the soldier.

ALS in DNA, 1, A-55; FC in DNA, 181, pp. 71–75.

From Callender Irvine, Philadelphia, 1/22. "Your favor of the 5th instant was duly received. I have instructed the Dep[ut]y Comm[issar]y of Purchases at Newport Kentucky [John McKinney] to add to the Contract prices of Army materials here, the cost of transportation from Phila[delphia] to Newport, conformably to the suggestion contained in your letter." ALS in DNA, 1, I-106; FC in DNA, 45, 387:300.

From John T. Lewis

Pendleton, So[uth] Ca[rolina], 22d Jan[uar]y, 1819

Your friend Capt. John Simpson at my elbow requests me to make his best respects to you and ask that you will have forwarded to him or me Land warrants for Richard & Duncan Presley, soldiers of the late war & of Regiment not known. The Location is desired to be made in the Illinois or Mis[s]ouri.

By having this immediately attended to you will much oblige Capt. Simpson & the soldiers.

[P.S.] Capt. Simpson desires a description of the Lands if you can give it him.

ALS in DNA, 1, L-77. NOTE: Calhoun's answer to this request appears herein under date of 2/8.

From D[avid] B. Mitchell, "Mount Nebo," [Ga.,] 1/22. He has returned from Ala., intends soon to travel to Washington to settle his accounts and to confer with Calhoun in person, and informs Calhoun that [William] McIntosh wants to accompany Mitchell to Washington. McIntosh's desire was not prompted by Mitchell, but to yield to it may do no harm and much good. Mitchell refutes in writing the charges against him concerning high prices charged within the Creek area for corn, fodder, and bridge and ferry tolls; but he will discuss these points in detail with Calhoun. LS in DNA, 77 (M-271:2, frames 1489–1494); PC in Carter, ed., *Territorial Papers*, 19:543–545.

To Hugh Nelson, [Representative from Va. and Chairman of the Committee on the Judiciary,] 1/22. Answering his letter of 12/30/1818 enclosing the petition of Henry Strider, encloses "a report from the Ordnance Department, [received today from Decius Wadsworth,] which contains the information you have requested." Asks that Congress enact a law to authorize the War Department to sell certain land to a Mr. Peacher, who has agreed to pay a fair price. FC in DNA, 3, 10:232.

From Decius Wadsworth, 1/22. Pursuant to Heman Allen's letter to Calhoun from Burlington, Vt., dated 1/4 (ALS in DNA, 1, W-174), which Calhoun, by an AEI, referred to Wadsworth, Wadsworth recommends that the supply of arms and shot at Vergennes, Vt., be retained there to supply the fort beside Lake Champlain when that fort shall have been completed. ALS in DNA, 1, W-174; FC in DNA, 32, 2:173–174.

From D[ecius] Wadsworth, 1/22. Repeats the information he gave on 12/23/1818 and 1/8/1819 concerning the sale of the furnace tract of land near Harpers Ferry; adds what he has learned since then; concludes that the sale was proper and that Henry Strider has no proper claim to the land. FC in DNA, 32, 2:175–178.

Robert Bogardus, Newark, to C[hristopher] Vendeventer, 1/23. Bogardus urgently reminds Vandeventer to try to settle the pending purchase of the land on which the fortifications at Hell's Gate stand "while Gen[era]l [Joseph G.] Swift & the Vice President [Daniel D. Tompkins] be at Washington. They can give all the required information." ALS in DNA, 1, B-24.

To Capt. [René] E[dward] De Russy, New York [City], 1/23. Answers his letter of 1/18 (ALS with Ens in DNA, 1, D-56), which pledged that he would carry out Calhoun's orders in regard to permitting the pilots of New York Harbor to land at and to use Sandy Hook. But De Russy also submitted evidence of their destruction of public property there; enclosed copies of his regulations against which they protested; argued that these most recent ones, of 11/1818, were sufficiently liberal and might well be reconsidered and approved because of apparent misrepresentations by the pilots against them; and pleaded for an understanding of his course in respect to the pilots. In reply, Calhoun says that he is willing to reconsider the problem: "In viewing your proceedings toward the Pilots of New York, I could perceive nothing on your part but a desire to promote the public interests. Every privilege compatible with the public interest ought to be granted to a class of people so useful as the pilots, but if any injury will arise to the public property on the Hook by extending the privileges beyond what are contained in your last regulations, you will report the particulars to the Chief Engineer [Walker K. Armistead], for my consideration." FC in DNA, 3, 10:233.

To E[dmund] P. Gaines, "Fernandina via St. Marys," 1/23. Encloses a copy of a letter [of 1/6] from Governor [William Rabun] of Ga., together with a resolution adopted in the Senate of Ga. [on 11/25/1818] seeking the assignment of a U.S. Army guard to the area west of Okefenokee Swamp in Southwest Ga., in order that surveyors and settlers there might be protected, and authorizing Rabun, as an alternative, to station some Ga. militiamen there. Calhoun asks Gaines whether it is practicable for the Army to afford the requested aid. LS with Ens in DNA, 11, 13390; FC in DNA, 3, 10:232. In reply on 2/12 (LS in DNA, 1, G-114; CC in DLC, Andrew Jackson Papers, 8565), Gaines explained how he would propose to spare some men for that duty.

To [James Monroe], 1/23. Submits a "list of promotions and appointments for the Army." LS with En in DNA, 156, 15B-A2; FC in DNA, 6, 1:344.

To Th[omas] Morris, New York [City], 1/23. "You will as early as practicable report the period for which each member of the Gen[era]l Court Martial of which Gen. [Gerard] Steddiford was President, has charged in the account rendered to you and amount paid to each." FC in DNA, 3, 10:234.

To William Rabun, [Governor of Ga.,] Milledgeville

Department of War, 23d January 1819

I have received your Excellency's letter of the 6th inst[ant (CC with En in DNA, 11, 13390)] and have submitted it to the President of the United States [James Monroe].

It will give the President pleasure to afford as far as practicable the aid required by the Senate of Georgia [which requested that an Army guard unit be stationed west of Okefenokee Swamp]. Gen. [Edmund P.] Gaines has been ordered to report on all the points to this Department and so soon as that report reaches me, I will communicate, more in detail, with your Excellency on the subject.

FC in DNA, 3, 10:232.

To John Sergeant, [Representative from Pa.]

Department of War, 23d January 1819

I have laid the memorial [dated 4/30/1818] of the American Philosophical Society, which you transmitted to me on the 12th instant [ALS with Ens in DNA, 1, S-209, together with an ALS dated at Philadelphia on 1/10 from Dr. R.M. Patterson, Secretary of the

Society, to Sergeant], before the President of the U[nited] States [James Monroe].

It would afford the President much satisfaction to comply with the wishes of the Society, but he is of opinion that, as the instruments were purchased for a specific purpose, under an act of Congress, it will require a similar authority to enable him to grant their request.

FC in DNA, 3, 10:233. NOTE: The Society's memorial stated that the Society had been granted by the City Council of Philadelphia the use for seven years of a centrally located building in that city "for an Astronomical Observatory." The memorial asked for the use for an equal term of some of the astronomical instruments that had been purchased by the U.S. in London for the use of [Ferdinand Rudolf] Hassler in the survey of the coast. More specifically, the memorial requested a loan of a duplicate set of instruments intended for observations at a fixed location—a set that was already in Philadelphia; and the Society claimed that Hassler had given assurance that the loan could be made without interfering with the progress of his survey.

Robert Bogardus, Newark, to [Joseph G.] Swift, [Washington,] 1/24. Bogardus reminds Swift not to forget to press for purchase of the Hell's Gate land. ALS in DNA, 1, S-219.

From Joseph McMinn, Murfreesboro, Tenn., 1/24. Informs Calhoun about commitments made by McMinn to almost 12 individual Cherokees, some of whom Calhoun will see as members of the tribe's delegation in Washington, in order to purchase their support for the emigration plan. To some McMinn gave cash payments ranging from $150 to $500 each; to some he promised that he would recommend to Calhoun that they be allowed to enlarge their reservations by 400 to 600 acres each of grazing land in coves otherwise unclaimed; to some he promised that their reservations might be given in fee simple. Some, but not all, of these gifts and promises have been, in McMinn's judgment, good investments in buying friendship. ALS in DNA, 77, (M-271:2, frames 1312–1316); LS in DNA, 75 (M-208:14).

James Stubblefield, Harpers Ferry, to [Decius] Wadsworth, 1/24. Stubblefield has completed the production of a gun lock embodying Wadsworth's improvement. ALS in DNA, 1, S-212.

From James Ervin, [Representative from S.C.]

Washington City, Jan[uar]y 25, 1819

Some time back I presented to your attention Mr. Samuel [*sic; actually* James] S. McCall, a young gentleman in the State of South Carolina whom his friends are desirous of getting admitted [as] a Cadet at West Point. He is now about nineteen years of age. From information [available to me,] he has studied the Latin and Greek languages, arithmetick, geography, and the English grammer [*sic*] and judging from the honorable mention of his name in the annual publication of the examination of the Scholars at Lodebar Academy he must have distinguished himself.

His manners from my own knowledge are not only conciliatory but exemplary, correct.

The gentleman who makes the application for him although for several years a member in the Legislature of So[uth] Carolina yet I suppose is unknown to you but is an intimate acquaintance of General [David R. ?] Williams, with whom you are acquainted. Although the encouragement ["of talents" *interlined*] is and ought to be a consideration of primary importance with myself yet it would be uncandid in me to endeavour to disguise from you the great anxiety which I feel to oblige a much respected friend who patronises this young gentleman. He [the patron] has been married for a number of years and although Heaven has given fortune and every thing to make life desirable has denied him children.

This young man, his nephew, he has made the object of his bounty & love; and finding that he possesses great talents is desirous of affording him every opportunity of improvement.

I with pleasure embrace this opportunity of giving you the assurance of the great esteem and respect of your friend, James Ervin.

ALS in DNA, 15, 1819, 79.

To Gen. A[quila] Giles, New York [City], 1/25. Answering his letter of 1/9 (ALS in DNA, 1, G-71) reporting that his son, George [Washington] Giles, went to the Military Academy on 12/30/1818 but was denied admission, Calhoun says: "Maj. [Sylvanus] Thayer has not reported the objections to admitting Cadet Giles and, as there are only four months to June, the period of the next examination, it appears to me advisable for him to remain [at home] until that time." FC in DNA, 3, 10:234.

To F[erdinand] R[udolf] Hassler, Newark, N.J., 1/25. "The enclosed is a copy of a letter from Maj. [Stephen H.] Long, who is anxious to obtain the chronometers now with Mr. [Henry] Vo[i]gt. Should these instruments not be absolutely necessary in your operations the ensuing summer, I will give Maj. Long an order for them. You will therefore inform me whether you can dispense with them." FC in DNA, 3, 10:234.

From R[eturn] J. Meigs, Jr. [Postmaster General,] 1/25. Because of "the negligence of the Post Master at Edgefield," S.C., "there was a partial failure of the Willington [S.C.] mail." However, "the Post Master at Edgefield" has written to Meigs an assurance "that the mail for the route started the first week in this month, in the care of an energetic man on whom reliance can be placed." FC in DNA, 161, 1817–1819:374.

From Edmund P. Gaines, Fernandina, E[ast] F[la.], 1/26. Encloses a letter of 1/18 in Spanish, with a translation, from José Coppinger to Gaines about the capture of Sgt. Augustus Santee and three other men by the Spanish. Also encloses a copy of Gaines's reply to Coppinger dated 1/24, which claims that Santee and the other men were without blame. ALS with Ens in DNA, 1, G-113; ALS in DNA, 11, 13234.

From Joseph McMinn, Murfreesboro, Tenn., 1/26. Because it was impossible for him to accompany the Cherokee delegation to Washington, he wishes to inform Calhoun through this letter of some of his opinions. [Charles] Hicks, [the prince regent,] may be ranked as the standard of opposition to the execution of the treaty. His opposition has recently been tempered by noting the number of Cherokees who are moving west. Fully one-half of the tribe is now reconciled to the government's plans. He advises Calhoun to press now for total emigration while opposition is at such a low ebb. ALS in DNA, 77 (M-271:2, frames 1310–1311, including only the last page of the ALS); FC in DNA, 75 (M-208:14); PC and PEx in *American State Papers: Indian Affairs,* 2:482–483, 500; PC's in Senate Document No. 63 and House Document No.

127, 18th Cong., 1st Sess.; PEx in House Report No. 109, 18th Cong., 1st Sess.

From E[LDRED] SIMKINS, [Representative from S.C.]

Washington City, 26 Jan. 1819

I do not enclose you the certificate of [former ?] L[i]eutenant [Allen B. ?] Addison under any hope of altering your determination in refusing to discharge Ira Youngblood, but as it is evident from this certificate that he ought *in good faith* to have been discharged at the end of the War, and as he is unable to do duty, & may perhaps be of some use to an innocent and suffering family (wife and three or four children) now in the Alabama territory, I enclose it and make this representation formally in the hope that it may be compatible with even a stern sense of duty to give some order that may facilitate his legal trial and discharge. Otherwise it will be necessary for Capt. Addison, who is much engaged in business ["will have" *canceled*] to go all the way to Savannah &c. Could you not prescribe some method of taking his testimony, &c.

P.S. Let me hear from you as speedily as possible on this subject. E.S.

ALS in DNA, 1, S-216.

From J[AMES] L. E[DWARDS]

War Department, Pension Office, January 27th 1819

Since writing the letter of the 22nd Ultimo to Ezra Bartlett, Esq., of Grafton, New Hampshire, I have had satisfactory evidence of Bedel's regiment having been on the Continental Establishment from and after January 1776.

FC in DNA, 91, 6:200.

From J[AMES] L. EDWARDS

War Department, Pension Office, January 27th 1819

The papers in the case of Experience Fisk are herewith returned, with General [Abner] Lacock's letter. If the applicant became disabled in consequence of injuries received *while in the line of his duty,* the law will authorise the Secretary of War to place his name on the roll of Pensioners, on his conforming to the enclosed regulations.

ALS in DNA, 1, E-36; FC in DNA, 91, 6:201.

From Wilson M.C. Fairfax, Thomas Ragland, Nathaniel H. Loring, Charles R. Vining, and Charles R. Holmes, Committee in Behalf of the Corps of Cadets, Washington, 1/27. [Upon a suggestion made orally to them by Calhoun,] this Committee's members "declare, that, notwithstanding the respectable precedents which exist of similar committees [representing Cadets], we cheerfully acquiesce in the President's [James Monroe's] condemnation of this mode of proceeding, if by that we are to understand a principle adopted by your Department applicable not only to our case, but to all similar cases in the military service." PC in *American State Papers: Military Affairs,* 2:19; PC in House Document No. 14, 16th Cong., 1st Sess.

To Wilson Lumpkin, Madison, Ga., 1/27. Acknowledges his letter of 1/7 [ALS in DNA, 77 (M-271:2, frames 1216–1217)] sending maps of the two tracts of land ceded by the treaty of 1/22/1818 [with the Creeks], stating that Lumpkin had received no replies to his communications, and saying, "I should be glad to hear from you on the subject of [the surveying of] the Florida line, as the land embraced by Jackson's Treaty cannot be surveyed until that line is run out." Calhoun answers that on 12/27/1818 he remitted a refund of Lumpkin's expenses reported in Lumpkin's letter of 12/10/1818. "You will report to this Department what time in your opinion is the most suitable to run out this [Fla.] line so that preparatory measures may be taken through Gen[era]l [Edmund P.] Gaines to afford the necessary protection to yourself & others who may be employed in that business." FC in DNA, 3, 10:235.

From Joseph McMinn

Murfreesboro, Tennessee, 27th January 1819

I had the honor to receive your two letters of the 30 Dec[embe]r last on the 18th Inst[ant], and that of the 27th of the same month, just as I had closed mine of yesterday[']s date. In neither of your letters do you give any intimation of my advising you of the Cherokee deputation, which I presume, will reach the City [of Washington] in a few days.

It is probable, that you would not think it advisable, that any steps should be pursued, in relation to taking the census, until you advise me of the result of the Cherokee visit, as I am fully persuaded they contemplate coming to a final understanding on the subject of an exchange of Countries ere they return home.

In consequence of my declining a trip to the City I dispatched an express to the Agency which returned on yesterday. The Sub-Agent reports, that Colonel Glass with his party 167 in number, weighed anchor on the 16th Inst[ant], previously to which he hoisted the American flag, and moved off under martial music in good spirits and perfectly pleased with the Government. The Sub-Agent further states that 52 heads of families had enrolled subsequent to the 20th Decem[be]r and that many were awaiting my arrival at the date of his letter, who hearing that I was not coming on, determined to return home without enrolling. When we add the above report to former enrol[l]ments the gross number is nine hundred and twenty-eight heads of families.

Under a belief that you will approbate my absence from the Cherokee Agency until the result of the Cherokee visit is known, I will decline going on, although I had determined on a contrary Course. I could not be there without being actively employed in purchasing improvements and entering into other arrangements of expenditure, which would be unnecessarily incurred, provided you enter into the general plan of exchanging Countries.

LS in DNA, 77 (not filmed in M-271:2); variant FC in DNA, 75 (M-208:14).

To Maj. ABRA[M] R. WOOL[L]EY, Pittsburgh

Department of War, 27th January 1819

I have received your letter of the 16th instant [ALS in DNA, 1, W-176, in which you reviewed your belief that you have been "a stag at bay for six years" because accusers want to procure your removal from Ordnance work at Pittsburgh and in which you revealed resignedly your presentiment that success will crown their efforts whether a court of inquiry investigates you or not]. Since

I have been in this Department my first object has been to promote & protect the public interest connected with it, and the second has been to sustain every officer, so far as his conduct deserves it, in the good opinions of the Army and the people.

The Department can have no object to remove you from the command at Pittsburgh, so long as your duty is promptly & faithfully performed; and it is my sincere wish & belief that nothing may occur which may make such a step necessary.

FC in DNA, 3, 10:235.

William Corry, Mayor, Cincinnati, to William H[enry] Harrison, [Representative from O.,] 1/28. Corry reluctantly requests again Harrison's intervention to obtain orderly conduct on the part of soldiers in and near Cincinnati, specifying several complaints that indicate that Calhoun's order concerning the behavior of soldiers there "has been either revoked or entirely disregarded." ALS in DNA, 11, 14021.

From William Lee and Peter Hagner, 1/28. They submit in duplicate a statement of funds transferred by order of President [James Monroe] during the recess of Congress from one appropriation to another and of the application of such funds. LS in DNA, 1, L-87; FC in DNA, 51, 2:465; FC in DNA, 53, 9:208.

To [James Monroe], 1/28. Calhoun submits "for your approbation the appointment of John Overton, Newton Cannon, and Robert Weakley, Esquires, of Tennessee, as Commissioners to negociate [*sic*] with the Chickasaw tribe of Indians for the cession of a tract of Land four miles square" that includes a salt spring reserved by the Chickasaws in the Chickasaw treaty of 10/19/1818. FC in DNA, 6, 1:344.

From [Daniel Parker], 1/28. Reports the Army's use of Fort Scott [in Ga.]: in 6/1816 the 4th Infantry Regiment first encamped on the site and in 9/1816 began to construct the fort; in 12/1816 it was abandoned; in the spring of 1817 a Company of Artillery occupied it; in 12/1817 two Infantry Regiments joined the Artillery there, "and it has ever since been occupied." FC in DNA, 12, 5:173.

From Jasper Parrish, Washington, 1/28. In 1793 he was appointed Interpreter to the Six Nations. When Callender Irvin[e] became the Agent, in 1803, Parrish was appointed Sub-Agent and Interpreter at $450 per year and two rations per day; he continued to serve as such under Agent Erastus Granger until last April, [when Parrish was designated as the Sub-Agent to the Iroquois]. Throughout these years his travel expenses for official business in Washington were always paid by the U.S. He asks that he be appointed Interpreter as of 4/1/1818 at $400 annually—which salary will be considered to cover all his official travel. ALS in DNA, 11, 13771.

From Decius Wadsworth

Ordnance Office, January 28th 1819

I do not find that any authority has been given from this Office to the Superintendant [*sic*] at Harpers ferry Armory, to apply any part of the funds of that institution towards the support of a Chaplain. There is some recollection of permission having been given by Lieut[enant] Col. [George] Bomford to occupy some of the Buildings there for the performance of divine Worship, there being no church in the vicinity. The Superintendant at Springfield has probably been erroneously informed respecting the matter.

FC in DNA, 32, 2:179.

To T[homas] W. Cobb, [Representative from Ga.,] 1/29. Answering his letter of 1/27 (ALS in DNA, 1, C-154) seeking bounty land for Samuel Goolsby, who enlisted in the Army in upland S.C. before he knew that the Treaty of Ghent had been concluded in 1815, Calhoun states flatly that no enlistee after the date of the arrival of the proposed treaty in New York [City] is eligible for the bounty. If this War Department rule in any instance "appears to have other than an equitable bearing, an application to Congress will be the only means of obtaining redress." FC in DNA, 3, 10:236.

To JOHN W[AYLES] EPPES, Chairman, Senate Committee on Finance

Department of War, 29th January, 1819

I have the honor to transmit herewith a draft of a bill, making appropriations to carry into effect treaties concluded with the several Indian tribes therein mentioned.

The item of $25,000 is to carry into effect sundry stipulations contained in said treaties, such as paying for improvements, building of mills, furnishing horses to emigrants &c. &c., the exact amount of the expenses for which cannot now be ascertained, but the above sum, it is thought, will be sufficient to cover them for the present year.

The compensation to the Agents is left blank, but I would propose that it be filled with the sum of $1,200, which is the lowest grade of salary given to Indian Agents, and is deemed a sufficient compensation to the two now proposed to be appointed.

LS in DNA, 158, 15A-D4; FC in DNA, 4, 2:90.

From Thomas S. Jesup, 1/29. "In my opinion one light Howitzer and one light field piece, will be sufficient for each Steam Boat employed on the Mississippi, and the Missouri [in connection with the Yellowstone Expedition]; and I have to request that orders be given to the Ordnance Department accordingly." LS in DNA, 31, War Department; FC in DNA, 42, 1:171.

From H[ugh] Maxwell, Washington, 1/29. He argues that his claim to extra compensation as one of the Judge Advocates of the court-martial for the trial of N.Y. militia delinquents, first organized in 1814, is "neither immoderate nor unmerited." Since 9/1817 he has "continued to devote very considerable time to the proceedings of the Court," and he states, "It is confessed on all hands that the whole labour and responsibility of the proceedings have been sustained by the President [Gerard Steddiford] and Judge Advocates." He believes that Calhoun's order of 12/23/1817 justifies his claim. He testifies that H[enry] B. Hagerman's services, "since his appointment . . . [as a Judge Advocate,] have been constant and zealous." ALS in DNA, 1, M-198.

To [James Monroe], 1/29. Proposes five promotions in the Corps of Engineers, each to be as of 11/12/1818: Lt. Col. Walker K. Armistead to become Col. in the place of [Joseph G.] Swift, resigned; Maj. William McRee to become Lt. Col. in the place of Armistead; Capt. Joseph G. Totten to become Maj. in McRee's place; 1st Lt. T[heodore] W. Maurice to become Capt. in Totten's place; and 2nd Lt. George Blaney to become 1st Lt. in the place of Maurice. LS with En in DNA, 156, 15B-A2; FC in DNA, 6, 1:344.

From Thomas Morris, New York [City], 1/29. Answering Calhoun's request of 12/23/1818, he states that no member of the court-martial for N.Y. militia delinquents has yet supplied Morris with a complete account of the compensation claimed by its members. Morris itemizes partial payments totaling $11,597. He wants Calhoun's approval as to both the period of service claimed by each member and the amount of pay to each before any account "is finally liquidated." Because [Gerard] Steddiford "is now in Washington," Morris suggests that Calhoun settle Steddiford's claims in conference. ALS in DNA, 1, M-157.

To G[erard] Steddiford, "New York [City]," 1/29. "You are permitted to select & retain two Judge Advocates for the term of two months. On reaching New York you will give public notice that all applications for remission of fines" imposed by your [N.Y. militia deliquents'] court-martial "must be presented within two months & that after that period none will be received. In cases where the Militia-man was returned a defaulter & has been fined but served a portion of his time you may remit so much of the fine as is in proportion to the time served." FC in DNA, 3, 10:236.

Col. Robert Butler, Washington, to Andrew Jackson, [Washington,] 1/30, "Private." Butler argues that he was honored in 1815 with a brevet rank too low. An AEI by J[ames] M[onroe] refers this claim to Calhoun for a study and report. ALS in DNA, 1, B-234.

From J[ames] L. Edwards, Pension Office, 1/30. Discusses the meaning of the words "term" and "period" in the statute of 3/18/1818 granting pensions to Revolutionary veterans who served "for the *term* of nine months, or longer, at any *period* of the war." Concludes that the interpretation that has been given "is correct, viz: that those who did not serve at least nine months under one term of enlistment, or to the end of the war, do not come under the provisions of the law." LS in DNA, 2, E-1819; FC in DNA, 91, 6:205–207.

From Edmund P. Gaines, Fernandina, E[ast] F[la.], 1/30. Encloses a copy of Gaines's letter of 1/27 to Comptroller Richard Cutts giving further proof, as requested by Cutts, of the failure of contractor Benjamin G. Orr to supply rations in sufficient quantity during the Seminole campaign of 1817–1818. ALS with En in DNA, 1, G-107; draft (dated 1/31) in DNA, 11, 13377.

From Edmund P. Gaines, Fernandina, E[ast] F[la.], 1/30. The resignation of Surgeon's Mate [Robert Carr] Lane left the troops at St. Marks without any medical officer. Dr. Selah Kirby has been employed and is proving satisfactory. Gaines asks that Kirby be appointed as Post Surgeon. Calhoun's letter of 11/25/1818 was received after being enroute for two months, whereas some other letters from Washington arrive in 11 days. ALS in DNA, 1, G-106; draft in DNA, 11, 13377.

To Roswell Lee, Springfield, Mass., 1/30. "I enclose for your information a copy of a letter of the Col. of Ordnance [Decius Wadsworth] in relation to the employment of a chaplain at Harpers Ferry. By it there appears to be an error in the impression that authority had been given to the Sup[erintenden]t [of the arsenal] at Harpers Ferry to apply a part of the funds of that establishment to the payment of a chaplain. I should be glad to grant your request but have not the power under the laws to do it." FC in DNA, 3, 10:237.

From Joseph Lovell, 1/30. Suggests the appointment as a Post Surgeon of Dr. Selah Kirby, who has been recommended by Post Surgeon Jabez W. Heustis, [Andrew] Jackson, [George] Gibson, and [former] Maj. [George P.] Peters. ALS in DNA, 11, 13572.

To [James Monroe], 1/30. Pursuant to a House resolution of 1/28, Calhoun submits the journal of the Commissioners who negotiated the treaty of 10/19/1818 with the Chickasaws and a copy of that treaty, which, he reports, has been ratified. FC in DNA, 6, 1:345.

From Thomas Morris, New York [City], 1/30. Two members of the court-martial [for N.Y. militia delinquents] cannot prepare their accounts without having at hand a copy of the proceedings of the court; they thought their accounts had been prepared already by others for them. ALS in DNA, 1, M-196.

To Jasper Par[r]ish, Sub-Agent and Interpreter to the Six Nations of Indians in N[ew] York

Department of War,
1st April, 1818 (Issued 30th Jan[uar]y 1819)

You are hereby appointed with the approbation of the President of the U[nited] States [James Monroe], ["appointed" *interlined*] Interpreter to the Six Nations of Indians, residing within the State of New York.

Your compensation will be at the rate of four hundred dollars per annum, commencing with the date hereof.

Given under my hand at the War office of the U[nited] States this 1st day of April, 1818, and of the Independence of said States the forty-second. J.C.C.

FC in DNA, 72, D:245. Note: The date of the issuance of this retroactive commission appears in the margin of the letterbook. This commission was presumably issued as a means of supplementing the $500 annual salary of Parrish due to him as a Sub-Agent. See *The Papers of John C. Calhoun*, 2:286–287.

From Henry Shaw, Zabdiel Sampson, and Joshua Gage, [Representatives from Mass.,] 1/30. They recommend Bvt. Capt. Joseph Gleason for appointment as an Assistant Commissary of Subsistence at Detroit. An AES by Marcus Morton, [Representative from Mass.,] approves this recommendation and identifies Gleason as formerly a newspaper editor in Mass. LS in DNA, 11, 13403.

From J[esse] Slocumb, [Representative from N.C.,] 1/30. For an appointment as an Indian Agent, Slocomb recommends Gen. Calvin Jones of Raleigh, whose reputation "as a Literary, Military & professional character" is excelled by "but few in our State." ALS in DNA, 11, 13538.

From Lt. L[ewis] G[ustavus] De Russy, New York [City], 1/31. Requests that he be allowed to serve as an Assistant Topographical Engineer or surveyor in the "expedition" that is to be commanded by Gen. Peter B. Porter. ALS in DNA, 11, 13286.

From N[icholas] Boilvin, Prairie du Chien, 1/——. Flour that has been furnished by the contractor for the soldiers there is unfit for their use and is about to be thrown away. Boilvin requests permission to give it to the Indians. ALS (in French) in DNA, 1, B-284. (An EU indicates that this letter was received or filed in 3/1819 or 5/1819. It bears also a date-stamp at St. Louis, March 29.)

FEBRUARY 1819

THIS MONTH, LIKE OTHERS THROUGH THE PAST YEAR, BROUGHT to Calhoun's desk additional evidence that Benjamin G. Orr was still failing to fulfill his contract for delivery of rations to Southern troops. Army and Navy Engineers presented to Calhoun a major report, which had been a year in the making, proposing new fortifications for defense of the Chesapeake Bay. A delegation of Cherokees from the mountain coves of the Southeast spent most of the month in Washington, conferred often with Calhoun and Monroe, signed a new treaty on the 27th, and wrote friendly notes before they departed. By then a Creek deputation had also arrived. On the 26th Calhoun sent to General Edmund P. Gaines news that the Spanish were said to be willing to ratify the pending treaty under which the two Floridas would be ceded to the United States. The rumor was premature by two years: the inevitable can evolve slowly.

Loring Austin, Boston, to C[hristopher] Vandeventer, 2/1. Congress having authorized a payment to Austin, he asks if Calhoun has yet initiated it. "It is of great importance to me" that the suits against me "should be completely settled, and all claims against me on this account finally barred." ALS in DNA, 1, A-66.

To Speaker [HENRY CLAY]

Department of War, 1st February, 1819

In pursuance of the resolution of the House of Representatives of the 26th ult[im]o directing the Secretaries of War and of the Navy, "to lay before the House a copy of the military orders in virtue of which the Negro Fort within the territory of East Florida was destroyed in the month of July, 1816, together with the correspondence of Colo[nel Duncan Lamont] Clinch and Commodore

[Daniel T.] Patterson in relation to that event; and any other information which may be in his possession in relation to the movement of the Indians in the Seminole Country," I have the honor to transmit a copy of the order of this Department, in virtue of which the Negro Fort, within the Territory of Florida, was destroyed in July, 1816, and copies of letters addressed to this Department by Major Gen[era]ls [Andrew] Jackson and [Edmund P.] Gaines; which comprehend all the information required by the resolution, relative to the destruction of the fort, in the Department of War.

LS with about 20 Ens in DNA, 201, 15A-F3; FC in DNA, 4, 2:90; PC with Ens in House Document No. 122, 15th Cong., 2nd Sess. NOTE: The Ens include letters of 3/15–6/15/1816 between Secretary of War William H. Crawford, Clinch, Gaines, Jackson, and David B. Mitchell, the last-named of whom was Governor of Ga. at the time.

From J[oseph] Du Commun, Teacher of French, Military Academy, West Point, 2/1. Applies for appointment as the proposed new Professor of Chemistry in the Academy; encloses a summary of his career since 1793. ALS with En in DNA, 14, 8, with an AEI by Calhoun referring this application.

To [John Gaillard] and [Henry Clay], 2/1. Transmits a statement of funds transferred from one appropriation to another during 1818 and, as a statute of 3/3/1809 requires, evidence showing how such funds were applied. LS (Gaillard's copy) in DNA, 154, 15A-F4; LS (Clay's copy, slightly variant) with En in DNA, 201, 15A-F3; FC in DNA, 4, 2:90.

To E[dmund] P. Gaines, Amelia Island, 2/1. Acknowledges his letter of 1/19 (ALS in DNA, 1, G-78; ALS in DNA, 11, 13377) enclosing a sketch of St. Augustine. Answers his report of 1/18 (ALS with 3 Ens in DNA, 1, G-94; LS in DNA, 11, 13509) of the detention of the schooner *Independence* of Philadelphia for an infraction of port formalities by enclosing "a copy of a letter addressed to me" by [William H. Crawford on 2/1 (ALS in DNA, 1, C-159; CC in DNA, 11, 13509)], "which will inform you of the only course by which relief can be obtained." LS in DNA, 11, 14021; FC in DNA, 3, 10:239.

From Capt. Nathaniel N[ye] Hall, Albany, 2/1. Requests permission to exchange positions with Capt. [William Robert] Duncan of the Southern Division—an exchange approved by J[acob] Brown. Asks also for a furlough of four months for personal reasons "of too delicate a nature to be mention[ed] in an official letter." ALS in DNA, 11, 13431.

Callender Irvine, Philadelphia, to C[hristopher] Vandeventer, 2/1. Maj. Thomas Martin, Military Storekeeper at Newport, Ky., died last month. Irvine asks Vandeventer to persuade Calhoun not to fill the vacancy immediately, in order that Irvine may ascertain whether one of his own relatives, [probably a brother-in-law, Peter Fayssoux, Jr., son of the Charleston, S.C., physician who is noted for Revolutionary service,] would accept the position. Regardless of that concern within his family, Irvine says: "I am desirous to effect the appointment of a person . . . at Newport, who will aid in effecting a change in the quality of the supplies provided there, & in some other matters." ALS in DNA, 1, I-111.

From Andrew Jackson, Washington, 2/1. Encloses a copy of a letter from Col. William King to Col. R[obert] Butler dated at Pensacola on 12/7/1818; pursuant thereto, Jackson requests prompt action to get Quartermaster funds sent to King and adds his "approbation" to King's praise of a Captain's "meritorious conduct." LS with En in DNA, 1, J-108.

From Joseph Lovell, 2/1. Encloses his quarterly report on the causes of illnesses and deaths in the Army, this one covering the third quarter of 1818 and based upon returns from Post Surgeons that are commended in quantity and quality. More care should be taken to recruit soldiers in good health. "The management of the recruiting service has always been defective, because the importance of the duty has not been duly appreciated by Officers of any grade. A man has too often been made a recruiting Officer because he is fit for nothing else, or for his own convenience, it being frequently considered a kind of furlough, a licence to frolic rather than an order for duty." LS with En in DNA, 2, L-1819; FC with En in DNA, 243, 1:30–40.

From John Lowry, McGovern's Hotel, Washington, 2/1. As Secretary of the [Eastern] Cherokee Deputation that has now largely assembled in the capital, Lowry requests for it an initial interview with Calhoun. ALS in DNA, 1, L-91.

To Hugh Nelson, [Representative from Va.,] 2/1. "I enclose copies of letters which relate to the subject of the petition of Mr. [Henry] Strider, received at this Department since the letter to you enclosing a report of the Ordnance Department thereon, of the 22d ult[im]o." FC in DNA, 3, 10:238.

From D[aniel] Parker, 2/1. Reports that four men enlisted in La. during 11/1818 and 145 in Pa. during [12/1818]. No returns of recruits have been received from Ala. and Miss. LS in DNA, 1, P-112; FC in DNA, 12, 5:176.

From Thomas Ragland and Wilson M. C. Fairfax, in Behalf Also of [Charles R. Holmes, Nathaniel H. Loring, and Charles R. Vining,] Committee in Behalf of the Corps of Cadets

[Washington, February 1, 1819]

We have considered the further alteration suggested by you, this day, of our letter to the [War] Department of the 27th ultimo, and regret that we cannot adopt the same. To go further than the modification before suggested, and agreeably to which that letter was handed in, would be, to admit that *we only* have been wrong, as a committee, notwithstanding numerous precedents; or that the Cadets, as a body, were in error in acting, in an extreme case, *by committee*: when, at the same time, they are not allowed to consider your condemnation of this mode, as a general principle; altho' the Rules & Art[icle]s of War, under which they are acknowledged to be, contain no distinction against them. The Cadets who lately composed that committee are sensible, Sir, that they are not to expect a change, in their favour, of the course w[hi]ch the Executive Gov[ernmen]t may have determined upon as proper. But they are also too sensible of what belongs to themselves, to make an acknowledgm[en]t of misconduct, where they are conscious only of having acted correctly, from pure motives, and with a disinterested aim, which, upon the most mature reflection, they cannot but approve. Serious, indeed, is the loss we sustain by relinquishing forever our hopes and prospects at the Academy; but presuming that the proposed letter is your ultimate condition of our return, we cannot, for a moment, hesitate between *interest* and *honour*.

We should, however, be unworthy of the cause in which we suffer, did we not experience unfeigned satisfaction, in knowing that for the Corps to which we belong, substantial redress has been granted; with a fair prospect of being hereafter exempt from injuries, such as those of which they were lately obliged to complain. It was for this, that, without personal grievance, we consented to relinquish individual ease and comfort: it is for this we yield ourselves a sacrifice to what the authorities to which we are bound to submit deem expedient—that we should remain under arrest, without a formal exhibition of charges against us, and be condemned without a trial.

LS in DNA, 1, R-97; PC in House Document No. 14, 16th Cong., 1st Sess.; PC in *American State Papers: Military Affairs*, 2:20.

Pension Certificate of Artemas Reed, 2/1. Calhoun certifies that this former Pvt. in the Revolutionary forces is to receive $8 per month in Va. from 5/23/1818. DS in DLC, United States: Finance, U.S. Banks, Box 2.

To C[aesar] A. Rodney, Wilmington, Del., 2/1. "Your letter of the 18th ult[im]o, and also one from your son Cadet Thomas M. Rodney of the 25th ult[im]o tendering his resignation, have been received. The resignation is accepted." FC in DNA, 3, 10:238; CC in DLC, Carnegie Institution of Washington Transcript Collection.

To William Smith, [Senator from S.C.,] 2/1. Answering his inquiry of 1/25 (ALS in DNA, 1, S-210), Calhoun informs him that [Col.] Simeon Knight was nominated and has been confirmed by the Senate to fill the position of Battalion Paymaster that was left vacant when the nomination [in 1817] of Capt. B[eaufort] T. Watts was rejected by the Senate. FC in DNA, 3, 10:238–239.

From ALEXANDER STUART

Washington City, Febr[uar]y 1st 1819

My mind has had no little exercise, in selecting the most eligible mode, of presenting the subject of this letter, to your favourable consideration. A plain tale, being more congenial to the feeling of the writer, and best suited, to the object, has been adopted.

Capt. John Campbell, a verry [*sic*] worthy and truly respectable gentleman, has written me, a letter, desiring that I should apply to you for a Cadet's appointment for his son William G. Campbell. The youth is about fourteen years old, considerably advanced in the classics, and a tolerable proficient, in the English branch of education, of an active, sprightly mind and good moral habits.

The Capt. is well known to several members of Congress, who on being acquainted with his wish, would render any aid, in their power, to accomplish, his object. He, directed me to persue [*sic*], that plan; but as in all the vicissitudes of my life, I have received from him and his family, so strong, and undeviating a friendship I concluded, that if I could place him under obligations, to you only, it ["would" *interlined*] shew him how sincerely, I appreciated, his civilities. Thus, impressed I solicit, the appointment, of the son of my friend, well satisfied, his conduct, will reflect credit, on himself and the service.

If, Sir, my unsupported recommendation, is not thought sufficient, I will call in the assistance of those gentlemen, whos[e] aid, he has directed me to ask. But if the appointment should be granted, on my application, I shall be peculiarly gratified, as it will evince, that altho' unfortunate, I am not insensible to acts of kindness.

ALS in DNA, 15, 1819, 39.

From W[illiam] A[llen] Trimble, Columbus, O., 2/1. He resigns his commission as a Lt. Col. in the 8th Infantry Regiment, as of 3/1, because he will begin on 3/4 to serve as a Senator from O.; his accounts have been settled, and he is not now in active duty. An AEI by Calhoun records the acceptance of this resignation. 2 ALS's (one formal, the other explanatory) in DNA, 11, 13987.

From Decius Wadsworth

Ordnance Office, 1 Feb[ruar]y 1819

From a cursory View of Major [Abram R.] Woolley's Accounts which have not yet been taken up for Settlement at the Auditor's Office, it may be presumed, if the Charge he has made of a per diem Allowance of $2½ per day during the Years 1816 and 1817 and $1½ per day for a part of 1818 be admitted, there will not be found any considerable Balance pro or con on the Settlement of his Accounts to the Close of 1818, provided the Expenditures stated to have been made in the 4th Quarter of 1818 shall appear to be supported by proper Vouchers.

There can be no objection therefore arising from the State of his Accounts to his receiving an Advance of $5,000 which is the Amount of his Estimate for the 1st Quarter of the present year.

It ought to be observed that the Estimate of Major [James] Dallaby of the Expences at the three [N.Y.] Posts of Watervliet, Rome and Vergennes (at each of which there is a Gang of Armourers employed in repairing small arms) for the first Quarter of the present year amounts to no more than $4,500. The current Expences at Pittsburgh are equal to those at the three Establishments abovementioned; and it has long been evident to me that Major Woolley feels anxious rather to augment than retrench the Expences at Pittsburgh. If he can be induced to change his Course I shall be much gratified, but do not expect it.

ALS in DNA, 1, W-177; FC in DNA, 32, 2:179–180.

From J[ames] L. E[dwards], 2/2. As he was ordered on 2/1 by Calhoun to do, Edwards submits a draft of a bill by which Congress might authorize Calhoun to appoint a second agent in Tenn. for paying U.S. pensioners, those who reside east of the Tennessee, Clinch, and Powell Rivers. FC (of both the letter and the draft) in DNA, 91, 6:208.

To E[dmund] P. Gaines, Fernandina, [East Fla.,] 2/2. A claim for $250 as rent for "land adjoining the City of Savannah now occupied by barracks for Troops of the United States" for the year 1818 has been received from Charles Harris of Savannah. Calhoun reiterates his order that Gaines shall "decide on the propriety of sustaining or abandoning the barracks at Savannah." LS in DNA, 11, 13877; FC in DNA, 3, 10:239.

From Lt. Col. James House, Governor's Island, New York Harbor, 2/2. Reports that the walls of the Battery [at the southern tip of Manhattan Island] have been damaged by a recent storm and that the city government wants the coöperation of the U.S. in rebuilding those walls, because some land involved has been ceded to the U.S. for defense. ALS in DNA, 221, 19, with an AEI by Calhoun asking [Walker K.] Armistead to report the probable cost of the rebuilding to the U.S.

From D[aniel] Parker, 2/2. Recruiting efforts resulted in 90 enlistments in N.Y. and Vt. during the most recent month for which reports have been received. "I believe the recruiting generally, between this [day] and the 1st of June, will not exceed what it has been for the last Quarter, and that the rations required of the several Contractors, on that account, will not excede [*sic*] those of the last Quarter." LS in DNA, 1, P-109; FC in DNA, 12, 5:177.

From the Rev. George Colton

Westford, County of Otsego, N.Y., [*ca.* February 3, 1819]

Mr. A[lvan] Stewart of Cherry Valley [N.Y.] delivered your compliments. Tho' you are exalted by your country to one of the most honorable posts which she had to bestow, yet you did not forget that we were once classmates at Yale College; that we once walked together in "the Academic Groves"—those days are past—we are dispersed far & wide. Tho' you are Sec[retar]y of War & a great man, you kin[d]ly remembered me, an obscure parson; and you will always have my thanks & best wishes. I live in obscurity; have but little money; no great ambition, except to excell [*sic*] in literature, knowledge of divinity & dooing [*sic*] good. As you, I think, was fond of Latin & mathematics, and greatly excelled, especially in the latter, it may give you some pleasure to know that I have had good opportunity to persue [*sic*] them to considerable advantage, for several years.

But "ad rem."

Mr. Charles Holt is a son of Maj. [Charles] Holt of Cherry Valley. He is a young gentleman of good tallents [*sic*] & morals. He is 16 years of age. [Actually, he was not yet 14.] He wishes to obtain the appointment of Cadet in the military school at West Point; and it is my real desire that you, dear Sir, will gratify his request. I must recommend him in strong language. I should have observed, that he belongs to a highly respectable family. But prolixity is needless; for I am credibly informed that recommendations have been sent to you from the most respectable quarters. But you will confide in my [*one word illegible*: word ?]. You know I'm a blunt, honest man that speaks right out. I really wish I could see you, expecially at Washington; I ever had much respect for you, and was glad when I heard of your appointment: though we had not the happiness to see exactly alike in politicks. But how much farther did you see than the obscure clergyman who, instead of debating with great men great political questions, was preaching, was reading the Latin & Greek folios.

You must write—and direct your letter to Cooperstown & C[herry] Valley [N.Y.]. Yours, with love & regard, George Colton.

ALS in DNA, 15, 1818, 86.

From [Thomas S. Jesup], 2/3. Answers Calhoun's letter of 2/2 by protesting that, when Deputy Quartermaster General [Milo] Mason was sent to the South in 1818 to take charge of Quartermaster operations in the Seminole War, Mason had adequate funds and that $40,000 remain in his and Capt. [Richard J.] Easter's hands, subject to orders from [Andrew] Jackson rather than Jesup. The financial shortage of which Col. [William] King complains cannot, therefore, be corrected by Jesup. Indeed, with the exception of the abovementioned $40,000, Quartermaster appropriations were entirely exhausted on 11/30/1818; and "I have been compelled on my own responsibility to apply funds of a different appropriation" to certain Quartermaster expenses. LU with 7 Ens in DNA, 1, J-119; FC in DNA, 42, 1:175–176.

From A[bner] Lacock, [Senator from Del.,] 2/3. In behalf of the Senate committee appointed to ascertain whether or not Andrew Jackson justifiably conquered Spanish posts in the two Floridas during 1818, Lacock states the substance of some testimony given to the committee by Col. [Robert] Butler and asks for certain relevant documents. LS in DNA, 1, L-89; CC in DLC, Andrew Jackson Papers, 8540–8541; PC in Bassett, ed., *Correspondence,* 2:410.

From D[ecius] Wadsworth, 2/3. He has requested of Lt. [Charles] Ward information concerning the character of Maj. [Richard] Oldham and Oldham's suitability for the position of Military Storekeeper that has been made vacant by the death of Maj. [Thomas] Martin. "Although it is believed the Services of a Military Storekeeper might be dispensed with at Newport, [Ky.,] yet should the information I have asked of Lieut[enant] Ward prove Satisfactory, as respects the fitness of Maj. Oldham, I should recommend his being appointed." FC in DNA, 32, 2:180.

From Ephraim Bateman, [Representative from N.J.,] 2/4. Encloses a memorial addressed to Calhoun by Daniel Garrison and dated 1/30. Garrison recites that the U.S. contracted with him on 2/11/1815 to supply 273 logs at stipulated prices, that 73 were bought, and that the news of peace caused him to lose the sale of the remaining 200 for $1,400. He asks for relief and suggests that the logs in question should be needed in the construction work that is being done at the Pea Patch, near to them. ALS (by Bateman) with ADS (by Garrison) in DNA, 1, B-205, with an AEI by P[eter] H[agner] stating that the contract does not require the U.S. to buy more logs than it needs.

From Capt. William Bradford, Commanding Officer, Fort Smith, Bell Point, [Ark. Territory,] 2/4. Explains that Calhoun's letter of 8/7/1818 "was received" via Natchez "by the last mail." Former Army Capt. Nathaniel Pryor, now a trader with the Osage Indians, reports that war is likely to break out again between the Cherokees and the Osages, because the former have been aggressors in stealing 40 horses from the latter. The Osages want peace but are being urged by four other tribes to make war upon the Cherokees. "I shall visit the Osages again and endeavour to prevent their resorting to hostile measures." ALS with En in DNA, 1, B-286; PC in Carter, ed., *Territorial Papers,* 19:33–34.

To [John Gaillard], President [Pro Tempore] of the Senate

Department of War, 4th February, 1819

In pursuance of the resolution of the Senate of the 29th Jan[uar]y, 1819, [ADS by Charles Cutts in DNA, 1, S-214,] referring the petition of Mary Cassin to the Secretary of War, to consider and report thereon, I have the honor to transmit a report, which states "the rules in auditing such accounts, and the objections to the claim of Mrs. Cassin," made by the 3d Auditor of the Treasury Dep[artmen]t [Peter Hagner].

I would respectfully suggest the propriety of passing an act for the relief of Mrs. Cassin, provided it is thought there is sufficient evidence of the claim being well founded.

FC in DNA, 4, 2:91.

From [Thomas S. Jesup], 2/4. Submits the report of the Quartermaster Department for the last quarter of 1818. As to the exact status of its funds, Jesup thinks it advisable to rely upon a Comptroller's report; but he encloses a statement of the amounts received and disbursed by Quartermaster officers. He reports confidentially how these officers have served. FC in DNA, 42, 1:176–177.

From former Capt. D[aniel] Kincheloe, Clarksburg, [Va. (later W.Va.),] 2/4. Reviews his efforts since the close of the War of 1812 to settle his accounts; claims that he has ever been willing to return to Washington for the purpose and that the true balance may be found to be in his favor rather than the government's; attributes the recent demand that he pay what he owes to an untruthful letter written by B. Wilson, Jr., who is an enemy of the administration. R[eturn] J. Meigs, Jr., can inform Calhoun reliably about Kincheloe. ALS in DNA, 1, K-27.

To Rufus King, [Senator from N.Y.,] 2/4. Calhoun answers his request of 2/3 for remission of the fine imposed upon Walter Burling as a N.Y. militia delinquent by stating that this case will be investigated as usual. FC in DNA, 3, 10:240.

To ABNER LACOCK, Chairman, Senate Committee on Pensions, and JOHN RHEA, Chairman, House Committee on Pensions

Department of War, 4th February, 1819

I have the honor to lay before you for the information of the Committee on pensions [in each of your respective houses], the last quarterly report of the state of the business in the Pension office.

FC in DNA, 4, 2:91.

To [James Monroe], 2/4. Complying with a Senate resolution of 1/25, Calhoun submits reports covering the regulations, entrance requirements, enrollment, etc., of the Military Academy. LS with Ens in DNA, 152, 15A-E5; FC in DNA, 6, 1:345; PC with Ens in *American State Papers: Military Affairs,* 1:838–848.

From Maj. W[illoughby] Morgan, St. Louis, 2/3. Acknowledges Calhoun's letter of 12/22/1818. "On my arrival at this place (about two weeks since) I learned that the suit commenced against me for the seizure of [Russel] Farnham and —— Darling had been discontinued. I am, therefore, happily rid of the necessity of giving you any further trouble in relation to this business." ALS in DNA, 77 (M-271:2, frames 1536–1537).

From C[harles] Tait, [Senator from Ga.,] 2/4. Encloses a letter to himself [dated 1/18] from "a former neighbour of mine in Georgia," Thomas W. Williams, seeking the appointment as a Cadet of Williams's nephew and ward, Matthew R.T. Harrison, who will become 14 next 12/7. "I shall feel obliged if you will state to me what prospect there is to get his ward into the Military Academy at the present or any future [time]." ALS in DNA, 15, 1819, 110.

To Thomas White, Richmond, 2/4. Answers his letter of 1/19 (ALS in DNA, 1, W-136, with AEI's by Calhoun, Peter Hagner, and Decius Wadsworth) protesting that Hagner has approved only part of the sum claimed by White for the storage of some lead for the government. Calhoun sustains Hagner's decision that the U.S. should not pay White for having delivered from storage more lead than he received for storage, because there is insufficient evidence as to this alleged fact and because the price of lead is not well established. If White wishes, he can ask Congress for relief. FC in DNA, 3, 10:240–241.

To John Wilson, "Civil Engineer," Charleston, S.C.

Department of War, 4th February 1819

I have received your letter of the 14th ult[im]o. Feeling every disposition to facilitate the execution of the important objects committed to you by the State of So[uth] Carolina, you have permission to make use of the public buildings at Rocky Mount in the prosecution of the works which you are about commencing on behalf of the State of South Carolina. It is expected every attention to the preservation of the Barracks will be given while they remain in your possession. As it is believed the tools and materials at those barracks are not immediately wanted, if you will call upon two disinterested persons in that quarter, to value them, and send to me their report, orders will be given for the sale of them to the State.

FC in DNA, 3, 10:241–242. Note: Wilson's letter of 1/14 is printed herein under that date.

From [the Cherokee Delegation], Washington, "Feb[ruar]y 5th 1818 [*sic*; 1819]." With the awkward but moving eloquence of ambitious aboriginies, these deputies of the Eastern Cherokees give assurances of their eagerness for education and civilization; they foresee that, when the dark cloud of superstition, prejudice, and ignorance shall have vanished from among them, "propelled by the dictates of Reason, restrained by prudence, education, & science, we may with confidence assure ourselves that we shall participate with our white Brothers in the enjoyment and advantages of the best of all earthly Governments." They explained: "It is to the want of education and not to a defect in nature" that "we must ascribe nearly all of our evils. Natural man is in every country and in every age nearly the same." They announce that their national laws "are now recorded in a book" but are communicated to their people orally; they want, therefore, a printing office and a periodical. They plead for complete fulfillment of the treaty of

7/8/1817, the deadline for its being made effective (June, 1818) "having passed without its accomplishment." They protest [Joseph] McMinn's having leased "our Lands, contrary to the Sperit [*sic*] and meaning of the treaty and in positive contradiction of its express Stipulations." "We have a strong desire to Hold Seperate [*sic*] property in our Lands, & to Give testimony in courts of Justice under certain Regulations. We wish to act with liberality towards our Brothers over the Missi[ssi]ppi and trust the Great Sperit will direct them in the straight path." LU (incomplete) in DNA, 77, 3913 (M-271:2, frames 575–579).

From Nathaniel Cutting

Section of Bounty Lands, Feb[ruar]y 5th 1819

I have the honor to hand you herewith a statement of the Transactions in this Branch of the Department over which you preside, embracing the period from the 1st of November 1818 to the 31st of January 1819 inclusive.

In conformity with your directions, it should have been presented to you on the 1st instant; but, although the several subdivisions of the business were then completed, yet the concourse of Members of Congress and others at the office, has hitherto prevented my forming the general Abstract. Having, likewise, some other Manuscripts to prepare which required thought and mature Reflection, I have remained at my "*Wigwam on Pleasant Hills*" to make a finish of it; [this has been] the first day that I have been absent from my Post on *a working* day for a long period.

ALS with En in DNA, 2, C-1819.

From Edmund P. Gaines

Amelia Island, E[ast] F[lorida], February 5th 1819

I have received your letters of the 18th and 19th of the last month. The orders of the President of the United States [James Monroe], with which I am honored in your last, shall be scrupulously obeyed.

I have heard little or nothing of the Seminole Indians for some weeks past, except that a small number of warriors have surrendered themselves with their families at St. Marks and Fort Scott in the last month.

In compliance with your instruction upon the subject of a cession by the Creek Nation of their reservation at Fort Hawkins, and requiring me to report "whether the occupation of that Post by the United States, is necessary in a military point of view, and if not whether it would be advisable to abandon it altogether," I have the honor to state:

That, independent of all considerations connected with our Indian neighbours, and with the establishment of an arsenal as heretofore suggested, I should not hesitate to say that the occupation of that Post is not necessary in a military point of view and that it ought to be abandoned.

1st. Because it is too distant from the national boundary or sea coast for the establishment of permanent Barracks for Troops destined for the national defence in a war against any foreign power.

2nd. Because it is destructive to discipline, and dangerous to the morals of officers and men, to be detached from their Corps and stationed for any considerable length of time at small interior Posts—and the Army is too small to afford entire Battalions or large detachments to garrison such Posts.

3rd. Because every member of the Army in time of peace should have an opportunity of devoting a part of his time to the construction of Fortifications (and these to be useful must necessarily be placed upon the best selected sites upon the sea coast and national boundary, and built upon the most approved plans with a view to the permanent defence of the country); thus employed, the officer will not only possess the advantage of acquiring knowledge necessarily connected with his profession, but will moreover contribute with the aid of the soldier to the erection of works of defence, which, bidding defiance to an invading foe, will stand as monuments of the foresight and wisdom of the Government and people, and of the skill and industry of the Army; & thus it will be proven that our country possesses the native talent, as well as the moral and physical powers necessary for every branch of her defence, whereas, at a post like that of Fort Hawkins, neither the skill of the officer or artificer nor the industry or labour of either can be employed to any valuable purpose upon works of defence.

But I am by no means prepared to say that our friendly Indian neighbors have arrived at that point of civilization at which we can safely abandon the only military Post upon their border.

It is not perhaps expected that I should touch upon this subject. I will, however, take the liberty in a few days to offer you my views upon such points as appear to have an immediate connection with our military arrangements.

ALS in DNA, 1, G-104; LS in DNA, 11, 13361.

From Andrew Jackson, Washington, 2/5. Acknowledges Calhoun's letter of 2/5 (LS and 5 CC's in DLC, Andrew Jackson Papers, 47:8544–8558; FC in DNA, 3, 10:242; PC in *American State Papers: Military Affairs,* 1:768; PC in Senate Document No. 73, 16th Cong., 1st Sess.; PC in Carter, ed., *Territorial Papers,* 18:555), which enclosed a request of 2/3 from A[bner] Lacock for information [about Jackson's invasion of the Floridas]. Jackson refers Calhoun to a letter of 5/19/1818 to Jackson from [William W.] Bibb, [Governor of Ala. Territory,] and mentions reports of Indian concentrations and atrocities that caused him to march to Pensacola. Jackson also refers Calhoun to a report of Jackson's military activities sent by him after reaching Pensacola and offers to provide further information about his operations if it is desired. 2 CC's in DLC, Andrew Jackson Papers, 47:8552, 8554; PC in *American State Papers: Military Affairs,* 1:747; PC in Bassett, ed., *Correspondence,* 2:410–411; PC in Senate Document No. 73, 16th Cong., 1st Sess.

From [Thomas S. Jesup], 2/5. Submits an estimate of the distance, time, and expense involved in moving a Regiment from Plattsburg, N.Y., to Pittsburgh. FC in DNA, 42, 1:177.

From Return J. Meigs, Washington, 2/5. Pursuant to Calhoun's letter of 12/8/1818, Meigs signed at Maryville, Tenn., on [1/18] a contract with [James] Turk & [Thomas] Henderson for rations to be supplied to the Eastern Cherokees who emigrate and to those at the Agency; Meigs encloses it. It complies with Calhoun's wishes, "with the addition of [a] *provisional* condition of delivering rations at the Chickasaw Bluff[s], if required, being apprehensive that such conditional arrangement may be found advantageous to the Government & of convenience to the emigrants, as considerable numbers may cho[o]se to remove by land; in such case it will lessen the expense of Boats." An AES indicates Calhoun's approval of the contract. ALS with Ens in DNA, 77 (M-271:2, frames 1343–1349); FC with En in DNA, 75 (M-208:8).

Eldred Simkins, [Representative from S.C.,] to [Christopher] Vandeventer

H[ouse of] Rep[resentative]s, Thursday [*sic*], 5 Feb. 1819

I rec[eive]d your note in which you mention that the Sec[retar]y of War could not discharge Ira Youngblood, but that in case of application to civil authority ["every facility" *interlined*] should be afforded him. I wish you had been a little more explicit about the facility to be given, what it is to be, how to be obtained &c. From the certificate given by [former] Lieut[enant Allen B.] Addison who enlisted him, it is most evident that he has been detained against good faith, and however blameable the ["enlisted" *interlined*] officer might be, yet from his own shewing Ira Youngblood ought not to have been detained an hour after the conclusion ["of the War" *interlined*]. My opinion of the officer who now presides in the War Department will not permit me to arraign his decision, and an application should not have been made to *him,* but [for the fact] that a confined soldier had applied for ["& obtained" *interlined*] his discharge through Mr. [George] McDuffie, [later a Representative and Senator from S.C.,] (papers presented by me,) and it was thought that this case might be as strong a one; and if so, equally entitled to the Sec[retar]y[']s consideration.

As for his [Youngblood's] serving out his time I cannot advise him to it, as seems to be thought best by the Sec[retar]y because 1. the hardships of his situation as a soldier and the impaired state of his health will likely kill him before the 14 Sept[embe]r, 2dly Because he may now perhaps be of some service to his family, and 3dly Because I have no hope whatever of further good being produced upon him by the discipline incident to a soldier, even were his health ["good" *canceled*] strong enough to be [*sic*] bear it. I must therefore intrude upon your goodness so far as to inform me ["how" *canceled*] what facility and in what way ["it" *interlined*] will be given so as to give him the advantage of it, in case it can be afforded compatibly with a sense of duty; for permit me to express my admiration for the stern principles of justice as guiding the course of a high public officer, and I ought not to claim *any thing* but what may comport with such a rule.

ALS in DNA, 1, S-211.

From John Williams, [Senator from Tenn.,] 2/5. Encloses a letter written to himself today in Washington by Maj. John Walker of the Cherokee Deputation, which says that "it would please them [the Indians] very much, if the Secretary [of War] would give each of them a few dollars" for their entertainment and that it "will do them much good." Williams comments: "Walker has been & is faithful to the promises he made you last winter. His suggestion is entitled to respect, and will no doubt have the effect he supposes it will." ALS with En in DNA, 1, W-179.

To William Wirt, 2/5. "The certificate of the County Court is required by the rules of this Department, to establish the heirship of deceased soldiers, where the heirs claim under the laws of Virginia. Will you inform me whether you consider the enclosed certificate sufficiently authenticated, without the seal of the court? I will thank you for your opinion as early as convenient. I enclose the written regulations." LS in DNA, 111, 163; FC in DNA, 3, 10:242.

From [Simeon] Baldwin, New Haven, 2/6. Encloses certificates for three pension applicants; inquires about delay in awards to two others. ALS in CtY.

From Nathaniel Cutting

Washington City, D.C., Feb. 6th 1819

Early in the present Session of Congress, I communicated to you my intention to *memorialize* that honorable Body on the Subject of the inadequate Salary which the appropriation for Clerk hire in the War Dep[artmen]t enabled you to award for that Vigilance and incessant Toil which I have always exercised in the humble station allot[t]ed me. The opinion and Counsel you were so good as to impart to me on *that* occasion, induced me to suspend my intended application; and the Memorial I had then prepared, still sleeps quietly in my Port Folio. You kindly took the trouble of perusing that Memorial, and were pleased to object to its *length,* and to its *stile* [*sic*]. With the highest deference for your superiour judgment, I must plead in defence of its *prolixity* that it was scarcely possible in fewer words to state the chilling neglect with which my assiduity in Public Service was treated during the Presidency of *Mr.* [James] *Madison*; nor could I well more briefly indicate my consequent mortification. But, as *"my Necessities"* though *"not my will,"* oblige me still to throw myself on the Bounty of the Sovereign, I have prepared a very concise sketch of the humble Duties I have been called to perform and the paucity of the remuneration that has been accorded me; the whole Representation of my case, is comprised in a single page of Small *Fool's-cap* Paper.

Allow me, Sir, to solicit *your Patronage* and *Support* in this application, and, through your kind intervention, the Patronage of *the President of the United States* [James Monroe]. *He* has formerly honored my exertions in public service with marked approbation, and has given me flattering indications of Amity, which I have uniformly endeavoured to deserve *"by a patient perseverance in the ways of well doing"*: but, as few or none of the ingredients which form the *obsequious Courtier,* enter into the composition of my Republican frame, it seems that other more plausible Friends and apparent Favorites, have stept [*sic*] between me and Presidential notice, until, perhaps, my name and the public services I have performed, even under his immediate direction, are obliterated from the Scroll of his Memory.

In the Memorial which I now contemplate, I have but slightly suggested a change in the denomination attached to my present Employ, which I now beg leave more fully to submit to your consideration; it is, that the appellation of *"Auditor of Claims for Bounty Land,"* be adopted in future as the ["official" *interlined*] *designation* of that Person who may be charged with the immediate care of that Branch of the War Department which has been for nearly *ten tedious* years confided to my management. I hope you will do me the justice to believe that this proposal is not the offspring of *a vain desire on my part* to introduce a useless distinction: if *that* were the case, it is not probable that one who had been honored with the appointment of *"Secretary of Legation, Consul of the* United States," and "*Secretary to the Commission of the United States at Paris under the Louisiana Convention,*" would have sat down quietly, *during more than nine years,* in quality of a *secondary Clerk* in the War Office. The fact is, that, as imperious circumstances rendered it necessary for me to seek Employment, and that the higher Powers who had the distribution of the "*Loaves and Fishes,*" did not appear disposed to allot me a more competent share of them, excepting, perhaps, through the medium of an humiliating solicitation at which my proud Republican Spirit always revolted, I have crept on, undistinguished, in a lowly station where, I presume, my Talents have been found useful; chearfully [*sic*] performing such Tasks "*as were set before me, asking no questions for conscience*['s] *sake.*"

I have long seen and felt that the *innovation,* if you please to term it so, which I now propose, would be productive of much public utility; as well as offer a fair occasion of affording me a compensation more analogous to the importance of my public Transactions, than that scanty pittance which has hitherto been so sparingly dealt out to me from the abundant *Cornucopia* of the United States.

The *utility* of the proposed change may be in some measure illustrated by calling to your recollection the late occurrence in *the Section of Bounty Lands,* when one of the Clerks *there* employed pointedly *rebelled* against the *nominal pre-eminence,* with which you were pleased to invest me, "*You are nothing but a Clerk, any more than me,*" was one of the young man's remarks, consonant to his obstreperous behavior. The weight of character & authority that would have attached to me in quality of "*Auditor of Bounty Land Claims*" would probably have prevented, not only *this impertinence,* but *the error* in his previous proceedings which elicited it.

I have at different times perceived indications of a similar spirit of self-sufficiency in others of the young men in this Office, although the symptoms of it did not so violently explode: however, it plainly spoke the same language; "*you are nothing but a Clerk.*"

It would be an ungracious and an humiliating Task for *me,* to be continually running *to you* with complaints that *this,* or *that Clerk,* did not punctually attend to the *opening Office-Hour*; or that he *quit the Office* before the usual hour of *closing it*[;] but, as *Auditor* I could exercise an immediate control, and should, probably, soon correct such aberrations from the established ro[u]tine of public duty; and, I flatter myself, I should thus obtain *much more* public service in course of the year, than is now rendered.

Nor is it arrogance in me to say that *my Duties* are now more *arduous* than those in *any other secondary* Branch of Public Service under the Government of the United States, those of [Peter Hagner,] the *3d Auditor of the Treasury, only excepted*: and there are few offices of that Class ["where" *interlined*] *the estimated value* of United States Property *alienated,* or *expended,* is equal to these Lands. For example: during the three years last past, the Grants on the average will be found to pass *one million of acres per annum*: or two millions of dollars value, each year!

Other Reasons, of less cogency in a public point of view, although equally valid, might be urged in favor of the new arrangement; but I forbear further intrusion on those valuable moments which I know you consciencíously [*sic*] devote to public service of a more important description: I must, however, take the further liberty on this occasion to request you will have the goodness to view this Representation with your accustomed candour, and that you will communicate to the President of the United States such portion of it as you may think will convey to him a just idea of the subject.

ALS in DNA, 1, C-213.

From CALLENDER IRVINE

Philad[elphi]a, Feb[ruar]y 6th 1819

Proposals have been [received] at this office from manufacturers, in various parts of the United States, to provide materials for Army Clothing for the service of the present year, and taking the most favorable of which, when there is certainty that the proposers have it in their power to execute contracts faithfully, I find that Clothes for Great Coats, kerseys for Jackets & overalls, & in short all the materials required for service this year, to be manufactured of Wool & Cotton, can be procured of Domestic manufacture, of good & unexceptionable quality, & upon nearly as reasonable terms, as the same quality of foreign goods can be purchased on, excepting Blankets & Blue Clothes.

The most favorable proposals to furnish domestic made Blankets are at $3 each. Foreign Blankets of the best kind & of proper sizes & weights, may be had at $2.80 each, and if the duty of 15 pr ct. paid to Government is taken into consideration the actual cost will be $2.38—difference 62 cents on each Blanket. The most favorable proposal to furnish blue Clothes as above, for uniform

Coats, of domestic manufacture—6/4 wide are at	$2.50	pr. yard
Foreign Clothes of excellent quality may be had at	$2.30	” ”
Deduct duty p[ai]d Government	.57	” ”
Actual Cost	$1.73	
difference	.77	” ”

The American Blankets procured last year were of excellent quality. If any objection can be made to them, it is that the Knap was not sufficiently raised upon them. This may be imputed in some measure to the short staple of our Wool.

The blue Clothes were also good and durable. Yet there was a want of uniformity as to *shade* of colour, & [they] were somewhat deficient as to their dressing & finishing. However, in these respects they are much improved within two years, and are improving. Foreign Blankets & Blue Clothes might be purchased at much lower prices than those above stated, but the quality, sizes & weights of the first and the quality, dye, finish & width of the latter, are such as to render them entirely unfit for Army purposes.

I have conceived it to be my duty to make to you the foregoing report, and I shall defer making Contracts for blue Clothes & Blankets, 'till I shall receive your instruction on the subject of them.

ALS in DNA, 1, I-114; FC in DNA, 45, 387:319. NOTE: Calhoun's answer to this letter appears herein under 2/10.

To Abner Lacock, Chairman of the Senate Committee on the Seminole War, 2/6. Encloses a copy of an exchange of letters between the War Department and Andrew Jackson; these, "together with the letter of Governor [William Wyatt] Bibb [of the Territory of Ala.] already transmitted to you, furnish all the information in the possession of the Department, in relation to the several points of inquiry embraced in your letter of the 3d instant." LS in DLC, Andrew Jackson Papers, 8558; variant FC in DNA, 4, 2:91; PC from the FC in Carter, ed., *Territorial Papers,* 18:556.

James Monroe to the House of Representatives, 2/6. The President transmits a copy of a letter from Governor [William W.] Bibb [of Ala. Territory] to [Andrew] Jackson [dated 5/19/1818], "connected with the late military operations in Florida. This letter had been mislaid, or it would have been communicated with the other documents at the commencement of the session." LS with En in DNA, 202, 15A-E1.

From ELDRED SIMKINS, [Representative from S.C.]

Ho[use of] Rep[resentative]s, 6 Feb[ruar]y 1819

I am requested by Mr. Charles Mayson of Cambridge So[uth] Ca[rolina] to get information from your department relative to an application made by Rob[er]t F. Griffin for a land warrant. He states that "Griffin had lost his discharge, but has furnished as he thinks sufficient evidence of its having been once in his possession and accounted for its loss." The papers did not go to the war office. Will you be so good as to give this letter that direction wh[ich] may [as] promptly as convenient furnish the information[?]

P.S. The papers I suspect must have been committed to you. E.S.

ALS in DNA, 1, S-233.

From Lt. Col. T[ALBOT] CHAMBERS

Saint Louis, 7th February 1819

I conceive it my duty to apprize you that I have received the most authentic information, that a civil officer is now awaiting the arrival of Mr. Johnstons [*sic*; James Johnson's] Steam boats, at this place, (which are intended to transport the troops to Yellow Stone) for the purpose of arresting them on account of a sum of money—which is due from Mr. Johnston to the Saint Louis bank. In notifying you of this circumstance, I have no other view, than to evade any detention which might be produced to the expedition, as it is all important that they should move as early in the spring as may be practicable.

ALS in DNA, 1, C-193.

To Capt. S[amuel] Babcock, Newcastle, [Del.,] 2/8. "I enclose a memorial of Daniel Garrison, by which you will perceive he states a part of the logs he is yet to deliver. You will report to me whether these logs will be required in the construction of the works at the Pea Patch, and if they are worth the price stated in the memorial." FC in DNA, 3, 10:243.

From JOHN W[AYLES] EPPES, [Senator from Va.]

Feb. 8th 1819

Jno. W. Eppes with his respects returns to the Secretary at War the enclosed letter.

ALU with En in DNA, 1, S-215. NOTE: The En is an ALS from Isaac Shelby to Henry Clay dated 3/22/1818 in which Shelby explains various cessions of land south of the Ohio River made by the Cherokees and by the Six Nations—for example, by treaties in 1744, 1768, and 1775, the treaty of this last date having been between the Cherokees and [Richard] Henderson & Co.

From Ch[arles] Hicks, Washington, 2/8. He and other members of an authorized Cherokee Delegation have arrived to negotiate "for a definitive adjustment" of the Cherokee treaty of 7/8/1817, which has not been fulfilled in accordance with its stipulations. The Cherokees "have a right to claim the fatherly & benevolent protection" of the U.S., look to the federal government "as the source of their happiness & future prosperity," and profess their favorable attitude toward the U.S. They want to "render justice" to those Cherokees who have emigrated to Arkansas; "we cordially agree that their just rights should be secured to them." The arts of civilization are making rapid progress among the Eastern Cherokees; a few more years of benevolent help will transform these Cherokees from a savage into a Christian people. All leases of land within the Eastern Cherokees' territory, made in defiance of treaty stipulations, should be annulled. In proof of other violations of the treaty, they have brought documents, copies of which [Joseph] McMinn has doubtless already sent to Calhoun. Hicks asserts that the Eastern Cherokees are not guilty, as charged, of "opposition or hostility to the fair execution of the late Treaty." He asks that the national debts of the Eastern and Western Cherokees be paid by the U.S. before annuities are distributed to either;

"most of these debts have been incurred by the Arkansas Cherokees." He seeks also a more generous arrangement for the Eastern Cherokees who live on land to be ceded to the U.S. in exchange for the land occupied by the Western Cherokees. He states that the annual assemblage of the Eastern Cherokees to receive annuities is a "great national evil"; and he asks, therefore, that payments be made to the national treasurer, with the value of the rations usually received to be added in money. He seeks an adjustment, too, of a long-term dispute involving an unauthorized cession of some Cherokee land to Ga. ALS, attested by J[ohn] Lowry, in DNA, 77 (M-271:2, frames 1100–1105).

From A[BNER] LACOCK

Senate Chamber, Monday Morning [February 8, 1819]

Agreeably to your request I spoke to the Pres[iden]t [James Monroe] last evening relative to G[enera]l [Andrew] Jackson, & orders to G[enera]l [Edmund P.] Gain[e]s when he left Florida & your answer. He says he wishes that nothing should be kept back, & is anxious that we [of the investigating committee] should be in possession of the whole official correspondence of the G[enera]l with the [War] department. Since G[enera]l Jackson has himself mentioned the subject it will be the more necessary for us to have the facts. Will you be so good as to send the copies as soon as convenient.

ALS in DNA, 1, L-90. NOTE: An EU dates this letter as having been written on 2/8/1819. Calhoun's reply to this request appears herein under its date, 2/10.

To JOHN T. LEWIS, Pendleton, S.C.

Department of War, 8th February 1819

I have received your letter of the 22d ult[im]o concerning the issue of land warrants to Rich[ar]d & Duncan Presley, soldiers of the late war.

If these men were discharged at the close of the war, their honorable discharges must be forwarded to this office, upon which land warrants will issue. If they died before the close of the war, the land warrants will issue to the heirs, upon certificates of heirship granted by the Ordinary.

Whether they died in the service or not cannot be ascertained at this Department unless the name of the officer by whom they were enlisted or under whom they served or the name of the Company or Regiment to which they were attached be mentioned.

FC in DNA, 3, 10:243–244. NOTE: The letter from Lewis of 1/22 appears herein under that date.

From Alexander Macomb, Georgetown, D.C., 2/8. Reports about the 5th Military Department and makes several recommendations. Suggests the establishment of a post at the falls of the St. Marys [River], partly to protect and to secure the Indian trade. Macomb would like to be appointed a commissioner to negotiate for the necessary land cession there and for another at Green Bay; and he cites, in support of this request, the fact that Indians show an extra respect toward Army men. For the same reason, he even suggests that the commanding officer of each remote Army post in the West should be given charge of Indian affairs within his command; to do so would also save the expense of an Indian Agent's salary and would relieve the commanding officers of the considerable trouble of dealing with such Agents. Macomb revives a 20-year-old idea that an ammunition and arms depot should be built at the mouth of the Detroit River. In addition, he suggests that a story should be added to the storehouse in Detroit for Quartermaster supplies. For the next vacancy in his own staff he suggests the appointment of Capt. Henry Whiting. ALS in DNA, 221, 25.

From WILLIAM REED,
[former Representative from Mass.]

Marblehead, [Mass.,] February 8, 1819

Permit me to introduce to your acquaintance, the Rev[eren]d Samuel Worcester D.D. of Salem in this vicinity, Sec[retar]y of the A[merican] B[oard of] C[ommissioners for] F[oreign] Missions, who goes to Washington, on business of the Board with the Ex[ecutiv]e. Doctor Worcester is a Gentleman of the first Talents & respectability in his profession, and from a long intercourse & particular acquaintance with him, [I] can assure you that he [is] deserving [of] your entire confidence.

ALS in DNA, 77 (M-271:2, frames 1569–1570).

To G[erard] Steddiford, New York [City], 2/8. Acknowledges his detailed report of 1/18 (LS with En in DNA, 1, S-208) of the proceedings of the court-martial since 1814 against about 12,000 N.Y. militia delinquents; requests specific information about the time spent by Steddiford himself and by the two Judge Advocates, in order to determine the correct amount of extra pay due to them. As Steddiford requested on 2/2 (LS in DNA, 1, S-217), Calhoun sends the approved proceedings of the court for three counties. FC in DNA, 3, 10:243.

To Cadet George Stickney, West Point, 2/8. Accepts his resignation of 1/31 (ALS in DNA, 15, 1818, 140), which had been proffered on the ground that "it is peculiarly necessary, on account of a recent occurrence." FC in DNA, 3, 10:243. Stickney wrote another letter of resignation, expressing his [mother's] consent, on 2/10. ALS in DNA, 14, 1819, 13.

To William H. Crawford, 2/9. Requests that $1,537,179.17 be made available for expenditure; itemizes 21 accounts to which the intended payments will be charged. FC in DNA, 171, 1:319–320.

From George Gibson, 2/9. "I have to request that Col. James Johnson be ordered to have in deposit at Bellefountain [*sic*] on or before the first day of May next two hundred and fifty thousand rations in addition to the four hundred and thirty thousand already ordered." FC in DNA, 191, 1:9.

From John W. Johnson, Factor, Pra[i]rie du Chien, 2/9. Corrects the erroneous report made by N[icholas] Boilvin to Calhoun in person last year that, while Boilvin was away, no one could serve as Indian Agent there. Johnson claims to have been a Sub-Agent since 1810; John Mason of Georgetown, [D.C.,] and George Graham know Johnson. He stresses a need for regulations at Prairie du Chien, to prevent contention between the military and civil officials. The Army's commanding officer there claims jurisdiction over nine miles square—an area including more than 50 civilian families; they are quite discontent "at being under Martial Law" and at being unable under civil law to collect debts and to compel "a compliance to Contracts." ALS in DNA, 1, [J-161]; PC in Carter, ed., *Territorial Papers,* 10:812–814.

From Stephen Pleasonton, 2/9. Answers Calhoun's letter of 1/29 requesting information about the disbursements made by Indian Agents during the last two years exclusive of payments made because of Indian treaties. "As the accounts of some of the Agents have not been received for the last quarter of 1818, and some that have been received are not yet adjusted, and as the disbursements of the Agents do not comprise all the expences relating to the Indians, I considered that the best mode to come at your object would be to extract from the Treasury books the several payments made to the Agents & others, out of the appropriation for the Indian Department, commencing with March 1817, when this Office went into operation, and ending the 31 December 1818. A Statement of these payments is accordingly enclosed." When funds "were advanced to individuals, on requisitions by the War Department, and not on settled accounts, I am ignorant of the objects to which it was intended they should be applied. In all other cases the object of expenditures is expressed." LS with Ens in DNA, 1, P-122; FC in DNA, 58, 1:107–108.

To Callender Irvine, Philadelphia

Department of War, 10 Feb[ruar]y, 1819

I have received your letter of the 6th instant in relation to the proposals received for materials to clothe the Army.

By reference to the instructions of the Acting Secretary of War [George Graham] dated the 2nd of January 1817, you will perceive that a small difference of price in favour of foreign fabrics, is not a sufficient reason for giving the preference to them over domestic ones. On the contrary, domestic fabrics are to be encouraged, provided the price be only "something enhanced." But, in the case reported by you, there appears a very considerable difference of price, which, if the domestic should be preferred, would materially enhance the expenditure. Under this view of the case, I shall decline giving orders to contract for the domestic articles of Blankets and Blue Cloths referred to in your letter.

LS in ScU-SC, John C. Calhoun Collection; FC in DNA, 3, 10:244. NOTE: Irvine's letter of 2/6 appears herein under that date.

To James Johnson, Great Crossing[s], Ky., 2/10. "You will have in deposit at Belle fontaine [Territory of Mo.] on or before the 1st day of May Two hundred & fifty thousand rations in addition to the four hundred and thirty thousand [*actually* 420,000] already ordered [on 12/10/1818]. FC in DNA, 3, 10:245; PC in House Document No. 110, 16th Cong., 2nd Sess.

To Abner Lacock

Department of War, 10th February, 1819

Agreeably to the request, made in your letter of the 8th instant, I now transmit, an extract of Gen[era]l [Andrew] Jackson's letter of the 10th of August last, and a copy of Gen[era]l Jackson's order to Gen[era]l [Edmund P.] Gaines, of the 7th of last August, in relation to St. Augustine; a copy of the order to Gen[era]l Gaines, of the 1st of Septem[be]r, and an extract of the answer to Gen[era]l Jackson's letter of the 10th of August, 1818; which comprehend all the information required by the Committee.

FC in DNA, 4, 2:91; PC in *American State Papers: Military Affairs,* 1:743.

From Joseph Lovell, 2/10. Pursuant to a report of Dr. [Benjamin Franklin] Harney, Lovell requests that all Army officers shall be prohibited from detaining medical supplies short of their destinations and from altering their destinations except in cases of absolute necessity. FC in DNA, 242, 2:35–36; FC in DNA, 243, 1:40–41.

From Wilson Lumpkin, Madison, [Ga.,] 2/10. Submits his claim for a refund of expenses incurred by him in surveying a part of the boundary line between the Creeks and Ga. that he was employed "to designate & run"; itemizes outlays totaling $1,201.35, which bears an AEI by Calhoun reading, "Allowed"; explains that

Lumpkin failed to procure vouchers in proof of many small expenditures, that he is not seeking a refund of what he spent for alcoholic beverages for himself and others, and that he will be content with any adjustment of this claim that "you deem to be right." Announces that he has employed a surveyor to extend the line at a cost of $5 per mile; wants about $200 for that surveyor. Georgians are urging Lumpkin to proceed to survey the boundary between Ga. and the Floridas; "I shall therefore proceed as soon as practicable." He asks for an advance remittance of $1,000 to cover part of the expenses of that survey. "I am at loss to determine what number of [Army] men [to be furnished by Edmund P. Gaines to serve as a guard unit] will be sufficient, but will exercise discretion according to the information I may obtain. At this time I am entirely uninformed to what extent danger is to be apprehended in the performance of said business, or whether the variegated society who inhabit that section are to be considered friendly or hostile." ALS with ADS in U.S. General Accounting Office, Indian Tribal Branch, Fifth Auditor Accounts, no. 626, "5th Auditor's Report on the Account of Wilson Lumpkin on account of the Indian Department (Creek), 1819."

From Return J. Meigs

Washington City, 10th February 1819

I ask permission to make some observations on the subject of the Cherokee mission now in the City. As I mentioned in a former letter that a strong party cherishes the Idea of continuing in the present local situation & under their present form of Government. I may be mistaken; they are silent on that point at present. If they wish to remain here, I mean on the present ground, it appears to me indispensable that they should receive laws from Georgia and Tennessee, mild laws adapted to their state of information, and this ought to be considered by them as a benevolent indulgence. It is time that their present customs, containing within their practical effect the destruction of life, should be abolished. If this is done and complete enfranchisement accorded to all those whose merit and information will justify it, it will be making a benevolent experiment in compliance with their wishes to retain the greatest part of their people on this side of the Mississippi: But it will in my opinion be only a temporizing expedient on their part to gain time; it will not stop the current of emigration to the west of the Mississippi river. Their country on the east of that river will not support them without industrious habits of labour, & this they will not submit to. They can be neither hunters or herdsmen on their old ground. On the west of the Mississippi those advantages are abundant; & they will realize them, unless emigration shall be interdicted; & even in such case they will evade it. There is no doubt in my opinion that the Cherokee nation, as a Nation, will be eventually located west of Mississippi river. Those who make an election to remain on the east must lose their distinctive character & name. They must be incorporated, or rather blended, with American citizens. Their feelings will revolt even at the gentle restraints of our civil polity & they will turn their eyes to the west.

If it is desirable to perpetuate their national existence & Name (& I think they strongly desire it), they must take new ground where the pressure of white population will not be great for many years to come. Everything short of a general movement will be ineffectual. It will be only temporizing, to gain time. From the bottom of my heart I wish them well. If I was their natural father, I would say to them: My Children, let us never break the bond of union; while united we are respectable; let *us all* go to the west. Let us carry with us the benevolent institutions, so liberally offered us by [religious] societies and especially by the Government. There our children may acquire those ideas & habits that will induce them understandingly to embrace civilized life & manners. It will perhaps be reply'd, Why may not this be done on our present ground? I answer, experience has demonstrated its impracticability. Cast our eyes on the line of Coast from Nova Scotia to South Carolina, a line of five hundred leagues, once covered by perhaps fifty tribes of Indians. Where are they? The same cause may be expected to produce the same effects.

If the Cherokees ever triumph over Barbarity, it will be done on the west side of the Mississippi river; but to effect this desirable object, the Cherokees must take the advice of the Government. If every tribe of Indians be permitted to put their Veto on the measures advised by the Government, it will be impossible to save them from extinction. They have had erroneous ideas on the subject of their relations with the Government. Their safety depends on their dependence, but it is difficult to make them comprehend this.

By extending the laws of Georgia and Tennessee, according to their Chartered limits, would at once put an end to intruders on their lands. At one stroke, all intrusion will cease. The calm, silent opperation [*sic*] of law would opperate to the complete removal of Intruders; & they at this moment amount to thousands. Military measures to remove intruders has [*sic*] completely been found ineffectual; intrusion on the Indian lands has increased & will increase untill the Indians are overwhelmed unless the civil law shall be made to opperate in those districts.

The Cherokees are this moment capable in point of information to receive the laws of the States to which they locally belong; but whether they receive them or not, it will not prevent the emigration to the west.

LS in DNA, 77 (M-271:2, frames 1350–1353).

To STEPHEN PLEASONTON, Fifth Auditor

Department of War, 10th Feb[ruar]y 1819

I will thank you to examine the enclosed account of Mr. [Samuel] Houston [for his services as an Indian Sub-Agent], and report whether the allowance, which he claims, was made to Richard Graham, as stated in the letter which accompanies the account.

FC in DNA, 72, D:245. NOTE: Pleasonton answered on 2/11.

Resolution by the Senate, 2/10. Confirms the promotions of five officers in the Corps of Engineers as of 11/12/1818: Walker K. Armistead to be a Col. in the place of [Joseph G.] Swift, resigned; William McRee to succeed Armistead as Lt. Col.; Joseph G. Totten to succeed McRee as Maj.; Theodore W. Maurice to succeed Totten as Capt.; and George Blaney to succeed Maurice as 1st Lt. ADS by Charles Cutts in DNA, 1, S-207.

To Ethan Stillman, Brookfield (Madison County), N.Y., 2/10. Answers the letter of 2/1 (ALS in DNA, 1, S-196) from this gunsmith "respecting your contract [in 1808] with the late Purveyor of Supplies, Tench Cox[e]," and seeking an additional payment to Stillman of $4,875. "It is one of those cases which it is not in the power of the Department to relieve. If you have sustained any damage, Congress alone can grant the relief." FC in DNA, 3, 10:245.

From H[UGH] YOUNG, Assistant Topographical Engineer

Washington, Feb. 10, 1819

I am sorry to be obliged to own, that a late unfortunate affair in which I was engaged, has consumed, in the last four days, the time which I intended for the completion of my official business in the City. In consequence of this, I will decline accompanying the General [Andrew Jackson ?] farther than Baltimore; at which place I shall see my parents, from whom I have been absent four years.

In Baltimore, I intend making out my requisitions, and preparing my accounts for settlement; and as soon as possible I will return to Washington to make the final arrangements for ["the commencement of" *interlined*] my Southern duties.

Maj. [John H.] Eaton of the Senate informs me that my map of E[ast] Florida was returned along with my report to the War Dep[artmen]t. As the map is not completed I should like to have it with me in Baltimore, where in the quiet of my family, I shall have abundant leisure to finish it. Col. [George] Gibson will take charge of it and have it forwarded.

ALS in DNA, 223, 28.

To the CHEROKEE DELEGATION

Department of War, 11 February, 1819

In order to avoid mistakes and to present my views more fully on some of the points which were touched on at our last interview, I have judged it proper to make the following written communication.

The Cherokees [are] to make a cession in proportion to the estimated number of their nation on the Arkansas and the emigrants who are enrolled to go there. The United States prefer the cession to be made in the States of Tennessee and Georgia and in the latter State, it would be desirable that it should be made as near and convenient to the present settlements in Georgia as possible.

The reservation which the Cherokees wish to make of a portion of their land, for a school fund must be in the Alabama territory, as the cession which will be made in Georgia will belong to that State; and that which may be made in Tennessee will be subject to the location of the warrants granted by the State of North Carolina. It is also understood, that the reservation so to be made is not to constitute any part of that portion of land which the Cherokees may cede in conformity to the principle which is contained in the preceding paragraph, but is to be made in addition to such cession as it will be wholly for the benefit of the Cherokee nation.

The United States will extend its kindness and protection to both branches of the Cherokee nation: to that which is West as well as that which may choose to continue to the East of the Mississippi; but as the Cherokees on the Arkansas are unrepresented no particular stipulation in regard to them, can be binding, and therefore must be waived. The land which has been granted to them on the Arkansas they will hold in the same manner and by the same title by which the [Eastern] Cherokees now hold theirs.

It is understood that the delegation, in behalf of their nation, wishes to strengthen the guarantee of that portion of the land which may be left to them after making the proposed cessions, so that it may be to them a permanent and lasting home without farther [*sic*] cessions. To secure such great benefits, it is indispensable that the cessions which they may make should be ample, and the part reserved to themselves should not be larger than is necessary for their wants and convenience. Should a larger quantity be retained, it will not be possible by any stipulation in the treaty, to prevent future cessions. So long as you may retain more land than what is necessary or convenient to yourselves, you will feel inclined to sell and the United States to purchase; the truth of what I say you know cannot be doubted, as your own experience and that of all Indian nations, proves it to be true. If on the contrary you only retain a suitable quantity, no more cessions will be asked for or made, and they will be settled down permanently. You are now becoming like the white people; you can no longer live by hunting but must work for your subsistence. In your new condition far less land is necessary for you. Your great object ought to be to hold your land separate among yourselves as your white neighbors; and to live and bring up your children in the same way as they do, and gradually to adopt their laws and manners. It is thus only that you can be prosperous and happy. Without this, you will find you will have to emigrate or become extinct as a people. You see that the Great Spirit has made our form of society stronger than yours—and you must submit to adopt ours; if you wish to be happy by pleasing him. I believe you know what is right and feel disposed to do it; and it is our wish that you should be happy and prosperous. We take an interest in your fate as you were the first proprietors of this happy country and are our near neighbours, but it is proper you should put confidence in our government, and take the advice which is offered sincerely for your good.

FC in DNA, 72, D:246–248; CC in DNA, 153, 15B-C4; PC in *American State Papers: Indian Affairs,* 2:190.

From Levi Colbert and Samuel Seeley, Chickasaw Nation, 2/11. They enclose a copy of the talk made by Andrew Jackson and Isaac Shelby that led the Chickasaws to cede lands to the U.S. in the treaty of 1818. They explain that George and Levi Colbert have agreed to sell their salt spring for $20,000 in a way deemed acceptable to the U.S. and have subsequently refused to accept higher offers. This letter gives evidence that some Chickasaws were trustfully in total harmony with the wishes of the U.S.: because Agent [Henry] Sherburne "had informed us of the wishes of our father the President of the United States," speculators from Nashville who offered more money "were told that the land could not be sold at present on any terms they might offer, which put an end to the business & they returned home." LS (signed with their marks) with En in DNA, 1, S-248.

To W[illiam] Crawford, District Attorney, St. Stephens, [Ala. Territory,] 2/11. A lawsuit against Capt. George P. Peters has been decided against him at Mobile but is appealed to a superior court. "You are requested" to defend Peters in behalf of the U.S. FC in DNA, 3, 10:246. Crawford's reply dated 3/6 accepted this assignment and expressed confidence that he could get the lower court's verdict reversed. ALS in DNA, 1, C-216; PC in Carter, ed., *Territorial Papers,* 18:575–576.

From W[ILLIAM] H[ENRY] HARRISON, [Representative from O.]

Washington, 11th Feb[ruar]y 1819

It is with great regret that I ask your immediate attention to the unpleasant circumstances detailed in the enclosed letter.

ALS in DNA, 11, 14021. NOTE: An EU reads: "Encloses letter from the Mayor of Cincinnati on the subject of the Soldiers."

From [Bvt. Maj.] E[lijah] Montgomery, Cantonment Montgomery, Ala., 2/11. Because a contractor has failed to deliver rations, Montgomery has issued a draft for $450 in order to buy, under an order of Col. W[illiam] King, food for use at Montgomery's post. ALS in DNA, 1, M-239.

To Capt. George P. Peters, Washington, 2/11. Answers his appeal of 2/2 (ALS in DNA, 1, P-116; PC in Carter, ed., *Territorial Papers,* 18:551–552) by giving him assurance that the U.S. will defend him at its expense in a lawsuit brought against Peters for seizing a raft of cedar logs at Mobile in 1817 in obedience to a War Department order. FC in DNA, 3, 10:245–246; PC in Carter, ed., *Territorial Papers,* 18:562–563.

From S[tephen] P[leasonton], 2/11. Answers Calhoun's letter of 2/10: as an Indian Agent, Richard Graham was paid until 4/20/1818, when a statute began to regulate such salaries, at the rate of $1,200 annually, plus allowances for two servants (pay, clothing, and rations) totaling $406, plus a subsistence allowance of $547.50, to make a total of $2,153.50; as a Sub-Agent [Samuel] Houston has been paid at the rate of $1,000 per annum plus four rations per day. Pleasonton does not recall that any Sub-Agent has ever been granted additional allowances claimed by Houston, whose account is returned. FC in DNA, 58, 1:108–109.

From John Scott, [Delegate from Mo. Territory,] 2/11. Calhoun's letter [of 11/4/1818] to [Frederick] Bates, concerning Osage depredations sought Bates's *opinion* concerning the case of James James alone. "I thought I understood you [to say] that the orders to Mr. Bates on this subject should be general, to examine and adjust *all* claims of a similar character," making actual payments to claimants. "I wish you would give such orders, if you think with me that they would be proper." ALS in DNA, 1, S-234. (Calhoun answered on 2/17/1819.)

To S[MITH] THOMPSON, Secretary of the Navy

Department of War, 11 Feb[ruar]y 1819

I have the honor to hand you, herewith an extract of a letter from Capt[ai]n Geo[rge] P. Peters, relative to certain cedar logs seized by him on Mobile River.

LS in DLC, Gideon Welles Papers, 2:18836; FC in DNA, 3, 10:246.

From Decius Wadsworth, 2/11. "I consider Major [Samuel B.] Archer's [musket] Lock to be materially inferior to the Common Lock, and as the Difference of a few Cents in the Price ought to weigh Nothing in Comparison with Perfection in the Qualities of a thing of this kind, I cannot recommend its Adoption." Wadsworth encloses, in support of this conclusion, the following letters or copies of letters: James Stubblefield, Harpers Ferry, to Col. [Nathan] Towson, 12/31/1818; S[amuel] B. Archer, Washington, to Burwell Bassett, [Representative from Va.,] 1/17/1819; D[ecius] W[adsworth] to Lt. Col. [Roswell] Lee, [Springfield, Mass.,] 1/20/1819; Adonijah Foot, Jacob Perkins, John Stebbins, Justin Murphy, and Elisha Toby, [Armorers, Springfield, Mass.,] to Roswell Lee, 1/28/1819; two letters from Roswell Lee, to Decius Wadsworth, both dated 1/30/1819; and [1st Lt.] C[harles ?] Ward, Greenleafs Point, [D.C.,] to [Samuel B.] Archer dated 2/8/1819. ALS with Ens in DNA, 1, A-70; FC in DNA, 32, 2:181.

To T[homas] H[ill] Williams, [Senator from Miss.,] 2/11. Answers his request of 2/5 (ALS in DNA, 1, W-180) that the denial of a license to trade with the Chickasaws to a certain person by the Chickasaw Agent [Henry Sherburne] be reversed, on the ground that the seventh article of the 1816 treaty with the Chickasaws was intended only to prevent peddling. Calhoun retorts that "the prohibition extends to every kind of trade, and I do not therefore feel myself at liberty to grant the license without the consent of the nation." FC in DNA, 3, 10:245.

To Henry Clay, [Representative from Ky.,] 2/12. Calhoun has received from "John Norvall [that is, Norvell, later a Senator from Mich.,]" of Lexington, [Ky.,] an application for an appointment as a Clerk in the War Department "and asking the favor of an answer to his application through you." Calhoun regrets "that there is no vacancy" but gives assurance that the application will be filed for consideration if any vacancy occurs. FC in DNA, 3, 10:246; PC in Hopkins and Hargreaves, eds., *The Papers of Henry Clay*, 2:669.

From N[INIAN] EDWARDS, [Senator from Ill.]

Senate Chamber, Feb[ruar]y 12, 1819

Agre[e]ably to an intimation, which I had the honor to make to you in our last interview, I beg leave to recommend for the appointment of a Cadet in the military academy, Master James [W.] Stephenson, the son of Colo[nel] Benjamin Stephenson who was one of the Delegates in Congress, from the Territory of Illinois & with whom you are acquainted.

This youth is about fourteen or fifteen years of age, pretty well educated, now engaged in the study of the Latin language, and possesses, in my opinion, talents of the first order, with a predilection for a military profession, that affords the most flattering prospects of his future usefulness in that profession, provided the opportunity of improvement which I solicit, should be afforded him, which I sincerely hope may be the case.

ALS in DNA, 15, 1819, 45. NOTE: Benjamin Stephenson served as the Ill. Delegate in the U.S. House of Representatives during 1814–1816.

From Ch[arles] Hicks, Washington, 2/12. Calhoun's communication of 2/11 "is now before us," the Cherokee delegation, which is disposed to be liberal in making a cession of part of the Eastern Cherokees' land to the U.S. "for the benefit of our fellow Citizens of the Arkansaw [*sic*] Country" and not less inclined to comply with the government's wish for cessions of land in both Ga. and Tenn. For "the purpose of raising a fund for the education of our youths, we propose to make a reservation in the Alabama Territory adequate for that purpose." The area they intend to retain "we conceive not to be larger than what is actually necessary for our wants and convenience," and they hope, therefore, to have it secured to them by a permanent guarantee for "our lasting homes. It is true we cannot live much longer by hunting, and that we must work for our subsistence. This we have been aware of for some time, and [we] find that domestick pursuits are much more agreeable than the pursuit of the chase." This "we assert from experience. But the present condition of our people, cannot permit us to possess seperate [*sic*] property in our lands with success; policy and prudence require that the change should be gradually adopted, as the situation of the people will admit; but we flatter ourselves that the time is not far distant when the Cherokee people will be in a situation to adopt the habits, customs, and laws of our white brethern [*sic*] of the United States. We have full confidence in the wishes and good intentions of the government towards the Cherokee people, and are fully sensible that the promotion of our future happiness is desired." Hicks proposes and outlines an area of 25 miles square for the support of schools among the Eastern and the Western Cherokees. He defines proposed boundaries for a more northern tract to be surrendered to the U.S.—a tract that they are convinced is larger "than the just proportion due to the Arkansaw Cherokees." Even so, Hicks and others of the Eastern Cherokee delegation feel "disposed to act with Liberality, from the generosity of the sentiments manifested by yourself towards our people. This Cession will disturb a large portion of our Citizens but we confide in the Liberality of the Government in providing for them by Reservations, & [in giving to them] compensation for their improvements" on the lands to be vacated. ALS, attested by John Lowry, in DNA, 77 (M-271:2, frames 1106–1109).

From James Johnson

Great Crossing[s, Ky.,] 12th Feb. 1819

I have been much engaged making preparations for the expedition up the Mississippi and Missouri. I have already nearly accomplished all my purchases of provisions. I shall have the small balance provided before the time of its departure.

I have also provided three steam boats which will be ready in March. I do believe another steam boat will be necessary. I can make a calculation as to the weight of the rations because a certain number 420,000 is ordered to be deposited the 21st March at Head quarters (Belle Fontaine).

But I have no data to calculate on the amount of munitions baggage &c. The weight is ["uncertain" *canceled*] with me yet uncertain. It would help me considerably to know the probable weight of munition baggage detachment &c. also what will be ordered up each river as both must be provided. I have it in my power to obtain another steam boat if wanted. I have not selected the largest steam boats. Prudence I thought dictated from something like from 100 to 150 tons burthen as these rivers are untryed [*sic*] with steam boat navigation. In making the various arrangements it will readyly [*sic*] occur to you that very heavy expen[s]es are incur[r]ed. I shall employ over a hundred thousand dollars of capital in the naked steam boats, besides the common equipment. I must necessarily incur considerable additional expense over and above Mississippi or Ohio voyages. And the times are so hard here that money cannot be had by any negociations [*sic*]. Banks and individuals are hard run.

It will therefore greatly oblige me besides promoting the public good in making me as liberal advances as the nature of your official duties admit. Rest assured I shall do my duty and sir will balance your advance by exertions in the public service to accomplishing the desired object. I have authorised my Brother [Richard M. Johnson] to receive any advance you may make to me as my agent. Excuse me for these p[o]ints [?]. The importance of having money to effect the great object has induced me to make this appeal to you.

[P.S.] If another steam boat should be directed it will still increase my expen[s]es and want of funds. I do believe another will be necessary.

ALS in DLC, United States Army: Quartermaster Department; PC in House Document No. 110, 16th Cong., 2nd Sess.

From Gideon Morgan, Jr., Washington, 2/12. Reviews the negotiations that led to "a conditional treaty" accepted by "a few Cherokees" at a place "within the Chickasaw Nation" in 9/1816 or 9/1817, by which [Andrew] Jackson and other treaty commissioners obtained a cession of almost two million acres of Cherokee land for only $60,000, payable in installments. Asks for a reconsideration of these terms, "when we believe perfect Justice will be rendered to us." ALS in DNA, 77 (M-271:2, frames 1525–1526).

Resolution by the Senate, 2/12. Requests [James Monroe] "to procure the cession of jurisdiction in and over such military and naval sites as have been, or may be purchased, for the use of the United States, and where such cession has not already been made." ADS by Charles Cutts in DNA, 1, S-231.

To Maj. Loring Austin, Boston

Department of War, 13 Feb[ruar]y, 1819

A compromise, under the act of Congress at the last Session, for claims against you, on account of nine judgements obtained against you, for the confinement of nine persons, in obedience to the orders of Gen[era]l [Zebulon Montgomery] Pike, has been made; and you are released from all demands on account of those judgements.

LS owned in 1953 by Walter N. Eastburn, East Orange, N.J.; photostat of the LS in ScU-SC; FC in DNA, 3, 10:248.

To William A. Burwell, [Representative from Va.]

Department of War, 13th February 1819

In reply to your letter of the 11th of February which I received yesterday I enclose a draft of a bill in conformity to your request. It is believed that the abuses under the late act [of 3/18/1818 for pensions to Revolutionary veterans] has [*sic*] been principally under that part of the act which described the ["reduced" financial] condition of the applicant; and has been caused principally by the vagueness of the words used. I understand it to be your wish to substitute in lieu of those words that of indigent circumstances, which is certainly much more precise, as it indicates a degree of poverty but little above pauperism. How far such a change is expedient must rest with Congress to determine. It will doubtless diminish much the number of pensioners.

FC in DNA, 3, 10:249.

To Robert Butler, Adjutant General [of the Southern Division, Washington,] 2/13. Answers his letter of 2/8 (LS in DNA, 1, B-206) submitting the claim of the "late Sub-Agent" to the [Eastern] Cherokees, Samuel Houston, to extra compensation on the ground that [Richard] Graham once received a similar allowance; replies that the precedent cannot be effective and that Houston "has been paid the full amount allowed him when he rec[eive]d the appointment." FC in DNA, 3, 10:247.

From T[HOMAS] FORSYTH

St. Louis, 13th February 1819

From information which I have recently rec[eive]d from the Salt River Country it appears that an Indian of the Fox Nation was most wantonly killed by a white man by the name of Samuel Thompson. This affair as related by Fleming (a mechanic of this place, and who was wounded by the Indians immediately after the Indian was killed by Thompson) is as follows.

Some Indians were ascending the Mississippi River about the begin[n]ing of the present month in their canoes. At a place about twenty miles above the mouth of Salt River, the Indians['] dogs run [*sic*] after some hogs. Thompson was sent from a house to tell the Indians to call their dogs away. Thompson took his gun, went to the canoes, and shot an Indian dead. The Indians put on shore and went a few steps into the woods, where Fleming and a mulatoe [*sic*] boy were at work, shot at and wounded Fleming in the hand, after which Fleming and the Boy made their escape to the house and the Indians proceeded on their journey. Since which the Indians have come into the settlements and had a meeting with the settlers, who have promised the Indians that Thompson would be punished for killing the Indian, yet they have allowed Thompson to leave that part of the Country and no doubt but he is long since out of the jurisdiction of this Territory.

It is said that the dead Indian was related to the Black Tobacco, one of the Chiefs of the Fox Nation of Indians, which Chief has always been much attached to the United States, and I am of opinion that when the Indians arrive at their different villages from their different hunting places (in May next) that the matter may be made up (should the government think it proper) by means of a few presents to the relatives of the deceased Indian.

ALS in DNA, 1, F-75; FC in WHi, Draper Collection, Thomas Forsyth Papers, 4:77–78.

To F[erdinand] R[udolf] Hassler, Newark, [N.J.,] 2/13. "Your claim for pay for services rendered in completing the business of the survey of the coast" during 4/14–27/1818 must be submitted to the Secretary of the Treasury [William H. Crawford] "for adjustment." [René Edward] De Russy has orders to receive at Newark from Hassler the public's instruments. "Your letters of the 5th of December last have been referred to the Engineer Department and are now mislaid. If they contained any thing which has not been answered by me, I will thank you to transmit duplicates of them, when they shall be attended to." FC in DNA, 3, 10:248.

[James Johnson to Thomas S. Jesup]

Great Crossings, [Ky.,] Feb[ruar]y 13th 1819

Haveing [*sic*] enter'd into a contract to transport to the St. Peters & Yellow Stone [Rivers] the detachments, munitions & provisions &c. ordered there by the Secretary of War, I feel an ardent desire to fulfill this engagement punctually.

I[n] order to effect this I beg here to ask for Information in some points. What will be the probable amount or number of rations required to ascend each river? What will be the probable weight of the munitions, Baggage &c.[?] What will be the probable number of Troops[?] This last may be an improper question; if so I hope you will excuse me for asking it. I know I am ordered to deposit 420,000 complete rations at Belle Fountaine [*sic*] by the 21st March. I have supposed that the whole of these rations would go up the two rivers, but I can give but a poor guess at the probable weight of the other branch of transportation. My contract[ual obligation] is to have two Steam Boats ready but provided that is not sufficient by 30 days['] notice I must furnish others. This would retard the movements of the provisions further. The size of the Steam Boats are [*sic*] not named in the contract; it is therefore very desireable [*sic*] to to [*sic*] receive information on the above enquiries if consistent, to be answered. I wish nothing to be lacking on my part, but to fulfill the most sanguine expectation & wishes of the War Department. I presume it is wished that the whole should go in mess [that is, en masse ?] compactly together. It is as easy for me to prepare for such a state of things as any other, provided I know in time. Another subject I beg leave to call your attention to in preparing for this undertakeing [*sic*]. The greater portion of expence is incurred before we start. My Steam Boats will be considerably over $100,000[;] the outlet [that is, outlay?] & extra arrangements for navigating unknown waters is very great. I request therefore that as liberal an advance be made as the nature of the case will admit. I pledge myself that it shall be [earned] promptly by every exertion in my power. I flatter myself that this request will be granted when it is reccollected [*sic*] that I have given such ample security for the faithful discharge of my contract and the reccolection [*sic*] that few if any individual[s] particularly in the West would be able to undergo the expences without considerable aid from his employer. I have made my Brother R[ichard] M. Johnson my agent who will receive for me any advance which may be made. I incline to think that in order to accomplish the views & wishishes [*sic*] of the Department that a fourth Steam Boat will be necessary. If so I have it in my power to purchase a fine Boat just finishing. I however shall wait till I receive further information from you on the above enquiries. I may appear troublesome but your generous mind will forgive me when I tell you my heart & soul is on this subject.

LU in DNA, 43, James Johnson, 126; PC in House Document No. 110, 16th Cong., 2nd Sess.

[JAMES JOHNSON] to THOMAS S. JESUP

Great Crossings, [Ky.,] 13th Feb. 1819

I have the pleasure to inform you that by this morning[']s mail I received your favour of the 21st Ult[im]o. I have so far anticipated the wishes of the Secretary of War in early movements up the Missouri, that I have now nearly ready for shipment the whole of the requisition of 420,000 complete rations ordered by him. Early in March I shall have three Steam Boats ready for the service;

arrangements are made to fortify each Boat to be bullet proof. I am happy to learn that two small guns of artil[l]ery, gunners and am[m]unition will be furnished by Government for each; the Boats will be prepared for their reception so as to opperate [*sic*] succesfully if found necessary. Should the gover[n]ment want more provisions than was first expected by the Forces being increased in that quarter it will be very agre[e]able to receive the Order as soon as suits the conveniance [*sic*] of the department as this is the Best season to procure them, particularly the meat part of the Ration when it may be difficult at a later season to procure them in such quantities and qualities as might be wished.

Salt Pork is universally ship[p]ed to Orleans unless engagements are made pretty early; at a late season new purchases cannot easily be made to put up this article in this way. It will afford me much pleasure to communicate at all times such information as may be thought interesting.

CC in DLC, United States Army: Quartermaster Department; PC in House Document No. 110, 16th Cong., 2nd Sess.

To President [James Monroe]

Department of War, 13 Feb[ruar]y 1819

Thomas Tupper, Assistant Deputy Quarter Master Gen[era]l of the United States Army, stationed at Sackets Harbour, [N.Y.,] has conducted himself in a very unsatisfactory manner to this Department. He was ordered to this place several months ago, to settle his accounts, and has neither obeyed the order, nor rendered any reasons why he did not. I, therefore, recommend that he be dismissed [from] the Military service of the United States.

LS in DNA, 2, C-1819; FC in DNA, 6, 1:346.

From Alexander Richards, Georgetown, D.C., 2/13. He has examined [Nathaniel] Cutting's records concerning land warrants issued under the Canadian Volunteers act of 3/5/1816. At least half of these grants are based, he has concluded, upon fraudulent claims. The law itself was defective in not defining clearly what U.S. citizens resident in Canada were eligible. Nearly 60% of 267 warrants granted have been issued to six agents for claimants, James

L. Edwards and Lewis Edwards, government Clerks, being among the six; and all such agents have probably received spurious claims from speculators, not from claimants directly. Richards suggests that 174 pending claims should be "most critically scrutinized before warrants are granted on them." ALS in DNA, 1, R-120.

From Waller Taylor, [Senator from Ind.,] 2/13. Encloses a letter from a Baptist minister, the Rev. [Isaac] McCoy, who wishes to settle among the Miami Indians for a "benevolent Purpose." ALS in DNA, 1, T-85.

From William McIntosh, Washington, 2/14. Announces the arrival today of himself and others constituting a delegation from the Creeks. They are staying in Strother's Tavern. When Agent [David B. Mitchell] arrives, in a day or two, they will want to confer with President [James Monroe]. ALS in DNA, 77 (M-271:2, frames 1234–1235).

From Eldred Simkins, [Representative from S.C.]

Ho[use of] Rep[resentative]s, 14 Feb. 1819

Mr. Charles Mayson of Cambridge, S.C., writes me to know something of an application I suspect might have been made through you on the part of one Rob[er]t F. Griffin for a land warrant. He states that Griffin has lost his discharge but has furnished sufficient evidence of its existence and loss. I wrote you before [on 2/6] on this subject, but have rec[eive]d no answer. Will you be so obliging as to give this letter such direction as to shew where & in what situation this application is.

ALS in DNA, 1, S-233.

From Capt. S[amuel] Babcock, Philadelphia, 2/15. In reply to Calhoun's letter of 2/8 to him, Babcock states "that no timber of the kind described will be wanted for the public work at the Pea Patch" and that some logs such as those bought from [Daniel] Garrison [in 1815] "are lying useless at the Pea Patch." ALS in DNA, 1, B-205.

From James Gould, Litchfield, [Conn.,] 2/15. Recommends Greenbury W. Ridgely of Ky. for an appointment to serve in the Missouri expedition. ALS in DNA, 11, 13850.

To Th[omas] S. Jesup, 2/15. Answering his inquiry of 2/13 (FC in DNA, 42, 1:185), Calhoun states that, under "the invariable interpretation" of Quartermaster regulations, "officers who are ordered to this place to settle their accounts" are entitled to neither fuel nor quarters "while here for that purpose." FC in DNA, 3, 10:250.

To T[HOMAS] S. JESUP, Quartermaster General

Department of War, 15 February 1819

I transmit herewith a report of the Adj[utant] & Ins[pector] General [Daniel Parker] of the strength of the Regiments to be stationed hereafter upon the Missouri & Mississippi Rivers and the Estimate of the Colo[nel] of the Ordnance [Department, Decius Wadsworth,] of the Artillery Stores required to accompany the march of the Troops. From these documents you will be enabled to make the suitable arrangements for transportation and for the necessary disbursements required of the Quarter Master[']s Department.

FC in DNA, 3, 10:251.

To Return J. Meigs, Washington, 2/15. Calhoun asks Meigs's opinion about T[homas] L. McKenney's suggestion "that the merchandize provided in compliance with the requisition of the 30th of December last be forwarded to the Chickasaw Bluffs, not to the Cherokee Agency." LS in DNA, 75 (M-208:8); FC in DNA, 3, 10:251. (For Meigs's reply, see 2/18 herein.)

From D[aniel] Parker, 2/15. Estimates that 1,900 noncommissioned officers, musicians, and Privates of the 5th and 6th Infantry Regiments and the Rifle Regiment are now serving in the region of the upper Mississippi and the Missouri Rivers. LS in DNA, 1, P-124; FC in DNA, 12, 5:184–185.

To William Prince, Vincennes, 2/15. Encloses a copy of a letter from the Rev. Mr. "McKoy [Issac McCoy] in relation to permission to settle on the Miami reservation. If the Indians have ["no" *interlined*] objection you will grant the permission." FC in DNA, 3, 10:250.

To Waller Taylor, [Senator from Ind.,] 2/15. "Enclosed is a copy of a letter [of 2/15] from this Department to W[illia]m Prince, Esq., Indian Agent at Vincennes, from which you will see the direction that has been given to the application of the Rev. Isaac McCoy." FC in DNA, 3, 10:250.

From Daniel D. Tompkins, Washington, 2/15. Recommends that former Capt. Mangle M[arcellus] Quackenbos be appointed Military Storekeeper at New York [City], William Bloodgood of Albany as a Cadet, and James Engle of Bergen County, N.J., as a Cadet. ALS in DNA, 11, 13825.

To P[hilip] P[endleton] Barbour, [Representative from Va.,] 2/16. Answers his inquiry of 2/11 "respecting bounty lands supposed to be allowed" to soldiers of 1756–1757 by stating that no law permits such grants. FC in DNA, 3, 10:251.

From Nathaniel Frye, Jr., [Chief Clerk,] Paymaster General's Office, 2/16. Pursuant to a letter of 1/28 from J.H. Farnham at Frankfort, Ky., to R[ichard] M. Johnson, Frye points out that in 8/1818 the Cashier of the Branch Bank of the United States at Lexington, [Ky.,] had almost $11,400 of unexpended pension funds in hand and that two remittances totaling more than $4,000 have been sent to him for the half-pay pensioners since. If the Ky. Agent for Paying U.S. Pensioners had notified the Paymaster General [Robert Brent] that he needed additional funds, they would have been remitted promptly. But further remittances must now come "from the appropriations now under consideration in Congress, as those of the last year are reduced to about 800 dollars." ALS in DNA, 1, F-63.

From John Sergeant, [Representative from Pa.,] 2/16. Introduces his brother-in-law, John G. Watmough, who wishes to discuss with Calhoun a contract offered to Watmough by the Ordnance Department to supply saltpeter. ALS in DNA, 1, S-230.

From W[alker] K. Armistead, 2/17. Requests a remittance of $20,000 to Capt. James Gadsden for construction costs at Mobile Point. FC in DNA, 21, 1:46.

From Charles Hicks, in behalf of the Cherokee Delegation, and Return J. Meigs, Washington, 2/17. Pursuant to their conference of yesterday with Calhoun, they review various estimates of the number of Eastern Cherokees who have emigrated or will do so (one figure being 5,291) and claim that about 12,544 will not; they think the national debt should be paid from the annuities of both the Eastern and the Western Cherokees and that the Eastern Cherokees should then receive annually a share of the annuities proportionate to their population. Copy attested by John Lowry in DNA, 77 (M-271:2, frames 1110–1113).

General Order by D[aniel] Parker, 2/17. "Captain Thomas Tupper, Assistant Deputy Quartermaster General, having neglected his duty, and having failed to obey orders, is hereby dismissed [from] the service of the United States, to take effect on the 31st December last, when the order of the War Department, for the settlement of his accounts, should have been fulfilled." PC in House Report No. 69, 17th Cong., 1st Sess.; PC in House Report No. 28, 17th Cong., 2nd Sess.

To John Scott, [Delegate from Mo. Territory,] 2/17. [In answer to Scott's letter of 2/11, summarized herein under that date,] Calhoun says: "By the enclosed copies of letters you will perceive that Mr. [Frederick] Bates considered the accounts arising under the Osage Treaty to have been finally settled on the 1st of June last and I do not think proper to open the subject again. Should more claims arise Mr. Bates will be directed . . . to examine & report on them." FC in DNA, 3, 10:252.

From Henry Sherburne, Chickasaw Agency, 2/17. Reports in considerable detail his outlays for labor and materials for repairs made on his Agency house. LS in DNA, 1, S-251.

From Daniel D. Tompkins, [Washington,] 2/17. "The Farmer's & Mechanic's Bank of Albany entertain a hope that the Government will transfer a portion of their funds required for expenditure on the Northern & Western frontiers of New York to that bank. This institution was friendly & accommodating to the government of the U.S. in the late War," and Tompkins asks "a compliance with their wishes as far as may be consistent with the public good & the convenience of the [War] Department." ALS in DNA, 1, T-89.

From Decius Wadsworth

Ordnance Office, February 17, 1819

It will be in our power in the course of next summer to furnish a field piece for the use of the militia of the State of Tennessee under the Act of Congress for arming the militia, the consent of the Governor of the State, being implied, and an engagement to forward his receipt or acknowledgment for the same when delivered at the most convenient place which may be selected on the Ohio River. The reason why we cannot immediately order a piece to be sent is that all the field pieces at Pittsburgh will be required for the Expeditions up the Missouri and Mississippi. Indeed if it be thought worth while to incur the expense a 6-pounder may be sent immediately from Greenleafs Point [D.C.] to Pittsburgh to be forwarded from there down the river.

P.S. We use Iron field pieces and recommend them as being equal to Brass. D.W.

FC in DNA, 32, 2:184.

From J[ames] L. E[dwards]

War Department, Pension Office, February 18th 1819

On examining the declaration of Elijah Peters, forwarded by Mr. [Thomas Willis ?] Cobb, [Representative from Ga.,] I find that he is entitled to a pension, for his services under Gen[era]l [William] McIntosh. A certificate of pension has been issued & forwarded to Mr. Cobb.

In reply to Mr. Minott's letter, which is returned herewith, I have only to observe, that his statement is correct in regard to the case of Nathaniel Adams, who enlisted for eight, but served upwards of nine months. As to the other cases, I have to remark, that when a man leaves the service, without permission, he is always reported as a Deserter, and the rule adopted, concerning Deserters, has been to exclude them from every gratuity of the Government, unless they returned to their duty & were pardoned. I regret that any blunders should be made in this Office; but they are unavoidable, where there are so many new Clerks, and where the business is so much hurried, as it is in this Office.

The principle, on which James B. Fulton's claim is rejected is, that the character of the commanding officer, does not change that of the soldier. Mr. F[ulton] was drafted from the militia, to serve nine months, in consequence of a resolution of Congress, requiring each State to furnish it's [*sic*] Quota, to fill the ranks of the Continental Army. The States complied with the requisition of Congress, but the drafted men were not placed on the same footing as the regular troops, and are not considered as entitled to pensions, under the Act of last March.

FC in DNA, 91, 6:273.

From Edmund P. Gaines

Fernandina, E[ast] F[lorida], February 18th 1819

When I had the honor of addressing you on the 5th instant, I promised myself the pleasure of presenting you my views upon such points respecting our Indian neighbours, as should appear to me connected with the proper disposition of the troops, and the arrangement of Military posts, upon the Indian frontier of my command. I had then, indeed, but little hope that I should be able to add a single ray to the light which you already possessed upon this subject. Your reports in relation to Indian, as well as Military affairs, which I have since seen confirm me in what I had anticipated, and leave me scarcely any other apology for soliciting your attention, and giving you the trouble to read this letter, than that I had promised to write it.

I beg leave therefore, respectfully, to observe that, as all military views must be predicated on, or relate either directly or indirectly to a state of war, and as in the event of a war with any foreign power, experience proves that most of the Indians will take an active part, and that those who are not for us will be against us, there can be no good reason why we should not organize and instruct the young warriors of the friendly tribes and "in peace prepare them for war." May we not, at once, employ a number of them equal to the number of men wanting to complete each Corps, to serve in seperate [*sic*] Companies until relieved by recruits? Eighteen months or two years instruction under experienced officers of the Army, would render this description of force highly valuable as light Infantry or Rifleman, to act against Indians, or against the troops of any nation accustomed to employ Indians, or ["against" *interlined*] any other invading foe. And it would moreover have the effect of producing habits of civilization.

I think it can be established beyond dispute, that most of the friendly Chiefs and many of the principal warriors of the Creek nation who joined us in the war of 1813 and '14, against the "red sticks," were such as had been on terms of friendly intercourse with our troops at Forts Wilkinson, Hawkins and Stoddert: I am equally assured that this was not the case with many, if any of the "red stick" party; and yet, it is well known ["that" *interlined*] the fostering hand of the President of the United States had long been extended, through the Agency of the philanthropic [Benjamin] Hawkins, [the Creek Agent,] equally to all of that Nation. The Cherokees have, in like manner, derived no inconsiderable portion of their elementary views of civilization from the military posts at S.W. Point, at Tellico and Highwassee. The Cherokees have nevertheless had the benefit of Agents of the very first grade. The establishment of two of the last mentioned posts about the year 1796, forms the era from which we may reckon the termination of a long series of predatory war upon our frontier settlements in the then Territory, now the State of Tennessee. If the information given me upon these subjects be correct, (and I have good reason, from my own observation, for the last twenty years to believe it to be so) the conclusion follows, that, a military post should remain at the principal rendezvous of the Indians, until long after every indication of hostility shall have disappeared.

Faithful Agents may indeed acquire great influence, and may effect much good during a period of peace, so long as they have ample sums of money to distribute among the Indians, and more particularly among the influential Chiefs, who are often the most avaricious—but when the country is involved in war, and invaded by a foe able to compete with Agents in thus operating upon the avarice of the Chiefs, they will go over to the highest bidder if not restrained by considerations resulting more from the specimens of Military preparation, and military strength exhibited at our adjacent posts, than from all the reasoning and all other efforts of Agents.

Colonel Hawkins, who was justly distinguished for his patriotism, as well as for the zeal and ability with which he devoted many years of his life to the laudable work of civilizing the Creek Indians, laboured long under the impression that his efforts would be crowned with success; but at the moment when his hopes were most sanguine, the work of massacre commenced, in a manner calculated to prove that little or no favorable impression had been produced upon their minds—that nothing beyond the worst of the vices of civilized man, had been learned by a great part of the Nation.

I conclude that the establishment, within their limits, of military posts, with work-shops, and military artificers: instructing such as are disposed to learn the mechanic arts: enrolling the aspiring young warriors in military corps: teaching them the art of war, and placing the whole of their concerns under the controul of discreet field officers of the Army, would, not only be the most effectual means of producing a desirable change towards civilization, but would inevitably secure the ["Indians" *interlined*] in our ranks on the approach of a war.

Although strongly confirmed in the correctness of these opinions, I am by no means so vain as to imagine, even if it were practicable without the interposition of Congress to place the friendly Indians under military controul or to make any radical change in the established intercourse with those Indians, that it would be attempted without more information than I am able to furnish. I can only promise myself the pleasure of being instrumental in bringing the subject into view; and I persuade myself that the more it is investigated the less reason I shall have to apprehend that I can be charged with presenting to you, upon this occasion, views of a mere visionary character.

The objections (2nd and 3rd) contained in my letter of the 5th instant as applicable to Fort Hawkins were intended likewise to apply to all other small inland Posts, or such as are not intended to be fortified; and, should it not be deemed necessary for purposes connected with our friendly Indian affairs, to post a part of my command within or adjacent to the Creek Nation, I earnestly hope that I may soon have it in my power to withdraw the troops from all such posts, and give to the Corps the collected strength and proper position of each and I take this occasion to request that I may be authorised to post each Corps at, or in the immediate vicinity of the principal points to be fortified.

ALS in DNA, 1, G-123; ALS in DNA, 11, 13510. NOTE: Calhoun answered this letter on 3/4.

From George Gibson, 2/18. Encloses a letter from John Scott, [Delegate from Mo. Territory, to Calhoun dated 2/10] recommending Maj. Thomas Hempstead. Gibson urges that Hempstead be appointed as a Military Storekeeper as soon as possible. ALS with En in DNA, 11, 13458.

From [Thomas S. Jesup], 2/18. Requests that R[obert] M. Harrison be appointed an Assistant Deputy Quartermaster General in the place of the dismissed Capt. [Thomas] Tupper. FC in DNA, 42, 1:187.

From ROSWELL LEE, [Superintendent]

U.S. Armory, Springfield, [Mass.,] February 18th 1819

Since my Letter of the 13th I have understood that the Pay Master [John Chaffee] has not made up his mind to resign his office except in a certain Event, Viz the Death of his Father. Of course no calculation can be made for a Successor at present.

LS in DNA, 1, L-107.

From THOMAS L. MCKENNEY, "Unofficial"

"Weston," [Georgetown, D.C.,] February 18, 1819

I know you will excuse the liberty I now take, in volunteering a request in behalf of our Cherokee Indians. I have been led to hope that the *principle* of their mission will be recognized, as, ["also" *interlined*] in general, the details growing out of it. I speak of my *understa[ndi]ng* of their wishes—which, however, may not be critically correct. Should their proposal, as I understand it, be received, it will throw into the possession of Tennessee, & Georgia, a great body of fine land; and with it, a numerous body of *coarse, bad people.* My fear is, that this wretched set of men, finding their squatting places (Knickerbocker, I think it is, calls such folks squatters) to have fallen into the possession of men who will occupy them, themselves, will force themselves upon the lands which the present negotiation may reserve for the Indians. The impunity with which they have so long held the lands, now occupied by them, seems to warrant this apprehension. If they shall do so, there will still be no relief to the Indians, *whose principle* [*sic*] *curse has flowed from this source.*

If, in your adjustment of this affair, which promises so much good to the Cherokees, there can be devised any plan to make these interlopers diverge from the Indian reserve, a great acquisition to the peace of the Indians, & the quiet of our borders, will be realized; and this will not prove otherwise, I am sure, than a source of great consolation to both you & myself.

ALS in DNA, 77 (M-271:2; frames 1293–1295).

From Return J. Meigs, Washington, 2/18. [Answering Calhoun's request of 2/15,] Meigs approves Thomas L. McKenney's plans for sending goods to the Chickasaw Bluffs for the [Cherokee] emigrants [enroute to the Arkansas] but urges that at least 500 pounds of gunpowder, which McKenney can deliver from nearby places, should be added to the proposed goods. [Meigs dated his letter "1818," and it was therefore assigned erroneously to that year in *The Papers of John C. Calhoun,* 2:146. But two EU's on the manuscript date it as being of and received in 1819, and the fact that it answers Calhoun's letter of 2/15 in 1819 provides conclusive evidence that Meigs was incorrect when he wrote "1818."] ALS in DNA, 77 (M-271:2, frames 1354–1355).

To Thomas Morris, New York [City], 2/18. Explains that one member of the general court-martial for N.Y. militia delinquents has been allowed a total of $1,475.74 for his recent service, including $163 for transportation of his baggage a distance of 1,630 miles. His claims to allowances for servants and forage have not been allowed "because he has not actually kept in service servants or horses." Morris will pay all of the total allowed that has not already been given as an advance. "The principle of this settlement will govern the payments to be made to all other members of the Court." FC in DNA, 3, 10:253–254.

To B[ENJAMIN] RUGGLES, [Senator from O. and Chairman of the Senate Committee on the Militia]

Department of War, 18th February 1819

In answer to your note of the 16th instant [soliciting my suggestions as to possible improvements in a proposed bill to compel State officials to submit their militia returns promptly (ALS in DNA, 1, R-104)], I have the honor to state that the Act of March 2d 1803, relative to establishing an uniform Militia throughout the United States, seems fully to embrace the annual returns refer[r]ed to in the resolution of the Senate, enclosed in your letter. It is to be regretted that some of the Adjutants General of States, have failed to transmit the returns required by law, and for which forms were transmitted to all States soon after I came into this Department but it is doubtful whether the withholding of arms, as proposed, would enforce the provision of the law relative to returns, as the arms would remain in the Arsenals of the United States, where the arms would be well preserved for the States without expense.

I am not prepared to point out any mode satisfactory to my own mind to effect the object of the committee.

FC in DNA, 3, 10:253.

From D[ecius] Wadsworth, 2/18. A misunderstanding has arisen concerning arms furnished by the U.S. to the N.Y. militia. Lt. Col. [George] Bomford authorized Maj. [James] Dalaby to negotiate a settlement of the issue with Anthony Lamb, the representative of N.Y.; they agreed on 12/8/1817 that the U.S. owed to N.Y. a large amount of arms, and Bomford ordered that this balance be given in the form of cannon. But Dalaby "could not have been provided with the proper documents & Vouchers," which show a large debit against N.Y. "On my return to the Seat of Gov[ernmen]t in June last . . . I sent an order to Maj. Dalaby to issue no more Cannon to the State." Wadsworth submits to Calhoun for study copies of all papers relevant to this problem. FC in DNA, 32, 2:182–183.

From J[ames] L. Edwards, 2/19. Encloses a "pension certificate for John Laws, whose declaration was sent to you, by Judge [John] Marshall." Reports that a pension certificate for Spencer Edwards was issued on 1/9 and was sent to the pensioner through another person. As to the third and fourth persons for whom Marshall has sought pensions, the Pension Office has no evidence that any application has ever been received from either. LS in DNA, 1, E-47; FC in DNA, 91, 6:279.

From Nathaniel Frye, Jr., Chief Clerk, Paymaster General's Office, 2/19. Encloses a CC of a letter dated 12/12/1818 from Maj. John B. Hogan, Paymaster of the 4th Infantry, at Fort Montgomery, to Robert Brent complaining that the mails were being carried thereabout so carelessly that Hogan dared not trust his accounts to them. Encloses an ALS of 1/13/1819 from Hogan to Brent, which proved that Hogan was going to [New] Orleans under orders from Col. [William] King and Gen. [Edmund P.] Gaines; Frye remarks "that it is impossible for the Paymaster General to effect regular and punctual payments to the troops, if his deputies . . . are taken from their proper duties." Encloses also a CCEx from Hogan's letter of 1/20 to Brent complaining that the Treasury provides Hogan with depreciated paper money for the troops; on this subject, says Frye, "I wish to have a conference with you as soon as convenience will permit." LS with Ens in DNA, 1, F-64.

To D[aniel] Garrison, in the care of Capt. [Samuel] Babcock, Philadelphia, 2/19. "Capt. Babcock, the Engineer at the Pea Patch, reports to me that the logs" you intend to deliver "are not wanted for public works in the Delaware [River]. As these logs cannot be applied to any other purpose by this Department it is the wish of the Department that the contract be re[s]cinded." FC in DNA, 3, 10:254.

From Ch[arles] Hicks, Washington, 2/19. Answers, in behalf of the Cherokee Delegation, two proposals made "by yourself yesterday at our interview with you." Rejects Calhoun's proposal that the Eastern Cherokees should include in the land that they will cede an area along their southern boundary, which separates them from the Creeks; "we believe that the interest and future happiness of our Nation" require U.S. acceptance, instead, of the cession already offered by the Cherokees; "we trust you will admit, that a settlement formed all around our whole Nation, by such white neighbours as seek the disturbance of our peace and happiness, would be productive of destroying the seeds of civil[iz]ation which are so much desired to be sown on our Country; the removal of our Citizens on the frontier of North Carolina to the interior of our Country we conceive would ultimately be the cause of promoting their advancement towards civil[iz]ation." Answering Calhoun's second suggestion, concerning "future emigrations," the Cherokees retort that, "in surrendering to the U.S. the bounds we propose, we anticipate a definitive adjustment of the late Treaty and that the Nation shall not her[e]after be under obligations to surrender any more land in consequence of the removal of her Citizens to the West. We are fully impressed with a belief founded on reasonable calculation, that our Citizens will not make choice of leaving the lands of their nativity" if they receive proper guarantees of permanent possession of their Eastern reservations. They submit a list of the Cherokees whom they consider to be entitled to hold reservations in fee simple; this will help by indicating how many others will hold life estates in other reservations; they believe that the treaty should authorize the designation of some of these two kinds of reservations by decisions that will be made by the Cherokees and their Agent at home. It seems pointless to discuss now the boundary between the Creeks and the Cherokees because the Cherokees are "unwilling to surrender their Territory bordering on that line" and because [William] McIntosh and others of the Creek Delegation [now here] do "not feel themselves authorised to make a definitive adjustment" of that boundary. "As we have not conclusively agreed on the subject of the lands intended to be reserved for the use of schools, and the manner in which the sales are to be made, we wish to have a further conversation with you on that subject." They believe that the present negotiations are "near a close," and they propose to have decisions about Cherokees who may be entitled to a mere life estate in their reservations made, under a provision of the forthcoming treaty, "at home." LS in DNA, 77 (M-271:2, frames 1114–1117).

From Maj. S[TEPHEN] H. LONG

Washington City, February 19th 1819

Pursuant to your instructions I have the honor to draw on the War Department for $4,500, being the residue of the appropriation for making a survey of the water courses tributary to the Mississippi, $2,000 having been previously drawn. I have to request that the above $4,500 may be remitted to [me at] Pittsburg[h], previous to the 12th of March next.

LS in DNA, 1, L-106.

To Thomas L. McKenney, 2/19. Acknowledges his letter of 2/11 (LS in DNA, 1, M-*ca.* 206; FC in DNA, 73, E:199); approves his proposal that for three reasons goods for the emigrating Cherokees should be sent to the Chickasaw Bluffs, not to the Eastern Cherokee Agency. FC in DNA, 72, D:248–249.

To Joseph McMinn, Murfreesboro, Tenn., 2/19. "The articles which the Superintendent of Indian Trade was directed to forward to the Cherokee Agency for the use of the Emigrants to the Arkansaw, on the 30th Decem[be]r last, subject to your order, and of which you were informed by letter of that date, it is thought best by him to forward them to the Chickasaw Bluffs instead of the Agency, which arrangement is approved by Colo[nel Return J.] Meigs, who is now at the seat of the Government, and has been accordingly adopted." FC in DNA, 72, D:248.

From Capt. J[ohn] M. O'Connor, Paris, [France,] 2/19. Encloses a printed prospectus, in French, of "a very important addition that Gen[era]l Jomini proposes making to his famous work on the Seven Years['] War & on the Campaigns from 1792 to 1797." ALS with En in DNA, 1, O-20.

From Decius Wadsworth, 2/19. He can find no reason why the arms supplied to the N.Y. militia, reported in his letter of 2/15, should be considered more than the amount to which N.Y. is entitled; he blames the misconception on misinformation from the Department of the Treasury. ALS in DNA, 1, W-196; FC in DNA, 32, 2:184–185.

From D[ecius] Wadsworth, 2/19. Requests that $3,500 be sent to Lt. [William C.] Lyman at Augusta, [Ga.,] for the arsenal there. "That Officer has tendered his Resignation to be accepted by the last of March. He represents the foregoing sum to be necessary to pay some outstanding Accounts, and to enable him to Close the Business of his Agency, which will be taken up by Lt. [John Walter] Phillips, for the remainder of the Year." FC in DNA, 32, 2:186.

From William Woodbridge, [later a Delegate from Mich. Territory,] Gibson's Hotel, [Washington,] 2/19. Upon suggestion of [James Monroe], Woodbridge encloses some papers relating to "the petition of certain Indians concerning Dr. [William] Brown" and gives testimony to the usefulness of the Doctor. [Monroe] has also advised Woodbridge to inform Calhoun about Woodbridge's idea "of the value to our country of the lands possessed by the Saguina [Saginaw] Indians & the probability of being able by treaty to procure those lands." Woodbridge has been authorized to receive for [former] Capt. [James ?] McCloskey any payment due to McCloskey. "On these several topicks, Sir, I could wish to have had an opportunity to converse with you, & for that purpose have several times called at the War Office; but have at all times been so unfortunate as to have found your door so barricaded by attendants, having business perhaps more important, that I have felt obliged to relinquish that mode of pursuing the object & to solicit you Sir at your convenient leisure to advise me at what time I may have the pleasure to see you." ALS in DNA, 1, W-218; PC in Carter, ed., *Territorial Papers,* 10:815–816.

From W[ALKER] K. ARMISTEAD

Engineer Department, 20 February 1819

I have the honor of acknowledging the receipt of your letter of appointment conferring on me the rank of Colonel of Engineers, for which mark of distinction be pleased to accept my grateful thanks.

FC in DNA, 21, 1:47.

From W[alker] K. Armistead, 2/20. "Cadets [Wilson M.C.] Fairfax and [Thomas] Ragland are desirous to receive their pay here to enable them to proceed to West Point, where they will be ordered for trial by Court Martial." FC in DNA, 13 (M-91:1, p. 73).

To Charles Bullock, Fort Hawkins, 2/20. Pursuant to his letter of 1/27 (ALS in DNA, 1, B-196) expressing fear that loss in the mails had befallen his earlier, unanswered letter enclosing a draft in his favor issued by D[avid] B. Mitchell, Calhoun says that the $5,059.21 will now be paid and that earlier payment was impossible because a necessary appropriation did not become available until "this week." FC in DNA, 72, D:250.

From [Col.] Robert Butler

Philadelphia, February 20th 1819

I have the honor to inform you that I have remained here for the completion of the public business at this place, growing out of the late treaty with the Chickasaws, and that I am yet without your promised letter on that subject.

The Maj. General [Andrew Jackson] left this [place] on yesterday morning 4 o'clock for New York [City]. All well.

ALS in DNA, 1, B-209.

From the Cherokee Delegation

[Washington, February 20, 1819]

Father,

We have received your proposals for completing the object of our visit. We think the cessions proposed [by you] larger than we expected would be required of us. You know our circumstances in our relation to the Government from whom we receive protection. We do not doubt that you take into view the future prospects that are before us; & we will not entertain a doubt that what you propose you propose in the character of a father advising his children, and we will not throw away your advice. We request you as our father to take into your consideration the Treaty of Turkeytown, where, by not complying with your offer at Highwassee in 1817, we imprudently deprived ourselves of an annuity of $6,000 p[e]r annum in perpetuity. We hope our father will take this circumstance into consideration and place us at least on the footing with the Chickasaws, to whom we attribute the loss we feel. Father, we are your children: do with us as you think best; we confide in you to provide for us as you would for the youngest children of the great family. Need we to say more to a father? A.B.

Draft in DNA, 75 (M-208:8).

To E[LIAS] EARLE, [Representative from S.C.]

Department of War, 20th February 1819

In the case of Mr. Carouth [*sic*; Adam Carruth, a manufacturer at Greenville, S.C.,] an inspector has been directed to remain constantly at his establishment and arrangements have been made for the Ordnance office to make advances to him for the arms as fast as they are delivered.

FC in DNA, 3, 10:256.

From EDMUND P. GAINES

Fernandina, E[ast] F[lorida], February 20th 1819

The troops stationed in the Harbour of Charleston S.C. having been uniformly more healthy than at any other post within my command, and as that Harbour will require very extensive works of defence, I propose to assign to that post, as soon as the troops can safely be drawn from the southern frontier, three Companies of Artillery and one Regiment of Infantry, a part of this force to be occasionally detached to Savannah. I propose likewise to post one Company of Artillery and five Companies of Infantry at Point Petre: the Infantry to be detached, as occasion may require, towards Darien and Traders-hill. The residue of the Infantry will be sufficient (should Indian hostilities not be renewed) to garrison a Post upon the Appallachicola [*sic*] river, and, if it should be deemed necessary, within or near to the Creek Nation. The Battalion of Artillery under Lt. Colonel McCrea [William MacRea], will, when completed by enlistments, be sufficient for Norfolk, Va., and Fort Johnson, N.C.

From the extensive wilderness country comprehended in my command, the extraordinary movements rendered necessary by the repeated hostilities of the Indians, added to the failures of the contractor, and the extravagant prices demanded for every article purchased on public as well as private account, it has been expensive, and vexatious beyond what I experienced or witnessed during the war with England. And I learn from various sources that I have not been able to escape censure. I am not conscious of having merited this direful reward. The accusations having appeared principally in the least reputable of the newspapers, and without even a tolerably respectable name in support of them, I have not deemed it proper to trouble you upon the subject. Whatever impressions may have gone abroad to the contrary, I feel it to be my duty to state that, the regular troops of my command (with the exception of two or three unworthy individuals, who have been duly prosecuted) have discharged their duty honestly and faithfully, and whenever opportunity offered, have evinced a degree of energy, constancy and courage not to be surpassed by any troops under similar circumstances. The service has been extremely harassing to the fourth and seventh Regiments of Infantry, and I think it is time they should be so relieved as to afford them, and the public service, the benefit of the drill, in Battalion and Brigade.

Permit me to station my command as I have proposed; allow me six thousand dollars to purchase materials for building and repairing Barracks; and four thousand dollars to purchase materials for building boats to convey supplies and troops from Post to Post—and I promise, in return, to render my command useful in the construction of fortifications, healthful, highly disciplined, efficient, and always ready at a moment[']s notice to meet an enemy, without any expence for Barracks or transportation beyond the price of the *materials* necessary for the construction of boats and Barracks; excepting only when the service demands extraordinary movements.

ALS in DNA, 1, G-122; ALS in DNA, 11, 13292. NOTE: Calhoun answered this letter on 3/4.

From James Johnson

Great Crossing[s, Ky.,] 20th Feb. 1819

I beg leave to suggest the propriety of a number of swords being provided for each steam boat such as are generally used on board of our Navy. It ap[p]ears natural to me that if the Indians are excited to oppose us in our rout[e] up the Missouri &c. that it would at ["once" *interlined*] suggest itself to them or their councilors the Brittish [*sic*] to board & sink our boats by night. Cut off our supplies & the expedition is defeated.

A pair of Canoes loaded with Indians to be set afloat above us could very silently approach us by night and unless we were on our guard and well armed with proper instruments for such an attack they might succeed. I can conceive of nothing better than these [*sic*] kind of swords to defend ourselves. Let every man sleep with one by his side where danger ap[p]eared. In a moment he could be using this instrument of death, more successfully than fire arms. For a night attack I should prefer not a gun to fire unless a field p[i]ece with grape shot to loose among their small craft.

You will please to excuse me for any suggestions of mine. My heart is on this subject. I am determin[e]d if human exertions will effect it to suc[c]eed.

We may possibly not need any preperations [*sic*] for defence, but should we need it, it is every thing to be prepared for the worst.

ALS in DNA, 1, J-141.

From James Johnson, Burwell Bassett, and Thomas Newton, [Jr., Representatives from Va.]

City of Washington, Feb[ruar]y 20th 1819

We take leave to recommend Doct[o]r Wat Tyler of Charles City County Virg[ini]a as surgeon of the fort now constructing on Old Point Comfort Va. We believe Doct[o]r Tyler well qualified to discharge the duties of the office. He rec[eive]d a liberal education, & has been for many years engaged in the practise of medicine, & surgery.

He is a highly respectable gentleman. His connexions are as respectable as as [*sic*] any in Virginia.

ALS by Johnson, signed also by Bassett and Newton, in DNA, 11, 13998.

To A[bner] Lacock, [Senator from Pa.,] 2/20. Sends to him two letters from [David B.] Mitchell, recent Governor of Ga., "concerning the commencement of the Seminole War," one being addressed to the War Department and the other to [Edmund P.] Gaines. FC in DNA, 3, 10:256.

From ARTHUR LIVERMORE, [Representative from N.H.]

Feb. 20, 1819

Will the Secretary of War express an [opinion] as to [the] utility of a Post route from Fort Wayne in Indiana to Chicago?

ALS in DNA, 1, L-105. NOTE: Calhoun answered on 2/22.

From John McKee, Choctaw Agency, 2/20. Announces that he has issued a draft for $634.64, this sum "being the amount of Mr. [Cyrus] Kingsbury[']s account for the buildings for the Mission School in this Nation." ALS in DNA, 77 (M-271:2, frames 1254–1255).

To J[ohn] Marshall, Chief Justice, [U.S. Supreme Court,] Washington, 2/20. Acknowledges his letter of 2/18 (ALS in DNA, 1, M-213) verifying the Revolutionary services of four applicants for pensions who served in Marshall's command; sends to him a pension certificate for one of the four, John Laws, and a report as to the others. FC in 3, 10:256.

From PETER B. PORTER

Albany, Feb[ruar]y 20, 1819

The Directors & other officers of the *Mechanics & Farmers' Bank*, in this city have expressed to me a belief that it would be found convenient to the Government, and particularly to your Department, to make deposits, from time to time, at this place, of certain portions of the public monies, intended to be disbursed in the northern and western parts of this State, and on the [Great] Lakes, to be drawn for as the public exigencies might require; and that it would be extremely agreeable to them if the government would accord this mark of its favour and confidence to this institution.

I take great pleasure in stating to you that this Bank, as regards its credit & responsibility, has the highest standing—that its Bills are as current in every part of the State, including the city of N[ew] York, as those of any of the Banks of that city—That the officers, &, speaking generally, the Stockholders, are *distinguished* for their patriotism and devotion to the Government of the U[nited] States—and that during the most gloomy periods of the late war, *no* institution of this kind evinced a more unshaken confidence in the government, or went further in proportion to its capital, in accom[m]odations for its benefit.

ALS in DNA, 1, P-128.

From Alex[ander] Richards

Georgetown, D.C., Feb[ruar]y 20th 1819

The enclosed is as nigh the *date* and *substance* of a letter I refer[r]ed to in a conversation with you this morning, as I can recollect. I have had it Copied, that you might use it, and *my writing* not appear. If there was [*sic*] no impropriety in your requesting the original papers, sent to your [*sic*], to be examined, I should like to see them at your office on Monday, when I could give further explainations [*sic*].

[P.S.] This Envelope you will consider *confidential*—and the enclosed so far as respects my *name.*

ALS in DNA, 1, R-108. Note: EU's on this letter indicate that the enclosed letter related "to certain claims" and that it was "not filed."

To Henry Sherburne, Chickasaw Agency, 2/20. Remits $7,379 to be paid to specified individuals in accordance with the recent Chickasaw treaty, which was ratified on 1/7; the appropriation required "did not pass until a few days ago," however, and Calhoun hopes that the remittance will arrive in time to comply with the stipulated limit of 60 days after ratification. The recipients include Capt. John Gordon of Tenn., $1,115 in payment of a debt owed to him by Gen. William Colbert, a Chickasaw; Capt. David Smith of Ky., $2,000 in payment of a debt owed to him by the Chickasaws; Levi Colbert; and Maj. James Colbert, $1,089, "being a sum taken from his pocket in the Baltimore theatre in June 1816." FC in DNA, 72, D:249–250.

To Waller Taylor and James Noble, [Senators from Ind.,] and Jer[emiah] Morrow, [Senator from O.,] 2/20. Accepts their protest of 2/19 (LS in DNA, 1, T-104) against the appointments of [John] Johnston and [William] Conner to appraise the improvements on the Delawares' ceded lands, in accordance with the treaty of 10/1818, on the ground that Conner has an Indian family, that there may be a bias against the U.S., and that qualified men lacking prejudice are available; concurring in the objection, Calhoun says, "I will thank you to name two suitable persons to take that valuation." FC in DNA, 3, 10:256.

S[YLVANUS] THAYER to WALKER K. ARMISTEAD

Military Academy, West Point, Feb[ruar]y 20th 1819

Presuming that appointments will shortly be made out for the Cadets who will be ordered to join the Mil[itary] Acad[em]y in June next I take the liberty of enclosing herewith an estimate of the vacancies which will exist at that period. The number of Cadets appointed to join the Academy in September & October last was 185 of whom only 110 were admitted. Should the same proportion of those appointed the present year be admitted, then 125 new appointments will be necessary to fill all the vacancies.

Many Cadets have joined the Academy under an impression that they might be admitted at any time of the year provided they could render satisfactory reasons for delay. Would it not, therefore, be advisable to attach to the letters of appointment an extract from the regulations which were approved on the 23d July 1818[?]

ALS with several Ens in DNA, 1, T-92.

From D[ecius] Wadsworth, 2/20. Submits the usual quarterly returns for the Ordnance Department to the end of 1818. Attributes the delay to the tardy returns from Harpers Ferry. The estimated expenses for the first quarter of 1819 will be about $30,000. "Those [expenses] at Pittsburgh will exceed the Estimate on Account of the Stores required for the Expeditions up the Missouri & Mississippi." FC in DNA, 32, 2:186–187.

C[hristopher] V[andeventer] to Thomas Wilson at [N.G.] Dufief's [Bookstore], Philadelphia, 2/20. Answers Wilson's report of 2/15 (LS in DNA, 1, W-191) stating that Wilson has sent to the War Department the two-volume, 1817 edition of Boyer's French-English dictionary; that Wilson has written twice about them but that neither these letters nor the books have been acknowledged; and that Wilson assumes, nevertheless, that the books arrived and, therefore, that the $20.87 due for them should be paid. Promises that the remittance will be dispatched if the account is presented in the usual form for public accounts. Encloses a copy of a letter addressed to Wilson on 1/12. FC in DNA, 3, 10:254.

CALVIN JONES to [JAMES] MONROE

Raleigh, Feb. 21, 1819

I lately travelled among the Chickesaw [*sic*] and Cherokee nations of Indians, and while I felt an esteem and respect for their character which I was not prepared to expect, I was touched by the miseries of their situation. The observations I made satisfied me of the practicability of their civilization. Believing that whatever talents I possessed were of a kind to qualify me for an undertaking of this nature, and feeling a strong desire to employ them in that way, I lately made application [in person ?] to the Secretary of War for the appointment of Agent to some nation of Southern Indians. More lately a member of Congress advised me to address myself directly to your Excellency. I since learn a law has passed authorizing the President to adopt measures to favour the civilization of some of the Indian nations. I know not whether the plan contains a situation that I could ask to fill. I have a desire to promote the honour and interests of my country and the happiness of the human race and if your Excellency can employ me usefully my most zealous and faithful services are proferred [*sic*]. I only require that the emoluments of the place should be equal to the support of a family. My zeal must necessarily be limitted [*sic*] by circumstances, and I am not in a situation to enable me to make great sacrifices to advance any object however important and desirable.

ALS in DNA, 11, 13538.

From W[ALKER] K. ARMISTEAD

Engineer Department, Feb[ruar]y 22d 1819

I have the honour to report that the instruments alluded to by Capt. [Hugh] Young in his letter to you of Feb[ruar]y 18th 1819 cannot be furnished from any on hand.

I beg leave to observe that Capt. Young has never made any return of public property in his possession, nor reported himself to me, as it was his duty to do.

LS in DNA, 1, A-73; FC (dated 2/23) in DNA, 21, 1:48.

To the Cherokee Delegation, 2/22. "I transmit you propositions on which I am willing to close the Treaty of the 8th July, 1807 [*sic*; 1817]. The Session of Congress is drawing to a close, and it is desirable that the treaty should be formed as soon as practicable, so as to have it ratified by the Senate before the adjournment of Congress. If you are willing to adopt the terms proposed, they can be reduced to form immediately and the treaty be signed tomorrow or next day." FC in DNA, 72, D:251–252; CC in DNA, 153; PC in *American State Papers: Indian Affairs,* 2:190.

From T[IMOTHY] FORD

Charleston, [S.C.,] Febr[uar]y 22d 1819

I venture to presume a little on our old acquaintance in addressing you on a matter that concerns myself, & hope I shall stand excused for intruding a little on your time. I perceive that Congress are about to make some new organnization [*sic*] of the Judiciary—& that probably a Judge will be appointed to preside in the circuit courts of this, & of one or both of the adjacent States. After many years of steady practice in the courts of Law & Equity of this State, & the federal Courts, I feel disposed to offer my professional services to my country in a Judicial capacity. I have on different occasions been requested by my friends to offer for our State courts, but have hitherto, & recently, declined being a candidate, because our Judiciary arrangements separate a person from his family for too large a portion of the year in continued succession to suit my habits & views.

How far I may be qualified to fill the office now in the contemplation of Congress it becomes not me to say—that must rest on my reputation & the Opinions of those who know me. But presuming that a Salary will be annexed to the office, in some reasonable degree, commensurate with it's [*sic*] labours & duties I am desirous of being considered an applicant—and, if I infringe no rule of propriety or any habits or inclinations of yours in asking it, I will beg the favor of your announcing to the President [James Monroe] such my desire. Should it please him to call me to this Station I hope I should discharge its duties with fidelity to the public—and I am sure I should discharge them with alacrity under an Administration of which I most cordially approve.

ALS in DNA, 103, 1817–1825, Timothy Ford.

From CH[ARLES] HICKS, "in behalf of the [Cherokee] Delegation"

Washington City, February 22d 1819

Your communication of this date has been duly rec[eive]d and underwent a deliberate consideration of this Delegation, and we are sorry to say we cannot concur with your proposition relative to the boundary contained therein. We entertain a thorough belief that for want of a personal acquaintance with the situation of the population of our Country you are unapprised of the vast number of our Citizens who would be disturbed by this morning[']s proposition, and permit us on that point to assure you, that unless we are very much mistaken indeed, the bounds you ask for will include within its [*sic*] limits more than one-half of our people. We herein again take the liberty of assuring you that we feel desirous of liberally providing for the Arkansaw [*sic*] emigrants, and entertain the strongest conviction that the quantity of land contained in our first proposition on that point was making a liberal and generous provision for them. In this belief we are also strengthened by the opinion of our Agent Colo[nel Return J.] Meigs as transmit[t]ed to your Department, to which proposition on that point should you concur, the earliest possible time by you to be appointed to close the negotiation will be pleasing to us—but we have every confidence in the Government, and also in you as her agent, and verily believe that nothing but justice will be finally sought for by you, and this we think we have offered—besides the reservations intended for those of our people who may reside and own possessions within the territory intended to be ceded for whom we had understood provision was to be made by reservations. Our distinct understanding on the subject of reservations either for life or in fee simple, was that the reservee might either live on such estate, or move elsewhere and leave it for his benifit [*sic*] as he should think proper. On the subject of An[n]uities we think your proposition of this morning would ["not" *interlined*] be an equitable dividend in as much as the calculation will not leave us our just proportion, but we are willing that the Arkansaw people should have one-third, altho' that number according to the calculations heretofore made, for them, and which we think were exag[g]erated, leaves a balance of Six hundred & fifty more than they are entitled to, but we will consent to that division hereafter, provided the same will not be subject thereto until after our National debts are paid.

LS in DNA, 77 (M-271:2, frames 1118–1121).

From [Thomas S. Jesup], 2/22. Encloses a draft of Lt. Otis Fisher for $1,400 payable to Hurd & Sewall of New York [City]. FC in DNA, 42, 1:192.

To A[rthur] Livermore, [Representative from N.H.,] 2/22. "In answer to your letter of this day's date [actually of 2/20,] I have to state that the Mail is now carried by Military Express from Fort Wayne to Chicago. A regular Mail between those posts, would be a great accom[m]odation to the Army in the facility and celerity of transmitting orders." LS in DNA, 203, 15A-D11.1; FC in DNA, 3, 10:258.

To Thomas L. McKenney

Department of War, 22d Feby. 1819

Your note of the 13th [addressed to Christopher Vandeventer (LU in DNA, 1, M-214; FC in DNA, 73, E:199)] has been received.

To enable you to procure the supplies in time, I enclose a list of all the annuities which are to be paid in goods the present year. Many of the annuities formerly paid in goods are, by late treaties, hereafter to be paid in money.

The enclosed copy of a letter from Jasper Parrish, accompanied by an invoice of goods, will direct you as to the proportion of the annuity due to the Six Nations which is to be paid in goods and the kind of goods suitable for them.

A requisition for the amount of the enclosed list will be issued in your favor immediately on the passage of the bill to carry into effect the treaty with the Quapaw tribe and with the tribes of the Illinois nation of Indians.

[Enclosure]

List of Indian Annuities which are to be paid in goods.

Eel Rivers,	p[e]r act 6th May, 1796	$500	
Kickapoos,	" " " " "	500	
Piankeshaws [*sic*],	" " " " "	500	
Kaskaskias,	" " " " "	500	$2,000
Six Nations,	p[e]r act 25 Feb[ruar]y, 1799, $4,500, of this sum $2,200 to be p[ai]d in goods, balance in cash		2,200
Sacs	p[e]r act 3d March, 1805	600	
Foxes	" " " " "	400	1,000
Choctaws	p[e]r act 19 Feb[ruar]y, 1808		3,000
Great Osages	p[e]r act 3d March, 1811	1,000	
Little Osages	" " " " "	500	1,500
Quapaws	p[e]r act 3 March, 1819 [*sic*]	1,000	
Peoria, Kaskaskias, Mitchigania, Cahokia, & Tamarois tribes of the Illinois nation	" " " " "	300	1,300
			$11,000

FC with the list in DNA, 72, D:250–251.

To Stephen Pleasonton, 2/22. "I return the accounts of Augustus [*sic*] Chouteau, for his services as Commissioner [to negotiate the Quapaw treaty of 1818 and perhaps others], which you will settle agreeably to the enclosed letters and extract." LS in U.S. General Accounting Office, Indian Tribal Branch, Fifth Auditor Accounts, no. 627, "5th Auditor's Certificate on the account of Augustus [*sic*] Chouteau, one of the commissioners for treating with the Indians"; FC in DNA, 72, D:252.

From Winfield Scott

Richmond, Feb. 22nd 1819

I extremely regret to feel myself under the necessity of begging your attention, for a moment, to a subject which, at the first view, may appear to be altogether private and therefore improper to be submitted to your official cognizance. I allude to the correspondence into which I was accidentally drawn, some sixteen months since, with Major General [Andrew] Jackson of the Army.

The general order of the 21st Feb. 1818, or rather the first sentence of it, prohibits the publication of "transactions between officers of a private and personal nature," without qualification, as to the mode. Now the letters alluded to, either fall under this description, or they do not. On the first supposition, Major General Jackson has violated the order, by freely exposing (I understand in a garbled shape) the correspondence in question, to the members of Congress at Washington, & to others, without limitation or reserve; or on the other hand, he has but exercised a right common to us both, & I may, in self defence, lay the entire subject before the public. It is true, that my information does not state, that he has printed the correspondence. It seems, that he has only exposed such parts of it, as he thought proper, by multiplying & circulating manuscript copies or extracts, with a view to excite prejudice against me; and such is the peculiar nature of the case that that effect necessarily results from a substitution of a part for the whole. Accordingly, a Georgia paper some ten months since, made a very unfair allusion to the difference between us, on information derived, as was stated, from an officer who had served under the immediate orders of Maj. Gen[era]l J[ackson] & again, some time last week, as I learn, a Georgetown Gazette, no doubt under the direct influence of Maj. Gen[era]l J[ackson] made a similar allusion.

I can no longer be indifferent to the insiduous [*sic*] course pursued against me, & must, therefore, request leave, to resort to the press in self defence; for I cannot perceive, that there is any difference made by the order between publishing by manuscript & publishing by printing. If there be a difference between the measure I have in view, & the course actually adopted against me, I cannot fail to be the victim of a mere subtlety; for my positition [*sic*], duties & inclination, equally prevent me from hawking my papers among the visitors at Washington, & it is still more abhorrent to my pride & feelings to attempt to reply to every scurrilous paragraph & base insinuation which may be printed against me.

The request I have the honour to submit, is, in more precise terms, this: that should I print the entire correspondence, in question, in a pamphlet form, you will not sanction my arrest, should an application to that effect be made. I will barely add, that it is not my wish to circulate the corerspondence until the discussion of the Seminole War, before the Senate, is abandonned [*sic*] or ended.

ALS in DNA, 1, S-249; CC in NN, James Monroe Papers.

From H[ENRY] S[T.] G[EORGE] TUCKER, [Representative from Va.]

Feb[ruar]y 22 [1819]

I feel it my duty to enclose two applications for Cadetcies in the military academy. At the same time I beg leave to remark that neither of them is for the young gentleman for whom you obligingly promised me a warrant. The name of that applicant is Robert Y. Conrad. He is a lad of most conspicuous capacity and very considerably advanced in his Education. There is no doubt of his being qualified as the law directs for his admission into the academy. There are other reasons which I am sure will not be without their weight. He is fatherless and his mother in indigent circumstances, having been reduced ["from affluence" *interlined*] by her husband[']s death to her present situation. I have brought up one of her sons myself. He is now a fine, promising young man in the study of the law. They are the nephews of Judge [Hugh]

Holmes and of that Capt. [Maj. Andrew Hunter] Holmes who at nineteen years of age distinguished himself in an engagement with the British in Canada with the small force under his command. He afterwards fell in battle when advancing against Mackinaw [Fort Mackinac, Mich., 8/4/1814] with his gallant compeer [Lt.] Col. [George] Croghan. These boys are his nearest male relations.

If the rules of the department ever permit an appointment before a lad is full fourteen years of age the present case would be as little objectionable as any other on that score. Robt. Conrad is very large of [*sic*] his age & will be 14 in September. Submitting all these matters to your decision, I have the honour to be, Dear Sir, most respectfully your friend . . . .

ALS in DNA, 15, 1819, 78.

From W[alker] K. Armistead, 2/23. Requests a payment of $3,334 to Rufus King, [Senator from N.Y.,] for the maps sold by King to the U.S. FC in DNA, 21, 1:48.

From W[alker] K. Armistead, 2/23. Requests remittances of $40,000 to Capt. James Gadsden for fortifications at Mobile and of $30,000 to Nathaniel Cox for fortifications at New Orleans. FC in DNA, 21, 1:48.

From J[ames] L. Edwards, Pension Office, 2/23. Samuel Jacob Axon was a Surgeon's Mate in the 1st S.C. Regiment, but there is no record of how long or when he served. Certifies that there is no application from Axon in the Pension Office. LS in DNA, 157, 15A-G1.

From William McIntosh and three other Creek Chiefs, Washington, 2/23. They seek payment of an indemnity for the destruction of the Chehaw village in 1818; settlement by treaty of misunderstandings about the Creek ownership of the land on both sides of the boundary between the U.S. and Spanish Fla.; countermanding by Calhoun of an order by [Andrew] Jackson concerning cattle commandeered by Creek warriors from the Seminoles in 1818; payment to the Creeks who served in the Seminole War of $8 per month, which was what militiamen in that service received, rather than the $5 per month paid to the Creeks. LS in DNA, 77 (M-271:2, frames 1236–1240).

To [James Monroe], 2/23. Calhoun nominates two men for appointments: Richard Oldham as Military Storekeeper at the Newport, Ky., arsenal and Thomas Hempstead as Military Storekeeper "for the Commissary Department" at St. Louis. LS in DNA, 1, P-152, with an AEI by Monroe signifying his approval; FC (dated 2/25) in DNA, 6, 1:347.

From Gideon Morgan, Jr., Washington, 2/23. Urges that George "Harland [*sic;* Harlin]" be granted a reservation on lands ceded [by the Cherokees], because Governor [Joseph] McMinn had promised such a gift to Harlin. ALS in DNA, 77 (M-271:2, frames 1527–1528). (Morgan dated his letter "1818," and it was therefore assigned erroneously to that year in *The Papers of John C. Calhoun,* 2:156. An EU indicates, however, that the letter was written in 1819. An accompanying statement by Return J. Meigs [M-271:2, frame 1529], dated 2/23/1819, pressed Harlin's claim even more strongly, stating that Harlin's father "at the risk of his life steadily endeavored to dissuade the Cherokees from their acting under British influence" and that McMinn reputedly promised to George Harlin "a reservation of land of one mile square for his services" in promoting emigration by the Cherokees.)

To Maj. Richard Oldham, in care of R[ichard] M. Johnson, Washington, 2/23. Appoints him to be the Military Storekeeper at the Newport, Ky., Arsenal, with the compensations of a Capt. of Infantry. Asks for an immediate reply; if he accepts, he is to report to [Decius Wadsworth]. FC in DNA, 3, 10:258.

To George Read, [Jr.,]
U.S. District Attorney, Newcastle, Del.

Department of War, 23d February 1819

I have received your letter of the 16th instant [ALS in DNA, 1, R-103], relative to the title of the Pea-patch in the Deleware [*sic*]. As that position is considered the key to the defence of the Deleware and on that account highly valuable to the United States, I must request your particular attention to defence of the suit.

FC in DNA, 3, 10:259.

From Thomas Settle and James Owen, [Representatives from N.C.,] 2/23. They request permission for Dr. [Egbert H.] Bell to practice medicine [among civilians] in New Orleans, where he is to be stationed as Post Surgean. They are confident that he will not abuse the privilege, if it should be granted. LS in DNA, 1, S-239. (An AEI by Calhoun refers this request to Surgeon General [Joseph Lovell]. An AES by Lovell reads: "Doct[or] Bell is not a Post Surgeon at present." The sketch of Bell in Heitman, *Historical Register,* 1:207, indicates no interruption in Bell's career as an Army doctor, 1812–1815 and 1816–1821.)

To Henry Sherburne

Department of War, 23d Feby. 1819

Your letter of the 3d instant [LS in DNA, 1, S-235, concerning chiefly a reported intention of the Chickasaws to sell for $20,000 their reservation to a Maj. Lewis of Tenn. and to lease to him the Salt Spring] has been received.

The contract which you state that George Colbert has [been reported to have] made for the sale of the reservation and the lease of the Salt Spring, for a cession of which it is contemplated to hold a treaty with the Chickasaw nation, having been made since this determination on the part of the government, cannot be considered valid. John Overton, Newton Cannon, and Robert Weakl[e]y, Esquires, have been appointed commissioners for the purpose of holding this treaty.

You will inform the nation of these circumstances and take every measure you may deem politic and necessary to prepare the Chiefs for a friendly and favorable reception of the Commissioners.

Your letter [of 12/12/1818 (LS in DNA, 1, S-151)] forwarding the certificate of Mr. [John] Sommerville [Cashier, Nashville Branch, State Bank of Tenn.] for the $6,000 [that you deposited there, as instructed, to the credit of Thomas Tudor Tucker] was duly received.

FC in DNA, 72, D:252. NOTE: On 2/13 (LS in DNA, 1, S-248) Sherburne had written to Calhoun that Levi and George Colbert had not known of any desire on the part of the U.S. to buy the reservation and to lease the salt spring in question; that the commitment had not yet become binding, because no deed and no rental contract had actually been signed, no money paid; and that the Colberts and other Chickasaws would prefer that the U.S. should make the prospective purchase and that neither property should be owned by an individual.

Thomas Wilson, Philadelphia, to C[hristopher] Vandeventer, 2/23. Wilson sends the bill requested in Vandeventer's letter of 2/20 and gives assurance that N.G. Dufief will obtain in London, if the order reaches him there in time, a copy of the best Spanish–English or Spanish–French dictionary. LS in DNA, 1, W-200.

To W[ILLIAM] WIRT

Department of War, 23d February 1819

The enclosed opinion of the District attorney for Delaware, [George Read, Jr.,] is upon a case of great importance to the United States, involving the title of the military position, called the Pea-patch, which is considered the Key to the defence of the Delaware. Believing the validity of the title made out by the District Attorney, the United States purchased that important site. Since the purchase and the commencement of the fortifications on it, a suit has been commenced under a conflicting title derived from a New Jersey patent.

The opinion of the Dis[tric]t Att[orne]y contains all the facts, and I will thank you, at a convenient time, to examine the case and communicate to me your opinion.

LS with En in DNA, 111, 167 and 199; FC in DNA, 3, 10:259–260. NOTE: The enclosure is a CC of the letter to Calhoun from Read dated 9/7/1818.

To Capt. H[ugh] Young, Top[ographical] Eng[ineer], Baltimore, 2/23. Answers his appeal of 2/18 (ALS in DNA, 1, A-73) by authorizing him to purchase the instruments that will be needed in his frontier survey "on as good terms as possible, taking care to select them of as good quality as can be found in the Country." FC in DNA, 3, 10:258.

To Joseph Anderson, 2/24. Answers his letter of 2/19 (LS with Ens in DNA, 1, A-71; FC in DNA, 59, 19:56) expressing an opinion that U.S. Marshals will be able to collect fines from delinquent militiamen only after lawsuits, except in Pa., where a State court has upheld the validity of the decisions of the court-martial, and suggesting that the War Department rather than the Treasury Department can best pose this problem to [James Monroe]. Calhoun replies: "As the collection of the fines has hitherto been confided to the Treasury Department, and as Mr. [William H.] Crawford may probably be acquainted with the merits" of the particular case in question, Calhoun believes that Crawford should decide what is to be done. FC in DNA, 3, 10:260.

To [James Barbour], President [Pro Tempore] of the Senate, and Speaker [Henry Clay], 2/24. As required by a statute "concerning public contracts" enacted on 4/21/1808, Calhoun submits "statements exhibiting the contracts" made during 1818 by Commissary General of Subsistence [George Gibson], Commissary General of Purchases [Callender Irvine], the Ordnance Department, and the Engineer Department. LS with 4 Ens (Barbour's copy) in DNA, 154, 15A-F4; LS with 4 Ens (Clay's copy) in DNA, 201, 15A-F3; FC in DNA, 4, 2:92; PC with Ens in *American State Papers: Military Affairs,* 1:848–860.

From W[illiam] Eustis, Williamsburg, Va., 2/24. Encloses a letter to himself dated 1/5/1818 [*sic*] from his nephew, [Bvt. Lt.] Col. A[bram] Eustis, seeking the command of a Regiment and alleging that he has been overlooked unjustly when promotions were made. Confirming this contention, W[illiam] Eustis admits that, when he retired "from the War Department [as Secretary of War, about the end of 1812], I perceived that, from a misplaced delicacy, I had not done him [Abram Eustis] justice in his rank and preferment." CC with En in DNA, 159, 17B-D2.

Jo[seph] Gales, Jr., Washington, to [James Monroe], 2/24. Urges a reappointment for [1st] Lt. [Joseph P.] Bunting, "whose dismission from the service [on 1/8] I look upon as a case of the most aggravated hardship which has ever fallen under my observation." An AEU by W[illiam] W. Seaton expresses similar sentiments. ALS in DNA, 11, 13156.

From John H. Hall

Washington City, 24 Feb. 1819

On the 25 Jan. last, Col. [Decius] Wadsworth informed me that the compensation which had been formerly allowed me for personal services, must cease from the 31 Dec. previous, because it made the guns fabricated at Harpers Ferry appear to cost more than they really did. I immediately called on Lieut[enant] Col. [George] Bomford, mentioned the affair to him & asked his advice upon the subject—he observed that as the board of Officers would probably report upon my guns in a few days & would perhaps report upon my compensation also, I had better remain quiet. In conformity with his advice I have taken no farther [*sic*] steps in regard to it untill [*sic*] this moment. Yesterday I learned, for the first time, that Lieut[enant] Col. Bomford, when speaking of the expected report, in reference to my compensation, only had in view that which would be allowed for guns made on my plan for the public service.

Although it is extremely painful to me to be under a necessity of troubling you upon this subject, yet my duty requires that I should not acquiesce in the the [*sic*] privation of the pittance formerly agreed to be allowed to me.

In March last I received through Mr. Preble, U.S. Attorney for the District of Maine, an invitation from Lieut[enant] Col. Bomford, in consequence of which I repaired to this part of the Country for the purpose of attending to the introduction of my guns into the public service, &, in faith of the agreement entered into with Lieut[enant] Col. Bomford have continued here to the neglect of all other business, for the accomplishment of an object in which, a[s] I conceive, the public interest is as much concerned as my own.

Requesting your pardon for thus obtruding myself on your notice, I would respectfully solicit your interference in regard to this affair so that I may receive if not an adequate compensation for a person in my situation, at least the trifling amount to which by agreement I am entitled.

ALS in DNA, 1, H-188.

From Callender Irvine

Phila[delphia,] Feb[ruar]y 24th 1819

Your letter of the 18th instant is received, enclosing a Copy of a letter addressed to the Dep[artmen]t of War, by the 2d Auditor, [William Lee,] upon which you have desired my opinion. I correctly comprehend the views of the 2d Auditor, to wit, that the Deputy Commissaries of purchase [John McKinney and Darby Noon] shall transmit their accounts for disbursements through me for examination & sanction. I cannot object to the proposed arrangement, tho' its adoption will certainly give me considerable additional trouble. But if it be intended that I shall be charged with money advanced to the Deputy Commissaries of purchase, & held responsible for the application of it, I beg to be excused & hope that no regulation of the kind may be sanctioned. Those Deputies, I presume, have given Bonds & Sureties to Gov[ernmen]t for the correct discharge of their duties, for the faithfull [*sic*] application of public money to be rec[eive]d by them from time to time. Besides (and I mean no reflection upon either Gentleman by the remark) I have not had any agency in the appointment of those disbursing agents; on the contrary, they were unknown to me until I was advised of their appointment [by] Government. But, I will not add [further remarks] on this head, because I feel persuaded that you will not sanction the intention, if indeed it exists at all, of making me responsible for the acts of men, who are scarcely known to me personally, in the disbursement of large sums of money annually.

FC in DNA, 45, 387:334.

To John McKee, Choctaw Agency, 2/24. Calhoun acknowledges McKee's report of 2/1 [ALS in DNA, 77 (M-271:2, frames 1250–1251)] that the "Commissioners have it in contemplation . . . to make another effort as soon as possible to obtain the desired cession of Land" from the Choctaws—an effort that, McKee believes, will be futile unless the Indians are predisposed to accept the government's offer. Agreeing, Calhoun replies: "The President [James Monroe] is desirous to make a treaty with the Choctaws for the cession of the land in question, provided it can be done on reasonable terms, but unless there is a favorable prospect of success, the expenses always incident to an Indian treaty ought to be avoided. You will therefore ascertain the disposition of the Indians upon the objects of a treaty and if favourable report to this Department." FC in DNA, 3, 10:260.

From Return J. Meigs, Washington, 2/24. Suggests that a clause should be added, "in the treaty or convention with the Cherokees about to be concluded, to secure to the Government" the four or more log cabins that belong to the Cherokee Agency at Hiawassee; they "may probably be needed some time longer for public use." ALS in DNA, 77 (M-271:2, frames 1356–1357); draft, quite different and dated 2/22, in DNA, 75 (M-208:8).

From Henry Sherburne, Chickasaw Agency, 2/24. Several individuals who are entitled to receive $100 or $150 under the recent treaty have been calling on Sherburne for their payments. But how is he to obtain the funds? Cash payments are preferred and will therefore give maximum satisfaction to the recipients. Several named Chiefs are entitled by the treaty to more than $4,000. "Many of the nation appear this spring to be more desirous than usual for Implements of Husbandry." Consequently, Sherburne finds it necessary to buy additional iron [from Tenn. for use by his blacksmith]. To supplement a previous report, he explains that he found it necessary to construct anew a 14′ x 9′ gallery leading to a door of the Agency house. ALS in DNA, 1, S-257.

From Waller Taylor and James Noble, [Senators from Ind.,] 2/24. They recommend George Hunt and William Cotton, both of Ind., "to value the property of the Delaware Indians, as provided by the late treaty with that Tribe." LS in DNA, 1, T-88.

From D[ecius] W[adsworth], 2/24. Recommends approval of the claim of Kingsley & French to about $2 extra per musket produced for the U.S.; explains the difficulties they encountered in fulfilling their contract, which was signed about 1808. Wadsworth believes that there will be no hesitation in allowing their claim to a refund for their extra expenses incurred for flints, for packing cases, for making delivery at Charlestown, [Mass.,] instead of Boston, and for use of a toll bridge. FC in DNA, 32, 2:188–190.

From Lewis Cass, Washington, 2/25. Recommends the appointment of a commission, including [Christopher] Vandeventer, to negotiate for a cession of the Indians' title to lands in the area of the Saginaw River and Bay; the prospects are favorable for obtaining a large cession in return for about $10,000 worth of goods and money and for an annuity of $1,200 or $1,500. LS in DNA, 1, C-215; FC dated 2/24 in DNA, 76 (M-1:4, p. 64); PC in Carter, ed., *Territorial Papers,* 10:816–817.

To F[erdinand] R[udolf] Hassler, Newark, N.J., 2/25. His letter of 2/14, with copies of letters between himself and Lt. [John R.] Vinton (ALS with Ens in DNA, 1, H-163), has been received. "I regret to find from your statement that you and Lt. Vinton can no longer act together in harmony, and have therefore ordered him to report for another duty." Hassler can keep the instruments that he received on 2/13 from Capt. [René Edward] De Russy but is to account for them when Hassler returns from his survey of the Northern boundary line. FC in DNA, 3, 10:261.

From James Noble, [Senator from Ind.]

Washington, Feb[ruar]y 25th 1819

I have taken the liberty to address you on behalf of Mr. John Russell Thornton, a soldier in the Army of the U.S. and stationed at this time in Brookville Indiana under the command of Capt. [George Henry] Grosvenor. Mr. Thornton is the son of Mr. Joseph Thornton of Brownsville Penn[sylvani]a a respectable merchant and a man of fair and unblemished character. His son has been liberally educated; pains have been taken by his father to give him a classical education. Mr. Thornton being wealthy indulged his son, and as is to[o] common with young men he became dissipated and in one of his frolics, while on a visit to Cincinnati enlisted in March 1818 under [the then 2nd] Lieu[tenan]t [James Duncan *or* William Montrose] Graham. From Mr. Thornton's standing in Society, being the son of wealthy parents, and well educated, his acquaintance were astonished ["at the enlistment" *interlined*]. I heard [2nd] Lieut[enant George W.] Stall say that he was offered a discharge, but Mr. Thornton refused to accept it, upon the ground that it would attatch [*sic*] dishonor to his character. A letter from Capt. Grosvenor will be presented to you, ["under whose command Mr. Thornton now remains" *canceled*]. Mr. Thornton is perfectly the gentleman in his manner, and I have no doubt from his talents, he will make a very useful officer to the U.S. Should it be in your power to have him promoted to the rank of Lieu[tenan]t it will be thankfully rec[eive]d by Mr. Thornton & duly appreciated by his friends. I have thus hastily addressed you, on behalf of Mr. Thornton. My feeling[s] have compelled me to do so, and I have entered into all those feelings which are common to parents toward their son.

N.B. Mr. Thornton is now [a] first Sergea[n]t.

ALS in DNA, 11, 13976. NOTE: Four AES's were appended on 2/27 to this letter by Henry Baldwin, Robert Moore, and C[hristian] Tarr, [Representatives from Pa.,] and by A[bner] Lacock, [Senator from Pa.]. An AEU by Calhoun directed that this recommendation was "To be particularly attended to."

To William Rabun, [Governor of Ga.,] Milledgeville, 2/25. [Edmund P.] Gaines reports that "the security of Georgia will not require the establishment" of military posts along the southern boundary of Ga. west of the Okefenokee Swamp—this because of "the disposition of the Indians, & from the acquisition of the Floridas." Wilson Lumpkin, however, will be furnished with troops for his protection while surveying that boundary from Fort Scott to the head of the St. Marys River, if he applies for them to Gen. Gaines. FC in DNA, 3, 10:261.

From Decius Wadsworth, 2/25. The accounts of Ordnance officers are in good order, with few exceptions. One is Capt. [Joseph H.] Rees, who owes $6,000 to the U.S. and may have loaned that sum to a friend who lacks either the inclination or the ability to refund it. Another is Capt. [Edwin] Tyler, who owes about $4,000, was granted in 1/1819 a leave of absence for a week or two, and has not reported for duty since. [George] Bomford has

$5,000 outstanding, and Wadsworth suggests that Bomford's account should be settled before much time elapses. ALS in DNA, 1, W-199; FC in DNA, 32, 2:190–192.

From Capt. L[EWIS] WARRINGTON, U.S.N., Capt. J[ESSE] D. ELLIOTT, U.S.N., Brig. Gen. [SIMON] BERNARD, Col. W[ALKER] K. ARMISTEAD, [Lt. Col.] WILLIAM MCREE, and [former] B[vt. Brig.] G[enera]l J[OSEPH] G. SWIFT

George Town, [D.C.,] 25 February 1819

We the undersigned Commissioners appointed by the President of the United States, [James Monroe,] to survey, and examine Chesapeake Bay, and the Coast of the United States, East of that Estuary, for the purpose of selecting a position for a Naval Depot, and to plan a General System of Defence, have, this day, the Honor to submit to you, the result of their labors.

P.S. Captain Elliott, being absent, authorized Captain Warrington to subscribe his Name.

LS in DNA, 1, W-208; FC of the long En (dated 2/24) in DNA, 22, 1818:342–394. NOTE: The enclosed report proposed coastal fortifications in the Hampton Roads area, in the upper Chesapeake Bay, and to the southwest of Cape Henry at a total cost estimated at $4,258,890.845 for construction.

From JOHN WILLIAMS, [Senator from Tenn.]

Senate Chamber, Feb. 25th 1819

Your letter of yesterday was rec[eive]d to day. I have endeavoured without effect, to obtain the opinion of the whole delegation from Tennessee on the subject of the reservations. I am not apprised of any ["of any" *canceled*] substantial objection to any of the reservations except John Ross'. If his is ratified it will have a most pernicious influence on future negotiations with the Cherokees. Under my present impressions I will resist the ratification of the treaty with a reservation at Tellico Island for Jno. Ross.

ALS in DNA, 1, W-207.

To [William H. Crawford], 2/26. "Mr. [Ferdinand Rudolf] Hassler has applied to me several times for an adjustment of his claim for services rendered in completing the business of the survey of the coast, under his contract with the Treasury Department, after the act of the 14th of April last, which repealed the act under which he entered into the contract. As I have no means of judging of the extent of the duty performed by Mr. Hassler, I will thank you to adjust his claim, & inform me of the amount, if any, due him." FC in DNA, 171, 1:320–321.

To Edmund P. Gaines, Fernandina, via St. Marys, Ga.

Department of War, 26th February, 1819

The enclosed letter shews that Mr. [Benjamin G.] Orr has failed to comply with his contract. Under present circumstances, I am anxious that supplies should be procured upon as economical terms as possible. The state of his account renders vigilance very necessary.

I have the pleasure to inform you that the Floridas have been ceded to the United States by Spain: an event long desired, and which will have the most beneficial effects upon our affairs in that quarter.

LS in DNA, 11, 14021; variant FC in DNA, 3, 10:262.

To F[erdinand] R[udolf] Hassler, Newark, N.J., 2/26. Acknowledges his letter of 2/20 (ALS in DNA, 1, H-164). He is to notify Calhoun of the costs when Hassler receives the zenith sector and other "articles ordered." "I am obliged to you for your remarks in relation to the [surveying] instruments. I have no doubt but that they are of the first quality, and I shall give orders to have them preserved with the greatest care." FC in DNA, 3, 10:262.

From [Jonathan Roberts, Senator from Pa.,] 2/26. He encloses a letter to himself from John B.C. Lucas in St. Louis dated 12/19/1818 alleging that Benjamin and John O'Fallon, brothers who are nephews of [William] Clark, are unworthy to hold public offices. Lucas encloses extracts from records of the St. Louis Circuit Court, in its term of 2/1818, proving one conviction against each brother—against Benjamin in conjunction with Thomas F. Smith for misconduct during an 1817 election. Roberts identifies [Benjamin] O'Fallon as "an Indian Agent with the Sioux" and implies that O'Fallon's nomination to that position should not be approved. ALU with Ens in DNA, 1, R-115.

From Decius Wadsworth, 2/26. "The appropriations for the Ordnance Department having been made to include an Item" for $45,500 "to satisfy the Engagement entered into with Randolph Ross for Gunpowder, his Claim to receive that Sum by the supplementary Agreement concluded on the 13 August last becomes complete." To be paid, Ross's agent needs only to present the proper vouchers to Second Auditor [William Lee]. ALS in DNA, 1, W-212; FC in DNA, 32, 2:192.

Maj. Abram Eustis, Fort Independence, [Castle Island, Boston Harbor,] to W[alker] K. Armistead, 2/27. Eustis reports that heavy damage was done to the Fort by a "most violent gale of wind attended with an uncommon tide, on the night of the 25th inst[ant]." ALS in DNA, 223, 44, with an AEI by Calhoun directing that Eustis should be "advised to send an estimate of the money required [for repairs]."

From Edmund P. Gaines

Fernandina, E[ast] F[la.], February 27th 1819

I promised a few weeks ago, to send you in the early part of the present month, a chart of the River St. Johns, and of the coast to this place. [Because of] a desire to add to it a sketch of the country between this place and the Oakafonoka [*sic*] swamp, and at the same time to ascertain whether the Indians had returned, as had been apprehended by some of the inhabitants, near to the frontier, I detached a small active party under my aid[e] de camp, Lt. [Daniel E.] Burch, whose reports [to me dated 2/18 and 2/26] I enclose herewith. By which you will perceive that he found the late encampments and trails of several small parties, supposed to have been in pursuit of cattle. His sketch will be completed in a few days, when it will be forwarded.

Reconnoitring parties will be occasionally detached to scour the country and keep an eye to the movements of the Indians.

It is a fact not heretofore known or published, that the Oakafonoka swamp has no connection with the waters of the St. Mary's [*sic*] river. This has been ascertained by Generals [John] Floyd, [Wiley] Thompson and Blackshear, as well as by Mr. Burch, as will be seen by his report herewith.

ALS with Ens dated 2/26 in DNA, 1, G-127; LU with En dated 2/18 in DNA, 11, 13292.

From Edmund P. Gaines

Fernandina, E[ast] F[la.], February 27th 1819

By reports from the commandants of Forts Gadsden and Scott, up to the 28th ultimo and 1st instant, I learn that the requisitions made by Lieut. Col. [Mathew] Arbuckle in October last for four months['] supply of rations had been but in part complied with by the contractor [Benjamin G. Orr]; that Captain [Joel] Spencer had been ordered to purchase the quantity necessary to complete the supply required; that an additional supply of fifty-four thousand rations had been required on the 31st of December last; and likewise a supply for one month to be left in deposite [*sic*], as directed by the General order from the Department of War, at each post on the 1st of June; and that the troops are again compelled to rely upon purchases of corn, at a very high price, from the settlement on Chattahoochee, in lieu of bread, having on hand but a small supply of the other parts of the ration.

Under these circumstances, and uncertain whether the purchases will be effected in time to furnish a proper supply to send with the detachment intended as an escort, which has been requested by the commissioner [for surveying the southern boundary of Ga., Wilson Lumpkin,], I have notified him that a detachment of four Companies will be ordered to accompany him from this place, in running the line from the head of St. Mary's to the junction of the Flint and Chattahoochee between the U.S. and Spain.

ALS in DNA, 1, G-126; CC in DNA, 11, 13292.

From THOMAS L. McKENNEY

Weston [Georgetown, D.C.,] February 27th 1819

I beg leave very respectfully, to recommend to your notice, as an applicant for a Cadet's appointment, in the Academy at West Point, William G. Campbell, of Chester Town, Kent County, E[astern] S[hore], Maryland.

This young Gentlemen [*sic*] is now in his fifteenth year, is well grown, of sound health, and vigorous constitution. He is considerably advanced in the Classicks, and has attainments in other corresponding branches of learning. He is of good morals; and is the son of Capt. Jno. Campbell of that town, whose character and standing are known to me, to be excellent.

This application is made at the request of his Father, whose object is to prepare his son, by the sort of education, which that academy confers, for usefulness to his Country; and not for the sake of avoiding the ordinary expences of his education.

I feel a special interest in recommending this young Gentleman, and part of it arises from the belief that the E[astern] Shore of the State of Maryland shares but sparingly of this sort of notice:—but this would not act as an inducement, nor would any thing else, did I not believe the young Gentleman would do credit to himself, and be of future use to his Country.

ALS in DNA, 15, 1819, 39.

From Return J. Meigs, Washington, 2/27. Estimates that the expenses of paying the Cherokee annuity at the Agency, [including the cost of rations for the Indians gathered there,] have averaged $2,562 per year through the past 16 years. "I have no certain data to aid me here in making this result, but am confident it is not materially incorrect. These meetings [of the Indians] to receive their annuities have two almost contrary effects. Those effects are, to polish, and demoralize; the first is therefore acquired at the expense of the last. It appears to me that ["it" *interlined*] is very desirable that those meetings should be dispensed with in future." ALS in DNA, 77 (M-271:2, frames 1358–1359).

To the President of the Branch Bank of the United States and Agent for Paying U.S. Pensioners, Savannah

War Department, Feb[ruar]y 27th 1819

You will please to pay to the Half-pay Pensioner of the United States, who was placed on the Roll of your Agency, under the 2d Section of the Law of the 16th April 1816, prior to the 5th of September 1818, the semi-annual allowance due the said pensioner on the 4th of March 1819, amounting to twenty-four dollars.

Funds to meet this payment will be ordered to your credit, from the Treasury Department.

In the months of June & December in each year you will report any death or removal which may take place within your Agency, and which shall have come to your knowledge.

LS in PPL.

From N[ichola]s Van Dyke, [Senator from Del.,] 2/27. He recommends for an appointment as a Cadet a 15-year-old Wilmingtonian, William M. Reynolds, "whose attainments are equal to what would be expected at his age." ALS in DNA, 15, 1819, 54.

From [2nd] Lt. A[lexander] M. Houston

Montpelier Cantonement [*sic*], 28th February 1819

I have this day drawn a set of Bills of Exchange on you payable at sight, in favor of John H. Mallory or order, for one thousand four hundred and fifty dollars, it being the price of Five Thousand Rations of Meat and Flour which I was ordered to purchase by Col. William King, commanding [the] 8th Military Department East of the Alabama, the Contractor having failed to furnish the necessary Supplies.

I was ordered to purchase Five Thousand Complete Rations, but could only effect a purchase of that number of Meat and Flour, which I was authorised so to do by the Colonel.

LS in DNA, 1, H-206.

Decius Wadsworth to [Christopher] Vandeventer

[Ordnance Department, February ——, 1819]

Orders have been sent to Pittsburgh to have the Artillery and stores made ready as soon as possible. Some small Articles will be sent from this side [of] the Mountains for the sake of Dispatch.

ALS with En in DNA, 1, W-192. Note: An EU indicates that this note was received or filed in 2/1819. The En enumerates scores of items that were to be supplied "for the Expeditions up the Missouri and Mississippi."

MARCH 1819

CONGRESS ADJOURNED ON THE 3RD. CALHOUN SPENT MOST of March doing follow-up work. It was made more urgent by the fact that Monroe expected Calhoun to leave with him on a Southern tour about the end of the month. Meanwhile, Chief Clerk Christopher Vandeventer got away for a vacation; it was protracted when his bride became ill; Calhoun wrote best wishes for her recovery. General Gaines wrote on the 14th that he had restored Pensacola to Spanish control, in fulfillment of the administration's promise made last summer. Four days later Calhoun approved the defense plan for Baton Rouge proposed by Captain James Gadsden. Calhoun began to prod George Boyd, a brother-in-law of John Quincy Adams, to report for duty as Indian Agent at Mackinac, a quite northern outpost; but Boyd was so devoid of resources that he could not afford to travel even to Washington to get funds for the long trip.

From N[icholas] Boilvin, Prairie du Chien, 3/1. Warns that the Indians in the Northwest have been plotting for four years to attack all U.S. forts on that frontier. The British, Boilvin believes, are inciting the threat because British fur traders resent sharing the fur trade with the U.S. Boilvin has attempted to arrest the plot through dealings with the Sioux, but the effort has been in vain. He is sending his wife and children away from his post to ensure their safety. ALS (in French) in DNA, 1, B-219.

From LEWIS CASS

1 March 1819

I presume a removal of a portion of the Senecas to the reservation at Lower Sandusky would not be unacceptable to our Citizens in their neighbourhood, nor improper in itself. The reservation is sufficiently extensive for a considerable addition to their numbers, and the less they are scattered, the greater will be our chance in attaining any object connected with a melioration of their condition.

ALS in DNA, 1, O-17.

Charles Henry DuPasquier, Philadelphia, to [James Monroe], 3/1. This former Swiss industrialist proposes to establish a factory for the production of printed or painted textiles, especially linens; he describes in detail the history, nature, and prospects of this kind of production. LS (translated from the French original by Charles Le Brun) in DNA, 1, D-88.

From Thomas L. McKenney

Office [of] Indian Trade, March 1st 1819

Advices are just received from the U.S. Factor, Isaac Rawlings, who writes from the Illinois Bayou 400 miles up [the] Arkansas [River], confirming the report I made you in March last respecting the difficulty of the navigation. They were all hands, the military boat also, on the 11th January last, at a stand, the boat and her crew, 10 or 15 miles below the Bayou, for want of water to proceed.

Mr. Rawlings had obtained the sense of the Cherokee Indians respecting the location of the Factory. Where he is now located, he states, is the *heart* of the Cherokee Country. However important it is to have the Factory at or about the military post, yet it may be worthy of consideration how far policy, as well as success in its operations, may dictate that sort of Contiguity, when the military post shall itself prove to be on the outskirts of the nation or indeed beyond the Cherokee boundary. It appears to be very necessary if the Factory be intended to serve the commerce of the Indians, as it is, that it should be within their reach, and yet at the same time military protection is essential to its security. Can that be had this side of Belle Point? If so, I think it important to fix this commercial part of the arrangement where it will best suit the convenience of those for whose supplies it is intended.

Mr. Rawlings complains of great scarcity of food and the means of living.

LS with Ens in DNA, 1, M-238; FC in DNA, 73, E:206–207.

To [James Monroe], 3/1. Submits for approval a list of promotions and appointments in the Army. LS with En in DNA, 156, 15B-A2.

To E[dmund] P. Gaines, Amelia Island, 3/2. Acknowledges his report of 2/15 (ALS with Ens in DNA, 1, G-117; draft in DNA, 11, 13292). "You are mistaken in supposing that your report of the 31st of last May had escaped my notice or recollection." Gaines then "merely stated it as your opinion that the Barracks [at Savannah] ought to be abandoned." Calhoun revived the subject because Gaines never reported that he had given any specific orders to that effect. LS in DNA, 11, 13877; FC in DNA, 3, 10:263.

To Thomas Hempstead, St. Louis, 3/2. Appoints him Military Storekeeper in St. Louis, with the pay and emoluments of an Infantry Captain. Requests an immediate reply; if the position is accepted, orders him to report to the Commissary General of Subsistence, [George Gibson]. FC in DNA, 3, 10:264.

From Callender Irvine, Philadelphia, 3/2. "In obedience to your instructions I have to report that the services of Mr. James Ward, as Military Storekeeper at Wilmington N.C. are not required in this Department. It is proper for me, however, to repeat that Mr. Ward appears to have been appointed Storekeeper for the Ordnance Dept." FC in DNA, 45, 387:342.

To Callender Irvine, Philadelphia, 3/2. "You will furnish Maj. [Stephen H.] Long . . . on his requisition, three flags of the description he may require." FC in DNA, 3, 10:263. (Irvine promised on 3/5 to comply with this order. ALS in DNA, 1, I-145; FC in DNA, 45, 387:349.)

To Th[omas] S. Jesup, 3/2. He is to order a subordinate to furnish Maj. [Stephen H.] Long, Topographical Engineer, "with such funds as he may require, to enable him to transport instruments" from New York [City] to Philadelphia and thence to Pittsburgh. [These instruments were intended for use by Long in his expedition for exploration of the Mississippi and, more especially, of its tributaries.] FC in DNA, 3, 10:263.

[FRANCIS] ("FRANK") JONES, [Representative from Tenn.,] to JAMES MONROE

Washington City, March 2d 1819

I have received a letter from [former] Capt. Jno. Key, [Jr.,] late of the United States Army, in which he states that he is informed that the Agent of the Chickasaws [Henry Sherburne] intends to resign and he wishes to succeed hi[m]. I have known Capt. Key some time; he is a man of business and I have no doubt capable to the discharge of the duties of that office. As to his character, so far as I know it, [it] is unobjectionable.

ALS in DNA, 11, 13559.

To Wilson Lumpkin, Madison, Ga., 3/2. His letter of 2/10 is acknowledged. The Floridas have been reported to have been ceded to the U.S. Because doubt has been reported "as to the true head" of the St. Marys River, Lumpkin will suspend "the running of the line" between it and the Flint River. He is to discontinue all expenses incurred for that purpose and is to settle his accounts. FC in DNA, 3, 10:262.

James Monroe to [James Barbour], 3/2. Monroe submits to the Senate for ratification the treaty [of 2/27] concluded by Calhoun with the Eastern Cherokees. LS with Ens in DNA, 153, 15B-C4; PC with Ens in *American State Papers: Indian Affairs,* 2:187–194.

From James W. Paxton, Willington, [S.C. ?], 3/2. Declines appointment as a Surgeon's Mate, a position that he considers "of neither honour nor profit." ALS in DNA, 11, 13783.

To W[illiam] Rabun, [Governor of Ga.,] Milledgeville, 3/2. Calhoun has received Rabun's letter of 2/17 (LS with En in DNA, 1, R-113) indicating that the boundary between Ga. and East Fla. should lie to the south of what has previously been agreed upon with the Spanish as the head of the St. Marys River. Consequently, "and as the acquisition of the Floridas may change the character of the boundary," Calhoun has ordered [Wilson] Lumpkin to suspend the survey thence to the Flint River. FC in DNA, 3, 10:263.

To D[ecius] Wadsworth, 3/2. "You will order the Ordnance officer at Philadelphia [3rd Lt. Martin Thomas] to furnish Maj. [Stephen H.] Long on his requisition, such ordnance, and ordnance stores, as he may require" [for use in connection with his expedition of exploration of the Mississippi's tributaries]. LS (evidently sent to Thomas by Wadsworth, with an EU dated 3/2 signifying that Wadsworth was relaying this document as an order) in ScU-SC, John C. Calhoun Papers; FC in DNA, 3, 10:263.

W[illiam] Wigton, New York [City], to [Christopher] Vandeventer, 3/2. Wigton has been paid by Marshal [Thomas Morris], in cash and by check, $475.74 [for Wigton's services as a member of the court-martial for N.Y. militia delinquents] but protests that this is insufficient compensation for the sacrifices he has made. ALS in DNA, 1, W-225.

To William Clark and Talbot Chambers, each at St. Louis

Department of War, 3d March 1819

It has been represented to this Department by the agent of the American Fur Company [Ramsey Crooks] that the licenses granted to their traders by the Indian Agents at Green Bay, Chicago, & Michilimackinac have not been recognized by the civil & military officers of the Government on the Mississippi as sufficient authority to carry on their traffic with the Indians in that quarter of the country and that the company has sustained serious injury in consequence thereof; I have therefore to request that proper respect, in future, be paid to licenses issued to traders by these Agents and that they be considered as the protection of the traders and their people in every section of the Indian Country whilst in the lawful prosecution of their business.

FC in DNA, 72, D:253–254; CC in DNA, 76 (M-1:6, p. 22); PC in Carter, ed., *Territorial Papers,* 15:520.

To [James Monroe], 3/3. Nominates Benjamin O'Fallon, of Mo. Territory, as Indian Agent on the Missouri. LS in DNA, 156, 15B-A2.

From William Rabun, [Governor of Ga.]

Milledgeville, 3d March 1819

On the 17th ultimo, I had the honor to address you on the subject of the contemplated line between this State and the Province of East Florida; I stated, that the Legislature of this State had directed me to appoint Commissioners to ascertain the true head or source of the St. Marys river, and I promised to forward their report to you as soon as the same was received. The Commissioners have returned and reported, that after a careful examination, they found the head of that river to agree with the report made by Mr. [Andrew ?] Ellicott, and prove beyond the possibility of doubt, that the information received by the Legislature of this State relative to that subject was incorrect. I flatter myself that directions will be forwarded to Mr. [Wilson] Lumpkin ["immediately" *interlined*] to close that line, according to the treaty with Spain. And if the Gen[era]l Government can afford us assistance in guarding the Surveyors who will be engaged in laying out that country, it will be acknowledged as a great accommodation.

LS in DNA, 1, R-124.

From John Williams, [Senator from Tenn.]

State Chamber, March 3d 1819

You will probably want a Surveyor to lay off the reserves under the late Cherokee treaty. I would name our mutual friend Robert Houston for that purpose. His correctness as a Surveyor and fidelity as a man will insure a faithful execution of such a trust. In a few months he can be spared from his Quarter Master[']s duties. And I will prevail on him to undertake this business.

ALS in DNA, 11, 13485.

To E[dmund] P. Gaines, Fernandina, [East Fla.]

Department of War, 4 March, 1819

Your letter of the 18th Ultimo in relation to Indian Affairs has been received, and I coincide with you in the views you have taken of the subjects therein contained. The objects proposed must, however, necessarily be the work of time.

Since writing your letter of the 20th Ultimo, you will have been informed of the late treaty with Spain, ceding the Floridas to the United States. As, on the possession of that country, the character of your command will be entirely changed, you will make no material alteration in the present disposition of the Troops, until that event shall afford you the opportunity of obtaining the information necessary to determine their most eligible location.

LS in DNA, 11, 13511; variant FC in DNA, 3, 10:264–265.

From C[harles] Jouett, Washington, 3/4. Resigns; recommends Dr. William Madison of Ky., a relative of former President James Madison, to succeed to the position of Indian Agent at Chicago. ALS in DNA, 11, 13630.

From Thomas L. McKenney

Office [of] Indian Trade, March 4th 1819

The enclosed statement and letter received by today's mail from Col. [John] McKee will shew the arrangements proposed in the preparation of the Chaktaw [*sic*] annuity, also the amount which it embraces and the proportion which is required in Cash. The mode of assorting and packing the several parcells [*sic*] is quite easy; but the amount called for is more than the requisition which I have had the honor to receive from the Department of War by 8,850 Dollars, exclusive of what is stated to be due under former stipulations. The cash part called for is five hundred Dollars, leaving 11,350 Dollars to be provided in goods, implements of husbandry, &c., &c.

If this be in accordance with the intentions of the War Department, I will be glad to receive, at as early a period as may be convenient, authority to make a corresponding preparation, which will require an additional requisition for Chaktaw annuity, exclusive of cash, of 8,350 Dollars or, if it be intended to pay the former annuities as stated in the enclosed sheet, 19,750 Dollars, exclusive of the cash.

Puck-shun-nub-bie, the principal Chief, has set a liberal example, in his donation of $200 to aid the missionary establishment in the Chaktaw nation.

[P.S.] The act of the 3rd March 1817, alone, allows them $6,000.

LS in DNA, 1, M-231; FC in DNA, 73, E:208–209.

To Return J. Meigs, Washington, 3/4. "In the distribution of the Cherokee annuity, you are authorized to do it in any manner that may be satisfactory to the nation, provided the expense thereof does not exceed twelve hundred and eighty dollars." LS in DNA, 75 (M-208:8); FC in DNA, 72, D:254.

From Dr. T[obias] Watkins, Assistant Surgeon General, Baltimore, 3/4. Recommends Dr. S[amuel] B. Smith to succeed Dr. [James C.] Bronaugh, who intends to resign as Assistant Surgeon General. ALS in DNA, 11, 13917.

From William Woodbridge, [Delegate from Mich. Territory,] 3/4. Recommends Dr. William Madison of Ky. for appointment as Indian Agent at Chicago. ALS in DNA, 11, 13630.

From William Woodbridge, Washington, 3/4. Explains the importance of a military post at Detroit, emphasizing particularly its strategic relationship to the Indians and to the British. ALS in DNA, 1, W-253; PC in Carter, ed., *Territorial Papers,* 10:818–821.

To Heman Allen, [former Representative from Vt.,] 3/5. Acknowledges his letters of 2/20 (ALS with En in DNA, 1, A-76) and 2/22 (ALS in DNA, 1, A-78) reporting difficulties in obtaining from his predecessor, [David] Robinson, "the books, papers and balance of public funds appertaining to the office of Commissioner of Loans and Agent for paying Military Pensioners in the District of Vermont," which Robinson was ordered on 12/21/1818 to relinquish. "A division of the Agency was not contemplated by this Department. On enquiry I find the Pay Department omitted to give instructions to Mr. Robinson in relation to the Half Pay Pension. I have directed that this should be done immediately, and the rolls and necessary instructions will be transmitted to you" this week. FC in DNA, 3, 10:265.

To Paymaster General Robert Brent, 3/5. Directs him to send six months' pay in advance to the officers of the 6th Infantry Regiment, as its commander, Col. H[enry] Atkinson, has suggested, [because its participation in the Missouri Expedition will disrupt monthly payments]. FC in DNA, 3, 10:265.

To Ram[se]y Crooks, Agent of the American Fur Co., [Washington,] 3/5. Acknowledges his letter of 3/2 (ALS in DNA, 1, C-190); encloses a copy of the resultant instructions [of 3/3] to [William] Clark and [Talbot] Chambers. FC in DNA, 72, D:255.

From Richard Harris, Dauphin Island, [Ala., *ca.* 3/5]. This contractor for the building of fortifications there asks to be supplied with a small military force to prevent interference or depredations by pirates. Asks that the U.S. should buy about 100 to 150 slaves to assist Harris in building the fort there; if the purchase cost is advanced to Harris, the money might be entrusted to some person or company in whom "entire confidence" is placed, the Negroes could be shipped to the Army Engineer at the Island and covered enroute by hazard insurance, and they should "remain the property" of the U.S. until Harris's contract has been fulfilled. This letter was postmarked at Mobile on 3/6 and appears to have been written for Harris by one J. Cline. Copy in DNA, 1, H-202.

To [James Monroe], 3/5. Nominates Dr. William Turner to be the Agent to the Miami and Eel River Indians and to such of the Wea and Potawatomi Indians as "have heretofore been attached to the Agency at Fort Wayne." An AEI by Monroe reads: "Approved." LS in DNA, 2, C-1819; FC in DNA, 6, 1:348.

To Winfield Scott

War Department, 5th March 1819

The very great pressure of business, to which the Department is subject towards the termination of a session of Congress has delayed my answer to your letter of the 22d February till this time.

I have laid your statement before the President [James Monroe] in order to take his direction in relation to it; and it is his opinion that any relaxation in the order of the 21st February 1818 would in this case be improper. Publications of the kind prohibited are always injurious to the reputation and interest of the Army & Country; and when they come from officers of the standing and reputation of yourself or Gen. [Andrew] Jackson they cannot but have the most injurious effects. In this case I cannot but think, that those who are opposed to the Army would seize on the publication and wield it with effect against our military establishment. Whether Gen[era]l Jackson has done any act in violation of the order in this case I am not apprized, but admitting he has the Department would find in such violation a reason for enforcing & not for rescinding or relaxing the order.

FC in DNA, 5, 1:102–103; CC in DNA, 1; CC in NN, James Monroe Papers; PC in Jameson, ed., *Correspondence*, p. 152.

From D[ecius] Wadsworth, 3/5. Requests an advance of $2,000 to Adam Carruth of Greenville District, S.C., on his contract for manufacturing 10,000 stands of arms. FC in DNA, 32, 2:193.

From D[ecius] Wadsworth, 3/5. Requests that $5,000 be sent to Maj. [Abram R.] Woolley at Pittsburgh "to enable him to provide the Stores required for the Expeditions to the Missouri and Mississippi." FC in DNA, 32, 2:193.

To George Boyd, Indian Agent, Mt. Pleasant near Port Royal, Va., 3/6. "As the season has arrived when it is important that you should be at your post, you are requested to report yourself immediately to this department and to state at what time you will be prepared to set out for the Agency at Michilimackinac." LS (with the signature removed) in DNA, 76 (M-1:70, pp. 85–88); FC in DNA, 72, D:255.

From William A. Coleman, 61 Stone St., New York [City], 3/6. Seeks payment of $18.75 each from the War and Navy Departments for "the 6 first vol[ume]s" of the *North American Review*, sent to each. An AEI by L[ewis] E[dwards] states that "we have not rec[eive]d the books." ALS in DNA, 1, C-221.

To W[illiam] H. Crawford, 3/6. Requests that $146,925 be placed in the hands of Thomas Tudor Tucker and thus made available for expenditure under 12 laws, here itemized, for the payment of annuities to the Indian tribes. FC in DNA, 171, 1:321.

To W[illiam] H. Crawford, 3/6. "Be pleased to place in the hands of Thomas Tudor Tucker Esq., as Agent for the Department of War, the sum of one hundred thousand Dollars, on account of the appropriation per act 15th February 1819, for the Indian Department." FC in DNA, 171, 1:321.

To A[NDREW] JACKSON, [Washington]

Department of War, 6th March, 1819

You are already informed of the motives of the President [James Monroe], and of the arrangements which have been made to occupy in force the contemplated posts on the Missouri. It is believed, that our principal post ought to be at the Mandan Village, or in its neighbourhood, and, for the present, no attempt ought to be made, until it is strongly occupied, to ascend the river to a more remote point. The Missouri there approaches nearest to the establishment of the Hudson Bay Company on Red River, and holds, in its descent to the Mississippi from that point, a more southerly direction, both of which will render the position permanently important. You will, accordingly, give orders to render it, with the means which may be in possession of the detachment, as strong as practicable. Whether an attempt ought to be made to push our troops during the next summer to this remote position, will depend on circumstances to be judged of by the officer charged with the command of the [9th Military] Department, [Henry Atkinson]. Should it be deemed practicable, without exciting Indian hostilities, to occupy the position at so early a period as to afford time to render it sufficiently strong and to construct the necessary buildings to protect the troops against the inclemency of the winter in that high latitude, it ought to be attempted; but, should a contrary impression exist, some strong position less remote ought to be occupied. The Council Bluff or the Great Bend will probably afford such positions, and, as one or both of these will probably have to be permanently occupied in considerable force, the labour which may be bestowed to render the troops secure will not be lost. It is hoped and believed, that, with proper caution, the contemplated movements may be made, without exciting Indian hostilities; yet, it will be necessary to be so prepared, at all times, should they be excited, as to experience no disaster. To effect these important objects, much will doubtless depend on the character of the officer charged with their execution. The selection of Col[one]l [Henry] Atkinson has been made with much reflection. It is believed, that he possesses all the requisite qualities. You will, however, inculcate on him the necessity of the greatest caution and vigilance. No pains ought to be spared to conciliate the various Indian Tribes by kind treatment, and a proper distribution of presents. Gov[erno]r [William] Clark will be directed to furnish the means of making the presents. Mr. [Benjamin] O'Fallon, the Agent for the Missouri, will accompany, or precede the expedition. He is represented as eminently qualified for his office. [Brevet] Major [Stephen H.] Long with his command, accompanied by several citizens eminent for scientifick acquirements, will ascend the river, about the same time, in a Steam-boat of light draught, in order to acquire a more enlarged and accurate knowledge of the country between the Rocky Mountain[s] and the Mississippi. You will give orders to afford to the expedition under him every aid and protection which may be practicable. Strict orders will also be given to treat with kindness and justice such citizens as may be permitted by the Government to carry on trade among the Indians. Should the necessary protection be afforded to our traders, it will, in addition to the profits of the Fur Trade, afford the means of greatly extending our influence over the various tribes within our limits.

LS in DLC, Andrew Jackson Papers, 8617–8619; FC in DNA, 3, 10:266; CC in NjMoN, L.W. Smith Collection; CC in DLC, Jacob Brown Papers, Letterbooks, 2:139–141; PC in Jameson, ed., *Correspondence,* pp. 152–154.

To Joseph McMinn

Department of War, 6 March, 1819

I have the pleasure to inform you that a treaty has been concluded with the [Eastern] Cherokee Delegation, which it is hoped will be satisfactory to all parties; and you are requested, as no further encouragement will be given to the emigrations to the Arkansaw [*sic*], to take immediate measures to wind up the business in which you have been engaged [since the autumn of 1817] under the former treaty [of 7/8/1817] in the most economical manner.

Your communications which were intended to be here before the delegation, did not reach the Department until after the arrangement was made, but it is believed that it has been made on the best terms that could be effected. So soon as the treaty is printed you will be furnished a copy.

I will thank you to furnish a statement of your expenditures, in order that I may know the state of the appropriation to carry into effect the Cherokee treaty; and you will also furnish an estimate of the sums necessary to close the business.

LS in DNA, 75 (M-208:14); FC in DNA, 72, D:255–256; CC in DNA, 153; PC in *American State Papers: Indian Affairs,* 2:190. NOTE: By the treaty which Calhoun concluded with the Chiefs of the Eastern Cherokees in Washington on 2/27, the Eastern Cherokees ceded to the U.S. most of their land in return for money and for a reservation on which they might live in the East instead of being forced to emigrate to the Arkansas River area. A PC of the treaty is in the *American State Papers: Indian Affairs,* 2:187–189.

From W[ILLIAM] MCREE

Washington, 6 March 1819

I have the honor to resign my Commission of Major in the Corps of Engineers; to take effect the first instant.

The circumstance, of my having determined on this measure previous to my appointment to be Lt. Col. in the Corps; has been the reason of my not accepting it; and of not giving an earlier answer to the letter of appointment which I had the honor to receive from you on the occasion.

ALS in DNA, 11, 13691. NOTE: An EU indicates that this resignation was accepted on 5/9.

From JAMES MONROE

March 6, 1819

I wish you to place [Alfred Beckley,] the son of the late Mr. [John] Beckley, at the accademy [*sic*] at West point. Mr. [John] Beckley was Clerk of the House of Rep[resentative]s, from the commencement of the gov[ernmen]t, for many years, & Clerk of the H[ouse] of Delegates of Virg[ini]a, for many years before. You will give the warrant to Gen[era]l [William Henry] Harrison, who will forward it to his [Alfred Beckley's] mother, who resides in Kentucky.

ALS in DNA, 15, 1819, 61. NOTE: John Beckley served as the Clerk of the U.S. House of Representatives from 1789 until 5/1797. EU's on the manuscript indicate that [Alfred] Beckley was appointed as a Cadet on 3/6 but that the appointment was not sent to Harrison until 7/23.

[To MARK MORS, Me.]

WAR DEPARTMENT.
REVOLUTIONARY CLAIM.

I CERTIFY That, in conformity with the Law of the United States, of the 18th of March, 1818, Mark Mors, late a Private in the Army of the Revolution, is inscribed on the Pension List, Roll of the District of Maine Agency, at the rate of eight dollars per month, to commence on the twenty-eighth day of April one thousand eight hundred and eighteen.

GIVEN at the War Office of the United States, this sixth day of March one thousand eight hundred and nineteen.

J.C. Calhoun
Secretary of War.

DS in ScU-SC, John C. Calhoun Papers.

From [1st] Lt. G[arston] Powell, Cincinnati, 3/6. Requests permission to pay to [John H.] Piatt the rent due on barracks there before Powell's unit moves away. ALS in DNA, 11, 13815.

Pension Certificate of Thomas Rathbun, 3/6. Calhoun certifies that this former Pvt. in the Revolutionary Army is to receive $8 per month in Pa. from 4/10/1818. DS in WHi.

To [Dr.] William Turner, 3/6. Appoints him Indian Agent at Fort Wayne, to serve the Miami and Eel River tribes and those of the Wea and Potawatomi tribes who are attached to that Agency, at an annual salary of $1,200; sends him instructions; will send his commission if the Senate ratifies this appointment. FC in DNA, 72, D:256–257.

From Edmund P. Gaines

Fernandina, E[ast] F[la.], March 7th 1819

By a communication from Colonel [William] King dated the 4th of February, and received not until yesterday, I am informed that a Spanish force destined for the reoccupancy of West Florida, had but just appeared off the Harbour [of Pensacola], at the Barrancas.

ALS in DNA, 1, G-132.

From [former Col.] J[ames] R. Mullany, Washington, 3/7. Appeals for an Army appointment, preferably somewhere along the Eastern seaboard, reviewing autobiographically his years of previous service. ALS in DNA, 1, M-226.

To Col. H[enry] Atkinson, Plattsburg, [N.Y.,] 3/8. "Your letters of the 23d & 28th ult[im]o (ALS's in DNA, 1, A-79 and A-83, respectively; FC's in DNA, 181, pp. 91–92 and 95–96, respectively) respecting advance pay for the officers of your Regiment [because they have been ordered to begin a march to new duty at a distant post] have been received. I have instructed the Pay Master General [Robert Brent] to remit the necessary funds without delay & to direct the Paymaster to make the advances requested." FC in DNA, 3, 10:268; FC in DNA, 181, pp. 98–99.

To John "Bowyer [*sic*; Boyer], Ag[en]t for C[amillus] Griffith," Norfolk, 3/8. Answers his appeal of 3/4 (ALS in DNA, 1, B-218) for an advance of $2,000 to permit Boyer to make additional purchases, because the number of soldiers in the area of Griffith's contract to supply rations has increased: "The advances already made together with the purchases on account of the failure of the contractor of which I have been informed since the last advance to him will it is believed leave no balance in his favor and I must therefore decline complying with the request." FC in DNA, 3, 10:269.

Cadets Wilson M.C. Fairfax and Thomas Ragland, [Washington,] to Chief Engineer [Walker Keith Armistead], 3/8. "If we are ordered to West Point we desire the privilege of drawing our transportation at this place as our funds are so low at present as to render it necessary." LS in DNA, 14, 16, with an AES by Lt. George Blaney referring this application from the Engineer Department to Calhoun.

From George Gibson, Washington, 3/8. Encloses a list of five men nominated for appointment as Military Storekeepers and of one Bvt. Capt. and 37 Lts. nominated to become Assistant Commissaries [of Subsistence]. An AES by James Monroe certifies his approval. ALS with En in DNA, 2, G-1819.

To Luke Lea, Cashier of the Bank of Knoxville and Agent for Paying U.S. Pensioners in East Tenn.

War Department, March 8th 1819

You are hereby appointed Agent for paying the Pensioners of the United States, residing within the District of East Tennessee, under the Law of the 3rd of March, 1819, entitled, "an Act to authorize the Secretary of War to appoint an additional Agent for paying Pensioners of the United States, in Tennessee." You are, therefore, enjoined to do and perform all the duties appertaining thereto, by conforming to the instructions, which may, from time to time, be given you from this, or the Treasury Department, and by accounting to the United States, for all monies, that may be placed in your hands, in pursuance of this appointment, for the payment of the said Pensioners; and in order, that the Laws relating to the appointment of Agents, & the established usages may be complied with, you are requested to transmit to this Department, as soon as may be, your Bond, to the U[nited] States, with two good & sufficient securities, for the sum of five thousand dollars, conditioned, that you will faithfully, discharge the above defined duties.

Instructions will be given you from the Treasury Department, with regard to the manner, in which your accounts will be kept & rendered, and information, also, given therefrom, relative to the compensation, you are to receive, for performing the duties, imposed on you, by this appointment. A copy of the circular letter, from the Treasury Department, with a set of the forms of receipts, accounts &c. alluded to in it, are now enclosed to you.

FC in DNA, 91, 6:314.

To S[TEPHEN] H. LONG, "Pittsburg[h] or Philadelphia"

Department of War, 8th March 1819

You will assume the command of the expedition to explore the country between the Mississippi and the Rockey [*sic*] Mountain[s]. You will first explore the Missouri and its principle [*sic*] branches and then in succession Red river, Arkansas and Mississippi above the mouth of the Missouri.

You are authorized to make requisition on any officer in the Quarter Masters, Commissaries, Ordnance, Engineer or Medical Department for the requisite supplies; and to incur any expense which you may deem necessary to the complete success of the expedition; to cover which you will draw on this Department. Instructions have been given through the Maj. Gen[era]l of the Southern Division [Andrew Jackson] to the officers of the ninth Military Department to extend to you and your party every aid and protection and the Indian Agent for the Missouri, Mr. [Benjamin] O'Fallon, has been directed to accompany you up that river, if his duty in relation to the military expedition on the Missouri, will admit of the arrangement. He is authorized to purchase such articles as he may deem suitable for presents to the Indians, not exceeding in value $5,000.

Previous to your departure both from Pittsburg[h] and St. Louis you will report the number and names of your party, with the arrangements made for the expedition and the expenses incurred.

The object of the expedition is to acquire as thorough and accurate knowledge as may be practicable of a portion of our country which is daily becoming more interesting but which is as yet but imperfectly known. With this view you will permit nothing worthy of notice to escape your attention. You will ascertain the latitude and longitude of remarkable points with every possible precision. The extreme bend of the Missouri to the north is thought to be a very interesting point. You will ascertain it with particular care. You will if practicable ascertain some point on the 49th parallel of latitude, which seperates [*sic*] our possessions from those of Great Britian [*sic*]. The extent of our limits being known will tend to prevent collision between our traders & theirs.

You will enter in your journal everything interesting in relation to soil, face of the country, water courses and productions whether animal, vegetable or mineral.

You will conciliate the Indians by kindness & by presents and will ascertain as far as practicable the number and character of the various tribes with the extent of country claimed by each.

Great confidence is reposed in the acquirements and zeal of the citizens who will accompany the expedition for scientifick purposes, and a confident hope is entertained that their duties will be performed in such a manner as to add both to their own reputation and that of our country.

The instructions of Mr. [Thomas] Jefferson to Capt. [Meriwether] Lewis, which are printed in his travels will afford you many valuable suggestions of which as far [as] applicable you will avail yourself.

I have examined the forms of Vocabulary and the Meterological register transmitted by you and think them judicious.

You will seize every safe opportunity to report the progress and the striking incidents of the expedition to this Department.

FC in DNA, 3, 10:267–268; CC in PPAmP; PEx in Edwin James, compiler, *Account of an Expedition from Pittsburgh to the Rocky Mountains, Performed in the Years 1819 and '20* . . . (3 vols. Philadelphia: H.C. Carey and F. Lea, 1822–1823), 1:3–4.

By J[ames] M[onroe], 3/8. Remits the fines imposed by court-martial upon 20 delinquent militiamen of N.Y. DI in DNA, 2, P-1819.

To Benjamin O'Fallon, 3/8. "You have been appointed to an Indian Agency [on the Missouri River] which will require an uncommon degree of industry, discretion, and abilities. The important military movements which are contemplated on the Missouri will be greatly facilitated or impeded by the friendship or hostilities of the Indians." He is "to precede the military expedition, in order to prepare the Indians for it, by a representation of our pacific views and by a judicious distribution of presents" worth as much as $5,000, preferably traveling with [Stephen H.] Long's probable advance party. "No measure ought to be taken to excite the suspicion of such [British and illicit] traders or to come in collision with them 'till the military posts are finally established, at which time you will give notice that all trade except that which is duly licensed by [the U.S.] government will be prohibited under the penalty provided by law." FC in DNA, 72, D:257–258; PC in Carter, ed., *Territorial Papers,* 15:520–521.

Pension Certificate of Thomas Roberts, 3/8. Calhoun certifies that this former Pvt. in the Revolutionary Army is to receive $8 per month in Ga. from 6/6/1818. DS in GAHi.

From Winfield Scott

Richmond, Mar[ch] 8th, 1819

I had the honour to address you on the 22nd ultimo on a subject of deep importance to me but have not been complimented with a reply. In the meantime I have received without solicitation much additional information in support of the facts and inferences then relied upon and which demonstrate the necessity of some prompt movement on my part.

Had Major General [Andrew] Jackson laid before the public the *entire* correspondence which has taken place between us, I should have been the last individual in the Army to call your attention to the general order of the 21st Feb., 1818. He would have been entitled to my thanks. But he has chosen to publish such parts of it only as were calculated, in his judgment, to produce a strong excitement against me, in direct proof of which, I beg leave to refer you to the accompanying letter, written by an officer of honour & intelligence.

It appears by this evidence, that Major General J[ackson] has, in his publication at New York, as elsewhere, omitted to give a copy of my concluding letter, the last in the series, which ridicules & repels the gross abuse of that which immediately preceded it. Perhaps he thought it was sufficient, that he had caused me to be represented, (in the Aurora, whilst passing thro' Philadelphia) as having, in that letter, declined fighting him, on the ground of *religious scruples.* Whether this will turn out to be the fact, in respect to my past or future conduct, is a question altogether irrelevant to this communication.

I think, then, Sir, it is clearly shown, that Major General J[ackson] has violated the general order, in question; unless, indeed, it be decided in defence of him that since the discovery of the art of printing, *publication* can only take place thro' the medium of the press; and even were this absurd construction admitted, I am persuaded it would be easy for me to trace the ex parte newspaper articles (paragraphs and letter) before alluded to, to the same source. On my part, I do most solemnly aver, that no copy of the correspondence, entire or in parts, has ever gone out of my possession; that I have only shown it to a few friends, always under the injunction, that no allusion to it should be made in the public papers; that I have never so alluded to it myself, and that to the best of my knowledge & beleif [*sic*], no such allusion has been made by those friends; except in a single instance, in The Enquirer (whilst I was to the North) & that to the best of my recollection, was made in a spirit of fairness & conciliation, in reply to the article in the Georgia paper, mentioned in my last letter.

Having, therefore, obeyed the law prescribed for the government of the Army, I feel that I have a right to complain of the injury done me by its infraction, & which could not have been done, but for the law. Obedience & protection I have always supposed to be reciprocal duties. Yet, in the present state of the public mind, I do not offer myself as [what] is technically called the *private prosecutor* of Maj. General Jackson. Perhaps I may think it would be in vain to seek redress in that mode. The odium which he has known so well how to excite, whilst it crushes me, would, in the case of this arrest, but serve to elevate him above the law. What I have asked & what I still desire is, that the Executive will not drive the weaker party to ["his" *canceled and* "the necessity of" *interlined*] hazarding his commission by placing himself in opposition to its declared will. The poison already infused in the public mind, to my prejudice, can only be neutralized by a *fair* publication. When this shall be essayed, I shall then be at liberty, in honour & in conscience, according to the necessity of the case, either to resort to my legal claims, or those other rights which are prior & paramount to all human institutions.

Permit me to request, Sir, thro' you, that the President [James Monroe] will have the goodness to review the general order in question, (also called, on the face of it, a "regulation,") in connection with the 8th section, 1st article of the Constitution, & perhaps, he may recal[l] it. Perhaps he may decide that a publication by manuscript is a casus omissus under the order or regulation, & if so, it may be safely assumed, that a publication in a pamphlet form is not prohibited. And above all, if it be decided, that the prohibition is valid, as to both these points, it cannot escape his attention that it is in the hands of Major General J[ackson], at once an instrument of offence & defence.

I beg you, to believe, Sir, that in presenting the foregoing strong view of a case of peculiar hardship, it has been my intention to treat both you & the Executive, with the most perfect respect; & I am happy in being at liberty, to add, that my feelings and my duty are, on this point, in perfect accordance.

P.S. It may be necessary to state in addition to the foregoing facts that Major General Jackson has sent to a member of the Virginia Legislature a "copy" of the correspondence in question to be shown &c., &c. Whether it be certified, as in other instances, or whether it be *entire,* I have not had an opportunity of ascertaining.

I have this moment been honoured with your letter of the 5th instant, literally since the above was signed. I am sorry to add that I feel myself compelled to adhere to the views already developed whilst I anxiously await a more favourable result.

ALS in DNA, 1, S-255; CC in NN, James Monroe Papers. NOTE: Calhoun answered on 3/11.

From John Vaughan, Philadelphia, 3/8. As expected, he has placed two chronometers in the care of a craftsman for repairs. [Ferdinand Rudolf] Hassler expected to receive them next. [Stephen H.] Long has also applied for them. Hassler has insisted that one of them, a box chronometer, is "the only one [of its type in the U.S. that] he could use if he went out [on his intended boundary survey] next summer" and seems to want both; and Calhoun's instructions appear to indicate that Hassler has first claim on the instruments if he considers them necessary. [René Edward] De Russy has taken from Long "all the other Chronometers, & left him without any." Vaughan has found three that can be purchased in Philadelphia at $350 each. ALS in DNA, 1, V-14.

From Decius Wadsworth, 3/8. Advises against making any further advance to Alexander McRae of Richmond on his contract to supply arms; the only security the U.S. has for the present advances is a mortgage on McRae's property on Fine Creek, [near Richmond,] which, if it had to be sold, probably would not repay these advances. ALS in DNA, 1, W-229; FC in DNA, 32, 2:194–195.

From Jacob Brown, Philadelphia, 3/9. Since he left Washington, he has realized that he forgot to confer with Calhoun about the application by Lt. [Lewis Gustavus] De Russy last winter for permission to serve as Assistant Surveyor in the running of the boundary line between the U.S. and Canada. Brown has postponed giving his consent until he can first obtain Calhoun's, which can be mailed to Brown at New York [City]. LS in DNA, 11, 13286.

To William Clark, St. Louis, 3/9. Maj. [Benjamin] O'Fallon has been appointed Indian Agent on the Missouri and authorized to purchase $5,000 worth of goods to be used as presents to the Indians; Clark is to get this sum from the Receiver of Public Monies at St. Louis. FC in DNA, 72, D:258; PC in Carter, ed., *Territorial Papers,* 15:522.

From Ch[arles] Hicks

Washington Hotel, March 9th 1819

As there is yet a number of the spoliation claims unpaid, we hope you will place in the hands of our Agent [Return J. Meigs] the balance of the money due the Cherokees on that appropriation to the end that our people may get their just claims without farther [*sic*; "trouble" *interlined*] and delay, as it is anticipated by them on our return. The delegation avail themselves of this opp[ortuni]ty to express their sincere regard for your happiness and welfare, and take leave of you for their homes.

ALS in DNA, 1, H-180.

To John Johnston, Indian Agent, Piqua, [O.]

Department of War, 9th March, 1819

I have to inform you that Dr. William Turner has been appointed Agent for the Miami and Eel River tribes of Indians, and such of the Wea and Potawatomie tribes as have heretofore been attached to the Agency at Fort Wayne; your duties, therefore, as Agent at that place cease, and you will hereafter, in addition to the duties of Indian Agent at Piqua, perform those of Agent for the Shawnese [*sic*] at Wapaghkonetta, agreeably to the stipulation contained in the 9th article of the treaty concluded with the Wyandot, Seneca, Delaware, Shawnese, Potawatomie, Ottawa and Chippeway tribes of Indians on the 29th Septem[be]r 1817.

You are also required to act as Agent for the Delawares until their removal to the West of the Mississippi conformably to the treaty concluded with them at St. Marys in Ohio, on the 3d of October, 1818.

The books, papers, and public property belonging to the Agency at Fort Wayne, you will cause to be delivered to Dr. Turner on his application for them.

FC in DNA, 72, D:260; CC in DNA, 76 (M-1:6).

To Col. William King, Pensacola, 3/9. Acknowledges his letters of 2/2, 2/3 (ALS with En in DNA, 1, K-31), and 2/4 (ALS in DNA, 1, K-32). "I have learned with much regret [of] the arrival of the Spanish expedition destined for the reoccupancy of West Florida, as both that [province] and East Florida [which] have been ceded to the United States, by the late treaty with Spain, will probably be reoccupied by our troops by the month of August next, at farthest. In the removal of the troops you will adopt the measures best calculated to effect the necessary movements at the least expense. I regret to learn [of] the failure of the contractor. You will take the proper means to hold him responsible and will make the necessary contracts on the most eligible terms possible." Answering King's report of 2/3 that families of Spanish officers were hungry, Calhoun says: "The issue of rations to distressed inhabitants of Pensacola is approved in extreme cases, and in such only; and, it is hoped that these will be few and that the expenses will not be great." FC in DNA, 3, 10:270.

To Reuben Lewis, Indian Agent on the Arkansas River

Department of War, 9th March, 1819

I enclose a copy of a letter written by Capt. [Charles] Hicks of the Cherokee nation on the Tennessee, to Colo[nel Return J.] Meigs, their Agent, who has submitted it to this department. It is not the wish of the Dep[artmen]t to interfere with the Cherokees on the

East and West of the Mississippi on the subject to which this communication refers, but as it is probable that the former will make a representation to the latter, with a view to procure an arrangement on this point, I have to request that you will use your endeavors to induce them to make such a one as may be just and equitable.

A treaty has been concluded with the Cherokee Delegation, at the seat of government, and I enclose you a copy of the 6th article, which relates to the division of the annuity [on the basis of two-thirds to the Eastern Cherokees and of one-third to the Western Cherokees, without the taking of an actual census, if this proportion is accepted by the Western Cherokees], of which you are required to give them notice, and, if objections are made, to enter into such explanations on the subject, as you may think necessary to satisfy them as to the justice of the distribution, and inform this Department of their decision.

A copy of the treaty will be sent to you after it is published.

FC in DNA, 72, D:259–260; CC in DNA, 153; CCEx in DLC, Andrew Jackson Papers, 8629, with an added "Note" in the same hand: "To the above letter no answer was received from Mr. Lewis, and it was presumed the arrangement had been acquiesced in"; PC in *American State Papers: Indian Affairs,* 2:190.

From William McIntosh and three other Chiefs in the Creek Delegation, Washington, 3/9. They review much of the Creeks' history since the opening of the War of 1812, explaining that McIntosh and some other Creeks remained friendly toward the U.S. but that other Creeks, also known as Seminoles, believed British promises, accepted and used British arms, and "became enemies to you." The friendly Creeks were promised payment for the lands and property they lost during the war; but the $85,000 received "did not pay us half what we lost." They protest, in particular, that it is wrong for the U.S. to claim the Seminoles' lands in the Floridas by conquest without making payment to the Creeks for those lands. Nor does justice accompany any proposal that the Creeks will have to make room for the surviving Seminoles when the latter are removed from the Floridas. LS in DNA, 77 (M-271:2, frames 1241–1246).

Alexander Macomb, Detroit, to Capt. [William] Whistler, Green Bay, 3/9. Orders him to make ready the 12 batteaux that are at Green Bay and to "construct and engage" 20 more, in order that the 32 may be used as early as 5/20 to transport the 5th [Infantry] Regiment thence to Prairie du Chien "on its way to the Missis-[s]ippi." CC in DNA, 2, M-1819.

To Thomas Morris, Marshal, New York [City], 3/9. Encloses an order by President [James Monroe] remitting the fines imposed by the N.Y. militia court-martial against 18 named individuals and reducing the fines of two. LS in NhHi, Morris and Stark Papers; FC with En in DNA, 3, 10:269.

To Benjamin O'Fallon, 3/9. "I enclose you a commission as Indian Agent on the Missouri. Your compensation will be at the rate of $1,800 per annum, in full for your services." FC in DNA, 72, D:259.

From [William H. Crawford]

Treasury Department, March 10th 1819

Mr. Crawford presents his compliments to the Secretary of War, and informs him, that agreeably to the usage of the Treasury, Governor [William] Clark must be instructed to draw his bills on the Department of War in favor of the receiver of public monies at St. Louis.

LU in DNA, 1, C-197.

Ch[arles] Hicks to [James Monroe]

Wednesday morning, 10th March 1819

The Cherokee Delegation respectfully take their Father the President of the United States by the hand, to take leave. The early starting of the Steam Boat will excuse them from personally presenting themselves. While transacting the business of their Mission they have, also, experienced the kindest attention of the War Department.

In behalf of the Delegation. Ch[arles] Hicks.

LS in DNA, 1, H-179.

Calhoun and Smith Thompson to [James Monroe], 3/[*ca.* 10]. They submit the report [dated 2/25] of a system of defense for the Chesapeake Bay and of a suitable site for a Naval depot that has been prepared by J[oseph] G. Swift, S[imon] Bernard, L[ewis] Warrington, J[esse] D. Elliott, Walker K. Armistead, and William McRee. Calhoun and Thompson call attention to the fact that the report requests Monroe "to cause to be resumed & completed the survey heretofore commenced" in preparation for the establishment of two Navy arsenals; suggests that Army Engineers be added to the Navy officers detailed for that survey, in order that proper fortifications for the arsenals may be suggested and the cost of constructing the fortifications may be estimated; and requests Monroe "to cause such a survey of the Chesapeake Bay to be made, as may be requisite to ascertain what points are necessary to be fortified, for the protection of the commerce of said Bay, and a report of the same with a plan of the works necessary to be erected with an estimate of the expense of the same, to be made to Congress at their next session." FC in DNA, 6, 1:347.

From D[ECIUS] WADSWORTH

Ordnance Office, 10th March 1819

Mr. Robert L. Stevens with whom there is a Contract for elongated Shells and who left the City a few days ago, represented to me before his Departure, that owing to many Difficulties and Delays inseparable from a new Undertaking, and the Experiments he has been compelled to make, to ensure the Perfection of his Work, he Should probably be delayed a month or two beyond the Time Stipulated in the Contract for the Delivery of the first Parcel of Shells, which I told him was of little consequence, and it was further understood between us that if it should meet your approbation the sum of Five Thousand Dollars should be remitted to him, to be reimbursed out of the first Parcel of Shells to be delivered. I request therefore you should think it proper that the sum of Five Thousand Dollars may be remitted to him out of the Appropriation for Cannon & Shot.

FC in DNA, 32, 2:195.

From Col. H[ENRY] ATKINSON, 6th Infantry Regiment

Plattsburgh [*sic*; N.Y.,] March 11, 1819

I have the honor to enclose, herewith, letters from Brevet Maj[o]r [Gerard D.] Smith of the 2nd Reg[imen]t & Capt. [Newman S.] Clarke of the 6[th] Reg[imen]t soliciting a transfer. It meets my entire approbation, as well as that of Colonel [Hugh] Brady, which is signified by his assent in the accompanying letter. The Gentlemen rank alike in each Regiment, which precludes any objection on that score, and are both excellent officers. The first has no family, but the latter is encumbered with a wife, in a delicate situation, and one child: Therefore, the exchange will be beneficial to us & to the service in executing the duty before us. Should you think proper to order the transfer to be made, which I have earnestly to request you will; It is desireable [*sic*] the order should reach us by the 26th ins[tan]t at Albany, whence Capt. Clarke will march with the Reg[imen]t & where Maj. Smith will join to relieve him.

The whole country is covered with from two to three feet of snow: Notwithstanding, we shall take up our line of march about the 18th ins[tan]t and without some untoward circumstance, which should not be anticipated, every thing being in the best order for the march, we shall reach Pittsburgh by the first day of May.

As I informed you in a previous letter, as soon as the troops pass Albany, I shall set out for Washington City.

ALS in DNA, 11, 13046.

To [Dr.] W[ILLIAM] BALDWIN, [Surgeon, U.S. Navy]

Department of War, 11th March [1819]

Your letter of the 8th instant [ALS in DNA, 1, B-221, asking if he is to receive an Army appointment and on what financial terms he is to serve,] has been received:

The immediate object of the expedition under the command of Maj. [Stephen H.] Long is to obtain an accurate knowledge of the geography of the country. With a view, however, of advancing the sciences, I authorized Maj. Long to associate with him[self] such scientifick gentlemen as he might think proper to accompany him and he was authorized to allow such moderate compensation as he might judge proper.

You are therefore considered in the light of a volunteer at[tached as a specialist in botany] to the expedition and will make your [financial] arrangements with Maj. Long.

FC in DNA, 3, 10:272. NOTE: For a summary of Dr. Baldwin's distinguished achievements in botany, of his illness throughout the early stages of Long's travels in connection with the Missouri expedition, and of his death on August 31, 1819, see the sketch of Baldwin in the *Dictionary of American Biography*.

To GEORGE BOYD, King George Courthouse, Va.

Department of War, 11th March 1819

Previous to the receipt of yours of the 2d instant [ALS in DNA, 1, B-219], a letter was addressed to you at Port Royal, Virginia, on the 6th stating the necessity of your being at your post; and I now repeat it, with a request, that you will hasten your departure, as the season of the year has actually arrived when the presence of the Indian Agent is indispensable. When you have set out for the purpose of undertaking the duties of your office, funds will be furnished; until then no advance can be made.

Your request to be transferred to some more Southern post cannot be complied with, as all the new Agencies were filled before your letter came to hand.

Your Commission is enclosed.

LS in DNA, 76 (M-1:70, pp. 89–92); FC in DNA, 72, D:264.

To JACOB BROWN, Brownville, [N.Y.]

Department of War, 11th March 1819

I enclose a copy of the order to Maj. Gen. [Andrew] Jackson in relation to the expedition on the Missouri, which were [*sic*] drawn up in conformity to the direction of the President [James Monroe] after the deliberation with yourself and the General in relation to it and the expedition on the Mississippi. The same principle will govern both of the expeditions which have the same objects, the complete security of our frontier and the extension of our trade with the Indians. If the expeditions are conducted with prudence it is believed that there will be no hazard of Indian hostilities. Suitable presents will be sent up the Missouri in the Steam boat and one of the [Indian] Agents, probably Mr. [Thomas] Forsyth at Fort Armstrong, will be directed to accompany the expedition for the purpose of distributing presents and preparing the Indians for the establishment of our post at the mouth of the St. Peters. Whether that position can be safely occupied the next summer will depend on circumstances to be judged of by the officer charged with its establishment. It is conceived to be the most commanding position on the upper Mississippi and ought to be rendered proportionally strong. It was intended to order an Engineer to accompany the expedition but the engagements of that Corps is [*sic*] so extensive at present that no officer of that Corps can be spared from other duties.

Should an Indian war take place the Regiments on the Missouri & the Mississippi ought to coöperate, and to produce the effect you will in that event order the commandant of the 5th Regiment to report to and receive orders from the officer in command of the 9th Military Department, [Henry Atkinson].

P.S. Enclosed is an extract of Maj. [Stephen H.] Long's Journal in relation to Fort Crawford & the mouth of the St. Peters—[an extract from a report by Long addressed to Brig. Gen. Thomas A. Smith and dated at Bellefontaine, Mo. Territory, 5/12/1818].

FC in DNA, 3, 10:272; CC with CCEx in DLC, Jacob Brown Papers, Letterbooks, 2:138–142; CC in DLC, Andrew Jackson Papers, 8634; CC in MHi; PC in Jameson, ed., *Correspondence,* pp. 155–156.

To William Clark, St. Louis, 3/11. Modifying Calhoun's letter of 3/9 to him, directs him to issue his drafts *on* the War Department *in favor of* the Receiver of Public Monies at St. Louis, not *on* the Receiver. FC in DNA, 72, D:265.

To [William H. Crawford], 3/11. Requests that $888,209 be made available for expenditure under seven appropriations: for the pay of the Army; for subsistence; for the forage of officers' horses; for clothing the Army; for bounties and premiums; for the Hospital Department; and for the Quartermaster Department. The first, second, fourth, and seventh requested amounts are each to be in six figures. FC in DNA, 171, 1:322.

From John Gaillard, [Senator from S.C.]

11th March 1819

Permit me to trouble you with the enclosed letter for the President [James Monroe]. As you are well acquainted with the Gentlemen named therein who are applicants for offices it is unnecessary for me to say any thing about them.

ALS in DNA, 103. Note: This letter was franked at Charlotte, N.C., on 3/15. An EU refers this letter to Monroe and reads: "Mr. Gaillard recommends Mr. [John D.] Heath as Judge in Florida."

To E[dmund] P. Gaines, Fernandina

Department of War, 11 March, 1819

Your letters of the 24th [concerning lots leased at Fort Hawkins (ALS with Ens in DNA, 1, G-125; CC in DNA, 11, 13361)] & 27th ultimo [two in number, transcribed under that date] have been received.

The President of the United States [James Monroe] having directed the suspension of the [running of the] boundary line between the Flint and St. Marys River, the troops detailed by you as an escort for the Commissioner [Wilson Lumpkin] will not be necessary. The Governor of Georgia [William Rabun] and the Commissioner have been informed of this determination.

I note the attempts made to discover the sources of the St. Marys, and view with much satisfaction the disposition evinced to increase our knowledge of the topography of the country.

The leases of the lots within the reservation at Fort Hawkins, will, it is thought, be good.

It would be desirable to obtain a cession of the tract of country on which Fort Hawkins is situated. The Creek Agent [David B. Mitchell] has been instructed to endeavour to effect this object, which may affect the leases. He has, also, been directed, should it be found necessary, to apply to you to remove the intruders on the Creek Land. You will, in such event, furnish the requisite force. He has been further instructed to use his influence with the Creeks, to effect the removal of the Seminoles up into the body of the Creek Nation, in which event, you will instruct the officers commanding at Forts Gadsden and St. Marks to afford every necessary aid in effecting this object.

LS in DNA, 11, 14021; FC in DNA, 3, 10:273.

To Erastus Granger, "Late Agent to the Six Nations, N[ew] York," 3/11. Directs him to deliver to [Jasper] Par[r]ish all bonds, mortgages, etc., belonging to the Iroquois and any U.S. property still in Granger's hands. FC in DNA, 72, D:264.

To F[erdinand] R[udolf] Hassler, Newark, N.J., 3/11. S[tephen] H. Long has been authorized to obtain immediately, "as circumstances do not admit of delay," a certain chronometer; but Hassler can requisition any other chronometers that the War Department may possess. FC in DNA, 3, 10:270–271.

To S[tephen] H. Long, Philadelphia, 3/11. Acknowledges his report of 3/8 (ALS in DNA, 1, L-124) as to personnel recruited for his exploring expedition and his plea for permission to use certain chronometers that [Ferdinand Rudolf] Hassler could use instead for Hassler's survey of the northern boundary. Calhoun authorizes Long to take possession of "any chronometers" owned by the War Department that "you may deem useful for the purposes of the expedition." FC in DNA, 3, 10:271.

To Wilson Lumpkin, Madison, Ga., 3/11. Having informed him on 3/2 that President James Monroe "has thought it best to suspend the running of the line between East Florida" and Ga., Calhoun now encloses an explanation of the reasons for that order. Appoints him the commissioner to survey the boundaries of lands in Ga. ceded by the new treaty with the Eastern Cherokees; directs him to correspond with [Return J.] Meigs as a means of learning what reservations to survey; encloses a printed copy of the treaty; promises a remittance of $1,000 as an advance for his expenses. He is to be paid $8 per day while engaged in surveying the [Cherokee boundary] line [within Ga.] and "the usual surveying fees" in full "for your services in locating the [Indians'] reservations." FC in DNA, 72, D:262–263; CC in DNA, 153, 15B-C4; CC in DNA, 75 (M-208:8); PC in *American State Papers: Indian Affairs,* 2:191.

To D[avid] B. Mitchell, Creek Agent

Department of War, 11th March, 1819

It being desirable to the government to obtain a cession of a tract of Country on which Fort Hawkins is situated, you are requested to ascertain the terms on which such cession could be obtained, and report them to this department.

It is important, for the more permanent security of the peace and safety of the inhabitants of the frontier, that the Seminole Indians should be moved up into the body of the Creek nation, and you are therefore authorized to take such steps as may be necessary to effect this object in the most expeditious and economical manner. The government will furnish the provisions that may be required for the support of the Seminoles during their removal, and until they are in a situation to provide for themselves.

FC in DNA, 72, D:263.

To Jasper Par[r]ish, [Canandaigua, N.Y.,] 3/11. As he requested on 3/2 (ALS in DNA, 1, P-135), Calhoun encloses an authorization to former Agent [Erastus] Granger to deliver to Sub-Agent Parrish the stock certificates representing an investment held in trust for the Senecas and, for that matter, all other property belonging either to the Six Nations or to the U.S. As Parrish requested on 2/2 (ALS with En in DNA, 1, P-123), the annuity due to the Iroquois for this year is being sent in the forms of $2,300 in cash and of $2,200 worth of goods. FC in DNA, 72, D:263–264.

To Winfield Scott, [Richmond]

Department of War, 11th March 1819

I yesterday received your letter of the 8th ins[tan]t and have stated its contents to the President [James Monroe].

The President concurs with me in opinion that any relaxation of the order of the 21st February 1818, as it relates to the correspondence between yourself & Gen[era]l [Andrew] Jackson, would be improper. The reason of the order applies with particular force at this time to the correspondence referred to; and its publication could not fail, as I have already stated to you, to produce most unhappy effects. No one can regret more sincerely than I do the unfortunate misunderstanding between you & the General. It is to the President also a source of much regret; and he felt very solicitous if any opportunity had presented itself, to have healed the difference between you. In refusing to yield to your solicitation on a subject in which you take so much interest, I am satisfied your candour will see in it, no other motive, but a sincere desire to promote the interest of the Country and the Army. How far General Jackson may have transcended the letter or the spirit of the order of the 21st February would be premature in me to decide at this time, but I cannot but remark that there is a wide difference *in effect* in reading the correspondence, or even furnishing copies of it to individuals, & going before the public through the public prints. Whether such qualified publication, if such it may be called, is a breach of the order or not, I do not think any argument in either view can be drawn from it to justify a relaxation. The breach of an order is a good reason to enforce it, but is very far from being a sound reason for suspending it. On the contrary supposition, that such publication is consistent with the order, the means of vindicating your character would be equally open to yourself and General Jackson. As to the insinuations of the newspapers they have but little effect with the community, and are of such a nature that it is difficult to render the authors amenable to any tribunal civil or military.

[P.S.] I return the letter of Maj. Picton. J.C.C.

FC in DNA, 5, 1:103–104; CC in DNA, 1; CC in NN, James Monroe Papers; PEx in Jameson, ed., *Correspondence*, pp. 154–155.

To Robert Walsh, [Jr.,] Philadelphia

Department of War, 11th March 1819

I transmit to you a copy of the instructions to Maj. [Stephen H.] Long which will indicate the object of his expedition, and the country which it is intended to explore. The immediate object of the expedition is to acquire a more accurate geographical knowledge of an interesting portion of our country; but it is also the desire of the government to render it extensively useful to the sciences. As you take a deep interest in the advancement of knowledge, particularly in our country, I have transmitted the copy of the instructions, in order to receive any suggestions from you or the literary societies with which you are connected, by which the expedition may more completely effect the objects proposed. Maj. Long is now in Philadelphia, making his arrangements, the details of which he would readily communicate.

LS in PPAmP; FC in DNA, 3, 10:271.

From RAM[SE]Y CROOKS, Agent, American Fur Company

Washington, 12th March 1819

Fearing that in the present pressure of business, your intended communication to the authorities on the Mississippi prohibiting entirely the introduction of Spirituous Liquors into any part of the Indian Country, may possibly escape your recollection, I beg leave to remind you of its importance, trusting my duty to the American Fur Company, will apologize for this seeming importunity.

My avocations will not permit me to transmit immediately on my return to New York [City], the remarks you requested; but I shall with pleasure avail myself of the first leisure I can command, to meet your wishes.

ALS in DNA, 1, C-199.

To Capt. JAMES GADSDEN, Mobile

Department of War, 12 March 1819

You will report to the [War] Department as early as practicable to whom the sites of the Forts at Mobile, Dauphin Island, Petite Coquille and Chef Menteur belong, and upon what terms they can be obtained. You will also state your opinion as to the terms and should any doubt exist as to title you will refer to the District Attorney of New Orleans.

FC in DNA, 3, 10:274; PC in Carter, ed., *Territorial Papers,* 18:580.

To Robert Houston, Knoxville, 3/12. Appoints him the commissioner to survey lands in Tenn., N.C., and Ala. ceded to the

U.S. by the Cherokee treaty of 2/27, of which a copy is enclosed; directs him to correspond with [Return J.] Meigs as a means of ascertaining what reservations to survey; promises to remit $1,000 as an advance toward his expenses. FC in DNA, 72, D:265–266, with the commission itself on p. 479; CC in DNA, 153, 15B-C4; CC in DNA, 75 (M-208:8); PC in *American State Papers: Indian Affairs,* 2:191.

To [James Monroe]

Dep[artmen]t of War, 12th Mar[ch] 1819

Secretary of War [Calhoun] presents his respects to the President, and informs him, that in a conversation with Gen[era]l [Andrew] Jackson on the subject of the line between Tennessee & the Chickasaws, he suggested to Gen[era]l Jackson that one commissioner would be sufficient, to which the Gen[era]l assented, and named Gen[era]l [James] Winchester, who is appointed, himself.

FC in DNA, 6, 1:348.

To Patrick Noble, Abbeville, S.C.

War Dep[artmen]t, 12th March 1819

It was ["with" *interlined*] deep sorrow that I heard of the death of your brother [probably John Noble]. Few men had a warmer heart; or have passed through life with a more unblemished character. It has been his good fortune to leave, I suppose, not an enemy behind him.

Mr. [Langdon] Cheves has been appointed President of the U[nited] States bank, and there will consequently be a vacancy on the bench. I think you ought to offer for it; as it appears to me your prospect of success must be good. It would in many respects suit you well.

It is strange that there is no evidence of the administration on the estate of Isaac Teasdale in the Ordinary's office; as by a recurance [*sic*] to the letter of Adm[inistratio]n filed with the papers, it appears to be granted by T[homas ?] Livingston. I hope you will cause another examination to be made. I send you five patents, for Harris, Roddam [?; possibly Leanner Roden of Abbeville], Wilson, [Joshua ?] Franks [of Laurens ?], & Means, which I wish you to transmit to the proprietors.

We will set out about the 1st of next month and will proceed in company with the President [James Monroe] by the way of Norfolk to Charleston, and will probably ["be" *interlined*] in Abbeville early in May.

We are all well. James [Edward Colhoun] leaves this [place] in a few days for the Congress Frigate. Floride joins her love to you & Elizabeth. Remember m[e] to all of my friends.

ALS in ScCleA; variant PC in *The Journal of Southern History,* vol. XVI, no. 1 (February, 1950), pp. 69–70. NOTE: John Noble (1769–1819) is the only brother of Patrick Noble who is known to have died in 1819. George Wesley Clower, "Notes on the Calhoun-Noble-Davis Family," *The South Carolina Historical Magazine,* vol. LIII, no. 1 (January, 1952), pp. 51–52.

To [WILLIAM] RABUN, Governor [of Ga.], Milledgeville

War Dep[artmen]t, 12th March 1819

In my communication of the 2d Inst[ant] I stated to you that the President [James Monroe] had directed me to give orders to suspend for the present the running of the line from the Apilachicola [*sic*] to the head of the St. Marys. The President has given to the subject farther [*sic*] reflection; and has come to the conclusion that it would be improper to run the line till the subject is laid before Congress. The instruction originally given to Mr. Lumkins [Wilson Lumpkin] was to run it out provisionally; and subject, consequently, to be run at some future time by American & Spanish Commissioners according to the provision of the treaty between the U[nited] States & Spain dated the 27th of October 1795.

The U[nited] States has now acquired the rights of Spain in the Floridas; & Congress may order the line to be run definitively, whenever they may judge proper; and as they will probably authorise it to be done at the next session, it would scarcely be worth the trouble and expense to run it provisionally at present.

Mr. Lumkins has been informed of the determination of the President; and I hope that the State of Georgia will experience no inconvenience from the decision.

A very considerable cession of land has been acquired to Georgia under the treaty lately concluded with the Cherokees; and Mr. Lumkins has been instructed in order to ascertain its limits to run the line mentioned in the treaty from the point where the Unicoi turnpike intersects the Blue Ridge to the nearest main source of the Chistatee & to lay off the reservations within the State of Georgia. Accept the assurance of my respects.

ALS in NcD; FC in DNA, 3, 10:273. NOTE: In the ALS the words "27th of October 1795" were added by someone other than Calhoun, probably by one of his Clerks.

From [1st] Lt. J[OHN] H[OLMES] WILKINS, Light Artillery

Fort Wolcott, [R.I.,] March 12th 1819

Having understood that an expedition to explore the waters of the Missouri and Mississippi is about to be organized and that a Train of Artillery will accompany it, I beg leave to offer my services provided a command suitable with my rank can be obtained and that it will not be incompatible with your arrangements to have one allot[t]ed me.

ALS in DNA, 1, W-243.

To Gen. James Winchester, 3/12. Appoints him commissioner to survey the southern boundary of Tenn. in accordance with the Chickasaw treaty of 10/19/1818. LS in DLC, John C. Calhoun Papers; FC in DNA, 72, D:267.

To William Clark, St. Louis, 3/13. An Army post is to be established where the St. Peters River empties into the Mississippi. Clark is to instruct [Thomas] Forsyth to accompany the expedition as Indian Agent, "to explain the views of the government and, by a judicious distribution of presents, to keep quiet the Indians." Clark is also to buy $2,000 worth of goods for this distribution, have them delivered to the steamboat for the trip, and bill the War Department. FC in DNA, 72, D:267; Ex in WHi, Draper Collection, Thomas Forsyth Papers, 5:10; PC in Carter, ed., *Territorial Papers,* 15:527.

To [William H. Crawford], 3/13. "The Secretary of War has the honor to enclose the petition and documents in the case of Mons[ieu]r Poirey to the Hon[orabl]e Sec[retar]y of the Treasury, requesting that he would be pleased to designate the proper officer to whom to refer it for settlement & direct adjustment as soon as convenient." FC in DNA, 171, 1:323.

From Peter Hagner

3d Aud[itor's] Office, March 13th 1819

I have the honor to state that in the examination of the Accounts of Contractors for Subsistence of the Army it is found, that, issues of provisions have been made to Indians which are chargeable to [the] Indian Department, and the Vouchers in many cases are so connected with those for the Army issues, as to make it impracticable to separate them. The public convenience would therefore in my opinion be promoted if an Authority were given by the President of the United States [James Monroe] under the act of Congress passed at the last Session, for the 3d Auditor to audit such part of the Accounts of [the] Indian Department as connect themselves with the Contractors['] Accounts now the duty of that Office to audit, and which would be promotive of the public convenience.

ALS in DNA, 1, H-193; FC in DNA, 53, 10:56. Note: Normally, Indian accounts were subject to audit by Fifth Auditor Stephen Pleasonton.

To A[ndrew] Jackson, Nashville, 3/13. Encloses for his information a copy of a letter to [Jacob] Brown, "the subject of it having an intimate connection with the contemplated operations on the Mississippi and the Missouri." LS in DLC, Andrew Jackson Papers, 8640; FC in DNA, 3, 10:274.

From Edmund P. Gaines

Fernandina, E[ast] F[la.], March 14, 1819

By a report which I have but just received from Colonel [William] King, it appears that Pensacola and Barrancas were delivered on the 8th ultimo to the Spanish Major General John M. Echeverri, pursuant to instructions given in conformity with yours of the 14th of August 1818.

The accompanying package marked A, contains copies of the instruction, Colonel King's report, with the correspondence between the Colonel and Spanish General numbered 1 to 4 inclusively.

Upon the subject of a deposite [*sic*] of rations at Fort Crawford it may be proper to state, that, the supply was required in the expectation that the reoccupancy of Pensacola by the Spaniards would have taken place in November last, and that two Companies might be stationed at Fort Crawford, where it was desirable to have an abundant supply, and to have the deposite made whilst the water communication remained under our controul. I have however directed Col. King early in last month to reduce the requisition if not previously complied with, to 15,000 rations. My order upon this subject must have reached him about the 20th or 25th of February.

ALS with Ens in DNA, 1, G-140; draft in DNA, 11, 13292.

From Brig. Gen. [Simon] Bernard, New York [City], 3/15. Explains faults that he finds in [Joseph G.] Totten's plans for a proposed fort at Rouses Point, [N.Y.]. Argues that a fort in such an isolated area may be useless and that the whole plan for fortifications along the Canadian boundary needs to be reconsidered. LS in DNA, 1, B-228.

To William Clark, St. Louis, 3/15. He is to do all he can to prevent the illegal distribution of spiritous liquors among the Indians within Mo. Territory, "either by licensed or other traders, and to enforce the law on this point strictly against all offenders." Lewis Cass "has adopted the most rigid measures on this subject within his Superintendency, and it is just and proper that they should be equally rigid in every portion of the Indian country, that the trader in one part may not have an unfair advantage over the traders in another by the sale of an article forbidden by law and which carries with it vice & calamity." FC in DNA, 72, D:268; CC in DNA, 76 (M-1:6, pp. 22–23); PC in Carter, ed., *Territorial Papers,* 15:527–528.

To Richard Cutts, Second Comptroller of the Treasury, 3/15. "I have examined with great care, in the presence of the Comptroller and [Benjamin G.] Orr, the Contractor, the points submitted by them, growing out of Mr. Orr's Contract of 1817 for [supplying rations to the troops in] South Carolina and Georgia and have refused to overrule the decision of the 3d Auditor [Peter Hagner] for the following reasons," which Calhoun explains at length and point by point. Calhoun finds that all requisitions made by Army officers for rations needed in the Seminole War of 1818 were legitimate demands upon Orr; that Orr's failure to send a reliable representative into the area was tantamount to his having ignored his contractual obligations after having received an advance of $20,000 from the U.S.; and that Orr should be held accountable for the purchases of food that were made by Army officers because the expected rations were not delivered. FC in DNA, 3, 10:275–278.

To Thomas Forsyth, Indian Agent

Department of War, 15th March, 1819

Your letter of the 13th ultimo has been received. I regret to hear of the murder committed by a white man on an Indian and hope you will use every measure in your power sanctioned by the laws, to bring the perpetrator to justice. In the mean time, in order to prevent the Indians from resorting to retaliatory measures, by which injury might be inflicted on the peaceable and unoffending Citizens, you are requested to state to them the horror with which this and similar acts are viewed by the government and to assure them of its protection, and that you are authorized to use every effort for the apprehension of the murderer, that he may be tried and punished agreeably to the laws of his country. You are also authorized to make such presents to the relatives of the deceased as you may think proper and necessary to satisfy them for the outrage committed against them.

I enclose a copy of a letter addressed to Governor [William] Clark, by which you will perceive that it is intended you shall accompany the expedition to the mouth of the St. Peters, and that you are to receive your instructions on this subject from him.

FC in DNA, 72, D:269.

From H[ug]h Holmes, Winch[este]r, [Va.,] 3/15. "Anticipating many calls upon me by the old Revolutionary soldiers within my [judicial] circuit whose declarations have been forwarded to the War Office," Holmes apprises Calhoun of the dates and route of the appointments that Holmes expects to keep in the near future. He has delivered all pension warrants that he has received except one; "I have forgotten where" the recipient of that one lives. "Francis Hughes of Orange was with me this day and says he was told by one of the Clerks in the War Office that his warrant was sent to me. I have not received it, and presume, as the applicants are probably as troublesome at the War Office as they are to me, one of the gentlemen [in the Pension Office] may have said so to free himself from importunity." An AEI by Calhoun directs [James L.] Edwards to furnish Holmes with appropriate information. ALS in DNA, 7, Box 581 (Letters Received, 1808–1849).

To James Johnson, Great Crossings, Ky., 3/15. Answering his letter of 2/28 (ALS in DNA, 1, J-154, in which Johnson acknowledged the new order of 2/10 for 250,000 rations but referred erroneously to the earlier order of 12/10/1818 as having been for 450,000), Calhoun states that his order of 2/10 was intended to be for 250,000 in addition to the 420,000 ordered on 12/10/1818. FC in DNA, 3, 10:278.

D[aniel] Parker to Col. H[enry] Atkinson, 3/15. Pursuant to an order from Calhoun, Parker directs Atkinson to come to Washington as soon as Atkinson shall have completed the making of necessary arrangements for marching his [6th Infantry] Regiment to St. Louis. The purpose of his visiting Washington is to become better acquainted with the War Department's desires concerning his "future command, &c.," [in connection with the Missouri Expedition]. "The sooner you arrive at this place the better, as it is probable the Secretary of War may leave this city for a few weeks early in April." PC in House Document No. 110, 16th Cong., 2nd Sess.

From Henry Sherburne, Chickasaw Agency, 3/15. He issued a draft for $200 on 3/13 for his blacksmith's supplies and for repairs to the Agency house. ALS in DNA, 1, S-264.

To Col. T[albot] Chambers, St. Louis, 3/16. Encloses a copy of Joseph Rolette's complaint [of 1/15] against Chambers [for having ordered Rolette to leave Prairie du Chien]. "It is with regret that I so frequently receive communications from the 9th Military Department [Chambers's area] of personal grievances." The order has been canceled until Chambers reports "the circumstances of the case & the reason for your order." He is also to submit a report about Ezra Youngb[lood]. FC in DNA, 3, 10:280.

From John H. Hall

Washington City, 16 March 1819

By all the intimations upon the subject which have, from time to time, been received by me from the Ordnance Department, I was induced to believe that when the Government should have tested my guns by proper Officers, they would then proceed to adopt them to a large extent & that a purchase of a right to make at least 10,000 would be immediately effected. Under this impression I had formed expectations which I now begin to perceive will not, at present, be realized. Relying however upon the intention of the Government to give the guns a full & fair trial, in regard to the only points upon which any doubts can now be entertained viz. the expense of fabrication & their ability to maintain their superiority under all the variety of circumstances which may occur while in the hands of soldiers, I submit in silence to the painfull [*sic*] disappointment.

The suggestion which you made to me on Friday last relative to fabricating 1,000 of my Rifles for farther [*sic*] trial, in service, is such as I would have gladly embraced while my workmen were with me & it was in my power to execute such a contract. In my letters to the Ordnance Dep[artmen]t, at that time, I earnestly solicited such an one, but could not obtain it, nor even one for common Rifles, which I asked for, assigning as my motive the advantages which would be derived from it in making my improved Rifles. In his reply to my request, Col. [Decius] Wadsworth remarked "If your patent Rifle should be introduced into the United States service we shall expect to abolish altogether, in the Army, the use of the common Rifle" & for that reason refused to contract with me for any common ones.

Your other suggestion for me to superintend the construction of 1,000 of my Rifles at one of the Public Armories, I am ready to close with, for such a compensation for my personal services as the Government may think proper to allow. I would however suggest that $3 per day is as small a sum as I can maintain my family upon, with the decency to which they have been accustomed.

By taking from a reservoir at one of the Armories, a quantity of water, sufficient for moving such simple machinery as will be necessary for the new guns, & erecting a snug wooden building & smiths' [*sic*] shop for the men to work in, by themselves, who may be employed upon the guns, the business may be kept entirely distinct & separate from the other affairs at the Armory, so as to occasion little or no inconvenience to them in any respect. By such an arrangement the expences of fabrication may be ascertained to great exactness. As there is no reason for doubting that the guns will be generally adopted, hundreds of them having already stood the test of several years['] service in a variety of hands, under a variety of circumstances, with increased reputation, & they have equally well sustained the severe experiments, by order of Gov[ernmen]t, at Charlestown, [Mass.,] at Harpers Ferry, & at Greenleafs' [*sic*] point, it may be safely concluded that the buildings & machinery which may be necessary for giving the fabrication of them a fair trial will always continue to be usefull [*sic*].

The expense of arms constitutes so small a portion of the whole expense of troops, that an improvement in them by which the efficiency of troops is increased, cannot prove expensive in service, at any price which does not exceed the usual one in a proportion far greater than that in which the efficiency of the troops is increased by it. The board, in their very guarded report, admit that my rifles are full[y] as accurate as the common Rifle, & throw with as much force, & that they may be loaded with ease in every situation (which is far from being the case with common Rifles) & that in respect to celerity they are to other Rifles as two to one. These things being so (& more is true), would it not be more economical to arm troops with them even at twice the price of common Rifles, $17, than to use the latter, when by this additional expense of $17 per man the troops are rendered twice as effective in all cases where their fire can be used? But the expense of these Rifles will not exceed that of common Rifles more than $2 & they possess other advantages of very great importance, such as admitting the application of a bayonet to them with as much advantage as to a musket (in consequence of their celerity). They never can become useless in action by the sticking of a ball part way down the barrel as frequently happens with other rifles, nor by being overcharged & getting burst, for they can take in but one heavy charge at a time, nor by the breaking of a ramrod, for they are loaded without it—& that which is of the first importance to *American troops,* those guns throw their blast from their vent holes upwards instead of side-wise as other guns do. This circumstance I have always considered of as much importance, for troops of the line as that of their celerity. By firing in the ranks, with common guns which throw the blast from their vents against the cheeks & faces of the men, even our best gunners soon contract such a habit of flinching as is very destructive of their accuracy. In those independent Companies of Militia which are in the habit of frequent firing, not an individual can be found, who has done duty in their ranks twelve months, that can discharge his piece without flinching.

I would take the liberty of remarking that as Portland (my home) is much nearer to the Armory at Springfield than to that at Harper's Ferry, I should upon that account, greatly prefer superintending the fabrication of my guns at the former.

ALS in DNA, 35, In-6-18. NOTE: An AEI by Calhoun referred this letter to the Ordnance Department.

From F[erdinand] R[udolf] Hassler, Newark, N.J., 3/16. Acknowledges Calhoun's letter of 3/11 and thanks him for permission to retain certain chronometers for use in the Canadian boundary survey. Asks that two box chronometers, now in Washington, shall be carefully packed and sent to [Henry] Voigt in Philadelphia for cleaning. ALS in DNA, 221, 38; CCEx in DNA, 221, 42.

Richard M. Johnson, Great Crossings, Ky., to [Christopher] Vandeventer, 3/16. A note evidently written by Johnson on the cover of a letter from which the note is now separated reads: "As this communication is to Mr. Calhoun on matters not official my friend Maj. Vandeventer will direct it to the Sec[retary] if he has left the City of Washington." ALS in DNA, 1, J-107.

To [James Monroe]

Department of War, 16 March 1819

The Secretary of War presents his respects to the President of the U.S. and submits for his approbation & signature the enclosed order.

Copy of Order

It is ordered by the President of the United States in pursuance of the authority vested in him by act of Congress passed at the last session, that the 3d Auditor [Peter Hagner] do audit such part of the accounts of the Indian Department as connect themselves with the Contractors['] accounts now the duty of that officer. 16 March 1819.

FC in DNA, 6, 1:348. Note: A DS of the enclosed order, signed by Monroe on 3/16, is filed in DNA, 1, P-139.

From David A. Ogden, [former Representative from N.Y.]

New York [City], March 16th 1819

Previous to my departure from Washington, the President [James Monroe,] as well as yourself, requested me to commit to writing, my views as to the [proposed] concentration of the Seneca Indians upon the Allegany [*sic*] Reservation, & you were both pleased to say, that the subject should receive your early consideration after the adjournment of Congress.

I had originally intended to suspend the present communication until I reached Albany, where our State Legislature are in Session, in order to have first ascertained the views of the Executive of New York, [Governor De Witt Clinton,] in relation to the other Tribes of Indians, resident within this State; but the period of the President's departure to the Southward & Westward is so near approaching, that I have concluded not to delay it, particularly as the State of New York in their cession to the Commonwealth of Massachusetts [in 1786] expressly stipulated that they would not interfere in the extinguishment of the Native right to the Lands included in that cession, but delegated that power exclusively to Massachusetts & her Grantees.

Since my arrival in this City, I have received a printed copy of a report [no. 90, dated 3/4/1819,] on the subject of all the Indian Tribes in this State, lately made to the house of Assembly by a Committee of that Body. This document will be found to possess but little merit in point of style, & indeed the framers of it, who are understood to be Farmers, appear to have a very imperfect knowledge of the situation of the Reservations occupied by the Senecas, which they seem to consider, as belonging to the United States. It however exhibits a striking picture of the present condition of our Indians, & furnishes strong evidence of the justice of the remarks contained in your Report of the 5th De-c[em]b[e]r last [addressed to Speaker Henry Clay], & of the necessity of adopting some course similar to that, which is there recommended.

I am gratified to find that several Individuals of high respectability, with whom I have conversed, decidedly approve of the plan suggested in your report as affording the best, if not the only means of effecting the object in view, & that among the number, is the pious & highly respected Bishop of the Protestant Episcopal Church of this diocese.

I have now the honor to enclose a copy of the printed report above referred to, & also a copy of a Memoir on the subject of the New York Indians, [dated 3/17,] which I have prepared, in order to submit to some of the members of our State Legislature, with a view to aid the passage of the Resolution [for adoption by the N.Y. legislature, a printed copy of which is also enclosed], grounded in that Report. This paper may serve to exhibit some details, which may possibly be found useful to you, in the progress of this business.

Considering the speedy departure of the President & yourself from the seat of Government, & the improbability (from want of time) of any previous communication from the Executive of this State, founded on the pending resolution, I take the liberty to suggest, whether with a view to avoid unnecessary delay, it would not be proper & useful, now to inform Governor Clinton of the late act of Congress, & to apprise him of the general views of the President in relation to Indians, circumstanced as those are, in the State of New York.

The interest which the State has in the Reservations occupied by the Oneidas & other Tribes will no doubt lead the Governor to take part in the measures proposed & will probably induce a wish to unite those Tribes, with the Senecas on the Allegany Reservation, contiguous to which, the State possesses about One hundred Thousand acres of land, lately conveyed by the Holland Land Company for the benefit of the Canal fund.

I find a general disposition among the Gentlemen associated with me, to conform to the views of the General Government, as regards the Seneca Indians, upon just & liberal principles, & if it shall be deemed desirable, that the absolute title to the Allegany Reservation shall be vested in Trustees for their use & benefit, we should acquiesce in this measure, expecting however to be allowed a fair consideration for the fee of this land, in reduction of the price to be paid for the release of the Indian right to the remaining Reservations.

I believe you are fully acquainted with the value of the Allegany Reservation; in point of soil, it is not surpassed by any lands in the State. It is sufficiently extensive as to all the purposes of cultivation for the accommodation of all the Seneca Indians. Its value may be estimated at from 6 to 8 dollars p[er] acre. It is of all the Reservations least liable to interference from the White Settlements, & must remain so, as the Allegany Mountains on each side are not calculated for improvement or cultivation & will present a constant barrier between the two populations. Under the preceeding [*sic*] statement, I have to solicit,

1. That a Commissioner may be appointed to hold a treaty with all or any of the Tribes, composing the Six Nations of Indians residing in this State.

2. That the Commissioner be instructed to apprise the Indians of the object of his appointment & of the general views of the Government, preparatory to a Treaty or Council to be held, as soon as circumstances will admit.

3. That a *Talk*, under the hand of the President & the formality of a Seal be prepared & sent to the Commissioner, to be delivered by him to the Indians, explaining the late proceedings of Congress & the views of the President, as to the proposed concentrations, enforced by such remarks, as may be calculated to operate favorably on the minds of the Indians & accompanied by such other instructions to the Commissioner, for his own government as you may think expedient.

I beg leave to add, that I think it of essential importance, that the Commissioner should be instructed to renew to the Six Nations, the assurance of a gratuitous seat to the West, for the accommodation of such, as may not be inclined to continue in this State. The enclosed letter from Governor [Lewis] Cass [to yourself dated 3/1], handed to me at the moment of my departure from Washington, will serve to show that no objection is apprehended on the part of the people of Ohio, to their removal to that State, & as the Senecas, who hold a tract at Lower Sandusky, under the late Treaty, are willing to receive a part of those of their Nation in this State, who may incline to join them, it might be important that this circumstance should be particularly noticed by the Commissioner in his communication with the Seneca Nation in this State.

LS with Ens in DNA, 1, O-17. NOTE: The letter from Lewis Cass to Calhoun written on 3/1 appears herein under that date.

To JOSEPH ROLETTE, Prairie du Chien

Department of War, 16 March, 1819

Your letter of the 15th of January last in relation to the order of Col[one]l [Talbot] Chambers, of the 25th of December for your departure from Prairie du Chien, has been received.

You are allowed to return to your family and property, at Prairie du Chien, and to continue there until further orders from the Department.

The officer commanding [at Prairie du Chien] has been instructed to this effect, and directed to report on the circumstances of your case to this Department.

FC in DNA, 3, 10:280; CC in DLC, Carnegie Institution of Washington Transcript Collection. NOTE: Rolette's long complaint of 1/15 against Chambers is an ALS in French, with a translation into English, in DNA, 1, R-123.

To W[alker] K. Armistead, Robert Brent, Joseph Lovell, and D[ecius] Wadsworth, 3/17. "At the request of the Secretary of the Treasury [William H. Crawford], you will make your requisitions on that Department for the contingent fund of your office quarterly in equal proportions, unless the disbursements shall require a larger sum." FC in DNA, 3, 10:281; LS (Armistead's copy) in DNA, 221, 40; LS (Lovell's copy) in DNA, 245, 1:55; CC (Lovell's copy) in DNA, 244, A:5; LS (Wadsworth's copy) in ScU-SC, John C. Calhoun Papers.

From Thomas L. McKenney

Office [of] Indian Trade, March 17th 1819

I beg leave respectfully to represent that in conformity to the provisions contained in the 2d article of the Treaty of Fort Wilkinson entered into June 16th 1802 (see Colvin's digest, Laws U.S. vol. 1, page 371) Ten thousand Dollars were stipulated to be paid over to the U.S. Factory then at that place, for the considerations therein mentioned, which Ten thousand Dollars have never been received, nor any part or parcell thereof.

To illustrate the nature of this claim, I enclose a true Copy of the list of debts for which that consideration was inserted; to which is added the joint report of the Agent and the Factor.

I shall be excused for expressing a hope that a warrant may be directed on account of this claim as soon as practicable, as the Indian Trade Department needs the use of all its resources.

I avail myself of this occasion to solicit the favor of your attention to the contents of a letter which I did myself the honor to address to the War Department bearing date 23d Sept[embe]r 1817—and to which no answer has been received. If the claims therein referred to shall prove correct, as I am entirely satisfied they are (the vouchers accompanied that letter to the War Department), it will be serviceable to the [Indian] Trade Department to have this claim adjusted also.

LS with Ens in DNA, 1, M-245; FC in DNA, 73, E:229–230.

From Thomas L. McKenney

Office [of] Indian Trade, March 17th 1819

I beg respectfully to state that the act approved March 3d 1809, entitled an act supplemental to an act for establishing trading houses wih the Indian Tribes, appropriated $40,000, in addition to sums previously appropriated, for the carrying on trade and intercourse with the Indians, only $30,000 of which were drawn from the Treasury, leaving a balance of $10,000. I am aware of the course which this $10,000 has taken; and that it is not within the reach of this office in the regular way. But it has occurred to me that in so plain a case, when it cannot be the intention of one branch of the Government to absorb the essential and legally appropriated means for the prosecution of [the work of] another, that some transfer of some other appropriation might be made, so as to give to this office the use of this money, untill [*sic*] a law of Congress should restore it, or that you could devise some plan for its restriction more direct than this.

I beg leave respectfully to state that it would come in aid of the operations of this office much to the advantage of the object for which it was intended, and to ask the favor of you to act upon it, if there be any way in which you can do so consistent with the laws &c.

FC in DNA, 73, E:230–231.

To Smith Thompson, Secretary of the Navy, 3/17. Answers his letter of 2/25 enclosing one from William H. Crawford to Thompson of 2/23 (LS with CC in DNA, 1, T-98) indicating a desire on Thompson's part to be prepared whenever the Army can pursue jointly with the Navy the survey of the coasts, in accordance with the statute of 4/14/1818. In reply to Thompson's inquiry as to the balance available for the project, Calhoun says nothing. He states simply "that the officers of the Corps of Engineers are so entirely employed upon fortifications, the designation of depots, and other duties that none of them will be dispensable for the abovementioned purpose the present year." FC in DNA, 3, 10:281.

To Thomas Waide, Washington, 3/17. Answers his appeal of 2/25 (ALS in DNA, 1, W-238) that justice be done to his client, John Miller of Mass., whose misfortune it has been to have served in the same Company and Regiment with a John Miller of N.Y., the latter of whom has received by mistake a warrant for 160 acres of bounty land due to the John Miller of Mass. Calhoun replies that "if a mistake exists, it is believed that it was not made in the

Office of Bounty Lands but in the General Land Office, where application must be made for its correction." FC in DNA, 3, 10:281.

From Chris[topher] Andrews

Mar[ch] 18, 1819

Permit me to renew the recollection of the application I made last summer [written on 8/27/1818] in favor of my brother George Andrews for a Cadet's warrant. I am induced to give you this trouble from the circumstance that, you remarked in the course of the conversation I then had with you, that sometimes among the multiplicity of applications, some were forgotten, from having lain a long time upon the files of the office, while those of more recent date were recollected. Judge [Joseph] Anderson informs me that he has addressed you a letter [dated 3/18] recommending my brother.

ALS in DNA, 15, 1818, 179.

To W[alker] K. Armistead, Engineer Department

Department of War, 18th March 1819

Enclosed is Capt. [James] Gadsden's report upon the defences of Baton Rouge & plans of the fortifications. You will furnish the Quarter Master General [Thomas S. Jesup] & Colonel of Ordnance [Decius Wadsworth] with copies of plan No. 1, which has been adopted.

LS in DNA, 221, 41; FC in DNA, 3, 10:282. Note: The FC has the following additional words after the word "adopted" in the LS: "and inform Capt. Gadsden of its adoption."

From S[amuel] R. Betts, Newburgh, [N.Y.,] 3/18. Having been away for several weeks, he asks if the court-martial [for N.Y. militia delinquents] has been dissolved and whether his compensation as a Judge Advocate therein has been approved. A Deputy Marshal has been collecting fines and may have funds enough to provide the payment to Betts. ALS in DNA, 1, B-235.

Capt. James Gadsden, Mobile Point, to [Walker K.] Armistead, 3/18. Gadsden corrects the misimpression, apparently held by both the Chief Engineer and by Congress, that the funds already appropriated for fortifications at Mobile Point, Dauphin Island, and Rigolets are sufficient to permit their completion. He explains that ditches dug for the foundations fill with water before firm foundations can be constructed. If inspectors cannot study the problem at the site, Gadsden offers to travel to Washington to present facts concerning the cost and difficulty of building these fortifications. ALS in DNA, 223, 61.

From P[eter] H[agner], 3/18. Acting under the [recent] statute for the relief of Monsieur Poirey, Hagner has audited Poirey's account and has decided that Poirey is entitled to be paid, at the rate of $60 per month from 1/1/1779 to 11/4/1783, $3,486 for his services as secretary and aide-de-camp to Lafayette. No approriation has been made by Congress for this purpose. Calhoun should decide if the payment can be taken from any other funds. FC in DNA, 53, 10:111.

To T[homas] S. Jesup and D[ecius] Wadsworth, 3/18. Informs them that Capt. [James] Gadsden's plan No. 1 for fortifications at Baton Rouge has been adopted; [Walker K.] Armistead will send a copy of it to each. FC in DNA, 3, 10:282; LS (Jesup's copy) in ScU-SC, John C. Calhoun Papers.

JAMES PITCHLYNN to [JOHN C. CALHOUN ?]

Choctaw Nation, March 18, 1819

Dear Sir: I take this [*sic*] pleasure to inform you I have got several families of the Choctaws who are willing to move west of the Mississippi; and, I believe, if there was a treaty held in the nation, there would be one-third or half of the nation would move in the fall. I find all the rich white people living in the nation; they give bad talks to the Indians; they tell them not to exchange lands, and some public men in the nation. Some of the Indians has [*sic*] threatened to knock me in the head on this account. I have never heard from you nor the President of the United States about my business. You wrote for me at your house. I hope you will write to me soon as you receive answer. Excuse my bad writing, as I told you I never went to school but six months.

CC in DNA, 153, 16B-C2; PC in *American State Papers: Indian Affairs,* 2:229.

From the Rev. Lewis D. Schweinitz

Salem, Stokes County, North Carol[ina,] March 18th 1819

Circumstances having put it out of my power, when lately passing thro' Washington on my return from Europe, to do myself the honor of waiting upon you personally in order to acquit myself of a duty imposed on me, by my Colleagues the Directors of the Society of United Brethren in North Carolina, I now beg leave by letter to tender you their most cordial acknowledgements for the highly valued present of One Hundred Dollars, which Mr. Th[omas] L. McKen[ne]y, Superintendant [*sic*] of Indian Trade, has by your direction transmitted to the Rev. John Gambold, our missionary among the Cherokee nation at Springplace, Conessago: a donation not only requiring in itself our sincerest thanks, but still more estimable as a testimony of your friendly consideration towards the poor Indians, unto whom we are, in our small degree, striving, under the divine favor to make known the saving truths of the gospel & installing into their minds principles conducive to their temporal & eternal welfare.

Charles Hicks, one of the Chiefs of the Cherokee nation, and one of those who by the instrumentality of our brethren, have embraced Christianity, and, we trust imbibed truly Christian principles, has lately been at Washington with others of the nation on business; and from him we have received information, that the perplexities in which the nation had been involved are now terminated to their perfect satisfaction, in consequence whereof there is now a fair prospect that they will remain in their present situation. We must sincerely rejoice thereat, because the contrary event must have terminated our endeavors for them, which after nearly twenty years of great expence and apparently fruitless toil, now begin to wear a promising aspect.

We make bold, Honor'd Sir, to address an enquiry on the subject to you, which we conceive of importance to our establishment as well as to the great work of civilization among the Indian nations in general; videlicet whether in the arrangements made with the Cherokees provisions have been introduced tending to secure to each, individual property in the lands & thus preparing the way for a gradual incorporation with other Inhabitants of this country, believing, as we have been taught to do by nearly twenty years of observation, that features of this kind would remove the greatest obstacles which have hitherto stood in the way of success of our endeavors as well as those of others.

If such should be the case, we beg leave further to enquire whether measures could be taken to obtain for our missionary establishment where it is now situated, and where houses and improvements at a vast expence considering our small means, have been erected, a permanent seat by securing the landed property thereof, even in case it should be within the limits of the Cherokee country.

Sensible that you, honor'd Sir, occupied by so many important avocations of duty, could not without impropriety on our part be requested to transmit to us the necessary information, we beg leave only to ask the favor that you would point out to us the proper person to address on this subject, if it in any way meets your approbation.

In the meantime I have the honor to assure you, that your kind notice of our mission evinced by the present to Mr. Gambold has in no small degree encouraged our hopes that the praiseworthy endeavors of Government to effect an amelioration among the Indians by means of civilization—an object which doubtless can never be better advanced than by their being brought to a conviction of religious truth—are in a fair way of succeeding under the auspices of a gentleman who like yourself is so actively & zealously disposed to aid the important work.

Accept, honor'd Sir, the just tribute of particular respect which we feel gratified in having an opportunity to offer to you, subscribing ourselves The Directors of the Society of United Brethren or United Fratrum in North Carolina and in their behalf, Honor'd Sir, [I am] Your most obedient Servant, Lewis D. Schweinitz.

ALS in DNA, 1, S-263.

To [Walker K. Armistead], 3/19. Asks where the two box chronometers mentioned in the letter [of 3/16] from F[erdinand]

R[udolf] Hassler to Calhoun are to be found. LU with En in DNA, 221, 42.

To W[alker] K. Armistead, T[homas] S. Jesup, and Decius Wadsworth, 3/19. "Enclosed is a copy of an act of Congress authorizing the sale of certain Military sites. You will take the necessary steps to ascertain and will as early as practicable report to this Department the Military sites attached to your Department no longer necessary for Military purposes, according to the provisions of the act." FC in DNA, 3, 10:283; LS with En (Armistead's copy) in DNA, 221, 44; LS (Wadsworth's copy) in DNA, 31, with EU indicating an answer on 8/31.

To Maj. J[OHN] T. CHUNN, Ft. Wayne ("Duplicate sent to Detroit")

Department of War, 19th Mar[ch], 1819

The extraordinary issue of rations at Fort Harrison to the Indians by your order, an abstract of which showing the amount is enclosed, requires explanation, in as much as there appears to be no order on the Books of this Department, which authorizes you to issue rations to Indians.

An order was issued by this Department on the 7th May, 1816, which requires "that all abstracts for issues to the Indians shall be signed and certified by the officer commanding the post at which the rations shall be issued." This regulation was made "imperative from the date of its reception," and a circular letter was written on the next day (8th May 1816) notifying the commanding officers of the posts in the Indian country and at stations to which Indians usually resort, of this order, and stating that "the Agents are required to make daily reports to them of the number of Indians present, and for whom rations are to be issued. In default of such report the abstracts are not to be certified and will not be allowed." This circular was addressed to "Major W[illia]m [*sic*; Willoughby ?] Morgan, or officer commanding at Fort Harrison," at that time, and it is presumed, that when you took the command you were placed in possession of it. It is therefore necessary that the daily reports required to be made by the Agents, and the abstracts to be certified agreeably to such reports, should be forwarded to this department. You will furnish such other information as may be in your power, of the necessity for this unusual issue of rations, as will be satisfactory, otherwise you will be chargeable with the amount.

In April and May 1818, there appear to have been rations issued to an amount equal to a daily issue of nearly 3,000, a number that it is scarcely possible could be required for any assemblage of Indians in that quarter of the country, particularly for two months continuance.

You are requested to return the enclosed statement with the evidence and explanations required, as early as practicable.

FC in DNA, 72, D:271–272.

To William H. Crawford, 3/19. Encloses a list of annuities that are to be paid in specie; requests the names and addresses of the Receivers of Public Monies and/or banks on which it would be most convenient to issue drafts for these funds; requests that these be ordered to honor such drafts. FC in DNA, 72, D:270. Crawford's reply of 3/20 [LS in DNA, 1, C-222; CCEx in DNA, 76 (M-1:6)] gives assurance that arrangements will be made to have the needed specie available for annuities and for other War Department expenses at places where revenues from public land sales accumulate and provides instructions how Indian Agents can withdraw such funds.

From Brig. Gen. Adam Lynn, 2nd Brigade, Militia of D.C., Alexandria, [D.C.,] 3/19. Nominates about 20 men for promotions and appointments in his unit. An AES by James Monroe certifies his approval. ALS in DNA, 11, 13700.

To Benjamin Parke, Vincennes, Ind., 3/19. A contractor has submitted a bill for $44,813.74 for rations allegedly issued by him to Indians at Fort Harrison between 6/1817 and 6/1818 under orders of Maj. J[ohn] T. Chunn, the commanding officer there. This amount seems extraordinary for such a period, unnecessarily large. Calhoun asks Parke to submit promptly any information that Parke has concerning why so many rations were issued. FC in DNA, 72, D:269–270.

To D[aniel] Parker, 3/19. "You will keep the Pay Department regularly and early informed of the movement of the Troops in order to enable the Paymaster Gen[era]l [Robert Brent] to make arrangements for their regular and prompt payment." LS in DNA, 11, 14021; FC in DNA, 3, 10:282.

To William Prince, Vincennes, [Ind.,] 3/19. Gives Prince the same information that Calhoun has written today to Benjamin Parke and, similarly, asks for a report as to "the necessity for issues [of rations] to so great an extent"; but Calhoun wants Prince to explain, in particular, "those for the months of April and May 1818." FC in DNA, 72, D:270.

From D[ecius] Wadsworth, 3/19. Requests a payment of $1,000 to John H. Hall "for the privilege of fabricating at the United States Armory one thousand Patent Rifles." FC in DNA, 32, 2:197.

From [2nd] Lt. George Blaney

Engineer Department, 20 March 1819

I have the honor to state that one of the Chronometers referred to in Mr. [Ferdinand Rudolf] Has[s]ler[']s letter is in the possession of Major [Isaac] Roberdeau—the other is with Capt. [René Edward] De Russy at New York [City] and will be forwarded to this Department with the Instruments &c. which Mr. Has[s]ler delivered to Capt. De Russy by the order of the War Department.

FC in DNA, 21, 1:50.

From George Boyd

King Geo[rge] Court House, Va., March 20th 1819

I have the honor to acknowledge the receipt of your letter of the 11th instant, inclosing my Commission as Indian Agent for the post of Mac[k]inac, and to inform you that I have by this mail, inclosed to my friend Mr. E.M. Caldwell, the paper which I hold as part of the proceeds of the sale of my House in Washington, which has Eleven months to run, with a request that He will endeavour to negotiate the same, at a loss of twenty per cent, & even more, should more be exacted, to enable me to commence my journey to Mac[k]inac. This I hope, Sir, will satisfy you of my desire to be at my post, without loss of time, and will s[er]v[e] to convince you that my departure is delayed alone for the want of funds: indeed at this moment, I have not wherewithal to defray my own Expences to Washington, much less to meet the accumulated expenditure of myself & a large family to the distant point of my destination. I am in great hopes however to be on my journey by the 15th of April. With many thanks for your kind attention as regards the early date of my Commission, I have the Honor to remain with great respect & Consideration, Sir, your . . . .

ALS in DNA, 1, B-236.

From [William H. Crawford], 3/20. "If the Agents of the several tribes in the North west should be authorized to draw upon the War Department for their salaries or such contingent expenses as cannot be regulated so as to admit of the transmission of Treasury drafts in their favour previous to the expenditure, I have the honour to suggest the propriety of authorizing them to draw upon the War Department for such sums in favour of one of the following Receivers of Public Money, viz, at Detroit, at Wooster, at Vincennes, and at Kaskaskias. Those west of the Mississippi may be supplied in like manner by the Receivers at St. Louis and at Franklin." CCEx in DNA, 76 (M-1:70, p. 93).

To M[ARTIN] D[AVIS] HARDIN, [former Senator from Ky.,] Frankfort, Ky.

War Dep[artmen]t, 20th March 1819

I have no other apology to offer for the long interval between the date of this communication and yours of the 19th of Dec[embe]r, but that continual pressure of official duties, to which the War Dep[artmen]t is subject during the session of Congress, and which compelled me almost entirely to suspend my private correspondence.

I am very favourably impressed with Judge [William] Logan's character both as a man and politician. Your delegation, even those who had been politically opposed to him, speak in very respectable terms of him.

I am glad to hear that on the great doctrine of construction he thinks so correctly. This doctrine with an air of freedom & plausibility is by its votaries in many instances a mere cover for weakness & tergiversation. The people have made their constitution, have given in other words their letter of instructions, and within their limits, till changed as solemnly as they were adopted, it is left to judgment & counsel [?].

I shall be very happy to be made acquainted at the next session through you with the Judge.

The acquisition of the Floridas has I think put a new aspect on our affairs both at home & abroad. It is intimately connected with the South American question, and will enable the government, to persue [*sic*] in relation to it, that policy which our present & future interest may require, undisturb[ed] by those inelated [?] feelings, which the state of things ["in Florida" *interlined*], for many years past, were calculated to produce.

You promise to let me hear from you occasionally. I will be happy to receive your opinions at all times, on our publick affairs. Nothing is more gratifying to me, than to receive the opinions of those, on whose candour & judgment I can rely. Those who look on have many advantages over the actors and availing myself of the observation, I can not but think, that some of our old friends, have pushed the bank question too far in your State legislature. Every day's experience more powerfully impresses me with the opinion, that the National bank, in the present state of our currency, is indispensable, and I trust its future administration under Mr. [Langdon] Cheves will be governed by the strictest integrity and enlightened intelligence. I feel the magnitude of the subject, and hope the country will take council of its coolest & most deliberate judgment. Yours sincerely, J.C. Calhoun.

ALS in ICHi. NOTE: This letter was postmarked on 3/21. William Logan had been elected a Senator from Ky. for a term that began on March 4, 1819.

TO THOMAS JEFFERSON

War Dep[artmen]t, 20th March 1819

The statement of Mr. [Peter] Hagner of the amount due to M. Poirey and such of the documents as he [that is, Poirey] requested to be returned to him are herewith enclosed. If it is the wish of M. Poirey, that the amount may be paid to you, by transmitting evidence of it to this Department it will be paid to you, as his agent. A formal power of attorney will not be necessary. A request in the form of a letter for you to receive or transmit it to him will be sufficient; or if he omitted to make such a request and you should think proper, to secure, what is due to him in our account, it can be paid to you and his receipt or power to receive it be hereafter obtained.

I hope your health is entirely restored. Your indisposition has strongly evinced the deep hold which you have on the sympathy of your country. To your friends, it was the source of great satisfaction to observe that all party animosity towards you had subsided to respect & esteem for your great and illustrious services. That the continuance of your life may long afford our country an opportunity to express these sentiments towards you, is my most ardent desire.

ALS in DLC, Thomas Jefferson Papers, 215:38333–38334.

From H[ENRY] SHERBURNE

Chickasaw Agency, Mar[ch] 20th 1819

Your letters of the 20th & 23d Ult[im]o are received, the first saying that the sum of $73.79 will be remitted to me by the Treasurer of the United States [Thomas Tudor Tucker] to pay the several sums stipulated, by the late Treaty with the Chickasaw Nation; when it comes to hand, which I presume will be by a draft on some of the Banks, it must be sent to Nashville to be exchanged for bank bills, as it will be useless in its original form; for this purpose I have engaged Major James Colbert, who is trusty & well acquainted with the road; this measure I am induced to take for the greater safety of the money, altho' it will be some expence to the U[nited] States, as mail robberies have become too frequent to hazard so large a sum by mail. I have mentioned to the Chiefs the cause of the delay of payment, as observed by you, with which they are fully satisfied.

Major Colbert has notified me that his engagements in his farming business, & attention to a large stock of cattle, are such that he cannot serve any longer than to the end of this quarter, as

U[nited] States Interpreter without great injury to himself; I am now looking out for a successor & have a prospect of obtaining a person who will fully answer the purpose; this determination of his does not arise from any difficulty with me or dissatisfaction to the United States, but merely from the above reasons; as the calls of the Indians on me have been the Two last quarters unusually frequent, I have laboured under some disadvantages, in getting on with my duty, by his absence, which he confesses he well knows, & is therefore perfectly willing to resign, rather than the public business should be embarrassed, which determination of his I fully acquiesce with, as I believe it will be to his interest & my accommodation.

The Treaty soon to be holden for the purchase of the reservations & Salt Spring by John Overton, Newton Cannon, & Robert Weakley Esquires, Commissioners on the part of the United States, shall meet with every attention in my power to carry the wishes of Government into effect, & no doubt if the Commissioners want any particular aid from me in the intended negotiation, I shall soon hear from them, & will most cheerfully give it.

Before this you have received my letter of the 13th Ult[im]o which particularly mentions the substance of the Talk I had with George & Levi Colbert relative to the reservations and Salt Spring, [which was that] they appeared desirous to sell to the United States, altho' they had agreed to sell & lease to Major Lewis soon after the Treaty was signed; which sale & lease, as you say, having been made since the determination on the part of Government, to treat for them, cannot be considered valid; if this be the case, I think if the amount to be given for the purchase can be agreed on, no great time will be required to accomplish the business.

LS in DNA, 1, S-256.

From Roger Skinner, Albany, 3/20. Recommends Alexander Duer of New Orleans for appointment as the U.S. Marshal in La. Illness caused him to emigrate from N.Y., leaving "a lucrative practice in the law for a climate better suited" to his health. An AEI by Calhoun identifies Skinner as the U.S. Attorney for the Northern District of N.Y. and as "a gentleman of respectability." ALS in DNA, 103.

To Maj. C[hristopher] Vandeventer

War Department, 20th March 1819

I have heard with extreme regret that Mrs. Vandeventer was so much affected by the fatigue of travelling. I hope that your anticipation of the effects of the season on her health will be realized; but it appears to me that you ought not to venture on ["the rest of" *interlined*] your journey with her till you are fully assured of her increased strength. I must entreat ["of" *canceled*] you, not to hurry your movements on account of the Department. Were you to do so it would be to me a source of much regret. The business of the Department will all be completed before I will leave this [city], & I will make such arrangements that there will be no embarras[s]ment from your absence. Yours sincerely, J.C. Calhoun.

ALS in DLC, Christopher Vandeventer Papers.

From Edmund P. Gaines

Fernandina, Amelia Island, March 22nd 1819

I have the honor to acknowledge the receipt of your letter of the 26th ultimo, with an enclosure shewing that Mr. [Benjamin G.] Orr had failed to comply with his contract; and announcing the cession of the Floridas.

Colonel [Duncan Lamont] Clinch acted under General regulations requiring purchases to be made on the failure of the contractor; in whom I had ceased to repose confidence.

The purchases by Major [Hugh] McCall in Savannah have been made with great promptness, and upon the most economical terms—the supplies purchased were of good quality, and for the most part at lower prices than had been recently given for similar articles by the contractor's agent. The expiration of the contract system, added to the acquisition of the Floridas, equally & long desired, cannot but be viewed by the Army and our country as events of the greatest importance to both.

ALS in DNA, 1, G-144; draft in DNA, 11, 13292.

From Th[omas] S. Jesup, 3/22. Submits proposed regulations to govern all Quartermaster accounts and returns. LS in DNA, 1, J-163.

To A[bner] Lacock, [former Senator from Pa.,] Washington, 3/22. Answers his letter of yesterday, dated "Sunday" (ALS in DNA, 1, L-131). Gives assurance that Cadet [Joseph] Pentland is to receive his pay and subsistence from the date of his arrival at the Military Academy. "Notwithstanding the reasons stated by you" for the reinstatement of Lt. [Joseph P.] Bunting, "I still consider the view taken of the subject by me in my conversation with you to be the correct one." FC in DNA, 3, 10:284.

From Edmund P. Gaines

Fernandina, Amelia Island, March 23rd 1819

I have been honored with your letters of the 2nd and 4th instant.

The extraordinary ill health of the troops upon this Island—the sick amounting to near one-fourth of the whole number of men present—has induced me to direct the movement of the Infantry to Traders-hill. They marched this morning.

The news of the cession of the Floridas must have the effect of disarming the Semonola [*sic*] Indians of their hostility, restoring the fugitive blacks, and giving entire security to this frontier.

Under this persuasion I have concluded, until authorised to post my command at such points as, on the possession of the ceded territory may be deemed proper, to visit the Posts at Savannah and in the harbour of Charleston, where I shall be happy to receive your communications during the next month.

ALS in DNA, 1, G-145; CC in DNA, 11, 13292.

From Jac[ob] Brown

Albany, March 24th 1819

I have the honor to inform you that I have ordered the 6th Reg[iment,] with the detachment of recruits for the 5th, direct from this place to Olean upon the Allegany [*sic*] River, where they will take water transportation for Pittsburgh. The season being favorable for a march upon this Line will enable us to gain ten days by moving upon it.

Colo[nel Henry] Atkinson will soon be with you and explain every thing, I hope, to your satisfaction.

P.S. I leave this [place] for Brownville to-day.

ALS in DNA, 1, B-237; variant FC in DLC, Jacob Brown Papers, Letterbooks, 2:143.

From Ramsey Crooks and Robert Stuart, New York [City], 3/24. "In a letter addressed by us to John Jacob Astor, Esq., on 24th January 1818, which we understand was by that Gentleman transmitted to the Department of War, it is stated that 'we are told the concern of David Stone & Co. includes a man by the name of Bellows and others equally notorious for feats by no means praiseworthy on the frontiers of Canada during the late war.' We at the time felt fully authorized to make the above statement, but information lately obtained has satisfied us of our having been misinformed on this subject; and any unfavorable impression that portion of our communication may have created ought therefore no longer to exist." LS in DNA, 1, C-211; CC in DNA, 76 (M-1:6, p. 23).

To [the Rev.] J. H. Hobart, New York City

Department of War, 24 March 1819

I have received your communication of the 20th Inst[ant] in relation to the civilization of the Indians; and it is a source of real gratification to find that your opinions accord with those of the government. It is to my mind perfectly clear, that our system in relation to the Indians ought to undergo an entire and radical change. The great point is, by instruction to prepare them to become a part of our community. Any thing short of that desireable [*sic*] state will expose them to annihilation, and ourselves to great inconvenience. It is most desireable to make use of the Indians themselves to bring about so great a change; and where a native so intelligent as Williams, can be found, much good may be effected by giving a proper direction to his zeal.

The President [James Monroe] is not yet in possession of the requisite information to apply the fund appropriated at the last session to improve the condition of the Indians. Measures have been taken to acquire farther [*sic*] information, which however, will probably not be obtained, till after his return from his Southern tour. In the mean time, the Department of War will engage to contribute at the rate of $100 annually for four years towards the education of the Onondago youth to whom you refer. Accept of the assurance of my respect and esteem.

FC in DNA, 3, 10:385–386.

From Th[omas] S. Jesup, 3/24. Asks that the Ordnance Department be directed to deliver, to a place to be designated later, one six-pounder and one five-and-one-half-inch howitzer for the Missouri and Mississippi Expeditions. CC in DNA, 32, War Department.

From Joseph McMinn

Murfreesboro, Tennessee, 24th March 1819

I have had the honor to receive your letters of the 19th February and 6th Inst[ant] and in reply to the latter have to observe, that I will with great pleasure enter on the duties assigned, as soon as I regain a sufficient proportion of lost health to enable me to sustain the fatigues of the tour. This I hope may be some time in the latter part of April or first of May next.

I very much regret that my communications did not arrive at an earlier period, tho: I trust a recurrence to their dates will evince, that their passage has been protracted by a failure in the mail.

A part of those papers having special relation to the sales of emigrant improvements, renders it very desirable that I should be apprised of your opinion touching the propriety of the measure, and also what disposition shall be made of the Notes taken for payment in the different cases. They now stand endorsed to me by an error committed in the clerk['s] department, which had been carried to such an extent before I had an opportunity of correcting it as to justify its continuance through the whole transaction. You will please advise me whether I am or not, to endorse the notes to you, as I first intended they should be, and also to whom I may deliver them.

It further becomes my duty to state that in several instances an adverse possession has been held against the Lessee, in which cases they have asked me for a surrender of the Notes and I in answer have stated to them, that I would represent their situation to you and ask for your instructions as my guide. Which please address to me at Washington, Rhea County, Tennessee, so as to enable me to avail myself of your instructions on my arrival in the [Cherokee] Nation.

LS in DNA, 77 (M-271:2, frames 1317–1319); FC in DNA, 75 (M-208:14).

To Charles [R.] Marshall, [Charleston ?], S.C., 3/24. Appoints him to be a Cadet. DS in DNA, 15, 1818, 183.

From David A. Ogden, [former Representative from N.Y.,] Washington, 3/24. He and his associates claim the right of preemption to about 220,000 remaining acres of land in about nine reservations now claimed by the Seneca Indians. He traces this right back to a treaty by which N.Y. relinquished it to Mass. in 1786. He and his associates expect to hold a treaty with the Senecas next summer in an effort to obtain a cession of these remaining acres. They want the U.S. to send someone to attend the treaty. LS in DNA, 1, O-17.

To Decius Wadsworth, 3/24. Orders him to deliver to James Johnson one six-pounder and one five-and-one-half-inch howitzer, in addition to the ordnance "already provided for the use of the Steam boats on the Mississippi." LS in DNA, 31, War Department; FC in DNA, 3, 10:285.

To John Williams, [Senator from Tenn.,] Knoxville, 3/24. Calhoun cannot find in War Department files the regulations for the government of the Military Academy proposed by its academic staff. He does remember having loaned them to Williams during the recent session of Congress. He asks Williams to return them or to report what he can. FC in DNA, 3, 10:286.

To Lewis Cass, Detroit

Department of War, 25th March 1819

A warrant has this day been issued in your favor for ten thousand five hundred and fifty dollars to pay the Annuities due to the following tribes of Indians for the present year, viz: Ottawas, three thousand three hundred dollars; Chippewas, two thousand eight hundred dollars; and Pottawatomies, four thousand four hundred and fifty dollars, which is to be paid to them in specie, and arrangements have been made with the Treasury Department to place the amount to your credit at Chillicothe.

The appropriation for the Indian Department requires that a due regard be paid to economy in all of its disbursements; and it is hoped that you will be able to distribute the annuity in the present form of payment without incurring the expence of making considerable issues of provisions. I would suggest whether payment could not be made more conveniently at their several villages and thereby avoid those large assemblages which are both expensive and injurious to their morals.

LS in DNA, 76 (M-1:6, pp. 25–26); FC in DNA, 72, D:273.

To Auguste Chouteau, St. Louis, 3/25. Appoints him a commissioner to negotiate a new treaty with the Kickapoos and with "any other tribe who may have a title to the land ceded by the treaty" of 9/25/1818; gives him instructions, especially as to the issuance of any necessary rations under the most economical contract he can obtain. LS and CC (the latter in French) in MoSHi, Auguste Chouteau Papers; FC in DNA, D:272.

To Capt. James Gadsden, Mobile Point

Department of War, March 25, 1819

I will leave this [place] on the 29th inst[ant] in company with the President [James Monroe] for South Carolina. It was the wish of the President to proceed as far as New Orleans, but he has declined under the apprehension that the season will not permit him to proceed so far along the coast.

The acquisition of the Floridas gives a new character to our South Western frontier and will greatly enlarge the duties of your Corps, as well as that of the Topographical Engineers. We will probably have formal possession of them in August, and it is intended, as soon as it can be conveniently done, to have the coast and country carefully examined. If your duties will admit of it, yourself and Capt. [Hugh] Young will be selected for the exploring party.

Since I received your communication of the 27th December certain information has been received through General [Edmund P.] Gaines, as well as Commissioners appointed by the State of Georgia, that the St. Marys, except in very wet seasons, is not connected with the Okafanokee [*sic*] Swamp. It would seem by a reference to the maps of Florida, that a water communication might be formed at no great expense between the Atlantic and the Gulph [*sic*] of Mexico, by the St. Johns, and that the connection would be, either in peace or war, of the first importance to the country.

You suggest the propriety of employing Capt. Young to examine the inland communication between Mobile Bay & Lakes Borgne and Porchartrain [*sic*]. I deem it very important to have a survey of the communication and hope that Capt. Young will have it in his power, to give it his early attention.

FC in DNA, 3, 10:286.

To E[dmund] P. Gaines, Fernandina, 3/25. "Your letter of the 12th instant enclosing a sketch of the inhabited part of East Florida, with Field Notes by Lieut[enant Daniel E.] Burch, has been received. The Sketch is an interesting one, and affords fuller and more correct information of the country than any previously in the possession of the Department." LS in DNA, 11, 14021; FC in DNA, 3, 10:288.

To Dan[iel] Garrison, Salem, N.J., 3/25. Answers his acceptance of 3/8 (ALS in DNA, 1, B-205) of Calhoun's proposal on 2/19 to cancel Garrison's contract for supplying logs to the U.S.; refuses to grant Garrison's plea for interest as compensation for his alleged loss on logs that U.S. agents refused to buy because they were not needed but which Garrison made no other effort to sell. FC in DNA, 3, 10:287.

To George Gibson, T[homas] S. Jesup, and Decius Wadsworth, 3/25. Encloses a copy of the sixth section of the statute of 7/16/1798 concerning contracts; orders them, in compliance, to send to Second Comptroller [Richard Cutts] "the original contracts made by your Department." FC in DNA, 3, 10:288; LS with En (Gibson's copy) in DNA, 43, 25; LS with En (Wadsworth's copy) in DNA, 31, War Department, 3.

To Richard Graham, Indian Agent for Ill. Territory, 3/25. Arrangements have been made for the Receiver of Public Monies at Edwardsville to provide Graham with $1,000 in specie for this year's annuity payments to the Ottawas, Chippewas, and Potawatomies residing on the Illinois and Milwaukee Rivers and their tributaries and near the southwestern shores of Lake Michigan. FC in DNA, 72, D:275.

From Peter H. Green, Boston, 3/25. Transmits his accounts for the quarter that ended on 2/28. More than $10,000 will be due to him as a rations contractor by 5/31, and he has issued a draft for that sum; he will need it to fulfill his commitments, especially because his contractual obligations are to be extended through June. ALS in DNA, 1, G-136.

From [Bvt. Col.] J[acob] Hindman, Fort McHenry, [Md.,] 3/25. As a test, he has kept five pairs of the shoes manufactured by one Young in constant use since 1/13 and has concluded that Young's shoes are good for Army use, although some pairs now need mending. LS in DNA, 1, H-201.

From Gerard T. Hopkins and Andrew Ellicott, Baltimore, 3/25. Last year they visited Calhoun to recommend John Shaw for appointment to the proposed position of Indian Agent at Sandusky, [O.]. In behalf of the Baltimore Yearly Meeting of the Society of Friends (Quakers), they reiterate their recommendation of Shaw, who has been the Society's employee in work with the Indians. LS in DNA, 11, 13888.

To John Johnston, Indian Agent, Piqua, O.

Department of War, 25 March, 1819

A Warrant has this day been issued in your favor for $17,225 to pay the annuity due the following tribes of Indians for the present year, with the amount specified to each, viz: Wyandots, $6,725; Delawares, $5,500; Shawnese, $4,000; Seneca, $1,000; as also for the sum of $14,480.13 to reimburse certainly [*sic*] friendly Indians for losses sustained during the late war with Great Britain, provided for by the 12th article of the treaty of the 29th Septem[be]r 1817, to wit: to the Wyandots, at Upper Sandusky, $4,319.39; Senecas at Lower Sandusky, $3,989.24; to the Indians at Lewis and Scoutash's towns, $1,227.50; to the Delawares for the use of the Indians who suffered losses at Greentown and at Jeromestown, $3,956.50; to the representatives of Henibis, a Delaware Indian, $348.50, to be paid at Wapaghkonetta; and to the Shawnese an additional sum of $420 to be paid at Wapaghkonetta; and to the Senecas the additional sum of $219 to be paid at Wapaghkonetta, which is to be paid in specie, and arrangements have been made with the Treasury Dep[artmen]t to forward the whole am[oun]t to you accordingly at your Agency.

The appropriation for the Indian Department &c., &c., &c., &c., [a marginal note at this point in the letterbook beside the FC shows that this letter was concluded with the appeal for economy in Indian expenses that was written on this day to Lewis Cass].

FC in DNA, 72, D:274; CC in DNA, 76 (M-1:6).

From Dr. James Mease

Philadelphia, March 25 1819

Your letter [of 3/11] to Mr. [Robert] Walsh [Jr.] requesting hints for subjects of inquiry by the scientific members of the expedition under Major [Stephen H.] Long, was referred to the Amer[ican] Philos[ophical] Soc[iety], and a Committee appointed to take the subject into Consideration. What they have done, I do not know; but as some ideas occurred to me in relation thereto, I put them on paper, and herewith have the pleasure to send them, as a volunteer offering, not doubting of their being received in the same good part, in which they are written. Permit me to add that the measure of attaching the naturalists to the expedition has met with the warmest praises of every friend to science in this City.

ALS in DNA, 1, M-259.

To R[eturn] J. Meigs, [Sr.,] Washington, 3/25. A[ndrew] Jackson has been ordered "to remove the intruders on the Cherokee land, on a requisition from you for that purpose, should it be found necessary." Meigs is to "require their departure, within a fixed period," and then "select some of the most wealthy and influential from among them for prosecution" under statutes of 3/30/1802 and 4/29/1816. Certain pension applications will be submitted to a Congressional Committee on Pensions. Meigs is to make careful reports about the Cherokees' claims for indemnities for alleged damages done by the militia during the War of 1812. Richard Riley's claim should be made against the Cherokee nation, not the U.S. LS in NcD; FC in DNA, 3, 10:287; PC in Carter, ed., *Territorial Papers,* 18:591–592.

To Pierre Menard, Sub-Agent for Ill. Territory, 3/25. Arrangements have been made for the Receiver of Public Monies at Kaskaskia to provide Menard with $300 in specie for this year's annuity payment to the Piankashaws. FC in DNA, 72, D:275.

From Jo[seph] Jo[nes] Monroe, Washington, 3/25. Recommends that Robert C. Jones, son of former Capt. Thomas Jones of Nelson County, Va., be given an Army commission. The son is now serving as a Quartermaster Sgt. in the 4th [Infantry] Regiment at Pensacola. Monroe encloses a letter to himself from Jones [dated 1/27], expressing Jones's desire for advancement. ALS with En in DNA, 11, 13544.

To William Prince, Indian Agent, Vincennes, 3/25. In accordance with a treaty's stipulation, arrangements have been made for the Receiver of Public Monies at Vincennes to provide Prince with specie for this year's annuity payments of $3,500 to the Weas and $500 to the Kickapoos. FC in DNA, 72, D:275.

From David Robinson, Bennington, [Vt.,] 3/25. Acknowledges Calhoun's letter of 3/12. Robinson has delivered to [Heman] Allen the [pension] rolls that were in Robinson's possession; he will send to Washington promptly the few accounts and vouchers that remain in his hands. ALS in DNA, 1, R-127.

To Benjamin "Stevenson [*actually* Stephenson]," 3/25. Appoints him [the Sub-Agent at Edwardsville, Ill.] a commissioner, jointly with Auguste Chouteau, who has instructions, to negotiate a new treaty with the Kickapoos "and other tribes of Indians who may have a claim to the land ceded to the United States by the treaty" of 9/25/1818. "Your compensation will be at the rate of eight dollars per diem for the time actually engaged, and will be paid on your certificate of honor to that effect." FC in DNA, 72, D:272–273.

To S[ylvanus] Thayer, 3/25. Asks for a copy of the regulations of the Military Academy adopted on 7/23/1818, to replace the copy loaned recently to Senator John Williams and not returned; wants the replacement copy because "a new Edition . . . is about to be issued." FC in DNA, 3, 10:288.

To William Turner, Indian Agent, Fort Wayne, Ind., 3/25. He is to receive at Cincinnati and to pay $17,300 to the Miami Indians and $600 to the Eel River Indians for their annuities for 1819. FC in DNA, 72, D:274.

From [2nd] Lt. George Blaney, 3/26. Requests a remittance of $25,000 to Nathaniel Cox at New Orleans for construction costs for fortifications at Chef Menteur and the Rigolets and a remittance of $26,500 to Capt. James Gadsden for such costs at Dauphin Island and Mobile Point. FC in DNA, 21, 1:51.

To George Hunt and William Cotton, 3/26. Commissions them to appraise the improvements on the land ceded by the Delaware Indians under the treaty of 10/3/1818; Hunt and Cotton will receive "reasonable compensation." FC in DNA, 3, 10:289.

To John Overton, [Nashville,] 3/26. Appoints him a commissioner to negotiate with the Chickasaws for a cession of their reservation mentioned in an enclosed Senate resolution, which, with an enclosed copy of a treaty, will serve as instructions to the commission. FC in DNA, 72, D:252–253.

From D[ecius] Wadsworth, 3/26. Recommends the purchase at $500 of a 10-volume French treatise on artillery, of which only 30 copies were published. FC in DNA, 32, 2:201.

From D[ecius] Wadsworth, 3/26. Answering Calhoun's letter of 3/25, Wadsworth states that he has always obeyed the regulation that requires copies of contracts to be deposited in certain proper places. FC in DNA, 32, 2:200–201.

To Robert Weakley and [Newton] Cannon, 3/26. Appoints them commissioners to serve with John Overton in seeking to obtain from the Chickasaws a certain reservation. FC in DNA, 72, D:253.

From Col. H[enry] Atkinson

Greenbush, [N.Y.,] March 27th 1819

I have the honor to inform you that my [6th Infantry] Regiment arrived at this post yesterday in good condition; we lost but one man on the march, occasioned by an unfortunate, or rather accidental death. Only two desertions have occur[r]ed since the order for the march was rec[eive]d, and to judge from the good spirits manifested by all grades, we shall have a successful movement. I had caused all our supplies to be in readiness on our arrival here, and as transportation can be had at the shortest notice, we shall be able to recommence our march as soon as the recruits arrive, who are expected in two days; when, I shall take my departure for Washington City, with a hope of reaching there by the 3rd of April, & at the furthest, by the 5th.

LS in DNA, 1, A-91.

To Col. Henry Atkinson, Washington, 3/27. Calhoun regrets that he will not be in Washington when Atkinson visits there before taking command of the very important 9th Military Department. His first objective, in his new command, will be to protect the Northwestern frontier and to maintain, if possible, friendly relations with the Indians. The proposed posts on the Missouri should help to control these tribes and to protect the U.S. fur trade. Foreign traders are to be excluded from the area. FC in DNA, 3, 10:291–292; PC in Jameson, ed., *Correspondence*, pp. 159–160.

To Lewis Cass, Detroit, 3/27. Encloses his commission to negotiate a treaty with the Chippewas, at costs as small as possible, for a cession of their land in the Saginaw Bay area of Mich. Territory, preferably in exchange for other land west of Mich. or beyond the Mississippi. "The rapid and close settlement of the peninsula of Michigan is considered important in a national point of view, and this can best be effected by an entire extinguishment of the Indian title if it can be effected on fair terms; but if it can not, it will only remain to contract their population on reservations of reasonable extent." Because annuities paid to Indians "encourage idleness," Calhoun hopes that Cass will be able to persuade the Chippewas to accept any annuity in such a way that the U.S. would apply it "to the support of schools, or some other purpose useful to the nation." LS with En in DNA, 76 (M-1:6, pp. 37–43); FC in DNA, 3, 10:290–291; PC in Jameson, ed., *Correspondence*, pp. 157–158.

To A[NDREW] ELLICOTT, Baltimore

Department of War, 27 March 1819

The letter [dated 3/25] from yourself and Mr. [Gerard T.] Hopkins on the part of the Committee of the Society of Friends of Baltimore recommendatory of Mr. [John] Shaw has been received.

The Department is of opinion that the Act of Congress does not authorize the appointment of an Agent at Sandusky in addition to the two Agents at Fort Wayne [and] at Piqua, and is disposed to assign the duties at Sandusky to Mr. [John] Johns[t]on, the Agent at Piqua.

FC in DNA, 3, 10:293.

From R.W. Gill, Washington, 3/27. Itemizes $33,122.08 of claims by the city of Baltimore against the War Department that originated in the War of 1812—at Fort McHenry, for example; acknowledges that $15,000 have been paid so far; seeks a further payment of $8,000 for claims that have already been allowed, plus money for any additional items that Calhoun can now approve. An AEI by Calhoun referred this letter to [Richard] Cutts. ALS with En in DNA, 63, 1817:43.

From George Graham

Washington, March 27th 1819

I must take the liberty of soliciting of you, a Cadet[']s appointment for Mr. Peter [*actually* Daniel] Walker so soon as he shall attain the proper age, he being now about 12 years old. He is a fine intelligent lad, and is the son of Mr. Joseph Walker, who lives near Alexandria in Louisiana.

ALS in DNA, 15, 1820, 62.

To Th[omas] S. Jesup, Quartermaster General

Department of War, 27 March 1819

The important movements on the Mississippi and Missouri render your presence necessary at St. Louis, to which place you will repair as soon as your official duties will admit. In discharge of your duties of your office as connected with the movements referred to, you are vested with full and discretionary powers; and its [*sic*] confidently expected from your energy and discretion, that measures which you may adopt will be economical and effectual. You will keep the Department informed of all your measures. You will cause to be purchased the laws of the United States with the acts since pass[e]d for the use of Colo[nel Henry] Atkinson, the Commander of the 9th Military Department.

LS in ScU-SC; FC in DNA, 3, 10:290; PC in House Document No. 110, 16th Cong., 2nd Sess.

To Reuben Lewis, [Indian Agent and Commissioner in Ark., Mo. Territory,] 3/27. Orders him to survey the land reserved to the Quapaws by the treaty of 8/24/1818 with them, to ban and have expelled all intruders from the reserved area after the survey, and to serve as Agent to the Quapaws in addition to the [Western] Cherokees. FC in DNA, 72, D:277; PC in Carter, ed., *Territorial*

Papers, 19:57; PC in *American State Papers: Indian Affairs,* 2:179–180.

To A[lexander] Macomb, Detroit, 3/27. Calhoun protests that there is frequent evidence of extravagance and irregularity among the Army posts under Macomb's jurisdiction along the Upper Great Lakes. "Nothing is so calculated to render the Army unpopular." In particular, Calhoun disapproves a recent requisition for Quartermaster stores for the post of 195 men at Mackinac for the year 1819, which seems to be excessive "both in amount and kind" and does not comply with regulations. "You will institute an immediate enquiry in the present case, correct the evils complained of, and report thereon to this department." FC in DNA, 3, 10:293.

To Morris S. Miller, Utica, N.Y., 3/27. Commissions him to represent the U.S. "as the general protector of the Indian tribes" in forthcoming negotiations between N.Y. proprietors, some Mass. commissioners, and the eastern Senecas. If the proposed, 30,000-acre Allegheny reservation is as suitable for the Senecas as the proprietors allege, Miller should urge their acceptance of it; but Miller can also assure these Senecas that any who can obtain land among the western Senecas of the Lower Sandusky reservation or from other western Indians will receive U.S. encouragement to emigrate thither. Miller is to make certain that the eastern Senecas understand everything that the proprietors may propose and give their assent freely to any treaty. The expenses of the negotiations are to be paid by the proprietors; but the U.S. will pay Miller $8 daily. FC in DNA, 3, 10:289–290; PC in House Document No. 70, 16th Cong., 2nd Sess.; PC in Jameson, ed., *Correspondence,* pp. 156–157.

To G[erard] Steddiford, New York [City], 3/27. "The two months having elapsed for which you and the two Judge Advocates were retained in service [after the adjournment of the court-martial for N.Y. militia delinquents], it is desireable [*sic*] that the accounts of the Members for their services on the Court should be adjusted." Calhoun asks Steddiford to procure the submission of each member's charges to Marshal [Thomas Morris], who has been ordered to "transmit them to this Department for a final allowance." FC in DNA, 3, 10:294.

To Lawrence Taliaferro, 3/27. Appoints him "Indian Agent at St. Peters on the Upper Mississippi, where you will repair so soon as a military post shall be established at that place, and should the Senate at their next session advise and consent thereto, you will be commissioned accordingly." Instructs him to execute and submit an enclosed bond. "In discharging the various duties of your office, you will be governed by such instructions as you may hereafter receive from this Department. Your compensation will be at the rate of $1,300 per annum." FC in DNA, 72, D:276; PC in Carter, ed., *Territorial Papers*, 10:823.

To Dean Weymouth, Washington, 3/27. On 6/1 he will succeed William S. Washington as a Clerk in Calhoun's office, at the same salary that Washington receives. Until then, Weymouth, at his own present salary, will "perform duty in the Bounty Land Office," effective "immediately." FC in DNA, 3, 10:293.

To Alexander Wolcott, Jr., Indian Agent, [Vincennes]

Department of War, 27 Mar[ch] 1819

Under an act of Congress of the 3d of March last, authorizing the President of the United States to transfer Indian Agents, you are hereby assigned to the duties of the Agency at Chicago, where your presence is immediately required; you will therefore repair to your post as soon as practicable, and on your arrival report to this Department.

FC in DNA, 72, D:277.

From Maj. William Bradford, Fort Smith, Ark. [Territory], "Private," 3/28. Some Spaniards recently came within U.S. territory, "whether for trade, or to sound the feelings of the Indians in respect to their disposition for hostilities, I have not yet learned." Bradford has employed a spy to ascertain their object and will attempt to arrest any who may repeat the invasion. A large council of Indians (Osages, Pawnees, Arapahoes, and other tribes) should be allowed to visit "Washington, that they may see the strength of our government, & enter into some treaty with it, as they do not acknowledge themselves under the protection of the

U[nited] States. I am the more strongly induced to make this suggestion, as, should a war at any time occur with Spain, they might prove the same auxiliary force to that country, as did the Northwestern Indians to the British during the late war." ALS in DNA, 1, B-287; PC in Carter, ed., *Territorial Papers,* 19:59–60.

To the CREEK DEPUTATION (a Talk)

Department of War, 28 Mar[ch], 1819

I have listened with attention to what you have said in relation to your claim to the land in Florida occupied by the Seminoles. You say you are one people, and that you only have the right to dispose of their land: But we cannot assent to this argument. The Seminoles have long inhabited the country, and you know that they are our enemy; they have made war on us, and we have been compelled to incur very heavy expense to protect our people from their cruelty. We have a right to dictate the terms on which we will give them peace; and it is conceived to be for the advantage of us all, of you, the Seminoles and ourselves, that they should remove from their present settlements, and form new ones within the limits of your country. Should they be permitted to remain where they now are, you well know the consequences. Emissaries will again come among them, and under the deceitful character of friends, again excite them to war against us. It is our wish to avoid these consequences, and we expect your coöperation in the good work. We expect that you will assign them a tract of country for a new home and take them under your protection. We, on our part, will furnish the necessary means and expense of transportation, and will also contribute to their subsistence 'till they can support themselves in their new residence. You will on your return, I hope, communicate these views to them, and use your influence to bring them to a determination which will ultimately be to the benefit of all.

Brothers, You state that the sum which has been paid is not equal to the damages which you sustained in the late war, and that in justice, you ought to receive the remainder. The power to remunerate you belongs solely to Congress, and when they appr[opr]iated the sum of $85,000, it was estimated that it was sufficient. Whether an additional sum will be voted to remunerate you for your losses rests solely with the justice and wisdom of Congress.

Brothers, To what I am now going to say I wish for your most serious attention, as it is very nearly connected with your prosperity and happiness. You know that you can no longer live by hunting. The game has gradually disappeared, and there is not now sufficient for your people. What will be the consequence? Either you must dwindle away, or you must submit to work and live like your white neighbours. Your own experience ought to convince you, that our mode of living is greatly preferable to yours. Look at the difference! We, from a handful, have become a great and happy people. The Indians, on the contrary, have become few, feeble and miserable. As your friend, it is my sincere wish to see you prosperous and happy; and it is for this reason that I desire to see you abandon your old customs and imitate your white neighbors. To effect this great change, you must establish schools, learn to spin and weave and cultivate the ground. We are willing to give you aid, if you will but adopt our advice. The Cherokees have listened to our talk. They have set apart a large tract of land, which is to be sold and the proceeds to be applied under the direction of their father, the President of the United States, to learn [*sic*] their young people to read, write and support themselves by their own labour. Were you to do the same, or were you to apply a part of your annuity to so good an use, your people would soon experience its good effect. On your return, I hope, you will communicate this advice to the Big Warrior and the Creek nation. He is said to be a wise man; and I am sure he will see that what I have said is good. Should he and you adopt it, you will do much for yourselves and children; but should the advice which is given from a regard for your happiness be neglected, I see no other alternative, but that you must gradually dwindle away and disappear as a people.

FC in DNA, 72, D:278–280.

To Callender Irvine, Philadelphia, 3/29. Encloses a copy of a Senate resolution of late 1/1819 indicating a desire to require by law that the Army should be clothed in the products of U.S. manufacturers only; orders Irvine to report comparatively the cost, durability, and quality of U.S. and foreign clothing. FC in DNA, 3, 10:292.

To A[ndrew] Jackson, Nashville, 3/29. Appoints him to serve with John McKee and Daniel Burnet as commissioners to negotiate a treaty with the Choctaws, if the commissioners feel that "there is a strong probability of success." Encloses Jackson's commission, dated 3/29 and signed by both James Monroe and Calhoun (DS in DLC, Andrew Jackson Papers, 8671). Gives to Jackson the usual instructions as to such negotiations, including a reminder that economy should be practiced; and directs him specifically to use as a guide the instructions given last year to McKee and Burnett "as far as they are now applicable." FC in DNA, 3, 10:294; PC in Bassett, ed., *Correspondence*, 2:414.

From Richard M. Johnson

Great Crossings, [Ky.,] 29th March 1819

The Steam Boat Calhoun was lau[n]ched at Leestown on Friday; the novelty of the scene attracted the attention of the citizens of Frankfort and its vicinity. An account of the lau[n]ch will I presume he noticed in the papers. Leestown is only one mile below Frankfort on the Kentucky River. It is impossible to describe to you the distress of this Country on account of circulating medium. Loans cannot be obtained from B[an]ks or individuals—both are calling in their debts by wholesale, & nothing can be purchased on credit. This will produce much difficulty ["with" *interlined*] all classes of the community; and those under contract with the Gov[ernmen]t will feel it to their disadvantage, and the Gov[ernmen]t also without very liberal policy as to the payment of money. For ordinary years your policy has been liberal, & if you did not know that facts which I state in relation to the universal pressure of the times are correct, I should be unwilling to press this subject upon you at this time. On the Army [rations] Contract with Col. Gipson [George Gibson] the two last quarters will be $70,000, 35,000 each. Provisions to the amount of the two first advances have been provided & arrangements making for the whole year as this spring furnishes the last good opportunity for supplies the remainder of the year even to next January. On the transportation Contract with the Gov[ernmen]t from the estimate of Gen[era]l [Thomas S.] Jesup it amounts to upwards of $120,000. When the last advances were made a ballance [*sic*] remained of about $30,000.

I now enclose to you the evidence that justifyed [*sic*] my declarations to you that ["more than" *interlined*] double that expence would be incurred on that point the first year, & what is $50,000 to the nation compared with the object of these establishments[?] The proof to which I allude is the certificate of the two Maj[o]rs of [*one word illegible*] Col. [James] Morrison['s] letter &c. who speak from calculation & long experience. I also enclose you the Tonnage upon which Gen[era]l Jesup made his calculation, by which you will ["see" *interlined*] that he predicates his calculation upon $6 per hundred to the Yellow Stone, whereas the certificates forwarded establish $10 to the Martain [that is, Martin] Cantoonment [*sic*] 450 miles. I am ignorant of this matter & have no personal knowledge on this subject. I am certain of one thing, that my Brother [James Johnson] wishes nothing unreasonable & hereafter under all the facts & circumstances the price can be fixed by the parties or disinterested referees. The object of this letter is to seriously impress on your mind the impossibility of discharging the debts which my Brother has incur[r]ed under his Engagement without an advance of 50 or $60,000 at least. He has been devoted to the objects of the Gov[ernmen]t for 6 months past. I may say 12 months: for he was preparing as soon as the papers announced your determination ["to establish Posts at Yellow Stone &c." *interlined*]; he was convinced of two facts. 1st that without Steam & Keel boats united the establishments could never be made.

2[nd]ly. He was certain that no man in the Western Country, or indeed in the U.S. could effect the object of the Gov[ernmen]t without long previous preparation. These things he anticipated & he ["is" *interlined*] now nearly ready to commence this grand expedition: His steam boat "Johnson" has been ready for a considerable time[;] the "Calhoun" is lau[n]ched & will be ready in ten days. The Thomas Jefferson is hourly expected from Wheeling with the stores of Gov[ernmen]t. The whole expence direct & incidental have [*sic*] been incurred[;] much has been paid, considerable is now becoming due. My Brother has gone to Louisville to make final arrangements with his steam Boats & provisions &c. And while he is devoted wholely [*sic*] & exclusively ["to these objects" *interlined*] the payment of demands & his other arrangements have devolved upon me and I find I shall be obliged ["to" *interlined*] put off the payments of debts now due, without some arrangements with Richard Smith Esq. Cashier; & with that view I have this day given him power & authority to receive all such monies as may be advanced to him from the War Department on the Contracts of my Brother James. I can assure you of one fact, that the time & the resources of my Brother will be exclusively devoted to the public business, & he has made his arrangements positively to accompany the expedition in person to the highest point of distination [*sic*], & the execution of his other duties ["here" *interlined*] public & private will devolve upon me & nothing shall suffer in relation to his duties to the Gov[ernmen]t. The establishment of these military Positions will cost 3 or $400,000 more the first year over any other year, and the Government must not permit those who bear the brunt to suffer in credit; & without your timely assistance that will be the case. One circumstance alone constitutes a sufficient inducement to advance at least $100,000 more this than any subsequent year, that the whole expence of the means of transportation for subsequent years falls upon this year & at this time the pres[s]ure is felt on that account. For the advances made this year any subsequent year would be sufficient [to cover all expenses for] the 12 months & make all things easy; for another year the steam boats, Keels &c worth $150,000 will be paid for & ready for the business. If you were to advance $100,000 more on the transportation contract the Gov[ernmen]t would be perfectly safe; for rest assured Sir if there is not a perfect willingness to meet this expence the expedition had better stop short, far short of its distination, a thing that I should much regret as the public mind has contemplated this matter with delight and the whole administration [has been] strengthened by it in the Western Country. In fact the whole Western community is alive on this subject. All things are ready, to accomplish the object. Nothing is wanting but resources & these the Gov[ernmen]t alone can ["alone" *interlined*] furnish at this time; I shall conclude by a recapitulation of money matters. Two last quarters on contract with Col. Gipson [George Gibson] not yet advanced will make the sum of [$]70,000[;] the whole of former advances expended & this now expending in preparing for last deposits. On transportation contract by statement of Gen[era]l Jesup $30,000 due all of which & more expended in preparation &c. making $100,000. But add for transportation at least $100,000 in addition, the expence incur[r]ed by providing all the means total [$]200,000. The transportation [advance] ought to be perhaps on the St. Louis Contract, a great part of it at least. The advances made my Brother were upon requisitions, which have all been provided & altho advances have been liberal, the whole am[oun]t has been expended for the Gov[ernmen]t. I refer you particularly to the papers sent with this.

ALS with En in DNA, 1, J-220. NOTE: The enclosure is a letter from James Johnson at Louisville to Richard M. Johnson dated 3/26.

From ALEXANDER KERR

Bank of the Metropolis, [Washington,] March 29th 1819

As you are about leaving the City for some time I beg leave to address you on the subject of Mr. [Benjamin G.] Orr's draft for $3,102—that you may leave such direction respecting it as you may think necessary, in case he may be allowed any part of his claim in your absence.

My understanding, when he gave the bill & when I left it in the [War] Office, [was] that his funds were pledged to the Br[anch] Bank [here of the Bank of the United States] for $12,000 & that my bill w[oul]d come next after—& that [I might ultimately receive a payment] from his funds on the old contract. I hope you will so direct it, that I may have a chance of getting the bill paid, as it has placed me in a very disagreeable situation.

Wishing you & Mrs. C—— a pleasant journey & safe return, I have the honor to [be] . . . .

ALS in DNA, 1, K-34.

To John McKee, Choctaw Agency, 3/29. Informs him that Andrew Jackson has been commissioned to join McKee and [Daniel] Burnet, under their commissions dated 5/2/1818, to negotiate a treaty with the Choctaws. Nevertheless, it "is the wish of the government that a Treaty should not be held unless there is a strong probability of obtaining a successful one. You will report" to Jackson "on such probability," and Jackson will decide if, when, and where any negotiations shall begin. FC in DNA, 3, 10:294–295; CC in DLC, Andrew Jackson Papers, 8674.

From William Wirt

Office of the Attorney General, March 29th 1819

Assuming the facts stated by the [U.S.] District Attorney for Delaware touching the title to the Pea-Patch, as being correctly stated, and as being *all* the facts involving the title, there can be no doubt that the title derived by the U.S. from the State of Delaware is compleat [*sic*]. It would be more satisfactory to me, however, to inspect the various charters, grants and conveyances on which the title of Delaware and [New] Jersey to the island in question, respectively rest, before I give an opinion on which your Department may think it proper to act. If those Documents are not in your office or in that of the Department of State, I submit to you the propriety of instructing the District Attorneys of Delaware and Jersey to procure and forward a full & compleat deduction of the title of each State, severally.

LS in DNA, 1, W-256; FC in DNA, 112, A1:59–60; FC in DNA, 112, A2:52–53.

From William Wirt

Off[ice] of the Atto[rney] Gen[era]l, March 29th 1819

I took it for granted that the verbal answer I had the honor of giving you, as to the necessity of the seal of the County Court of Virg[ini]a [being added to certain documents that you discussed with me], was sufficient to the purpose, and trust that no inconvenience has resulted from this impression. The papers are now returned, and I have the honor to be . . . .

FC in DNA, 112, A1:59; FC in DNA, 112, A2:52.

From Henry W. DeSaussure

Charleston, [S.C.,] 30th March 1819

Dr. Findlay [James E.B. Finley, M.D.,] of this City requests that I would make known to you the wishes & the claims of a young gentleman of Beaufort, to be admitted to the Military Academy at West Point. His name is [Richard Laboulardrie De] Treville. He is a grandson of an old Revolutionary officer, who served in the South Carolina line, during the Revolutionary war, with reputation. I believe it was in the Regiment of artillery. He is represented to me to be a young gentleman of good character.

I told the Doctor that I was sure of your desire to serve the descendants of the old officers, if there was room in the Establishment. He will explain the claims of the young man more fully, when he has the pleasure of seeing you here, on the arrival of the President [James Monroe].

I regret that I shall not be here on the arrival of the President. It w[oul]d have given me much pleasure to have paid my respects to him; as well as to have greeted you on your return to your native State, which feels no ordinary Interest in you. May I not hope that the President & yourself will return by the upper rout[e], & take Columbia, in your way to Washington? He w[oul]d be rec[eive]d as well as yourself with the respect due to the talents & patriotism, which have rendered distinguished services to our Country.

ALS in DNA, 15, 1819, 68.

Lewis Edwards, Acting Chief Clerk, War Department, to Capt. Samuel Babcock, Philadelphia, 3/30. Orders him to obtain and to transmit copies of the charters, grants, and conveyances on the basis of which Del. and N.J. claim the Pea Patch. Attorney General [William Wirt] wants to inspect these documents before giving an opinion as to the "right of the United States" to that island. FC in DNA, 3, 10:295.

From R[ICHARD] GRAHAM

Indian Agency, Illinois State, March 30th 1819

Since the Territory of Illinois has passed into a State Government many applications have been made for licenses to trade with the Indians on the East side of the Mississippi. Never having the power to grant licenses, I have in every case refused, but have advised the persons making applications to continue their trade under their old licenses untill I should hear from you on that subject.

I have been applied to by some of the Chiefs of the Potawatamie [*sic*] Nation of Indians for permission for them to visit the President of the U[nited] States [James Monroe].

The Wampum has been sent to the Chiefs of the Confederacy inviting them to council, as I understand to consolidate more closely the different bands of Chippeways, Ottaways & Potawatamies forming the Confederacy—with a view to their residence on the lands ceded by the U.S. to them by [the] Treaty of St. Louis of Aug[us]t 1816—the com[missione]rs for running the Indian Boundary line on the part of the Indians requested of me to obtain for them previous to the meeting of their Council answers to the following queries. Does the President intend they shall make war on the Sacs & Foxes in case they refuse to give up the Country they now live on, & which was ceeded [*sic*] to the Confederate Nation by the United States? If war becomes necessary to obtain possession of the Country thus ceeded what aid are they to receive from the President? In case of war will all supplies be withheld from the Sacs & Foxes?

When running by the Indian Boundary line I was followed by a large band of Win[n]ebagoes to Rock Island, who del[ivere]d to me the enclosed speech on the part of their Nation, which, they wish should be communcated to the President.

ALS in DNA, 1, G-68.

From Richard M. Johnson, "Not Official"

Blue Spring, near Great Crossing[s, Ky.,]
30th March [1819]

The papers will give an eligant [*sic*] account of the Launch[ing] of the Steam Boat "Calhoun," the first in the bosom of the State [of Ky.], & christened amidst the acclamations of a numerous & intelligent audience. Altho I was in hopes that my Brother could go on with his engagements without asking further advances, since my arrival [here after the adjournment of Congress] I have discovered the fal[l]acy of my hopes in this respect.

I had no conception of the pressure of the times here, nor the great expence of the steam boats which must be employed under the transportation arrangement. I have transmitted to you the certificates of honorable men to prove that the estimate of Gen[era]l

[Thomas S.] Jesup upon which your advances have been predicated was the ordinary price upon our best & most frequented rivers. If you should think yourself justifyed [*sic*] in making a liberal advance under the transportation contract, the expedition will go on with dignity, honor, success, & brilliancy. I never have known any measure of the administration in the West [to] give half the interest & satisfaction. I feel such an anxiety on the occasion I declare before God, if I could sell $50,000 worth of property (every thing but my house & a few family servants) to difray [*sic*] the expedition for the present at a fair price I would freely do it: but this cannot be done; and unless you can make a considerable advance on the transportation acc[oun]t which ought to be charged to the St. Louis contract I fear discredit must be the consequence! What would this produce? Difficulties in every respect, and injure in some way the expedition & I am willing to sacrifice every thing but life to see your wishes accomplished in this thing.

I know you are willing to make the advance if public duty demands it. To prove this I refer you to the letters of Col. [James] Morrison and the certificates of the Messrs. [Benjamin and John] O'Fallon. In case of a Paymaster you have to advance very often $100,000 under a securityship of $10,000. In this case you have $50,000 securityship. You will have 3 steam boats worth $200,000 chartered to you the Gov[ernmen]t for my Brother is now in Louisville & will have to purchase an additional Steam Boat, without which it will be impossible to accomplish the object, at least without hazard. The only object is to find what will certainly be due for transportation. I am certain that no calculation upon the lowest value & the least quantity of Tons with $100,000 in addition to what has been advanced on transportation will be due: but I wish to ascertain what is the smallest advance I can get along without going to Jail or being discreditted [*sic*]. I have come to this conclusion that $50,000 advance more on the transportation account, with such sums as may meet the payments that my Brother may have to make in the purchase of the New Steam Boat would make all things easy untill the result of the expedition is known. In the event of this advance, the provisions & supplies for the Army can be meet [*sic*] with the advances from Col. Gipson [George Gibson] at the usual periods.

Now, Sir, I have put the case of prosperity, ease & happiness in one scale & on the other discredit & ruin, and if the papers do not make it as clear as holy write [*sic*] that you can make the advance then let ruin be the consequence. I expect my Brother at home in a few days at which time he will give an account of his preparations & outfit.

Wishing you health and happiness I remain as usual yours sincerely, R[ic]h[ard] M. Johnson.

ALS in DNA, 1, J-220.

From JOHN TAYLOR, [former Representative and Senator from S.C.]

Columbia, [S.C.,] March 30th 1819

Believing that the taking possession of the Floridas agre[e]ably to the late Treaty (if ratified by Spain) will fall within the Direction & Controul of your Department, as well as the organization of a Tempor[ar]y Government for the same after it has been accepted, I venture to solicit your kindness & patronage for Doctor Elias Marks of this Town, who is desirous of some appointment in that Territory & intends permanently to reside at either St. Augustine or Pensacola. He is a Gentleman of about 25 or 30 years of age, a scholar & a Physician of considerable reputation & skill, a graduate of the University of New York, speaks both the French & Spanish languages with fluency; not supposing a medical appointment within the List of your Semi Diplomatic Corps for receiving said Territories, I have suggested to him the propriety of attaching himself as secretary or otherwise to the Retinue of our public agents who go to receive the the [*sic*] Country from Spain, after which by being acquainted with the officers of Government on the spot, he will stand the better chance of obtaining the appointm[en]t of Port [*or perhaps* "Post"] Physician for one or other of these places, or if he obtain it may continue in any civil office. For e[i]ther of which he is unquestionably well qualified.

Any assistance you can give Dr. Marks in his present views will greatly oblige your most ob[e]d[ien]t serv[an]t, John Taylor.

ALS in DNA, 11, 13639. NOTE: An AES by Joseph Lovell states: "No appointment of this nature will probably be made."

From Robert Walsh, Jr.

Philadelphia, March 30th 1819

At the first stated meeting of the American Philosophical Society, held after the receipt of the communication with which you honored me, in relation to the expedition [under Stephen H. Long] for exploring our western waters, I made the Society acquainted with your wishes, and found it eager to promote them by all the means in it's [*sic*] power. A committee consisting of Mr. P.S. Duponceau, Dr. Samuel Brown, Dr. Thomas Cooper, Dr. R.M. Patterson and myself was immediately appointed ["by the Society" *canceled*] to prepare, in conformity with the object of your letter, such suggestions as might seem appropriate. The members of the Committee—with the exception of Dr. Cooper unfortunately sick—assembled yesterday evening, and presented respectively the papers which I now ["enclose" *canceled and* "send herewith" *interlined*] under the direction of the Committee. It is thought well to transmit without retrenchment or modification, to the Department of War, the heads of inquiry proposed by each member; in order that the Department may ["throw" *canceled and* "use" *interlined*] them [*illegible words canceled and* "in" *interlined*] the ["form and convert them to the use" *canceled and* "manner" *interlined*] which it may deem most eligible. Dr. Cooper had already put into the hands of one of the gentlemen composing the expedition a schedule of queries in geology and mineralogy. The Society has full confidence in the knowledge and sagacity of the men of science attached to the exploring party, and has therefore rather intended by what it offers, to testify it's [*sic*] disposition to co-operate in the liberal aims of the Government, than expected to contribute any material aid.

ALS in PPAmP; Ens in DNA, 1, W-245. Note: The enclosures include suggestions, information, and queries by Brown, Duponceau, and Walsh concerning such matters as the vocabulary of the Osage Indians, the medical experience of Indians, meteorology, topography, and the determination of correct latitudes and longitudes.

From James R. Baird, Abbeville District, S.C., [*ca.* 3/31]. Recommends Dr. E[lias] Marks of Columbia, S.C., for some appointment in the Floridas. ALS in DNA, 11, 13639.

L[EWIS] EDWARDS to [JAMES MONROE]

War Department, 31st March 1819

The Secretary of War has the honor to represent to the President of the U.S. that the appropriation for half-pay pensions is inadequate to the accomplishment of its object; it is therefore necessary for the public service, that the sum of one hundred and twenty-two thousand Dollars be transferred from the appropriation for Revolutionary pensions to the credit of the first mentioned appropriation.

FC in DNA, 6, 1:349. NOTE: A notation reads: "Approved J.M."

From B[enjamin] W. Hopkins, Mobile Point, 3/31. Pleads that Calhoun will sustain him in his understanding of the advances that are payable to him under his contract for the construction of the fort there; alleges that the smaller advances payable under the recent interpretation by Capt. James Gadsden would have prohibited Hopkins from bidding for the contract in the first place and that Hopkins had a satisfactory, oral agreement with [Joseph G.] Swift concerning the larger advances claimed by Hopkins. ALS in DNA, 1, H-228; PC in Carter, ed., *Territorial Papers*, 18: 597–598. (For Gadsden's interpretation and Calhoun's decision sustaining it, see PC's in Carter, ed., *Territorial Papers*, 18:588–589 and 640–642. Hopkins's letter of 3/31 was acknowledged in Calhoun's absence on 5/13 by Lewis Edwards, who stated that because Calhoun was away "no other construction can be put on your contract than the one literally expressed therein" and promised to lay Hopkins's appeal before Calhoun "immediately on his return." FC in DNA, 3, 10:304.)

From Adam Lynn, Alexandria, [D.C.,] 3/31. Withdraws four names from his list [of 3/19] of nominees for promotion in the 2nd Brigade of the D.C. Militia. ALS in DNA, 11, 13700.

From Dr. ELIAS MARKS

Columbia (So[uth] Carolina), March 31st 1819

The assurance which my friend, Mr. [James R.] Baird, has given me of the benignity of y[ou]r feelings, has emboldened me to address you on the present occasion. For, I feel assured, whatever be the result of the present application, y[ou]r answer will be dictated by a humane & liberal feeling. In soliciting [your] influence for the procurement of an agency in any important sea-port of the Floridas, I am chiefly influenced by a desire of residing in the vicinity of the ocean; as I have, from past experience, found such a situation congenial with my health. I feel, furthermore, desirous, Dear Sir, of entering upon an active & successive course of duties, no matter how responsible or laborious.

As I have an intimate knowledge of the French and a tolerable acquaintance with the Spanish languages (the latter of which opportunity will improve) I am induced to solicit y[ou]r kind exertions in my favour for the office of Collector of the Port of Pensacola, or, any other respectable sea-port. Or, I would most willingly enter upon any *professional* duty [as a physician] which government would assign.

As I have a family immediately dependent upon me for support, it is only by this or similar means that I shall be enabled to obtain a location so congenial with my choice.

Y[ou]r kind exertions, D[ea]r Sir, in my favour will be ever gratefully acknowledge[d] by Y[ou]rs most Respect[full]y, Elias Marks.

ALS in DNA, 11, 13639.

From Seth Otis, Egbert Ten Eyck, Charles E[zra] Clarke, O[rville] Hungerford, [the three last named later becoming Representatives from N.Y.,] and 38 other residents of Jefferson County, N.Y., 3/31. They argue that the road between Plattsburg and Sackets Harbor would be more direct and useful if it were routed through Jefferson County rather than through St. Lawrence and Franklin Counties, as is now planned. (This letter was postmarked at Watertown, N.Y., on 4/1.) LS in DNA, 1, M-263.

From Lawr[ence] Taliaferro, Fredericksburg, [Va.,] 3/31. Accepts his appointment as U.S. Agent for Indian Affairs at [the mouth of the] St. Peters [River]. ALS in DNA, 1, T-105.

From [Stephen H. Long, 3/——]. This document comprises sheets on which the vocabularies of Indian tribes could be recorded, and it bears an AES by Long reading: "Form of a vocabulary prepared for Western Expedition." A simple key to pronounciation is printed at the top of every page. In a column on the left of each page appear English words in common use, almost 100 of them; and beside each word there is blank space into which an Indian equivalent could be written. PC in DNA, 1, L-122.

SYMBOLS

The following symbols have been used in this volume as space-savers to designate the natures or forms in which these papers of John C. Calhoun have been found and the depositories and record groups in which they are preserved. The plurals of these symbols have been formed by adding an apostrophe and an "s," except in the single instance of a plural that appears below, which is "Ens" for "enclosures."

A-Ar —Alabama Department of Archives and History, Montgomery, Alabama
Abs —abstract (an editor's summary)
ADI —autograph document, initialed
ADS —autograph document, signed
ADU —autograph document, unsigned
AEI —autograph endorsement, initialed
AES —autograph endorsement, signed
AEU —autograph endorsement, unsigned
ALI —autograph letter, initialed
ALS —autograph letter, signed
ALU —autograph letter, unsigned
CC —clerk's copy (usually not for retention in the office of origin)
CCEx —clerk's copy of an extract
CLU —University of California at Los Angeles Library, Los Angeles, California
CSmH —Henry E. Huntington Library and Art Gallery, San Marino, California
Ct —Connecticut State Library, Hartford, Connecticut

CtLHi —Litchfield Historical Society, Litchfield, Connecticut
CtW —Olin Memorial Library, Wesleyan University, Middletown, Connecticut
CtWa —Watertown Library, Watertown, Connecticut
CtY —Yale University Library, New Haven, Connecticut
CU —University of California Library, Berkeley, California
DCI —Carnegie Institution of Washington, Washington, D.C.
DI —document, initialed
DLC —The Library of Congress, Washington, D.C.
DNA —The National Archives, Washington, D.C.

In citations within this book, the first number following each use of "DNA" is an editorial device referring to a specific series of records within a specific Record Group. For example, a document cited as being "in DNA, 3, 10:223–224" can be found on pages 223–224 of volume 10 in the series known as Letters Sent by the Secretary of War Relating to Military Affairs within Record Group 107, which consists of Records of the Office of the Secretary of War. The editor's code numbers like the "3" of this example are identified in the following list.

Any effort to locate a specific document, in person or by mail, by referring to such an editorial code number will provide the staff of the National Archives with insufficient information to enable it to render promptly the service desired. Instead, every such request should cite the Record Group by both name and number, the name of the specific series of records within that Record Group, and all document or file numbers or volume and page numbers that follow the editorial code number. For instance, one should not ask the National Archives staff for "DNA, 11, 13771"; instead, one should ask for the letter from Jasper Parrish to John C. Calhoun dated January 28, 1819, which is to be found in file number 13771 in the series of manuscripts known as Letters Received that comprises part of Record Group 94, consisting of the Records of the Adjutant General's Office.

DNA *(continued)*

Certain series of records in certain Record Groups have been published, in whole or in part, in microcopies that are offered in the *List of National Archives Microfilm Publications, 1965,* and by some supplementary announcements. In these instances the corresponding microcopy number appears in the following list parenthetically after the name of the series of records—for example, "(M-222)" or "(T-494)." When such a reference in this volume is followed by a colon and an additional number—for instance, "(M-91:1)"—the second number specifies the relevant roll of microfilm in the indicated microcopy. Some users of this volume will find it more convenient to locate a wanted document on such a microfilm than in manuscript.

Some editorial code numbers and corresponding names of series of records have been included in the following list that are not cited within this book. These inclusions have been made for their value as a record of manuscripts within which documents related to other periods of Calhoun's life have been discovered. Correspondingly, if inclusive dates appear immediately after the name of a series of records, the specified years may indicate the period for which that series has been searched for Calhoun documents or microfilmed rather than the years with which that series begins or ends.

For the most comprehensive information that is available within one set of covers about the Record Groups, see the *Guide to the Records in the National Archives* (Washington: U.S. Government Printing Office, 1948). More detailed analyses of the contents of seven Record Groups relevant to Calhoun have been published by the National Archives in its series of near-print releases entitled *Preliminary Checklist* and *Preliminary Inventory.* These seven, listed in the order in which they appear below, are Record Groups 107, 94, 75, 59, 45, 46, and 233. When an "Entry" number appears parenthetically in the following list, it refers

DNA *(continued)*

to the description in the corresponding *Checklist* or *Inventory* of the series of records thus designated.

Record Group 107—Records of the Office of the Secretary of War

1—Letters Received by the Secretary of War, Registered Series, 1801–1860 (M-221; Entry 33. The corresponding Registers have been published in M-22 and are described in Entry 34.)
2—Letters Received by the Secretary of War, Unregistered Series, 1789–1860 (M-222)
3—Letters Sent by the Secretary of War Relating to Military Affairs, 1800–1861 (M-6; Entry 2)
4—Reports to Congress from the Secretary of War, 1803–1870 (M-220; Entry 21)
5—Confidential and Unofficial Letters Sent by the Secretary of War, 1814–1847 (M-7; Entry 7)
6—Letters Sent to the President by the Secretary of War, 1800–1863 (M-127; Entry 5)
7—Miscellaneous Papers Relating to Accounts, 1829–1865 (Entry 49)

Record Group 94—Records of the Adjutant General's Office

11—Letters Received by the Adjutant General's Office, 1805–1821 (M-566; Entry 12)
12—Letters Sent by the Adjutant General's Office (Main Series), 1800–1890 (M- 565; Entry 1)
13—Records Relating to the U.S. Military Academy, 1812–1867 (M-91; Entries 206, 207, 219), consisting chiefly of letters sent by the Engineer Department
14—Correspondence Relating to the Military Academy, 1819–1866 (Entry 212), consisting chiefly of letters to the Engineer Department from the Superintendent of the Academy
15—Application Papers of Cadets, 1814–1866 (Entry 243)

DNA *(continued)*

16—Letters Received by the Adjutant General's Office (Main Series), 1822–1889 (M-567; Entry 12)
17—Record of Regulations and Orders Received from the Secretary of War, 1821–1829 (Entry 50)
18—Military Academy Orders, 1814–1867 (Entry 219)
19—Orders and Circulars, 1797–1910 (Entry 44)

Record Group 77—Records of the
Office of the Chief of Engineers

21—Miscellaneous Letters Sent, 1812–1848
22—Reports of the Corps of Engineers, 1812–1824
23—Miscellaneous Letters Received, 1813–1818 (File B)
24—Bulky Package Files
25—Miscellaneous Papers Received, 1789–1831 (File G)
26—Plans for Removal of Obstructions from the Mississippi and Ohio Rivers, 1824–1826
27—Letters Received by the Board of Engineers for Fortifications, 1824–1825
28—Letters Sent by the Office of the Chief of Engineers Relating to Internal Improvements, 1824–1830 (M-65)
29—Letters Received "A," Fortification Papers, 1815–1818
30—Letters Referred, 1819–1825
(Additional series within this Record Group begin with editorial code number 221.)

Record Group 156—Records of the
Office of the Chief of Ordnance

31—Letters Received, 1817–1825
32—Letters to the War Department, 1817–1825
33—Letters Relating to Mineral Lands, "Lead Mines," 1821–1825
34—Lead Mines: Leases, vol. I, 1824–1825
35—Records Relating to Inventions
36—Records Relaaing to Experiments

DNA *(continued)*

37—Letters Sent by the Military Storekeeper, Springfield, Mass., Armory
38—Letterbook of the Watervliet Arsenal, 1819–1824
39—Letters Sent by the Superintendent, Springfield, Mass., Armory

Record Group 92—Records of the Office of the Quartermaster General

41—Letters Received, 1818–1825
42—Letters Sent, 1818–1825
43—Consolidated Correspondence File
44—Maj. James H. Hook's Papers: Letters, 1818–1821
45—Commissary General of Purchases: Letters Sent, 1817–1825

Record Group 217—Records of the United States General Accounting Office

51—Second Auditor: Letters Sent
52—Second Auditor: Letters Sent Relating to Property, 1818
53—Third Auditor: Letters Sent
54—Third Auditor: Congressional Letterbooks
55—Fourth Auditor: Letters Received
56—Fourth Auditor: Letters Sent
57—Fourth Auditor: Letters from the Secretary of the Navy, 1818
58—Fifth Auditor: Letters Sent
59—First Comptroller: Miscellaneous Letters Sent, 1817–1844
60—First Comptroller: Miscellaneous Letters Received
61—First Comptroller: Diplomatic, Consular, and Miscellaneous Letters
62—First Comptroller: Letters from the Third Auditor
63—Second Comptroller: Letters Received
64—Miscellaneous Letters and Papers, *ca.* 1804–1899
65—Records of Richard Bland Lee, Commissioner of Claims

DNA *(continued)*

66—Miscellaneous Records of the Third Auditor
67—Second Comptroller: Letters Received Relating to Pensions

Record Group 75—Records of the Bureau of Indian Affairs

71—Letters Received by the Office of Indian Affairs, 1824–1881 (M-234 and Entry 79, with the Registers as M-18 and Entry 75)
72—Letters Sent by the Secretary of War Relating to Indian Affairs, 1800–1824 (M-15; Entry 2)
73—Letters Sent by the Superintendent of Indian Trade, 1806–1823 (M-16; Entry 4)
74—Letters Sent by the Office of Indian Affairs, 1824–1881 (M-21; Entry 84, with the Registers as Entries 80–82)
75—Records of the Cherokee Indian Agency in Tennessee, 1801–1835 (M-208; Entries 1041–1057)
76—Records of the Michigan Superintendency of Indian Affairs, 1814–1851 (M-1; Entries 1120–1139)
77—Letters Received by the Office of the Secretary of War Relating to Indian Affairs, 1800–1823 (M-271; Entry 1)
78—Special Files of the Office of Indian Affairs, 1807–1904 (M-574; Entry 98)
79—Letters Received by the Superintendent of Indian Trade, 1806–1824 (T-58; Entry 3)
80—Documents Relating to the Negotiation of Ratified and Unratified Treaties with Various Tribes of Indians, 1801–1869 (T-494; Entries 103–104)

Record Group 49—Records of the General Land Office

81—Miscellaneous Letters Received, 1838–1842
82—Miscellaneous Letters Sent, 1796–1889 (M-25)
83—Letters Sent: Indian Lands, 1840–1842
84—Letters Sent: Preëmption Bureau, 1846–1847

DNA *(continued)*

85—Journal and Report of James Leander Cathcart and James Hutton, Agents Appointed by the Secretary of the Navy to Survey Timber Resources between the Mermentau and Mobile Rivers, November, 1818–May, 1819 (M-8)

Record Group 15—Records of the Veterans Administration

91—Letterbooks of the Pension Office: General, 1812–1831

92—Letterbooks of the Pension Office: Original Cases, 1827–1832

93—Revolutionary War Pension Files

Record Group 59—General Records of the Department of State

101—Miscellaneous Letters (Received), 1789–1906 (M-179; Entry 102)

102—Domestic Letters (Sent), 1784–1906 (M-40; Entry 99)

103—Applications and Recommendations for Office: Letters Received, 1797–1901 (M-439; Entry 331)

104—State Department Territorial Papers: Florida, 1777–1824 (M-116; Entry 879)

105—Accounting Records: Miscellaneous Letters Sent, 1832–1916 (Entry 202)

106—Diplomatic Instructions of the Department of State, 1785–1906 (M-77; Entry 1)

107—Diplomatic Despatches, 1789–1906 (a different microcopy for each distinct country or area from which the despatches were sent; Entry 8)

108—Consular Despatches, 1789–1906 (a different microcopy for each distinct country or area from which the despatches were sent: Entry 78)

109—Notes from Foreign Legations, 1789–1906 (a different microcopy for each distinct nation or area having a legation in Washington, D.C.; Entry 26)

DNA *(continued)*

Record Group 60—General Records of the Department of Justice

111—Letters Received in the Office of the Attorney General, 1818–1845
112—Letters Sent by the Office of the Attorney General, 1818–1820
113—Opinions of the Attorney General, 1818–1844
114—Drafts and Copies of Opinions, 1818–1824

Record Group 45—Naval Records Collection of the Office of Naval Records and Library

121—Letters Sent by the Secretary of the Navy to Officers, 1798–1868 (M-149; Entry 1)
122—Miscellaneous Letters Sent, 1798–1886 (Entry 3)
123—Letters to Federal Executive Agents: Nominations for Appointment of Officers, 1798–1824 (Entry 4)
124—Letters to Federal Executive Agents: Letters to the Secretary of the Treasury, 1798–1821 (Entry 4)
125—Letters to Congress, 1798–1886 (Entry 5)
126—Letters to Members of Congress, 1820–1831 (Entry 9)
127—Letters Sent by the Secretary of the Navy to the President and Executive Agencies, 1821–1886 (M-472; Entry 10)
128—Miscellaneous Letters Received by the Secretary of the Navy, 1807–1884 (M-124; Entry 21)
129—Letters from Federal Executive Agents, 1837–1886 (M-517; Entry 29)
130—Reports of the Secretary of the Navy to Congress, 1811–1820 (Entry 174)
131—Board of Navy Commissioners: Miscellaneous Letters Sent, 1815–1842 (Entry 217)
132—Letters Received by the Secretary of the Navy from Commanders, 1804–1886 (M-147; Entry 23)
133—Letters Received by the Secretary of the Navy from Captains, 1807–1861, 1866–1885 (M-125; Entry 24)

DNA *(continued)*

134—Letters Received by the Secretary of the Navy from Officers below the Rank of Commander, 1802–1886 (M-148; Entry 22)
135—Board of Navy Commissioners: Miscellaneous Letters Received, 1814–1842 (Entry 219)

Record Group 53—Records of the Bureau of the Public Debt

141—Legal Papers in the Office of the Register of the Treasury, 1784–1876
142—Second Bank of the United States, Baltimore Branch: Letterbook, 1817–1835
143—Estimates and Statements, 1811–1839

Record Group 46—Records of the United States Senate

151—President's Messages Suggesting Legislation or Submitting Specific Information or Documents
152—President's Messages Transmitting Reports
153—President's Messages—Indian Relations
154—Reports and Communications Submitted to the Senate
155—President's Messages Transmitting Reports from the Secretary of the Navy
156—President's Messages—Executive Nominations
157—Petitions and Memorials, Resolutions of State Legislatures, and Related Documents
158—Committee Reports and Papers
159—Other Records

Record Group 28—Records of the Post Office Department

161—Letters Sent by the Postmaster General, 1789–1836 (M-601)

Record Group 203—Records of the Office of the Chief of Finance (War)

171—Letters Sent to the Secretary of the Treasury, 1817–1819

DNA *(continued)*

Record Group 98—Records of United States Army Commands

181—6th U.S. Infantry: Letters Sent, 1817–1826
182—Division of the North: Militia Delinquents Reported to the Secretary of War, 1818–1819

Record Group 192—Records of the Office of the Commissary General of Subsistence

191—Letters Sent, 1818–1820

Record Group 233—Records of the United States House of Representatives

201—Reports and Communications Submitted to the House
202—President's Messages
203—Committee Reports and Papers
204—Petitions and Memorials, Resolutions of State Legislatures, and Related Documents Which Were Referred to Committees

Record Group 206—Records of the Office of the Solicitor of the Treasury

211—Letters Received: War Department
212—Letters Received: Miscellaneous
213—Letters Written
214—Letters Sent
215—Letters of Debts and Suits

Record Group 77—Records of the Office of the Chief of Engineers

221—Miscellaneous Letters Received, 1819–1825
222—Miscellaneous Letters Relating to the Military Academy, 1813–1818 (File F)
223—Letters from Engineers, 1819–1825
224—Letters Received, 1826–1866 (File C)
225—Buell Collection of Historical Documents Relating to the Corps of Engineers, 1801–1819 (M-417)

DNA *(continued)*

Record Group 26—Records of the United States Coast Guard

231—Lighthouse Bureau: Miscellaneous Correspondence, 1785–1852

Record Group 112—Records of the Office of the Surgeon General (Army)

241—Letters Received, 1818–1889
242—Letters and Endorsements Sent, 1818–1889
243—Reports to the Secretary of War Relating to Office Activities, Personnel, and Expenditures, 1818–1894
244—Orders Issued by the Surgeon General, the Secretary of War, and the Adjutant and Inspector General ("Orderly Book"), 1818–1819
245—Orders from the Secretary of War, Forms, and Resolutions of Congress, 1816–1837

Record Group 125—Records of the Office of the Judge Advocate General (Navy)

251—Records of General Courts-Martial and Courts of Inquiry of the Navy Department, 1799–1867 (M-273)

DNDAR —Daughters of the American Revolution Library, Washington, D.C.
DS —document, signed
DU —document, unsigned
EI —endorsement, initialed
En —enclosure
Ens —enclosures
ES —endorsement, signed
EU —endorsement, unsigned
Ex —extract
ExU —extract, unsigned
FC —file copy (usually in the form of a letterbook copy retained in the office of origin)
FU —University of Florida Library, Gainesville, Florida

GAHi —Atlanta Historical Society, Atlanta, Georgia
G-Ar —Georgia State Department of Archives, Atlanta, Georgia
GEU —Emory University Library, Atlanta, Georgia
GHi —Georgia Historical Society, Savannah, Georgia
GU —University of Georgia Library, Athens, Georgia
Ia-HA —Iowa State Department of History and Archives, Des Moines, Iowa
ICHi —Chicago Historical Society, Chicago, Illinois
ICN —The Newberry Library, Chicago, Illinois
IHi —Illinois State Historical Library, Springfield, Illinois
In —Indiana State Library, Indianapolis, Indiana
InHi —Indiana Historical Society, Indianapolis, Indiana
InNd —University of Notre Dame Archives, Notre Dame, Indiana
InU —Indiana University Libraries, Bloomington, Indiana
KyLoF —The Filson Club, Inc., Louisville, Kentucky
KyU —University of Kentucky Library, Lexington, Kentucky
LI —letter, initialed
LNHT —Howard–Tilton Memorial Library, Tulane University, New Orleans, Louisiana
LS —letter, signed
LU —letter, unsigned
MB —Boston Public Library, Boston, Massachusetts
MBAt —Boston Athenaeum, Boston, Massachusetts
MdBJ —Johns Hopkins University Library, Baltimore, Maryland
MdBP —Peabody Library, Baltimore, Maryland
MdHi —Maryland Historical Society, Baltimore, Maryland
MeHi —Maine Historical Society, Portland, Maine
MeLB —Bates College Library, Lewiston, Maine
MH —Harvard University Library, Cambridge, Massachusetts
MHi —Massachusetts Historical Society, Boston, Massachusetts
MiD —Detroit Public Library, Detroit, Michigan
MiDW —Wayne State University Library, Detroit, Michigan
MiU-C —William L. Clements Library, University of Michigan, Ann Arbor, Michigan
MnHi —Minnesota Historical Society, St. Paul, Minnesota
MnM —Minneapolis Public Library, Minneapolis, Minnesota
MoHi —State Historical Society of Missouri, Columbia, Missouri
MoSHi —Missouri Historical Society, St. Louis, Missouri
MWA —American Antiquarian Society, Worcester, Massachusetts

MWelC —Wellesley College Library, Wellesley, Massachusetts
MWiW-C —Chapin Library, Williams College, Williamstown, Massachusetts
N —New York State Library, Albany, New York
NBu —Buffalo and Erie County Public Library, Buffalo, New York
Nc-Ar —North Carolina Department of Archives and History, Raleigh, North Carolina
NcD —Duke University Library, Durham, North Carolina
NcU —University of North Carolina Library, Chapel Hill, North Carolina
NhD —Dartsmouth College Library, Hanover, New Hampshire
NhHi —New Hampshire Historical Society, Concord, New Hampshire
NHi —New-York Historical Society, New York, New York
NIC —Cornell University Library, Ithaca, New York
NjHi —New Jersey Historical Society, Newark, New Jersey
NjMoN —Morristown National Historical Park, Morristown, New Jersey
NjP —Princeton University Library, Princeton, New Jersey
NN —New York Public Library, New York, New York
NNC —Columbia University Library, New York, New York
NNPM —Pierpont Morgan Library, New York, New York
NPV —Vassar College Library, Poughkeepsie, New York
NRU —University of Rochester Library, Rochester, New York
NWM —United States Military Academy Library, West Point, New York
O —Ohio State Library, Columbus, Ohio
OCHP —Historical and Philosophical Society of Ohio, University of Cincinnati, Cincinnati, Ohio
OClWHi —Western Reserve Historical Society, Cleveland, Ohio
OFH —Hayes Memorial Library, Fremont, Ohio
OMC —Marietta College Library, Marietta, Ohio
PBL —Lehigh University Library, Bethlehem, Pennsylvania
PC —Printed Copy
PCarlD —Dickinson College Library, Carlisle, Pennsylvania
PEx —Printed extract
PHarH —Pennsylvania Historical and Museum Commission, Harrisburg, Pennsylvania
PHC —Haverford College Library, Haverford, Pennsylvania

PHi —Historical Society of Pennsylvania, Philadelphia, Pennsylvania
PLS —Printed letter, signed
PPAmP —American Philosophical Society, Philadelphia, Pennsylvania
PPiU —University of Pittsburgh Library, Pittsburgh, Pennsylvania
PPL —Library Company of Philadelphia, Philadelphia, Pennsylvania
PU —University of Pennsylvania Library, Philadelphia, Pennsylvania
PWbWHi —Wyoming Historical and Geological Society, Wilkes-Barre, Pennsylvania
PWcHi —Chester County Historical Society, West Chester, Pennsylvania
R-Ar —Rhode Island State Archives, Providence, Rhode Island
RHi —Rhode Island Historical Society, Providence, Rhode Island
RPJCB —John Carter Brown Library, Brown University, Providence, Rhode Island
Sc-Ar —South Carolina Archives Department, Columbia, South Carolina
ScC —Charleston Library Society, Charleston, South Carolina
ScCleA —Clemson University Library, Clemson, South Carolina
ScFHi —Florence County Historical Society, Florence, South Carolina
ScGF —Furman University Library, Greenville, South Carolina
ScHi —South Carolina Historical Society, Charleston, South Carolina
ScSpW —Wofford College Library, Spartanburg, South Carolina
ScU-SC —South Caroliniana Library, University of South Carolina, Columbia, South Carolina
T —Tennessee State Library and Archives, Nashville, Tennessee
THi —Tennessee Historical Society, Nashville, Tennessee
TKL —Knoxville Public Library, Knoxville, Tennessee
TxDaHi —Dallas Historical Society, Dallas, Texas
TxGR —Rosenberg Library, Galveston, Texas
TxU —University of Texas Library, Austin, Texas
Vi —Virginia State Library, Richmond, Virginia
ViHi —Virginia Historical Society, Richmond, Virginia

ViLxW	—Washington and Lee University Library, Lexington, Virginia
ViU	—University of Virginia Library, Charlottesville, Virginia
ViW	—College of William and Mary Library, Williamsburg, Virginia
ViWC	—Colonial Williamsburg, Williamsburg, Virginia
VtU	—University of Vermont, Burlington, Vermont
WaPS	—Washington State University, Pullman, Washington
WHi	—State Historical Society of Wisconsin, Madison, Wisconsin

BIBLIOGRAPHY

Adams, Charles Francis, ed., *Memoirs of John Quincy Adams, Comprising Portions of His Diary from 1795 to 1848.* 12 vols. Philadelphia: J.B. Lippincott & Co., c. 1874–1877.

American State Papers: Documents, Legislative and Executive, of the Congress . . . . 37 vols. Washington: various printers, 1832–1861.

Ames, Herman V., *The Proposed Amendments to the Constitution of the United States during the First Century of Its History,* in *American Historical Association Annual Report for 1896* (2 vols. Washington: U.S. Government Printing Office, 1897), vol. II.

Bassett, John Spencer, ed., *The Correspondence of Andrew Jackson.* 7 vols. Washington: Carnegie Institution of Washington, 1926–1935.

Biographical Directory of the American Congress, 1774–1949 . . . . House Document No. 607, 81st Congress, 2nd Session. [Washington:] U.S. Government Printing Office, 1950.

Brooks, Philip Coolidge, *Diplomacy and the Borderlands: the Adams–Onís Treaty of 1819.* Berkeley: University of California Press, c. 1939.

Carter, Clarence E., ed., *The Territorial Papers of the United States.* 25 vols. to date. Washington: U.S. Government Printing Office, 1934–present.

Clower, George Wesley, "Notes on the Calhoun-Noble-Davis Family," *The South Carolina Historical Magazine,* vol. LIII, No. 1 (January, 1952), pp. 51–53.

Correspondence between Gen. Andrew Jackson and John C. Calhoun, President and Vice-President of the U. States, on the Subject of the Course of the Latter, in the Deliberations of the Cabinet of Mr. Monroe, on the Occurrences in the Seminole War. Washington: printed by Duff Green, 1831.

Crallé, Richard K., ed., *The Works of John C. Calhoun.* 6 vols. Columbia, S. C.: printed by A.S. Johnston, 1851, and New York: D. Appleton and Company, 1853–1857.

Dangerfield, George, *The Era of Good Feelings.* New York: Harcourt, Brace and Company, c. 1952.

Gordon, William A., *A Compilation of Registers of the Army of the United States, from 1815 to 1831 (Inclusive), to Which Is Appended a List of Officers on Whom Brevets Were Conferred by the President of the United States, for Gallant Conduct or Meritorious Services during the War with Great Britain.* Washington: printed by James C. Dunn, 1837.

Hamilton, Stanislaus Murray, ed., *The Writings of James Monroe, Including a Collection of His Public and Private Papers and Correspondence Now for the First Time Printed.* 7 vols. New York: G.P. Putnam's Sons, 1898–1903.

Heitman, Francis B., *Historical Register and Dictionary of the United States Army, from Its Organization, September 29, 1789, to March 2, 1903.* 2 vols. Washington: U.S. Government Printing Office, 1903.

Hopkins, James F., and Mary W.M. Hargreaves, eds., *The Papers of Henry Clay.* 3 vols. to date. [Lexington:] University of Kentucky Press, c. 1959, 1961, 1963.

James, Edwin, compiler, *Account of an Expedition from Pittsburgh to the Rocky Mountains, Performed in the Years 1819 and '20 . . .* (3 vols. Philadelphia: H.C. Carey and F. Lea, 1822–1823).

Jameson, J. Franklin, ed., *Correspondence of John C. Calhoun,* in *American Historical Association Annual Report for 1899* (2 vols. Washington: U.S. Government Printing Office, 1900), vol. II.

Johnson, Allen, and Dumas Malone, eds., *Dictionary of American Biography.* 22 vols. New York: Charles Scribner's Sons, 1928–1944.

Lieber, G. Norman, *Remarks on the Army Regulations and Executive Regulations in General.* War Department Document No. 93. Washington: U.S. Government Printing Office, 1898.

Lyford, S.C., *Report on the Participation of the War Department in the International Exhibition, Held at Philadelphia, Pa., 1876, . . .,* in *Report of the Board on Behalf of United States Executive Departments at the International Exhibition, . . .*

(2 vols. Washington: U.S. Government Printing Office, 1884), vol. I, pp. 21–1007.

Meriwether, Robert L., and W. Edwin Hemphill, eds., *The Papers of John C. Calhoun.* 2 vols. to date. Volume I, *1801–1817;* Volume II, *1817–1818.* Columbia: University of South Carolina Press for the South Caroliniana Society, c. 1959, 1963.

Miller, Stephen F., *The Bench and Bar of Georgia: Memoirs and Sketches, with an Appendix, Containing a Court Roll from 1790 to 1857, Etc.* 2 vols. Philadelphia: J.B. Lippincott & Co., c. 1898.

Mills, Robert, *Atlas of the State of South Carolina, Made under the Authority of the Legislature; Prefaced with a Geographical, Statistical and Historical Map of the State.* Baltimore: F. Lucas, Jr., 1825.

Morse, Jedidiah, *A Report to the Secretary of War of the United States, on Indian Affairs, Comprising a Narrative of a Tour Performed in the Summer of 1820 . . . .* New Haven: printed by S. Converse, c. 1822.

Niles' Weekly Register, Baltimore, 1811–1849.

Owen, Thomas M., ed., "Letters from John C. Calhoun to Charles Tait," *The Gulf States Historical Magazine,* vol. I, no. 2 (September, 1902), pp. 92–104.

Prucha, Francis Paul, *American Indian Policy in the Formative Years: the Indian Trade and Intercourse Acts, 1790–1834.* Cambridge: Harvard University Press, c. 1962.

Prucha, Francis Paul, *A Guide to the Military Posts of the United States, 1789–1895.* Madison: State Historical Society of Wisconsin, c. 1964.

A Register of Officers and Agents, Civil, Military, and Naval, in the Service of the United States, on the Thirtieth Day of September, 1817; Together with the Names, Force, and Condition, of All the Ships and Vessels Belonging to the United States, and When and Where Built. Prepared at the Department of State, in Pursuance of a Resolution of Congress, of the 27th of April, 1816. Washington: Printed by E. de Krafft, 1818.

Richardson, James D., *A Compilation of the Messages and Papers of the Presidents, 1789–1902.* 10 vols. [Washington:] Bureau of National Literature and Art, 1903. (Other editions are also available, one being as House Miscellaneous Document No. 210, 53rd Congress, 2nd Session.)

[Swift, Joseph G.,] *The Memoirs of Gen. Joseph Gardner Swift, LL.D., U.S.A., First Graduate of the United States Military Academy, West Point, Chief Engineer U.S.A. from 1812 to 1818,* [Covering the Years] *1800–1865, to Which Is Added a Genealogy of the Family of Thomas Swift of Dorchester, Mass., 1634, by Harrison Ellery, Member of the New England Genealogical Society.* Privately printed, c. 1890.

Waring, Alice Noble, ed., "Letters of John C. Calhoun to Patrick Noble, 1812–1837," *The Journal of Southern History,* vol. XVI, no. 1 (February, 1950), pp. 64–74.

White, Leonard D., *The Jeffersonians: a Study in Administrative History, 1801–1829.* New York: The Macmillan Company, c. 1951.

Wiltse, Charles M., *John C. Calhoun.* 3 vols. *Nationalist, 1782–1828; Nullifier, 1829–1839; Sectionalist, 1840–1850.* Indianapolis: The Bobbs-Merrill Company, Inc., c. 1944, 1949, 1951.

INDEX

Abbeville County, S. C.: election in, 88, 165.
Abert, John J.: about, 22; from, 74, 83; to, 83.
Adams, Edwin: about, 505.
Adams, Isaac A.: about, 83; from, 74, 505.
Adams, John Quincy: about, xv, xix–xx, xxxii, 14, 97; absence of, 81, 82, 108, 112; from, 31, 43, 58, 65, 157, 274–275, 312; to, 32, 83, 101, 134–135, 141, 303–304, 341, 491.
Adams, Nathaniel: about, 581.
Addison, Allen B.: about, 522, 548.
Adjutant and Inspector General: office of, 162–163, 194, 447; staff of, 21–22, 416, 509. *See also* Parker, Daniel.
Adkins, Hiram: about, 256.
Alabama Department of Archives and History: documents in, 106.
Alabama Territory: appointments in, 165; Cherokees in, 565, 569–570, 656; Governor of (*see* Bibb, William W.); immigrants into, 15, 334, 337; land claims in, 170; Pension Agent in, 284; rations contractor for, 86; recruiting in, 535; roads in, 106, 173–174; U. S. District Attorney in (*see* Crawford, William).
Albany, N. Y.: bank at, 580–581, 596–597.
Alcoholic beverages: and Army rations, 62–63, 69–70, 231, 273, 492; and Indians, 48, 178, 222, 656, 661.
Alexander, Edward Henry: about, 286.
Allanson, Dudley W.: about, 157.
Allanson, John Sylvanus: from, 157, 218.
Allanson, Richard: from, 157.
Allen, Heman: about, 415, 455, 459, 693–694; appointment of, 414; bond of, 484; from, 333, 448, 516, 630; to, 412–413, 630–631.
Allen, William: pension of, 262.
Allowances to Army officers: regulations for, 21–22, 119. *See also* Forage allowances.
Ambrister, Robert Christy: court-martial of, 12, 18, 58, 81, 87, 92, 108, 109, 131, 274, 275, 331.
Amelia Island, Fla.: about, 144–145, 167, 504, 511–512, 685.
Amelung, Ferdinand Louis: petition of, 448; resignation of, 508.
American Board of Commissioners for Foreign Missions: order from, 430; Secretary of, 557.
American Fur Company: about, 478, 627, 631, 656.
American Philosophical Society: about, 35, 134, 692, 711; documents in, 35, 640, 656, 711; Librarian of (*see* Vaughan, John); request by, 388, 399, 435, 455, 460, 518–519; Secretary of (*see* Patterson, R. M.).
Anderson, Joseph: Clerk to, 481; from, 36–37, 106, 119–120, 199, 324, 510, 610, 673; to, 199, 510, 610.
Andrews, Christopher: from, 673.
Andrews, George: about, 673.

Angus, Samuel: about, 223, 300.
Annesley, William: invention by, 244.
Annin, Samuel: from, 196.
Apalache Indians: census of, 16; lands of, 305–306.
Apothecary General: assistant to, 210. *See also* Le Baron, Francis.
Arapaho Indians: visit by, 699–700.
Arbuckle, Mathew: about, 206, 340, 619; from, 91, 193; order by, 163.
Arbuthnot, Alexander: court-martial of, 12, 18, 58, 81, 87, 92, 108, 109, 131, 274, 275, 331; from, 206, 356.
Archer, Robert: about, 185.
Archer, Samuel B.: from, 568; to, 568.
Arkansas, Mo. Territory: Indian Agent in (*see* Lewis, Reuben); rations contract for, 295.
Arkansas River: exploration of, 424; navigation of, 624; settlements beside, 272–273.
Armistead, Walker Keith: about, 130, 301, 356, 517, 528, 563, 648, 674; from, 333, 370, 392, 432, 435, 436, 451, 452, 490, 580, 591, 592, 600, 606, 616; to, 286, 322–323, 429–430, 432, 434, 494, 505–506, 591, 598, 618, 637–638, 670–671, 673, 674, 676–677.
Armistead, Wilson Cary Nicholas: about, 286.
Armories, U. S.: proposed Western, 288, 297, 333, 335–336, 406, 507. *See also* Harpers Ferry, Va.; Springfield, Mass.
Armstrong, Thomas: about, 334.
Army, U. S.: Chaplains in, 251, 526, 529; funds for, xxi–xxiii, 249–250, 265; general staff of, 208–209, 375–381, 413–414, 416, 447; size of, xviii–xix, 162, 187–188, 193–194, 277–278, 374–381, 484, 491. *See also* Artillery; Deserters; Infantry Regiments; Military Departments; Recruiting service; Rifle Regiment; Roads.
Artillery, Corps of: reforms in, 413–414; regulations for, 506.
Artillery, Regiment of Light: appointment in, 232; clothing for, 152, 290; regulations for, 506.
Asbury College: about, 68–69.
Ashley, Richard H.: about, 136.
Aspinwall, Thomas: from, 245; to, 245.
Astor, John Jacob: from, 29, 222; to, 686.
Atkinson, Henry: about, xxx, 218, 492, 631, 697; commands held by, 359, 633–634, 651, 695; from, 163–164, 166, 189, 195, 291–292, 359, 416, 486, 501, 512–515, 637, 649, 695; reports by, 315, 474; to, 99, 166, 189, 359, 416, 637, 663, 695–696.
Atlanta Historical Society: document in, 641.
Atlantic (brig): sale of, 275, 305.
Attorney General, U. S. *See* Wirt, William.
Auditors, U. S. Treasury Department: 2nd (*see* Lee, William); 3rd (*see* Hagner, Peter); 4th (*see* Freeman, Constant); 5th (*see* Pleasonton, Stephen).
Augusta, Ga.: arsenal at, 17, 402, 409, 591; physician at, 484–485.
Aury, Luis: about, 280.
Austin, Henry: to, 234.
Austin, Loring: about, 136, 147; from, 19, 532; to, 19, 572.
Axon, Samuel Jacob: about, 606.
Ayer, Theodore: about, 508.
Aylwin, William C.: duty of, 433.

Babcock, Samuel: about, 109, 387, 588; from, 577; to, 555, 577, 707.
Backus, Christopher: about, 158.
Bagot, Sir Charles: about, 87, 108.
Bailey, John: orders to, 97.
Bainbridge, William: about, 179, 397; from, 398, 432–433; to, 333, 389, 432–433.
Baird, James R.: about, 712; from, 711.

Baker, Edward: invention by, 370, 372, 393–394; petition of, 334, 357–358, 361.
Baker, Isaac L.: from, 448.
Baker, Samuel: pension of, 479.
Balch, Nathaniel: about, 286.
Balch, Samuel Y.: about, 286.
Baldwin, Henry: about, 615; from, 175, 247; to, 214, 247.
Baldwin, James M.: about, 389.
Baldwin, Oliver B.: about, 228.
Baldwin, Simeon: from, 549.
Baldwin, William: about, 423; from, 249, 649; to, 649–650.
Ballio, Paul: about, 235, 287.
Baltimore, Md.: indemnity to, 696–697; Quakers in, 691.
Banger, Timothy: from, 131.
Bangor, District of Me., Mass: road from, 228.
Bank of the United States: Baltimore Branch of, 116, 269; Cashier of, 484; Lexington, Ky., Branch of, 579; Nashville Branch of, 182; New Orleans Branch of, 118, 191, 194, 455; New York City Branch of, 387; personal accounts in, 482, 484; Pittsburgh Branch of, 341; President of, 473, 657; Savannah Branch Branch of, 621; Washington Branch of, 104, 705.
Bankhead, James: about, 249; from, 67, 510, 512.
Barbour, James: from, 166; to, 166, 610, 626.
Barbour, Philip Pendleton: from, 281, 304, 317–318, 371, 579; to, 281–282, 317, 371, 452, 579.
Barker, J. N.: from, 103.
Barlow, Willis Burn: heirs of, 432.
Barnes, Wheeler: from, 263.
Barnett, William: from, 174; to, 174.
Barraud, Cary: about, 237.
Barron, John, Jr.: from, 450.
Barron, William A.: about, 161, 387; from, 67.
Barry, William Taylor: from, 122–123.
Bartle, Andrew: from, 479, 481-482.
Bartlett, Ezra: to, 522.
Bassett, Burwell: from, 237, 595–596; to, 568.
Bateman, Ephraim: from, 541.
Bateman, Henry: from, 169; to, 169.
Bates, Frederick: from, 580; to, 567.
Bates, William D.: from, 277.
Baton Rouge, La.: arsenal at, xxi, 111, 265, 488; bank at, 455; barracks at, 67, 102, 111, 128, 297, 492; fortifications at, 673, 674; funds for, 191, 194, 253, 254, 260; public land at, 334, 393; sheriff at, 508.
Beach, F. Helen: about, xi.
Beall, Benjamin Lloyd: from, 439; to, 439.
Beall, Robert: about, 128, 211–212, 508.
Beaulieu, Joseph: pension of, 245.
Beckham, Armstead: from, viii.
Beckley, Alfred, about, 635–636.
Beckley, John: son of, 635–636.
Bell, Egbert H.: about, 608.
Bell, John R.: duty of, 500.
Belle Point, Ark., Mo. Territory: about, 329, 624.
Bellefontaine, Mo. Territory: funds for, 196; rations for, 367, 372, 374, 558, 560; stores at, 417.
Bellinger, Joseph: from, 102; to, 102.
Bellona Arsenal, Va.: about, 27, 259.
Bellona Foundry, Va.: about, 25.
Bender, George: about, 136, 434.
Benson, James Henry: about, 201, 217.
Benson, Peregrine: from, 201, 217.
Bernard, Simon: from, 288, 461, 482, 616, 661; reports by, 296, 497, 509, 648.
Bettle, Samuel: about, 499.
Betts, Samuel R.: about, 399; from, 282, 283, 398, 400, 430, 673; to, 282, 363, 398, 400, 430.
Bibb, William Wyatt: about, 152, 275; from, 331, 547, 553, 554; to, 331.
Bicker, Walter, Jr.: about, 19.
Biddle, Nicholas: about, 204; to, xxxi.

Biddle, Thomas, Jr.: about, 505; from, 149–150; to, 138, 149.
Binney, Horace: about, 402.
Blackshear, David: about, 619; to, 90.
Blair, John: campaign of, 186.
Bland, Theodorick, about, 135.
Blaney, George: about, 257, 528, 563, 638; from, 74, 292, 392, 679, 694.
Bliss, John: about, 293, 317, 322–323, 415, 492, 500; from, 425.
Bloodgood, Francis: about, 117, 481.
Bloodgood, William: about, 117, 481, 579.
Blount, John: accounts of, 148.
Blount, William G.: about, 17; from, 18, 333–334.
Boden, Andrew: from, 150.
Bogardus, Robert: from, 461, 517, 519.
Boilvin, Nicholas: about, 558; from, 83, 222, 324, 439, 531, 623; to, 83, 130.
Bomford, George: about, 526, 587, 611; accounts of, 615–616; allowances to, 158.
Bose, Philip: to, 131.
Boston, Mass.: fortifications at, 175; Paymaster at, 166.
Bounds, William: trial of, 433.
Bounty lands: eligibility for, 526, 579; reports about, 271, 545.
Bounty Lands, Section of, War Department: Chief Clerk of (*see* Cutting, Nathaniel); Clerks in, 549–552, 699; laws concerning, xxiv.
Bowditch, Nathaniel: book by, 437.
Bowen, William W.: from, 136.
Bowie, George: about, 89, 165.
Bowyer, John: from, 222, 315; to, 130, 222.
Boyd, George: about, 7, 31, 70, 87, 101, 104, 154, 302; from, 25, 118, 650, 679–680; to, 27–28, 111, 632, 650, 679.
Boyer, John: from, 637; to, 637.
Boyle, James H.: son of, 77.
Bradford, James H.: about, 232.
Bradford, William: about, 279; from, 67, 541, 699–700; to, 67, 112–113, 541.
Bradley, Abraham, Jr.: from, 42, 94, 123; to, 57.
Bradley, Bradford: about, 228, 393.
Brady, Hugh: about, 359, 649.
Brainerd, Cherokee Nation: school at, 430.
Branch, Richard Hayes: about, 252–253, 404, 456.
Brearley, David: about, 57; from, 74, 217–218.
Brent, Robert: about, 67, 163, 579; from, 107; orders to, 15, 637; to, 42, 79, 104, 150, 161, 166, 189, 190, 282, 482, 588, 631, 670–671.
Brethren, Society of United: schools of, 675–676.
Brewer, M.: campaign of, 186.
Brewerton, George D.: from, 452; to, 452.
Brigham, Paul: about, 391.
Briscoe, R. S.: from, 491.
Brockman, John: draft to, 163.
Bronaugh, James C.: about, 19, 630.
Bronaugh, Jere W.: from, 69.
Brooke, George Mercer: about, 92.
Brooks, Caleb: petition of, 334.
Brooks, James: about, 303.
Broom, Charles R.: from, 288–289.
Broom, James M.: from, 392.
Broom, Thomas R.: about, 191–192.
Brown, Cox & Allison: debt to, 119–120; payment to, 184.
Brown, Jacob: about, 142, 151, 534; from, 26, 58–59, 68, 99, 133, 150, 161, 182, 189, 208–209, 218, 257, 277, 293, 315, 358–359, 371, 472, 479, 503, 644, 685–686; to, 24, 26, 68, 74–75, 99, 133, 151–152, 189, 208, 209, 214–216, 257, 277, 284, 293, 358, 425–426, 445, 479–480, 503, 650–651, 660.
Brown, James: about, 407, 448.
Brown, Samuel: about, 711.
Brown, Thomas: to, 389.
Brown, William: about, 139, 155, 591.
Buchanan, James A.: from, 116, 269; to, 269.
Buckner, William Horace: about, 502.

Bulfinch, George S.: to, 341.
Bullock, ——: death of, 144, 254.
Bullock, Charles: from, 592; to, 592.
Bullock, W. B.: from, 240.
Bunting, Joseph P.: about, 610–611, 685.
Burbank, Sullivan: about, 136.
Burch, Daniel E.: about, 502, 618, 690.
Burckhartt, Nicholas L.: from, 176.
Burd, John A.: about, 254.
Burgess, Richard: about, 91.
Burley, Jacob R.: about, 360.
Burling, Walter: fine against, 542.
Burn, Willis: heirs of, 432.
Burnet, Daniel: about, 702, 705; from, 319, 482; to, 119, 482.
Burrill, James, Jr.: from, 461.
Burwell, William A.: from, 572; to, 572.
Bussard, David: bond of, 11.
Butler, Paul D.: about, 360.
Butler, Robert: about, 242, 245, 541; from, 94, 107, 116, 140, 145, 182–184, 304, 472, 528, 573, 592; to, 453, 534, 573.

Caddo Indians: boundaries of, 309; census of, 16; Factory for, 162.
Cadets: appointment form for, 44. *See also* United States Military Academy.
Cahokia Indians: annuities of, 603; treaties with, 209, 306.
Caldwell, E. M.: about, 679.
Calhoun (steamboat): launching of, 702, 703, 708.
Calhoun, Andrew Pickens (1812–1865): about, 186, 257.
Calhoun, Anna Maria (1817–1875): health of, 89, 165, 257.
Calhoun, Floride Colhoun (Mrs. John C.): about, xxxii, 165, 275, 705; miscarriage by, 257, 276.
Calhoun, James Edward. *See* Colhoun, James Edward.
Calhoun, John Caldwell (1782–1850): bills drafted by, 526–527, 572; crops of, 185–186; runaway slave of, 9, 179; Southern trip of, 473, 658, 663, 666, 684, 689, 705, 707, 712.
Calhoun, William (1776–1840): about, 256, 275, 415.
Call, Samuel: from, 228.
Callis, Otho W.: about, 57, 80.
Cambridge, Mass.: epidemic in, 155–156.
Cambridge, T. P.: from, 103.
Campbell, Hugh G.: to, 301.
Campbell, John: about, 537, 620.
Campbell, Quinton: from, 234.
Campbell, William G.: about, 537, 620.
Canada, Dominion of: boundary of, 238, 355–356, 408, 478, 614, 644, 653, 661, 666; outrage against, 99, 163–164, 189, 218.
Canadian Volunteers Act: fraudulent claims under, 418, 576–577.
Canals: construction of, 461–473; limitations of, 226–227; proposals for, 427–428, 690; resolution about, 228.
Cannon, Newton: about, 500, 525, 608, 683; to, 695.
Carroll, William: from, 142; to, 119.
Carruth, Adam: about, 303, 593, 632; from, 123; to, 123.
Carter, William, Jr.: about, 267–268.
Cass, Lewis, about, 28, 100–101, 247, 282, 476, 661; from, 123–127, 138–139, 146–147, 177–178, 189, 200, 209, 222, 229–230, 359, 365, 456, 480, 490, 510, 614, 623–624, 670; orders to, 56, 78; to, 42–43, 90, 102–103, 119, 123, 127, 365, 480, 689, 696.
Cassin, Mrs. Mary: petition of, 542.
Castle Pinckney, S. C.: about, 510.
Catawba River: proposed canal at, 493.
Cathcart, James Leander: about, 253, 264, 266–267, 271, 289; from, 259–260, 271, 284; to, 264.
Catlett, Hanson: from, 35, 70, 306; to, 11, 35.
Caton, Lewis: about, 371–372.

Caton, William: son of, 371.
Cavan & Co.: about, 291.
Chaffee, John: about, 323, 585; from, ix.
Chambers, Talbot: about, 8, 316, 664, 670; from, 59, 69, 85, 210, 374, 416, 443, 453, 454, 554; to, 69–70, 85, 210, 297–298, 374, 416, 417, 498, 627, 631, 664.
Chaplains, Army: about, 251, 526, 529.
Chaplains, Navy: charges against, 303.
Charleston, S. C.: fortifications at, 91, 510, 593–594, 685; Military Storekeeper at, 67, 83 (*see also* Wilson, Robert); Navy officer at, 301; ordnance at, 510; sickness at, 23; trial at, 395, 396–397.
Charlestown, Mass.: about, 241, 397, 614, 665.
Chase, William Henry: about, 89.
Chateaugay County, N. Y.: road through, 24, 292, 358, 472, 513–515.
Chauncey, Christopher: from, 402.
Chauncey, Commodore Isaac, U.S.N.: about, 299; from, 284, 304, 316, 325, 355, 402; to, 222–223, 304, 325, 355, 363, 400, 402.
Chauncey, Wolcott: about, 314.
Chef Menteur, La.: fortifications at, 656, 694.
Chehaw Indians: about, 170, 258–259, 606.
Cherokee Indians: annuities of, 241; census of, 429, 524; hotel bill of, 481; treaties with, 76, 113, 170, 428–429, 555
Cherokee Indians, Eastern: Agency for, 20, 613; Agent to, 583 (*see also* Meigs, Return J.); annuities of, 447, 555–556, 580, 592–593, 620, 630, 646; claims of, 644; Creek boundary of, 589; delegation from, 364, 407, 412, 447, 477, 490, 519, 521, 524, 534–535, 544–545, 549, 561–566, 580, 592–593, 600, 644, 647 (*see also* Hicks, Charles; Lowry, John; Morgan, Gideon, Jr.); emigration by, 20, 117, 197, 200, 266, 316–317, 364, 407, 424, 428–429, 430, 438, 447, 477, 488, 519, 521, 524, 544–545, 547–548, 555–556, 561–566, 580, 586, 589, 590, 634–635, 687–688; indemnities to, 693; intruders among, 317, 585–586, 693; rations for, 197, 332–334, 337, 360, 364–365, 505; road through, 331, 424, 489–490; schools for, 272, 430, 456, 544, 599–600, 675–676, 701; Sub-Agent to (*see* Houston, Samuel); treaties with, xxiii, 555–556, 564–566, 569–572, 585–586, 588–589, 600–602, 613, 616, 626, 628, 634–635, 645–646, 653, 656–657, 659.
Cherokee Indians, Western: about, 67, 107, 495, 541; Agent to (*see* Lewis, Reuben); annuities of, 555–556, 580, 646; boundaries of, 112–113, 133, 272–273; census of, 16; delegation from, 223; Factory for, 624; intruders among, 394; treaty with, 247.
Chesapeake Bay: fortifications at, 616, 648. *See also* the names of bordering sites.
Cheves, Langdon: about, 473, 657, 681.
Chew, John: from, 90; to, 90.
Chicago, Ill.: canal survey at, 190; Factory at, 124; Indian Agents at, 224, 389, 480, 627, 629, 630, 699; mail to, 596, 602; rations for, 318, 362, 368.
Chicago Historical Society: documents in, 28, 103, 681.
Chickasaw Indians: about, 339, 682–683; Agency of, 64, 67, 93, 281, 580, 613, 663; Agent to (*see* Sherburne, Henry); annuities of, 27, 34, 40, 41, 64, 105, 132, 134, 162, 164, 170, 182–183, 188, 231, 234, 235, 238–239, 241, 246, 252, 288, 304, 613; census of, 16, 322; civilization of, 599–600; road through, 201; Sub-Agent to (*see* Cook, David Godfrey); treaties with, 38–40, 69, 93–94, 119, 140, 145, 182–184, 213,

242, 244–245, 264, 269–270, 280–281, 306–307, 319, 320, 322, 349, 361, 408, 475–477, 492, 500, 525, 529–530, 566, 568, 592, 597, 608, 613, 659, 682, 694, 695.
Chief Engineer, Army: about, 591. *See also* Armistead, Walker Keith; Swift, Joseph G.
Childs, Charles B.: trial of, 332.
Childs, Enos R.: to, 365–366; trial of, 332.
Chippewa Indians: about, 138, 456, 696; annuities of, 689, 691; from, 155; treaties with, 68, 119, 194, 306, 645, 696, 708.
Choctaw Indians: about, 476; Agent to (*see* McKee, John); annuities of, 388, 410, 603, 629–630; census of, 16; delegation of, 326; emigration by, 674; Factory for, 8, 331; payments to, 318; schools for, 195–196, 243, 596, 630; Sub-Agent to, 117; treaties with, 66, 69, 119, 142, 243, 265–266, 319, 331, 388, 436, 482, 612–613, 702, 705.
Chouteau, Peter: about, 247.
Chouteau, René Auguste (1749–1829): about, 33, 67, 604, 694; from, 107, 136, 209, 495; to, 119, 689.
Christie, William: about, 195.
Chunn, John T.: to, 677–678.
Cincinnati, O.: barracks at, 636; complaint from, 525, 567; Mayor of, 567 (*see also* Corry, William).
Clark, George Rogers: followers of, 198, 221.
Clark, Isaac: claim of, 337–338.
Clark, William: about, 33, 67, 136, 176, 245, 334, 634, 647; from, 23, 37, 107, 111, 127, 247, 398, 440, 476; nephews of, 617; to, 37, 102–103, 119, 127, 247, 627, 631, 644, 651, 659, 661, 662.
Clarke, Charles Ezra: from, 713.
Clarke, John: contract of, 402.
Clarke, Newman S.: about, 649.
Claxton, Alexander: about, 267; from, 289; to, 264.
Clay, Henry: about, xxxii, 668; from, xxxi, 109, 133, 298; to, 36, 274, 277–278, 286, 293, 298, 301, 341–355, 366, 374–386, 398, 420, 448, 461–473, 490, 491–492, 501, 506–507, 509, 532–533, 555, 569, 610.
Clemson, Anthony: about, 18.
Clemson, Eli B.: about, 417; from, 210, 316; to, 210.
Clemson University Library: documents in, xxxii, 89, 257, 276, 474, 658.
Clinch, Duncan Lamont: about, 504, 532–533, 684; from, 167.
Cline, J.: about, 631.
Clinton, De Witt: about, 667; from, 386; to, 386–387.
Clitherall, George C.: about, 330.
Clothing, Army: contracts for, 403, 415; domestic fabrics for, 366–367, 403, 406, 411, 510, 552–553, 559–560, 701; funds for, xxi, 17, 409; purchasing policy for, 431; quality of, 131, 171–172, 253, 278–279, 388, 450, 493, 552–553, 691; reports about, 285, 364; stockpiles of, 457–459, 483. *See also* Irvine, Callender.
Coast, survey of the: about, 66, 356, 503, 519, 672; finances of, 36–37, 574, 617; report of, 115.
Cobb, Thomas Willis: about, 581; from, 526; to, 526.
Cocke, William: from, 41.
Cohea, Perry: account of, 93.
Colbert, George: about, 608, 609, 683; land of, 307, 566; visit to, 182.
Colbert, James: about, 598, 682–683.
Colbert, Levi: about, 307, 598, 609, 683; from, 269–270, 566.
Colbert, William: annuity of, 34, 132; debt of, 598.
Colburn, Reuben: petition of, 477.
Coleman, William A.: from, 632.
Colhoun, Floride (Mrs. John Ewing, Sr.): regards to, 257.
Colhoun, James Edward: about, 15, 658; to, 185–186.

Colhoun, John Ewing, Jr.: from, 256; to, 256–257.
Colquhoun, William S.: to, 341.
Colston, Edward: from, 481.
Colton, the Rev. George: from, 539–540.
Columbia, Tenn.: road from, 24, 94, 140, 472, 492.
Comanche Indians: census of, 16; traders with, 173.
Commissary General of Purchases: contracts by, 403, 415. *See also* Clothing, Army; Irvine, Callender.
Commissary General of Subsistence: duties of, 384–385; salary of, 413. *See also* Gibson, George.
Commissioner of Public Buildings: from, 66.
Commissioners of the Navy. *See* Navy Commissioners, Board of.
Comptrollers, U. S.: 1st (*see* Anderson, Joseph); 2nd (*see* Cutts, Richard).
Comstock, Oliver Cromwell: from, 435; to, 435.
Congress (U. S. frigate): about, 406, 658; commander of (*see* Henley, John D.); crew for, 285, 299–300, 373.
Connecticut: militia of, 246, 391; politics in, 237.
Conner, Samuel S.: from, 405.
Conner, William: about, 421, 598.
Conrad, Robert Y.: about, 605–606.
Constitution, U. S. S.: about, 397.
Cook, David Godfrey: about, 27, 38, 322; from, 103; to, 103.
Cook, John: about, 499.
Cooper, Samuel: about, 22; from, 140–141.
Cooper, Thomas: about, 711; from, 102, 402; to, 95, 101, 102.
Coppinger, Don José: about, 426, 433, 448, 486, 501–502; from, 521; to, 521.
Cornelius, the Rev. Elias: from, 195.
Cornwall, Conn.: school at, 195.
Corry, William: from, 525.
Cotton, William: about, 613; to, 694.
Council Bluffs (now Ia.): proposed post at, 633.
Cox, John: about, 106.
Cox, Nathaniel: funds for, 606, 694.
Coxe, Edward D.: from, 103.
Coxe, Tench: about, 564.
Craig, James: from, 201.
Crawford, Joel: from, 90; to, 90.
Crawford, William: from, 566.
Crawford, William H.: about, xv, xxxii, 157, 218, 574, 610, 670; as Secretary of War, 8, 32, 324, 533; from, 37, 149, 204, 253, 254, 260, 455, 533, 647, 672, 678, 680; reports by, 226, 512; to, 16–17, 79–80, 83, 161, 169, 184, 191, 194, 228, 237, 247, 249–250, 251, 253, 260, 265, 270, 334, 355, 366, 399, 455, 460, 499, 558, 566, 617, 633, 651, 660, 678.
Creek Indians: about, 151, 152, 218, 583; Agents to (*see* Hawkins, Benjamin; Mitchell, David B.); annuities of, 211, 236, 410; boundaries of, 69, 96, 99, 235, 261, 434, 560–561, 589, 606; delegations of, 577, 646, 700–701 (*see also* McIntosh, William); Factory of, 8; Fla. land claims of, 700; indemnities to, 501, 606, 646, 700–701; lands of, 10, 507, 546–547, 652, 654; merger of Seminoles with, 193, 646, 652–653, 654, 700; rations for, 340; schools for, 170–171, 701; treaties with, 14, 207, 475, 523, 606.
Crittenden, John J.: to, 325.
Croghan, George: about, 606.
Crooker, Turner: about, 486.
Crooks, Ramsay: about, 222, 229, 627; from, 631, 656, 686; to, 631.
Cross, George Warren: from, 23.
Cross, Trueman: from, 334.
Crowell, John: to, 450.
Crowninshield, Benjamin W.: about, xiv–xvi, 397; to, 12, 83, 263, 331, 395, 401.
Crozet, Claudius: about, 141.
Cruger, Daniel: from, 435.
Cudworth, Nathaniel: to, 113.

Cue, Robert: certificate by, 250.
Cullens, George: certificate by, 250.
Cummins, Francis D.: from, 3.
Cummins, Joseph: from, 240.
Cunningham, Thomas S.: from, 332.
Cutbush, James: about, 210.
Cutting, Nathaniel: about, 281, 338, 432, 576; decisions by, 419, 434; from, 198, 221, 271, 303, 403, 545, 549–552; to, 104.
Cutts, Charles: attestations by, 363, 374, 484, 492, 510, 542, 563, 572.
Cutts, Richard: about, xxv, 403, 691, 697; from, 218; to, 166, 168, 529, 662.

Dailey, James: pension of, 252.
Dalaby, James: about, 341, 538, 587; from, 187; to, 187.
Darlington, Benjamin: from, 37–38, 70; to, 11, 37.
Darragh, Alexander P.: about, 406.
Darrington, John: from, 66.
Dauphin Island, Ala. Territory: fortifications at, 175, 427, 451, 631, 656, 674, 694.
Davies, William: from, 240.
Davis, John M.: about, 18–19.
Davis, John W.: from, 275, 304–305, 366; to, 275, 304, 366.
Davis, Matthew L.: from, 392–393; to, 369.
Day, Sylvester: about, 80–81.
Dean, Edward: petition of, 329.
Dearborn, Henry: policy of, 459.
Delafield, Richard: about, 356.
Delavan, Benjamin: about, 209, 214, 359.
Delaware: Pea Patch claim of, 109, 706, 707; U. S. District Attorney for, 706.
Delaware Indians: about, 138, 326, 692; annuities of, 692; appraisal of improvements of, 598, 613; emigration by, 247; treaties with, 71, 119, 189, 194, 306, 420–421, 483, 613, 645, 694.
Dennison, Elisha: claim of, 147.
Depew, Jesse: about, 393.
Dering, Henry: orders to, 169.
De Russy, Lewis Gustavus: about, 644; from, 31, 65, 531; to, 31, 65.
De Russy, René Edward: about, 386–387, 574, 614, 643, 679; from, 370, 503–504, 517; to, 392, 494, 517.
DeSaussure, Gabriel E.: from, 263.
DeSaussure, Henry W.: from, 706–707.
Deserters, Army: about, 128, 230–231; capture of, 68, 166, 168, 373, 449; care of, 256; outrage by, 189, 433; punishment of, 14, 294–295, 312, 440; reports about, 26, 307, 695.
Desha, Robert M.: from, 371.
De Treville, Richard Laboulardrie: recommendation of, 706–707.
Detroit, Mich. Territory: Army post at, 216, 630; depots at, 265, 557; Receiver of Public Monies at, 680; road from, 24, 472–473, 492.
Detroit Public Library: documents in, 8, 251.
de Villemont, Charles: about, 107.
Dexter, Daniel S.: death of, 204.
Dickerson, Mahlon: to, 305.
Dieterich, John Philip: recommendation of, 150, 165–166.
Dietrich, Peter F.: about, 223.
Digges, Thomas A.: from, 35, 130; to, 130.
District of Columbia: banks in, 104, 705; militia of, 678, 712.
Diven, James: from, 141.
Diven, James, Jr.: about, 141.
Dixon, Jared: pension of, 265.
Donelan, Mary Esther: about, xi.
Donelson, Andrew J.: about, 115.
Dorman, James: from, 179; to, 179.
Dougherty, Thomas: about, 491; attestations by, 305, 329, 334, 386, 420, 440, 501; from, 150–151.
Downes, John: about, 225.
Downs, William F.: from, 120; to, 120.
Doyle, Edmund: claim by, 356.
Dozier, Evans: about, 488–489.

Duane, William: about, 14; from, 71; to, 71–72.
Du Commun, Joseph: from, 533.
Duer, Alexander: recommendation of, 683.
Dufief, N. G.: about, 490, 599, 609; to, 338.
Duke University Library: documents in, 80, 659, 693.
Duncan, William Robert: about, 534.
Dunlap, William: from, 120.
DuPasquier, Charles Henry: from, 624.
du Plessis, Chevalier Thomas de Mandiet: claim of, 303–304.
Duponceau, P. S.: about, 711.
Dusenberry, Samuel: about, 404–405, 412, 416.
Dysentery: epidemics of, 155, 502.

Earle, Elias: to, 593.
Eastburn, Walter N.: document owned by, 572.
Easter, Richard J.: about, 40, 182, 540; from, 454.
Eaton, John H.: about, 564.
Eaton, William: from, 451.
Echeverri, John M.: about, 661.
Edgefield, S. C.: Postmaster at, 521.
Edwards, James L.: about, xxiv, 159–161; charge against, 576–577; Clerks under (*see* Pension Office, War Department: Clerks in); from, 8, 245, 253, 284, 293, 298–299, 325, 387, 446, 482–483, 522–523, 528–529, 538, 581–582, 588, 606; orders to, 164, 538, 663; reports by, 325, 328; to, 104, 151, 325.
Edwards, Lewis: about, 319, 632; charge against, 576–577; from, 712.
Edwards, Ninian: about, 245, 260, 433, 503; from, 209, 398–399, 494–495, 569; to, 102–103.
Edwards, Spencer: pension of, 588.
Edwardsville, Ill.: Receiver of Public Monies at, 691.
Eel River Indians: Agent to, 631, 636, 644; annuities of, 603, 694.
Ellicott, Andrew: about, 628; from, 691, 696; reports by, 158–159, 428; to, 696.
Ellicott, James: visit by, 71.
Elliot, Howard: discharge of, 320.
Elliott, Jesse D.: from, 616; report by, 648.
Elliott, Moses H.: about, 330.
Emerson, Mrs. William: bounty land for, 338.
Engel, Mary Lynn (Mrs. Douglas H.): about, xi.
Engineers, Board of: meeting of, 109.
Engineers, Corps of: Chief of, 591 (*see also* Armistead, Walker Keith; Swift, Joseph G.); contracts issued by, 505–506, 610; funds for, 196, 198–199, 493; office of, 21–22, 199, 494; officers of, 293, 333, 425–426; printing and stationery for, 432, 490; promotions in, 527–528, 563; reforms in, 413; uniform of, 436.
Engineers, Topographical. *See* Coast, survey of; Long, Stephen H.; Young, Hugh.
England: U. S. Minister to (*see* Rush, Richard).
Engle, James: about, 579.
English, D.: from, 302.
Enterprise (U. S. brig): about, 395.
Eppes, John Wayles: from, 555; to, 506, 527.
Erie, Pa.: Naval Station at, 204.
Erie Canal: construction of, 468.
Ervin, James: from, 520.
Erving, George W.: from, 81, 98.
Essex, U. S. S.: about, 147.
Esterbrook, Alvin: about, 391.
Eustis, Abram: about, 373; from, 610, 618.
Eustis, William: from, 270, 323, 610; to, 610.
Evans, Samuel: about, 223; from, 329; to, 333.
Evarts, Jeremiah: from, 456–457.

Factory system of Indian trade: changes in, 38, 44–56, 123–127,

177–178, 310, 341–355, 443. *See also* Indian trade.
Fairfax, Wilson M. C.: about, 592; from, 293, 317, 415–416, 523, 535–536, 637–638.
Fanning, Alexander C. W.: about, 143, 426.
Fanning, John B.: from, 406.
Farnham, J. H.: from, 579.
Farnham, Russel: arrest of, 418, 543.
Fate, John M.: about, 363.
Fay, Heman A.: from, 172.
Fayssoux, Peter: about, 534.
Fayssoux, Peter, Jr.: about, 534.
Fell, Frederick S.: about, 131.
Fenwick, John R.: about, 166; from, 128, 196, 252, 290, 506; to, 196.
Fifth Auditor. *See* Pleasonton, Stephen.
Finch, Isaac: testimony by, 418.
Finch, William B.: about, 427; orders to, 291, 302.
Finley, Clement Alexander: about, 508.
Finley, James E. B.: about, 706–707.
Fire Brand (U. S. schooner): about, 332, 404.
First Comptroller, U. S. *See* Anderson, Joseph.
Fisher, Otis: about, 287, 602.
Fisk, Experience: pension for, 522–523.
Fisk, James: to, 391.
Fitch, Thomas: about, 191; from, 184.
Florance, William: from, 103, 139.
Florida, East: canal proposed in, 428, 690; Ga. boundary of, 95, 96–97, 99, 143, 158–159, 186–187, 261, 523, 561, 615, 619, 626, 628, 652, 653, 658; Governor of (*see* Coppinger, Don José); map of, 564, 618–619; Negro Fort in, 532–533; sketch of, 690.
Floridas, East and West: applicant for position in, 652; defense of, 109; rations contractor for, 86; Spanish reoccupation of, 645; topographical survey of, 107; U. S. acquisition of, 3, 427–428, 431, 617, 626, 629, 681, 684, 685, 690, 710. *See also* Seminole Indians; Spanish posts in the Floridas.
Floyd, John; about, 619; charges by, 267, 301; from, 257, 259; to, 257–258, 366.
Folsom, David: from, 195–196.
Folsom, Israel: education of, 195.
Folsom, McKee: education of, 195.
Folyard, John: pension of, 159–161.
Foot, Adonijah: from, 568.
Fooy, Benjamin: from, 327.
Forage allowances: about, 39–40, 57, 190, 220; funds for, 241, 651; regulations for, 109, 116.
Ford, John: from, 170.
Ford, Timothy: from, 600–601.
Forman, Judge ——: arms produced by, 475.
Forsyth, John: about, 98, 141, 179; from, 243.
Forsyth, Robert M.: about, 98.
Forsyth, Thomas: about, 245, 651, 659; from, 389, 573–574, 662; to, 130, 662.
Fort Armstrong, Ill.: about, 61, 215, 362, 651.
Fort Bainbridge, Ala. Territory: road from, 173, 174, 221.
Fort Barrancas, West Fla.: about, 29–30, 152, 637, 660–661.
Fort Calhoun, Va. *See* Rip Raps Shoal.
Fort Claiborne, Ala. Territory: rations at, 324; road to, 137, 173, 221, 326.
Fort Covington, Md.: about, 401, 414.
Fort Crawford, Ala. Territory: rations at, 661.
Fort Crawford, Prairie du Chien (now in Wisc.): about, 215, 651; rations at, 362.
Fort Diamond, N. Y.: construction of, 140–141.
Fort Fayette, Pa.: sale of, 284.
Fort Gadsden, East Fla.: about, 30, 205; Negroes at, 193.
Fort Gratiot, Mich. Territory: reservation of, 57, 193, 199.

Fort Harrison, Ind.: rations at, 677–678.
Fort Hawkins, Ga.: about, 57, 94, 123, 507, 546–547, 583, 654; leases at, 207, 299, 652; mail from, 131; road from, 24, 66, 174, 326, 328, 435.
Fort Independence, Mass.: about, 373, 618.
Fort Johnson, S. C.: about, 510.
Fort McHenry, Md.: about, 211, 450, 696.
Fort Meigs, O.: about, 108; road to, 472–473, 492; Treaty of, 421.
Fort Mifflin, Pa.: reports about, 138, 149–150; Surgeons at, 80–81.
Fort Mitchell, Ala. Territory: road from, 174.
Fort Monroe, Va. *See* Old Point Comfort.
Fort Moultrie, S. C.: about, 510.
Fort Norfolk, Va.: about, 477.
Fort Pickering, Chickasaw Bluffs, Tenn.: about, 327.
Fort St. Charles: retention of, 488.
Fort St. Marks, East Fla.: commandant of, 92; physicians at, 529; rations for, 260; restoration to Spain of, 14, 29–30, 32, 87, 143, 152, 255, 511–512 (*see also* Spain).
Fort Scott, Ga.: history of, 525.
Fort Smith, Mo. Territory (now Ark.): commanding officer at, 541.
Fort Stoddert, Ala. Territory: about, 583; road to, 24, 66, 137.
Fort Sullivan, Mass. (now Me.): rations for, 166.
Fort Warburton. *See* Fort Washington.
Fort Washington, Md.: about, 481; contractor for, 479; fishery near, 35, 130.
Fort Wayne, Ga.: danger at, 240.
Fort Wayne, Ind.: Indian Agent at, 282, 444, 480, 510, 636, 644–645, 694, 696 (*see also* Johnston, John); mail from, 596, 602; rations for, 318.
Fort Wilkinson: about, 583; Factory at, 671; Treaty of, 211, 671.
Fort Wool, Va. *See* Rip Raps Shoal.
Fortifications, Army: appropriations for, xxi; plans for, 175; reports about, 205. *See also* Engineers, Corps of, and the names of specific forts.
Foster, Daniel: pension of, 198.
Foster, William B.: from, 38, 65, 70; to, 11, 38.
Fourth Auditor. *See* Freeman, Constant.
Fowler, Abram C.: about, 195.
Fowler, John: from, 162, 216, 224.
Fox Indians: about, 245, 573–574, 708; annuity of, 603.
Foxall, Henry: from, 302.
France: U. S. Minister to (*see* Gallatin, Albert).
Francisco, Peter: pension of, xxi.
Frankford Creek Arsenal, Pa.: repairs at, 32.
Frankfort, Ky.: arsenal at, 409.
Franklin County, N. Y.: road through, 713.
Franklin, Mo. Territory: Receiver of Public Monies at, 680.
Franks, Joshua: warrant for, 658.
Fraser, Donald: from, 389.
Freelon, Thomas W.: about, 389.
Freeman, Constant: report by, 398; to, 153, 299, 305, 366.
Freeman, Edgar: from, 363; to, 363.
Freeman, Thomas: about, 264.
French, George P.: about, 318.
Friends, Society of. *See* Society of Friends.
Fromentin, Eligius: about, 448.
Frost, John Earle: debt to, 403.
Frye, Nathaniel, Jr.: about, 191, 509; from, 107, 133–134, 189, 230, 254, 271, 278, 325, 579, 588.
Fulton, James B.: about, 582.
Fur trade: companies engaged in, 440–443; Northwest, 60, 623.
Fürst, Mority: about, 226, 235.

Gadsden, James: about, 14, 20, 33, 58, 81–82, 87, 110, 128, 426, 427,

712; from, 3, 12, 19–20, 41, 275, 427–428, 674, 690; funds for, 580, 606, 694; reports by, 42, 109, 673, 674; to, 656, 689–690.
Gage, Joshua: from, 530.
Gaillard, John: about, 511; from, 338, 652; to, 289, 446, 490, 506–507, 509, 533, 542.
Gaines, Edmund P.: about, 14, 217–218, 235, 275, 523, 561; court-martial of, 303; from, 8, 17, 86, 143–145, 148, 152, 173, 191–192, 205–207, 230, 234, 252, 254–255, 294–295, 299, 312, 331, 338–340, 396, 405, 426, 433, 440, 448–449, 476, 486, 501–502, 504, 507, 518, 521, 529, 533, 545–547, 582–585, 593–594, 618–619, 625, 628–629, 637, 652, 660–661, 684, 685, 690; orders by, 167, 484–485, 588; orders to, 96, 99, 114, 121, 193, 518, 556, 560; reports by, 186, 615; to, 19–20, 29–30, 33, 43, 58, 85–87, 95, 106, 143, 152, 158, 173, 184–185, 192, 207, 230–231, 234–235, 252, 260, 294, 299, 331, 338, 405, 504, 507, 517–518, 521, 529, 533, 538–539, 545, 596, 617, 625, 628–629, 652–653, 684, 685, 690.
Gaines, George S.: about, 8.
Gale, Anthony: about, 278, 371.
Gales, Joseph, Jr.: from, 610–611.
Gallatin, Albert: from, 88, 98; report by, 227.
Galveston, Tex.: privateers at, 280, 403–404; tornado at, 305.
Gambold, the Rev. John: about, 675, 676.
Gantt, Edward A.: about, 325.
Gardens, vegetable: Army labor for, 513–515.
Gardiner, John: from, 199, 218, 225.
Gardiner, the Rev. John D.: from, 80; to, 80.
Gardner, John L.: about, 330.
Garlington, John: from, 120.
Garrison, Daniel: about, 555, 577; from, 541, 690; to, 588, 690–691.
Gassaway, John: from, 371–372.
Geddes, John: testimony by, 489.
Gedney, Samuel: from, 59.
Gedway, Samuel: about, 508.
General Accounting Office, U. S.: documents in, 94, 136, 154, 444, 481, 494, 503, 561, 604.
General Land Office, U. S.: Chief Clerk of (*see* Gardiner, John); Commissioner of (*see* Meigs, Josiah); mistake made by, 672–673.
General Macomb (merchant brig): detention of, 395.
Genius of Liberty: about, 154.
Georgia: Cherokee lands in, 565, 585–586, 653, 659; Fla. boundary of, 37, 95, 96–97, 99, 143, 158–159, 186–187, 261, 523, 561, 615, 619, 626, 628, 652, 653, 658; Governors of (*see* Mitchell, David B.; Rabun, William); map of, 32; militia of, 366; ordnance bought from, 337; pensions in, 621, 641; request by, 517–518; Senate of, 517–518; Tenn. boundary of, 317.
Gibbes, William: about, 194.
Gibbs, George K.: about, 257.
Gibson, George: about, xxviii, 19, 21, 91, 112, 362, 369, 529, 564, 625; absence of, 64, 75, 77; contracts issued by, 300, 702, 704, 709; from, 295, 318, 360, 436, 558, 585, 638; to, 22, 40, 104, 232, 340, 403, 429–430, 507, 691.
Gibson, James: from, 39, 70; to, 11, 39.
Giles, Aquila: claim by, xx; from, 192, 258, 372, 495, 520; son of, 283; to, 192, 495, 520–521.
Giles, George Washington: about, 192, 258, 283, 372, 495, 520–521; from, 394, 504.
Gill, R. W.: from, 696–697.
Glassell, James M.: about, 192, 486; from, 192, 501–502.
Gleason, Joseph: about, 481, 530.
Glenn, Hugh: about, 69–70, 85.
Gloster, Dr. ——: death of, 491.
Gloster, Arthur B.: about, 443, 505.

Good Hope (flatboat): sinking of, 213, 241.
Goolsby, Samuel: bounty for, 526.
Gordon, John: payment to, 598.
Gordon, William: to, 341.
Gould, James: from, 578.
Graham, George: about, 21, 68, 157, 280, 281, 320, 419, 558, 559; from, 59, 501, 697; to, 448.
Graham, James Duncan: about, 615.
Graham, John: about, 65, 135.
Graham, Richard: about, 567, 573; from, 68, 245–246, 260, 707–708; to, 68, 130, 405–406, 433–434, 691.
Graham, William Montrose: about, 615.
Granger, Erastus: about, 301, 526; to, 653, 654.
Gratiot, Charles: from, 196.
Gray, French Strother: about, 502.
Great Britain: treaty with, xv; U. S. Minister to (*see* Rush, Richard).
Great Swamp Indians: gift to, 222.
Green Bay (now in Wisc.): boats at, 647; Factory at, 49, 124; Indian Agent at, 315, 627; land sought at, 222, 557; rations at, 318, 362, 368.
Green County, N. Y.: militia of, 194.
Green, Duff: appointment of, 414; recommendations of, 176, 398–399.
Green, George: about, 73.
Green, Peter H.: about, 405, 505; from, 225, 504, 691; to, 369, 504.
Greenbush Cantonment, N. Y.: about, 277, 477.
Greenleafs Point, D.C.: about, 258, 665.
Gregory, Luther: petition of, 329.
Griffin, Robert F.: about, 554, 577.
Griffith, Camillus: about, 320, 637; contract of, 86, 260, 299; from, 66; to, 366, 369.
Grimbrede, Thomas: from, 292, 480; to, 292, 451.
Grimké, Charles F.: about, 68, 107; from, 3.
Grimké, J. F.: from, 68.
Grimké, Thomas S.: about, 68; from, 107; to, 107.
Grosvenor, George Henry: about, 614, 615.

Habersham, Robert: from, 240.
Hagerman, Henry B.: about, 133, 527.
Hagner, Peter: about, xxv, 71, 160, 541; accounts of, 36, 154, 258, 681; charges against, 479, 481–482; decisions by, 543, 662; duties of, 552, 660, 667; from, 91, 415, 419, 451, 486, 487, 525, 660, 674; reports by, 368, 477, 491–492, 542; to, 91, 147, 187.
Hajo, Hillis: about, 206.
Hall, Bolling: from, 435.
Hall, Harrison: from, 147.
Hall, John: about, 133–134, 288, 392, 407–408, 418.
Hall, John H.: about, 679; from, 274, 406, 507, 611–612, 664–666.
Hall, Joseph C.: about, 389.
Hall, Nathaniel Nye: court-martial of, 4–5, 58, 98, 208, 216, 315, 340, 445; from, 534.
Hambly, William: about, 206, 356, 428.
Hamilton, Alexander: from, 242.
Hamilton, Mrs. Alexander: application by, 242.
Hamilton, Archibald W.: about, 3, 260.
Hamilton, James A.: about, 223.
Hamilton, John: warrant for, 242.
Hamm, John: about, 250.
Hammond, C.: from, 250.
Hampton Roads, Va.: fortifications at, 227, 616 (*see also* Old Point Comfort, Va.).
Hanes, John: from, 284; to, 284.
Hansell, William Young: from, 57, 80; to, 57, 80.
Hardehy, John: about, 160–161.
Hardin, Martin Davis: to, 680–681.
Harlin, George: about, 607.
Harney, Benjamin Franklin: about, 560.
Harpers Ferry, Va. (now W. Va.): furnace tract at, xxv, 479, 516–517;

public land at, 420; stores at, 102, 122, 128–129; U. S. Armory at, viii, xxi, xxv, 17, 18, 129, 168, 196, 202–204, 274, 283–284, 288, 297, 302, 323, 333, 335–336, 370, 394, 402, 526, 529, 599, 611, 665–666.
Harris, Charles: about, 153–154, 538.
Harris, Richard: from, 631.
Harris, William L.: about, 318.
Harrison, Benjamin: from, 491.
Harrison, Charles: about, 182.
Harrison, John: from, 176.
Harrison, Matthew R. T.: about, 543.
Harrison, Robert M.: about, 585.
Harrison, William Henry: about, 79, 181, 253, 636; from, 360, 567; to, 282, 525.
Harvard University Library: document in, 140.
Hassler, Ferdinand Rudolf: about, 370, 392, 454, 478, 503, 519, 643, 653, 679; accounts of, 36–37, 617; from, 238, 239, 355–356, 387, 574, 614, 617, 666, 676-677; to, 238, 387, 521, 574, 614, 617, 653, 666.
Havana, Cuba: prisoners at, 312.
Haverford College Library: document in, 40.
Hawkins, Benjamin: about, 583–584.
Hay, Richard: affidavit by, 172.
Hayden, Jeremiah D.: about, 90, 259.
Hayes, Joel: from, 263.
Hayes Memorial Library: document in, 115.
Hayne, Arthur P.: from, 416; resignation by, 20, 82.
Heath, John D.: about, 489, 652.
Hector (a slave): about, 9, 179.
Heele, William: from, 175.
Hegins, Charles: about, 27, 138, 168–169, 175, 419; to, 369.
Heileman, Julius Frederick: about, 131, 172, 392.
Hell Gate, N. Y.: fortifications at, 461, 517, 519.
Hempstead, Thomas: about, 585, 607; to, 625.
Henderson & Co.: treaty with, 555.
Henderson, Archibald: from, 243, 265, 278, 282–283.
Henderson, Richard: about, 555.
Henderson, Thomas: contract of, 505; from, 332–333. *See also* Turk & Henderson.
Hendrick, Solomon U.: from, 483.
Henley, John D.: from, 278, 299–300, 406; to, 285, 406.
Henry E. Huntington Library and Art Gallery: document in, 151.
Henshaw, John H.: to, 341.
Hepburn, John M.: about, 509.
Herrick, Samuel: about, 250.
Heustis, Jabez W.: about, 330, 529.
Hickey, William: about, 325.
Hicks, Charles R.: about, 200, 407, 521, 675; from, 555–556, 569–570, 580, 588–589, 601–602, 644, 645, 647.
Higgins, Charles. *See* Hegins, Charles.
Hill, William: from, 246; to, 11, 246.
Hills, John: about, 27, 33.
Hindman, Jacob: about, 493; from, 211, 691.
Hines, Jacob: about, 491.
Hobart, the Rev. J. H.: from, 686; to, 686–687.
Hodges, Samuel, Jr.: 39, 60, 72, 75, 99–100, 239–240; to, 72, 99, 239.
Hogan, John B.: about, 123, 265, 319; from, 588.
Holding, John W.: about, 136.
Holland, John: about, 26.
Holmes, Andrew Hunter: about, 606.
Holmes, Charles R.: from, 293, 317, 415–416, 523, 535–536.
Holmes, Hugh: about, 605–606; from, 663.
Holmes, John: about, xxxii.
Holmes, Oliver W.: about, x–xi.
Holt, Charles: about, 540.
Holt, Maj. Charles: son of, 540.
Homans, Benjamin: about, xvi–xvii, 101, 267–268, 308; from, 43, 300, 390; to, 221, 242, 363, 373.
Hook, James H.: about, 401.
Hook, Thomas: petition of, 329.
Hooker, Samuel F.: about, 299.

Hopkins, Benjamin W.: about, 151, 418–419; from, 712.
Hopkins, Gerard T.: from, 691, 696.
Horlbeck, John: from, 91.
Hornet (U. S. schooner): order to, 368, 424; repair of, 373.
Hornet, U. S. S.: about, 369, 389; repair of, 373.
House, James: from, 539.
House of Representatives, U. S.: Clerks of (*see* Beckley, John; Dougherty, Thomas); Speaker of (*see* Clay, Henry).
Houston, Alexander M.: appointment of, 164; from, 621.
Houston, Robert: recommendation of, 628; to, 656–657.
Houston, Samuel: about, 115; accounts of, 563, 567, 573.
Howard County, Mo. Territory: militia of, 176.
Hoyt, the Rev. Ard: from, 272, 430; to, 272.
Hoyt, Gates: from, 75; to, 75.
Hoyt, Moses: about, 451.
Hudson, Dawsey P.: road contract of, 26, 92, 201, 326–327.
Hughes, Daniel: from, 132.
Hughes, Francis: pension of, 662.
Hugo, Samuel B.: court-martial of, 64, 87.
Humbert, Jean Joseph Amable: about, 280.
Humphreys, Gad: about, 416, 486.
Humphreys, May: about, 291.
Hungerford, Orville: from, 713.
Hunt, George: about, 613; to, 694.
Hunt, Thomas: about, 19, 481.
Hunt, Thomas F.: about, 476, 508; from, 5.
Hunt, W. S.: heirs of, 419.
Huntington, Ebenezer: from, 246, 391; to, 391–392.
Huntington, George: from, 263.
Huntsville, Ala.: road from, xxv.
Huntt, Henry: from, 258.
Hurd & Sewall: draft to, 602.
Hutton, James: about, 253, 264, 266–267, 271.
Hyde, ——: about, 188, 255, 295–296.

Illinois: Delegate from, 569; Indian Agent for (*see* Graham, Richard); Indian lands in, 209, 260, 405–406; statehood of, 707; Sub-Agent for (*see* Menard, Pierre); Superintendent of Indian Affairs in (*see* Edwards, Ninian).
Illinois Indians: annuity of, 603.
Inabinett, E. L.: about, xi.
Independence (schooner): detention of, 533.
Independence, U. S. S.: crewman of, 433.
Indian Agents: appropriations for, xxii.
Indian trade: audits of, xxv; corporations in, xvii–xviii, 440–443; licenses for, 64, 222. *See also* Factory system.
Indian Trade, Office of: creation of, 343; funds of, 199, 559; Superintendent of (*see* McKenney, Thomas L.). *See also* Factory system.
Indiana: Indian lands in, 189.
Indiana Historical Society: document in, 103.
Indians: annuities of, xxiii–xxiv; civilization of, xxiii–xxiv.
Infantry Regiments: 1st, 259, 393; 2nd, 358–359, 474, 649; 3rd, 215, 257; 4th, 230, 476, 525, 588, 693; 5th, 136, 474, 578, 647, 651, 685; 6th, 292, 359, 474, 492, 513–515, 578, 631, 649, 663, 685–686; 7th, 502; 8th, 259, 321, 393, 405, 537.
Ingersoll, Charles J.: to, 8–9, 179, 334.
Internal improvements: constitutionality of, xix–xx, 472; proposals for, 226–227. *See also* Canals; Roads.
Iroquois Indians: about, 295–296, 555; Agents to (*see* Granger, Erastus; Parrish, Jasper); annuities of, 447, 603, 654; census of, 336; emigration by, 11, 42–43, 56–57,

90, 188, 255, 336, 670; Interpreter to, 526, 530; property of, 653, 654; Sub-Agent to, 451. *See also* the names of individual Iroquois tribes.
Irvine, Callender: about, 17, 131, 460; Clerk to, 131; duties of, 103–104; from, 32, 171, 207–208, 210, 231, 240, 243, 262, 265, 272, 278–279, 289–290, 305, 364, 366–367, 400–401, 416–417, 431, 450, 452, 457–459, 483, 502–503, 508, 515, 534, 552–553, 559, 612, 625; Indian Agency of, 526; to, 79, 103–104, 120, 121–122, 131, 167, 172, 173, 207, 210, 219, 240, 253–254, 278, 289, 305, 316, 360, 388, 400–401, 403, 406, 415, 417, 431, 436, 440, 452–453, 483, 502, 515, 559–560, 612, 625, 701.
Irving, Washington: brother of, 223, 508.
Irving, William: from, 223; to, 508.
Irwin, Jared: about, 419.
Isett, Samuel L.: about, 175.

Jackow (a Miami Chief): plea of, 326.
Jackson, Andrew: about, xv, xxi, xxxi–xxxiii, 14, 33, 37, 41, 58, 64, 79, 121, 164, 242, 269, 275, 288, 304, 307, 317, 390, 426, 427, 454, 508, 529, 540, 566, 657; enmity of Scott toward, 604–605, 632, 641–643, 654–655; from, 18–19, 19–20, 24–25, 39, 40, 43–44, 60, 81–82, 85–86, 87, 91, 94, 109, 113–114, 115, 116, 123, 131, 145–146, 169, 223, 224, 229, 244, 245, 270–271, 274–275, 312–314, 318–319, 331, 360–361, 417, 420, 431, 436, 439, 533, 534, 547, 560; Indian services of, 182–184, 231, 571, 705; Northern trip of, xxxii, 564, 592; orders by, 339, 512, 606; orders to, 639, 650, 693; Seminole campaign of, 8–9, 105–106, 540–541, 547, 556, 596 (*see also* Lacock, Abner); to, 3, 20, 23–24, 30–31, 39–40, 43, 60–61, 74–75, 91–92, 94, 109–111, 115, 116, 119, 145, 152, 158, 164, 169–170, 223–224, 265–266, 270, 272–273, 314, 318, 327, 331, 362, 394–395, 417–418, 431–432, 453–454, 528, 547, 553, 554, 633–634, 660, 702.
Jackson, Epenetus H.: about, 159–161.
Jamaica: specie from, 291.
James, Ashabel: debt to, 256.
James, James: about, 567.
Jamison, John: from, 173, 305, 320, 476; to, 102–103, 130, 305–306, 476.
Jamison, Titus T.: about, 286.
Janners, William: resignation by, 112.
Java, U. S. S.: about, 397.
Jefferson (steamboat): about, 703.
Jefferson County, N. Y.: road through, 713.
Jefferson, Thomas: about, xx, 331, 640; from, 306; to, 511, 681–682.
Jenkins, Elisha: from, 117.
Jenkins, Lemuel: from, 252, 399, 504; to, 399, 504.
Jennings, Jonathan: from, 189, 200, 240; to, 119.
Jennings, Samuel K.: from, 68–69.
Jesup, Thomas S.: about, xxvii, 5, 21, 40, 68, 79, 128, 277, 329–330, 373, 393, 453, 673, 702–704, 708–709; from, 3–4, 28, 57, 83, 189–190, 219–221, 260–261, 287, 334, 372, 411, 434, 483–484, 490–491, 508, 527, 540, 542, 547, 575, 578, 585, 602, 685, 687; to, 22, 79, 104, 120, 150, 158, 161, 190, 221, 271, 334, 372, 387, 429–430, 440, 484, 540, 574–576, 578, 625, 674, 677, 691, 697.
John Adams, U. S. S.: crew for, 261, 285, 304, 363, 389, 404–405, 412, 416.
Johnson (steamboat): about, 703.
Johnson, Henry: about, 298, 330.
Johnson, James, of Ky.: about, xxx–xxxi, 330, 488, 554, 688; advances to, 321–322, 702–705, 708–710; from, 446, 570–571, 574–576, 595, 663, 705; Navy contract of, 321–

322; orders to, 374, 558; ordnance contract of, 311, 328–329; rations contract of, 295, 300–301, 318; recommendations of, 72–73, 122–123, 129, 133, 152–153, 180–181, 233–234; to, 367–368, 369, 372, 560, 663; transportation contract of, 298, 329–330.
Johnson, James, of Va.: from, 432, 595–596; to, 432.
Johnson, Joel: about, 298, 330.
Johnson, John T.: about, 298, 330.
Johnson, John W.: from, 558–559.
Johnson, Richard M.: about, xxx–xxxii, 122, 180, 300–301, 322, 370, 394, 489, 571, 575, 607; from, 288, 290, 333, 334–335, 361, 411, 436, 446–447, 450, 495, 666, 702–705, 708–710; to, 288, 335–336, 361, 368, 372, 411, 413–414, 436, 461, 488–489, 495–497, 579, 705.
Johnson, Thornton F.: about, 166; from, 5.
Johnston, John: about, 59, 365, 421, 480, 598, 696; from, 199–200, 282, 420–422, 510; to, 130, 200, 510, 644–645, 692.
Johnston, Thomas: about, 330.
Jones, Calvin: from, 599–600; recommendation of, 531.
Jones, Francis: from, 434, 626; recommendation by, 106; to, 434.
Jones, George: from, 240.
Jones, Godfrey: accounts of, 64, 117–118.
Jones, R. C.: to, 341.
Jones, Robert C.: from, 693.
Jones, Roger: appointment of, 58.
Jones, Thomas: son of, 693.
Jones, Thomas ap Catesby: from, 401.
Jones, Walter: to, 95–96.
Jones, William: about, 153.
Jouett, Charles: about, 389, 480; from, 476, 629; to, 130.
Jouett, Mrs. Charles: illness of, 476.
Judson, Elnathan: about, 264.

Kaskaskia, Ill.: Receiver of Public Monies at, 680, 693.
Kaskaskia Indians: annuity of, 603; treaties with, 209, 306.
Kearney, Lawrence: from, 395; to, 395; trial of, 396–397.
Kearney, Robert: duty of, 267.
Keep-Tryst Furnace: sale of, xxv, 479, 516–517.
Keiser, Christopher: about, 258–259, 337.
Kelley, Diana Bliss: about, xi.
Kendall, Amos: from, 152–153.
Kennerly, James: boat for, 127.
Kent, Joseph: from, 28, 86; to, 28–29.
Kentucky: Chickasaw lands in, 244; depression in, 702, 708–709; pensions in, 579.
Kerr, Alexander: from, 319, 705.
Kerr, John L.: to, 17.
Key, John, Jr.: about, 626.
Kiblee, Walter R.: from, 43.
Kickapoo Indians: about, 495; annuities of, 83, 603, 693; treaties with, 689, 694.
Kimball, Hazen: from, 240.
Kincheloe, Daniel: from, 542.
King, Benjamin: about, 86.
King, John, Jr.: from, 128.
King, Rufus: about, 486, 606; from, 58–59, 494, 542; to, 11, 542.
King, William: about, 476, 567, 588, 621, 661; from, 86, 164, 312, 534, 540, 637, 645; report from, 660–661; to, 86, 92, 241, 387–388, 645.
Kingsbury, the Rev. Cyrus: about, 430, 596; to, 171.
Kingsley & French: claim of, 613–614.
Kinzie, John: about, 282, 389, 480.
Kirby, Selah: about, 529.
Knight, Moses: pension of, 179.
Knight, Simeon: about, 510, 536.
Knoxville, Tenn.: bank in, 276, 283, 287, 638; prices in, 337.

Lacock, Abner: about, 11, 615; from, 70, 486, 522, 540–541, 547, 553, 556, 560, 685; to, 70, 486–487, 543, 553, 560, 596, 685.
Lacy, John T.: about, 389.

Lafayette, Gen. ——: aide-de-camp to (*see* Poirey, Monsieur ——).
Lafitte, Jean: about, 332, 404.
Lake Pontchartrain: fortifications at, 115.
Lamb, Anthony: about, 587.
Lambert, William: from, 325, 340; to, 325, 340.
Land office. *See* General Land Office.
Landreth, John: about, 253, 264, 266–267, 271; to, 287.
Lane, Robert Carr: about, 529.
Lane, Sam: from, 66.
Lassalle, Stephen B.: from, 179.
Lauck, Joseph D.: about, 404; from, 44, 153, 197; to, 44, 153.
Laurens District, S. C:. applicant from, 485.
Laval, John: from, 397–398.
Lawless, James: about, 256.
Lawrance, Mrs. Eleanor: land of, 461.
Lawrence, William: petition of, 329.
Laws, John: pension of, 588, 596.
Lea, Luke: to, 638.
Lea, Squire: about, 330.
Lead: offer of, 503, 504–505, 508; storage of, 543–544.
Leavenworth, Henry: from, 136–137, 481.
Leavitt, Joseph: from, 228.
Le Baron, Francis: about, 103–104, 192.
Le Brun, Charles: translation by, 624.
LeConte, John: from, 434.
Lee, Charles E.: about, xi.
Lee, Ludwell: from, 147–148.
Lee, Roswell: about, 394; from, ix, 449, 585; to, 529, 568.
Lee, Stephen: application for, 137.
Lee, Thomas: from, 137.
Lee, William: accounts of, 259, 311, 445, 618; from, 285, 368, 373, 487, 507, 525, 612; report by, 455; to, 166, 168.
Lewis, Maj. ——, of Tenn.: about, 608, 683.
Lewis, John: son of, 147.
Lewis, John James Howell: recommendation of, 147–148.
Lewis, John T.: about, 434; from, 515–516, 556; to, 556–557.
Lewis, Meriwether: about, 640.
Lewis, Reuben: from, 223, 279; survey by, 112–113; to, 102–103, 113, 130, 279, 645–646, 697–698.
Lewis, William B.: accounts of, xxi.
Lewis, William Lynn: about, 71.
Library Company of Philadelphia: documents in, 172, 198, 247, 252, 621.
Library of Congress: about, 35; Librarian of, 485.
Light Artillery. *See* Artillery, Regiment of Light.
Little Eyes (a Miami Chief): speech by, 326.
Livermore, Arthur: from, 596, 602; to, 602.
Livingston, Thomas: about, 657.
Lloyd, Thomas: from, 70.
Locke, John: from, 225–226.
Logan, William: about, 680–681.
Long, Stephen H.: about, xxii, xxx, 84, 133, 199, 643, 651, 653; explorations by, 249, 452, 505, 625, 627, 634, 639–640, 649–650, 655–656, 692, 711; from, 35–36, 422–424, 436–438, 454, 521, 590, 653, 713–714; orders to, 37, 89; to, 74, 395–396, 639–640, 653.
Loring, Nathaniel H.: from, 293, 317, 415–416, 523, 535–536; to, 414.
Lorman, William: from, 401.
Louisiana: emigrants to, 448; map of, 320; militia of, 229; rations contractor for, 86; recruits in, 535; timbers in, 253; U. S. Marshal in, 683.
Lovell, Joseph: about, xix, xxvii, 21, 103, 208; endorsements by, 86, 232, 608, 710; from, 61–63, 80–81, 168, 185, 186, 192, 210, 246, 248–249, 273–274, 287, 301, 306, 330, 438, 529, 534, 560; to, 79, 104, 150, 162, 429–430, 438, 670–671.
Lovely, Persis (Mrs. William L.): about, 113.

Lowndes, Caleb: about, 12, 72, 82, 83.
Lowndes, William: regards to, 198.
Lowry, George: about, 407.
Lowry, John: attestations by, 556, 570, 580; from, 534–535.
Lucas, John B. C.: from, 316, 617.
Lumpkin, Wilson: about, 143, 615, 619, 628, 652, 658–659; from, 69, 235, 261, 434, 523, 560–561, 626; surveys by, 14, 95; to, 9–10, 69, 96–97, 99, 158–159, 186–187, 235, 261, 434, 523, 626, 653.
Lyman, William C.: funds for, 591.
Lynch, James: from, 263.
Lynn, Adam: from, 678, 712.
Lynz (U. S. schooner): Purser of, 406.

McArthur, Duncan: from, 138–139; to, 119.
McCall, Hugh: about, 684; from, 131, 153–154, 396; to, 153–154.
McCall, James S.: about, 520.
McCall, Richard: to, 336.
McCalla, John M.: from, 13; to, 13.
McCandless, William: from, 40, 70; to, 11, 40.
McCloskey, James: debt to, 591.
McCoy, the Rev. Isaac: from, 577, 579.
McCoy, John Boyle: about, 77.
McCreedy, Charles: about, 333.
McDuffie, George: about, 89, 276, 548.
McGavock, James: unit of, 256.
McGee, Malcom: about, 67, 93.
McGuire, William: about, 283; from, viii.
McIntosh, James Simmons: about, 35.
McIntosh, William: about, 149, 171, 218, 235, 516, 581, 589; from, 577, 606–607, 646.
McKee, John: about, 265, 318–319, 331, 503, 702; from, 4, 20, 117, 319, 326, 388, 596, 612, 629; to, 102–103, 119, 130, 319, 326, 388, 612–613, 705.
McKeever, Isaac: about, 280.
McKenney, Thomas L.: about, 40, 164, 322, 508; from, 41, 44–56, 59–60, 69, 71, 104, 132, 162, 179, 196, 216, 226, 231, 235–236, 239, 241, 252, 319, 331, 364, 440–443, 503, 504–505, 585–586, 590, 620, 624, 629–630, 671–672; funds of, 34, 287; praise of, 125; sales by, 319–320; suggestions by, 578, 586; to, 38, 41, 44, 59, 69, 104, 162, 246, 252, 319–320, 331, 388, 438, 503, 590, 603.
McKinney, John: about, 450, 515, 612; from, viii, 411.
McKnight, G. B.: about, 198.
McLean, John: from, 133; to, 133.
McLeod, Collin: trial of, 98, 211.
McMahon, Bernard: book by, 204.
McMahon, Thomas P.: from, 204.
McMinn, Joseph: about, 407, 438, 545, 555, 607; from, 76–77, 200–201, 266, 316–317, 364, 412, 428, 447, 477, 487–488, 519, 521–522, 523–524, 635, 687–688; to, 4, 76–77, 117, 200–201, 266, 428–429, 438, 523–524, 590, 634–635, 687.
McNeill, William Gibbs: about, 83; from, 66; to, 22, 66.
McRae, Alexander: about, 16, 18, 25, 643.
MacRea, William: about, 185, 594; from, 477; to, 26, 477.
McRee, William: about, 109, 509, 528, 563; from, 288, 461, 616, 635; reports by, 296, 497, 648; to, 287.
McWhorter, Dr. ——: about, 484–485.

Macedonian, U. S. S.: cruise of, 95, 101, 221; officers of, 221, 225.
Mackay, James: book by, 437.
Mackinac, Mich. Territory: expenses at, 698; Indian Agents at, 27–28, 31, 627, 632 (*see also* Boyd, George; Puthuff, William Henry; Tipton, Jacob); officers at, 23; rations at, 267, 318, 362, 368.

Macomb, Alexander: about, 100, 199, 267; from, 107–108, 193, 216, 250–251, 472–473, 557, 647; to, 24, 77, 111, 193, 698.
Macon, Nathaniel: from, 443, 505; to, 491, 505.
Madison, James: relative of, 629.
Madison, John R.: to, 406–407.
Madison, William S.: recommendations of, 224, 629, 630.
Madisonville, La.: road to, xxv, 24, 94, 140, 170, 472, 492.
Magee, Matthew J.: about, 35.
Mails, U. S.: delays or losses in, 12, 18–19, 20, 41, 42, 57, 58, 60, 81–82, 87, 92, 94, 109, 123, 131, 270–271, 280, 284, 314, 408, 456, 521, 529, 541, 592, 682, 687.
Maine, District of, Mass.: pensions in, 479, 636.
Mallory, John H.: payment to, 621.
Mandan Indians: village of, 60, 215, 633.
Mansfield, Jared: about, 238.
Manufacturing: textiles, 624. *See also* Armories, U. S.; Clothing, Army; Ordnance, Corps of.
Marine Corps, U. S.: Commandant nominees for (*see* Hall, John; Henderson, Archibald; Miller, Samuel; Smith, Richard); Commandant of (*see* Wharton, Franklin); funds for, 243, 251; hospitals of, 204; rations for, 265; regulations for, 265, 286.
Marks, Elias: about, 710, 711; from, 712–713.
Marshall, Charles R.: to, 688.
Marshall, John: about, 588; from, 596; to, 596.
Marshall, Samuel R.: from, 331, 389; to, 389.
Marshall, William P.: about, 502.
Marsteller, Ferdinand: about, 479, 481.
Marston, Morrill: from, 100–101.
Martin Cantonment, Mo. Territory (now Kan.): transportation to, 703.
Martin, John: about, 407.
Martin, Thomas: death of, 534, 541.
Martin, Wyly: about, 416, 453; from, 498.
Maryland: Cadets from, 620; militia of, 17; pensions in, 116, 269; University of, 86.
Mason, Armistead Thomson: about, 181; from, 111–112, 233–234, 263; to, 111–112.
Mason, John: about, 181, 558; from, 302.
Mason, John T., Jr.: from, 180–181.
Mason, Jonathan: from, 504; to, 505.
Mason, Milo: about, xxviii, 40, 92, 158, 540; from, 258; to, 258–259.
Masot, Don José: about, 29.
Massachusetts: Adjutant General of, 410; militia of, 410; pensions in, 499 (*see also* Maine, District of); Seneca land claims of, 667–670, 688, 689.
Massachusetts Historical Society: documents in, 24, 68, 75, 151, 161, 216, 257, 277, 284, 293, 426, 480.
Massias, Abraham A.: from, 511.
Maupin, George W.: about, 237, 330.
Maurice, Theodore W.: about, 528, 563.
Maxwell, Hugh: about, 133; from, 527.
Mayson, Charles: about, 554, 577.
Mead, William: about, 21.
Mease, James: from, 692–693.
Medical and Hospital Department, Army: about, 19, 33; funds for, 162, 168, 192, 241, 409, 651; printing for, 438; reforms in, 287, 413; regulations for, 141. *See also* Lovell, Joseph.
Meigs, Josiah: about, 221; from, 57; to, 57, 199.
Meigs, Return J.: about, 117, 266, 272, 456, 505, 590, 602, 607, 653, 657; from, 20, 197, 407, 424, 459, 489, 547–548, 561–563, 580, 586, 613, 620; to, 42, 102–103, 130, 197, 264, 331, 364–365, 424, 430, 459, 547, 578, 586, 630, 645, 693.

Meigs, Return J., Jr.: about, 110, 542; from, 521; to, 41, 58, 92, 94.
Melish, John: from, 32.
Melven, George Washington: about, 131.
Menard, Pierre: from, 86, 162; to, 162, 693.
Menominee Indians: lands of, 222.
Merchant, Charles Spencer: about, 13.
Merrill, Orsamus Cook: from, 454, 459; to, 454–455, 459.
Miami Exporting Company: Cashier of, 199–200.
Miami Indians: about, 326, 483; Agent to, 282, 631, 636, 644; annuities of, 694; from, 326; missionary to, 577, 579; treaties with, 189, 194, 240, 306, 421–422.
Miami River, O.: road to, 108, 250–251.
Michigan Indians: annuity of, 603; treaty with, 306.
Michigan Territory: extension of, 61; Governor of (*see* Cass, Lewis); Secretary of (*see* Woodbridge, William); Superintendent of Indian Affairs in (*see* Cass, Lewis).
Michilimackinac. *See* Mackinac.
Mickasukee Indians: about, 207.
Middleton, Henry: from, 97; to, 393.
Milbert, ——: about, 292, 451.
Military academy: proposed Western 495–497. *See also* United States Military Academy.
Military Departments, Army: 1st, 19, 84; 2nd, 19, 260; 3rd, 19, 84; 4th, 59; 5th, 19, 100, 107, 557; 8th, 259, 621; 9th, 633, 639, 651, 664, 695, 697.
Military Storekeepers: of Ordnance, 231, 311–312, 625; of Purchasing Department, 120, 265, 417.
Militias of the States and Territories: arms for, 391–392; funds for, 17, 403; pensions for, 419–420; returns of, 228, 246, 289, 301, 440, 587; reliance upon, 463; service by not wanted, 144, 148–149, 152. *See also* New York State: militia court-martial in; Pennsylvania: militia court-martial in.
Milledgeville, Ga.: mail from, 123.
Miller, Albert S.: about, 17–18; from, 18.
Miller, Amosa: from, 332.
Miller, George: invoice of, 481.
Miller, James: about, 156, 157, 218; from, 13; to, 13.
Miller, John, of Mass.: bounty land for, 672.
Miller, John, of N. Y.: bounty land of, 672.
Miller, John Henry: about, 89.
Miller, Jonathan P.: about, 251.
Miller, Morris S.: to, 698.
Miller, Pleasant M.: from, 17–18.
Miller, Samuel: from, 270, 323; recommendations of, 243, 244, 263, 290, 291, 302, 304; to, 270.
Mills, George R.: about, 147.
Milon, Monsieur ——: from: 331.
Minnesota River. *See* St. Peters River.
Mushulatubbe (a Choctaw): from, 243.
Mississippi: rations contractor for, 86; recruiting in, 535; timbers in, 253.
Mississippi Expedition: boats for, 647; Indian Agent for, 659, 662; ordnance for, 687; plans for, 527, 697, 702–705. *See also* Missouri Expedition.
Missouri Expedition: about, xviii, xxix–xxxi, 60–61, 554; commander of, 431–432; Indian Agent for (*see* O'Fallon, Benjamin); plans for, 116, 214–216, 279, 297–298, 318, 329–330, 395–396, 416, 423, 443–444, 453–454, 474, 478, 527, 558, 560, 570–571, 574–576, 578, 581, 595, 599, 622, 631, 632, 633–634, 639–640, 649–651, 660, 663, 685–686, 687, 695–696, 697, 702–705; rations for, 300, 374; recruits for, 218, 356, 578, 659; units for, 257. *See also* Johnson, James, of Ky.; Johnson, Richard M.
Missouri Historical Society: documents in, 247, 420, 689.

Missouri River: navigation of, 498.
Missouri Territory: bank in, 478; Governor of (*see* Clark, William); Indian Agents in, 440, 627; judge in, 195; militia of, 176, 398–399, 414; Superintendent of Indian Affairs in (*see* Clark, William).
Mitchell, Andrew C.: to, 66, 340.
Mitchell, David B.: about, 132, 218, 475, 533, 577, 592; from, 24–25, 137, 148, 170, 173–174, 193, 236, 356, 501, 516, 596; orders to, 258, 652; to, 24, 66, 102–103, 106, 130, 137, 148, 170–171, 193, 211, 221, 236–237, 259, 299, 326, 328, 356, 435, 501, 654.
Mitchell, George E.: about, 401; from, 59, 77, 131, 166, 505; to, 80–81, 167, 171–172.
Mitchill, Samuel Latham: from, 228, 451; to, 292.
Mix, Elijah: contract of, 15–16.
Mix, Timothy: pension of, xxi.
Mobile, Ala. Territory: jail at, 128, 212; lawsuit at, 566, 567; map of, 218, 225; ordnance at, 110; road to, 24.
Mobile Point, Ala. Territory: fortifications at, 115, 151, 175, 427, 451, 580, 606, 656, 674, 694.
Monefon, Carlos: from, 82–83.
Monroe, James: about, xiii–xx; as Secretary of War, 71–72; commission signed by, 702; from, 8, 9, 43, 58, 96–97, 98, 101, 108, 113–115, 121, 134–135, 137, 223–224, 270, 331, 390, 445, 499, 512, 554, 626, 635–636; likeness of, 226, 235; message of, xiv, xxxi, 276; militia fines remitted by, 640; Southern tour of, 658, 687, 689, 707; talk by, 499; to, 4–5, 14, 20, 32–33, 37, 43–44, 58–59, 64, 65, 81–82, 87–88, 92, 97–98, 101–102, 104, 108–109, 112, 115–116, 121, 128, 141–142, 148–149, 152, 155, 175, 192, 195–196, 221, 226–227, 241, 243, 244, 249, 252, 262–263, 270–271, 275, 277, 278, 282–283, 290, 291, 301, 302, 304, 306–307, 323, 326, 327, 360–361, 390, 401, 414, 438–439, 451, 483, 484, 511–512, 518, 525, 528, 529–530, 543, 576, 599–600, 607, 610–611, 624, 625, 626, 627, 631, 647, 648, 652, 657, 667, 712.
Monroe, Mrs. James: health of, 4–5, 14, 58–59, 88.
Monroe, Joseph Jones: from, 693; to, 693.
Montgomery, Elijah: from, 567.
Montgomery, Richard: widow of, 97.
Montgomery, Mrs. Richard: request of, 97.
Moore, David: trial of, 284, 355.
Moore, Jesse: to, 10.
Moore, Robert: endorsement by, 615.
Mordecai, Alfred: about, 340, 491, 505.
Mordecai, Jacob: from, 340, 491, 505.
Morgan, Gideon, Jr.: about, 407; from, 571–572, 607.
Morgan, Willoughby: from, 418, 543; to, 418, 543, 677.
Morin, William: about, 436.
Morris, Charles: about, 267; to, 333.
Morris, Thomas: about, xxvi–xxvii, 398, 399, 400, 432, 627, 698; from, 18, 33, 390, 401, 528, 530; to, 18, 33, 237, 518, 528, 586–587, 647.
Morrison, James: about, 703, 709.
Morristown National Historical Park: document in, 634.
Morrow, Jeremiah: to, 598.
Morrow, William: about, 250.
Mors, Mark: to, 636.
Morton, John: report by, 509.
Morton, Marcus: about, 530; from, 291.
Mossey, Peter: about, 307.
Mott, Noah: pension of, 172.
Mount Dearborn, S. C.: U. S. property at, 493.
Mühlenberg, Peter, Jr.: about, 136.
Mullany, James R.: about, 483; from, 637.
Mullins, Jack S.: about, xi.
Munroe, Thomas: from, 491.
Murphy, Justin: from, 568.

Murray, Alexander: to, 333.
Murray, Francis: about, 26.

Nacogdoches (now in Tex.): Spanish march toward, 173, 198, 228–229.
Nashville, Tenn.: banks in, 182, 234, 391, 608, 682; Military Storekeeper at (*see* Tatum, Howell); newspaper at, 287.
Natchitoches, La.: disbursements at, 162; road to, 320; Spanish threat against, 198.
National Archives, U. S.: records in, ix–x, 716–726.
National bank. *See* Bank of the United States.
National Historical Publications Commission: about, x–xi.
National Intelligencer, Washington, D. C.: ads in, 77; news in, 87.
Navy Commissioners, Board of: about, 274, 406; contracts issued by 307, 321; President of (*see* Rodgers, John).
Navy Pension Fund: reports about, 286, 290, 366; revenue for, 305.
Navy, U. S.: Acting Secretary of the, ix; agents of, 414–415; building of, xxii–xxiii, 491; captures by, 398; Chaplains in, 251; Chief Clerk of (*see* Homans, Benjamin); funds for, 237, 251, 366, 444; hospitals of, 389; increase in, 307–308, 366, 438–439; printing for, 424–425; proposed arsenals for, 648; rations for, 316, 400, 404, 406–407; recruiting service of, 261; regulations of, 241, 261, 286, 305; Secretary of the (*see* Crowninshield, Benjamin W.; Thompson, Smith); timbers for, 253, 259–260, 264, 266–267, 287, 307–308.
Neel, John M.: from, 151.
Negro Fort, East Fla.: about, 532–533.
Negroes: claim to, 173; hostilities by, 313–314; importation of, 193, 218, 237; runaway (*see* Hector); U. S. purchase of, 631.
Nelson, Hugh: from, 516; to, 516, 535.
Nesbitt, Nathan: from, 201.
New Brunswick, N. J.: railroad from, 227.
New Hampshire Historical Society: documents in, 179, 499, 647.
New Jersey: Pea Patch claim of, 706, 707; U. S. Attorney for, 706.
New Jersey Historical Society: document in, 305.
New London, Conn.: Navy depot at, 332.
New Orleans, La.: bank at (*see* Bank of the United States); barracks at, 488; fortifications at, 606; road to, 24; war operations near, 60.
New Stockbridge Indians: petition of, 483.
New-York Historical Society: documents in, 11, 244, 419.
New York, N. Y.: cession by, 539; harbor fortifications at, 142, 175, 285, 288, 296–297, 539; harbor pilots of, 370, 386–387; 494, 517; Navy hospital at, 389.
New York Public Library: documents in, 5, 14, 20, 33, 59, 79, 88, 92, 96, 109, 121, 149, 472, 605, 632, 643, 655.
New York State: Agent for (*see* Pell, Ferris); fortifications in, 66–67, 296–297; internal improvements in, 713; Marshal of (*see* Morris, Thomas); militia court-martial in, xxv–xxvii, 18, 33, 39, 59, 133, 252, 363, 435, 542, 558, 640, 698 (*see also* Betts, Samuel R.; Hagerman, Henry B.; Jenkins, Lemuel; Maxwell, Hugh; Morris, Thomas; Steddiford, Gerard; Wigton, William); militia of, 587–588, 590; pensions in, 307; recruits in, 539; Seneca lands in, 667–670, 688, 698; U. S. Attorney for the Northern District of, 683.
Newberry Library: document in, 188.
Newport, Ky.: clothing at, 388; Deputy Commissary of Purchases at (*see* McKinney, John); Military

Storekeeper at, 534, 541, 607; physician at, 488–489.
Newport, R. I.: fortifications at, 142, 175.
Newton, Thomas, Jr.: from, 302, 595–596.
Nicholls, David Charles: court-martial of, 98; from, 249.
Nichols, Benjamin: from, 176.
Nichols, Robert H.: about, 303.
Nicholson, Edward L.: about, 293.
Noble (a riverboat): about, 327, 439.
Noble, Elizabeth (Mrs. Patrick): about, 89, 165, 275, 473, 658; to, xxxii.
Noble, James: from, 598, 613, 614–615; to, 420–422, 598.
Noble, John (1769–1819): death of, 657–658.
Noble, Patrick (1787–1840): from, 88, 164, 473; to, 88–89, 164–165, 275–276, 473–474, 657–658.
Nonsuch (U. S. schooner): about, 264, 267, 284, 289.
Noon, Darby: about, 612; from, viii, 172; to, 172.
Norfolk, Va.: fort at, 13; Marine barracks at, 243.
Norris, Andrew: from, 185–186.
North American Review: subscriptions to, 632.
North Carolina: Cherokee cession in, 656; constitutional amendment sought by, 473; land warrants by, 565; Military Storekeeper of Ordnance for, 508.
Northern Division, U. S. Army: boundaries of, 61, 116, 164, 214–215, 474; commander of (*see* Brown, Jacob); Judge Advocate of, 208.
Norvell, John: from, 569.
Nourse, Charles J.: about, 22; from, 447.
Nuttall, Thomas: about, 95, 101.

O'Bannon, Jennings: about, 102.
O'Connor, John Michael: about, 137, 141, 175; from, 590.
O'Fallon, Benjamin: about, 440, 476, 634, 639, 644, 709; charges against, 617–618; nomination of, 627; to, 640–641, 647.
O'Fallon, John: about, 8, 42, 709; charges against, 617–618.
Office of Indian Trade: funds for, 633. *See also* Bronaugh, Jere W.; Factory system of Indian trade; McKenney, Thomas L.
Ogden, David A.: about, 136; from, 10–11, 255, 295–296, 667–670, 688; to, 10–11, 20–21, 56–57, 78, 90, 147, 255.
Ohio: Pension Agent in, 250.
Old Point Comfort, Va.: fortifications at, 16, 115, 175, 370, 595.
Oldham, Richard: about, 541, 607; to, 607.
Oliver, William: draft to, 199.
Oneida Indians: about, 668; emigration by, 262–263; from, 262–263.
Onís, Don Luis de: about, xxxiii, 14, 29, 31, 32, 98; to, 43, 58.
Onondago Indian: education of, 687.
Ordnance, Corps of: assistant to Chief of (*see* Bomford, George); Chief of (*see* Wadsworth, Decius); Clerks in, 509; clothing needed by, 400; contracts by, 19, 405, 456, 610; funds of, xxi, 17, 205, 265, 409, 599, 618; inventions for, 274, 277, 357–358, 370, 449, 519, 664–666; Military Storekeepers of, 231, 311–312, 625; office of, 21–22; production by (*see* Harpers Ferry; Springfield); reports of, 268–269, 285, 599; specifications of, 23, 42.
Orr, Benjamin G.: about, xxviii, 57, 80, 91, 92, 241, 260, 529, 617, 619, 684; accounts of, 324, 662; defaults by, 163, 179, 187; drafts by, 319, 705; from, 491; to, 369.
Osage Indians: about, 495; Agent to, 247; annuities of, 603; depredations by, 309, 567–568; enemies of, 67; proposed delegation of, 699–700; theft by, 541; trade with, 53;

treaties with, 247, 272, 306, 394, 580, 711.
Otis, Harrison Gray: from, 142.
Otis, Seth: from, 713.
Ottawa Indians: annuities of, 689, 691; from, 155; treaties with, 68, 119, 138–139, 194, 306, 645, 708.
Overton, John: about, 500, 525, 608, 683, 695; to, 694.
Owen, James: from, 608.

Palmer, William Adams: to, 484.
Panic of 1819: onset of, xiv, 702, 708–709.
Parke, Benjamin: from, 12, 72, 82, 189, 200, 449; to, 72, 82, 119, 449, 678, 679.
Parker, Daniel: about, 21, 301, 417; from, 121–122, 193–194, 210, 211–212, 214, 226, 228, 259, 307, 362, 373, 401, 440, 443–444, 447, 474–475, 492, 509, 512, 525, 535, 539, 578, 663; orders by, 81, 218, 340, 580; orders to, 14, 185, 474; reports by, 278, 454, 484, 578; to, 22, 104–105, 133–134, 162–163, 164, 187–188, 193, 226, 416, 429–430, 679.
Parker, Thomas: about, 395; to, 396–397.
Parrish, Jasper: about, 255, 301, 451, 653; from, 188, 279, 336, 447, 526, 603, 654; to, 188, 279, 530, 654.
Parrott, Richard: from, 302.
Partridge, Alden: from, 175, 190, 238, 276; to, 238, 276.
Pascagoula Indians: about, 476; census of, 16; lands of, 305–306.
Pasteur, Edward: from, 36.
Patterson, Daniel T.: about, 264, 289, 424, 532–533; from, 280, 332, 403–404, 427; to, xvi, 217, 266–267, 291, 302, 332, 427.
Patterson, R. M.: about, 460, 711; from, 388, 399, 455, 518–519.
Pathkiller (a Cherokee): about, 407.
Pavatt, Isaac: from, 201.
Pawnee Indians: about, 309; proposed delegation of, 699–700; treaties with, 33, 306.
Paxton, James W.: about, 415; from, 415.
Paymaster General, Army: Chief Clerk to (*see* Frye, Nathaniel, Jr.); Clerks to, 482, 509; funds for, 17, 161, 190, 265, 408, 651; report to, 679; reports from, 271, 282. *See also* Brent, Robert.
Payne, Daniel N. C.: from, 142; to, 142.
Payne, John: injury to, 436.
Pea Patch Island, Delaware River: Army Engineer at (*see* Babcock, Samuel); fortifications at, 115, 175, 541, 555, 577; title to, 109, 607–608, 609, 706, 707.
Peale, Charles Willson: son of, 396.
Peale, Titian Ramsay: about, 396, 423.
Pearce, George: from, 204.
Pearson, Amos: pension of, 267.
Pell, Ferris: from, 66–67, 296, 297; to, 296–297.
Pennsylvania: auction in, 247; lawsuit by, 214; militia court-martial in, 610; pensions in, 636; rations contractor for, 419; recruits in, 535; Revolutionary muster rolls of, 188; Secretary of State of, 188; U. S. District Court of, 5.
Penobscot County (District of Me.), Mass.: road in, 228.
Pensacola, West Fla.: defense of, 17; Governor of, 92 (*see also* Masot, Don José); Quartermaster expenses at, 476, 534; regulations for, 512; relief at, 645; restoration to Spain of, 4, 14, 29–30, 32, 79, 87, 105, 152, 255, 313, 361, 637, 660–661 (*see also* Spanish posts in the Floridas); testimony from, 229; U. S. occupation of, 511–512, 547; visitor to, 387–388; war operations near, 60.
Pension Office, War Department: about, viii, xxi, xxiv, 25, 250, 281,

483, 487, 663; Chief Clerk of (*see* Edwards, James L.); Clerks in, 66, 282, 325, 328, 340, 341, 439, 582; funds for, xxii, 151, 218, 221, 250, 403, 712; regulations of, 5–8, 10, 154–155, 284, 371, 387, 419–420, 452, 482–483, 486–487, 528–529, 582; reports about, 142, 159–161, 253, 293, 298, 301, 305, 325, 446, 448, 543; statutes for, 368, 572.
Pensions, Navy. *See* Navy Pension Fund.
Pentland, Edward: from, 175.
Pentland, Hegins & Heele: about, 175.
Pentland, Joseph: about, 685.
Peoria, Ill. Territory: Indian Agency at, 245.
Peoria Indians: annuity of, 603; treaties with, 209, 306.
Percival, John: from, 321.
Perkins, Jacob: from, 568.
Perry, James: about, 34, 38.
Peter, George: from, 302.
Peters, Elijah: pension of, 581.
Peters, George P.: about, 529, 566; from, 567, 568; to, 567.
Peters, Richard: decision by, 5–8.
Peters, Thomas R.: to, 5–8.
Pettygrove, George: from, 269–270.
Peychaud, Anatole, Jr.: about, 508.
Philadelphia, Pa.: bank at, 234; Museum at, 396.
Philips, Joseph: from, 260; to, 433–434.
Phillips, John Walter: about, 591.
Piankashaw Indians: annuities of, 86, 162, 603, 693.
Piatt, John H.: rent to, 636.
Pickens, Andrew, Jr.: about, 89, 257, 276.
Pickens, Andrew, Sr.: will of, 89.
Picton, Maj. ——: from, 655.
Picton, John M. W.: about, 276.
Picton, the Rev. Thomas: from, 276.
Pike, Zebulon Montgomery: about, 21, 572.
Pillard, James: from, 176.
Pinkney, Ninian: about, 4, 89.
Piqua, O.: Indian Agent at, 644–645, 696 (*see also* Johnston, John).
Pitchlynn, James: about, 436; from, 674–675.
Pittsburgh, Pa.: arsenal at, 242, 265, 424; Ordnance officer at (*see* Woolley, Abram R.); sale of lots at, 284.
Platte River: exploration of, 423.
Plattsburgh, N. Y.: ordnance at, 501; roads from, 472, 479–480, 492, 713; roads to, 315, 359, 371.
Pleasants, James, Jr.: from, 414; to, 414–415.
Pleasonton, Stephen: about, xxv, 34, 130, 184, 324, 444, 660; from, 475, 559, 563, 567; to, 320, 494, 503, 559, 563, 567, 604.
Plumer, Nathan: from, 373.
Poinsett, Joel R.: from, 134–135; journal of, 141.
Point Peter, Ga.: about, 122, 338, 340.
Poirey, Monsieur ——: claim of, xx, 306, 511; payment to, 660, 674, 681–682.
Polk, Edward: about, 286.
Pooshemullaha (a Choctaw): from, 243.
Pope, John: from, 224.
Pope, LeRoy: records for, 284.
Porter, Augustus: from, 451; to, 451.
Porter, John: about, 267; from, 390; to, 390.
Porter, Moses: about, 13; from, 14, 172, 197–198, 373; to, 14–15, 172, 197, 373.
Porter, Peter B.: about, 531; from, 597–597.
Portsmouth, Va.: Surgeon at, 237.
Postmaster General. *See* Meigs, Return J., Jr.
Postmaster General, Assistant. *See* Bradley, Abraham, Jr.
Potawatomi Indians: about, 138; Agent to, 631, 636, 644; annuities of, 689, 691; from, 155; proposed delegation of, 708; theft by, 503; treaties with, 68, 119, 189, 194, 306, 645, 708.
Powell, Garston: from, 636.

Prairie du Chien, Mich. Territory (now in Wisc.): Factory at, 124; Indian Agent at (*see* Boilvin, Nicholas); lead at, 503, 508; officials at, 558–559; rations at, 531.
Preacher, John: sale to, xxv.
Prentis, Ebenezer: from, 332.
Presley, Duncan: warrant for, 515–516, 556–557.
Presley, Richard: warrant for, 515–516, 556–557.
Preston, James P.: from, 373, 491; to, 373, 491.
Pride, David: deposition by, 175.
Prince, William: from, 83; to, 130, 579, 679, 693.
Princeton College: student at, 362.
Privateering: about, 280, 332, 403–404, 631.
Prometheus (U. S. brig): about, 291, 302, 308, 427.
Pryor, Nathaniel: report by, 541.
Puckshunnubbie (a Choctaw): gift by, 630.
Purchasing Department, Army: contracts by, 610; Deputy Commissaries in (*see* McKinney, John; Noon, Darby); funds for, 167, 207–208, 253–254, 265, 289–290, 406, 409, 460, 651; Military Storekeepers of, 120, 265, 417. *See also* Clothing, Army; Commissary General of Purchases; Irvine, Callender.
Puthuff, William Henry: about, 28, 222, 230; to, 31.

Quackenbos, Mangle Marcellus: recommendation of, 579.
Quakers. *See* Society of Friends.
Quapaw Indians: Agent to, 697; annuities of, 603; treaties with, 107, 119, 136, 247, 272, 306, 394, 604, 697.
Quarles, Tunstall: from, 72–73, 320; to, 320.
Quartermaster Department: baggage allowances in, 119; debts of, 260; funds for, 17, 39–40, 162, 189, 220–221, 265, 411, 434, 506, 540, 651; officers in, 33, 493, 585; printing for, 434; reforms in, 413; regulations for, 685; report of, 542. *See also* Quartermaster General.
Quartermaster General: office of, 21–22; recommendation for, 19. *See also* Jesup, Thomas S.; Quartermaster Department.

Rabun, William: about, 14, 37, 96, 390, 652; charges by, 365–366; from, 397, 420, 439, 517, 518, 626, 628; to, 99, 332, 397, 518, 615, 626, 658–659.
Ragland, Thomas: about, 592; from, 293, 317, 415–416, 523, 535–536, 637–638.
Railroads: proposal for, 226–227.
Ramage, James: to, 368, 424.
Ramsey, James: about, 150.
Randall, Richard: about, 301, 502.
Randolph, David W.: about, 227.
Randolph, Edward B.: about, 8.
Rangers, Regiment of: about, 312.
Rathbone, P. H.: to, 368, 369.
Rathbun, Thomas: pension of, 636.
Rations, Army: changes in, xix, 74–75, 133, 145–146, 208, 273–274, 381–384, 474; components of, 61–64, 231; contractors for, xxviii–xxix, 27, 384–386; for Indians, 449; funds for, xxi–xxii, 336–337; new supply system for, 167, 318, 362, 369, 384–386, 392, 409; quality of, 531; requisitions for, 318; specifications for, 112.
Rations, Navy: about, 316, 397, 400, 404, 406–407.
Rawlings, Isaac: report by, 624.
Raymond, P.: from, 112.
Read, George, Jr.: from, 109, 607, 609; to, 607–608.
Read, George C.: about, 389; from, 369, to, 369.
Read, J. Bond: from, 240.
Recruiting service, Army: about, 262, 535, 539; bounties for, 167; critic-

isms of, 262, 388, 534; funds for, 194, 410, 651.
Reed, Artemas: pension of, 536.
Reed, William: from, 251, 557–558.
Rees, Joseph H.: accounts of, 615.
Reid, Samuel C.: from, 165–166.
Reily, J. H.: payment to, 320.
Renshaw, James: about, 223, 264.
Reynolds, James B.: from, 326–327; to, 26, 92.
Reynolds, William M.: about, 621.
Reynoldsburg, Tenn.: road from, 92, 201.
Rhea, John: from, 276, 283; to, 276, 283, 287, 477, 543.
Rhodes, Hillary: about, 106.
Rich, Charles: from, 390–391.
Richards, Alexander: about, 136; from, 418, 576–577, 597.
Richards, George H.: from, 332.
Richardson, Joseph: campaign of, 186.
Richardville, John Baptiste (a Miami Indian): about, 240.
Riddle, James W.: to, 11.
Ridgely, Greenbury W.: about, 578.
Rifle Regiment: about, 35, 274, 432, 443–444, 453–454, 474, 578.
Rigolets Pass, La.: fortifications at, 674, 694.
Riley, Richard: claim of, 693.
Ringgold, Tench: from, 491.
Rip Raps Shoal, Hampton Roads, Va.: fortifications at, 175. *See also* Hampton Roads, Va.
Ripley, Eleazer W.: about, 28, 40; from, 128, 191, 194, 198, 228–229, 312, 320–321, 393, 427, 488, 508; to, 67, 77, 102, 128, 194, 224, 297, 312, 320, 321, 393, 427.
Roads: construction of, 23–24, 26, 66, 92, 94, 106, 108, 137, 170, 173–174, 201, 221, 228, 263, 292, 315, 320–321, 326–327, 331, 358–359, 371, 424, 460, 461–473, 486, 492, 513–515, 713; cost of using, 435; funds for, xxi–xxii; proposals for, 479–480. *See also* Turnpikes.
Roberdeau, Isaac: about, 679.
Roberts, Jonathan: from, 314, 617–618; to, 617.
Roberts, Thomas: pension of, 641.
Robertson, Thomas Bolling: from, 198; to, 198.
Robertson, William H.: about, 321.
Robeson & Wallace: about, 295.
Robinson & Taylor: to, 369.
Robinson, David: about, 414, 630; from, 407, 459, 693–694; to, 415, 693.
Robinson, Hamilton Edward V.: application for, 244.
Robinson, John H.: from, 244.
Rock River, Ill.: Indian Agency at, 245.
Rockwood, C. L.: petition of, 368.
Rocky Mount, S. C.: U. S. property at, 493, 544.
Roden, Leanner: warrant for, 658.
Rodger, Mathew: about, 222–223.
Rodgers, John: from, 241, 253, 274, 307–308, 321–322, 336, 373, 397, 404; report by, 438; to, 244, 253, 308, 336, 397, 404.
Rodgers, Matthew: about, 222–223.
Rodney, Caesar Augustus: about, 65, 135; from, 15, 29, 264, 407–408, 418, 536; to, 29, 536.
Rodney, Mrs. Caesar Augustus: nephew of, 15.
Rodney, Thomas M.: from, 536.
Rogers, John: about, 200–201.
Rogers, Thomas S.: about, 508.
Rolette, Joseph: from, 664, 670; to, 670.
Romaine, Benjamin: from, 362.
Romaine, Washington: about, 362.
Romayne, James T. B.: about, 161.
Rome, N. Y.: armory at, 538; road from, 263.
Ross, Daniel: from, 169–170.
Ross, John: about, 407, 616.
Ross, Randolph: about, 27; payments to, 491, 618; to, 33–34.
Rouse, James W.: from, 338.
Rouses Point, N. Y.: about, 68, 238, 239, 408, 513–515; fortifications at, 175, 291–292, 661.

Ruden, Jacques: about, 301.
Ruggles, Benjamin: from, 587; to, 587.
Rundlet, James: from, 415.
Rush, Richard: about, 247; from, 81, 108, 115, 212–213, 244.
Russell, Joseph P.: from, 267.
Russell, M. M.: from, 103; testimony by, 489.

Sabine River: exploration of, 424.
Sabine, W. H.: about, 475.
Sac Indians: about, 216, 245, 708; annuity of, 603.
Sackets Harbor, N. Y.: barracks at, 26, 190, 359; boat at, 392; road from, 24, 263, 315, 358–359, 371, 472, 492, 713.
Sag Harbor, N. Y.: arsenal at, 80, 149, 169.
Sage, Ebenezer: from, 149; to, 149.
Saginaw Bay: about, 614, 696.
Saginaw Indians: about, 591.
St. Augustine, East Fla.: about, 501–502; Governor at (*see* Coppinger, Don José); proposed attacks against, 20, 85–86, 87, 560; sketch of, 533.
St. Charles County, Mo. Territory: militia unit of, 176.
St. Lawrence County, N. Y.: road through, 713.
St. Louis, Mo. Territory: Army depot at, 417; Assistant Commissary of Issues at (*see* Clemson, Eli B.); bank at, 554; lead at, 503, 508; military reservation at, 37; Military Storekeeper at, 607, 625; Receiver of Public Monies at, 644, 647, 651, 680; schools at, 74.
St. Marks. *See* Fort St. Marks.
St. Marys, Ga.: trial at, 256, 258, 259, 267, 302.
St. Marys, O.: building at, 277; road to, 24; treaties at, 12, 69, 83, 240, 282, 483.
St. Marys River: Ga. boundary terminating at, 37, 95, 96–97, 99, 143, 158–159; navigation of, 428.
St. Peters River: Indian Agent at mouth of, 478, 699, 713; post at mouth of, xxix, 60–61, 215–216, 318, 329, 651, 659.
Saltpeter: contract for, 579.
Sampson, Zabdiel: from, 530.
Sands, Abraham L.: about, 450; to, 186.
Sandusky, O.: Indian Agent at, 360, 480, 691, 696; Indians at, 282; road to, 24.
Sandy Hook, N. Y.: fortifications at, 175, 517.
Santee, Augustus: about, 449, 502, 521.
Saranac (U. S. brig): crew of, 304, 325; sale of, 363.
Saratoga County, N. Y.: militia of, 194.
Sault Ste. Marie, Mich. Territory: visit to, 107.
Saunders, Henry: about, 112.
Savannah, Ga.: about, 684, 685; barracks at, 538–539, 625; fort at, 240; newspaper at, 92, 94, 131; ordnance at, 396; Postmaster of, 131; trial at, 522.
Saxon, Lewis: son of, 120.
Saxon, Lydall: recommendations of, 118, 120, 485.
Say, Thomas: about, 95, 101, 423.
Scarbrough, William: from, 240.
Schenectady County, N. Y.: militia of, 194.
Schweinitz, the Rev. Lewis D.: from, 675–676.
Scott, James: about, 36.
Scott, John: about, 478; from, 198, 221, 244, 567–568, 585; to, 221, 580.
Scott, Winfield: deposition by, 84; employment of, xxix, 141–142; enmity toward Jackson of, 631–632, 641–643, 654–655; from, 22, 93, 104, 137, 604–605; 631–632, 641–643, 654; to, 151, 631–632, 654–655.
Seaton, William W.: about, 611.
Second Auditor. *See* Lee, William.
Second Comptroller. *See* Cutts, Richard.

Secretary of State. *See* Adams, John Quincy.
Secretary of the Navy. *See* Crowninshield, Benjamin W.; Thompson, Smith.
Secretary of the Treasury. *See* Crawford, William H.
Section of Bounty Lands. *See* Bounty Lands, Section of.
Seeley, Samuel: from, 269–270, 566.
Selkirk, Lord: about, 215; from, 23.
Seminole Indians: claims by, 173; fears of, 20, 143–144, 148–149, 152, 158, 173, 184, 205–207, 234–235, 252, 254–255, 312–314, 339–340, 360–361, 426, 431, 433, 545–546, 561, 615, 685; hostilities by, 96, 99, 356; lands of, 646, 700; merger with Creeks of, 193, 236–237, 299, 652–653, 654, 700; slaves of, 237.
Seminole War of 1817–1818: about, xxxi–xxxiii, 4, 8–9, 508, 529, 540, 547, 662; reports about, 275, 331.
Senate, U. S.: President of (*see* Tompkins, Daniel D.); President Pro Tempore of (*see* Barbour, James; Gaillard, John); Secretary of (*see* Cutts, Charles).
Seneca Indians: annuity of, 692; emigration by, 78, 623–624, 698; indemnity to, 692; lands of, 667–670, 688; stock owned by, 654; talk to, 499; treaties with, 119, 138–139, 306, 421, 645, 698.
Senter, German: about, 330.
Sergeant, John: from, 399, 404, 455, 460, 488, 518, 579; to, 388, 404, 455, 460, 488, 518–519.
Sergeant, Thomas: to, 188.
Settle, Thomas: from, 608.
Seybert, Adam: from, 402.
Shannon, Samuel: about, 66.
Shaw, Henry: from, 327, 477, 530; to, 327, 477.
Shaw, John: about, 691, 696.
Shaw, John, U. S. N.: about, 259, 302; from, 268; to, 256, 267–268.
Shaw, Joshua: about, 396, 423.
Shaw, Samuel: about, 327, 394; from, 388.
Shawnee Indians: annuity of, 692; emigration by, 247; indemnity to, 692; treaties with, 71, 119, 138–139, 194, 306, 421, 645.
Shelby, Isaac: about, 64, 145, 182, 269, 304, 319, 325, 566; from, 242, 244, 245, 555; to, 119.
Sheldon, William: about, 489; from, 449.
Sherburne, Henry: about, 182–184, 361, 475, 566; decision by, 568; drafts by, 234, 246; from, 26–27, 34, 64, 67, 93–94, 105, 117–118, 132, 134, 154, 162, 188, 213, 238, 264, 280–281, 287–288, 322, 327, 391, 408, 439, 580, 608–609, 613, 663, 682–683; orders to, 235–236; report by, 364; rumored resignation by, 626; to, 26, 34, 38–39, 41, 64, 102–103, 105, 117–118, 130, 134, 164, 213, 238–239, 264, 280, 287, 322, 327, 408, 477, 597–598, 608–609, 682.
Shields, Samuel B.: from, 326, 327–328.
Shubrick, William B.: about, 412; from, 401.
Sibley, John: from, 198.
Simkins, Arthur, Jr.: to, 369.
Simkins, Eldred: about, 88; from, 363, 415, 484, 522, 548–549, 554, 577; to, 369, 484–485.
Simpson, John: about, 515–516.
Sioux Indians: about, 215, 216, 222; Agent to, 618.
Skinner, Roger: from, 683.
Slater, E. F.: document owned by, 91.
Slaves. *See* Negroes.
Slocumb, Jesse: from, 531.
Smallpox: deaths from, 16.
Smith, Ballard: from, 71.
Smith, Daniel D.: from, 190.
Smith, David: payment to, 598.
Smith, Gerard D.: about, 649.
Smith, Henry: ward of, 151.
Smith, James: about, 508.

Smith, John: about, 150.
Smith, Jonathan: from, 455.
Smith, Joseph Rowe: about, 151.
Smith, Richard: about, 704.
Smith, Richard, U.S.M.C.: recommendations of, 278, 304, 328, 329, 331; to, 278.
Smith, Robert: from, 19.
Smith, Samuel: certificate by, 70; from, 78, 154, 175, 201, 217, 408, 460, 492–493; to, 154–155, 201, 217, 336–337, 408–410, 415, 455, 460, 492–493.
Smith, Samuel B.: about, 80–81, 246, 630.
Smith, Samuel C.: about, 420.
Smith, Sidney: about, 147.
Smith, Thomas A.: about, 417; from, 35; to, 59, 60–61, 77, 116, 210, 651.
Smith, Thomas F.: about, 618.
Smith, William: from, 485, 536; to, 536.
Snelling, Josiah: about, 95, 218; from, 189; to, 163–164.
Snoddy, John: from, 176.
Society of Friends (Quakers): adherent of, 67; friendship for Indians of, 499; missionary efforts of Baltimoreans, 71; recommendation by Baltimoreans, 691, 696.
Society of United Brethren in N. C.: schools of, 675–676.
Solomon, H.: from, 103.
Sommerville, John: about, 608–609.
South Carolina: Civil Engineer of, 493; constitutional amendment proposed by, 473–474; Department of Archives and History of, xi; 1st Regiment of, 606; internal improvements in, 473, 493, 544; judicial appointment in, 600–601; pensions in, 434; U. S. Attorney for, 395; University of, xi, 120 (*see also* South Caroliniana Library).
South Carolina Historical Society: documents in, 113, 193.
South Caroliniana Library, University of S. C.: documents in, 79, 186, 267, 288, 405, 479, 560, 572, 627, 636, 671, 674, 697.
South Caroliniana Society: about, xi.
Southard, Henry: to, 478.
Southern Division of the Army: Adjutant General of (*see* Butler, Robert); boundaries of, 61, 116, 164; commander of (*see* Jackson, Andrew).
Southwest Fur Company: about, 222.
Spain: alleged cession of the Floridas by, 645, 658, 684, 685, 690, 710; claims of, 173; prisoners of, 312, 486, 502; reoccupation of the Floridas by, 637, 645; restoration of Fla. posts to, 8–9, 20, 29–30, 37, 43, 58–59, 85–86, 88–89, 110–111, 149, 255 (*see also* Fort Barrancas; Fort St. Marks; Pensacola, West Fla.); Southwest raids by, 173; treaty with, xv, xxxiii, 96; U. S. Minister of, 97 (*see also* Onís, Don Luis de); U. S. Minister to (*see* Erving, George W.).
Spence, Robert T.: to, 333.
Spencer, Joel: about, 363, 619; from, 163, 283, 363, 369; to, 363, 369.
Spring Place, Cherokee Nation: school at, 675.
Springfield, Mass.: U. S. Armory at, viii–ix, xxi, 17, 129, 168, 202–204, 288, 297, 302, 323, 333, 335–336, 394, 402, 526, 585, 666.
Stall, George W.: about, 615.
Stark, Caleb: from, 499; to, 499.
Stark, John: pension of, 499.
Starr, Charles H.: from, 314–315.
State Department: building of, xxii–xxiii, 491; Clerk of (*see* Bailey, John); Secretary of (*see* Adams, John Quincy).
State Historical Society of Missouri: document in, 35.
State Historical Society of Wisconsin: documents in, 25, 103, 574, 659.
Steamboats: navigation of the Missouri by, xxx, 498. *See also* Johnson, James, of Ky.; Long, Stephen H.
Stebbins, John: from, 568.

Steddiford, Gerard A.: about, xxvi, 59, 282, 398, 400, 504, 518, 527, 528; from, 39, 133, 149, 168, 194, 363, 432, 455, 558; to, 39, 133, 149, 168, 194, 252, 283, 363, 399, 418, 432, 455–456, 485, 528, 558, 698.
Stelle, William: to, 328.
Stephenson, Benjamin: son of, 569; to, 694.
Stephenson, James W.: about, 569.
Sterrett, John: from, 42.
Steuart, William M.: debt to, 403.
Stevens, John: from, 226–227.
Stevens, Robert L.: about, 648.
Stewardson, Thomas: about, 499.
Stewart, Alexander: to, 341.
Stewart, Alvan: about, 539.
Stewart, Charles: about, 336.
Stewart, Levi B.: about, 329.
Stickney, Benjamin F.: about, 282, 442, 444, 510; from, 122.
Stickney, George: from, 558; to, 558.
Stillman, Ethan: from, 563–564; to, 563–564.
Stockbridge Indians: about, 483.
Stone & Co.: about, 686.
Stone, David: about, 686.
Stone, Ruth Elizabeth Clark (Mrs. Richard G., Jr.): about, xi.
Storrow, Samuel A.: about, 19, 208, 315.
Story, Horace C.: about, 293, 425.
Stout, Ebenezer: to, 341.
Stout, Nathan B.: about, 109.
Stow, Silas: from, 232.
Strider, Henry: lease by, 420; petition of, 516, 517, 535.
Strong, Amos: about, 298.
Strong, William: from, 390–391.
Strong, William, U.S.M.C.: complaint against, 303.
Stuart, Alexander: from, 195, 537.
Stuart, Robert: about, 222, 229; from, 686.
Stubblefield, James: from, 370, 519, 568; report by, 393.
Stubbs, James R.: about, 133.
Subsistence Department, Army: contracts by, xxviii–xxix, 403, 507, 610, 691; funds for, 17, 265, 336–337, 409, 493; printing for, 436; reforms in, 413; staff of, 19, 163, 167, 232, 384–385, 417, 638. *See also* Commissary General of Subsistence; Rations, Army.
Sugg, William: about, 117.
Sulphur Fork, Red River: Factory at, 162 (*see also* Fowler, John); Indian Agent at, 320.
Sumner, William H.: from, 410.
Superintendent of Indian Trade: office of created, 343. *See also* McKenney, Thomas L.
Surgeon General, Army. *See* Lovell, Joseph.
Surprise (U. S. ketch): about, 280.
Suwanee River: canal along, 428.
Swett, Moses: from, 84; to, 84.
Swift, Joseph G.: about, 74, 264, 432, 451, 517, 563, 712; allowances to, 21; charges against, 175, 190, 238; from, 11, 13, 22, 84, 89, 109, 151, 175, 198–199, 205, 227, 283, 285, 328, 410, 416, 418–419, 616; orders by, 435, 436; orders to, 67; reports by, 12, 648; resignation of, 277, 528; to, 15–16, 22, 73, 79, 89, 105, 141, 142, 150, 151, 162, 196, 198, 229, 238, 239, 258, 270, 277, 285, 340, 362, 418, 461, 491, 505, 519.
Swift, William R.: about, 270.

Tait, Charles: from, 105, 444, 543; to, 105–106, 543.
Talcott, Andrew: about, 356.
Taliaferro, Lawrence: from, 713; to, 699.
Taliaferro, William: about, 114.
Tallmadge, Charles B.: from, 166.
Tallmadge, James, Jr.: about, 475.
Talontuskey (a Cherokee): funds for, 223.
Tamarois Indians: annuities of, 603; treaties with, 306.
Tampa, East Fla.: proposed expedition to, 144–145, 207, 313–314.
Tanner, ——: aid to, 111.

Tanner, John: capture of, 23.
Tarr, Christian: about, 615.
Tatum, Howell: about, 227–228, 400–401, 440; from, 89, 194, 229, 241, 288; report by, 373; to, 229, 241, 288, 445.
Taylor, James: from, 488–489.
Taylor, Lt. James B., U.S.N.: to, 259, 302; trial of, 258, 267, 301, 390.
Taylor, John: from, 710.
Taylor, John C.: about, 68–69.
Taylor, John W.: to, 419.
Taylor, Richard (a Cherokee): about, 266, 407.
Taylor, Robert: about, 477; from, 13, 26.
Taylor, Waller: from, 577, 598, 613; to, 579, 598.
Taylor, Zachary: from, 388; order by, 98, 211.
Teal, Harvey S.: document owned by, 262.
Teasdale, Isaac: estate of, 657.
Tellico Island, Cherokee Nation: reservation of, 616.
Ten Eyck, Egbert: from, 713.
Tennessee: Cherokee lands in, 585–586, 656; Chickasaw boundary of, 657, 659; Chickasaw cession in, 244; Ga. boundary of, 317; Governor of, 316 (*see also* McMinn, Joseph); Military Storekeeper in (*see* Tatum, Howell); militia of, xxi, 4, 116, 581; pensions in, xxv, 276, 283, 287, 538, 638; prices in, 333–334, 337; Quartermaster agent in, 194; Quartermaster claims in, 89; salt in, 34, 475, 477, 492, 528, 566, 608–609, 683; State Bank of, 608.
Texas area: exploration of, 163, 213, 224–225, 268; hostilities in, 431; Spanish threats from, 198, 228–229, 312, 320–321; unsettled boundaries of, xxxiii, 309, 352.
Thayer, Sylvanus: about, 44, 451, 520; charges against, 175, 190, 238, 317; from, ix, 73, 151, 163, 192, 285, 322–323, 598; orders by, 197; orders to, 166, 358; report by, 112; to, 227, 285–286, 293, 492, 500, 694.
Third Auditor. *See* Hagner, Peter.
Thomas, Charles: from, 402.
Thomas Jefferson (steamboat): about, 703.
Thomas, Martin: order to, 627.
Thomas, Owen: about, 448.
Thomas, Philip E.: visit by, 71.
Thompson, Jacob: about, 26.
Thompson, Samuel: murder by, 573–574.
Thompson, Smith: about, ix, 286, 402, 420; from, 481, 648, 672; to, 301, 314–315, 373, 398, 407–408, 491, 568, 672.
Thompson, Wiley: about, 619.
Thornton, John Russell: about, 614–615.
Thornton, Joseph: son of, 614.
Thorpe, Thomas: from, 302.
Thruston, Charles Mynn: from, 493.
Thruston, Robert A.: from, 59.
Thweatt, Archibald: from, 252, 404, 456; to, 252–253.
Tilghman, William: about, 70.
Tipton, Jacob: about, 31.
Tobias, Solomon: from, 489.
Toby, Elisha: from, 568.
Tompkins, Daniel D.: about, 517; from, 579, 580–581.
Toncray, Lewis: from, 256.
Tone, William T. Wolfe: from, 450.
Topographical Engineers, Army. *See* LeConte, John; Long, Stephen H.; Young, Hugh.
Torrey, John: about, 423.
Totten, Joseph G.: about, 238, 370, 387, 528, 563, 661; to, 239.
Towcash Indians: about, 309.
Townsend, David S.: from, 166.
Townsend, Peter: contracts of, 22–23, 25, 89–90.
Towson, Nathan: about, 78; from, 94; to, 94, 568.
Treasurer, U. S. *See* Tucker, Thomas Tudor.
Treasury Department: accountability to, 268–269; offer to, 149; quarters

of, xxii–xxiii; Secretary of, xxii (*see also* Crawford, William H.).
Treat, Joseph: from, 228.
Trenchard, Edward, U. S. N.: about, 223.
Trenton, N. J.: railroad from, 227.
Trescot, George: about, 427.
Trezevant, Peter: son of, 23.
Trezevant, Peter Dunlop: about, 23, 97; from, 102.
Trimble, David: from, 73; to, 73.
Trimble, Isaac: about, 73.
Trimble, William A.: from, 16, 163, 213, 224–225, 268, 302–303, 308–311, 537; to, 163, 213–214, 224, 302–303, 308.
Trinity River: about, 431.
Trist, Nicholas P.: about, xvi, 98, 114, 121; from, 139–140.
Troup, Robert: from, 301.
Tucker, Henry St. George: from, 605–606.
Tucker, John: to, 341.
Tucker, Thomas Tudor: from, 78–79; funds of, 16, 36, 79–80, 104, 161, 239, 265, 391, 609, 633; remittance from, 682; to, 78.
Tupper, Thomas: about, 372, 483; dismissal of, 576, 580, 585; to, 373.
Turk & Henderson: about, 334; bids by, 340, 360, 364; contract of, 505, 547–548; from, 332–333; to, 369. *See also* Henderson, Thomas; Turk, James.
Turk, James: about, 333–334, 337, 505; from, 142, 332–333; to, 142. *See also* Turk & Henderson.
Turner, Samuel, Jr.: from, 175.
Turner, William: about, 59.
Turner, William, M.D.: about, 510, 631, 644–645; from, 194; to, 636, 694.
Turnpikes: about, 226–227.
Twiggs, David Emanuel: from, 20.
Tyler, Edwin: accounts of, 615.
Tyler, Wat, M.D.: recommendation of, 595–596.

Union College: student at, 117.
United Brethren in N. C., Society of: schools of, 675–676.
United States Armories. *See* Harpers Ferry, Va. (now W. Va.); Springfield, Mass.
United States Military Academy: about, 358, 495–496, 533; Academic Staff of, 163, 227, 285–286; bill for, 509; Commandant of Cadets at (*see* Bliss, John); curriculum of, 461; documents in library of, 277, 500; Drawing Master at, 292; funds for, xxi, 199; graduates of, 363, 370; hospital at, 285; regulations for, 688, 694; reports about, 543, 598; Superintendent of (*see* Thayer, Sylvanus); student discipline in, 293, 317, 322–323, 415–416, 500, 523, 535–536; uniforms at, 264, 416–417, 435.
University of Georgia Library: documents in, 66, 211.
University of South Carolina: about, xi, 120. *See also* South Caroliniana Library.
University of Virginia: proposed establishment of, 511.

Vandeventer, Christopher: about, xxviii, 66, 149–150, 175, 398, 614; from, 15–16, 75, 76–77, 338, 369, 430, 439, 548, 599; to, 67, 78–79, 122, 150–151, 175, 231, 235–236, 241, 283, 284, 338, 374, 461, 475, 490, 493, 517, 532, 534, 548–549, 603, 609, 622, 627, 666, 684.
Vandeventer, Mrs. Christopher: illness of, 684.
Van Dyke, Nicholas: from, 621.
Van Rensselaer, Solomon: pension of, xxi.
Vaughan, John: from, 35, 134, 643; to, 35, 134.
Vegetable gardens at Army posts: labor for, 513–515; seeds for, 204. *See also* Rations, Army.
Vergennes, N. Y.: armory at, 538.
Vergennes, Vt.: ordnance at, 516

Vermont: Commissioner of Loans in, 414, 415, 448, 484, 630; ordnance in, 516; pensions in, 307, 407, 412–413, 414, 415, 448, 454–455, 459, 484, 630, 693-694; recruits in, 539; U. S. Marshal in, 407, 455, 459.
Veterans' benefits. *See* Bounty lands; Bounty Lands, Section of; Pension Office.
Vickery, Edward: about, 307.
Vincennes, Ind.: Indian Agent at, 699; Receiver of Public Monies at, 680, 693.
Vining, Charles R.: from, 293, 317, 415–416, 523, 535–536.
Vinton, John R.: about, 356, 370, 387, 461, 614; from, 478.
Virginia: Governor of (*see* Preston, James P.); heirship in, 432, 549; legislative Clerk of, 635–636; militia of, 392; ordnance for, 90; pensions in, 281–282; University of, 331; verification of documents in, 706.
Voight, Henry: about, 437, 454, 521, 666.
Voorhees, Samuel S.: son of, 15.
Voorhees, Sillsby: about, 15, 29.

Waddel, the Rev. Moses: recommendation by, 415.
Wade, William: report by, 291.
Wadsworth, Capt. Alexander S., U. S. N.: from, 261, 404–405, 412, 416; to, 261, 416.
Wadsworth, Decius: about, 21, 90, 543, 607, 611, 664, 673; from, 11–12, 16, 18, 22–23, 25, 27, 31, 39, 89–90, 128–129, 134, 168, 199, 201–204, 205, 227–228, 241–242, 251, 256, 259, 264, 268–269, 274, 283–284, 288, 291, 297, 303, 311–312, 323, 328–329, 333, 335, 337, 341, 357–358, 370, 391–392, 393–394, 400, 402, 420, 456, 475, 479, 489, 508, 516–517, 526, 529, 538, 541, 568, 581, 587–588, 590–591, 599, 613–614, 615–616, 618, 622, 632, 643, 648, 679, 695; orders to, 80, 94, 110, 169, 240; reports by, 372, 484, 516, 578; to, 22, 42, 79, 105, 150, 251, 288, 405, 429–430, 519, 568, 627, 670–671, 674, 677, 688, 691, 695.
Wager, Catherine (Mrs. John): claim of, 128–129, 481; from, 102, 122; to, 140.
Wager, John: about, 128, 140.
Waide, Thomas: from, 159–161, 164, 281, 672; to, 164, 281, 672–673.
Wakefield, Henry: about, 361.
Walker, —— (of N. C.): bounty land for, 361.
Walker, —— (of the Northwest): about, 365.
Walker, Daniel: about, 697.
Walker, Felix: to, 489–490.
Walker, Isaac: about, 365.
Walker, John (a Cherokee): about, 266, 407, 549.
Walker, Joseph: son of, 697.
Wallace, Edwin R.: to, 341.
Wallace, James: from, 240.
Wallace, Joseph, M.D.: about, 80.
Walsh, Robert, Jr.: from, 711; to, 655–656, 692.
Walsh, Samuel A., M.D.: from, 285.
War Department: books and maps in, 11, 32, 35; Clerks in, 302, 318, 323, 325, 328, 340, 373, 403, 439, 493, 509, 569 (*see also* Vandeventer, Christopher); funds for, viii, xxi–xxiii; office expenses of, 250, 424–425, 490, 491, 506–507; quarters of, xxii–xxiii; Superintendent of buildings of, 491.
Ward, Charles: from, 568; request of, 541.
Ward, James: about, 625; from, 508.
Ward, William: about, 298, 330.
Warrenton, N. C.: about, 505.
Warrington, Capt. Lewis, U.S.N.: from, 616; report by, 648.
Washburn, Samuel: about, 260–261.
Washington, Lund: about, 481.
Washington, U.S.S.: commander of, 284. *See also* Chauncey, Isaac.

Washington, William S.: about, 699.
Washington, William T.: about, 403.
Waterford, Pa.: arsenal at, 291.
Waterhouse, Benjamin, M.D.: from, 155–157, 172; to, 157, 172.
Waters, Asa: contracts of, 201–204.
Waters, George Washington: recommendation of, 73.
Watertown, Mass.: arsenal at, 17, 241–242.
Watervliet, N. Y.: arsenal at, 187, 265, 538; church at, 187.
Watkins, Tobias, M.D.: from, 630.
Watmough, John G.: recommendation of, 579.
Watson, Lt. William H., U.S.N.: about, 412.
Watterston, George: from, 485–486.
Watts, Beaufort Taylor: about, 536; from, 83, 118.
Watts, John: about, 83.
Waupagkanetta, O.: mission at, 71.
Wayne, James M.: from, 240.
Wea Indians: Agent to, 631, 636, 644; annuities of, 693; cession by, 83; treaties with, 189, 194, 306.
Weakley, Robert: about, 500, 525, 608, 683; to, 695.
Webb, Edward: about, 405.
Weeks, Thomas D. L.: claim of, 494, 503.
Weightman, Richard, M.D.: about, 502.
Wells, ——: about, 21.
Welton, Caleb: about, 237.
Weymouth, Dean: about, 229, 494; to, 699.
Wharton, Col. Franklin, U.S.M.C.: death of, 244, 290.
Wheat, Gothedon (Mrs. James Thomas): about, xi.
Wheaton, Joseph: about, xxi; from, 13, 84.
Wheaton, Seth: from, 281; to, 281.
Whetten, John: about, 29.
Whetten, William: about, 29.
Whistler, William: to, 647.
White, Lt. John, U.S.N.: from, 397, 398.
White Rock Indians: gift to, 222.
White, Thomas: from, 543; to, 543–544.
Whiting, Henry: about, 557.
Whitman, Lemuel: from, 237.
Wickliffe, Robert: from, 129.
Wideman, ——: sale to, 275.
Wiggins, George B., & Co.: draft to, 154.
Wigton, William: from, 410, 627.
Wilberforce, William: about, 58.
Wilkins, John: from, 228.
Wilkins, John Holmes: from, 659.
Williams, Brooke: about, 509.
Williams, David R.: about, 520.
Williams, John: from, 79, 121, 337, 358, 475–476, 500, 509, 549, 616, 628; loan to, 694; report by, 283; to, 358, 509, 549, 616, 688.
Williams, Lewis: from, 337; to, 337–338.
Williams, Thomas Hill: from, 568; to, 568.
Williams, Thomas W.: from, 543.
Williamson, John P.: from, 240.
Williamson, William D.: from, 228.
Willington, S. C.: about, 521.
Willis, Perrin: from, 447–448.
Wilmington, N. C.: Military Storekeeper at, 625.
Wilmot, Allen: fine against, 283.
Wilson, ——: warrant for, 658.
Wilson, B., Jr.: from, 542.
Wilson, Charles: claims of, 164–165.
Wilson, James Jefferson: about, 432; from, 424–425, 429.
Wilson, John: from, 493, 544; to, 341, 491, 544.
Wilson, Robert: about, 67, 83, 508.
Wilson, Thomas: from, 338, 397–398, 490, 599, 609; to, 338, 490, 599.
Winchester, James: about, 657; to, 659.
Winder, Rider Henry: resignation of, 79.
Windsor County, Vt.: Cadets from, 391.
Wingate, J. F.: from, 405.
Winnebago Indians: about, 246, 708.

Winston, William O.: from, 79.
Wirt & Clark: contract of, 11–12, 25, 39, 409.
Wirt, William: about, xv; from, 112, 195, 214, 247, 706; opinions of, 4, 6, 58, 65, 96, 98, 216, 315, 332, 707; to, 186, 549, 609.
Wise, George S., U.S.N.: from, 300; to, 300.
Wistar, Thomas: about, 499.
Wolcott, Alexander, Jr.: to, 130, 699.
Wood, George: to, 341.
Woodbine, George: about, 314.
Woodbridge, William: from, 214, 591, 630.
Woodruff, Joseph: to, 122.
Woodside, John: about, 271; from, 491.
Wool, John E.: about, 156–157; from, 19.
Woolley, Abram R.: about, 11, 35, 37–38, 39, 40, 65, 70, 78–79, 242, 246, 256, 291, 311, 328, 341, 538, 632; from, 27, 168, 232, 311, 338, 524; to, 27, 168–169, 232, 315, 338, 524–525.
Woolsey, Capt. Melancthon T., U.S.N.: from, 303; to, 303, 392.
Wooster, O.: Receiver of Public Monies at, 680.
Worcester, Samuel, D.D.: introduction of, 557–558.
Worth, William Jenkins: from, 394.
Wright, Benjamin: from, 263.
Wright, Clinton: about, 74.
Wright, Francis: to, 341.
Wright, Obed: about, 65, 112, 390, 439.
Wright, Robert: about, 286; from, 74; to, 74.
Wright, Uriel: recommendation of, 318.
Wright, William: about, 286; from, 263.
Würtemburg: King of, 88, 109.
Wyandot Indians: Agent to, 282, 365, 480; annuities of, 241, 692; indemnity to, 692; tour by, 365; treaties with, 71, 119, 138–139, 146–147, 194, 306, 421, 645.

Yale College: Calhoun's classmate in, 539.
Yale University Library: documents in, 186, 450.
Yazoo River: exploration of, 424.
Yellowstone Expedition. *See* Missouri Expedition.
York River: limestone near, 227.
York, S. C.: college at, 103.
Yost, Henry: about, 28–29.
Young, ——: heirs of, 88.
Young, Hugh: about, 158, 205, 690; from, 564, 600, 609; surveys by, 107, 427–428; to, 609–610.
Young, John: about, 214, 247.
Youngblood, Ezra: about, 664.
Youngblood, Ira: discharge of, 522, 548.
Younglove, Ezra: from, 8.

Zantzinger, William P.: from, 323.

Colophon

The type face used in setting the text of this volume is Linotype Caledonia. It is chiefly of the ten-point size, leaded two points. The type face used for display purposes is of the Bodoni family. The letterpress paper is Warren's Olde Style, Antique Wove, substance 50.

Typesetting, presswork, and binding have been done by The R. L. Bryan Company of Columbia, South Carolina, under the general supervision of William B. Harley.